3.89

MW00655320

$10

Behavioral Consultation and Therapy

APPLIED CLINICAL PSYCHOLOGY

Series Editors:
Alan S. Bellack, *Medical College of Pennsylvania at EPPI, Philadelphia, Pennsylvania,*
and Michel Hersen, *University of Pittsburgh, Pittsburgh, Pennsylvania*

Current Volumes in this Series

THE AIDS HEALTH CRISIS
Psychological and Social Interventions
  Jeffrey A. Kelly and Janet S. St. Lawrence

BEHAVIORAL CONSULTATION AND THERAPY
  John R. Bergan and Thomas R. Kratochwill

BEHAVIORAL CONSULTATION IN APPLIED SETTINGS
An Individual Guide
  Thomas R. Kratochwill and John R. Bergan

HANDBOOK OF BEHAVIOR MODIFICATION WITH THE MENTALLY RETARDED
Second Edition
  Edited by Johnny L. Matson

HANDBOOK OF THE BRIEF PSYCHOTHERAPIES
  Edited by Richard A. Wells and Vincent J. Giannetti

HANDBOOK OF CLINICAL BEHAVIORAL PEDIATRICS
  Edited by Alan M. Gross and Ronald S. Drabman

HANDBOOK OF SEXUAL ASSAULT
Issues, Theories, and Treatment of the Offender
  Edited by W. L. Marshall, D. R. Laws, and H. E. Barbaree

HANDBOOK OF TREATMENT APPROACHES IN CHILDHOOD
PSYCHOPATHOLOGY
  Edited by Johnny L. Matson

PSYCHOLOGY
A Behavioral Overview
  Alan Poling, Henry Schlinger, Stephen Starin, and Elbert Blakely

A Continuation Order Plan is available for this series. A continuation order will bring delivery
of each new volume immediately upon publication. Volumes are billed only upon actual ship-
ment. For further information please contact the publisher.

Behavioral Consultation and Therapy

John R. Bergan
University of Arizona
Tucson, Arizona

and

Thomas R. Kratochwill
University of Wisconsin–Madison
Madison, Wisconsin

Plenum Press • New York and London

Library of Congress Cataloging-in-Publication Data

Bergan, John R., 1931-
    Behavioral consultation and therapy / John R. Bergan and Thomas R.
Kratochwill.
        p.   cm. -- (Applied clinical psychology)
    Rev. and updated version of Behavioral consultation / John R.
Bergan. c1977.
    Companion v. to Behavioral consultation in applied settings /
Thomas R. Kratochwill and John R. Bergan. c1990.
    Includes bibliographical references.
    ISBN 0-306-43345-1
    1. Mental health consultation. 2. Behavioral assessment of
children.   I. Kratochwill, Thomas R. II. Bergan, John R., 1931-
Behavioral consultation. III. Kratochwill, Thomas R. Behavioral
consultation in applied settings. IV. Title. V. Series.
    [DNLM 1. Child Behavior. 2. Child Psychiatry. 3. Problem
Solving--in infancy & childhood. 4. Referral and Consultation.   WS
350 B494b]
RJ503.45.B47 1990
618.92'89--dc20
DNLM/DLC
for Library of Congress   90-6728
                                                                CIP

To
David, John and Kathy,
Tyler and Carol

Preface

This book is a revised and updated version of *Behavioral Consultation* (Bergan, 1977). The book is written for individuals interested in procedures for increasing consultation skills to assist parents, teachers, and other socialization agents to solve mental-health and educational problems of children and youths. The book is a basic text to be used in developing consultation skills in students entering the various fields in which consultation techniques are applied. In addition, we intend that the companion volume, *Behavioral Consultation in Applied Settings: An Individual Guide* (Kratochwill & Bergan, 1990), serve as a skill development resource for professional practitioners whose work involves consultation services. School psychologists, school counselors, community psychologists, child clinical psychologists, counseling psychologists, child psychiatrists, and social workers are among the many types of professionals for whom both works are intended.

As the title indicates, the text is behavioral in its orientation. We present a problem-solving model designed to make principles derived from behavioral research available to consultees engaged in socialization. Through application of the model, consultants can learn to assist consultees to define problems, apply psychological principles in the development of plans to solve problems, implement plans designed to achieve problem solutions, and evaluate goal attainment and plan effectiveness.

We emphasize the development of communication skills for use in consultation. Readers are provided with a consultation analysis procedure for coding the verbal interactions occurring during consultation. They are then shown how to use the consultation analysis technique in conducting effective problem-identification, problem-analysis, and problem-evaluation interviews.

The book is divided into three parts. In Part I, basic concepts and techniques in behavioral consultation are presented. In Chapter 1, we discuss the nature of consultation and provide an overview of the problem-solving model described in the text as a vehicle for rendering behavioral consultation. In Chapter 2, we present verbal interaction techniques that can be applied in behavioral consultation, and we discuss procedures for acquiring skill in using those techniques.

Part II elaborates the problem-solving model presented in the text. In Chapter 3 we discuss problem identification. Chapter 4 deals with problem analysis. Plan implementation is described in Chapter 5, and problem evaluation is discussed in Chapter 6.

Part III describes applications of behavioral consultation in applied settings. In Chapter 7, we present and analyze interview transcripts from case studies in behavioral consultation. In Chapter 8, we discuss applications of consultation within the context of consultative problem-solving systems designed to advance the utilization of scientific knowledge in the socialization process.

Chapter 9 includes a discussion of future research directions in behavioral consultation. Specifically, we review methodological, conceptual, and research issues in behavioral consultation and chart some research priorities for the future.

The material presented in the book represents over 15 years of research and demonstration work in behavioral consultation. All of the techniques discussed have been applied in many field settings. For example, grants from the National Follow-Through program and the Office of Special Education and Rehabilitative Services made it possible to demonstrate a number of the techniques in both urban and rural school districts across a variety of geographic regions ranging from the Atlantic seaboard to Alaska. The many examples of consultation problems in the text have been taken from a file of over 4,000 cases accumulated through the work done in Follow-Through and through subsequent research and demonstration projects in Arizona, Iowa, and Wisconsin.

In addition to having been tested in field settings, the principles and techniques described in the book have been used in graduate instruction and in in-service training programs for practicing psychologists for close to two decades. Thus, there has been an opportunity to refine the material to increase the effectiveness of the book in assisting readers to acquire consultation skills.

The ideas presented in this book evolved over a period of several years, and in the course of developing them, we received help from many people. A number of people contributed to the early development of the consultation model in Arizona. We wish to thank Ronald Henderson, Ralph Wetzel, and Robert Egbert for encouraging and supporting the initial research and demonstration program set up to determine the effectiveness of consultation services of the type presented in this text. We owe special thanks to Richard Brown, Sara Currin, Dal Curry, Steven Gray, Karen Haberman, Carol Hillyer, Huntley Hoffman, Richard Koussa, Elaine Nicholson, and Margaret Ronstadt, each of whom played a key role in implementing various early research and demonstration projects used in Arizona to field-test the consultation techniques described in the book. In addition, we wish to express our thanks to the many psychological consultants who demonstrated the effectiveness of behavioral consultation in communities participating in the Follow-Through implementation program and in communities receiving research and demonstration services through the Office of Psychoeducational Research at the University of Arizona. Special thanks go to Joel T. Tudor, Superintendent of the Tombstone Public Schools, for his early interest in and support of the research and demonstration programs set up to develop and evaluate innovative consultation techniques.

In Wisconsin, a large number of individuals contributed to the current text. First, our sincere appreciation goes to Susan M. Sheridan, Pamela Rotto, and Mary Ann Ford for their thoughtful comments on the text and especially for their work in developing consultation training materials. Special thanks also go to Diane Salmon for her many contributions to the consultation training project at the University of Wisconsin–Madison. We also wish to thank the many individuals who served as consultants to teachers of emotionally handicapped children.

Several individuals provided a review and offered critical commentary on earlier versions of the text. We extend special thanks to Sandy Christenson, Steve Elliott, Mark Shinn, and Joe Witt for their time and efforts in reviewing the work.

Contents

I

Concepts and Techniques in Behavioral Consultation

Basic Concepts in Behavioral Consultation

Behavioral psychology has emerged as a major force influencing the socialization practices used in guiding the development of the young. Behavioral principles have been applied widely both in the home and in the school (Kazdin, 1978, 1988; Kratochwill & Bijou, 1987). Moreover, the scope of behavioral applications has been extremely broad, encompassing efforts to accelerate social, emotional, and intellectual development as well as attempts to remediate significant learning and adjustment problems in children and adolescents (Kratochwill & Morris, 1990; Morris & Kratochwill, 1984; Ollendick & Cerny, 1981).

As the massive body of research evidence on the use of behavioral principles in psychology and education was accumulated, psychologists, providing consultation services to parents, teachers, and other socializing agents, have increasingly incorporated behavioral techniques into their services. The application of behavioral theory and research in consultation services may be referred to as *behavioral consultation*. In this chapter, we introduce the basic concepts of behavioral consultation. In the first section, we discuss the general nature of consultation services, and then we present a model for conducting behavioral consultation.

THE NATURE OF CONSULTATION

Consultation has many varied meanings (Reschly, 1976). Based on a review of the medical, organizational, and mental health literature, West and Idol (1987), for example, noted that there are three general meanings of the term *consultation*. In the medical literature, the term refers to the process by which a physician requests and receives expert advice from a colleague. In the organization literature, the meaning of *consultation* relates to change at the system level. In the mental health literature, *consultation* refers to a process through which a consultant works with a consultee (e.g., a professional, a paraprofessional, or a parent) to provide services to a client (a child). In this regard, consultation is often regarded as a triadic relationship (Tharp, 1975; Tharp & Wetzel, 1969). This triadic relationship involves a consultant, a consultee, and a client.

Based on their review of the literature, West and Idol (1987) identified 10 different models of consultation (see Table 1-1). Each model was listed and evaluated through five questions:

1. Does the consultation model rely on a theory?
2. Does the consultation model rely on a knowledge base?
3. What is the implied or observed goal of the consultant within the consultation process?
4. Does the model have particular stages of progression through the consultation process?
5. What are the responsibilities of the consultant and the consultee within the consultation model? (West & Idol, 1987, p. 390)

Our purpose here is to focus on the behavioral consultation model and its associated characteristics. Readers interested in the other models of consultation should review the references in Table 1-1.

Defining Characteristics of Behavioral Consultation

A number of characteristics are associated often enough with consultation generally and behavioral consultation specifically, to be thought of as defining features. Some of these are not always present in consultation activities, but taken together, they provide a relatively accurate description of what is usually involved in consultation.

Consultation as Problem Solving

One of the most fundamental features of consultation is that it is a problem-solving venture (Gutkin & Curtis, 1982). Consultation typically involves an attempt to alter an existing set of circumstances in the direction of a desired set of circumstances. Moreover, it is generally not clear at the start of consultation how the needed alterations can best be effected. The alterations may involve a focus on the teacher or parent, the child, the physical environment (e.g., curriculum or space), or any combination of factors.

TABLE 1-1. Analysis of 10 Consultation Models in Response to Five Criterial Questions

Consultation model	Theory for the consultation relationship	Knowledge base for problem solving	Goals	Stages/steps	Responsibilities
Mental health Caplan (1970) Meyers *et al.* (1979)	Assumes that consultees have the capacity to solve most of their work problems and that consultants can help them increase their range of effectiveness (Gallessich, 1982). Theories that have been applied to how the consultant treats the consultee include neoclient-centered psychology (Rogers, 1942, 1951, 1959) and Adlerian psychology (Adler, 1964; Dreikurs, 1948, 1967). No single theory of communication has been applied.	Psychodynamics; clinical skills; crisis concepts; specialized diagnostic and decision-making skills; theme interference reduction; onedownmanship; avoidance of therapy; relationship building.	Consultant chooses one of four possibilities: client-centered, consultee-centered, program-centered, or administrative or consultee-centered. Success is measured by the degree to which the consultation expands the consultee's capacity to diagnose, cope with, and solve emotional or technical problems of the consultee or the client.	Consultant chooses type of consultation for the problem and primary target of interventions. *Example* 1. Consultant seeks information on nature and scope of work problem, consultee's capacity for problem solving, and ways the consultation may be useful. 2. Consultant "treats" the consultee by offering *expert* opinion, or shared, straightforward problem-solving is used.	Consultant is responsible for gathering information on the nature of the problem and for providing solutions to problems. The consultant/consultee relationship is egalitarian (Gallessich, 1985)

(continued)

TABLE 1-1. (Continued)

Consultation model	Theory for the consultation relationship	Knowledge base for problem solving	Goals	Stages/steps	Responsibilities
Behavioral Bergan & Tombari (1975, 1976); Kratochwill & Bergan (1978a); McNamara & Diehl (1974); Tombari & Bergan (1978)	Assumes that consultant's application of behavioral or social learning theory will help consultee solve problems. Behavioral learning theory has been more consistently applied to methods for problem solving than to how the consultant interacts with the consultee, although the latter would also be applicable.	Flexible knowledge of behavioral programming and principles of social learning theory and applied behavior analysis.	To reduce the frequency of an undesirable client or consultee behavior; to increase the frequency of desirable client or consultee behavior.	1. Problems identification. 2. Problem analysis. 3. Plan implementation. 4. Problem evaluation. (Bergan, 1977)	Consultant serves as an expert; consultee is the recipient, although sometimes mutuality of problem solving is emphasized.
Organizational A. Human relations model Argyris (1964); Bennis (1969a, 1970); Homans (1950); Lippitt (1969)	Organizational theory: problems of organizations must be solved in a manner that incorporates into the process all those individuals in the organization because of the focus that they bring to bear on one another (Lewin, 1951);	Communication skills; decision-making skills; force-field analysis approved, data collection and feedback, social and psychological, cognitive behaviorism, psychodynamic systems, ecology, psychodynamic systems, statistical models	To bring about planned change by focusing on individuals and their attitudes and values and group processes in the organization (Brown, Wyne, Blackburn, & Powell, 1979); to increase organizational productivity and	1. Orientation. 2. Contract setting. 3. Reconnaissance. 4. Problem and opportunity development. 5. Aspirations. 6. Analysis. 7. Experimentation. 8. Results analysis. 9. Program design.	Consultant facilitates the group's progression through all stages.

the influence of environment on personal growth (Rogers, 1942, 1951, 1959)	and methods, humanistic values and assumptions (Gallessich, 1985).	morale (Gallessich, 1982).	10. Implementation. 11. Evaluation and feedback. 12. Recycling. (Gardner, 1974)	Consultant facilitates process, demonstrates interventions, and provides training.
B. Organizational thinking Schmuck & Runkel (1972)	Same as for the human relations model.	Group conflict, inter- and intragroup communication, decision making, methods of goal setting, defining roles.	1. Working with subsystems of the organization as groups. 2. Developing communication skills. 3. Working with subsystems to develop problem-solving skills. 4. Developing a series of training exercises, which start with simulation and evolve to a point where the real issues of the school are the focus (Schmuck & Runkel, 1972).	1. Entry phase. 2. Diagnosis of organization's functioning. 3. Selection of a subsystem of the organization. 4. Demonstration of the intervention (Brown et al., 1979). 5. Organizational training.	
C. Advocacy	Any practitioners of other models may use advocacy consultation; based on conflict theory (i.e., Chesler, Bryant, & Crowfoot, 1981).	Knowledge of law, organizing people, organizing events, media use, negotiation, parent partnership, persuasive writing and speaking, building support networks,	To seek due process for various types of clients; to facilitate group process to help people work together; to organize events; to develop partnerships with parents of clients.	None specified.	Consultant facilitates effectiveness of others.

(continued)

TABLE 1-1. (*Continued*)

Consultation model	Theory for the consultation relationship	Knowledge base for problem solving	Goals	Stages/steps	Responsibilities
		tolerance for ambiguity and conflict; known for what they believe in *not* by particular methodologies. Some advocacy consultants have both expert content knowledge and advocacy process knowledge (Conoley & Conoley, 1982).			Consultant analyzes interactions of the group or organization; consultant and consultee work collaboratively to identify problems and to generate solutions; consultee provides information on organizational structure, climate, and norms.
Process Schein (1969)	Systems change theory (von Bertalanffy, 1950).	Understanding of process phenomena; process observation, interaction analysis; decision-making rules; data gathering; role identification; use of empirical approaches; reference for the unique (Conoley & Conoley, 1982; Neel, 1981).	Consultants work to make consultees more aware of events or processes that affect work production and social emotional atmospheres of the system (Schein, 1969); to leave a consultee (organization) with new skills (Conoley & Conoley, 1982).	1. Process observation. 2. Analysis of group interactions.	

Clinical (doctor–patient)	The general characteristic is that it is patterned after psychiatry and adapted for use when consulting with colleagues about client's problems. No specified theory.	Expert diagnosis of a client's mental or emotional condition and an authoritative recommendation of how staff (consultees) should treat the patient (Gallessich, 1982); problems are conceived of as patient's (or program's, team's, organization's) problems; generally, goals are limited to the particular case; to increase consultees' coping effectiveness.	1. Diagnosis. 2. Prescription. 3. Treatment.	Consultant assumes responsibility for the case, determines data to be gathered and how to gather them, directly examines client, treats or prescribes treatment; consultant–consultee relationship is hierarchical.
Program	No specified theory.	To help agencies design, develop, implement, and evaluate programs. Methods are difficult to define because of the diversity in the nature of the consultation (Gallessich, 1982).	*Example* 1. Consultee clarifies goals and objectives. 2. Consultant proposes ideal theoretical approaches to objectives. 3. Consultee explains organizational constraints and resources. 4. Both "brainstorm" to develop practical implementation strategies.	Consultants may assist in all aspects of the program or may be limited to a highly specific task.

(continued)

TABLE 1-1. (*Continued*)

Consultation model	Theory for the consultation relationship	Knowledge base for problem solving	Goals	Stages/steps	Responsibilities
				5. Together develop a research and implementation plan. 6. Consultee implements the plan (Gallessich, 1982).	
Education and training	No specified theory.	Knowledge of open-systems operations; task analysis; needs assessment; instructional design; evaluation of training (Gallessich, 1982).	To transmit needed knowledge, information, and skills to consultees to alleviate problems (usually client-centered).	No specific stages or steps.	Consultant serves as an expert.

Model	Theory base	Knowledge requirements	Goal	Stages	Description
Collaborative Idol et al. (1986); Kurpius & Robinson (1978); Sarason (1982)	Generic principles of collaboration and consultation have been hypothesized (Idol et al., 1986); no formal testing for theory development has been done.	Consultants possess knowledge of social learning theory, classroom assessment, learning processes, child management, and applied behavior analysis; consultees possess knowledge of scope and sequence of curricular instruction, theories of child development, and techniques for large group instruction.	To develop parity between special and classroom teachers, resulting in shared ownership of learning and management problems of exceptional and nonachieving students participating in regular classroom instruction.	1. Gaining mutual acceptance. 2. Assessing causes of problems, problems themselves, and outcomes of problems. 3. Formulating goals and objectives matched to assessment outcomes. 4. Implementing teaching and learning procedures. 5. Evaluating program outcomes, including clients, consultants, consultees, parents of clients, program administrators, and overall programs (Idol et al., 1986)	Emphasizes mutuality and parity in the consulting relationship, with the consultant serving as a learning specialist and the consultee serving as a curriculum and child development specialist; consultee is primarily responsible for program implementation; all other stages reflect mutual responsibility.

In most cases, consultation focuses on the difficulties that a consultee faces in working with a client or a group of clients for whom he or she is responsible (Caplan, 1970; Lambert, 1974). For example, a teacher may seek consultation services to reduce the level of disruptiveness of the children in a class, or a parent may ask for consultative assistance to eliminate a child's temper tantrums. However, in some instances, consultation may focus on more general concerns, such as providing teachers with skills to enable them to communicate effectively with their colleagues (e.g., see Broskowsi, 1973).

Consultation as Indirect Service

Another feature that is generally characteristic of consultation is the indirect influence of the consultant on the client. Generally, the consultant does not have direct contact with the client during consultation; rather, he or she works with the consultee, who in turn works with the client (Caplan, 1970; Tharp & Wetzel, 1969). For example, when a consultant provides services to a parent or a teacher with respect to the behavior of a child, it is the parent or the teacher who assumes the responsibility for working with the child to alter his or her behavior.

The tactic of providing indirect services to clients has long been regarded as one of the most attractive features of consultation. Providing direct services to children has been challenging. The need for psychological services is far greater than the ability of society to provide services. For example, the Joint Commission on the Mental Health of Children (1970) estimated that 1.5 million childrn under 18 years of age were in need of immediate professional assistance; at that time, less than 30% of this number were receiving the assistance. More recently, it has been estimated that 20%–30% of all children enter elementary school with behavior problems that are moderate to severe, and that of this group approximately half have severe problems that require professional intervention (Weiner, 1982).

Consultation provides a tool that can extend the reach of psychological services to many more individuals than could be served by direct contact with professionals. When a psychologist provides consultation services to a teacher or a parent, he or she spends less time than would be required to give direct services to a child. This model allows many more children to receive services than would be the case otherwise. In addition, the consultee (parent or teacher) may well acquire skills in the course of consultation that can be used with children other than the client.

An indirect service-delivery approach is not without some potential disadvantages (Martens & Witt, 1988; Witt & Martens, 1988). One criticism leveled against the indirect-service approach to consultation is that it generally works for the power structure of the social system of which the client is a member (see Pearl, 1974). It is true that consultation services are typically rendered to consultees who have some authority over the clients with whom they are working. This concern is certainly the case when the consultee is a parent or a teacher.

Obviously, there is a need to represent the interests of those individuals within a social system who have little or no power. This issue is the central assumption underlying the child-advocacy movement that gained momentum in the 1970s. However, it would be incorrect to assume that consultation provided to individuals in positions of authority invariably has a bad effect on clients. This kind of assumption would imply the unwarranted view that the goals and practices of socialization agents are generally inimical to the needs and interests of children.

Although consultees are usually people in positions of authority, this is not a necessary requirement of indirect service. For example, a 12-year-old boy was referred to a consultant by the principal of the junior high school that he attended. The principal described the boy as incorrigible, and all five of his teachers agreed on the accuracy of this description. The consultant discussed the matter with the boy and found that the child was deeply concerned about being continually "hassled" by his teachers. Together, the consultant and the child-consultee developed a plan to end the hassling. During the course of consultation, the boy recorded his teachers' behaviors, and within a short period of time after his plan had been put into effect, he was quite satisfied with the results. The boy's teachers, though unaware of the specifics of the plan, were also happy with the outcomes of consultation. As one teacher put it, "I just can't believe the change that has come over that boy!"

Although indirect service is a frequent characteristic of consultation services, consultation may not always involve an indirect relationship between the consultant and the client. As we shall discuss later in the chapter, some writers see the principal purpose of consultation as changing the social system in which the consultee functions (Schmuck, 1982; Schmuck, Runkel, Saturen, Martell, & Derr, 1972; see also Table 1-1). For example, consultation aimed at producing change in a school system may focus on increasing the clarity of communications among students and staff in the system. Consultation of the systemic variety is usually not targeted at a specific client or group of clients served by a consultee. It is often asserted that systemic change will influence a consultee's effectiveness in dealing with clients. For instance, it might be argued that increased clarity in communication between teachers and students would enable teachers to handle student problems more effectively than they otherwise could. Nevertheless, discussions held between consultants and consultees to produce system change do not necessarily include any attempt to evaluate the influence of consultation on clients. Thus, it would be stretching a point considerably to say that consultation of this kind is aimed at providing indirect service to clients.

Consultation as a Collegial Relationship

Ideally, consultation usually involves a collegial relationship between the consultant and the consultee (Bergan, 1977; Caplan, 1970; Lambert, 1974). That is, the consultant and the consultee function as "equals" in the consultation process. It should be noted that consultants may actually control the dyadic relationship across the stages of behavioral consultation (Erchul, 1987). To some extent, the equality that exists between consultant and consultee derives from the fact that both are often professionals in the same field, as when a teacher and a psychologist in a school work together in consultation. However, the principal basis for the equality relationship is the fact that the consultant generally has no authority over the consultee. For example, a consultee usually participates in consultation only voluntarily.

The specific nature of the collegial relationship that exists during consultation is generally defined by ground rules established before or at the time that consultation is initiated. Obviously, neither party should violate these ground rules. For example, if a consultee asks for assistance in dealing with the behavior of a child, then he or she has a right to expect that the consultant's efforts will be directed to providing the assistance requested.

The proviso that ground rules be adhered to may create certain limitations on the functioning of the consultant. For example, Caplan (1970) pointed out that a consultant committed to assisting the consultee with a client problem should not divert discussion from the client's problems to an examination of the consultee's problems. An attempt to uncover the consultee's problems could turn consultation into therapy. A therapist–patient relationship would replace the collegial relationship specified in the ground rules for consultation. Caplan (1970) argued that, if the consultee is looking for therapy rather than consultation, the consultant should refer the consultee to another professional. The roles of consultant and therapist cannot be simultaneously enacted with a consultee because the relationship between a therapist and a patient is not a collegial relationship.

Consultation as Knowledge Utilization

A consultee generally seeks consultation services because he or she believes the consultant has special knowledge and skills in the field of psychology that will be useful in problem solving. Thus, one of the consultant's major responsibilities is to draw on his or her knowledge of psychology and education to make relevant information available to the consultee. For example, research in behavior modification has shown repeatedly that behavior is often initiated by unnoticed environmental cues. A consultant could make this information available to a consultee in a variety of ways. He or she might begin by asking a question such as, "What generally happens right before Carol throws a temper tantrum?" A question such as this would probably alert the consultee to look for cues that might affect behavior.

The process of making knowledge available to the consultee involves three tasks. First, the consultant must have access to the kinds of information to be conveyed. The dominant method for ensuring that the consultant will have access to the needed information has been to require long years of rigorous professional training for psychologists who plan to engage in consultation. Although this strategy has much to recommend it and will undoubtedly continue to be used, it alone cannot provide the consultant with all the necessary information to be maximally effective in rendering services (Bergan, 1970).

We live in an age of unprecedented knowledge expansion. Toffler (1970) made this point dramatically two decades ago by stating, "The United States Government alone generates 100,000 reports each year, plus 450,000 articles, books and papers. On a world wide basis, scientific and technical literature mounts at a rate of some 60,000,000 pages a year" (p. 31). Although a psychologist may acquire much information of enduring value in graduate training, new and significant developments are continually occurring. Moreover, the sheer quantity of useful information is far too great for any one individual to process and retain. Dubin (1972) estimated that the half-life of psychologists' knowledge is approximately 10–12 years.

What is needed is a mechanism by which consultants can attain convenient, systematic, and continuous access to new information. At present, no easy mechanisms exist. There are, of course, information storage and retrieval systems such as the Educational Resources Information Centers (ERIC). However, it would be impractical from a time standpoint for a consultant to use existing storage and retrieval systems, such as ERIC, on a routine basis. The issue of how to solve the problem of information accessing will be discussed further in Chapter 8. In brief, one way to handle the problem is to make it possible for consultants to be part of a system (e.g., an organization) that includes information-accessing responsibilities and capabilities (Phillips, 1982). In addition, continuing professional education can be an effective means of keeping abreast of important knowledge and skills (Lindsay, Crowe, & Jacobs, 1987).

The second task that must be accomplished to make psychological information available to consultees is selecting specific principles from the psychological knowledge base for use in problem solving. To isolate principles applicable to solving a specific problem, the consultant must make a thorough study of the problem. Such a study may include an examination of conditions in the client's environment that may be affecting a client's behavior and/or characteristics and exerting a controlling influence on his or her actions. For example, in dealing with a problem involving a child's aggressive behavior, a consultant might uncover possible setting events or reinforcers that affect aggression. The consultant might also find that the child lacks the social skills necessary to interact effectively with other children. Information of this sort can provide the basis for developing procedures to solve problems.

In addition to communicating information in a usable form, the consultant must present psychological knowledge in a manner that enables the consultee to incorporate the information into his or her views on how to interact with the client. In the collegial relationship that occurs in consultation, the consultee is not required to accept information that the consultant presents. He or she generally evaluates the information conveyed and may reject it if it does not seem acceptable or if it seems incompatible with his or her value system (Witt & Elliott, 1985). The folklore of consultation is replete with "horror" stories related to the rejection of consultant knowledge.

The central approach described in this book for increasing the likelihood that the consultee will accept the psychological information presented by the consultant is involving the consultee in the selection of interventions. For example, a consultant may present a number of principles that could be applied in solving a particular problem and may then ask the consultee to select from among them the ones that he or she feels would be most useful. The consultant may also ask the consultee for his or her ideas on how a particular principle could be applied in the problem-solving process. Techniques such as these will be discussed in detail in later chapters in the book.

Consultation and Counseling

Consultation can be distinguished from counseling in that consultation generally implies indirect service to a client whereas counseling does not. As indicated earlier, in consultation, a consultant usually works with a consultee, who in turn provides services to a client. By contrast, in counseling, a counselor generally renders services directly to a client. Consultation and counseling may also differ in terms of the verbalizations that occur within each approach (Henning-Stout & Conoley, 1987).

Although a distinction can be made between consultation and counseling, the distinction is not always adhered to in theory or practice. For example, consultation services are often labeled as counseling rather than as consultation. Krumboltz and Thoresen (1969) illustrated this practice. They regard consultation as a form of counseling in which the problem presented by the client involves changing another person's behavior.

An inversion of the Krumboltz and Thoresen point of view would depict counseling as a special form of consultation in which the consultee is the client. Under these conditions, the consultee-client seeks the services of the consultant for the purpose of effecting changes in his or her own behavior.

There may be a great deal of overlap in the kinds of activities described by the terms *consultation* and *counseling* and in the kinds of techniques used in rendering these services. The degree of overlap is particularly marked in behavioral consultation or counseling. For example, many of the techniques of behavioral consultation to be described in succeeding chapters can be used in offering services directly to clients. Case-study material illustrating this fact will be presented in Chapter 7.

Special Characteristics of Consultation for Children and Youths

The various characteristics of consultation described above apply to consultation rendered for the benefit of adult clients as well as to consultation for the preschool and school-aged child. However, the major focus of behavioral consultation is on the socialization of children and youths. Consultation for the young shares most of the features of consultation for adults; yet there are special characteristics that set consultation for children and youths apart from other forms of psychological consultation.

Children and Youths as Clients and Consultees

In most cases, children or adolescents are the clients in consultation for the young. The consultees are generally individuals responsible in some way for the development of the young. Parents and teachers are prime examples of individuals falling in this category. School administrators and leaders of youth groups in religious organizations and community agencies are also individuals who at one time or another may become consultees in consultation.

Although socialization agents are typically the consultees and children or adolescents are generally the clients in consultation, there are occasions in which these roles are reversed. As an illustration, consider the case of a young girl seeking to alleviate constant criticism of her actions by her parents. In this instance, consultation would be directed at changing parent behavior and the consultee would be the young girl. Of course, the young girl might find, as consultees sometimes do, that her own actions needed to be altered for her to be successful in changing her parents' (clients') behavior.

Consultation to Promote Mental Health and Educational Development

Consultation for children and youths emphasizes mental health and educational development. Thus, in consultation for the young, a consultant might assist a parent to eliminate potentially dangerous, aggressive acts by a child. A consultant might also help a teacher to use psychological principles to improve a child's reading skills.

The role of consultation for children and youths in promoting mental health has long been recognized (Cowen, 1973). Consultation related to mental health has two purposes. One is preventive; the other, remedial. Consultation aimed at preventing psychological and educational problems focuses on social and emotional development. Services of this sort are directed at such problems as providing children with skills to enable them to interact effectively in social situations and helping them to develop their own system of values to guide their behavior. The rationale underlying preventive consultation is that, insofar as it is possible to facilitate social and emotional growth, the likelihood of subsequent mental illness will be decreased.

One of the remedial functions of consultation is to reduce the severity and longevity of existing problems or disorders. Such a reduction is accomplished by attacking social and emotional problems through consultation before problems have been sufficiently severe to warrant psychotherapy and/or placement in a more restrictive setting. For example, one of the authors (TRK) has been involved in training behavioral consultants to work with teachers of children in the Wisconsin schools who have been labeled emotionally disturbed. One of the purposes of the project was to reduce the probability that children already identified as being in need of mental health services would be placed in even more restrictive settings.

A second remedial function of consultation is to reduce the incidence of residual effects resulting from social and academic disorders. Thus, for example, consultation can be useful in helping children who have been in residential treatment facilities to make an effective adjustment at home, in the neighborhood, and at school after their return to the communities in which they formerly lived.

For many years, consultation services have been dominated by mental-health concerns. However, during recent decades, there has been a growing recognition of the important role that consultation can play in promoting educational development (Bergan & Caldwell, 1967; Cutts, 1955; Ysseldyke, Reynolds, & Weinberg, 1984). The emphasis in consultation in the educational domain has been on promoting intellectual growth in children and youths. As in the case of mental-health consultation, efforts to promote intellectual development have included both preventive and remedial services.

Preventive services related to intellectual development have focused on forestalling the cumulative achievement deficits that generally occur over the years in children who enter school lacking the necessary preschool experiences to succeed academically. Consultation is one of the many forms of preventive service initiated in the massive social programs of the 1960s to reduce the intellectual deficits of the poor.

In most cases, preventive consultation has involved efforts to help educators apply psychological principles in the design and implementation of educational programs to promote academic achievement. For example, consultation has been used on numerous occasions to assist teachers to apply reinforcement principles to promote the mastery of academic tasks (Lentz & Shapiro, 1985).

Remedial consultation related to intellectual development generally involves services to children who manifest special learning problems. If, for example, a child were having difficulty acquiring basic mathematical skills, a parent or teacher might seek consultation services in an effort to help the child overcome his or her difficulty (see Rosenfield, 1987).

Roles of Participants in Consultation

As already indicated, the three main roles associated with consultation are those of the consultant, the consultee, and the client. These roles are defined within the context of classes of behavior that each of the participants in consultation is expected to perform. There may be substantial variation in the manner in which individual participants enact roles, and in some cases, what people actually do in consultation violates role expectations. Nevertheless, the roles defined for consultation do serve as effective guides for the behavior of those engaged in the consultation process.

The Consultant Role

There are a number of general expectations that the consultant has to fulfill. It is the consultant's responsibility to establish the stages in the consultation process and to guide the consultee through them. To accomplish these tasks, the consultant must exert some control over the consultee's behavior. As we shall discuss in detail in Chapter 2, the consultant achieves control largely by the application of certain kinds of verbalizations. For example, when a consultant says to a consultee, "Tell me what happens right after Ted cries," the consultee has, in effect, been cued to focus on environmental conditions associated with Ted's behavior. Likewise, the question "How intelligent do you think Ted is?" requires the consultee to focus on one of Ted's personal characteristics. The consultant uses verbalizations like these to lead the consultee through the consultation process.

There is empirical evidence that consultants control the dyadic relationship across all stages of consultation (Erchul, 1987). The consultant derives the authority to influence consultee behavior from the fact that the consultee has sought the services of the consultant. Moreover, the consultant typically has some professional status (e.g., school psychologist or social worker) that carries with it certain professional skills and responsibilities (e.g., behavior change). Because the consultant must attempt to influence the consultee to render services, it is essential that the nature of the services to be provided be fully understood by the consultee before consultation is initiated. This orientation usually occurs through in-service workshops or during the initial phases of consultation.

The second major function the consultant serves during consultation is making psychological and educational knowledge available to the consultee. For example, the consultant might assist the consultee to develop a method for assessing client behavior. In providing this kind of service, he or she would call on knowledge of principles of measurement and evaluation and especially the techniques and procedures of behavioral assessment. Likewise, the consultant might assist the consultee to find effective ways to communicate with the client. In accomplishing this task, he or she would rely on knowledge of principles drawn from social psychology.

Although the consultant generally has no direct authority over or relationship with the client, he or she does have a responsibility to the client. Specifically, the consultant should provide services that will benefit the client. However, in meeting this responsibility to the client, the consultant should not, at least in most cases, preempt the authority of the consultee.

The Consultee Role

The consultee may be expected to engage in at least four kinds of activities during consultation. The first is specification or description of the presenting problem or issue. As an initial step in the consultation process, the consultee usually describes a specific problem to the consultant. When this happens, the consultant controls the fact that discussion about a problem will occur, but the consultee specifies what the problem is. A consultant might begin the consultation by saying, "Tell me about Carol's problem." In response, the consultee might say, "Carol's been crying during recess for nearly a week."

A second kind of activity that is invariably required of the consultee is evaluation or decision making. The consultant usually suggests a plan to solve a consultee's problem, but the consultee has to decide whether to put the plan into effect. Similarly, during problem solving, a consultant may help a consultee to devise a means of measuring client behavior, but the consultee has to determine whether the measurements made indicate that a solution to the problem of concern has been attained. In many cases, the consultee functions as a joint problem-solver. For example, a teacher may engage in hypotheses about the factors influencing behavior and the development of a plan. Moreover, a collegial brainstorming of issues may occur when the consultee has training in psychology.

A third kind of activity generally required of the consultee is working with the client. If data are to be collected to assess the performance of the client, the consultee often has to collect them. If a plan is to be implemented to change client behavior, the consultee usually has to put it into effect.

The final type of activity a consultee may be expected to pursue is supervision. Often, the consultee is responsible for supervising the client's actions, as when a parent supervises the behavior of his or her child. In addition, the consultee may have assistants who work with him or her in providing services to clients. For example, if the consultee is the principal of a school, members of the staff may participate in one or more consultation activities that the principal has to supervise. Likewise, a consultee who is a teacher may have a teacher's aide who works under his or her supervision during consultation.

As the description of the consultee role indicates, the consultee has a great deal of influence over what happens in consultation. The consultee is not a passive agent. Rather, he or she makes a direct and vital contribution to the consultation process and to its outcomes.

The fact that both the consultant and the consultee influence the implementation and outcomes of consultation is one of the special strengths of this approach to intervention. The interdependent contributions that the consultant and the consultee make allow the client to reap the benefits of the combined knowledge and skills of both. For example, when a psychologist consults with a teacher concerning the behavior of a child, the child receives the benefits of combining educational and psychological knowledge and skill.

The Client Role

The client's role is to change in the direction of the goal established during consultation. Thus, if the problem is that a child is having temper tantrums, hopefully he or she will stop having them. If the problem requires achieving certain objectives in an academic area such as reading, hopefully the students for whom the objectives are intended will attain them.

In addition to having a role with regard to behavior change, the client should participate to varying degrees in establishing the goals of consultation and in designing and implementing plans to produce goal attainment (Ross, 1980). One way to initiate client participation is for the consultee to inform the client of his or her concerns and tentative plans related to consultation. Consider a teacher who was concerned about a child in her class who invariably complained whenever a new activity was introduced. If the teacher said, "It's time for us to work on social studies," the child would very likely mumble, "Oh no! Not that again." The teacher informed the child that her complaining was bothersome because it might have a negative effect on the motivation of the other students. The child could see the teacher's point and agreed that it would be beneficial to everyone concerned if she stopped complaining. The teacher then suggested a plan involving rewarding the child by allowing her to pursue an activity of her choice if she did not complain for a given period of time. To the teacher's surprise, the child wanted no part of the plan. In this regard, the little girl said something like, "If you give me a special privilege for not complaining, you'll be making a big deal out of my complaining to the other kids. I don't want to be made into a special case. I try not to complain, but the words just slip out of my mouth before I'm aware of what I've said." The teacher reported what the child had said, and after some discussion, the consultant and the teacher worked out a new plan. Whenever the teacher was about to introduce a new activity, she would signal to the child by establishing eye contact with her. This cue was the child's reminder not to complain.

There are often substantial benefits to be gained by involving children who are clients in the decisions made during the course of consultation. Most, if not all, theorists agree that a fundamental goal of socialization is to assist the child to acquire the ability to become an effective, self-directed individual. Involving the child in the decision-making process during consultation can afford the child valuable experiences in goal setting and in designing and implementing plans to achieve established goals. Although it is usually beneficial to involve children in consultation decisions, this may not always be the case. For example, a consultee may not want to call a child's attention to a problem because the child may not be able to interpret the problem accurately or because recognition of the problem may be emotionally upsetting to the child.

Goals of Consultation

Three goals have been advanced for behavioral consultation service (Bergan, 1977). One is to change client behavior. Another is to produce long-term positive change in the consultee (e.g., skills) and the third is to promote change in the social organization within which the consultee and the client are functioning.

Change in the Client

The principal goal of consultation is to produce a change in client behavior. When a mother seeks consultation services because her daughter overeats, she hopes that consultation will result in a reduction in such behavior. Similarly when a teacher seeks services because a child in his class cannot read, he hopes that consultation will promote the acquisition of the needed reading skills. Of course, it is assumed that socialization agents will have to change their own behavior or the environment to effect change in child behavior (see below).

Consultation for children and youths functioning as clients may cover a broad range of behaviors involving both the mental health and the educational development of the individual. Moreover, services may achieve the preventive as well as the remedial goals described earlier. The consultant may focus on the development of social or academic skills in children who are not currently having special learning or adjustment problems. On the other hand, consultation may be directed toward alleviating specific social, affective, or intellectual difficulties of a child or adolescent.

Change in the Consultee

Although the central objective of consultation is to produce change in the client, some writers in the field take the position that behavioral consultation should also focus on changing the consultee (Witt & Martens, 1988). Goals associated with changing the consultee may include modifications in the knowledge or skills of the consultee, changes in confidence in dealing with the client, or alterations in objectivity in relating to the client (Caplan, 1970; Meyers, Parsons, & Martin, 1979). For example, a teacher may acquire knowledge and skills by mastering a new teaching technique through consultation services. Likewise, consultation may focus on increasing a father's confidence in dealing with his son's aggressive behavior. Similarly, consultation may be directed at enhancing a teacher's objectivity regarding a child through a change in his or her feelings toward the child.

One basis for the view that consultation should focus on changing the consultee is the assumption that, in some cases, the principal source of client difficulties is the consultee. For instance, a consultee may seek services because he or she feels a lack of the necessary knowledge and/or skills to handle a particular problem (Meyers et al., 1979). Under these circumstances, the goal of consultation would be to provide the consultee with the missing information and/or competencies. Consider the case of a mother seeking to develop curiosity in her child and wondering how to go about it. A consultant might help the mother by teaching her to use modeling techniques to stimulate question asking on the part of the child (Henderson & Garcia, 1973).

A second basis for the position that consultation should focus on change in the consultee is the view that a change in the consultee may be beneficial to clients who are not directly involved in consultation. A young, inexperienced teacher, for example, may be having such extreme difficulties controlling a class that he or she seeks assistance from a consultant to learn classroom-management techniques. In a situation like this, the teacher's principal concern is not the behavior of a specific group of children. He or she hopes to acquire skills that will be applicable to a broad range of children in a variety of situations.

Organizational Change

Some theorists (e.g., Schmuck, 1982) take the position that a central goal of consultation should be to produce change in the social organization in which the client and the consultee function. Consultation, for instance, may be provided to educators for the purpose of changing organizational aspects of a school.

The major goals that have been advocated with respect to organizational change fall into two broad categories: communication and problem solving. Communication goals deal with the effectiveness of communication among different components of an organization. Attempts to increase communication effectiveness focus primarily on increasing the ability of individuals to interpret the messages of others accurately. For example, an administrator may have a totally inaccurate perception of teachers' views regarding some aspect of an educational program. In this case, consultation might focus on providing the administrator with skills in interpreting the teachers' communications. Efforts to improve communication may also focus on providing skills in communicating to others. For example, teachers might be taught techniques for increasing the level of participation of all individuals in group meetings with the principal.

Behavioral consultation incorporates several goals in the area of problem solving. Among these goals include providing organizational groups with skills in defining problems, actively attempting to solve problems, and evaluating whether problem solutions have been attained. For example, administrators and teachers in a school might be given training in the formulation of objectives for a school program and the measurement of performance with respect to these objectives. They might then be introduced to techniques of problem analysis and the design and implementation of intervention strategies. Finally, they might be given skills in evaluating problem solutions.

Consultation in Applied Settings

Consultation may be rendered to families in a community by private practitioners or by consultants employed in various community agencies. In addition, consultation is often provided in educational settings either by professionals working within such settings or by outside consultants. When rendered in an educational institution, consultation may be offered at different levels in the institutional hierarchy.

Consultation at the Administrative or Systems Level

In the simplest case, consultation at the administrative level is rendered to one administrator. The clients may be staff members and/or children. An example would be a school principal seeking consultation services with respect to the design of an in-service program for the teachers in proactive classroom management or regarding some aspect of child development.

In many instances, consultation at the administrative level involves several administrators as well as other staff members. Under these conditions, the administrators and the staff involved serve as consultees. A consultant, for example, might be called on to assist in the development and evaluation of a new mathematics program for a school. In a situation like this, the consultant would probably work jointly with administrators and teachers on the formulation of the program objectives, the specification of plans to achieve the objectives, and the design of evaluation procedures to measure the attainment of the objectives. Within institutions such as schools, some consultation at the administrative level is essential to the conduct of effective services. If, for instance, a consultant is to render effective services to teachers regarding the problems they face in working with children, it is useful to precede those services by consultation with the administrators of those schools (Ponti, Zins, & Graden, 1988). The focus of this consultation should be on the establishment of priorities and objectives regarding the services to be rendered. The consultant might meet with the school principal and staff to discuss objectives regarding the kinds of problems of most concern within the school. This kind of discussion would provide focus for consultation efforts and would do much to ensure administrative and staff support for the consultation services to be rendered.

The central consultation problem faced at the administrative level deals with possible conflicting expectations of the consultant held by administration, staff, and students (Hughes, 1987). For example, an administrator receiving consultation may believe that a consultant should openly discuss problems brought up in staff or student consultations. On the other hand, staff and students may believe that issues discussed in their respective consultation sessions should be treated as confidential. Guidelines governing the conduct of consultation should be spelled out in advance to minimize confusion regarding expectations in consultation. Consultees have a right to know what can be communicated in confidence and what cannot.

Consider the following situation. A consultant was rendering services at the administrative level aimed in part at reducing the use of drugs in a high school. One aspect of the program involved consultation at the student level to deal with individual drug-related problems. The guidelines established for services at the student level specified the conditions under which information given in consultation would be treated as confidential. In one case, a high-school girl sought consultation services to change the perception of her peers regarding her use of drugs. The girl quite reasonably conceptualized the school as being divided into two camps; students who used drugs and students who did not. She wanted to stop using drugs but noted that, if she did, she would have no friends. Her argument was that the drug users would not accept her because she had given up drugs and that the nonusers would not accept her because of her bad reputation. Thus, her goals were: (1) to stop using drugs, and (2) to change the views of her peers who did not use drugs. In one consultation session, the girl said to the consultant, "I want to tell you something in strictest confidence, so you must promise not to tell anyone, especially not Mr. Trueblood [the principal] or my parents." The consultant responded, "As long as I can be sure that what you tell me doesn't involve harm to you or to someone else, I will not reveal what you have told me, but if I feel that this is not the case, I will have to tell the appropriate persons what I know." As it happened, the information she communicated did not indicate possible harm to herself or to anyone else. The reader may or may not agree with the consultant's position in the above example. However, the consultant made her position clear to the consultee and to Mr. Trueblood.

Consultation at the Staff or Parent Level

In consultation at the staff and/or parent level, the consultees are individuals who function as change agents with respect to the behavior of children. Classroom teachers are the most obvious examples of professional consultees in this category. Specialists such as speech therapists, reading teachers, social workers, and nurses are also included in the category of staff consultees.

Consultation at the staff or parent level often involves a single consultee. However, in some instances, a number of consultees may be involved. For example, a junior- or senior-high-school student may have four or five teachers concerned about some aspects of his or her behavior. In these circumstances, all of the concerned teachers may be consultees. As another example, consultation may be implemented conjointly with teacher and parent, a procedure that is likely to facilitate generalization across settings (Sheridan, Kratochwill, & Elliott, 1990).

Similarly, consultation at the staff or parent level may focus on one client, a small group of clients, or a relatively large number of clients. For example, a teacher may be concerned about the behavior of one child in a class or may be concerned about the performance of the entire class. A parent may be concerned about managing the family environment, which includes several children.

The central advantage of consultation at the staff level is that it may increase the probability that the individual needs of clients will be met. For example, when a teacher seeks consultation to help a child develop greater self-confidence or to assist a child to learn socialization skills with other children, the results of consultation may have a direct and highly significant impact on the functioning of that child. By contrast, consultation given at the administrative level may do little or nothing to meet the special needs of any one child or specific group of children. Likewise, administrative consultation aimed at increasing communication skills in a school staff may have little impact on a child who has a fear of coming to school or who is trying to stop using drugs.

The main problem associated with consultation services at the staff or parent level is ensuring that services will be used when they are needed. Two critical related variables include the skills and efficiency of the consultant in rendering services (Bergan & Tombari, 1976). A consultant who is unsure of his or her consultation skills may avoid rendering consultation services whenever possible. Similarly, if teachers are aware that services are inefficient or that the consultant is not effective in interviewing or in applying psychological principles in problem solving, they may be reluctant to refer cases for consultation. When conditions like these prevail, the psychologist must find avenues to improve her or his functioning as a behavioral consultant in the schools (e.g., must supplement training or acquire information).

Consultation at the Student Level

Consultation services may be rendered directly to a child or an adolescent, usually when the individual has been referred or has sought services in an effort to solve a personal problem. An adolescent may be having academic problems or difficulties getting along with parents or peers and, as a consequence, may seek psychological services. The relationship becomes consultative when, in the course of problem solving, it becomes apparent that there is a need to change the manner in which others interact with the individual. For example, a seventh-grade girl was referred for psychological services because she was having difficulty getting along with her classmates. In the course of discussing her difficulties, the child indicated that her classmates were always talking about her behind her back and that this behavior was extremely annoying to her. After some discussion, it was decided that an attempt should be made to reduce the incidence of this noxious peer behavior. An analysis of the problem revealed that the child reacted to behind-the-back remarks by displaying anger toward her peers. The consultant pointed out that the child's anger might be reinforcing the noxious peer behavior. Thus, it was decided that the child should try to ignore her peers whenever they seemed to be talking about her behind her back. The girl indicated that this would be very difficult because she did not think she could control her anger. The consultant then asked her to name some experiences that were extremely pleasant and enjoyable to her and told the girl to try to think of those whenever she felt that peer behavior was about to make her angry. This plan worked quite well; within a few days, the girl's peers had almost completely stopped saying things behind her back.

Consultation at the student level has a number of advantages. First, it provides the child an adult support person who is willing to act on the child's behalf without an imposition of adult goals. Children are surrounded by adults who feel it is their responsibility to tell children what to do. In consultation rendered to a child consultee, the child is the principal determiner of what should be done.

A second advantage of consultation at the student level is that it affords the child the experience of working with an adult as a colleague. The child will probably regard the consultant as having authority by virtue of his or her status as an adult. Nevertheless, the collegial relationship characteristic of the consultant–consultee roles prevail: The child is the decision maker and plan implementer, and the consultant guides the consultation process and assists the child in principles of psychology that may be useful in problem solving.

Another advantage of consultation at the student level is that it gives the child the experience of controlling his or her environmental circumstances. For instance, in the example given previously, the child found out that she could do something to improve the quality of her experiences in school.

A final advantage of student-level consultation is that it may give a child skills that can be used in controlling his or her own behavior. These skills can also influence the reactions of others to the child. For instance, the above child learned a technique to control her own anger and to influence the reactions of her classmates.

One potential problem of consultation at the student level is that it may not provide the same efficiency of services as other forms of consultation. Consultation rendered at the administrative or staff level may affect a number of children, whereas consultation at the student level generally influences only a single individual.

A PROBLEM-SOLVING MODEL FOR BEHAVIORAL CONSULTATION

Consultation can be conducted in a variety of ways. Some theorists suggest the use of a mental-health model of consultation that emphasizes the role of internal pathological states in controlling behavior (Caplan, 1970; Lambert, 1974). Others view consultation as a tool for promoting the development of educational organizations (Broskowski, 1973; Rhodes, 1974; Schmuck, 1982). These theorists suggest that changes aimed at improving the functioning of educational systems have a beneficial effect on the children and youths served by such systems.

Behavioral consultation is conceived of in this book in terms of a problem-solving model (Bergan, 1970, 1977; Bergan & Dunn, 1976; Bergan & Tombari, 1975). This model was designed to help consultees define the problems they face in working with clients, to formulate and implement plans to solve problems, to assess the effectiveness of the plans implemented, and to evaluate the attainment of consultation goals.

Consultative problem-solving may be used in helping parents solve problems involving their children. It may also be applied in educational settings at all three levels in the institutional hierarchy. A consultant might use the model to assist an administrator and a school staff member to solve a problem relating to some aspect of an instructional program. Similarly, he or she might use the approach to work with a teacher in solving a problem involving an individual student. Finally, the consultant might work with a student on a problem that the child is having with friends, family, or teachers.

Distinctive Features of Consultative Problem-Solving

Several related features of consultative problem-solving can markedly affect the nature of behavioral consultation. First, the model depicts the consultee as a problem solver and involves him or her in the problem-solving process. The consultee is not merely the passive recipient of advice. The consultee defines the problem of concern in consultation and plays an active role in designing the plan to solve the problem. He or she is responsible for plan implementation, and for making the final decisions regarding the extent of problem solution and plan effectiveness.

A second feature of the model is that it encourages the development of problem-solving skills in the client. The client may be involved in the problem-solving process in essentially the same way as the consultee. The extent of his or her involvement may vary as a function of his or her developmental level, the nature of the problem, and the views of the consultee on how much responsibility children and youths should be given in managing their own affairs. Nevertheless, as noted in the previous section, the client may be involved to some degree in problem identification, plan design and implementation, and problem evaluation.

A third aspect of the model is that it provides a means of promoting the use of a broad range of psychological principles in the socialization of the young. The consultant in this case is engaged in a knowledge-linking role (Havelock, 1969). Consultants provide a medium through which knowledge producers can communicate information to knowledge consumers. Insofar as a consultant relies on knowledge associated with narrow theoretical positions, his or her ability to make useful information available to consultees is highly restricted. On the other hand, if the consultant is encouraged to make use of a broad range of principles in consultation, his or her ability to meet the needs of clients should be enhanced.

Another characteristic of the model is that it links decision making to empirical evidence. Decisions related to problem definition, plan effectiveness, and problem solution are all based on a direct observation of client behavior. Furthermore, decisions regarding plan design incorporate knowledge from scientific investigations of human behavior. As indicated earlier, the strategy of using scientific findings as a basis for formulating consultation plans should increase the likelihood of plan success. The approach of buttressing this strategy with empirical evidence regarding client behavior provides corrective feedback that further enhances the probability of goal attainment.

A fifth feature of the consultative problem-solving model is that it defines problems presented in consultation as being related to person–environment interactions. The strategy of describing a problem as requiring an elimination of the discrepancy between existing and desired behavior places problems within an environmental context. For example, in consultative problem solving, one could not legitimately say, "Bobby's problem is that he is mentally retarded" or "Bobby's problem is that he has a learning disability." These statements attempt to describe Bobby, but they do not state specifically what his problems are. To say that Bobby is mentally retarded or learning-disabled does not indicate in any precise way what his current behavior is or specify standards of acceptable behavior toward which he may aspire.

Placing problems within a behavioral framework puts the responsibility for achieving problem solutions on the participants in consultation. When problems are defined only as internal conditions, it may be assumed that little can be done to change the condition of the client. In these cases, participants in consultation may abrogate their problem solving responsibilities.

A sixth characteristic of consultative problem-solving is that it emphasizes the role of environmental factors in controlling behavior. The participants can alter some aspect of the environment in the hope of changing an internal state believed to control behavior, or they can attempt to influence behavior directly. For example, an attempt might be made to change a boy's academic performance by changing his attitude toward school or by changing what he does in school. The former of these two approaches is circuitous. Whenever possible, it is better to change behavior directly rather than indirectly. The large quantities of basic and applied research amassed in the field of behavioral psychology suggest that, in many cases, it is possible to bring about marked changes in behavior by altering environmental conditions. Consultative problem-solving is designed to take advantage of these research findings.

A final characteristic of the consultative problem-solving approach is that it focuses evaluation on goal attainment and plan effectiveness rather than on the individual characteristics of the client. This approach emphasizes what the participants in consultation have accomplished, rather than problems within the client. Psychological reports in consultation become a source of information regarding problem solution, rather than a repository of extended narratives about client deficiencies.

Goals of Consultative Problem-Solving

The consultative problem-solving approach assumes that the activities of consultation are goal-directed. In every case, the procedure in consultation is to find a way to alter an existing set of circumstances in the direction of goal attainment. Thus, if a teacher seeks consultation concerning a child in his class because the child is having severe spelling difficulties, the goal will be to alleviate these difficulties and the problem will be to find a way to achieve this goal.

Problem Solving to Promote Mental Health and Educational Development

One critical question regarding goals is: What kinds of goals ought to be pursued in consultation? The goals of consultative problem-solving are to promote the mental health and the educational development of children and youths. In pursuing its broad goals, consultative problem-solving may focus on issues involving prevention and/or remediation. The range of problems may include all phases of social, emotional, and intellectual growth. Thus, in carrying out consultative problem-solving, a consultant may find himself or herself helping a parent to control a child's aggressive behavior or helping a school use problem-solving techniques to enhance the academic accomplishments of students in one or more areas of the school curriculum.

Goals Defined in Behavioral Terms

Within the consultative problem-solving model, the immediate goals of consultation are defined in objective terms to the degree possible. Also, consultation is aimed at producing clearly specified changes in behavior. For example, the goal of reducing a child's aggressiveness might be defined in terms of reductions in hitting behavior.

The strategy of defining immediate consultation goals in behavioral terms stands in sharp contrast to the widely followed practice of conceptualizing goals in terms of the alleviation of pathological states or traits within the individual. Many writers have described the implications of conceptualizing problem behaviors in terms of pathological states rather than simply in terms of behavior change. The pathological-state approach is generally referred to as the medical model of behavior (Kazdin, 1978; Krasner & Ullmann, 1965). The central assumption underlying this model is that maladaptive behaviors are symptomatic of an underlying pathological condition within the individual. In accordance with this assumption, behavioral symptoms identified in consultation are often labeled to indicate the specific pathological state from which the individual is suffering.

The practice of conceptualizing consultation goals in behavioral terms may minimize the labeling of children. When goals are specified in behavioral terms, there is no assumption that behavior is symptomatic of an underlying pathological condition. Therefore, there is no need to label the children whose behavior is of concern in consultation. Behavioral goals describe the client as changing his or her behavior in a desired fashion. The emphasis is on what the individual accomplishes in the course of behavior change, not on a pathology presumed to underlie the position from which he or she started.

Types of Consultative Problem-Solving

Consultative problem-solving may focus on the achievement of long-range developmental goals for children and youths, or it may center on specific problems of immediate concern to the client and consultee. These differences require variations in the consultative problem-solving process.

Developmental Consultation

Developmental consultation is concerned with changes in behavior that generally require a relatively long period of time. For example, a parent concerned about the emotional development of his child might establish several goals that could take a number of months to achieve.

The focus of developmental consultation is invariably on the attainment of one or more long-range objectives. Moreover, the achievement of each of these long-range goals generally requires a mastery of subordinate objectives that are hierarchically related to the long-range goals. For example, one long-range objective in the area of emotional development might be a reduction in a child's school-related fear reactions. The achievement of this goal might involve a number of subordinate goals, such as minimizing a fear of interacting with other children and minimizing a fear of riding the bus to school. Each of these subordinate goals might be broken down further into subgoals. Thus, fear of interacting with peers might include interactions in the presence of an adult and interactions occurring without benefit of adult supervision.

Developmental consultation generally requires *reiterative* applications of the consultative problem-solving model. For example, consultation may focus initially on one or two specific behaviors related to a given subordinate objective. All phases of the problem-solving process would be implemented in an effort to achieve the goals established with respect to these behaviors. After goal attainment has occurred, problem solving aimed at changing other behaviors related to subordinate objectives would be undertaken. Hopefully, reiterative applications of the problem-solving process would continue until all of the objectives of developmental consultation have been achieved.

Problem-Centered Consultation

Many of the problems presented in consultation call for action regarding a limited number of specific behaviors of immediate concern to the consultee. Consultation for problems of this kind may be described as problem-centered consultation. Consider the following case. A teacher who was obviously extremely upset called a consultant to discuss the behavior of a girl in her class. During the initial interview with the consultee, the consultant found that the girl frequently made violent assaults on other children in the school. In the most recent assault, the girl had got into a fight with another girl and had slit the other child's throat with a razor blade. She then informed her teacher that, because she felt sorry for the other child, she had lifted her hair out of the way before she slashed her. "At least she won't have to get a new hairdo," she said. The injured girl was taken to the hospital immediately and treated for her wounds. The girl who had slashed the child was remanded to the custody of the juvenile authorities in the community. However, within a few days, both children were back in school; in the teacher's view, the probability of further explosive behavior was frighteningly high.

In cases such as this, the consultant's initial task is to deal with the immediate presenting problem. Thus, the consultant and the consultee in the above example chose to focus exclusively on eliminating the child's aggression.

Theoretical Influences on Consultative Problem-Solving

Consultative problem-solving is a form of behavioral consultation. Thus, it has been strongly influenced by behavioral theory and research (Kazdin, 1989). General systems theory has also played a major role in shaping the model.

The Influence of Systems Theory

Consultative problem-solving is one of a number of approaches based on systems theory notions concerning problem solving (e.g., Flanagan,

1970; Glaser & Nitko, 1971; Kaufman, 1971). Systems theory deals with the functioning of interrelated components comprising an organized structure. System theorists assume that system functioning is generally governed by feedback providing information on the extent to which system activities conform to constraints associated with system operations. System theory models of the problem-solving process conceive of problem solving as an activity in which feedback is used to produce operations conforming to the constraint of achieving a solution. Systems theory models describe the problem-solving process as a series of discrete steps. The steps generally include (1) the identification of the problem to be solved; (2) the formulation of a plan to achieve problem solution; (3) implementation of the plan; (4) an evaluation to determine whether a solution has been attained; and (5) revision in one or more phases of problem solving, when necessary, to increase the likelihood of achieving problem solution.

Systems concepts in the area of problem solving outline a basic approach to achieving the goals of consultation. When consultees seek consultation services, it is generally because they have a problem that they have not been able to solve. Often, they feel that more effective problem-solving will occur through consultation than would otherwise be possible. Systems theory provides detailed guidelines for approaching the problem-solving task to be pursued in consultation.

The Influence of Behavioral Psychology

The central contribution of the behavioral viewpoint to consultative problem-solving is a knowledge base that can be used in the design of plans targeted at the problems presented in consultation. Behavioral research covers an enormous domain, including both basic and applied studies. Results of behavioral investigations have provided an abundance of information that can be and have been effectively applied in socialization (Gelfand & Hartmann, 1984; Hughes, 1987; Kazdin, 1989; Morris & Kratochwill, 1984). At the heart of behavioral consultation is the application of the technology from applied behavior analysis. The premises on which the model of applied behavior analysis lies and that have direct relevance to the applications of behavioral consultation in applied settings have been advanced by Lentz and Shapiro (1985). These premises, with our revisions and extensions, are as follows:

1. A major goal of psychological service in the school and community is the prevention, identification, and remediation (or treatment) of educational, social, and behavioral problems of children and consultees (teachers and parents).
2. Children who are experiencing problems should receive psychological or psychoeducational services independent of labeling or placement in special-education settings.

3. To design effective treatments, the procedures of broad-based behavioral assessment should be used (Shapiro, 1987; Shapiro & Kratochwill, 1988). In this regard, the problems must be "(a) operationally defined and directly measured, (b) data must be collected
that allow analysis of the problem in terms of maintaining environmental events, (c) levels of problem behaviors must be compared to
desired levels and operational goals must be directly used to develop and implement remedial plans, and (d) performance data
should continue to be regularly collected so that treatment can be
evaluated" (Lentz & Shapiro, 1985, p. 199).

4. Following the behavioral assessment, treatment plans are implemented within the context of the resources needed to implement
them.

5. Traditional assessment strategies (e.g., IQ tests and norm-referenced tests) can be used to supplement behavioral consultation, but
they are primarily useful in describing legal eligibility for special
education.

6. A child's failure to perform adequately in the instructional environment is due to environmental events in the child's settings. A good
predictor of success in a classroom setting is the outcome from
interventions in that setting.

7. There is a sequence of events that can lead to logical decisions
related to remediation in appropriate settings and that meets the
spirit of Public Law 94-142. Figure 1-1 illustrates a flowchart of a
behavioral model of psychological services in schools. The model
presented in Figure 1-1 also illustrates an application of a procedure
for fitting behavioral consultation within prereferral interventions.
A more detailed discussion of the model is presented in Lentz and
Shapiro (1985) and in Shapiro (1987).

Use of the behavioral knowledge base in plan design has the advantage of producing plans based on principles that have been found to be
effective in controlled studies. Plans based on research findings should
have a greater likelihood of success than plans derived from informal
sources of knowledge, such as clinical experience.

Of course, a great deal of experimental research has been conducted
outside the behavioral tradition that has implications for intervention plan
design. Heavy reliance on behavioral research findings does not imply that
research outside the behavioral framework should be ignored. On the
contrary, research from a variety of theoretical positions may be usefully
applied in behavioral consultation. For example, Gettinger (1988) provided
an overview of classroom management strategies that extend beyond the
usual applications of applied behavior analysis.

A second contribution of behavioral psychology to consultative problem-solving is that it offers a technology for evaluating the effectiveness of

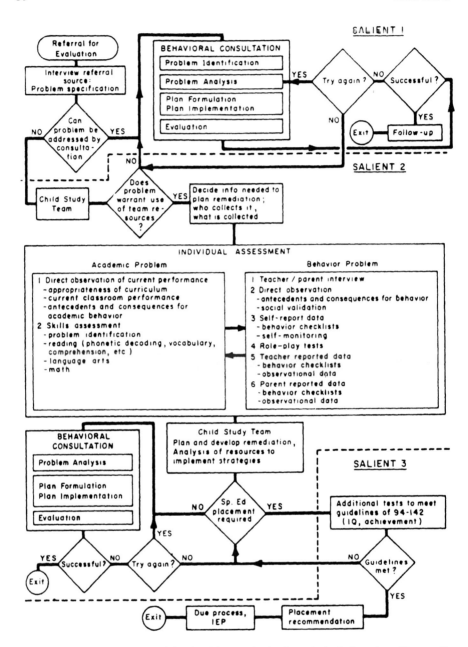

FIGURE 1-1. A behavioral model for the delivery of school psychological services. [Source: F. E. Lentz & E. S. Shapiro. (1985). Behavioral School psychology: A conceptual model for the delivery of psychological services. In T. R. Kratochwill (Ed.), *Advances in School Psychology* (Vol. 4, pp. 191–222). Hillsdale, NJ: Lawrence Erlbaum Associates. Reproduced by permission.]

implemented plans. Although the main concern of participants in consultation generally centers on achieving a problem solution, there may also be an interest in determining the influence of the plan on goal attainment. Of course, it is quite possible for a problem to be solved in the absence of any influence of the plan selected. For instance, a child whose reading difficulties are the focus of consultation may improve in reading as a result of watching educational television rather than as a consequence of a plan devised in consultation. If those involved in consultation wish to obtain some indication of plan effectiveness, they must find a means of separating plan influences from other sources of influence. The experimental methodology developed largely within the behavioral tradition provides a vehicle that can be used to evaluate plan effectiveness in consultation (Barlow, Hayes, & Nelson, 1984).

Stages in the Problem-Solving Process

As shown in Figure 1-2, there are four stages in consultative problemsolving: (1) problem identification; (2) problem analysis; (3) plan implementation; and (4) problem evaluation. These stages describe the steps necessary to move from an initial designation of the problem of concern through the development and implementation of a plan designed to achieve problem solution, to the evaluation of goal attainment and plan effectiveness. These stages often overlap in practice and are not discrete.

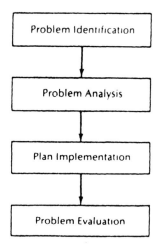

FIGURE 1-2. Stages in consultative problem-solving.

Problem Identification

Problem identification is the specification of the problem(s) to be solved in consultation. A problem is defined as the necessity of eliminating the discrepancy between observed behavior and desired or expected behavior (Kaufman, 1971). For example, if a child is throwing temper tantrums every night at bedtime and his parents wish that he would never throw a temper tantrum again, a problem exists. Their problem is to devise a way to stop the tantrums and thereby restore peace in their home.

Problem identification is achieved primarily by means of a problem-identification interview (PII). In the PII, the consultant assists the consultee to describe the problem of concern to him or her. In the case of the child having tantrums, the consultant might say, "Tell me some of the things that Bobby does when he has a temper tantrum." A request such as this leads the consultee to provide a precise description of the specific tantrum behaviors that are to be the focus of consultation.

After the concerns of the consultee have been explored in some depth, the focus of the PII shifts to a discussion of the procedures to be used in measuring the current status or baseline level of the behaviors to be changed through consultation so that (1) the existence of the problem can be validated, and (2) goals for assessing treatment efficacy can be established. In the case of the temper tantrum illustration, the consultant and the consultee would discuss procedures for measuring the incidence of tantrums over a period of a few days.

Problem identification is completed when it is established that there are sufficient data to determine if there is a discrepancy between the current and the desired level of incidence of the behaviors of concern. Thus, if our tantrum child were having an average of six tantrums a day and his parents felt that even one tantrum a day constituted an intolerable situation, it could be said that the goal had been defined.

Problem Analysis

When a problem has been identified, consultation proceeds to problem analysis. The purposes of problem analysis are (1) to identify variables that may facilitate the achievement of a problem solution, and (2) to develop a plan to solve the problem specified in the problem identification phase of consultation. Problem analysis is accomplished primarily through a problem analysis interview (PAI). In the PAI, the consultant and the consultee discuss client and consultee skills and/or environmental conditions that may influence client behavior. In this discussion, the consultant brings his or her knowledge of psychology to bear on the problem presented. For example, in the temper tantrum case, the consultant would draw on his or her knowledge of behavioral principles to ascertain the conditions that may be controlling the tantrum behavior. In this connection, he or she might ask the consultee what activities or behavior generally occur right before and right after the child has a tantrum. Questions regarding occurrences closely associated in time with tantrums will probably lead to hypotheses about environmental conditions that may be maintaining the tantrums. For example, the voluminous case histories in the behavior-modification literature suggest that tantrums are sometimes maintained by parents giving a lot of attention to the child (reinforcement) (Wolf, Risley, & Mees, 1964). Thus, the child's parents may have been reinforcing tantrums by reading him stories to quiet him down.

After hypotheses have been advanced regarding the kinds of factors that may influence client behavior, the discussion turns to the design of a plan to achieve problem solution. The consultee is generally the principal architect of the plan. The consultant assists the consultee to apply psychological and educational principles to the development of a specific set of tactics that will be put into effect to change client behavior. The consultant might say, "You indicated that your story reading might be a reward for Bobby's tantrums. How could you make story reading a consequence for appropriate bedtime behavior rather than for tantrums?" A question such as this would probably lead the consultee to specify a procedure that he or she would regard as an acceptable and appropriate step in the direction of solving the problem and, at the same time, would incorporate the insights of the consultant into the situation.

Plan Implementation

During the plan implementation phase of consultation, the consultee implements or supervises the implementation of the plan designed in problem analysis. Data collection generally continues so that the consultee will have some indication of the effectiveness of the plan.

The consultant's central task during plan implementation is to ensure that implementation will go as intended. To accomplish this task, the consultant usually checks briefly with the consultee to determine that there is agreement between the plan specified and the plan being implemented, and to deal with whatever unforeseen problems may have arisen in the implementation effort. Thus, the consultant in the tantrum case might call Bobby's mother or father to find out when story reading was occurring in relation to tantrums. If Bobby's mother said, "I tried not to read him a story, but he yelled for three hours. What could I do?" then the consultant would have either to attempt to get the parents to implement the plan as it was designed, or to face the problem of establishing a new plan.

Problem Evaluation

After a plan has been in effect for a suitable period, problem evaluation is undertaken to determine the extent of goal attainment and plan effectiveness. Problem evaluation takes place in a problem evaluation interview (PEI). In the PEI, the consultant and the consultee determine if problem solution has been achieved by comparing the data collected during plan implementation with the level of acceptable performance specified in problem identification.

If the goals established for consultation have been attained, consultation may terminate. However, other problems may be introduced. For example, in developmental cases, consultation may cover a series of problems, all of which are linked to a broad developmental goal. In a situation like this, each of the evaluation interviews in the series becomes a problem identification interview until all of the problems of concern have been addressed.

If the goals of consultation have not been achieved, consultation usually moves back to problem analysis so that the original plan can be revised or a new one constructed. For example, if the tactic of withdrawing story reading proved to be an impossible plan for Bobby's parents to implement, a new plan would have to be devised.

In some cases, even after one or more carefully developed plans have been implemented, there may still be virtually no progress toward goal attainment. Under these conditions, consultation may terminate, or the consultant and the consultee may go back to problem identification to define another problem related to client behavior.

In addition to evaluating the degree to which the consultation goals have been achieved, it also is usually advisable to evaluate the effectiveness of the plan used during the implementation phase of consultation. How plan evaluation is accomplished depends on the procedures that have been implemented to determine plan effectiveness. Some group experimental and quasi-experimental designs associated with research methods may be applied in consultation (Cook & Campbell, 1979; Kazdin, 1980d). However, many consultation cases involving the behavior of one client use a form of single-subject design. When this is the case, the evaluation generally involves making a judgment regarding changes in the level and the trend of the data series associated with plan implementation. For example, if the data collected indicated that Bobby's tantrums dropped off markedly during plan implementation, there would be some justification in assuming that the plan selected was an effective one.

If a plan seems to be working—that is, if behavior is clearly moving in the direction of goal attainment—the plan may be left in operation even if goal attainment has not yet occurred. Of course, if there is no suggestion that the plan has been effective, a change is warranted.

In the event that the goals of consultation have been attained and the evaluation suggests that the plan has had an influence on client behavior, the consultant and the consultee have gained information that may be useful in solving other problems. Knowledge that a plan has been effective generally has no direct influence on immediate decisions made in consultation. As discussion in the preceding paragraphs indicated, most of the decisions made during problem evaluation are based on information concerning goal attainment, not plan effectiveness. Nevertheless, if one looks beyond the problem of immediate concern, it is obvious that the evaluation of plan effectiveness provides important information to the consultant, the consultee, and the client. Without plan evaluation, the participants in consultation may persist in what is essentially superstitious behavior. That is, in the absence of plan evaluation, they run a significant risk of applying procedures that really had no effect on problem solution even though they happened to be associated in time with that desirable outcome. Insofar as they have been rewarded by goal attainment, they are likely to repeat the behaviors that led to that state of affairs in other similar situations.

2

Verbal Interaction Techniques in Consultation

Consultation, in large part, is a matter of verbal interchange between a consultant and a consultee. For example, a consultant may ask a parent about his or her child, and in response, the parent may say, "Ted is now 8 years old and he still has a bed-wetting problem." Despite the consultant's lack of direct involvement in the matter, what the consultant says to the parent and what the parent says to him or her may well determine whether the bed-wetting will continue. Because of its potential effects on treatment outcomes, *what* is said during consultation must be structured in some way. The consultant must have sufficient knowledge of the nature of his or her verbal behavior and must be able to control verbalizations in a manner that maximizes the probability that clear and appropriate information will be gathered that will increase consultation effectiveness.

Behavioral theory and research indicate that the first step toward achieving control of behavior is to specify it in measurable terms. In order to achieve control over the consultant's own verbal utterances emitted during consultation, the consultant must be able to measure the extent to which he or she uses various types of verbalizations during consultation interviews. For example, a question such as "What do you do immediately after Bobby begins to cry at bedtime?" is likely to be more useful in identifying consequent events than the query "How does Bobby's crying make you feel?" The first question would produce information about events controlling Bobby's crying behavior, but the second probably would not. The second question may still be a useful one, but for obtaining qualitatively different information. Insofar as questions about conditions associated with behavior contribute to the purpose of behavioral consultation, it is important for a consultant to be able to measure the extent to which he or she uses verbalizations of this kind in consultation. Likewise, insofar as questions about the feelings of the consultee do not generally contribute directly to achieving the goals of behavioral consultation, it is important for a consultant not to use questions of this type excessively or as the primary focus in interviews. Such questions may, however, be important during the initial phases of consultation when a relationship is being established.

Consultant control of verbal behavior during consultation necessitates not only recognition of the *types* of verbal utterances that have occurred during interviews, but also the ability to *produce different kinds* of verbalizations to meet specific interviewing needs. If a consultant is trying to elicit information about the conditions controlling client behavior, he or she must be able to produce the type of verbal utterance most appropriate for this particular goal. A question such as "What do you do when Bobby starts to cry?" will probably produce more information about conditions associated with Bobby's behavior than a question such as "Do you tend to ignore Bobby's crying?" The first question permits a range of possible answers; the second calls for one of two alternatives: yes or no. To be an effective interviewer, a consultant must be able to produce utterances that will elicit the specific information needed. In this chapter, we discuss procedures that consultants can use to increase their ability to control their production of the different types of verbalizations used in behavioral consultation.

MESSAGE CLASSIFICATION

Methods for classifying verbal interactions in interviews have a long history in psychology. They evolved from an interest in gaining an increased understanding of verbal interchange in psychotherapy. Not surprisingly, the various systems developed to categorize verbal statements occurring during therapy sessions have reflected the particular interests of the investigators who designed the systems. For example, Porter (1943) developed a system to explore the degree of responsibility assumed by the therapist in an interview, Bales (1950) constructed a system that focused on problem solving, and Dollard and Mowrer (1947) developed a system to investigate the level of drive revealed by a client in a therapy session.

The classification system described in this book reflects our point of view regarding the importance of verbal behavior during behavioral consultation. The system is intended to articulate with the four-stage problem-solving model described in Chapter 1. It was designed both as a research tool and as a training tool. The classification system has been useful in studies of the relation between what is said during consultation and the outcomes of consultations. We also believe that individuals attempting to learn how to be effective consultants benefit from a system that enables

TABLE 2-1. Message Classification Categories and Subcategories

Categories	Message source	Message content	Message process	Message control
Subcategories	Consultant Consultee	Background environment Behavior setting Behavior Individual characteristics Observation Plan Other	Specification Evaluation Inference Summarization Validation	Elicitor Emitter

them to analyze the verbal behavior that occurs during consultation (Kratochwill, VanSomeren, & Sheridan, 1989). More will be said about training and models of training consultants in Chapter 9. At this point, we emphasize that specific training in the consultation-analysis coding system introduced in this chapter is very helpful in the training of consultants. Other training procedures are available and are discussed in more detail in Chapter 9.

The consultation analysis system allows the classification of verbal interchange in terms of four categories: (1) source; (2) content; (3) process; and (4) control. These four categories and the subcategories associated with them are shown in Table 2-1. The *source* category indicates the person speaking. *Content* refers to what is being talked about. *Process* indicates the kind of verbal action conveyed in a message, and *control* refers to the potential influence of a verbalization by one participant in consultation on what will be said or done by another participant.

Message Source

There are generally only two roles for individuals involved in a consultation interview: consultants and consultees. A brief description of each of these sources of verbal messages is presented next.

The Consultant Source

As indicated in Chapter 1, a psychological consultant is a professional who renders psychological services to a consultee, who is responsible for some phase of the learning or development of a client. Individuals who function in the consultant role are classified as consultants in the source category.

The many readers who either are psychological consultants or aspire to this role may question the need to belabor the matter of labeling consultants further. However, there are cases in which it is somewhat difficult to determine who should be classified as a consultant. For example, suppose that a school psychologist, a counselor, a speech therapist, and a teacher are discussing a child's learning problems. Who should be categorized as a consultant in this situation? The answer is that those people who are rendering professional services to individuals functioning as change agents with respect to the child should be labeled consultants. Any or all of the professionals described here could function as consultants. For example, the teacher might be providing professional advice to the speech therapist, who is giving direct educational services to the child. On the other hand, the speech therapist might be advising the counselor concerning speech difficulties that may be associated with emotional reactions in the child. The key factor in determining whether an individual should be classified as a consultant is the kind of responsibility the individual has in the situation. If his or her responsibility is to provide services to a change agent, then he or she is a consultant.

As this example implies, there may be more than one consultant in an interview session. Under these conditions, each consultant is assigned a number for coding purposes.

The Consultee Source

Individuals who function as change agents with respect to the behavior of a client are classified as consultees. Parents and teachers are among the most frequent consultees when services are rendered to children and youths. However, professionals such as school psychologists or counselors may function as consultees in those instances in which they provide direct services to a client and receive consultation from another professional. This latter option may occur in cases of professional supervision roles in consultation (Knoff, 1986; Kratochwill, Bergan, & Mace, 1981).

In some cases, the consultee and the client may be the same individual. This situation arises when the client takes the responsibility for effecting changes in his or her own learning or development. In this case, clients participating in consultation interviews are coded within the consultee category.

As in the case of the consultant classification, more than one consultee may participate in an interview. When this happens, each consultee is assigned a number for coding purposes.

Message Content

It is reasonable to assume that what a consultant and a consultee talk about during consultation will have a substantial impact on the outcome of consultation. The range of topics that may be discussed is, of course, unlimited. However, there are certain constraints that tend to narrow the scope of conversation considerably and thereby make it possible to code interview content. For example, in part as a result of the consultee's concern and in part as a result of the consultant's professional responsibility, consultants and consultees generally focus the majority of their comments on the client's problem or on matters at least tangentially related to it. There may be a few asides about the recent teacher strike, the rising crime rate, how difficult it is to raise children today, each other's good health, and so on; yet, the discussion tends to gravitate toward the problem at hand.

One of the major factors that may influence interview content is the theoretical orientation of the consultant. If the consultant favors one of the cognitive or psychodynamic theories that views behavior as a manifestation of controlling mechanisms operating within the organism, then his or her conversation will probably focus on topics relating to such mechanisms. On the other hand, if the consultant adheres to one of the behavioral viewpoints that emphasizes environmental determinants of action, then his or her conversation will probably focus on behavior and the environmental conditions that may control it.

The content categories selected for use in consultation analysis have been chosen to represent the broad range of theoretical perspectives that consultants bring to the consultation process and to reflect the things that need to be discussed to implement the consultative problem-solving model described in Chapter 1. As shown in Table 2-1, there are seven content categories. The "Background environment" and "Individual characteristics" classifications were included in deference to the interests of organismic theorists. (The behavior-setting and behavior categories are of special interest to organismic theorists.) The "Behavior setting" and "Behavior" categories are also of special interest to the various types of behavioral theorists. The "Observation" and "Plan" categories are intended to represent the proclivities of consultants of many theoretical persuasions to gather data on client behavior and to formulate a plan to solve the client's problem. The "Other" category was included to handle those few utterances that may occur in an interview about matters that do not fall in the other six content classifications.

The Background Environment Subcategory

Verbalizations concerning "remote" environmental conditions related to behavior are categorized in the background environment subcategory. Background-environmental conditions may be remote in time or location or both. For example, a consultant might ask about some event that occurred earlier in the life of the child that may affect his or her current behavior. On the other hand, the consultant might show an interest in current home conditions that could influence the child's actions at school. In either case, the consultant's verbalizations would be coded in the background environment subcategory.

Some examples of background environment verbalizations should enable the reader to code them accurately when there is occasion to do so. Each of the examples that follow has been coded in the process and control categories as well as in the content category so that readers may have a broad range of illustrations to refer to.

As a first illustration of the use of the background environment subcategory, consider an organismically oriented consultant concerned with the possible physical causes of attention problems. An individual with a theoretical persuasion of this sort might say, "Tell me something about the conditions surrounding Bob's birth" (background-environment-specification elicitor). The intent of this type of question may be to ascertain possible sources of brain injury. The assumption underlying the question is that brain injury may cause excessive activity in the child.

As another illustration, consider the psychodynamically oriented consultant concerned with Freudian concepts such as sibling rivalry. A consultant with this viewpoint might open a discussion of sibling relationships with an innocuous question such as "How many brothers and sisters does Carol have?" (background-environment-specification elicitor). Or in response to probes about sibling relations from a consultant, a consultee might say, "I am unhappy about the way Alice's sisters treat her at home" (background-environment negative-evaluation emitter).

Explorations of parent–child relationships, which, like sibling rivalry, are a major concern of psychodynamically oriented theorists, might lead to a consultee question such as "Why do you think Bob's father used to beat him?" (background-environment-inference elicitor). Or after a prolonged discussion of parent–child relationships, a psychodynamically oriented consultant might say, "You indicated that when Carol gets home after school there generally isn't anyone around" (background-environment-summarization emitter).

The Behavior Setting Subcategory

The behavior setting subcategory includes verbalizations referring to antecedent, consequent, and sequential conditions occurring contiguously with a client's behavior. Antecedent conditions are those events which occur before a client behavior. Consequent conditions are events that occur immediately after client behavior. Sequential conditions indicate the time of the day or the day of the week when the behavior of concern typically occurs or the patterning of antecedent and/or consequent conditions across a series of occasions.

Behavioral consultants view conditions in the immediate environment in which behavior occurs as the central determinants of behavior. Accordingly, they are generally interested in obtaining information regarding all three of the types of conditions represented in the behavior setting subcategory. They are often concerned about *antecedent conditions* that identify factors that may signal the occurrence of behavior (Skinner, 1953). For example, through questioning, a consultant might establish that a student's complaining behavior generally follows a teacher's instructions to begin a new activity; the teacher's instructions may serve as a signal for the occurrence of complaints. Sometimes, consultant verbalizations regarding antecedent events are aimed at the discovery of variables that may affect the observational learning of the client (Bandura, 1969). For example, consultant questioning might reveal that a parent is modeling behavior that he or she is trying to eliminate in a child, such as a mother's angrily scolding her child, saying: "You have no right to throw a temper tantrum to get what you want."

Behavior therapists generally take great pains to determine *consequent conditions* in order to identify variables that may control the probability of occurrence of a behavior of concern. A behaviorally oriented consultant might ask what happens immediately following a behavior in order to identify possible reinforcers that may control the behavior.

Sequential conditions are of interest to the environmentally oriented consultant and help in acquiring information about such matters as sequential variables that could affect retention or response rate (Lentz & Shapiro, 1985).

A behavioral consultant often inquires about the scheduling of reinforcement across a series of occasions in order to identify sequential influences on the rate of occurrence of a behavior. For instance, it is well known that different response rates occur when reinforcement follows every response and when reinforcement is periodic (Ferster & Skinner, 1957). By asking when reinforcement occurs across a series of occasions, the consultant may be able to glean useful information about the scheduling of reinforcement.

The following examples will help the reader to become familiar with verbalizations in the behavior setting subcategory. Examples of specification elicitors include "What happened just before Ted hit Bob?" (behavior-setting specification elicitor); "Under what conditions would the children have to perform in order to achieve this objective of your reading program?" (behavior-setting specification elicitor); and "What steps do you generally follow in teaching addition?" (behavior-setting specification elicitor). Examples of summarization emitters include "I scolded Alice this morning" (behavior-setting specification emitter); "Ted generally throws tantrums on Mondays" (behavior-setting specification emitter); "The classroom is generally quite hot when Ted gets sleepy" (behavior-setting specification emitter); "You said that Alice tends to do her best work in the

afternoons" (behavior-setting summarization emitter); and "I like the way
the other children praise Alice when she reads well" (behavior-setting
positive-evaluation emitter). An example of a positive validation elicitor is
"Did you say that Carol spoke to Ted just before he tore up Alice's paper?"
(behavior-setting positive-validation elicitor).

The Behavior Subcategory

The behavior subcategory concerns what the client does. Included in
the discussion are utterances dealing with the client's covert processes
(e.g., thinking and feeling) and overt actions (e.g., talking and walking).
Also included are tasks currently performed by the client, the strength of
the behavior, records of the behavior (e.g., graphs or anecdotal reports),
and behavioral goals.

Client behavior is of major concern to consultants of all theoretical
persuasions. However, behavior therapists place particular emphasis on
this subject. A major goal of consultants operating out of the behavioral
tradition is to specify behavior in sufficiently precise terms to ensure its
objective measurement (Mash & Terdal, 1989).

Precise specification of behavior is useful because it allows the consultant to interpret the consultee's evaluations of the client. For example,
when a consultee states, "Bob's immaturity really bothers me," the consultant is faced with the task of guessing precisely what is of concern to the
consultee. On the other hand, if the consultee says, "Bob's hitting really
bothers me," the consultant has a relatively specific understanding of at
least one important aspect of the client's behavior.

A second reason for the precise description of client behavior is that
precise description allows for the investigation of inferences regarding the
environmental factors controlling behavior. For example, it is difficult to
identify the specific environmental conditions that influence a student's
poor attitude toward classroom activities, but it is quite possible to determine conditions that may influence the student's verbal complaints.

The following examples are provided to help the reader become familiar with verbalizations in the behavior subcategory. Examples of behavior
specification elicitors include "What does Alice do to demonstrate her
anger toward the other children?"; "What are some examples of things
that Carol might do to improve her group participation?"; "Let's look at
the data on Carol's hitting behavior"; "What are the general goals of your
mathematics program?"; "We need to establish a goal for Alice"; "Show
me Ted's homework papers"; "How often does Carol hit other children?";
and "How long does it usually take for Carol to begin her work after she
has been told to do so?" Behavior specification emitters include "I want to
concentrate on Ted's multiplication skills"; "I know that Ted thinks he's
smart"; "Bob hits Ted very hard when they fight"; "On Wednesday, Bob
swore at Alice 10 times"; "Bob thinks about his misdeeds long and hard

before he carries them out"; "Is it possible that Bob yells in class to get your attention?" (behavior inference elicitor); "Carol's screaming is really upsetting to me" (behavior negative-evaluation emitter); and "Why do you think Bob reads so poorly?" (behavior inference elicitor).

The Individual Characteristics Subcategory

The central tenet of organismic theories of behavior is that the unique constellation of characteristics of an individual determine how he or she will behave in a given situation. This viewpoint is so deeply ingrained in Western societies that it is reflected in everyday speech. Thus, someone may say to a boy who has broken something, "How can you be so stupid?" In effect, we assign the cause of his behavior to his intelligence rather than to the roller skate over which he has just tripped.

Historically, individual characteristics that have been identified as playing a central role in the control of behavior cover a wide variety of attributes. These attributes include personality characteristics described as traits (Allport, 1937) or states (Freud, 1927); intellectual characteristics defined as abilities or aptitudes (Guilford, 1967); and physical characteristics such as sex (Freud, 1938); age (Gesell, 1940), and neurological functioning (Hebb, 1949).

The individual characteristics subcategory deals with verbalizations about individual attributes of the client. Thus, utterances referring to individual characteristics describe conditions or states of the individual, rather than verbalizations about behavior. In English, one of the variants of the verb *be* is often, though by no means invariably, used to specify individual states or conditions.

The following are examples of verbalizations in the individual characteristics subcategory: "How old is Alice?" (individual-characteristics specification-elicitor); "Why do you think Bob is overweight?" (individual-characteristics inference-elicitor); "Eight is a good age" (individual-characteristics positive-evaluation emitter); "You said that Alice is 15. Is that right?" (individual-characteristics summarization-emitter and individual-characteristics positive-validation elicitor); "Bob has a hot temper" (individual characteristics specification-emitter); "Alice always was hyperactive" (individual-characteristics specification-emitter); "Do you believe that Carol is immature?" (individual-characteristics inference-elicitor); "What do you think causes Carol to be so shy?" (individual-characteristics inference-elicitor); "You said Ted is aggressive and anxious, didn't you?" (individual-characteristics summarization-emitter and individual-characteristics positive-validation elicitor); "Are these the personality traits that you are interested in working on?" (individual-characteristics positive-validation elicitor); "Carol is ready to read now" (individual-characteristics specification-emitter); and "Ted's personality verges on the obnoxious" (individual-characteristics negative-evaluation emitter).

The Observation Subcategory

Consultation requires gathering data on client behavior. For example, in the consultative problem-solving model, data are collected during the entire time consultation is in effect. Verbalizations in the observation subcategory refer to observations and recording activities such as those involved in gathering data on client behavior.

Examples of utterances in the observation subcategory include "Can you get some data on Ted's behavior at recess?" (observation specification elicitor); "You could record Alice's behavior by tallying it on an index card" (observation specification emitter); "How would it be most convenient for you to observe Ted?" (observation specification elicitor); "How do you like the interval method of recording?" (observation positive-evaluation elicitor); "I don't think you'll be able to record effectively after school" (observation inference emitter); "Do you think you'll be able to collect data all week?" (observation inference elicitor); "I don't like taking data" (observation negative-evaluation emitter); "You said that you would observe Alice at bedtime for the next week" (observation summarization emitter); and "Did we agree that you will take data on Carol's eating behavior this week?" (observation positive-validation elicitor).

The Plan Subcategory

Consultation often includes a consideration of one or more plans to solve the problem or problems presented by the consultee. As indicated earlier, planning is a key feature of the consultative problem-solving model. Planning is necessary during the problem analysis phase of consultation. Thus, during this phase, verbalizations are heavily loaded in the plan subcategory. Post implementation planning may also occur during problem evaluation. Accordingly, there may be a significant number of verbalizations in the plan subcategory during the problem evaluation interview.

Planning may be of two types. The first is the specification of broad strategies to be used in solving a problem presented by a consultee. The consultant, who should be armed with an extensive knowledge of psychological principles, is generally in a good position to offer plan strategies to a consultee. For example, a consultant might say, "Peer modeling of socially desirable behaviors has been found to be effective in curbing a child's aggressive reactions. You might want to try something like that in this situation." This suggestion does not tie the consultee to a specific course of action. It merely presents a general approach to the problem that the consultee is trying to solve.

The second type of planning that occurs in consultation is the detailing of specific tactics for implementing a strategy. The consultee is usually in a much better position to generate tactics than the consultant because they know the client and the unique characteristics and constraints of the client's environment.

Utterances in the plan subcategory refer to procedures suggested to change client behavior, to maintain desired behaviors, or to generalize behaviors to new situations. In addition, plan verbalizations include procedures previously agreed on and implemented that are under discussion in a problem evaluation interview.

The following statements provide some examples of verbalizations that fall into the plan subcategory: "What are some ways in which you could reinforce Carol's good behavior?" (plan specification elicitor); "I am wondering if we could use the appropriate behavior modeled by the other children as a way of changing Ted's aggressive actions" (plan specification emitter); "Do you think that periodic review would help Alice to recall what she has learned in social studies?" (plan inference elicitor); "I don't like the idea of tangible rewards" (plan negative-evaluation emitter); "Ignoring Ted's fighting simply wouldn't be practical" (plan negative-evaluation emitter); "We said we would try to emphasize the distinctive features of each letter to improve Bob's letter-identification skills" (plan summarization emitter); and "Are we in agreement that reducing role conflict is the general strategy that we should follow in minimizing Ted's aggressive reactions?" (plan positive-validation elicitor).

The "Other" Subcategory

The range of conversation topics is virtually limitless in consultation. Therefore, it is necessary to have a catchall category to cover subjects not explicitly delineated in the other six content subcategories. The "other" subcategory serves this purpose. Examples of verbalizations in the "other" category include "Carol's clothes are generally dirty" ("other" specification emitter); "I like that dress" ("other" positive-evaluation emitter); "Why did the school bus break down?" ("other" inference elicitor); "You said that the walls in the room had just been painted green. Is that right?" ("other" summarization emitter and "other" positive-validation elicitor); and "Carol was absent Monday" ("other" specification emitter).

Message Process

Verbal utterances emitted during conversation include information about speaker actions or processes. This information is conveyed mainly, though not exclusively, in verbs. For example, a speaker may say, "Carol is immature." The verb *is* indicates, among other things, the speaker's act of specifying something about the topic of conversation (i.e., Carol). If the

statement had been "I think Carol is immature," there would be two verbs
conveying process information. As in the first example, the verb *is* indicates the specification of Carol's immaturity. However, the verb *think* adds
a qualification to that specification, namely that Carol's immaturity is not
an objective fact, but an inference made by the speaker.

The message-process category classifies verbal messages in accordance
with the kinds of speaker actions they describe *vis-à-vis* the content of
conversation. There are five subcategories within the process domain: (1)
specification; (2) evaluation; (3) inference; (4) summarization; and (5)
evaluation.

The Specification Subcategory

Specification utterances provide or elicit descriptive or definitional information regarding the various content subcategories under discussion in
consultation. Specifications describe client characteristics and behaviors,
the background environment and behavior setting associated with client
actions, the observation of client behavior, and plans generated to solve
whatever problems may have been presented by the consultee.

Utterances that call for nonverbal behavior rather than verbal specification are coded in the specification subcategory. For example, a verbalization such as "Let's look at the data" is coded as a specification even though
it calls for action rather than words. Verbalizations calling only for action
are rare and therefore do not warrant a separate coding subcategory. Moreover, from a communication standpoint, the information conveyed by a
nonverbal act is similar to the information conveyed by verbal specification. For example, the act of looking at data communicates the information
expressed by the verbal specification "I am looking at the data."

Some examples of verbalizations in the specification subcategory are
"How does Alice show her immaturity?" (behavior specification elicitor);
"Ted is compulsive" (individual-characteristics specification-emitter);
"How do you teach social studies?" (behavior-setting specification-elicitor); "When could you record Alice's behavior?" (observation specification
elicitor); "Tell me about Ted's early home life" (background-environment
specification-elicitor); and "Did he hit Carol or Alice?" (behavior specification elicitor).

The Evaluation Subcategory

In some cases, a verbal process may provide information about the
attitudes or emotional reactions of a speaker toward the things that he or
she is discussing. For example, a consultee may say, "Bob's masturbation
disgusts me," indicating not only that Bob masturbates, but also how the
consultee feels about it.

Verbalizations that convey or call for an attitudinal or emotional reaction are classified in the evaluation subcategory. Utterances of this sort invariably require a value judgment made in accordance with a value dimension. Polar terms such as *wise-foolish, good-bad, difficult-easy,* and *like-dislike* illustrate the dimensional character of evaluative judgments.

Evaluations may be either positive or negative. In the case of statements expressing an evaluative judgment, it is often blatantly obvious which of these two valences is intended. However, utterances calling for an evaluation on the part of the listener are almost always ambiguous with respect to valence. For example, if a consultant were to ask, "How do you feel about Bob's behavior?" either a positive or a negative evaluation could be made. Indeed, the intent of the question would presumably be to determine which of these two general feelings best expressed the consultee's reaction. Of course, if a consultant wanted to control the valence of a consultee's evaluative judgments, he or she could easily do so. For example, the consultant might say, "Tell me some of the things that you like about Bob's behavior."

In any case, because of the frequent ambiguity regarding the valence of utterances calling for an evaluation, such utterances are always coded as positive evaluations. In effect, this rule nullifies the valence aspect of an evaluation elicitor for coding purposes.

The central function of evaluations in consultation is to provide information regarding attitudes and feelings concerning the topics under discussion. For example, a consultee may express his or her feelings about client behavior, about collecting data, or about the possible effectiveness of a plan. Reactions of this sort provide the consultant with the information of most concern to the consultee, the willingness of the consultee to collect data on client behavior, and the kinds of plans that the consultee will be most comfortable implementing to achieve problem solution.

In addition to providing information about attitudes and feelings, evaluative utterances may be used as verbal reinforcers. For example, in order to encourage a consultee to continue collecting data during the plan implementation phase of consultation, a consultant might say, "I certainly appreciated your taking time to collect data on Alice's behavior last week."

The following examples of evaluative utterances are provided to illustrate verbalizations in this subcategory: "How do you feel about the changes that you have seen in Bob's behavior?" (behavior positive-evaluation elicitor); "I really like Alice" (individual-characteristics positive-evaluation emitter); "I am very happy with the change in Carol's attitude" (individual-characteristics positive-evaluation emitter); "It is important to collect data" (observation positive-evaluation emitter); "I like the way you implemented the plan" (plan positive-evaluation emitter); and "This plan is just plain poor" (plan negative-evaluation emitter).

The Inference Subcategory

Utterances coded as inferences usually contain verbs such as *think, assume,* or *feel* that suggest judgment. For example, a consultee might say, "I feel that Alice is compulsive." Verbalizations in the *inference* subcategory provide or call for judgments as opposed to statements of fact. The process of making inferences attests to the realization that many things are not known for certain and that some can probably never be known.

Some inferences take the form of predictions about future events. For example, a consultant might say, "This plan will work," thereby claiming a certain degree of clairvoyance. In other instances, an inference may express a probability judgment, as in the statement "Carol is probably unhappy."

Some inferences are inductive, involving generalization from specific instances. For example, in consultation, a consultant might say, "Since modeling worked with Carol, it would probably work with Alice." Other inferences are deductive. These statements require drawing conclusions about a particular class of events on the basis of information regarding a more general class. For example, a consultee might deduce that Bob hit Ted because he was angry. The generalization on which this deduction is based is the somewhat questionable assumption that anger causes aggression.

In consultation, inferences provide information about the kinds of assumptions that the consultant and the consultee make about client behavior, the conditions that may affect it, and the kinds of plans that may change behavior. The kinds of inferences made during consultation are probably influenced by the theoretical orientation of the consultant. A psychodynamically oriented consultant would probably focus on inferences related to underlying internal motives for client behavior. On the other hand, a behavioral consultant would very likely confine his or her inferences to such matters as the possible effects of environmental conditions on client behavior.

The following examples illustrate verbalizations in the inference subcategory: "I think Carol misspells words because she wants the attention of having me help her with her spelling" (behavior inference emitter); "Maybe Carol's reading difficulty stems from a lack of the prerequisite skills for reading" (behavior inference emitter); "What do you think might happen if you were to stop giving Carol extra help when she misspelled words?" (behavior inference elicitor); "Do you feel that Ted would be able to stay awake in class if he quit his evening job?" (behavior inference elicitor); "I don't have much hope about the effectiveness of this plan" (plan inference emitter); "I think this plan would take a great deal of time to implement" (plan inference emitter): "We probably ought to take more data" (observation inference emitter); "Alice seems insecure to me" (individual-characteristics inference-emitter); "Ted's excessive neatness suggests an almost compulsive nature to me" (individual-characteristics inference-emitter); and "Do you feel that Bob's hostility toward his brother is related to his feelings about his father?" (individual-characteristics inference-elicitor).

The Summarization Subcategory

In the course of an interview, it is often useful to review information discussed earlier in the interview or at some time before the interview. Verbalizations in the summarization subcategory provide or call for review of this kind.

One obvious function of the summary is to enhance recall of what has been said before. Participants in consultation say many things, and it is impossible to remember them all. The summary serves as a kind of rehearsal that reinstates previously discussed material and reduces the probability that it will be forgotten.

In addition to facilitating recall, summaries may help to establish focus in an interview. Summaries are invariably selective and do not always allow for a recounting of everything that has been said previously. Rather, they involve those things that the consultant considers of special importance. The selectivity in a summary may mark a particular topic for further discussion. For example, suppose that a consultee has made a number of statements on a variety of topics and that, in the course of these discussions, some things have been said that the consultant feels deserve further consideration. In this situation, the consultant may use a summary to initiate focus on those topics that he or she believes warrant further clarification. For instance, the consultant might say, "A moment ago you said that Ted usually runs out of the classroom when you are making a transition between learning activities." A statement of this kind would probably focus conversation on the relation between transitional periods and Ted's leaving the room.

A final function of the summary is reviewing material requiring agreement between the consultant and the consultee. For example, there should be agreement about the details of whatever plans are made to solve a problem presented in consultation. The process of ensuring agreement requires a plan summary.

Examples in the summarization subcategory include "You said that Carol's immaturity is revealed in her temper tantrums, in which she screams, kicks the walls and furniture in her bedroom, and breaks her toys" (behavior summarization emitter); "Tell me again what you said is Bob's most serious problem behavior" (behavior summarization elicitor); "You indicated that you would keep a record of the number of times that Bob wets the bed during the next seven nights" (observation summarization emitter); "Would you go over that recording procedure again?" (observation summarization elicitor); "You told me that Carol's crying usually begins Just after she has been put to bed in the evening" (behavior-setting summarization-emitter); "You indicated that you would help Carol with her reading only after she demonstrated that she could read two paragraphs without an error" (plan summarization emitter); "What did we say we were going to do about the hitting behavior?" (plan summarization elicitor); and "You told me that Bob's IQ was 84" (individual-characteristics summarization-emitter).

The Validation Subcategory

Validation utterances provide or call for agreement (positive validation) or disagreement (negative validation) with regard to matters of fact (Bergan & Tombari, 1975). For example, a consultant might say, "Am I correct in assuming that Alice cries only when she is put down for her nap?" A yes in response to this validation elicitor would indicate a positive validation; a no would suggest a negative validation. Validation elicitors can always be responded to with a yes or a no reply. This fact provides a useful clue to coding utterances that call for validation.

The central function of the validation utterance in consultation is to establish consensus between the consultant and the consultee. In consultative problem-solving conducted in accordance with the model described in Chapter 1, validation is required in all interviews in the problem-solving process. During problem identification, consensus achieved through validation is required to ensure agreement regarding the client behaviors of concern to the consultee, the conditions under which these behaviors occur, and the procedures established for recording these behaviors. In the problem analysis interview, agreement is necessary mainly in establishing the plan to be implemented in solving the problem presented by the consultee. In problem evaluation, agreement is necessary regarding such issues as whether or not the goals of consultation have been achieved.

Although establishing consensus is the central function of the validation utterance, inexperienced consultants sometimes use it to test hypotheses about the matters under discussion during consultation. For example, a consultant might say, "Is Ted aggressive before lunch?" If the consultant gets a negative response to this question, he or she will, of course, follow with "Well, then, is Ted aggressive after lunch?"

For a number of reasons, it is not advisable to use validation verbalizations to test hypotheses. First, these statements may prolong an interview. It may take several validation questions to get the information that could be obtained with a single specification question. A second disadvantage is that the use of validation for hypothesis testing may put the consultee in the position of having to say no many times during the course of an interview. Words tend to conjure up associations in the speaker and the listener. Few, if any, of the associations with the word *no* would be of any value in promoting an effective relationship between the consultant and the consultee. A third shortcoming of validation hypotheses is that they tend to call forth short responses, such as yes or no, from the consultee. Short responses tend to provide a very limited amount of information, and they may not give the consultant time to plan what to say next.

For all of the above reasons, it is advisable to use the specification elicitor rather than the validation elicitor when information beyond establishing consensus is required. Thus, for example, instead of saying, "Does Ted hit before lunch?" a consultant might say, "When does Ted hit?"

Verbalizations calling for validation are coded as positive. This is an arbitrary rule analogous to the previous rule regarding evaluation. As in the case of the evaluation rule, requests for validation tend to be ambiguous with regard to valence. Thus, the decision to code them as positive is tantamount to not coding valence at all.

Another provision regarding the coding of validation utterances is that polite requests such as "could you," "would you," and "will you" are not coded as validations even though they may be responded to with a yes or a no. For example, a question such as "Will you tell me about Alice's mother?" is coded as a specification even though it could be responded to with a yes or a no.

Examples of verbalizations calling for validation include "Does Bob make oral reading errors only when you are standing near him?" (behavior-setting validation-elicitor); "Did you say that Alice vomits only during social studies?" (behavior-setting validation-elicitor); "Did we agree that you would use tangible rewards to increase Bob's motivation to complete his assignments?" (plan validation elicitor); and "Did you say that you would record Ted's behavior during the first period after recess?" (observation validation elicitor).

In many cases, utterances calling for validation do not provide the information necessary to code content. This problem occurs most often in situations in which a validation verbalization follows a summary. Utterances such as "Is that correct?" or "Is that right?" are examples. When this problem occurs, content is coded in accordance with the antecedent utterance to which the validation refers.

Utterances providing validation rather than requesting it rarely contain enough information to allow the coding of content. In these cases, the content of the antecedent statement to which the validation refers is used for coding purposes. Examples of verbalizations providing positive validation include: "Yes," "OK," "all right," and "I agree." Some examples of negative validations are "No," "definitely not," "not on your life," and "not today."

Message Control

Verbalizations that occur during the course of conversation are not merely random events. They are controlled by internal mechanisms (such as the intentions of the speaker) and by environmental variables (such as the behavior of the listener). One of the major environmental factors controlling the verbal behavior of an individual is the verbal behavior of the person to whom he or she is speaking. The ability of one individual to influence the verbal behavior of another by the utterances that he or she emits comes from conventions of language that are instilled in the earliest phases of language learning (Skinner, 1957). It is these conventions that have provided the basis for the organization of the message control category.

The message control category allows the classification of the verbal behavior of a speaker on the basis of whether it is likely to have a direct effect on the subsequent verbal behavior of a listener. Those verbal behaviors presumed to have an influence on subsequent listener verbalizations are classified as elicitors. Those utterances that are not presumed to have a controlling effect on listener verbalizations are categorized as emitters.

The Elicitor Subcategory

An elicitor is an utterance that calls for a response in a particular content subcategory and a particular process subcategory. For example, the verbalization "Tell me what happens when Ted uses obscene language" calls for a response involving content in the behavior setting subcategory and a verbal process in the specification subcategory. In contrast, the utterance "Why do you think Carol is so immature?" calls for a response with content in the individual characteristics subcategory and a verbal process in the inference subcategory.

There are a variety of ways to elicit verbal responses from a listener. The most direct is the imperative statement. Imperative statements are used frequently in consultation. For example, a consultant might say, "Tell me about Bob's home life" (background-environment specification-elicitor). In effect, this statement commands the consultee to respond.

Although imperative statements can be used effectively in consultation, they do have the obvious disadvantage of being rather blatant in the manner in which they assert control. This blatancy may become more noxious as the response required of the listener becomes more demanding. Thus, an utterance such as "Tell me about Bob's home life" would probably not be offensive to most listeners because it requires nothing more than a verbal response. Moreover, it indicates consultant interest in the concerns of the consultee. On the other hand, an utterance such as "Collect data next week" (observation specification elicitor) might well be very offensive to the listener in that it calls for a highly effortful set of reactions. Indeed, these types of statements may result in resistance in consultation (Witt, 1990).

Fortunately, language provides a number of ways to soften the harshness of imperative control and thereby increases the likelihood that the listener will not take offense. One procedure that may be used is to exhort the listener to respond, as in "Let's make a plan" (plan specification elicitor). The attempt is to incite the listener to action by evoking a sense of cooperation and worthy purpose.

Another way to soften the implication of control is to use an indirect elicitor such as "I need more information on Carol's bed-wetting" (behavior specification elicitor), or "We ought to have some data on Bob's crying behavior" (observation specification elicitor). In these examples, the speaker does not come right out and demand what he or she wants. Yet, the intent is clear.

A distinctive characteristic of the disguised elicitor is that it provides a convenient way for the listener to reject the speaker's demands without affronting him or her and prevent embarrassment to both speaker and listener. For example, in response to the indirect elicitor calling for data on Bob's crying behavior, a listener might say, "That would be important. I wish I had the time to collect that kind of data, but unfortunately with my heavy schedule it just wouldn't be practical."

Sometimes a speaker attempts to reduce the noxious aspects of the elicitor by coupling it with appreciation. For example, a consultant might say, "Please continue recording Carol's behavior for another week." (observation specification elicitor); "I would really appreciate it if you could do that" (observation positive-evaluation emitter). The implication here, of course, is that the consultee would not receive the consultant's appreciation if he or she did not continue to collect data.

The use of positive consequences represents yet another approach to reducing the noxious aspects of elicitor control: "You continue to implement the plan as it was designed, and I'll come in on Thursday to observe Bob" (plan specification elicitor and observation specification emitter). In this example, the speaker is offering the listener a "deal," the attractiveness of which depends, of course, on how strongly the listener wants the speaker to observe Bob.

A final way to lessen the implication of control in the elicitor is to use a question to elicit the listener's reactions. For example, a consultant might say, "Could you tell me about Bob?" (individual-characteristics specification-elicitor). A question of this sort provides the listener with the effortless, though somewhat awkward, response of simply saying no.

Of course, not all questions can be responded to with a yes or no reply. Indeed, most questions require an elaborated response. However, even those questions tend to be less abrasive than the imperative elicitor, perhaps because a question requires the listener to focus on the search for an answer and distracts him or her from the realization that his or her behavior is being controlled. In addition, the acceptability of the question derives in part from the fact that people in our society are trained from their earliest years to respond without rancor to the countless questions that they are asked in the schools. In this connection, it is interesting to note that very young children often do tend to take offense when they are subjected to excessive questioning.

As the examples in the above paragraphs illustrate, the central function of the elicitor in consultation is to influence the verbal behavior of the consultee. In consultative problem-solving, the role of the consultant in directing consultee verbalizations is quite explicit. The consultant attempts to direct both the content and the process of the verbal messages emitted by the consultee. For example, it is the consultant who determines whether the consultee will talk about matters relating to the observation subcategory, the plan subcategory, or the behavior subcategory. Likewise, it is the consultant who influences the extent to which the consultee emits specifications, inferences, validations, and evaluations.

The consultant derives his or her authority to influence the consultee's verbal behavior from the request of the consultee for consultation services. The consultee desiring services will have made the decision to have consultant contact. What the consultee expects and what he or she should get is assistance from the consultant in applying the problem-solving model to those problems that are of concern to him or her.

Consultant control of consultee verbal behavior makes it possible for the consultee to use the consultative problem-solving model. What the consultant does by directing the consultee's verbal behavior is to provide the consultee with the necessary skills to use the problem-solving model to achieve problem solution. Consultant direction of consultee verbal behavior has the effect of making the consultee think like the psychologist trained in the use of the consultative problem-solving model. The consultee goes through the same problem-solving steps as if he or she had been trained specifically in the use of the model. Assuming that the consultee is working with a competent consultant, he or she has access to a broad range of psychological principles through the psychologist, who has had years of graduate training. Hopefully, the consultee's use of psychological principles will evidence a similar degree of sophistication, going beyond the stage of mastering abstract jargon and being able to apply psychological principles in concrete situations.

The Emitter Subcategory

An emitter is a verbalization that provides content and process information to a listener but does not call for a specific response on the part of the listener. For example, a remark such as "Carol has blue eyes" specifies one of Carol's characteristics, but it does not call for a reaction from the listener.

The most common type of emitter is the declarative statement. Sen-

tences such as "Bob has three brothers" (background-environment specification-emitter) and "I think Alice is shy" (individual-characteristics inference-emitter) are examples. In a few instances, marked by rare evidenc-
es of exuberance on the part of the consultant or the consultee, emitters
may take the form of exclamatory remarks. "Wow!," "oh boy!," and "gee
whiz!" are familiar examples. Exclamatory utterances usually do not provide direct information about content. However, content is implied and
may be coded from the antecedent to which the exclamation refers.

One major function of the emitter in consultation is to broaden the
extent of contact of the consultant with the environment of the consultee.
In most cases, the consultant enters consultation with little or no knowledge regarding such significant issues as the client's behavior and characteristics and the conditions in the environment that may influence what the
client does. Consultee emitters provide the consultant with a large part of
the information that he or she needs to comprehend the nature of the
problem presented by the consultee and to assist in the development of a
plan to solve it.

A second important function of the emitter is clarifying for the consultee various aspects of the problem under discussion. Even in cases in
which the consultee is seemingly desperate when seeking consultation
services, he or she may have no clear idea of the specific aspects of the
client's behavior that are most troublesome. Moreover, the consultee rarely
has a clear notion of what actions to take to solve the problem. In some
cases, the consultee's conception of the problem may be so vague that he
or she may not be able to recognize significant improvement in client
behavior.

During problem solving, a central function of the consultant is to assist
the consultee to produce emitters that will serve three purposes. First, it is
hoped that the emitters will clarify the nature of the problem under consideration. It is also hoped that the emitters will explicate plans that may be
implemented to solve the problem. Finally, they should assist the consultee in determining whether a solution has been achieved. For example,
at some point during problem identification, the consultee will hopefully
be able to make a remark that may begin with something like "What I am
really concerned about with respect to Bob's behavior is . . ." Similarly, in
problem analysis, the consultee should reach the point of having emitted
elements of a plan in which he or she has at least some confidence. Finally,
during problem evaluation, the consultee should be able to determine in a
precise way whether the problem of concern was solved.

THE CODING PROCESS

Applications of consultation analysis techniques in both training and
research require that the verbal interactions occurring during consultation

be coded.[1] It is best to code from written transcripts or video- or audiotapes. However, for some training purposes, it may be advisable to
code directly from observations of a "live" interview. Of course, live and
video interviews provide the coder with the option of examining nonverbal
behavior.

There are three aspects to effective coding. The first is determining
what to code, the second is selecting and using a coding instrument, and
the third is establishing observer agreement in coding.

Determining What to Code

Determining what to code requires dividing segments of verbal behavior into a series of discrete units of observation that may be assigned sets of
coding responses. The selection of a unit of observation is, of course, to
some extent an arbitrary matter. Nevertheless, linguistic convention does
provide certain breaks in the flow of speech that offer some basis for
dividing verbal output into units.

The Independent Clause as a Unit of Observation

The unit of observation selected for use in consultation analysis is the
independent clause or implied independent clause. Because the independent clause includes only those utterances that can be stated as sentences,
it has the advantage of segmenting verbalizations into units that can convey a complete subject–action–object relation even when standing alone.
The independent clause is preferable to the sentence as an observational
unit because sentences may contain more than one independent expres-
sion.

The sentence "Let's make a plan" provides a relatively simple illustration of a unit of observation. A somewhat more complex example is "Ted is
the one who overeats because he is frustrated."

When there are two independent clauses in one statement, they are
considered two units of observation. For example, "Alice swears, but Carol
does not" constitutes two units of observation. Likewise, "Alice swears
and therefore Ted drinks" includes two independent clauses and therefore
suggests two units of observation.

---

[1]The coding system described in the remainder of the chapter is based on the consultation
analysis record. An abbreviated method of coding may be based on the specific objectives
met in each phase of consultation interviews described in Kratochwill and Bergan (1990).
Some initial training research suggests that the objectives systems correspond generally to
categories of appropriate behavioral interviewing as determined through the consultation
analysis record (Kratochwill et al., 1989).

Incomplete and Interrupted Verbalizations

As indicated above, incomplete statements that imply independent clauses are coded as units of observation. For example, an utterance such as "Fine," implying, "That would be fine," would be coded as one unit of observation.

Interjections and short implied independent clauses such as "OK" and "uh-hum" occurring at the beginning of a sentence are coded as units of verbal behavior if they refer to a previous utterance and if the sentence that follows does not have the same content as the previous utterance. For example, suppose that a consultee said, "What really bothers me is that Ted leaves the room without permission." The consultant might then say, "OK, what happens right before Ted leaves the room?" "OK" in this example is coded as a unit of observation because it refers to the previous utterance and because the sentence following "OK" introduces new content. The "OK" may be regarded as an incomplete statement that might be filled in by something like "OK, I understand."

Suppose that the consultant had said, "OK, I see" rather than "OK, what happens right before Ted leaves the room?" In this case, "OK" would not be a unit of observation. It is part of the sentence "I see." Both "OK" and "I see" refer back to the consultee's remark rather than introduce a new content subcategory.

Even the most vehement of exclamatory remarks is not coded as a unit of observation when the content of the sentence that follows refers to a previous utterance. Thus, if a consultee said, "Alice is the one who stole the purse," and the consultant said, "Great balls of fire, she did do it," the interjection "Great balls of fire" would not be coded as a separate unit of observation. However, evaluative remarks such as "good" or "fine" are coded as units of observation regardless of the content that follows them.

Although incomplete utterances such as those given in the above examples imply independent clauses, there are many incomplete verbalizations that do not have this quality. It is common for people to start sentences that they never end. For example, a consultant may say, "You seem to . . . ," and the consultee may break in with "You know, the baby cried all night." Incomplete utterances that do not clearly imply an independent clause are not coded.

Another type of incomplete verbalization is a statement that is initially interrupted but subsequently completed. For example, a consultant might say, "What happens . . . ?" and be interrupted by the consultee with something such as "This all happened recently." In many cases, the consultant ignores the interruption and completes the statement. Interrupted utterances that are later completed are coded as units of observation. If the verbalization causing the interruption is an independent clause, it may also be coded. The verbalization that has been interrupted is coded in sequence after the utterance responsible for the interruption.

Coding Instruments and How to Use Them

Consultation analysis makes use of two types of coding instruments: consultation analysis records and consultation analysis checklists. Consultation analysis records provide the necessary data for in-depth examinations of consultant interviewing skills and verbal interactions between the consultant and the consultee. Consultation analysis checklists give an overview of the extent to which a consultant adheres to the specified purposes of problem identification, problem analysis, and problem evaluation interviews.

The Consultation Analysis Record

The consultation analysis record (CAR) is a form for coding units of observation in accordance with the message classification categories discussed earlier in this chapter. An illustration of a CAR is given in Figure 2-1.

Coding with the CAR requires that units of observation be determined and numbered on typed transcripts. It may be helpful to number all verbalizations on the transcripts. For most training applications, the reader will probably be concerned only with consultant verbalizations and therefore may limit her or his numbering to these. However, we recommend that both consultant and consultee records be coded whenever possible. It is convenient to number verbalizations from 1 to 25 and then start a new set beginning again with 1. This problem of locating a particular statement when utterances are numbered in sets of 25 is solved by assigning a record-form page number to each set of 25 verbalizations. The first set is called "page 1," the second set "page 2," and so on. A space is provided on the CAR for numbering pages.

As depicted in Figure 2-1, the use of the CAR calls for coding in all four message-classification categories. Thus, each unit of observation is coded four times in regard to source, content, process, and control. For example, the statement "I like Bob's attitude," when made by the consultant, is coded as consultant, individual characteristics, evaluation, and emitter under their respective categories.

The above procedure may appear simple to execute. However, some complications and qualifications may be involved. In cases in which more than one alternative is applicable to a given message classification category, only the first alternative is coded. For instance, the verbalization "When and why does Carol cry?" is coded as a behavior-setting specifica-

---

FIGURE 2-1. Consultation analysis record form. [Source: J. R. Bergan & M. L. Tombari. (1975). The analysis of verbal interactions occurring during consultation. *Journal of School Psychology, 13,* 212. Reprinted by permission of Human Sciences Press, 72 Fifth Avenue, New York, NY 10011. Copyright 1975.]

CONSULTANT _____   CASE NUMBER _____

CONSULTEE _____   INTERVIEW TYPE _____

                                                PAGE _____

CONSULTATION-ANALYSIS RECORD

	Message Source		Message Content							Message Process							Message Control	
	Consultee	Consultant	Background Environment	Behavior Setting	Behavior	Individual Characteristics	Observation	Plan	Other	Negative Evaluation	Positive Evaluation	Inference	Specification	Summarization	Negative Validation	Positive Validation	Elicitor	Emitter
1																		
2																		
3																		
4																		
5																		
6																		
7																		
8																		
9																		
10																		
11																		
12																		
13																		
14																		
15																		
16																		
17																		
18																		
19																		
20																		
21																		
22																		
23																		
24																		
25																		

tion-elicitor. The inference called for by the word *why* is not coded. The rule specifying that the inference should not be coded has the disadvantage of causing some loss of information. However, utterances of this kind are sufficiently rare so that the construction of the highly complex rules that would be required to provide for coding the inference may not be warranted.

Utterances such as validation elicitors and emitters (e.g., "OK") and evaluation elicitors and emitters (e.g., "good") that have content defined by an antecedent are coded according to the content of the immediately preceding verbalization. Consider the following example: "You said that Ted's outbursts always occur during reading, and you indicated that the other children reward Ted's disruptions by laughing. Is that correct?" The validation elicitor "Is that correct?" is coded in the behavior setting subcategory because the independent clause "you indicated that the other children reward Ted's disruptions by laughing" reflects content in the behavior setting subcategory.

The CAR has a number of applications. First, it provides the basis for analyses of the use of the content and process categories in an interview. Analyses of this sort can be very useful to the consultant in training. For example, consultation analysis might reveal that, during problem identification, heavy emphasis was placed on the behavior and behavior-setting content-subcategories but the observation subcategory was grossly neglected. Under these conditions, it might be expected that the consultee would lack sufficient information to record client behavior accurately and consistently. Information provided by consultation analysis would give valuable feedback indicating a need for greater concentration on observation verbalizations during problem identification.

Consultation analysis can also be used to obtain information on a consultant's control of an interview. As indicated earlier, it is the consultant's responsibility to guide the problem-solving process by controlling the verbal behavior of the consultee during consultation. Consultation analysis provides information on the extent to which the consultant uses elicitors to influence consultee verbalizations.

A third use of the CAR is to convey information on the extent to which a consultant focuses discussion on one topic of conversation before turning to another. Some consultants frequently move back and forth across content subcategories in their conversations; others tend to complete the discussion of one subject before turning to another. Bergan and Tombari (1976) found that the extent of consultant focus in an interview was significantly related to successful implementation of consultation.

The various applications of the CAR will be considered in greater detail in the chapters dealing with the problem-identification, problem-analysis, and problem-evaluation interviews. In these chapters, applications of the CAR will be considered in relation to the unique characteristics of each interview in the consultation process.

The Consultation Analysis Checklist

A consultation analysis checklist (CAC) is a list of the types of verbalizations usually required to achieve the purpose of a given interview. A CAC for the problem identification interview is illustrated in Figure 2-2.

As in the case of coding with the CAR, the first step in coding with a CAR is to number the units of observation on the transcript of the interview to be coded. The same numbering procedure as that used with the CAR may be used. Because only the verbalizations of the consultant are used in coding, only those verbalizations should be numbered.

It is possible to use a CAC without a transcript. However, it is not then possible to assign numbers to the units of observation.

To code a CAC, one simply enters the unit-of-observation number for an utterance beside the appropriate description of the utterance on the list. For example, suppose that unit-of-observation 13 on page 2 of a transcript is "How often does Carol chew her nails?" Because this utterance is a behavior specification elicitor (to determine behavior strength), the number 13-2 would be entered in the space beside "behavior specification elicitor" on the list. In the likely event that another behavior specification elicitor occurred, it would be entered next to the first one. When an utterance does not correspond to one of the categories on the list, it is not coded.

When coding is done from an observation of a live interview or directly from tape without a transcript, unit-of observation numbers are not available. Under these circumstances, tally marks are used for coding purposes.

Although the CAC does not provide the detailed information that can be obtained with the CAR, it is a highly useful instrument for training purposes. The CAC is easy to use and makes it possible to code an interview very quickly.

The central purpose of the CAC is to provide feedback to consultants regarding the extent to which the verbal behaviors emitted during an interview correspond to the objectives specified for the interview. For example, one of the purposes of problem analysis is to determine the conditions in the environment and/or the client skills that may contribute to problem solution. It is not uncommon for an inexperienced consultant to plunge into the design of a plan during problem analysis without exploring either the conditions or the skills potentially related to problem solution. The result of this kind of error is often the generation of an unimaginative and,

Problem-Identification Checklist
for Problem-Centered Consultation

Required Verbal Units	Frequency of Unit Use
1. Behavior specification or individual-characteristics specification elicitors (to introduce discussion)	_____
2. Behavior specification elicitors (to obtain a behavioral description of client behavior)	_____
3. Behavior specification elicitors (to determine behavior strength)	_____
4. Behavior summarization emitters (to summarize information about behavior)	_____
5. Behavior positive-validation elicitors (to establish agreement regarding specification and strength of behaviors)	_____
6. Behavior-setting specification elicitors (to establish antecedent conditions)	_____
7. Behavior-setting specification elicitors (to establish consequent conditions)	_____
8. Behavior-setting specification elicitors (to establish sequential conditions)	_____
9. Behavior-setting summarization emitters (to summarize conditions under which behavior occurs)	_____
10. Behavior-setting positive validation elicitors (to validate conditions under which behavior occurs)	_____
11. Observation specification elicitors and/or emitters (to establish performance assessment procedures)	_____
12. Observation summarization emitters (to facilitate recall of recording procedures)	_____
13. Observation validation elicitors (to validate recording procedures)	_____
14. Other specification elicitors or emitters (to arrange next interview and to ensure data collection)	_____

FIGURE 2-2. Consultation analysis checklist for a problem-centered problem-identification interview.

frequently, an unworkable plan. A CAC can provide feedback to a consultant that will minimize the occurrence of this kind of mistake.

A CAC has been constructed for all three types of interviews that occur in consultative problem-solving. The use of these checklists in specific interviews will be discussed in the following chapters on problem identification, problem analysis, and problem evaluation.

CONTROLLING VERBAL BEHAVIOR IN CONSULTATION

To use the message classification system, it is necessary to achieve a thorough mastery of the message classification concepts. This mastery requires practice. Two kinds of practice are useful: recognition practice and production practice. In the presentation that follows, the reader is given exercises involving each of these types of practice. These exercises are not sufficient to meet all practice needs, but they provide models for increasing skill in the use of message classification concepts to control verbal behavior in consultation.

Recognition Practice

Recognition practice refers to practice in recognizing the various categories of verbalization that may occur in consultation. This kind of practice is useful because it can help one to analyze one's own interviewing behavior and the interviewing behavior of others. As indicated above, analysis of one's own verbal behavior is useful in providing the necessary feedback to make productive changes in interviewing techniques. The analysis of a consultee's verbal behavior is useful in providing clues to how to work with the consultee. For instance, once able to discern that a consultee tends to describe a client in terms of individual characteristics rather than in terms of client behavior, the consultant may take special precautions to ensure the adequacy of problem identification. For example, a consultant may be especially careful to establish agreement regarding the precise behaviors to be recorded by the consultee.

Unit Recognition

The simplest kind of recognition practice involves the recognition of units of verbal behavior. Table 2-2 provides some examples of units that often occur during consultation. It is recommended that the reader code them at this time. Correct coding responses are provided at the right to allow a check on accuracy.

TABLE 2-2. Sample Units of Observation

Sample units	Correct coding for units
Tell me about Carol.	Individual-characteristics specification-elicitor
When during the day does this behavior generally occur?	Behavior-setting specification-elicitor
What are some of the kinds of skills that Bob would need to solve these math problems?	Behavior specification elicitor
What did the principal do when Bob said he would destroy the school and everything in it?	Behavior-setting specification-elicitor
Carol is a bright girl.	Individual-characteristics specification-emitter.
I have great admiration for Carol's intelligence.	Individual-characteristics positive-evaluation emitter
Could you take data during the morning?	Observation specification elicitor
I like the idea of using modeling.	Plan positive-evaluation emitter
What are the broad objectives of your reading program?	Behavior specification elicitor

TABLE 2-3. A Segment of a Problem Identification Interview (PII)

Consultant: (1) Mrs. Brody, can you tell me about Bob?

Consultee: (2) Do you have an hour? (3) For the last two years he's created quite a havoc in the other classes. (4) And in discussing this problem with his parents, he seems to have a big conflict with his mother. (5) He needs attention 100% of the time. (6) I'm not sure if he's trying to get attention or to show me who's boss. (7) I said something about, "Well, do you think you do this because you want to show me who's boss?" (8) and this big smile came over his face. (9) I think this is really an indication of how he feels; (10) and so he speaks out frequently all of the time.

Consultant: (11) This is the main thing he does that really bothers you?

Consultee: (12) This interrupting in class, yes. (13) Also his relationship with other children upsets me. (14) He does mean, nasty things. (15) If he doesn't like the way things are going, he'll just haul off and kick them, scratch them, or hit them over the head.

Consultant: (16) So he hits (17) and he interrupts the class very often.

Consultee: (18) Uh-hum.

Consultant: (19) And what does the child who's hit do?

Consultee: (20) Generally speaking, they get upset or teary-eyed.

Consultant: (21) What do you do when this happens?

Consultee: (22) I try to ignore it. (23) I think there are just so many fights that you can break up in one day without its being the main thing that happens during the school day. (24) But then I think my feelings come out some days if I see him hitting a girl or something like this for no reason I can figure out. (25) Then I take the situation in hand and set him down or put him outside.

TABLE 2-4. A Segment of a Problem Evaluation Interview (PEI)

Consultant: (1) Well, how was Bob's behavior last week?

Consultee: (2) Well, excellent. (3) We had a great week.

Consultant: (4) I have the data right in front of me.

Consultee: (5) Fantastically improved. (6) There weren't any fights that we needed to worry about all last week; (7) and interruptions decreased very much.

Consultant: (8) I can see. (9) Interruptions were 21 times before plan implementation and 5 times after the start of plan implementation. (10) How did you follow the plan?

Consultee: (11) The first thing we had planned on was finding a substitute behavior for the hitting. (12) Our way of doing this was to have a discussion, a group discussion, on this. (13) Several children came up with the idea that if you had a friend, a friend could help you, (14) and one of Bob's friends said that he could help Bob and Bob could help him stay out of trouble on hitting. (15) Then the next day we had a discussion on the nice things we do.

Consultant: (16) Great!

Consultee: (17) And each day we take time to find out what nice things we did that day.

Consultant: (18) So, as far as his hitting is concerned, are you satisfied that he won't go back to his hitting?

Consultee: (19) No, I'm not satisfied that he won't. (20) It just depends on if his friends are going to be around to stop him.

Consultant: (21) So, if you keep reinforcing good behavior on his part, will it keep him from hitting?

Consultee: (22) Yes.

Consultant: (23) Well, if this comes up again could you start another discussion?

Consultee: (24) Yes, right, by all means we will.

Recognition in an Interview Segment

Recognition, as used in consultation, takes place within the context of long sequences of verbal interactions occurring during an interview. To acquire the skills necessary to recognize the various message-classification subcategories associated with verbal interactions in an interview, it is useful for the consultant to have some experience in coding interview segments. Using a CAR, the reader should code the utterances in Table 2-3, which constitutes a portion of a problem identification interview. The units of observation have been numbered to assist in the coding task.

In addition to providing experience in the coding of an interview, Table 2-3 provides enough information to give an indication of the consultee concerns in this case. Table 2-4 includes a segment of the problem evaluation interview for the case. Figures 2-3 and 2-4 provide the authors' coding of these interviews, and they may be referred to on completion of the practice coding.

CONSULTATION-ANALYSIS RECORD

	Message Source		Message Content							Message Process							Message Control	
	Consultee	Consultant	Background Environment	Behavior Setting	Behavior	Individual Characteristics	Observation	Plan	Other	Negative Evaluation	Positive Evaluation	Inference	Specification	Summarization	Negative Validation	Positive Validation	Elicitor	Emitter
1		/			/						/						/	
2	/				/						/							/
3	/								/		/							/
4		/			/								/					/
5	/				/						/							/
6	/				/								/					/
7	/				/								/					/
8		/			/											/		/
9	/				/								/					/
10		/					/						/				/	
11	/						/						/					/
12	/						/						/					/
13	/						/						/					/
14	/						/						/					/
15	/						/						/					/
16		/					/				/							/
17	/						/						/					/
18		/			/											/	/	
19	/				/										/			/
20	/			/									/					/
21		/					/									/	/	
22	/						/									/		/
23		/					/									/	/	
24	/						/									/		/
25																		

FIGURE 2-3. Analysis of a problem-identification-interview segment.

CONSULTATION-ANALYSIS RECORD

	Message Source		Message Content							Message Process							Message Control	
	Consultee	Consultant	Background Environment	Behavior Setting	Behavior	Individual Characteristics	Observation	Plan	Other	Negative Evaluation	Positive Evaluation	Inference	Specification	Summarization	Negative Validation	Positive Validation	Elicitor	Emitter
1		/			/								/				/	
2	/								/							/	/	
3	/				/								/					/
4	/				/							/						/
5	/					/							/					/
6	/				/							/						/
7	/				/								/					/
8	/				/								/					/
9	/				/							/						/
10	/				/								/					/
11		/			/											/	/	
12	/				/											/		/
13	/				/					/								/
14	/				/					/								/
15	/				/								/					/
16		/			/									/				/
17		/			/									/				/
18	/				/											/		/
19		/		/									/				/	
20	/			/									/					/
21		/		/									/				/	
22	/			/									/					/
23	/			/								/						/
24	/			/									/					/
25	/			/									/					/

FIGURE 2-4. Analysis of a problem-evaluation-interview segment.

Production Practice

To use the message classification system described in this chapter to control interviewing behavior, the reader should be able to produce utterances that correspond to specific message-classification subcategories. The sections that follow illustrate how to practice producing single units of observation and longer interview segments.

Unit Production

Consultation requires the application of interviewing skills to meet an endless variety of needs and purposes. No two situations are exactly alike. Consequently, to be effective, one cannot simply mimic specific sets of verbal behaviors. What must be learned is the ability to generate examples of verbal concepts that meet particular consultation needs. Practice in unit production is intended to foster this kind of concept learning.

The reader's task in practicing unit production is to verbalize units of observation corresponding to message classification subcategories frequently used in consultation. During this task, the reader should keep in mind the fact that the message classification subcategories represent concepts, and that the examples are instances of those concepts. For example, the assertion that an elicitor is a verbalization that calls for a response in a particular content and process subcategory defines the concept of elicitor. To say, "Pass the butter," is to give an example that meets the defining specifications of that concept.

Table 2-5 provides a list of category descriptions of verbal behaviors. The reader should generate several utterances corresponding to each of these. It is desirable to have a friend or colleague check the accuracy of these productions.

TABLE 2-5. Verbal Subcategories
for Unit Production Practice

Behavior specification elicitor
Plan (tactic) specification elicitor
Observation specification elicitor
Behavior-setting specification-elicitor
Plan (strategy) specification emitter
Plan positive-validation elicitor
Observation validation elicitor
Behavior positive-validation elicitor

TABLE 2-6. Verbal Subcategory Sequences for Interview Segment Practice

A problem identification sequence
  1. Emit a series of behavior specification elicitors to identify a behavior of concern to a consultee.
  2. Follow these by a set of behavior-setting specification-elicitors.
  3. Conclude with behavior and behavior-setting summarizations.
A problem analysis sequence
  1. Emit behavior-setting specification-elicitors to identify antecedent, consequent, and sequential conditions that may influence goal attainment.
  2. Follow these with behavior setting summarization-emitters that summarize the conditions identified.
  3. Conclude with validation elicitors that validate what has been expressed in the summaries.
A problem evaluation sequence
  1. Emit the behavior specification elicitors to initiate an examination of data on client performance during plan implementation.
  2. Emit summarization emitters summarizing the goal(s) of consultation.
  3. Conclude with a validation elicitor to validate goal attainment.

Segment Production

To conduct consultation interviews effectively, it is necessary to link units of verbal behavior in an organized sequence. Table 2-6 provides subcategory descriptions and examples of sequences that occur frequently in consultation. The sequences presented are by no means exhaustive. Further discussion of sequences occurs in the chapters dealing with specific interviews.

The task in segment production is to generate strings of verbalizations in an interview corresponding to the subcategories given in Table 2-6. Research (see Goodwin, Carvey, & Barclay, 1971) suggests that, for this kind of task, efficacious results will be achieved if one proceeds in the following manner. First, observe an expert consultant emitting the sequences in Table 2-6 with another role-playing the part of the consultee. Next, ask a friend or colleague to role-play the consultee in an interview with you. Record the interview on video- or audiotape. Code the interview to obtain feedback on the extent to which the interviewing behaviors correspond to the sequences you were trying to emit. Finally, correct your mistakes in another interview segment.

After becoming familiar with the message classification categories described in this chapter, the reader can use them in conducting the various types of interviews in consultative problem-solving. The application of the message classification system in specific interviews will be discussed in detail in Part II of the book.

II

Consultative Problem-Solving

Problem Identification

Problem identification is the first step in consultative problem-solving. Problem identification plays a particularly critical role in consultation in that, when it goes well, there is a very good chance that a plan will be designed and implemented. And when a plan has been put into effect, the chances are extremely high that the problem presented in consultation will be solved (Bergan & Tombari, 1976). On the other hand, if problem identification is not executed correctly, the consultation process may break down and the consultant role itself will be in jeopardy. The consultee is deprived of access to psychological principles, and the consultant is placed in the position of having to find other activities or other consultees.

Two crucial factors in ensuring that problem identification will go as planned are the *knowledge* and the *skills* of the consultant. In this chapter, we discuss the knowledge and skills necessary to conduct the problem identification process and to convey the process to the consultee during the problem identification interview.

THE PROBLEM IDENTIFICATION PROCESS

As shown in Table 3-1, the problem identification process involves a series of steps designed to lead to the specification of the problems presented in consultation. The steps in the process eventuate in the designation of the goal or goals to be achieved through consultation, the measurement of current client performance, with respect to the target behavior and an assessment of the discrepancy between existing client performance and desired client performance.

TABLE 3-1. Steps in Problem Identification

1. Establish objectives.
2. Establish measures for performance objectives.
3. Establish and implement data collection procedures.
4. Display the data.
5. Define the problem by establishing the discrepancy between current performance, as reflected in the data collected, and the desired performance, as indicated in the performance objectives.

Establishing Objectives

The first step in the problem identification process is to specify the goal or goals to be achieved through consultation. The elaborate technology that has been developed in the fields of psychology and education for the specification of objectives can be of invaluable assistance in goal specification. Not all aspects of this technology are applicable to every case of consultation. Nevertheless, the match between consultation needs and instructional-objectives technology is close enough so that it will be useful to view goal specifications in terms of that technology.

Characteristics of Objectives

As indicated in Table 3-2, objectives may have a number of characteristics (Bergan & Dunn, 1976). One that is invariably present is a specification of the behavior or performance required to achieve the objective. For example, a mother might establish the goal of having a child get along well with a brother. The phrase "get along" (although ambiguous) indicates the kind of behavior that the mother is interested in promoting in her child.

Sometimes, the activity associated with an objective is designated much more specifically than it is in the above example. Thus, when a mother says that she wants a child to stop picking his nose or to stop spilling his food at meals, her goal is much more clearly communicated than when she says that she wants the child to get along with a brother.

TABLE 3-2. Characteristics of an Objective

Required characteristics	Optional characteristics
Specification of activity	Description of intended population
Specification of required performance level	Specification of performance conditions
Designation of attainment deadline	

A second essential feature of an objective is some indication of the level of performance required for attainment of the objective. In some cases, the specification of level may be quite general, as in the example of getting along well with one's brother. The term *well* is the only specification of performance level, and it does not indicate with any degree of precision what the mother really expects of the child. Precise designations of performance level are, of course, also possible and are more desirable. For instance, a mother might say that she wanted her little boy to see if he could avoid fighting with his brother for a whole day.

Sometimes, the required performance levels call for an increase in behavior, and sometimes they call for a decrease in behavior. Objectives related to academic accomplishments generally call for performance levels that are higher than those currently being displayed by students. A child who gets only 70% of his weekly spelling words correct may aspire to greater spelling accuracy. Similarly, a child who is doing poorly in such areas as reading and arithmetic generally desires to attain higher levels of skill in these areas. In contrast to academic objectives, objectives related to social behavior often call for a reduction in the current level of performance. For example, parents and teachers almost invariably desire to eliminate completely such behaviors as wetting the bed, hitting others, and disrupting the activities of others.

It is important to note whether an objective calls for an increase or a decrease in performance level because different sets of tactics are involved in accelerating performance and reducing it. For example, positive reinforcement can be used to increase behavior, but another procedure might be used when the goal is to reduce behavior.

One feature that is always implicit in an objective, but that is not always explicitly stated, is the specification of the individual or individuals for whom the objective is intended. In the typical consultation case in which a consultant is working with a parent or a teacher responsible for the development of a child, it is generally obvious for whom the objectives of consultation are intended. However, in some instances of consultation at the organizational level, it may be important to make explicit the specification of the population attempting to achieve a given set of objectives. For example, if a consultant is working with a school's administrator and staff on the formulation of objectives for the school reading program, it is useful to designate the population of children for whom specific sets of objectives in the program are designed.

A fourth desirable feature in an objective is the designation of the conditions under which performance of the objective is to occur. For example, a consultee may establish the goal of having a child achieve a certain level of accuracy in oral reading in a reading group to which the child has been assigned. The stipulation that achievement of the objective requires performance in the reading group indicates a required condition for the accomplishment of the objective.

The specification of conditions is generally desirable when a precise description of the objective is required. In contrast, when such precision is not needed, the description of conditions is usually not warranted. For example, when a consultant is explaining the broad goals of consultation services to a group of parents at a PTA meeting, there would be little value in dwelling on such minutiae as the specific conditions under which performance related to objectives must occur. On the other hand, when the consultant is discussing a specific case with a consultee, it is essential to deal with the matter of conditions.

A final characteristic that may be included in an objective is a deadline for achieving the objective. Deadlines are not generally specified in individual-case consultation; however, they are sometimes established in consultation at the administrative level. For example, in specifying the goals for a psychoeducational-services program in a school, it is usually advisable to specify time limits for the attainment of goals. In many cases, these may be of relatively long duration; for instance, goals might be set for an entire year.

The Specificity of Objectives

Objectives can vary widely in specificity (Duchastel & Merrill, 1973). For example, a father may hope that his child will learn to be a competent reader as a result of school experiences, whereas the first-grade teacher who is working with the child may hope that the child will learn the most common phonetic sounds for all letters and blends.

It is convenient to organize objectives in terms of three levels of specificity (Bergan & Dunn, 1976). These are shown in Table 3-3. Objectives representing the broadest level are called *general objectives*. Objectives of moderate specificity related to general objectives are called *subordinate objectives*, and the most specific objectives are called *performance objectives*.

A general objective is an objective that implies the attainment of all of the goals within a given category of objectives. For example, parents may express the goal that their child should be able to make friends with other children. This goal would be a general objective if it encompassed all of the subordinate goals with which the parents were concerned. Thus, goals involving issues such as the ability to share toys, good sportsmanship in game situations, and politeness in conversation might be included within the general goal of making friends with other children (e.g., McGinnis & Goldstein, 1984). Suppose, however, that the parents indicated that they wanted their child to become a socially competent individual. The objective of achieving social competence would include goals involving effectiveness in interacting with both adults *and* children. When viewed in relation to the

TABLE 3-3. Three Levels of Objectives

Level	Definition	Example
The general objective	An objective that implies attainment of all goals in a given category	The student shall achieve mastery of basic arithmetic operations.
The subordinate objective	An objective that is included in a superordinate category of objectives	The student shall achieve mastery of the operations required in division.
The performance objective	An objective characterized by a behavioral description of performance, conditions specification, and a designation of the required competency level	Given oral instructions, the student shall be able to count from 1 to 20 with 100% accuracy.

objective of achieving social competence, the goal of effective interaction with children is not a general objective. General objectives, then, are defined by their relation to the other goals that have been specified.

General objectives normally include only a broad description of the kinds of activity required for goal attainment and of the level of required performance. Moreover, there is usually no designation of the conditions under which performance is to occur or the deadline within which the objective must be attained. For example, the goal of interacting effectively with other children does not indicate what kinds of interactions are intended or what is meant by *effectiveness.* Nor does it indicate the conditions under which the interaction is to take place or the time allotted for achieving effectiveness. This lack of specificity in the general objective should not be regarded as unnecessary vagueness. It is required to produce the level of generality that the general objective is intended to represent.

The emphasis that has developed on performance objectives over the last several years has tended to overshadow the importance of the general objective. In addition, interest in the general objective has probably been adversely affected by evidence suggesting that highly specific objectives facilitate learning to a greater extent than broad, general objectives (see Dalis, 1970; Kaplan & Rothkopf, 1974). However, it should be noted that not all studies support the view that specific objectives produce greater learning than general objectives (Kaplan, 1974).

Despite that fact that, at least under certain circumstances, behavioral objectives may produce learning outcomes superior to those resulting from the use of general objectives, the general objective may fulfill a number of useful functions. The most significant of these is providing an organizational framework within which to conceptualize other goals. For example, when a school establishes the general goal of enabling students to achieve reading competence, it has established a superordinate category within which it may specify a large number of subordinate categories of objectives.

General objectives also help to ensure that objectives will be coordinated toward the attainment of an overall end. One of the criticisms frequently leveled at performance objectives is that they deal with trivia (Popham, 1968). This criticism may be justified when performance objectives are not organized into a framework that indicates their contribution to larger significant goals (Krathwohl & Payne, 1971).

A second function of the general objective is to provide a long-range focus for goals (Krathwohl & Payne, 1971). When a mother says that she wants her child to get along well with other children, she has set a goal that will probably take a considerable amount of time to achieve.

A third function of the general objective is reducing the number of objectives that an individual must keep in mind (Krathwohl & Payne, 1971). For example, suppose that a consultant were working with a school administrator to establish objectives for consultation services for the year. In such a situation, it would be important to agree on a few broad goals within which other more specific objectives could be delineated. The establishment of broad goals makes it possible for the consultant and the administrator to communicate the program to parents and teachers in a way that will ensure that they will recall what the program is designed to accomplish. Their ability to recall broad program goals can help them to use psychoeducational services effectively when they have a need for such services.

Several subcategories of objectives may be associated with a given general objective. These are referred to as *subordinate objectives*. Thus, for example, the goals described earlier of sharing toys, achieving good sportsmanship, and being polite in conversation would be regarded as subordinate objectives within the general objective of interacting effectively and making friends with children.

Several hierarchically related levels of subordinate objectives may be associated with a general objective. For example, in the area of sharing toys, one set of objectives might pertain to a recognition of the rights of property; another set might deal with the ability to appreciate the desires of others; and a third might be concerned with a recognition of the amount of time one has had possession of a toy.

Subordinate objectives, like general objectives, are expressed in rather broad terms. They do not usually contain a precise designation of activity type or required performance level, and they generally do not include a specification of conditions or deadlines.

Subordinate objectives serve many of the same functions as general objectives. They provide broad classification within which a number of subclassifications can be grouped, offer a relatively long-range focus in goal specification, and reduce the number of objectives that must be kept in mind in situations calling for goal specification.

The one unique function of subordinate objectives is linking performance objectives to general objectives. Performance objectives by themselves often seem trivial; they derive their significance from the manner in which they are linked together to further the achievement of broad goals. Subordinate objectives provide a key mechanism in the linking process. The use of hierarchically arranged categories of subordinate objectives makes it possible to link large sets of performance objectives into logical sequences. Sequencing of this sort not only serves the important function of specifying the relation between any one objective and the other objectives in an area but also provides guidelines for prioritizing specific sets of performance objectives. Consider once again the subordinate objective of learning to share toys and the subcategories of recognizing property rights, the feelings of others, and the length of time of toy possession. It would probably be easier to teach a child to share toys if he or she had some notion of the feelings and needs of other children with respect to toys than it would be if the child lacked such knowledge (Hetherington & McIntyre, 1975). This situation would suggest that objectives dealing with a recognition of the feelings of others be pursued before objectives involving toy sharing *per se*. Of course, other considerations might countermand this suggested ordering of the pursuit of objectives.

The most specific type of object i, is the performance objective, or, as it is often called, the behavioral objective. Mager (1961), whose classic book on preparing instructional objectives was largely responsible for the widespread interest in objectives, designated three defining characteristics of a performance objective: a behavioral description of the activity desired, a specification of the performance conditions, and a precise indication of the required performance level.

The first and most basic feature of a performance objective is a behavioral description of the activity required for attainment of the objective. A behavioral description is one that specifies in observable terms the actions to be taken in accomplishing an objective. The description must be sufficiently explicit so that independent observers would be able to agree on whether an individual had performed the actions required by the objective. For example, if one advanced the goal of achieving understanding of basic arithmetic concepts, there would obviously be room for a great deal of disagreement on what kinds of actions would be needed to demonstrate understanding. On the other hand, if one suggested that a child ought to be able to count out loud from 1 to 10, it would be relatively easy for independent observers to judge whether any given child had actually achieved the specified goal.

The second essential feature of a performance objective is a description of the conditions under which performance must occur. For example, a kindergarten teacher attempting to encourage a young child to talk at school might establish the condition that talking occur when the child was asked a question either by the teacher or by the teacher's aide in the classroom.

The third defining characteristic of a performance objective is a precise quantitative specification of the required performance level. This essential characteristic requires that phrases such as "will achieve mastery" be replaced by designations such as "with 90% accuracy" or "95% of the time."

One function of the performance objective is to provide a specific focus for goal-directed activities. When a goal is stated in performance language, it orients the attention of those seeking to achieve the goal toward the specific tasks requisite to goal attainment (Kaplan & Rothkopf, 1974; Kaplan & Simmons, 1974). Such an orientation is, of course, very important in consultation. It is vital that the consultant and the consultee focus their attention and efforts on the achievement of specific, mutually agreed-upon goals.

A second function of the performance objective is to relate goals to performance measures (Briggs, 1970). When an objective is stated in performance language, it is generally relatively easy to devise a way to measure the attainment of the objective. For example, in the case of the kindergarten teacher who is attempting to teach a young child to respond to adults' questions, goal attainment could be assessed simply by recording the number of times that the child responded to questions from the teacher or the teacher's aide.

A third function of the performance objective is to facilitate goal attainment. Many investigators hold the view that behavioral objectives may enhance learning and thereby promote the achievement of socialization goals. Findings on the extent to which behavioral objectives promote goal attainment have been somewhat inconclusive. Duchastel and Merrill (1973) pointed out that there are about as many studies that do not demonstrate the efficacy of behavioral objectives as there are studies that do. These inconsistencies appear to be traceable to a failure to consider potential influences on the effects of objectives on behavior related to goal attainment. For example, as mentioned above, a major function of the behavioral objective is orienting those seeking to achieve a goal toward tasks requisite to goal attainment. To the extent that situational cues other than objectives serve an orienting function, the contribution of objectives to goal attainment will diminish (Merrill, 1974). When conditions such as the presence of situational cues are taken into account, there is substantial support for the view that performance objectives facilitate goal achievement (Kaplan & Rothkopf, 1974; Kaplan & Simmons, 1974).

Objectives in Developmental and Problem-Centered Consultation

Consultative problem-solving may focus on the achievement of long-range developmental goals or on specific problems of immediate concern to the consultee and the client. These differences in focus require variations in the problem-solving process. One of the major differences between developmental and problem-centered consultation involves the specification of objectives.

Developmental consultation requires the establishment of general, subordinate, and performance objectives. The general and subordinate objectives are designated first. Then, the performance objectives are specified. In the initial problem-identification effort, only a limited number of performance goals are designated. These objectives are then pursued through consultative problem-solving. During the initial problem-identification phase of developmental consultation, provisions are made for the formulation of additional performance goals in reiterative applications of the problem-solving process.

In problem-centered consultation, general and subordinate objectives are not designated. Rather, discussion moves immediately to the specification of one or a limited number of behavioral goals that are of concern to the consultee. As mentioned earlier, problem-centered consultation is designed to deal with highly specific problems that often occur in crisis situations. In cases of this kind, the consultant should not dwell on long-range objectives. Thus, when a consultant is called in to deal with a case in which a student has just attempted to burn the school down, he or she would be well advised to deal with that problem immediately and to defer consideration of more general issues to a later time.

The specification of behavioral goals in problem-centered consultation is generally quite different from the designation of performance objectives in developmental consultation. In the problem-centered approach, the consultant's first task is to elicit behavioral descriptions of those aspects of client functioning that are of concern to the consultee. In contrast, in developmental consultation, the consultant focuses on a description of the behavior desired for the client. Thus, in developmental consultation, a consultant might ask, "What would Bob have to be able to do to demonstrate that he has achieved competence in oral reading?" A consultant examining the same type of behavior in problem-centered consultation might ask, "What are some of the things that Bob does that indicate that he is having difficulty in oral reading?"

Problem-centered consultation differs from developmental consultation in the description of conditions as well as in the specification of behavior. The conditions specified in a performance objective in developmental consultation indicate the circumstances that must prevail during performance aimed at mastery of the objective. Thus, an objective beginning with the phrase "Given a set of addition problems presented on worksheets . . ." indicates that the condition of presenting problems on worksheets must occur during performance of the objective. The description of conditions in problem-centered are now occurring. For example, a consultant might ask, "What generally happens right before Ted gets into a fight at school?"

The central purpose of describing conditions in problem-centered consultation is to identify environmental factors that may influence behavior. For example, the specification of antecedent and consequent conditions during problem identification may lead to the discovery of cues or reinforcers influencing behaviors that are targets for change in consultation.

Even though the basic reason for describing conditions in problem-centered consultation is to identify variables controlling behavior, a description of conditions also plays a role in defining the goals of consultation. As the consultant and the consultee explore the conditions under which the behavior of concern does occur, they also specify the conditions under which it must occur in order to meet the goals of consultation. For example, a consultant might ask, "Where does Ted get into these fights?" In response to this question, the consultee might say "They always take place on the playground. This is what I'm really concerned about, this incessant fighting on the playground." A statement of this kind may lead to the specification that the goal of consultation will be to eliminate fights occurring on the playground. The playground, then, would be a necessary condition of goal attainment.

Another difference between developmental and problem-centered behavioral goals involves the specification of a required competency level. In developmental consultation, a required competency level is generally established during the problem identification interview as a part of the discussion of the performance objective under consideration. In problem-centered consultation, the designation of a competency level is usually deferred until after the collection of baseline data. Deferring the specification of a competency level gives the consultee the opportunity to consider the client's current level of performance in making a decision concerning the desired level of performance.

Although the description of a desired competency level is deferred in problem-centered consultation, there is generally a discussion of the current strength of the client's behavior. The discussion of strength can give the consultant information about the severity of the problem under consideration, and it may be helpful in establishing procedures for assessing client performance. For example, if a parent were dealing with a behavior that occurred at a very high rate, it would probably not be practical to suggest a recording procedure that required the assessment of every instance of the behavior.

Even though the procedures for specifying objectives in problem-centered and developmental consultation are very different, in the end both forms of consultation arrive at the specification of concrete behavioral goals. Both varieties of consultation require objectives that include a behavioral description of client functioning. Both call for a specification of the conditions under which behavior is to occur during goal attainment, and both involve a quantitative specification of the required competency level.

The distinctions between developmental and problem-centered consultation regarding the designation of specific behavioral goals represent typical practice. They do not hold in every case. For example, a consultant dealing with a specific academic problem presented in problem-centered consultation might approach the problem by eliciting a set of performance objectives for the problem. Similarly, after having established general and subordinate objectives in developmental consultation, a consultant might switch to the problem-centered approach to explore the specific behaviors of immediate concern to the consultee.

Selecting Measures of Client Performance

The second step in problem identification is to select measures of client performance articulated to the goals of consultation. The choice of measures falls into three broad categories: tests, work samples, and naturalistic observations of behavior. An enormous amount of research and theory relevant to the assessment of client performance exists in the field of measurement. However, it would be far beyond the scope of this book to discuss this material in detail. What is necessary is to examine the issues related to the use of measures of client performance in the problem identification process. The reader unfamiliar with basic measurements concepts (e.g., reliability and validity) may wish to consult standard works on the measurement and evaluation field to supplement the discussion provided here (e.g., see Salvia & Ysseldyke, 1988).

Tests as Measures of Client Performance

Tests used as part of the problem identification process are intended mainly to provide a measure of the current performance of the client with respect to the objectives to be achieved through consultation. This purpose should be kept in mind continually in deciding whether or not to use a test or in determining what kind of test to use to measure client behavior.

Norm-Referenced Assessment. A norm-referenced test is a measure that describes an individual's performance by specifying his or her position relative to a norm group, that is, a group made up of a sample of individuals intended to represent a larger population (Glaser & Nitko, 1971).

Such tests are often referred to as nomothetic, or involving large numbers of subjects (Cone, 1986). Most of the tests that comprise the traditional armamentarium of consultants are norm-referenced tests. For example, many of the vocational aptitude and interest tests used by school counselors, the individual-intelligence tests and personality tests used by school psychologists, and the group intelligence and achievement measures widely used by a variety of types of consultants fall into the category of norm-referenced measures.

Even though norm-referenced tests may be useful to consultants for a variety of purposes, in general they are not appropriate as measures of client performance in problem identification. Norm-referenced tests generally purport to be measures of psychological constructs such as intelligence, academic achievement, or personality. They are not intended to assess the occurrence of specific behaviors (Barrett, Johnston, & Pennypacker, 1986) and are not linked to interactions. Ultimately, the objectives established during problem identification describe specific client behaviors of concern to the consultee. The measures selected to assess client performance should provide as precise an indication as it is practical to attain of the current level of occurrence of the specific client behaviors.

Although norm-referenced measures are generally to be avoided in assessing client performance during problem identification, there are circumstances in which they may be useful (Kratochwill, 1982; Nelsen, 1985), as when the consultant is providing consultation at the administrative level in an educational setting. Suppose that a consultant were working with an elementary school on the improvement of the school reading program from Grades 1 through 6. A norm-referenced achievement test might be used as a gross indication of performance *vis-à-vis* the objectives established for the group reading program. Individual teachers could supplement achievement test data with performance measures dealing with specific objectives for their own classes.

Another circumstance that might call for the use of a norm-referenced test during problem identification is a teacher's request for assistance in dealing with the academic problems of a new student about whom very little is known. Suppose that a sixth-grade boy has just moved into a school district from out of state. Assume further that it becomes obvious very quickly that the child lacks the necessary reading and math skills to do the work that he is being assigned in class. Under these conditions, it would be necessary to get some general idea of what the child did know in order to determine the point at which to begin working with him. Norm-referenced diagnostic tests in reading and math might be useful in providing a rough indication of where to start assessment with the child. The information provided by such tests might be augmented later by measures articulated to specific instructional objectives established for the child.

A number of norm-referenced psychoeducational tests are used by school psychologists. Goh, Teslow, and Fuller (1981) found that the Peabody Individual Achievement Test (PIAT; Dunn & Markwardt, 1970) and the Wide Range Achievement Test (WRAT; Jastak & Jastak, 1978) were the two most frequently used tests in psychoeducational assessment. However, when norm-referenced tests are used, the consultant should consider the overlap of the test content with the curriculum the child is exposed to (Shapiro, 1987a). For example, Jenkins and Pany (1978) examined first- and second-grade books from five basal reading series: *Keys to Reading* (Harris & Creekmore, 1972); *Reading 360* (Clymer, 1969); the *Bank Street Reading Series* (Black, 1965); the *SRA Reading Program* (Rasmussen & Goldbert, 1970); and *Sullivan Associates Programmed Reading* (Buchanan, 1968). Word lists in these tests were compared to reading recognition subtests from the WRAT, the PIAT, the Metropolitan Achievement Test, and the Slosson Oral Reading Test. Although the authors did not actually assess the children to examine actual differences, they did find large discrepancies across grade levels, tests, and curricula, a finding consistent with those of other writers (e.g., Armbruster, Stevens, & Rosenshine, 1977; Good & Salvia, 1988; Leinhardt & Seewald, 1981).

Criterion-Referenced Assessment. Almost as soon as it began, the performance objectives movement in education produced a concern about the development of criterion-referenced tests that would measure the attainment of objectives rather than the position of an individual in a norm group. Glaser and Nitko (1971) defined a criterion-referenced test as "one that is deliberately constructed to yield measurements that are directly interpretable in terms of specified performance standards" (p. 653).

There are very few commercially available criterion-referenced tests (Cancelli & Kratochwill, 1981). Among the more commonly used published criterion-referenced tests are the Brigance Inventory of Basic Skills (Brigance, 1977) and the Brigance Inventory of Essential Skills (Brigance, 1980). The content areas covered include reading, mathematics, language arts, and such specific skills as health and safety, vocational, and communication skills. Nevertheless, the Brigance inventories may not overlap closely with a specific curriculum, as they are constructed from many different curriculum-content areas (Shapiro, 1987a).

In educational settings, teacher-made tests may also be developed into a criterion-referenced format (Lentz & Shapiro, 1985; Shapiro & Lentz, 1986). In this instance, it is required that the items be constructed to measure specific performance objectives. Also, the conditions under which performance is to occur and the type of behavior assessed must correspond to the specifications described in the objective. For example, if an objective calls for the addition of two single-digit numbers presented on worksheets, then the criterion-referenced test items designed to measure attainment of that objective must be composed of paper-and-pencil problems involving the addition of two single-digit numbers. Presumably, these types of tests have more curriculum overlap than those measures constructed for general application.

The decision about whether to use a criterion-referenced test as a measure of client behavior during problem identification should be based on two considerations: the type of goal to be attained and the availability of a criterion-referenced test to measure it. For example, if the consultee's objective were to increase accuracy in solving division problems, then testing might be a useful tool for assessing client behavior. If the consultee had already constructed tests to measure division performance or were willing to construct such tests, then a criterion-referenced approach to measurement would be indicated. Suppose, however, that, like some teachers, the consultee objected to the use of tests to measure student performance. In this case, it would be necessary to find an alternative way to measure client behavior.

Curriculum-Based Assessment. Another option for the consultant is to rely on the curriculum in which the student is instructed to obtain data for problem identification and analysis. Curriculum-based assessment can be designed to yield technically adequate measurement, to make inferences about the curriculum in general, to discriminate growth in the curriculum, and to assess this growth repeatedly over time (Deno, Marston, & Tindal, 1986).

Currently, there are a number of models of curriculum-based assessment that are used in regular and special education. These include the Resource Consulting Teacher Model (e.g., Idol-Maestas, 1981, 1983), the Vermont Consulting Teacher Models (e.g., Christie, McKenzie, & Burdett, 1972; Knight, Meyers, Paolucci-Whitcomb, Hasazi, & Nevin, 1981), Directive Teaching (Stephens, 1977), Exceptional and Precision Teaching (Lindsley, 1964; White & Haring, 1980), and Curriculum-Based Measurement (Deno & Mirkin, 1977; Deno et al., 1986; Shinn, 1988).

Curriculum-based assessment in consultation problem-solving has at least three advantages over norm- and criterion-referenced testing (Shapiro, 1987a). To begin with, the problem of the test–text overlap is generally solved when the student is assessed on skills that he or she is learning in the classroom. However, this benefit is more salient when a curriculum-based model is in place in the school system. For example, Tindal, Wesson, Germann, Deno, and Mirkin (1985) described the Pine County model as a data-based system for educational assessment and planning. The system makes curriculum-based assessment easy to integrate into problem identification because the curriculum is implemented systemwide. Second, curriculum-based assessment can be linked to instructional planning. Again, this benefit is more likely when a curriculum is in place. Instructional planning can also be made more useful to students when a path-referenced system is developed (see discussion on pp. 156–158). Third, some curriculum-based assessment lends itself to repeated assessment before and after the treatment program. Therefore, this measurement strategy fits in nicely with the goal of behavioral consultation to evaluate interventions as they are implemented.

Integrating curriculum-based assessment into the behavioral consultation process is an important step in problem identification, analysis, and evaluation. Nevertheless, the consultant must consider a large range of variables that influence the instructional process (Lentz & Shapiro, 1985; Shapiro, 1987a). These variables include, for example, setting events, feedback, reinforcement, cueing, instructional pace, and the physical environment (e.g., heat, lighting, and noise).

Work Samples as Measures of Client Performance

Even when a comprehensive curriculum-based assessment format is not in place, a convenient and accurate way to measure client performance in educational settings is to use work samples. Ayllon, Layman, and Kandel (1975), for example, used work samples to measure the academic performance of three hyperactive children. They were able to obtain 100% interobserver agreement in judging the children's academic work. The work sample has several advantages. First of all, it provides objective evidence regarding client actions because it is a tangible product of client behavior. Second, the collection of work samples requires little or no effort on the part of the consultee. Third, work samples afford the consultant with an almost effortless opportunity to observe direct evidence of client behavior. Fourth, work samples often provide a nonreactive measure of client performance because the measures are unobtrusive (Kazdin, 1979).

The main disadvantage of the work sample as a measure of client performance is simply that many objectives do not lend themselves to a work sample format. For instance, a work sample articulated to the objective of reducing disruption may be too far removed from the behavior to provide useful information in the functional analysis of behavior. Nevertheless, even in this case, work samples may provide indirect data on the efficacy of an intervention.

Observational Measures of Client Performance

Perhaps, the most widely used procedure for measuring client behavior during problem identification is to record observations of behavior as it occurs in the natural environment (Hartmann, 1982; Shapiro, 1987a; Shapiro & Kratochwill, 1988). For instance, a parent or a teacher may record tantrum behaviors in a child, or a teacher may record sharing of toys at recess.

The advantage of behavioral observations is that they are easy to artic-ulate to the objectives formulated in consultation. This advantage is partic-ularly clear in the case of those objectives dealing with social interactions or affective states within the individual. Suppose that a mother says her child has a poor self-concept. Instead of measuring self-concept with a test that may be of questionable validity in behavioral assessment, the consultant might ask the mother what the child does to indicate that she has a poor self-concept. Suppose that the mother says that her daughter is continually making disparaging remarks about her schoolwork and about her abilities in playing the kinds of games that she engages in with her friends. On the basis of the mother's remarks, self-concept might be defined in one dimen-sion in terms of the number of disparaging comments that the mother observes the girl making during a given period.

Behavioral observations can be a highly useful tool in consultation in those cases in which it can be assumed that the observations made have adequate accuracy and reliability. However, when observations are inaccu-rate and unreliable, it is not possible to draw valid conclusions from them. For instance, if two people were to observe the child's "self-concept" be-havior in the above illustration and were to come up with markedly differ-ent estimates of the frequency of that behavior, it would be impossible to draw conclusions.

Many writers have suggested that the problem of accuracy or unre-liability be handled by training independent observers to record the behav-ior of concern (e.g., see Gelfand & Hartmann, 1984). Although the idea of obtaining independent recording of behavior is certainly a commendable one, in many instances, it is simply not practical in consultation. Under these conditions, one must simply accept with caution whatever data are provided. There is some justification for such acceptance. In consultation, a consultant must deal with the consultee's interpretation of the problem presented. The consultee's view may, to some extent, be inaccurate, and if the inaccuracy reaches significant levels, both the consultant and the con-sultee may wish to take steps to deal with the issue of accuracy. However, it would be foolish to assume that consultees generally come into consulta-tion with a totally distorted conception of the client's performance. On the contrary, they usually have real concerns related to concrete client behav-iors that they are able to judge with at least some degree of certainty. For example, a teacher might not know whether a child hit other children in the class five or eight times, but he or she would be aware that a significant amount of hitting did occur. Moreover, given assistance in devising a method of recording hitting behavior, the teacher would in all likelihood be able to record accurately enough to determine whether hitting was increas-ing or had decreased to the point where it no longer constituted a problem.

Although in some cases it may be impractical to assess the accuracy of reporting in consultation, a consultant can do a number of things to increase the probable accuracy of observations. First, the consultant should be sure that there is a behavioral definition of the client actions to be recorded (Baer, Wolf, & Risley, 1968; Gelfand & Hartmann, 1984; Hawkins & Dobes, 1975; Hawkins & Dotson, 1975). A behavioral definition clarifies what is to be observed and thereby increases the likelihood that the individual taking data will know precisely what he or she is to observe. As already suggested, the specification of behavioral definitions for actions to be observed during consultation may be accomplished through the use of behavior specification elicitors. Thus, for example, a consultant might ask, "What are some examples of things that Bobby does to demonstrate his poor self-concept?" The answer to a question of this kind usually provides a set of behavioral descriptions of client actions, some or all of which may serve to define the behavior of concern.

The second thing a consultant can do to increase the accuracy of observations is to make sure that the individual taking data is not saddled with an excessively demanding recording task (McLaughlin, 1975; Wetzel & Patterson, 1975). If the observer is required to record many behaviors under stringent time pressures, the likelihood of unreliability will be increased.

A third step that a consultant may take to increase accuracy is to monitor data collection activities. He or she should call the consultee on the telephone or, if possible, make a visit to the consultee to check on the recording procedures. This kind of monitoring shows concern on the part of the consultant that can influence the motivation of observers to take data accurately. In addition, it provides an opportunity to clear up any misunderstandings regarding the data collection process.

In monitoring data collection, the consultant should avoid giving evaluative feedback, as such feedback may adversely affect the accuracy of observations (O'Leary, Kent, & Kanowitz, 1975). For example, if the consultant were to say, "I'm glad to see that the data show so much improvement in Bob's behavior," it is not unlikely that the consultee's subsequent records would conform to the consultant's judgment, whether or not there was continued improvement in Bob's performance.

A fourth thing that a consultant can do to increase accuracy is to conduct training sessions to teach observers to record reliably (O'Leary *et al.*, 1975). It is not always practical to do this. However, in those instances in which it can be done, it is certainly advisable. One way to accomplish observational training in educational settings is to include it as part of teacher in-service training. In consultation with parents, it is sometimes possible to conduct training during home visits.

Selecting a Measurement Strategy

The behavioral consultant has available a wide variety of methods for gathering observational data. A first issue that the consultant must deal with is who will gather the data. In most cases, it will be desirable to have the consultee collect data for the purposes of problem identification and analysis. Under some conditions, however, it may be impossible to obtain data from the consultee. Several problems may emerge from having the consultee gather data. For example, the recording format may require extensive training or may be too complex or too intrusive, or the consultee may express philosophical objections to recording. Thus, for whatever reason, having the consultee gather data may be impossible or may yield data that are less than accurate given the conditions of consultation.

As a second option, the consultant might consider permanent product data or work sample data. Permanent product data are data that already exist or will come into existence as a natural by-product of behavior. For example, as noted above, a teacher may be willing to share a child's worksheets from math assignments because such assignments are a normal product of school activities and are therefore less intrusive.

A third option that the consultant can consider for data collection is to have the client collect data himself or herself. Such recording is often referred to as *self-observation* or *self-recording* (Gardner & Cole, 1988; Mace & West, 1986; Nelson, 1977a,b). Self-recording involves two components: discrimination of a behavior (overt or covert) and a record of its occurrence. Client recording is often feasible with children even when they are quite young (Risley & Hart, 1968). Self-recording may even have the advantage (or disadvantage, depending on the context) of being reactive on the behavior being recorded. For example, Piersel and Kratochwill (1979) implemented a self-observation procedure to gather baseline data on four children receiving behavioral consultation services. In the first case, the focus was on a child's assignment completion. Figure 3-1 shows data gathered by the teacher before and after the child's self-recording of her scores on a card taped inside her desk. In the second case, a child's disruptive talk was the focus of behavioral consultation. Following baseline recording by the teacher of teacher attention to loud talk, a self-charting program was implemented. The data reported in Figure 3-2 show that the self-charting reduced disruptive talk under teacher and student "unaware" and teacher and student "aware" of each other's conditions. In a third case, the number of interruptions of a 9-year-old girl were monitored across baseline and self-charting conditions. Figure 3-3 shows that the self-charting was effective in reducing interruptions under student unaware and aware conditions of teacher co-monitoring. Generally, data from the student and teacher correspond across the intervention phases.

In the fourth case, a 15-year-old male student was asked to self-record in Science Research Association (SRA) language arts and subsequently in math. Figure 3-4 suggests that the boy failed to complete any SRA or math assignments during baseline. Following the initiation of self-charting in language arts, his SRA performance began to increase, whereas his math

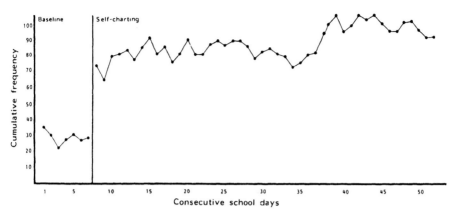

FIGURE 3-1. The cumulative frequency of assignment completion in Science Research Association (SRA) and math units across school days before and after self-charting. [Source: W. C. Piersel & T. R. Kratochwill (1979). Self-observation and behavior change: Applications to academic and adjustment problems through behavioral consultation. *Journal of School Psychology*, *17*, 151–161. Copyright 1979 the Journal of School Psychology Inc. Reproduced by permission.]

performance remained at zero. Following the introduction of self-charting in math, a similar positive effect was noted.

A fourth option that the consultant can entertain is to have individuals outside the consultee role take part in observational recording. Such individuals include teacher assistants or aides, relatives, peers, or other volun-

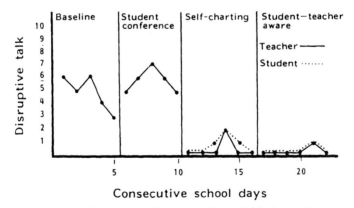

FIGURE 3-2. The number of times a teacher attended to a child's loud talk on consecutive school days before and after self-charting. A student conference was held before the initiation of the self-charting. [Source: W. C. Piersel & T. R. Kratochwill. (1979). Self-observation and behavior change: Applications to academic and adjustment problems through behavioral consultation. *Journal of School Psychology*, *17*, 151–161. Copyright 1979 the Journal of School Psychology, Inc. Reproduced by permission.]

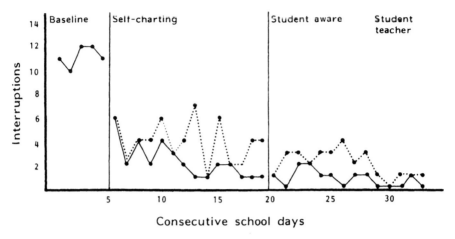

FIGURE 3-3. The frequency of interruptions of a 9-year-old girl across baseline and self-charting conditions. Following the first self-charting condition, the student was made aware that the teacher was also recording interruptions. [Source: W. C. Piersel & T. R. Kratochwill. (1979). Self-observation and behavior change: Applications to academic and adjustment problems through behavioral consultation. *Journal of School Psychology, 17,* 151–161. Copyright 1979 the Journal of School Psychology, Inc. Reproduced by permission.]

teers. This option may involve some training of the observer by the consultant outside the scope of typical consultation interactions. However, in the long run, this option may prove time-efficient. Client peers may be involved in data collection. A variety of studies have demonstrated that peers can be taught to collect reliable observations of behavior (e.g., see Fixsen, Phillips, & Wolf, 1972; Surratt, Ulrich, & Hawkins, 1969). In the event that consultation involves two or more clients, it may even be possible for each one to record the behavior of another. Checks on reliability can be obtained by comparing self-observations with peer observations.

A fifth option is for the consultant to gather the data directly himself or herself. It may not always be a good idea for the consultant to become involved in data collection, for three reasons. The first and most important is that it blurs the distinction between consultant and consultee responsibilities. Data collection is one form of commitment on the part of the consultee to take concrete steps to solve his or her own problems. If the consultant preempts this commitment by collecting data for the consultee, the consultee may infer that the consultant is going to take responsibility for solving the problem.

The second reason that the consultant should not assume the responsibility for data collection is that it is not an efficient use of time. As indicated in Chapter 1, one of the principal advantages of consultation is that it makes psychological knowledge available to many more clients than is possible when a psychological specialist renders services directly to clients.

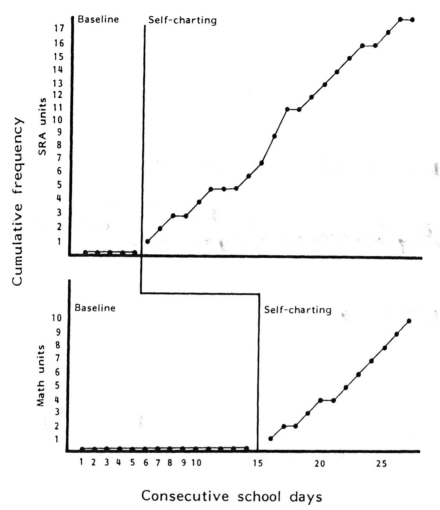

FIGURE 3-4. The percentage correct of assignment completion in phonics across school days before and after self-charting. [Source: W. C. Piersel & T. R. Kratochwill. (1979). Self-observation and behavior change: Applications to academic and adjustment problems through behavioral consultation. *Journal of School Psychology, 17,* 151–161. Copyright 1979 the Journal of School Psychology, Inc. Reproduced by permission.]

The instant that the consultant steps out of the consultant role and begins to provide direct services, this advantage is eliminated. Thus, for example, during the time when a consultant is recording client behavior, she or he could be providing consultation services to another consultee.

The final reason that the consultant should not become involved in data collection responsibilities is that, in most cases, it is simply impractical for him or her to do so. For example, suppose that continuous data collection is called for over a 5-day period. It may be impossible for the consultant to assume the responsibility of making a record of this kind.

Although a consultant should not take the responsibility for data collection, he or she should make an attempt to observe client behavior. Such observations may not be necessary in every case, but there may be circumstances in which the consultant will find it useful to observe the client in the environment in which the behavior of concern is occurring.

Collecting Data: Further Considerations

After observers have been selected to assess client performance, data on client behavior must be collected. Data collection requires careful planning involving several questions. Among these are: What shall be recorded? How shall recording occur? How many data shall be collected? When shall recording take place? How many observations shall be made? Who shall do the recording?

What to Record

In the case of tests, what one records depends on whether one is using a norm-referenced or a criterion-referenced instrument. If the test is a norm-referenced instrument, the manual invariably presents a variety of derived scores (e.g., IQs and percentile ranks), all of which indicate, in some way or another, the position of an individual in a norm group.

Because there are certain situations in which norm-referenced testing may be called for during problem identification, there are circumstances in which derived scores specifying group position may be used. The reader interested in a detailed explanation of these types of scores may consult any of the standard works on measurement and evaluation (e.g., Anastasi, 1976; Salvia & Ysseldyke, 1988).

If one is using a criterion-referenced test, a record is made of whether the objectives measured by the test have been mastered. When the test deals with the mastery of several objectives (as most test do), mastery may be summarized by indicating the number of objectives mastered or the percentage of objectives mastered.

In the case of the curriculum-based assessment or work samples, perhaps the most common measurement procedure is to record the frequency or rate of occurrence of the target response of concern. For instance, one might record the number of problems worked correctly on a homework assignment. Another measure often used on a work sample is the percentage of homework problems worked correctly.

Four recording techniques often assessed in naturalistic observations are event recording, duration recording, momentary-time sampling, and interval recording.

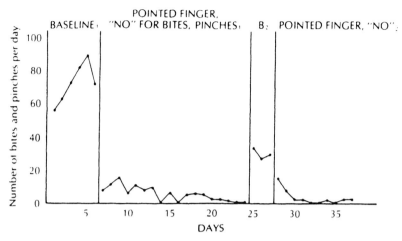

FIGURE 3-5. A child's daily rate of aggressive behavior. Baseline 1—Before the punishment procedure. Pointed Finger, "No" for Bites and Pinches—Teacher pointing and shouting "no" at the child contingent on bites and pinches. Baseline 2—Return to Baseline 1 conditions. Pointed Finger, "No"—Reinstatement of punishment procedures. [Source: R. V. Hall *et al.* (1971). The effective use of punishment to modify behavior in the classroom. *Educational Technology, 11*(4), 25.]

Event Recording. Event recording involves counting the number of behaviors observed during some observational period. Event recording is sometimes called *frequency assessment* and is one of the most common measures used in making behavioral observations. An investigation by Hall, Axelrod, Foundopoulos, Shellman, Campbell, and Cranston (1971) exemplifies the measurement of events (or events recording) in applied work with children. These investigators studied the use of verbal reprimands for aggressive classroom behavior. Their outcome measure involved assessing the number of times per day that a 7-year-old child hit or pinched another child. Figure 3-5 shows the outcome expressed as a percentage per day.

Duration Recording. Duration recording is used when the observer is interested in measuring some temporal aspect of behavior, such as duration, latency, or interresponse intervals (Gelfand & Hartmann, 1984). *Duration* refers to the length of time that a behavior or a set of behaviors occurs and is usually measured with some type of timing device such as a stopwatch. For example, a teacher may be concerned about the amount of time a child spends on a given task. A parent may be concerned about how long a temper tantrum lasts after they say, "No."

An experiment by Glynn, Thomas, and Shee (1973) illustrates the measurement of duration. These researchers were concerned with the effects of externally imposed contingencies and self-management techniques on "on-task behavior" in an elementary-school classroom. On-task behav-

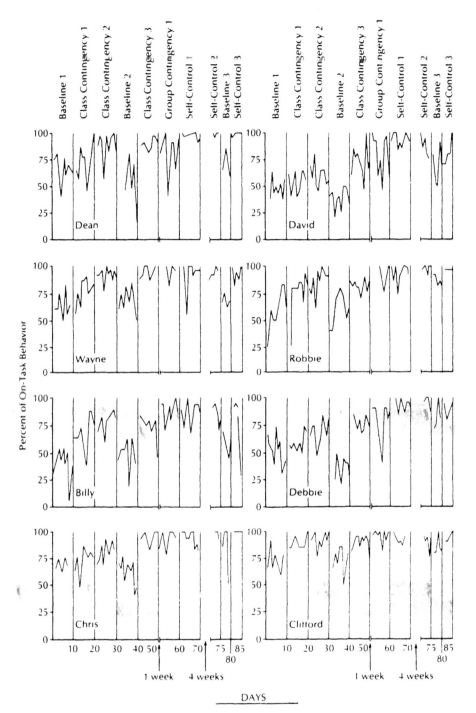

FIGURE 3-6. Individual daily on-task behavior scores. [Source: E. L. Glynn, J. D. Thomas, & S. M. Shee. (1973). Behavioral self-control of task behavior in an elementary classroom. *Journal of Applied Behavior Analysis, 6,* 111.]

ior was defined as the percentage of 10-second observation intervals in which a given child's behavior could be classified as on-task in terms of a particular academic assignment. Behaviors such as looking at the teacher, reading to the teacher, and writing were among the activities coded as on-task. As shown in Figure 3-6, Glynn and his associates summarized on-task behavior as the percentage of time per day that students spent on-task.

Latency of response refers to the time period between the end of a stimulus and the onset of the response signaled by the stimulus. In educational settings, latency is often an issue in flash-card drill sessions conducted for such purposes as learning to identify sight words. Walters, Parke, and Cane (1965) carried out an investigation illustrating the measurement of latency. They were interested in studying the effects of the timing of punishment on resistance to the temptation of playing with forbidden toys. One of the measures that they used was response latency. They calculated the amount of time from the moment that an adult experimenter left the room, affording the child the opportunity to engage in surreptitious play with forbidden toys, to the moment the child first touched one of the toys.

Momentary-Time Sampling. The momentary-time-sampling procedure is used when the observer is interested in determining whether a behavior occurs at some predetermined time. As Gelfand and Hartmann (1984) noted, this assessment technique is like taking a series of still photographs and examining them to determine if a particular behavior has occurred. The measurement can be signaled by some type of timing device.

Interval Recording. The interval-recording method involves breaking down an observation period into equal intervals and recording whether the behavior occurred at any time during the interval. The interval size is usually small, ranging from a few seconds to a few minutes. The interval size is based on three characteristics: the rate of the response, the average duration of a single response, and practical considerations (Gelfand & Hartmann, 1984). Gelfand and Hartmann recommended that in the case of high-rate target behaviors, the interval should generally be small so as not to include two complete responses in a single interval and at least as long as the average duration of a single response (p. 48).

How to Record

The issue of how to record (i.e., what behavior, what strategy, and how frequently) is of concern when performance is to be measured by means of behavioral observations. In contrast, published standardized tests indicate how recording is to be done and how scoring will be accompllshed. One way to record behavior is to use a mechanical counter. A number of inexpensive models are available. Mechanical devices are particularly useful when the behavior to be recorded occurs at a very high rate. Verbal interruption by students during classroom instruction is an example of a behavior that may occur at such a high rate that it is difficult to record it without the aid of a mechanical counter. In some cases, electronic devices may be used for recording.

Although mechanical devices are often useful, by far the most common method of recording is simply to mark the occurrence of behavior on paper. This procedure has the advantage of being inexpensive and convenient. It does take some time to prepare materials, but the amount of time required is usually minimal.

Again, a variety of observational codes have been developed that can be used in consultation. These include those appropriate for home settings (Patterson, Ray, Shaw, & Cobb, 1969), school (Alessi & Kaye, 1983; O'Leary, Romancyzyk, Kass, Dietz, & Santogrossi, 1979; Saudargas, 1983), and home and school (Wahler, House, & Stambaugh, 1976). The code developed by Wahler et al. (1976) provides 24 possible categories of behavioral observation. The observer marks one of six types of events preceding some behavior, followed by an appropriate response category that corresponds to the behavior; thus, scoring in multiple categories of behavior is possible. The Wahler et al. code has been used in several applied settings (e.g., Wahler, 1980; Wahler & Fox, 1980).

Another code, by Saudargas and Creed (1980), was developed for use by school psychologists and enables the observer to record 15 student and 6 teacher behaviors. The code is considered very useful in overall behavioral assessment efforts (Shapiro, 1987a; Shapiro & Lentz, 1986) and allows the recording of a wide range of teacher and child behaviors. The recording sheet used in the Saudargas observational assessment is reproduced in Figure 3-7. As can be observed in the figure, relevant information regarding conditions occurring at the time of observation are recorded by the observer. The various behavior categories are abbreviated in the lefthand column with various states followed by events. The Saudargas code has been the subject of rather limited research, but it is useful for observing teacher and child behavior. Nevertheless, the code was designed primarily to be used in classroom settings where some type of academic instruction occurs. Thus, it may be limited in terms of assessing a broader sample of childhood behavior in nonclassroom settings (Shapiro, 1987a).

Figure 3-8 provided another illustration of a form that can be used for compiling records of behavior whether they be mechanical, electronic, or written. The form indicates the dates during which recording is to take place, the behavior to be recorded, the conditions under which recording is to occur, and the method of recording. When conducting consultation, it is useful to have this kind of information written down to ensure that there

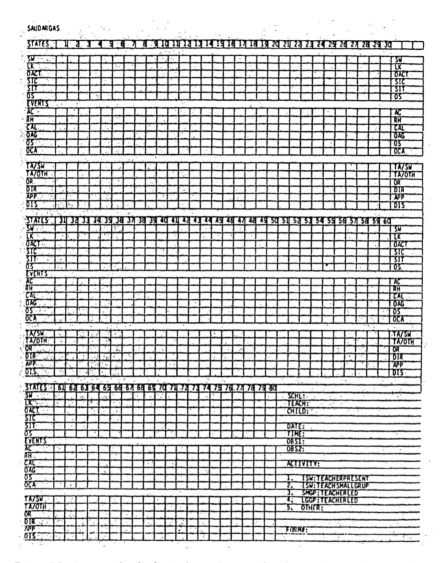

FIGURE 3-7. An example of a direct-observation recording format. [Source: R. A. Saudargas. (1983). *State-event classroom observation code.* Knoxville: University of Tennessee, Department of Psychology.]

will be no misunderstandings between the consultant and the consultee about what is intended. If the consultee does not understand how data are to be recorded, there will usually be a frustrating delay in getting to the problem-analysis and plan-implementation stages of the consultation process. Written records of information about recording can help to forestall the occurrence of this kind of delay.

DATA COLLECTION

Dates: From _____ to _____ Child's Name: _____

Behavior:

Conditions under which recording occurs:

Recording Procedures:

Time	Score	Antecedent Events	Consequent Events

FIGURE 3-8. Recording form. [Source: Adapted from J. R. Bergan & J. A. Dunn. (1976). *Psychology and education: A science for instruction.* New York: Wiley, p. 383. Copyright 1976 by John Wiley & Sons, Inc. Used by permission of John Wiley & Sons, Inc.]

Note that the data collection form provides for the recording of the time that a behavior occurred, the fact that it did occur, and the antecedent and consequent events related to it. It is not always necessary or useful to record all of these things. In some cases, it may be impractical to record anything other than the fact that the behavior of concern took place a given number of times. However, in other instances detailed information on time and conditions is warranted. This kind of information is particularly valuable during problem analysis in that it gives an indication of some of the factors that may be influencing the behavior of concern to the consultee.

Kubany and Sloggett (1973) devised the form shown in Figure 3-9, which they found to be particularly useful for teachers faced with the task of recording classroom behavior. The form is designed to be used with any recording-time schedules. These are indicated across the top of the record-

Date _____
Student _____
Teacher _____
Starting Time _____
Activity _____

Comments	Four	Eight	Sixteen
	2	12	12
	5	2	8
	7	10	28
	1	4	2
	3	6	24
	6	14	6
	4	8	24
	6	2	6
	4	10	30
	1	14	12
	2	8	16
	5	10	4
	3	6	8
	7	4	30
	2	12	28
	1	4	6
	7	12	24
	3	14	16
	4	2	12
	5	6	2

FIGURE 3-9. Teacher's observation code sheet including 4-, 8-, and 16-minute variable-interval schedules. [Source: E. S. Kubany & B. B. Sloggett. (1973). Coding procedure for teachers. *Journal of Applied Behavior Analysis, 6,* 341.]

ing sheet. As the reader can see in Figure 3-9, the recording schedules provide the option of recording on interval schedules that average out to be 4, 8, or 16 minutes. The columns of numbers for each recording schedule indicate the specific time intervals during which recording is to occur for each of the schedules.

To use the form, a teacher begins by setting a timer for the first time interval designated for the recording schedule that has been selected. For example, if the teacher decides to record on the 4-minute schedule, the given timer should be set for 2 minutes because that interval is the first interval given for the 4-minute schedule. When the timer goes off, the teacher simply records whether or not the behaviors of concern are taking place at that time. The timer is then set for the next interval, which, in the case of the 4-minute schedule, would be 5 minutes. This recording cycle is repeated throughout the time period that has been established for data collection.

DATA CHART

NAME *Scot* OBSERVER *L* DATE *2/11*

SPECIFIC BEHAVIORS PINPOINTED *"Swearing," for example, says G-d, says s-, says s-o-b and says b-.*

DATE	FREQUENCY	TIME INTERVAL	MINUTES OR HOURS	RATE	COMMENTS
2/11 Mon.	卌 /	8:30 am-4 pm	7½ hrs.	.8	
2/12 Tue.	卌 卌 ////	8:30 am-10 pm	13½ hrs.	1.03	

FIGURE 3-10. Data recording form for parents. [Source: G. R. Patterson. (1971). *Families: Applications of social learning to family life.* Champaign, IL: Research Press, p. 65.]

If the behavior of interest is occurring at a low rate, the above recording procedure may be modified by noting whether or not a behavior has occurred at any time during an interval rather than only at the time that the timer goes off. For example, a teacher using the 4-minute schedule might record whether a child has been on-task at any time during the first 2-minute interval.

The Kubany and Sloggett procedure has been used to record three kinds of classroom behavior: on-task behavior, passive behavior, and disruptive behavior. On-task behavior is described as doing what is required and is coded *A*. Passive behavior is defined as not doing what should be done, but not disrupting others. Passive behavior is coded *P*. Disruptive behavior includes such activities as being out of one's seat without permission, talking without permission, or making excessive noise; it is coded *D*.

Patterson (1971) reported the data chart shown in Figure 3-10 to be particularly useful for parents. As indicated in the figure, the form allows the observer to note for a given set of dates the frequency of occurrence of a behavior within a certain time interval. This information makes it possible to compute the response rate for the behavior of concern.

All the record forms presented in this chapter have in common the fact that they are generally easy to use. Simplicity is highly desirable in consultation. As we have indicated, keeping recording tasks simple may facilitate the reliability of the records. In addition, it may forestall negative reactions to data collection that can arise when recording demands on the consultee are excessive.

How Much to Record

The two principal variables that determine how much behavior is to be recorded during consultation are the number of clients involved in consultation and the number of behaviors of interest for each client. For example, if a consultee is concerned about a single behavior in a single child, then it may be necessary to record only one target behavior in one child. Suppose, however, that the consultee is a teacher who is concerned about a broad class of behaviors emitted by every student in the class. For example, the teacher might be concerned about the mastery of basic sight vocabulary in a group of 30 first-grade students. Under these conditions, a great deal of recording would be required.

As already noted, one of the continual problems facing consultants is making sure that recording demands placed on consultees do not get out of hand. Clearly, when the number of behaviors or the number of clients of concern is large, recording demands can quite easily become excessive. One way to deal with the problem of recording large numbers of behaviors and/or the behavior of a large number of clients is to use sampling techniques. For example, suppose that a first-grade teacher working with basic sight vocabulary is dealing with a pool of 300 words. He might sample 10 words a day for a period of 15 days. By this procedure, he would attain a fairly accurate estimate of the percentage of the 300 words mastered by the children whose behavior he was assessing. If he is dealing with a large number of children, he might sample children as well as words. For instance, he could assess five randomly selected children per day. If, as is usually the case in the schools, the teacher wants data on all the children, he would simply continue the sampling until all of the children had been tested.

How Many Times to Record

Because of the well-known fact that behavior may change as a function of time, it is generally useful to take some precautions to make sure that the behavior observed during problem identification is not simply a transitory phenomenon. Behavior therapists generally handle this problem by collecting data on a number of occasions over time. A series of data points of this kind provides a baseline against which to judge changes that accrue as a result of treatment. For example, if one were concerned with aggressive behavior in a child, one might record the number of fights the child got into over a 3-day period. Changes occurring during plan implementation could then be judged against this baseline. By contrast, if one were interested in assessing progress in reading achievement in 100 first-grade classrooms, one might randomly sample classrooms to obtain five samples, each conlaining 20 classes that could be tested over a period of 5 weeks. These data would provide a baseline against which to judge changes in reading resulting from plan implementation.

The first condition that should be considered in determining the length of baseline recording is the consistency of the behavior. If the rate of occurrence of a behavior is highly stable across a number of occasions, then the period of collecting baseline data can be quite short, for example, three or four recording sessions. On the other hand, if the behavior is highly unstable, then it is usually advisable to collect data over a longer period. (A more detailed discussion of this issue is provided in Barlow *et al.*, 1984.)

A final factor that must be taken into account in determining the length of baseline is the severity of the problem as judged by the consultee and/or the consultant. In the case of severe problems, it may be necessary to curtail or entirely eliminate the collection of baseline data. For example, if a child's aggressive actions are causing physical harm to other children, it would not be advisable to subject his or her peers to the torture of an extended period of baseline data collection.

Displaying Data: The Graph

After data have been collected, they should be summarized in a form that can be easily interpreted by the consultee. There are a variety of ways in which effective data display can be accomplished. Although it would be beyond the scope of this book to discuss all of these (see Parsonson & Baer, 1978, 1986), the following will give the reader some examples of procedures to be used to display the data obtained during consultation. We have chosen to use the line graph to illustrate data display procedures because this is the most common data display technique used in consultation.

Functions of the Graph

One reason for constructing line graphs is that they provide a visual representation of the behavior under study. The visual information presented in a graph is by and large easier to comprehend than a similar amount of information presented verbally or in a table. In a graph, one can see at a single glance both the quantity of behavior occurring at a given point in time (trend) and changes in the rate of behavior (trend) occurring over successive time periods. One can easily prove this to her or his satisfaction by looking at the graph in Figure 3-11 and then trying to describe in words what one sees.

A second reason for constructing graphs is that they can alert the consultant and the consultee to factors that may be influencing behaviors of concern in consultation. For example, changes in the rate of occurrence

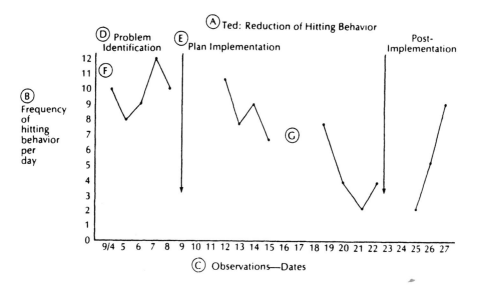

A. Title: Name and modification goal
B. Labeling of the ordinate
   1. Behavior—hitting
   2. Response strength measure—rate
   3. Unit of response strength—day
   4. Range of response strength—0-12
C. Labeling of the abscissa
   Dates on which data were collected
D. Labeling of case phases
E. Separation of case phases
   1. Draw vertical arrows to separate phases
   2. Do not connect data points between phases
F. Data points
   1. Connect data points, except
   2. between phases and
   3. when there is missing data
G. Example of missing data

FIGURE 3-11. A sample graph.

of behavior are much more apparent in a graph than they may be in a table describing behavior or in a verbal description of behavior. To the extent that a graph can call attention to changes in rate, it may alert the consultant and the consultee to search for variations in conditions occurring along with rate variations.

Essentials of Graphing

If the consultant and the consultee are to interpret a graph easily, it must have certain characteristics. These are summarized in Figure 3 11. As indicated in Figure 3-11, the first requirement for constructing an interpretable graph is a title that describes what the graph is about. The title

should include a behavioral description of what was recorded and a designation of the individual whose behavior was observed.

The second essential characteristic of an interpretable graph is appropriate labeling of the ordinate and the abscissa. The labeling of the ordinate
(the vertical axis) should include a designation of the behavior (e.g., hitting
behavior) that was recorded, a specification of the type of strength measure
used (e.g., frequency), and an indication of the period of time during
which recording occurred. In addition, the ordinate must be numbered in
units that include a broad enough range to accommodate expected variations in the behavior recorded.

The abscissa should indicate the times when observations were made.
It is generally best to specify these as dates rather than, for example, days.
When days are used, one loses information regarding the frequent cessa-
tions of recording that may occur on weekends or holidays.

The third essential characteristic of an interpretable graph is an indication of the phase in the consultation process during which the data were
collected. Graphs used in consultation may contain three phases. The first
presents the baseline data recorded during problem identification. The
second contains data taken during plan implementation, and the third
includes whatever postimplementation or follow-up data there may be.
Generalization data (e.g., across behaviors or settings) should be included
as well.

The phases in consultation are described first of all by being labeled on
the graph. In addition, vertical arrows may be drawn to show the separation between phases. Finally, lines connecting data points may be omitted
at transitions between phases.

Another essential feature of an interpretable graph is the designation
of missing data. One signifies missing data simply by omitting the line
linking the data points adjacent to the missing data.

A final essential feature of an interpretable graph is obvious: the accurate plotting of the data on the graph. All that is required is to place the
data points at the appropriate intersections on the ordinate and the abscissa, and then to draw a line connecting the data points. One should be
sure, however, to omit the line between phases and for missing data.

Variations in Graphing Format

The example given in Figure 3-9 is sufficient to meet graphing needs in
the kinds of cases typically encountered in consultation. However, there
are occasions on which alterations in format may be required.

In one situation that frequently arises in consultation and that calls for
some modification in graphing format, the consultee is collecting data that
involves sampling children and/or behavioral tasks. Consider the graphs
in Figure 3-12. These graphs illustrate one way to collect data on a sample

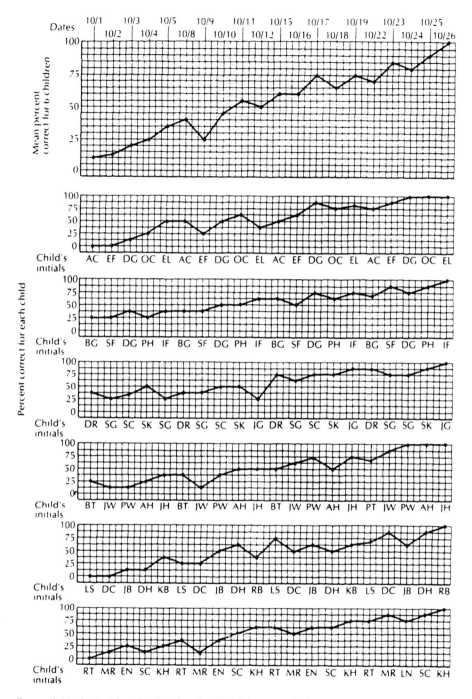

FIGURE 3-12. Letter identification data for 30 children sampled 6 at a time. Ten letters were sampled each day. [Source: J. R. Bergan & J. A. Dunn. (1976). *Psychology and education: A science for instruction.* New York: Wiley, p. 385. Copyright 1976 by John Wiley & Sons, Inc. Reprinted by permission.]

of children and a sample of tasks. In this example, six children were sampled each day. Their initials are given on the abscissas of the six graphs providing data on individual children. The children's task was to identify letters of the alphabet. Ten letters were sampled each day. The percentage of letters that each child identified correctly is represented on the ordinates of the graphs of individual behavior. The graph at the top of the figure summarizes the performance of all six children sampled each day.

Graphs such as in Figure 3-12 make it possible for a teacher to see overall class progress at a glance. In addition, with a little effort, one can observe the progress of individual children. The data in this example were collected for a period of 20 days, during which each child in the class was sampled at least three times. Thus, it was possible to observe trends in the performance of individual children. Consider child AC, the first child listed in the uppermost individual graph. He knew none of the letters the first time he was sampled. However, when he was asked to identify letters on 10/5, he was able to respond correctly to 50% of the letters presented, and when he responded on 10/22, he knew 75% of the letters presented.

A second case that requires a special graphing format is the attempt to record the relation between the acquisition of skills and a change in the behavior of concern in consultation. In this case, the graph should include data on the behavior of concern and on the skills related to that behavior. An example is given in Figure 3-13. In this example, the problem was to teach the child to read a list of 40 basic sight-vocabulary words. The basic method of instruction was the language experience approach to reading. In this approach, the teacher elicited oral language (for example, stories) from the children. The subject's words were written down by the teacher, and the child was given an opportunity to read them. Flash cards were constructed for each child containing words from dictated stories. These cards contained words that each child had difficulty reading. The children were encouraged to practice identifying the words on their set of cards to improve their reading skills. The consultee made no change in this teaching method throughout the period of consultation. The consultant and the consultee assumed that the basis for Bob's inability to read the words on his flash cards was that he lacked the prerequisite intellectual skills in word identification. Thus, the consultee continued to provide instruction in the usual manner. In addition, she introduced instruction in the hypothesized prerequisite skills. This tactic allowed the consultant and the consultee to examine the functional relations between skill acquisition and reading performance.

The skills-graphing format shown in Figure 3-13 makes it possible to represent visually the functional relation between skills and performance. The critical feature of this kind of graph is that data are presented on both performance and skills. Baseline data on the behavior of concern must be taken before skills instruction is introduced. The initial level of perfor-

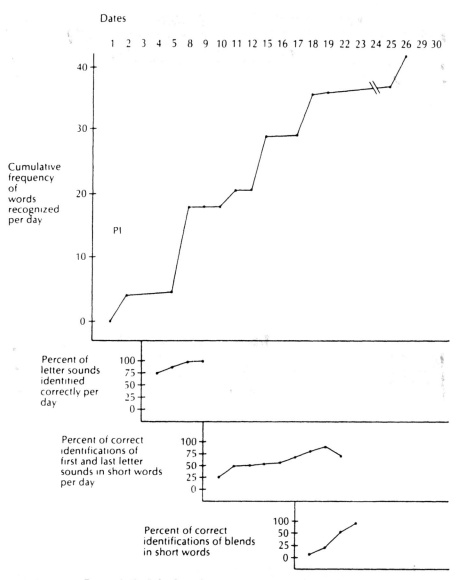

FIGURE 3-13. Bob: Cumulative increase in word recognition.

mance is usually taken as a baseline for each of the skills that are to be targets of instruction.

Defining the Problem

The visual display of data presented in graphic form provides some necessary but not sufficient information for problem definition. As indicated earlier, a problem can be defined, in part, in terms of the discrepancy between the observed performance and the desired performance. In determining this discrepancy, it is important to consider both the magnitude of the difference between performance and objectives and the trend in performance. For example, suppose that the extent of the difference between performance and objectives is relatively large, but that there is a sharp trend in performance in the direction of goal attainment. Under these conditions, the consultant and consultee would probably conclude, at least tentatively, that the problem of concern is a transitory one. As a result, they would very likely decide to defer problem analysis, at least for the time being. On the other hand, suppose that the magnitude of the discrepancy between performance and objectives is relatively small, but that the trend in baseline is not toward goal attainment. Under these conditions, the consultant and consultee would probably agree that there is a problem and would proceed to problem analysis.

THE PROBLEM IDENTIFICATION INTERVIEW

The problem identification process is initiated by means of the problem identification interview. In this interview, the consultant guides the consultee toward the specification of the objectives to be achieved through consultation and toward the designation of procedures for measuring performance with respect to objectives.

Interview Objectives and How to Achieve Them

The consultant's verbalizations during problem identification should be guided by the objectives established for the problem identification interview. These objectives are summarized in Table 3-4 and are discussed in detail below.

Goal-Specification Objectives for Developmental Consultation

In developmental consultation, the initial task of the consultant during problem identification is to attain a specification of the general, subordinate, and performance objectives. This specification can be achieved in a single interview when the number of objectives is small. However, when many objectives are involved, a number of interviews may be required. The interview objectives are the same regardless of the number of interviews. Thus, the problem identification interview in developmental consultation is treated as though it were one interview even though it may involve several sessions.

During the earliest phases of problem identification, the aim of the

TABLE 3-4. Objectives for the Problem Identification Interview

	Interview type	
Objective type	Developmental interview	Problem-centered interview
Goal specification objectives	Establish general objectives. Establish subordinate objectives. Establish a hierarchical classification for general and subordinate objectives. Establish performance objectives.	Obtain a behavioral description of client behavior of concern to the consultee. Obtain a description of the conditions under which behavior of concern occurs. Obtain an estimate of the level of incidence of behavior of concern.
Assessment objectives	Obtain agreement regarding the type of measure used to assess performance, what is to be recorded, how recording is to be done, how much behavior to record, the schedule of recording, and who is to collect data.	Obtain agreement regarding the type of measure used to assess performance, what is to be recorded, how recording is to be done, how much behavior to record, the schedule of recording, and who is to collect data.
Procedural objectives	Set a date for the next interview. Arrange to contact the consultee to check on data collection procedures.	Set a date for the next interview. Arrange to contact the consultee to check on data collection procedures.

consultant should be to establish general objectives and subordinate objectives. Little attention should be given to the hierarchical positioning of objectives. Discussion of position will usually come up, but the consultant should not make a specific effort to establish hierarchical relations in the beginning of problem identification. The initial phase of problem identification is essentially a brainstorming session in which the goal is simply to get a list of objectives. Dwelling on such matters as hierarchical relations among objectives may reduce the overall output of objectives produced by consultees during an interview.

After a list of fairly broad goals has been constructed, focus in the problem identification interview should shift to the hierarchical classification of objectives. The goal at this stage in problem identification is to construct a complete classification system for general and subordinate objectives. This system should specify what the objectives to be achieved are and what the hierarchical relations are among them.

In the advanced stages of problem identification, the interview focus should be on the establishment of performance objectives articulated to the various categories of subordinate objectives that have been designated.

This process sometimes takes place over an extended period of time. The goal of each session conducted in this phase of the problem identification process is to establish a limited set of performance objectives that are to be the focus of consultee intervention efforts in the immediate future. The strategy of focusing on a limited number of objectives prevents inundation of the consultee with so much planning that he or she is delayed excessively in getting to the task of effecting changes in client behavior.

Goal Specification Objectives for Problem-Centered Consultation

The initial objectives of problem-centered consultation are quite different from those for developmental consultation. In problem-centered consultation, the consultant's first objective leading toward goal specification is to get a precise description of the current behavior of concern to the consultee. The designation of goals to be achieved with respect to the behavior of interest is deferred until later in consultation. The consultant initiates the behavior specification process by eliciting behavioral descriptions of client functioning from the consultee. For example, if the consultee is concerned about client immaturity, some specification of what the client does to show his or her immaturity is needed.

The goal of attaining behavioral descriptions from the consultee involves, first of all, the obvious requirement that vague delineations of client actions be replaced by language indicating specifically what the client does in terms that would be understandable to an independent observer. Beyond this, the consultant must make sure that the behavior described is essential to the definition of the problem of concern to the consultee (Kazdin, 1985). When a consultee is asked to describe client behavior, he or she often touches on several behaviors, only some of which are really of concern in problem solving. Moreover, even in those instances in which only behaviors of significance from a problem-solving standpoint are mentioned, some of the actions described are of greater concern than others. For example, a first-grade teacher describing a child in her class might say, "Ted never gets his work finished, and he's always getting into fights, but what really concerns me is his constant daydreaming. He just isn't with us most of the time." In such a situation, it is the consultant's task to guide the consultee to assign priorities to the behaviors that she has described. Priorities can be used to determine which behaviors should be the immediate focus of problem-solving efforts.

After behavioral descriptions have been attained for those behaviors that are to be the immediate focus of problem solving, the consultant's goal should be to get a description of the conditions under which the behaviors of concern occur. This description should include the specification of antecedent, consequent, and sequential conditions related to these behaviors. Setting events should also be considered as the production and maintenance of child behavior are not guaranteed by an analysis of the immediate environmental contingencies (Wahler, 1975, 1980; Wahler & Graves, 1983). The specification of conditions gives the consultant tentative information that can be used in problem analysis to determine the environmental factors that may be influencing the behavior. It also can be used to establish the conditions under which client performance must occur before the consultee will agree that the goals of consultation have been achieved. For example, consider the case of a high-school teacher who is concerned about a group of female students who are smoking in the girls' lavatory. Her immediate objective may be to stop the smoking in that location. Location then becomes a condition of goal attainment.

The final objective leading toward goal specification in problem-centered consultation is to attain an indication of the level of incidence of the behaviors to be focused on. The specification of incidence can be only approximate at this stage. Nevertheless, it can provide the consultant with some indication of the severity of the problem with which he or she is dealing. For example, a child who gets into six or seven fights a day probably constitutes a greater threat to others than a child who is involved in altercations only two or three times a week.

The specification of incidence is also important in determining when to record behavior. As indicated earlier in this chapter, different recording strategies are required for high-rate problems and for low-rate problems.

Specification of the desired incidence of behavior is generally deferred until after baseline data have been collected. This time frame gives the consultee the opportunity to use information about the current level of performance in deciding on the specific goals to be achieved through consultation.

Performance Assessment Objectives

In both developmental and problem-centered consultation, one of the major goals in the problem identification interview is to arrive at procedures for measuring client performance. The specific objectives related to this goal follow directly from the measurement selection and data collection steps outlined earlier in the chapter in the discussion of the problem identification process.

The first interview objective related to the assessment of client performance is to achieve agreement on the measure to be used to assess client behavior. In some cases, agreement is implicit, requiring little or no discussion. For example, if the problem of concern is disruptive classroom behavior, behavioral observation is likely to be the method selected for assessing performance.

Whether or not an extended discussion of measures is required, the consultant should take the lead in determining the measures to be used.

That is, the consultant should suggest the kind of measure that he or she believes to be most suitable to the consultee's needs and then should seek approval for the suggestion from the consultee. The reasons for this approach is that the consultant generally has more knowledge of measurement and evaluation procedures than the consultee. This knowledge can be made available to the consultee through the use of suggestions. As the consultee must take responsibility for implementing whatever measures are decided on, the consultee must have the final decision regarding the selection of measures.

The second performance-assessment objective to be achieved during the problem identification interview is the specification of what is to be recorded. What must be agreed on is the type of strength measure to be used in recording behavior. As in the case of measurement selection, the consultant should assume the major responsibility for establishing the type of behavioral strength to be used in assessing client behavior. Once again, his or her strategy should be to suggest a strength measure and to seek consultee agreement on it.

The next assessment goal to be achieved in the problem identification interview is achieving agreement on how data are to be recorded. The consultant should indicate in a direct manner how this is to be done. He or she should establish whether recording should be done mechanically, electronically, or in writing. If a recording form is to be used, the consultant should explain its use to the consultee in detail.

The fourth interview objective related to assessment is to establish how much behavior is to be recorded. Once again, the consultant should take the lead in the specification process. However, as there is often a number of variables that could affect the decision and that are known only to the consultee, it is often advisable for the consultant to give alternative approaches to the problem of how many data to collect. The consultee may then choose among the alternatives that have been described. For example, suppose that a teacher is working with a large number of students on the achievement of a particular set of instructional goals. The consultant might suggest a sampling procedure as one alternative. However, it may happen that the tactic of assessing all of the students would also be practical. The teacher may point out that he has solicited the assistance of a number of parents in implementing the instructional program and that the parents would be willing to take over some of the assessment responsibilities associated with problem identification.

The next assessment goal is to establish agreement on the schedule of recording. The consultant should make an initial judgment about the type of scheduling required based on what he or she has learned about the problem and the rate at which the behavior of concern occurs. The consultant should then explain the strategy or strategies that may be appropriate and ask the consultee's approval for one of these. For example, if the problem occurred at a fairly high rate, the consultant might suggest a time-sampling recording procedure for the consultee's approval.

The final assessment objective during problem identification is to achieve agreement on who is to collect the data. Very often, it is taken for granted that the consultee is the one to collect data. However, as noted earlier in the chapter, there may be circumstances in which some other individual will be assigned data collection responsibilities. Even when this is the case, it is still generally the consultee's responsibility to see that data collection occurs.

Procedural Objectives

During each stage of the consultation process, a number of procedural details related to the mechanics of conducting the process must be given some attention. The first of these details is setting up the date for the next interview. The consultant should elicit from the consultee the time when it would be most convenient for him or her to meet again within the limitations imposed by the consultant's own schedule.

It is not usually advisable to let more than a week lapse between interviews. The consultation process is sustained in part by the interest of the consultant in the consultee's problem. One sign of interest is the willingness of the consultant to meet again in a relatively short period of time. Another even more important reason for scheduling the second interview soon after the first is that, in most cases, to do otherwise would unnecessarily delay problem solution. The collection of baseline data should generally take no longer than a week. After baseline data have been collected, the consultee is ready to go on to problem analysis.

A second procedural detail that should be handled during the problem identification interview is making arrangements to contact the consultee during the collection of baseline data to make sure that everything is going as planned. Such contacts are not necessary in every case. However, in most instances, it is highly advisable to get in touch with the consultee for a brief (e.g., 5-minute) conversation about data collection. This procedure provides a safeguard against the unfortunate consequences that may arise when the consultee has misunderstood what was to be done in collecting baseline data and has, as a result, collected inadequate and/or inaccurate data.

Outlines for the Problem Identification Interview

We have constructed outlines for two kinds of problem identification interviews. The first one is for the kind of interview used in developmental consultation focusing on a hierarchical set of general, subordinate, and performance objectives. The second is for the type of interview generally used in problem-centered consultation aimed at the pursuit of a limited number of specific objectives. These outlines should not be followed slavishly. They are not intended to cover all possible cases. Rather, they are designed to provide examples of general principles that can be used as guides for interviewing behavior in a wide variety of circumstances. Specific guidelines are also available in Kratochwill and Bergan (1990).

The Developmental Interview

The following outline describes the steps in conducting a problem identification interview involving the establishment of a hierarchically arranged set of general, subordinate, and performance objectives. The roman-numeral headings indicate the objectives to be achieved in the interview. The capital-letter headings describe the types of verbalizations required to achieve objectives, and the arabic-number headings provide examples of the kinds of verbal behaviors that a consultant might emit in an interview of this sort:

I. Establish general and subordinate objectives.
   A. Emit behavior specification elicitors to establish a list of general objectives.
      1. "What are your general concerns regarding Carol's behavior?
      2. "What are the broad goals that you have in mind for your career education program?"
   B. Emit behavior specification elicitors to establish a list of subordinate objectives.
      1. "What are some of the kinds of capabilities that Carol would need to acquire to achieve confidence in social situations?"
      2. "What are the broad areas of competency that you feel students should have in the three general categories of knowledge, attitudes, and skills related to vocations and avocations?"
   C. Emit behavior summarization emitters and behavior positive-validation elicitors to facilitate the recall of specified objectives and to establish agreement regarding what has been said.
      1. "You indicated that your main goal for Carol is to help her to display self-confidence in social situations."
      2. "You said that, for Carol to attain self-confidence, she would have to act in a self-confident way and to say things that suggested confidence in herself."
      3. "Is that an accurate summary?"
      4. "You indicated that your career education program has

three major goals: to enable students to achieve knowledge about vocational and avocational activities, to assist them to develop a value system to guide their decisions regarding occupational choice and leisuretime activities, and to help them to develop general skills applicable in a wide variety of career and avocational fields."

    5. "Does that summary reflect your views accurately?"

II. Establish hierarchical relations among general and subordinate objectives.

    A. Emit behavior specification elicitors to generate categories and subcategories of objectives.

        1. "What are some of the things we should list under the heading of verbal behavior displaying self-confidence?"

        2. "We need to arrange the career education goals we have listed by category."

        3. "Which of these goals would fall under the heading of building a value system to guide vocational and avocational decisions?"

    B. Emit behavior summarization emitters and behaviors positive-validation elicitors to facilitate recall of objectives and to establish agreement as to the composition of each category of objectives specified.

        1. "You said that, within the area of verbal behavior related to self-confidence, Carol would need to become less deprecating of her own abilities and achievements and also that she would need to display more tactful pride in her accomplishments."

        2. "Is that accurate?"

        3. "You indicated that, in the area of knowledge about careers, students ought to know the broad categories of occupations from which they may choose a career, the kinds of activities associated with those occupations, the societal functions served by the various occupations, the educational requirements for entry into various occupations, and the range of income levels associated with different occupational areas."

        4. "Have I reflected your views on knowledge goals accurately?"

III. Generate performance objectives related to subordinate goals of immediate concern to the consultee.

    A. Emit behavior specification elicitors to establish priority areas for generating performance objectives.

        1. "What would be the most important goal area to start working on with Carol?"

2. "Which one of the career-education-goal categories do you want to concentrate on first in instruction?"
B. Emit behavior specification elicitors to establish behaviors for performance objectives related to the subordinate objectives category of immediate concern to the consultee.
  1. "What would be some examples of things that Carol might do to show less self-criticism?"
  2. "How would students demonstrate their knowledge of occupations in the area of distributing goods?"
C. Emit behavior-setting-specification elicitors to establish the conditions under which performance is to occur.
  1. "In what kinds of situations would it be particularly crucial for Carol to avoid making disparaging remarks about her grades?"
  2. "Under what conditions would you expect the students to be able to recall examples of occupations related to the distribution of goods?"
D. Emit behavior specification elicitors to establish the level of acceptable performance for objectives.
  1. "What would be the maximum number of disparaging remarks that you would find acceptable?"
  2. "How accurate would the students have to be in listing occupations in order for us to say that they had achieved the goal?"
E. Emit behavior and behavior-setting-summarization emitters and behavior and behavior-setting positive-validation elicitors to enhance recall of performance objectives and to establish agreement regarding them.
  1. "You said that the first goal that you would like to pursue is to eliminate completely Carol's disparaging remarks about her grades."
  2. "You specified that, in order for us to say that Carol had achieved the goal, she would have to stop making critical comments at home, in informal social gatherings with her friends, and with her teachers."
  3. "Have I summarized your immediate goal accurately?"
  4. "You said that, for the unit on distributive occupations, you would like students to be able to list 10 occupations in the distributive category, to specify three activities associated with each of these occupations, to indicate the amount and type of education required for entry into each field, and to designate the wage or salary range for each field."

5. "You indicated that the students would display mastery of these goals when asked either in writing or orally,
6. and you indicated that, in every case, a 90% accuracy level would be required for goal attainment."
7. "Have I summarized your objectives correctly?"

IV. Establish assessment procedures for performance objectives.
   A. Emit observation specification emitters and elicitors and (when desired) evaluation emitters and positive validation elicitors to establish recording procedures.
      1. "We need to establish some procedures for collecting data on Carol's behavior."
      2. "You could observe the number of times that Carol makes disparaging remarks at home and record your observations on this form."
      3. "You could ask Carol to record her own behavior at school and with her friends."
      4. "I would suggest that data be collected for a week on Carol's behavior."
      5. "Do these suggestions meet with your approval?"
      6. "You will want to devise your own test to measure knowledge."
      7. "As your aim at this stage is for the students to recall what they have learned, you could devise a series of short-answer questions to go with each of the objectives that you have specified."
      8. "You could use the percentage correct as the measure of mastery, as that's how you indicated competency in your objectives."
      9. "I would recommend that you test a different group of children each day on a few of the questions from your pool of test items if you want to observe progress associated with instruction."
      10. "Do you find the suggestions that I have made acceptable?"
   B. When the recording procedures that have been suggested are at all complicated, which they almost invariably are, emit observation summarization emitters to facilitate the recall of procedures and positive validation elicitors to ensure agreement regarding the procedures that have been established.
      1. "We agreed that, for 1 week, you would record the number of disparaging remarks Carol makes at home and that Carol would keep track of her critical comments at school and with her friends."

    2. "Is that correct?"
    3. "We established that you would construct short-answer test items for each of the objectives you specified and that you would test five children a day using five items for the next five school days."
    4. "Have I got it right?"

V. Make arrangements for subsequent contacts with the consultee.
  A. Emit other specification elicitors to arrange for the next interview with the consultee.
    1. "When shall we meet next?"
    2. "Where shall we meet?"
  B. Emit other specification elicitors or emitters to arrange a contact to make sure that data collection is going as planned.
    1. "I'll call you on Tuesday to see how things are going with the data collection."
    2. "Could I see you sometime early next week to see how our data collection procedures are working?"

The Problem-Centered Interview

The following outline illustrates the interview typically used in problem-centered consultation aimed at the achievement of a limited number of specific goals related to some immediate crisis or difficulty faced by the consultee. The general format of the outline is the same as that used in the illustration of an interview involving a hierarchically arranged set of objectives.

  I. Determine the behaviors and the strengths of the behaviors of concern to the consultee.
    A. Emit a behavior specification elicitor or individual-characteristics specification elicitor to introduce discussion of the client and his or her problem.
      1. "Tell me about Ted."
      2. "Tell me about Alice's problem behavior in the classroom."
    B. Emit behavior specification elicitors to get a behavioral description of those characteristics of client behavior that are of concern.
      1. "What does Alice do when she annoys you?"
      2. "Give me some other examples of Ted's reading difficulties."
    C. Emit behavior specification elicitors to determine behavior strength.
      1. "How often during the week does this throwing paper occur?"

2. "About how many errors does Ted make during an oral reading session?"

D. Emit behavior summarization emitters and positive validation elicitors to summarize and to establish agreement regarding the specification and strength of the behaviors that are targets for change in consultation.

   1. "You have said that Alice throws paper at one of the lab tables."

   2. "She does this about three times a week."

   3. "Is that right?"

   4. "You said that Ted continually misreads and omits words during oral reading."

   5. "Is that correct?"

II. Determine the conditions under which the behaviors of concern occur.

A. Emit behavior-setting-specification elicitors to establish the antecedent conditions associated with the behavior of concern to the consultee.

   1. What is generally going on right before Alice throws paper in the classroom?"

   2. "What are you usually doing just before Alice throws paper?"

   3. "How do you introduce oral reading?"

B. Emit behavior-setting-specification elicitors to establish the consequent conditions associated with the behavior of concern.

   1. "What do you do when you discover that Alice has thrown paper?"

   2. "How do the other children react when Ted makes errors while reading?"

C. Emit behavior-setting-specification elicitors to establish the sequential conditions associated with the behavior of concern.

   1. "When during the day does this paper throwing most often occur?"

   2. "On what days of the week does paper throwing usually take place?"

   3. "What is the sequence of steps that you go through in teaching reading in the oral reading groups?"

D. Emit behavior-setting-summarization emitters and positive validation elicitors to summarize and validate the conditions under which the behavior occurs.

   1. "You have said that Alice usually throws paper in the room when your back is turned and you are writing on the blackboard.

2. "Afterward, the other kids giggle and laugh and in some cases treat her as though she has really done something great."
3. "Is that correct?"
4. "You said, that when you call on Ted to read, he volunteers eagerly and that, after he has finished, you always go over all of his mistakes with him, pronouncing the words for him and having him say the words correctly."
5. "Is that an accurate review of what happens?

III. Establish performance assessment procedures.
   A. Emit observation specification and, if desired, evaluation elicitors and/or emitters and validation elicitors to establish performance assessment procedures.
      1. "We need to get a record of Alice's paper-throwing activities."
      2. "The record will help us to establish a baseline against which to evaluate the success of our intervention plan."
      3. "I would suggest that you record the number of times Alice throws paper on this form throughout the rest of this week.
      4. "If you have the time to do it, you could also make a note of what happens before and after paper throwing."
      5. "Do these suggestions meet with your approval?
      6. "If you could record the number of errors that Ted makes during reading for the rest of the week, it would help us to establish a benchmark against which to judge the amount of improvement in his reading that we hope will soon occur."
      7. "You could use this form for recording,
      8. and if you have a chance, note the other children's reactions and your own when Ted makes a mistake."
      9. "Would these plans be OK with you?"
   B. Emit observation summarization emitters and positive validation elicitors to facilitate the recall of recording procedures and agreement regarding them.
      1. We agreed that you would record the number of papers that Alice builds during the rest of this week."
      2. "You're going to use this form,
      3. and if you have a chance, you're going to note what happens before and after the paper throwing."
      4. "Did I summarize our recording plans accurately?"
      5. "We said that you would record the number of errors that Ted makes during oral reading on this form for the rest of the week, and that, if you have the chance, you'll note your own reactions and those of the other children to Ted's mistakes."
      6. "Is that right?"

IV. Make arrangements for subsequent contacts with the consultee.
   A. Emit other specification elicitors to arrange for the next interview with the consultee.
      1. "Could we meet Monday or Tuesday of next week?"
      2. "Shall we meet in the teacher's lounge or in your classroom?"
   B. Emit other specification elicitors or emitters to arrange a contact to make sure that the data collection is going as planned.
      1. "When could I drop in to see how the data collection is going?"
      2. "I'll give you a call some time this week to see how the data collection is going."

Testing Interviewing Skills

At this point, you may wish to make an attempt at conducting a problem identification interview. If so, find a parent or a teacher who is willing to work with you on a problem and give your interviewing skills a try. Tape-record or videotape the interviewing session so that you can evaluate your performance using the techniques described below.

Checklist Evaluations for Problem Identification

Figures 3-14 and 3-15 list criteria for effective problem-identification interviews for developmental and problem-centered consultation, respectively. Score your interview using the appropriate checklist. Follow the scoring procedure discussed in Chapter 2. If you find that you have not met some of the criteria, correct your mistakes by role playing another interview with a friend.

Message Classification Analysis in Problem Identification

You may find it useful to do an in-depth study of the use of message classification categories during problem identification. Indices of consultant effectiveness have been developed for use in analyzing messages in interviews of the problem-centered variety (Bergan & Tombari, 1976). To analyze your use of the message classification categories, code your interviews using consultation-analysis record forms like the one shown in Figure 2-1 (Chapter 2).

You can begin your analysis of the kinds of messages used in problem identification by examining your use of the content. The content of messages emitted during problem identification should fall mainly in the *behavior*, *behavior setting*, and *observation categories*. Verbalizations in the behavior category are needed to attain a specification of the behaviors of concern to the consultee. Utterances in the behavior setting category are required to

CONSULTANT _____ CASE NUMBER _____

CONSULTEE _____ PAGE _____

Problem-Identification Checklist
for Developmental Consultation

Required Verbal Units	*Frequency of Unit Use*
1. Behavior specification elicitors (to establish general objectives)	_____
2. Behavior specification elicitors (to establish subordinate objectives)	_____
3. Behavior summarization emitters (to summarize general and subordinate objectives)	_____
4. Behavior positive-validation elicitors (to validate general and subordinate objectives)	_____
5. Behavior specification elicitors (to generate categories and subcategories of objectives)	_____

FIGURE 3-14. Consultation analysis checklist for a developmental problem-identification interview.

examine the conditions under which the behaviors of concern do or should occur, and messages in the observation category are needed to establish the recording procedures for collecting data on the client's behavior.

Two kinds of errors can be made with respect to the use of the content category. One is to focus the discussion on categories other than the three specified. For example, one could center discussion on individual characteristics and background environment rather than on behavior and behavior settings. Of course, if a consultant were committed to a theoretical orientation stressing the importance of individual characteristics and background environment, then he or she might deliberately choose to focus on those characteristics. However, from the standpoint of the consultative problem-solving model described in Chapter 1, an extensive focus on individual characteristics and background environment may be not warranted. This, of course, does not imply that some discussion regarding these content categories may not be necessary and useful. A discussion of background characteristics can expand on the range of the possible setting events that influence behavior (see Chapter 9 for a discussion).

Required Verbal Units	*Frequency of Unit Use*
6. Behavior summarization emitters (to summarize categories of objectives)	_____
7. Behavior positive-validation elicitors (to validate categories of objectives)	_____
8. Behavior specification elicitors (to establish priority areas for generating performance objectives)	_____
9. Behavior specification elicitors (to establish behaviors for performance objectives)	_____
10. Behavior-setting specification elicitors (to establish conditions for performance objectives)	_____
11. Behavior specification elicitors (to establish strength for acceptable performance)	_____
12. Behavior-summarization emitters (to summarize performance objectives)	_____
13. Behavior-setting summarization emitters (to summarize performance objectives)	_____
14. Behavior positive-validation elicitors (to validate performance objectives)	_____
15. Behavior-setting positive validation elicitors (to validate performance objectives)	_____
16. Observation specification elicitors (to establish recording procedures)	_____
17. Observation specification and/or evaluation emitters (to establish recording procedures)	_____
18. Observation summarization emitters (to facilitate recall of procedures)	_____
19. Observation positive-validation elicitors (to establish agreement regarding recording procedures)	_____
20. Other specification elicitors and emitters (to arrange next interview and to ensure data collection)	_____

FIGURE 3.14 (*Cont.*)

CONSULTANT _____ CASE NUMBER _____

CONSULTEE _____ PAGE _____

Problem-Identification Checklist
for Problem-Centered Consultation

Required Verbal Units	Frequency of Unit Use
1. Behavior specification or individual-characteristics specification elicitors (to introduce discussion)	_____
2. Behavior specification elicitors (to obtain a behavioral description of client behavior)	_____
3. Behavior specification elicitors (to determine behavior strength)	_____
4. Behavior summarization emitters (to summarize information about behavior)	_____
5. Behavior positive-validation elicitors (to establish agreement regarding specification and strength of behaviors)	_____
6. Behavior-setting specification elicitors (to establish antecedent conditions)	_____
7. Behavior-setting specification elicitors (to establish consequent conditions)	_____
8. Behavior-setting specification elicitors (to establish sequential conditions)	_____
9. Behavior-setting summarization emitters (to summarize conditions under which behavior occurs)	_____
10. Behavior-setting positive validation elicitors (to validate conditions under which behavior occurs)	_____
11. Observation specification elicitors and/or emitters (to establish performance assessment procedures)	_____
12. Observation summarization emitters (to facilitate recall of recording procedures)	_____
13. Observation validation elicitors (to validate recording procedures)	_____
14. Other specification elicitors or emitters (to arrange next interview and to ensure data collection)	_____

FIGURE 3-15. Consultation analysis checklist for a problem-centered problem-identification interview.

The second kind of error that one can make related to content is to minimize or eliminate discussion in one of the three critical content categories. For example, consider the following excerpts from a problem identification interview. The consultant began by emitting a string of verbalizations related to client behavior. Here is some of what he said:

"OK. What are some of the things that he does specifically, interrupts the other children, can you tell me some?"

"Tell me some more of the things in the committee."

"When he's working here at the committee, he tends to look out the window, and he does get out of his seat in committee."

"He tends to take other things from children, picks up their rulers and so forth."

"His eyes tend to wander away. He's pretty much inattentive to what he's supposed to be working on then. What are some of the things, Edith, that you would like for him to be able to do when he's working in the committees?"

"OK, so what you'd really like to work on, then, is at least initially keeping Bobby in his seat throughout the committee."

There were one or two more verbalizations dealing with behavior. Then the consultant turned his attention briefly to the behavior setting category:

"Let me ask you another question, Edith. Does that occur at all committees throughout the day, or does he do it in the morning or more in the afternoon?"

The consultant made one comment about where the behavior occurred and then went on to discuss the strength of the behavior and the recording procedures to be used to assess it.

The interview provides a fairly clear indication of what the child did that was of concern to the teacher, but because there was so little discussion in the behavior setting category, there is not the slightest knowledge of what might be influencing the child's behavior. To examine the effects of discussing conditions, compare the impression you got from the above interview with the following excerpt:

Consultant: You've said that Alice likes to irritate you and that she does so in various ways. Your biggest concern is that one of her ways is throwing papers in one of the labs and that she usually does this when you are writing on the board or involved in something where you really can't watch her all the time. And usually afterward, the other kids giggle and laugh and sort of, maybe, at least a few of them, treat her as though she had done something great.

Consultee: Uh-hum.

Consultant: Which she likes. Is this the problem as you see it?

Consultee: Yes.

Because the consultant used the behavior setting category appropriately, both she and the consultee left the problem identification interview with some notions about what might be influencing Alice's paper throwing. These notions set the stage for problem analysis.

To avoid the two kinds of content errors that can be made in problem identification, the consultant needs a fairly evenly balanced distribution of verbalizations in the behavior, behavior setting, and observation categories. In developmental consultation, there may be more verbalizations in the behavior category than in the other two classifications. However, in problem-centered consultation, the distribution of verbalizations across the three classifications should be very evenly balanced. The consultant can get a rough indication of balance by simply counting the number of utterances in each category.[1] If the numbers are relatively evenly distributed and if verbalizations in the behavior, behavior setting, and observation categories account for the bulk of what has been said in problem identification, then the consultant can be reasonably confident that use of the content category in problem identification is appropriate. If the consultant finds that he or she has omitted a relevant category or has placed undue emphasis on an irrelevant category, then steps must be taken in role-playing situations to change his or her interviewing behavior.

The consultant's analysis of message content should include not only an examination of the subcategories that he or she emphasizes, but also an examination of the extent to which he or she focuses the discussion on one topic before turning to another. He or she should stay on one topic long enough to explore it in some depth. There are things that the consultee will need to recall about each of the topics discussed. By focusing on a topic for an extended period, the consultant gives the consultee an opportunity to bring forth relevant associations on that topic.

You can get a rough estimate of the degree to which you maintain focus during problem identification by visually scanning the pattern of content changes in the interview. Group the verbalizations into sets of five. If most of the verbalizations in most of the sets are in the same content category, you are maintaining an adequate interview focus. If this is not the case, use role playing to improve your interview focus.

In addition to examining message content, also examine the way in which you handle the message process category. The aim of problem identification within the consultative problem-solving model is to establish certain matters of fact, for example, the behaviors of concern to the consultee and how those behaviors are to be measured. The message process subcategories used in problem identification should be those that contribute to establishing facts.

---

[1]Precise quantitative methods for assessing message content, process, control, and focus are discussed in Appendix A. These methods are intended mainly for use in research and are generally not used for training purposes.

Three message-process subcategories are useful in establishing matters of fact: the specification, the summarization, and the validation. The consultant can use specifications to call for factual information. He or she can use the summarization to facilitate a recall of the facts under discussion and can use the validation to establish agreement with the consultee regarding what has been said.

As in the case of message content, the consultant can make two kinds of errors in the use of the process category. The first is to emit verbalizations that do not fall mainly in the specification, summarization, and validation categories. For example, the consultant may focus heavily on evaluations by asking the consultee how he or she feels about the client's behavior and the consultee's attitudes, feelings, and emotions. A shift of this kind could cause a radical redefinition of the problem and a marked alteration in the relationships between the consultant and the consultee.

If the conversation is focused on consultee attitudes and emotions, the problem under consideration may very easily be defined not in terms of the client's behavior, but in terms of how the consultee feels about the client's behavior. The goal, then, would be to solve the consultee's problem, not the client's. For example, a mother and father who sought consultation because of their son's low grades in school might find themselves talking to the consultant about their overly high expectations with regard to the boy's achievement rather about how to improve his academic accomplishments.

The issue of how the consultee feels about the client is, of course, a matter of great importance, but within the framework of consultative problem-solving, it is an issue that is resolved mainly by the interactions between the consultee and the client, not by the interactions between the consultant and the consultee. For example, it could be that the parents in the above illustration did hold overly high expectations of their son. This view would very quickly become apparent by observing the boy's rate of progress toward the goals set in consultation. If one or more carefully conceived plans is tried to increase progress, and progress remains at the low level, the parents would have evidence to suggest that they revise their thinking about the boy's achievements. The boy's own feelings and his participation in setting standards for his achievement would also be crucial factors to consider in formulating goals and, if necessary, revising his parents' thinking about his achievement goals.

At the extreme, focusing on consultee feelings may have the additional effect of turning the consultation into a therapist–patient relationship rather than a consultant–consultee relationship. The collegial relationship in which both consultant and consultee fulfill their separate responsibilities in implementing the consultation process would be compromised. The consultee's responsibility to assist the client to achieve the goals of consultation would be eroded seriously, as would be the consultant's responsibility to provide psychological knowledge to assist the client to achieve consultation goals.

The second type of process error that may occur in problem identification is slighting or omitting specification, summarization, or validation utterances. The most common mistake is to fail to use a sufficient number of summaries and validations. The results of this error are sometimes disastrous. For example, the consultee may forget the specific behaviors to be recorded. In some instances, the result may be the remarkable consequences of a record of a different behavior during each day of baseline. When something like this happens, there is nothing to do but start over.

The consultant should strive for a reasonably balanced distribution of specification, summarization, and validation utterances. He or she will probably have more specifications than summarizations and validations. Nevertheless, the use of summarizations and validations should be extensive. In oral communication, messages cease to exist as soon as they are uttered. Thus, there must be much more redundancy than is the case in other forms of communication. Summarizations and validations provide that redundancy.

The final message-classification category that the consultant should consider is the control category. As indicated in previous chapters, it is the consultant's responsibility to control the content and the process of consultee verbalizations. He or she does this through the use of elicitors. As a general rule, there should be more elicitors than emitters in problem identification. The reader can check her or his use of elicitors simply by computing the percentage of elicitors used in the interview.

Problem Analysis

The consultant's task during problem analysis is to assist the consultee to identify factors that may influence the attainment of a problem solution and to help the consultee use those factors in the design of a plan to achieve a solution. To accomplish this task effectively, the consultant must first have the necessary knowledge and skills to analyze the problems presented in consultation. In addition, he or she must have the necessary communication skills to make this knowledge available to the consultee. In this chapter, we discuss the process of analyzing the problem presented in consultation and the skills required to communicate that process to the consultee effectively.

THE PROBLEM ANALYSIS PROCESS

The problem-analysis process, shown in Table 4-1, is comprised of a series of steps occurring in two broad phases. The first of these phases involves an analysis of the factors that may influence the attainment of problem solutions in consultation. The second involves the development of plans to solve problems.

The Analysis Phase

There are at least two ways to identify factors that may influence the behaviors of concern in consultation. One way is to focus on external and internal conditions that may affect the attainment of consultation goals. For example, if a young girl involved in consultation is trying to stop using drugs, a consultant and a consultee may attempt to assist her by exploring the environmental conditions that may be controlling her drug use. They may ask about the kinds of occasions that typically precede drug use,

TABLE 4-1. Steps in Problem Analysis

Choose an analysis procedure.
Conduct conditions and/or skills analysis.
Develop plan strategies.
Develop plan tactics.
Establish procedures for assessing
    performance during implementation.

whether the use occurs when she is alone or with others, and what generally happens after she takes drugs. They may also explore the possible effects of drug taking on covert behaviors that the girl emits. In this connection, they may ask about the kinds of images and covert verbalizations that generally precede and follow her taking of drugs.

The second way to identify the variables affecting the behaviors of concern in consultation is to analyze the kinds of skills the client and the consultee need to achieve the consultation goals. For instance, in the drug example, the girl may lack the social skills necessary to become accepted by that segment of her peer group that does not use drugs. If this is the case, a consultant and the consultee may identify the requisite social skills for participation in the nondrug culture and then teach these skills to the client.

In the case of the consultee, a teacher may need assistance in designing an instructional environment to facilitate learning in the children in a classroom. For example, there is a growing body of research that suggests that establishing and maintaining a positive instructional environment can reduce children's behavior problems that might otherwise be addressed only through behavior management strategies (see Gettinger, 1988).

The strategies of focusing on skills or on conditions are, of course, not mutually exclusive. Skills and conditions can be considered at the same time. Thus, the consultant and the consultee in the drug example may ascertain the conditions that may affect drug use and also try to identify the requisite social skills for acceptance by the nondrug segment of the girl's peer group.

Choosing an Analysis Procedure

The first step in problem analysis is to decide whether to focus on the analysis of skills or on the analysis of conditions, or on both. There are no hard-and-fast rules that one can invariably apply in making this decision. However, certain general guidelines may be helpful in selecting an appropriate analysis procedure.

If one of the purposes of consultation is to promote self-direction on the part of the client, problem analysis should generally include some consideration of the skills necessary to achieve self-direction. For example, suppose that the goals of consultation are to reduce a child's caloric intake and to assist the child to achieve an adequate level of control over his or her own eating behavior. In this situation, it would be useful to teach the child self-control techniques that can be used to control eating (Mahoney & Thoresen, 1974; Ollendick & Cerny, 1981).

When the goal of consultation is to increase or to maintain behavior, and when problem identification reveals variability in the level of behavior, problem analysis should generally focus on the conditions that may influence behavior rather than on skills. For example, suppose that a boy is doing poorly in spelling. An examination of four or five samples of his work reveals that, in some cases, he performs very well and, in other cases, he does not. Insofar as the child can meet high performance standards on some occasions, it seems reasonable to assume that he could meet them on most if not all occasions. Under such circumstances, the most likely variables to examine are the conditions that may influence his spelling behavior, such as his amount of studying.

Even if variability in performance is lacking, conditions may be a factor that should be considered in problem analysis. Preliminary explorations during problem identification may reveal environmental circumstances that could have a marked impact on the attainment of consultation goals. For example, in the case of a child having academic difficulties, poor work samples are often followed by extra attention from the child's parents. In circumstances such as these, the possible influences of environmental variables should be considered even if the child's academic performance is uniformly inadequate.

On occasion, the principal focus of problem analysis should be on the identification of the skills related to goal attainment. This is the case if the goal of consultation is to increase or to maintain behavior, if the level of performance is uniformly low, and if a preliminary exploration suggests that the existing conditions are generally supportive of goal attainment. For example, if all of the children in a class are having difficulty mastering multiplication, an examination might be made of the extent to which the children have attained mastery over the prerequisite skills in such areas as counting and addition.

Analyzing Conditions of Client Behavior

Research in experimental psychology has revealed a large number of conditions that can affect behavior. Tables B-1, B-2, and B-3 in Appendix B provide an extensive, though by no means exhaustive, list of variables that have been demonstrated to influence what people do. The principles listed in these tables represent not only a wide variety of research areas in psychology but also a high degree of theoretical diversity. In the paragraphs that follow, we discuss the use of these principles in consultation. However, a detailed explanation of the specific principles is beyond the scope of this book. Readers interested in a comprehensive review of child treatment procedures should consult some texts devoted to this topic (e.g., Kratochwill & Morris, 1990; O'Leary & Wilson, 1987; Ollendick & Cerny, 1981; Ross, 1981a).

In some instances, behavior is controlled by the actions of an external agent (e.g., the actions of an individual are influenced by reinforcers administered by some other person or persons). In other cases, the stimuli controlling behavior may be within the person whose behavior is being affected (e.g., a boy may control his studying behavior by covertly warning himself that he will probably receive a low grade if he does not study). Of course, these covert warnings may well be controlled by environmental factors (Skinner, 1953).

As implied in previous chapters, both internal and external conditions can be divided into three broad categories: antecedent conditions, consequent conditions, and sequential conditions. Antecedent conditions are events that occur just before a behavior, and consequent conditions occur just after a behavior. Sequential conditions indicate the patterning of events across a series of occasions.

Behaviorists have played a central role in classifying conditions in terms of their temporal relations to behavior. This strategy has marked advantages in consultation. The temporal classification of conditions makes it possible to relate experimental research directly to client behavior. For instance, as discussed in Chapter 3, a consultant may ask a consultee what generally happens just before or after the occurrence of a behavior of concern. Information of this kind can be linked directly to experimental findings identifying antecedent and consequent conditions that have the potential to affect behavior. Suppose that a young child is having difficulty acquiring concepts such as *middle, far, near, over,* and *under.* Research in cognition has shown that one of the antecedent conditions affecting concept learning is the degree to which relevant stimulus attributes are emphasized in concept-learning tasks (Trabasso, 1963). Assume that questioning during consultation reveals that relevant attributes of antecedent stimuli used in concept learning are not being emphasized in the existing teaching procedure. Under these circumstances, a plan developed in consultation could make use of research results on attribute emphasis. For example, in teaching the concept *middle,* objects in the middle of a group could be presented in a color different from other objects in the group.

The central task of the consultant in conditions analysis is to identify psychological principles that are related to conditions associated with client behavior and that can be used in the achievement of consultation goals. In performing this task the consultant should be able to call on the full range of psychological principles that may affect goal attainment. Moreover, he or she should be able to select from the vast array of available knowledge those principles that are pertinent to the particular problem.

In identifying the relevant psychological principles for use in consultation, the consultant may call on the store of knowledge that he or she has amassed through self-study and/or graduate training in the various fields of psychology. Study in such areas as learning, motivation, behavior modification, perception, memory, cognition, psycholinguistics, experimental social psychology, and experimental child psychology provides the consultant with fundamental knowledge that he or she can use in the attainment of consultation goals. However, knowledge provided through study of this kind is necessary but not sufficient to meet the consultant's and the consultee's needs.

The field of psychology is expanding at an extremely rapid rate, and the amount of information currently available in the field is far larger than any single individual could possibly integrate. Thus, knowledge gained through self-study or graduate training should be augmented by access to information storage and retrieval systems with a capability of providing consultants with up-to-date information on the psychological research relevant to the broad range of problems that may be encountered in consultation. At present, the opportunities for consultants to gain information are woefully inadequate. One approach to remedying this state of affairs is discussed in Chapter 8.

The consultant selects psychological principles for use in achieving the goals of consultation on the basis of discussions of antecedent, consequent, and sequential conditions currently related to client behavior. Through questioning of the consultee, the consultant is able to determine the match between existing conditions and conditions that psychological knowledge suggests ought to facilitate the attainment of the consultation goals.

Questioning during conditions analysis often reveals powerful psychological principles already operating in the client's environment, though these principles may not be affecting client behavior efficaciously. For instance, the behavioral literature is replete with examples of situations in which a parent or a teacher maintains undesirable behavior in a child by reinforcing it. In addition, there are cases in which a child may control parent or teacher behavior by manipulating positive or aversive stimuli. For example, a preadolescent boy diagnosed as schizophrenic successfully trained his father never to use the bathroom at home. Efforts to gain access to the bathroom in the house were severely punished by bizarre behavior. As a result, the father was forced to use the bathroom in a nearby gas station.

When conditions analysis reveals psychological variables in the client environment that are controlling behavior in undesirable ways, it is often beneficial to make use of those variables in problem analysis rather than relying on the introduction of new variables into the situation. For example, Pinkston, Reese, LeBlanc, and Baer (1973) reported a study in which teacher attention in the form of reprimands was maintaining a young child's aggressive behavior. To reduce aggression, teacher attention was removed as a contingency for aggressive acts. When the child choked, hit, or verbally assaulted another child, the teacher directed her efforts rescuing the "victim" rather than reprimanding the assailant. This strategy produced a marked reduction in aggressive acts. Subsequently, teacher attention was used to increase the incidence of the client's positive interactions with children.

The tactic of focusing problem analysis on variables already controlling client behavior may increase the likelihood of plan effectiveness. For example, in the above case, it would be reasonable to assume that teacher attention was a reinforcer capable of influencing the child's verbal behavior. The use of attention in the plan design would take advantage of the knowledge that, in all probability, this variable was one that would influence the child.

Another advantage of focusing problem analysis on variables already associated with client behavior is that it helps those involved to avoid the problem of dealing with unforeseen influences on client actions. For example, in the case described above, suppose that it was decided that, every time the child acted aggressively, he would lose free time. Under this plan, there would be two variables controlling the child's behavior: teacher attention and loss of free time. These variables would probably have opposite effects on the child. Teacher behavior might serve as a reinforcer increasing the use of aggressive acts, whereas loss of free time might be an aversive stimulus that would tend to reduce aggressive behavior. In a situation like this, teacher attention could cancel out the effects of the consequence of the loss of free time.

In some cases, variables that might have a beneficial influence on client behavior are not currently operating in the client's environment. For example, a teacher helping a child learn effective interaction skills may use children who have already developed such skills as models who can show the client how to interact appropriately in social situations.

In consultation cases, there are always a large number of variables that could influence client behavior. The consultant should focus problem analysis on all of the variables that may affect problem solution. However, the consultant should not consider more variables than can be incorporated into a practical plan to achieve the consultation goals. Nonetheless, it is better to err on the side of including too many variables in a plan rather than too few. Consultation differs from treatment or therapy research in this respect. The goal of the clinical researcher is typically to determine whether or not each of a small number of variables influences behavior. Accordingly, the researcher generally limits his or her efforts to isolating the individual effects of a few variables that can be studied under highly controlled conditions. The main goal of the consultant is to solve the problem at hand. In achieving this goal, the consultant often manipulates three or four variables at a time. If the plan developed in consultation is successful, there may be no way of knowing which of these variable manipulations has contributed to the success.

Because the number of psychological principles that may influence behavior is extremely large, the consultant must develop a strategy for classifying conditions that have the potential to influence client performance. Conditions classification reduces the strain on the consultant's memory as he or she attempts to select variables from the available knowledge base that is relevant to the specific problems encountered in consultation.

Tables B-1 through B-3 in Appendix B demonstrate one way of classifying conditions that may affect consultation. The classification is two-dimensional. First, conditions are classified on the basis of consultation goals. Conditions associated with the goal of increasing behavior are given in Table B-1. Conditions related to the objective of maintaining behavior are specified in Table B-2, and conditions dealing with the goal of reducing the strength of behavior are given in Table B-3. After conditions have been categorized in terms of goals, they are further subdivided into antecedent, consequent, and sequential conditions.

The potential functions served in consultation by antecedent, consequent, and sequential conditions vary in relation to the goals of consultation. When the goal of consultation is to increase behavior, antecedent conditions can be manipulated to help the client in stimulus discrimination. For example, a boy with a reading problem may be unable to recognize letters or words that he is called on to identify. Under these circumstances, identification may be enhanced by procedures that call attention to the distinctive features of the stimuli being presented (e.g., Bergan, 1972; Nelson & Wein, 1974; Samuels, 1973). For instance, a teacher might call attention to the distinctive features of letters by coloring those features differently from other parts of the letters. The DISTAR program uses different type set and then fades this stimulus dimension.

A second use of antecedent conditions is to enhance response capability. For example, children are often required to emit response chains that have been modeled for them. If a child is unable to make the kind of responses desired of him because the chain is currently too complex to perform, it may be desirable to reduce the complexity by such means as breaking the chain into component parts. Table manners, for instance, might be broken down into such behaviors as how to hold a fork, how to use it to eat, and what to do with the fork when it is not in use.

Third, antecedent conditions can be used as a source of information about stimuli to which the client is attempting to respond and about the kind of responses he or she is expected to make. For example, a boy may fail to control his behavior appropriately because he does not recognize cues in the environment that signal the probable occurrence of reinforcement. The obvious course of action in a situation like this is to alert the boy to the relevant cues.

A study by Kazdin, Silverman, and Sittler (1975) illustrates a procedure that can be used to alert children to reinforcing consequences in the environment. In this investigation, a teacher delivered nonverbal approval (patting approvingly) to two mentally retarded children when they were attending to the task at hand. In addition to noting the behavior of the target children, trained observers recorded the attending behavior of two other children who had the opportunity to observe that attending behavior was being reinforced. Nonverbal approval produced positive changes in the attending behavior of the target children. However, it did not affect the behavior of the two onlookers. Their attending behavior was enhanced when they were verbally prompted to notice the target children at the time of reinforcement.

When the goal of consultation is to increase behavior, consequent conditions can also be of assistance in altering the individual's performance of the desired behaviors. Performance may be increased by the time-honored techniques of adding a positive reinforcer or withdrawing a negative reinforcer.

The altering of sequential conditions is often the approach of choice when increasing behavior is related to reducing interference effects that may impair learning in complex verbal-learning tasks (Bower, 1974). If, for example, a student is having difficulty learning to read, it may be in part because the letters or words that she has learned previously are interfering with the stimuli she is currently attempting to master. Interference effects of this kind can be reduced in a variety of ways. The teacher might, for instance, reduce the similarity of the responses required of children in a paired-associate list (Marsh, Desberg, & Farwell, 1974).

The alteration of sequential conditions can also be an effective approach to the goal of building new discriminations and response patterns into an individual's repertoire of behaviors. For instance, a young child may be taught to discriminate stimuli in a concept-learning task by the reinforcement of responses emitted in the presence of relevant stimuli and the withholding of reinforcement on other occasions (Bourne & Dominowski, 1972). Thus, a child might be taught the concept *middle* by a reinforcement of responses to objects placed in the middle of a group and a withholding of reinforcement for responses made to objects in other locations. Shaping is the most common sequential condition used to build in new responses. It involves the reinforcement of successive approximations of a desired response.

In those cases in which the goal of consultation is to maintain performance capability, the central use of antecedent condition manipulation is to increase the strength of the associations between stimuli and responses. For example, if students are having difficulty remembering academic material that they have acquired previously, the antecedent conditions may be altered to increase recall. A variety of alterations are possible. One of these is to increase the meaningfulness of the stimuli to be recalled by pairing them with other stimuli familiar to the student. Thus, the meaningfulness of the term *antecedent* might be enhanced by pairing it with the word *before*. Verbal material can also be organized into categories to facilitate recall (e.g., see Gagné & Weigand, 1970; Tomlinson-Keasey, Crawford, & Miser, 1975). When facts and concepts are arranged in some orderly fashion, they are generally easier to recall than when their organization is haphazard.

The major use that can be made of sequential conditions in maintaining performance is to reduce interference effects associated with learning that occurs across a series of occasions. Interference can be reduced in several ways. For example, the repetition of material to be recalled can be increased by covert rehearsal between learning trials. Rehearsal may involve the use of imagery or covert verbalizations (see Levin, 1985). Periodic review sessions can be provided to enhance memory (Underwood, 1961), and overlearning in the form of additional trials beyond mastery can be used (Kratochwill, Demuth, & Conzemius, 1977; Kreuger, 1929).

In the many situations in which the goal of consultation is to reduce the strength of behavior, antecedent conditions can be manipulated to sever the relation between the response to be minimized and the stimuli that previously elicited it. This procedure can be accomplished in a number of ways. For instance, cues eliciting undesirable behavior can be removed, or a new response can be conditioned to stimuli that previously elicited undesirable behavior. The manipulation of antecedent conditions to reduce behavior is particularly useful in consultation because it provides a viable alternative to punishment.

Punishment is one of the two major consequent conditions that can reduce the strength of behavior. Punishment can be applied either by withdrawing a positive reinforcer or by adding an aversive stimulus. A boy may be punished by verbal reprimands for undesirable behavior. For example, sharp verbal reprimands have been found to be effective in reducing aggressive behavior in young children (Hall *et al.*, 1971). Soft reprimands may also be effective in modifying undesirable behavior. In fact, O'Leary, Kaufman, Kass, and Drabman (1970) found soft reprimands to be effective in reducing disruptive classroom behavior, whereas loud reprimands were not effective. However, punishment may produce a number of unfortunate side effects that can severely limit its usefulness (Kazdin, 1989; LaVigna & Donnellan, 1986; Sulzer-Azaroff & Mayer, 1977). These side effects can have particularly unfortunate consequences in consultation. For example, the act of punishing a child may become reinforcing to the consultee. In such a case, punishment may be administered in situations in which it is not warranted. The effects of punishment may also generalize to other responses that the consultee is attempting to increase rather than reduce. For instance, a child punished for using foul language in the classroom may stop talking in school altogether. One of the major goals of the school is to enhance language development. Another problem with the use of punishment is that it can make the consultee an aversive stimulus for the client. A child may quickly learn to dislike a teacher who continually punishes her, and the child's dislike may impair the teacher's effectiveness in instructional situations. For the reasons given above and for a number of others as well, it is often useful to avoid punishment.

The second major consequent condition that can be used to reduce the strength of behavior is extinction. Countless studies have demonstrated that if a positive reinforcer that has previously been maintaining behavior is withdrawn, the behavior will gradually diminish in strength (Kazdin, 1978; Ollendick & Cerny, 1981). For example, a child who screams at the top of her voice in a classroom may stop this behavior if reinforcement and/or peer attention is withdrawn.

Extinction can be a highly effective tool in consultation. However, it has three characteristics that may limit its usefulness. First, it generally requires the consultee to do nothing in an active way to alter the client behaviors of concern. Consultees often enter a consultation eager to solve client problems. A plan that admonishes a consultee to ignore client problems may not be very acceptable to him or her (see Witt & Elliott, 1985, for a review of acceptability issues in child treatment). Another difficulty associated with extinction is that behavior on extinction often increases sharply before it begins to diminish (Bandura, 1969). This characteristic of the extinction process may lead a consultee to conclude erroneously that a plan is not working. In such a situation, the consultee may abandon the plan before it has had a chance to exert its effects. The third problem with extinction is that it typically does not eliminate behaviors quickly. In some cases, extinction constitutes nothing more than a nuisance to the consultee. However, in other instances it can have serious consequences. For example, if a teacher is trying to stop a child from aggressive behavior that could seriously injure the child's classmates, the teacher may not wish to risk injury to the child's peers in order to give extinction a chance to work. The technique of rescuing the victim used in the Pinkston *et al.* (1973) study described earlier offers one solution to this problem. As the reader may recall, in this study aggressive behavior was reduced through an extinction procedure involving withdrawal of teacher attention in the form of reprimands following aggressive acts. The potentially harmful effects of aggression were controlled by protecting the victim.

The problems associated with the use of extinction can be ameliorated by combining extinction with other procedures for modifying client behavior. For example, to reduce aggressive behavior, a teacher may ignore aggression and at the same time reinforce an incompatible response, such as cooperative behavior. A plan of this kind allows the teacher to do something active to solve the hitting problem, and it generally produces results more quickly than extinction alone. In addition, it tends to forestall the temporary increase in behavior ordinarily associated with extinction.

Sequential conditions related to the goal of reducing response strength can be used to make extinction more effective. Extinction requires a continuous schedule to be effective. If positive reinforcement is introduced during the extinction process, the behavior will probably be strengthened rather than reduced. Thus, if the teacher in the hitting example given above ignored hitting behavior some of the time and reinforced it by attending to it on other occasions, hitting might actually increase.

The discussion to this point suggests a series of concrete steps that a consultant may take in conducting a conditions analysis:

1. Specify whether the goal of consultation is to increase, maintain, or decrease behavior.
2. Identify the antecedent, consequent, and sequential conditions currently associated with client behavior.
3. Determine the existing conditions that may affect behavior by matching existing conditions to conditions that research has indicated have the potential to control behavior. In achieving the match, the consultant should consider systematically the antecedent, consequent, and sequential conditions identified through research as influencing behavior. (Tables B-1, B-2, and B-3 can be of assistance in this regard.)
4. Identify conditions not currently associated with client behavior that nonetheless could influence behavior. The tables specifying the conditions influencing behavior may be used in accomplishing this task in essentially the same way as that recommended for Step 3.

Analyzing Client Skills

A number of investigators (e.g., Resnick, Wang, & Kaplan, 1973; Wang, 1973; White, 1973, 1974), following the lead of Robert Gagné (1970), have argued that the ability to perform various kinds of academic tasks is based to a large extent on the cumulative learning of hierarchically arranged sets of behavioral capabilities called *intellectual skills*. For example, it has been asserted that, before children can read words, they must be able to discriminate among them, and that, before they can discriminate among words, they must be able to distinguish among the letter groups used to make words (Gibson, 1969).

Gagné's hierarchy model holds that skills in a hierarchy form prerequisite relations. Each prerequisite skill is assumed to be necessary to the performance of the superordinate skills immediately adjacent to it in the hierarchy. For example, in a three-level hierarchy, Skill A may be prerequisite to Skill B, and Skill B may be prerequisite to Skill C, but Skill A may have no direct effect on Skill C. It may exert its influence only indirectly through its impact on B. In addition, there is no explicit recognition of the possibility that one subordinate skill may have a greater influence than another subordinate skill on superordinate skill learning.

Research using structural equation models[1] (Bergan, 1980) indicates that causal relations among subordinate and superordinate skills do not necessarily form hierarchies. The hierarchy is only one of a number of possible models for describing relations among skills. For example, in a model analogous to the one in the preceding paragraph, it may happen that A influences C both indirectly and directly. Skill A may affect C through its impact on B and also through a direct influence on C. Recent data also reveal that some subordinate skills may exert a much more powerful effect than others on superordinate skill learning. These findings suggest that it may be possible to develop more effective techniques than now exist for identifying those subordinate skills that have the greatest causal effect on the learning of superordinate skills.

Research on alternative models to Gagné's hierarchy model is still in an early stage of development. Accordingly, for the present, it seems advisable to continue identifying subordinate skills based on Gagné's views. This is the strategy followed in the present chapter.

Many problems that occur in psychological consultation can be analyzed in terms of Gagné's concept of intellectual skills. These problems include not only academic problems, but also social and motivational difficulties. For example, a child may have difficulty learning to multiply because she has failed to master the carrying operations associated with addition. Analogously, a child may have difficulty learning to interact effectively and appropriately with peers because (s)he lacks the prerequisite social skills for such interaction. By the same token, a child may have difficulty controlling motivation to stop using drugs or to stop overeating because (s)he lacks the self-management skills to govern these kinds of behaviors.

Skills analysis involves two tasks: identifying possible prerequisite skills and assessing skill mastery in the client. Both of these tasks may be accomplished by the consultant between the problem identification and the problem analysis interviews.

---

[1]Structural equation models are mathematical models for describing causal relations among a set of variables. Work on structural equations is an outgrowth of Wright's work on path analysis (1921). For a detailed introduction to structural equations, see Otis Duncan's book *Introduction to Structural Equation Models* (1975).

Skills analysis can be initiated by identifying potential prerequisite skills underlying the consultation goals. In some cases, one may rely on learning hierarchies validated through research in identifying prerequisite skills (White & Gagné, 1974). However, more often than not, skill hierarchies need to be constructed. These, of course, will be, at best, tentative approximations of the actual ordering of the prerequisite skills needed in the achievement of consultation goals.

To identify prerequisite skills, the consultant must specify the behaviors that are components of the goal behaviors (Gagné & Briggs, 1974) established in problem identification. For example, consider the case of Bob, a fourth-grader referred for consultation services because he was having difficulty in arithmetic. The consultant and the consultee established the following goal for Bob during problem identification: "Given worksheets containing problems involving the addition of two numbers, neither of which is greater than 9, Bob will be able to add the numbers correctly 100% of the time." In order to identify the prerequisite skills related to this goal, the consultant had to designate the behaviors involved in adding numbers presented on worksheets. For instance, the consultant identified the ability to read numerals as a prerequisite skill because reading numerals occurs as part of the process of adding numbers on worksheets.

The prerequisite skills identified through the process of specifying the components of the problem identification goals should be phrased as performance objectives. Specifying prerequisite skills as performance objectives facilitates the construction of test items to measure skill attainment. In addition, it clarifies for the consultee precisely what the client needs to learn to achieve skill mastery. For example, saying that Bob needs to learn to read numerals would not provide Bob's teacher with as much information as saying, "Given the numerals 1 through 20 presented in a random sequence on flash cards, Bob will be able to identify the numerals correctly 100% of the time."

Each of the performance objectives initially identified as a skill that is prerequisite to goal attainment can itself be broken down into components. The process of breaking down prerequisite skills into components is, of course, essentially the same as that of initially identifying the components of the goal behaviors established in problem identification. For instance, to establish the component behaviors associated with the identification of numerals, the consultant would ask what kinds of behaviors occur in the process of naming visually presented numerals. Two capabilities suggested immediately by this question are the ability to pronounce the numerals and the ability to discriminate visually among them.

The consultant may break down the skills that represent the lowest level of capabilities that have been identified. For example, the consultant knew that Bob could pronounce numerals, and he felt reasonably sure that

Bob could discriminate among them visually. Consequently, these skills were not included in the hierarchy finally established for Bob's arithmetic performance. However, it should be noted that a "bottom-up" task analysis is very time-consuming. As an option, the consultant can start at the terminal behavior and assess subskills only as far as necessary to create mastery.

In the process of breaking skills down into components, the hierarchical arrangement of the skills must first have been tentatively specified. The next task is to put the skills down on paper in a hierarchical form. It may be necessary to make a number of minor adjustments in the placement of skills in the hierarchy. The final product should be analogous in form to the hierarchy established for Bob's arithmetic skills as shown in Figure 4-1.

Gagné (1970, 1974) suggested that it is useful to categorize the skills in a learning hierarchy in terms of eight hierarchically related types of learning. These types are summarized briefly in Table 4-2. Applying Gagné's suggestion to Bob's addition performance reveals that identifying numerals presented visually is an example of multiple-discrimination learning.

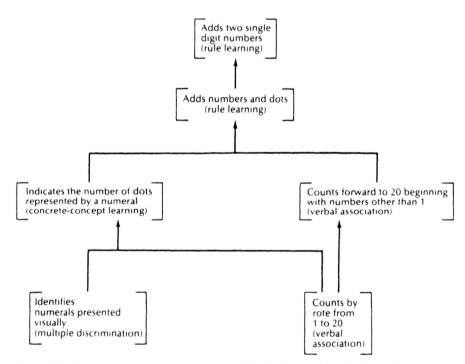

FIGURE 4-1. A tentative hierarchy of the prerequisite skills related to addition performance. The descriptions in parentheses classify the skills in accordance with Gagné's eight varieties of learning (1970).

TABLE 4-2. Gagné's Eight Types of Learning

Type	Description	
	Definition	Example
Signal learning	This is classical conditioning. A conditioned stimulus (signal) precedes an unconditioned stimulus and thereby gains the power to elicit the response elicited by the unconditioned stimulus.	A young child sees a dog (conditioned stimulus) before hearing a loud noise (unconditioned stimulus evoking a fear reaction). The presence of the dog subsequently evokes fear.
Stimulus–response learning	This is operant discrimination learning. A signal is followed by a response that results in reinforcement.	A child sees his teacher turn her back on the class (signal). He then yells. His peers reinforce him with laughter.
Chaining	Chaining is serial learning. A string of stimulus–response units is acquired.	Opening one's workbook to an assigned page is an example.
Verbal association learning	This is a form of chaining in which the stimuli and responses are verbal.	Reciting the letters of the alphabet illustrates verbal association learning.
Multiple-discrimination learning	This involves learning to distinguish among various stimuli in a set.	Visually identifying sight words is a familiar task in early reading instruction that involves multiple discrimination.
Concrete-concept learning	Concrete-concept learning is the acquisition of concepts defined by concrete stimulus attributes.	A child learns that a dog is an animal that has four legs and a tail and that barks.
Rule learning	Rules are concepts formed from other concepts.	The rule "Round things roll" is formed from the concept *round things* and *roll*.
Problem solving	Problem solving is the application of rules in the discovery of a higher order rule.	The many "story" problems given to children and youth in math classes illustrate problem solving.

The counting skills are forms of verbal association. Indicating the number of dots represented by a numeral is an example of concrete concept learning, and the addition skills in the hierarchy are forms of rule learning.

One reason for identifying skills in terms of Gagné's eight types of learning is that such an identification may be useful in determining the hierarchical arrangement of skills. Notice that, in the hierarchy for Bob's addition performance in Figure 4-1, multiple-discrimination and verbal-association skills are prerequisite to concrete-concept learning, and that

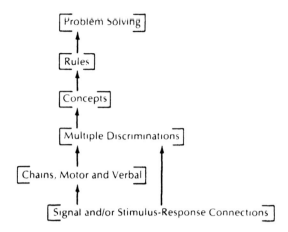

FIGURE 4-2. A general sequence for cumulative learning. [Source: Adapted from R. M. Gagné (1968). Contributions of learning to human development. *Psychological Review, 75,* 182. Copyright 1968 by the American Psychological Association. Reprinted by permission.]

concrete-concept learning, in turn, is prerequisite to rule learning. As shown in Figure 4-2, this ordering of skills is in accord with the ordering of Gagné's eight types of learning.

A second reason for categorizing skills in terms of Gagné's learning types is that the conditions influencing skill acquisition differ for the different types of learning (Gagné, 1974). For example, the ability to discriminate distinctive features of stimuli is crucial in multiple-discrimination learning, whereas this capability is not important in verbal association learning. Accordingly, plans designed to facilitate the acquisition of multiple discriminations may profitably include procedures of calling attention to the distinctive features of stimuli. Tactics such as underlining distinctive features or changing their size provide familiar examples of the ways in which teachers call attention to the distinctive characteristics of stimuli. For instance, a teacher may call attention to particular letters in a set of words by underlining the critical letters, as in Ran, Can, and Fan.

Once a tentative hierarchy of academic skills has been constructed, the consultant is ready to complete the skills analysis by assessing client mastery of the skills in the hierarchy. To do this, the consultant must obtain test items for each of the skills identified. If the consultant is fortunate enough to be working with a hierarchy validated through research, he or she may consult any of the standard works on test construction that include sections on criterion-referenced assessment to assist in the construction process (e.g., Thorndike, 1971). The following items provide examples for the hierarchy related to Bob's arithmetic difficulties:

1. While showing the child the numeral 6, the consultant asks, "What is this number?"

2. The consultant says, "Count from 1 to 2."
3. The consultant says, "Start with 6 and count up to 20."
4. While showing the child the numeral 3, the consultant says, "Make this many dots on your paper."
5. While showing the child a card with the problem 2 + 1 on it, the consultant says, "Add these."
6. While showing the child a card with the problem 3 + 4 on it, the consultant says, "Add these."

Skill assessment identifies those skills that the client currently does not possess and that therefore represent appropriate targets for instruction. For example, Bob was able to recognize numbers greater than 1. He could not represent numbers by dots, and he could not add numbers and dots. On the basis of this information, the consultant and the consultee decided to focus skill instruction on the three skills Bob lacked.

The Analysis of Latent Ability

The task analysis approach described above works well in those situations in which the goal is to establish the subordinate competencies related to a single type of task. In the example given above, the goal was to teach the child to add numbers involving relatively small sums. Task analysis proved to be a useful tool in achieving this goal. When the goal is to develop a broad range of skills, an entirely different approach is needed. For example, suppose that the goal is to improve the math skills of all of the children in a kindergarten class. This goal requires an analytic procedure capable of relating many different types of skills, including counting, numeral recognition, simple addition, and simple subtraction. Not only must the analytic procedure used be capable of relating different types of skills, but it must also be capable of accounting for large numbers of skills. When the number of skills being considered is large, the task-analytic approach may lead to diagnostic assessment procedures that are so time-consuming that they become impractical to implement. In the following paragraphs, we describe an approach involving the analysis of latent ability. The approach is useful in situations involving large numbers of skills of varying types. Some features of this approach can be implemented by a consultant using informal assessment techniques. However, full implementation of the approach requires professionally developed assessment instruments.

The Latent Ability Concept

Ability is typically regarded as an unobserved (latent) trait. Ability is generally defined operationally in terms of an individual's position in a norm group. For example, given an IQ test with a mean of 100 and a standard deviation of 15, a child with an IQ of 115 is one standard deviation above the average in the norm group representing the child's age-mates. The ability concept has generally been thought to be of little value in applied behavioral work. Behaviorists never tire of pointing out that knowing where an individual stands in a normal group tells one next to nothing about what the individual can or cannot do. As a consequence, information about ability is not very useful in identifying or analyzing problems, or in planning interventions to produce beneficial changes in behavior.

The difficulty with the ability construct as it has been used in the past lies in the effort to measure ability in terms of group position. There is another way to look at ability that can provide a great deal of information about what an individual can do. This approach defines ability in terms of an individual's position in a developmental sequence or path. Consider a set of skills that have been ordered along a scale by difficulty. The numbers on the scale tell how difficult each skill is. For example, consider a math scale devised for young children. Counting to 5 may have a difficulty value of 414. On the other hand, a simple verbal addition problem may have a difficulty value of 572. Latent-trait statistical-techniques (Bock & Aitkin, 1981; Lord, 1980) make it possible to determine the difficulty values of an ordered set of tasks. Moreover, these techniques can be used to place ability on the same scale as task difficulty. For instance, an ability of 414 would indicate that an individual had a 50-50 chance of being able to count to 5 correctly. Similarly, an ability of 572 would indicate a 50-50 chance of performing simple verbal addition correctly. Note that the mean and standard deviation for the scale are chosen arbitrarily just as they are in norm-referenced assessment instruments. For instance, suppose that an IQ test has a mean of 100 and a standard deviation of 15. It would be a simple matter to change the mean to 500 and the standard deviation to 50. Likewise, the mean and standard deviation for the hypothetical counting scale could be set to any values that the test constructor selects.

Path-Referenced Assessment

The approach described in the preceding paragraph references ability to an individual's position in a developmental sequence or path. Consequently, it may be referred to as a *path-referenced assessment* (Bergan, Stone, & Feld, 1985). Path-referenced assessment differs from norm-referenced assessment in that, in norm-referenced assessment, ability is defined in terms of position in a normal group.

Some authors would regard path-referenced assessment as a form of criterion-referenced assessment (see, for example, Hambleton, 1985). There are good reasons for including path-referenced assessment under the expanding umbrella of criterion-referenced assessment. There are so many definitions of criterion-referenced assessment that one more wouldn't hurt. Moreover, there would be one less construct to worry about in a field that is already overburdened with constructs. Finally, the earliest writings on criterion-referenced assessment (see, for example, Glaser, 1963) included the idea of skill sequences, which is central to the path-referenced approach.

There are two important reasons for not regarding path-referenced assessment as a form of criterion-referenced assessment. One has to do with the central role of the ability construct in path-referenced assessment. Path referring defines ability in terms of position along a path of development. The notion of ability has never been a part of the theoretical underpinnings of criterion-referenced assessment. Criterion-referenced assessment has its origins in behavioral psychology, and the ability concept has never been looked on favorably from the behavioral perspective. The second reason for distinguishing between path-referenced and criterion-referenced assessment is that there are large numbers of criterion-referenced assessment instruments that were not constructed by means of latent trait technology. To say that these instruments and path-referenced instruments are fundamentally the same invites confusion.

Advantages of the Path-Referenced Approach

There are a number of practical advantages in the path-referenced approach. These derive directly from the linking of the ability construct to the path position. The first advantage is that path referencing can increase the accuracy of estimates of skill performance. Path-referenced assessment uses the ability construct to take into account performance on an entire test in determining whether an individual can perform each of the various tasks on the test. For example, suppose that a child is asked to count to 10 and performs the task incorrectly. Suppose that, later on, the child is able to add 7 + 5 and to subtract 8 from 15 without difficulty. The observed ability to add and subtract suggests that the child may have made a careless mistake in counting to 10. The path-referenced approach would take addition and subtraction performance into consideration in determining whether the child can count to 10. The child's overall ability provides the basis for estimating the probability that the child can perform any particular task. By contrast, in criterion-referenced assessment, ability to perform a task is typically determined by performance on that task alone.

A second advantage of path referencing is that it reduces the number of skills that must be assessed. If one knows an individual's ability and the difficulty level of a task, one can estimate whether the individual will be able to perform the task in cases in which the individual has not actually been tested on that task. For example, suppose that a child has an ability of 600. Assume further that a teacher wants to know whether the child can count to 5 and that counting to 5 has a difficulty of 414. It would not be necessary to test the child further to get an estimate of counting skill. The child's ability level indicates that there is a high probability that he or she is able to count to 5 correctly.

A third major advantage of path referencing is that it provides a way to test the assumption that skills are ordered sequentially (Bergan, 1988). There are large numbers of assessment instruments on the market that, either implicitly or explicitly, assume that skills are ordered sequentially. Moreover, there are large numbers of curriculums that imply a sequential ordering of skills. Empirical validation of skill sequences used in assessment and curriculum design is lacking. As a result, the possibility of a lack of fit between the developmental level of the child and what the child is taught is increased.

The Head Start Measures Battery

The Head Start Measures Battery (HSMB) is an example of a path-referenced approach to assessment (Bergan & Smith, 1986). The HSMB is part of an assessment and planning system designed for use in the national Head Start organization. The battery is made up of six scales: language, math, nature and science, perception, reading, and social development. Each scale is composed of an empirically validated sequence of skills. The skills within each scale are grouped into categories. For example, in the math scale, the categories include numeral recognition, conservation of number, comparison of quantity, counting and ordering, addition, and subtraction. The categories are used to show the sequencing of highly related skills. For instance, addition skills are grouped together, so that it is possible to see the progression from recognizing that adding increases the number in a set to the ability to solve simple addition story problems.

The HSMB is used to plan learning experiences for children that are congruent with each child's developmental level. Following assessment, teachers receive a "Developmental Profile and Planning Guide" indicating for each child the skills that have been learned, the skills that are ready to be learned now, and the skills that the child will be ready to learn later. The readiness levels for each skill are based on the estimated probability that the child will be able to perform the skill correctly. For instance, if a child has a 50-50 chance of passing the items assessing a given skill, it is assumed that the child is ready for learning experiences that will increase the development of that skill. On the other hand, if the child has less than a 25% chance of performing the items assessing the skill, it is assumed that the child will be ready for learning experiences related to that skill later.

The Process of Analyzing Ability

Although the full implementation of path-referenced assessment technology requires professionally developed assessment instruments, it is possible to implement the process of analyzing ability during consultation without the aid of published assessment devices. The first step is to identify the different categories into which an ability area may be divided. For example, math might include geometry, arithmetic, and so on. The categories may be broken down into subcategories. For example, arithmetic may be broken down into counting, addition, subtraction, and so on.

The goal of the category division process is to arrive at a set of interrelated cognitive procedures describing the processes required for performing the tasks that make up the ability area. A cognitive procedure may be thought of as a set of actions (processes) carried out on objects to achieve a goal. The subtraction of whole numbers is a relatively simple example of a cognitive procedure in the math area (Brown & Burton, 1978). In this example, the action is subtracting, the objects are whole numbers, and the goal is to find the difference between two numbers.

A cognitive procedure generally governs the performance of a large number of tasks. For example, consider the procedure of counting. One can count forward, backward, by 2's, and so on. The ideal procedure includes all of the processes necessary to perform the various tasks in the procedure. For example, an ideal subtraction procedure would include processes for regrouping to perform subtraction tasks requiring borrowing. Of course, there may be less-than-ideal versions of a procedure that do not cover all tasks within a procedure. For instance, a child may lack the processes associated with regrouping.

The various versions included in a procedure reflect an ordered set of capabilities that define a developmental sequence for that procedure. The different versions of a procedure may be identified by delineating the attributes of the procedure that impose cognitive demands on the individuals. For example, the demand attributes of counting include the direction of counting (forward and backward), the range of numbers to be counted, the starting point (1 or a number greater than 1), and the increment (by 1's, by 2's etc.). Varying the demand attributes associated with a procedure produces variations in the difficulty of tasks related to the procedure. For example, counting forward is easier than counting backward. Likewise, counting by 1's is easier than counting by 2's, and counting starting from 1 is easier than counting starting with a number greater than 1.

The manipulation of demand attributes is the key to establishing the sequence of development in a given content area. One begins the process by identifying the hypothesized demands assumed to affect task difficulty. These hypotheses may be tested empirically by determining the relative difficulty of tasks associated with the various demands identified for study. For example, one can determine that counting forward is easier than counting backward by observing children's performance on these two types of tasks. Validation of the sequence of development is best done with the aid of statistical procedures such as latent-trait techniques. However, when statistical validation is lacking, as may be the case for some of the skill areas dealt with in consultation, validation may be undertaken through a careful observation of behavior using the procedures described earlier in the section on task analysis.

For most of this century, psychological thinking about the concept of ability has been dominated by a view that has defined ability in terms of position in a norm group. Changing the definition so that ability is defined in terms of what an individual can do makes it possible to change ability through intervention. Changing a child's ability is, after all, what most parents and teachers are concerned about. Although a parent may be delighted that a child has mastered specific objectives such as counting to 5, the parent's underlying wish is nonetheless to change the child's math ability. The mastery of isolated skills does not address that concern. For example, a teacher may teach a group of children a large number of specific skills without necessarily advancing the children developmentally. This would be the case if all of the skills were at about the same level of difficulty and did not lead to the acquisition of new and more complex skills. The linking of ability to developmentally sequenced skills opens the way to interventions aimed at affecting broad-scale changes in ability.

The Plan Design Phase

The second major phase of problem analysis is plan design. In plan design, the consultant and the consultee develop the procedures that are to be put into effect during the implementation phase of consultation.

Developing Plan Strategies

The first step in plan design is to specify broad strategies that can be used to achieve the goals of consultation. Plan strategies indicate, in general terms, possible courses of action that can be taken during the implementation phase of consultation. For example, a consultant might ask a teacher concerned about a child's ability to retain knowledge, "Would it be possible to give Ted some suggestions about how he might organize the material that he is to be tested on?" This question does not indicate specifically how organization should be applied; it merely suggests that the principle of organizing material to promote recall may be useful in making a plan to solve the student's recall problem.

Strategies may include the designation of conditions and/or skills that may influence goal attainment. For example, a consultant might suggest that peer modeling be used to promote prosocial behaviors in a child, or he or she might advocate that coaching be provided to teach a child the prerequisite skills for effective social interaction (see Gresham, 1981; Gresham & Evans, 1987).

The specification of strategies provides a way to introduce psychological principles based on research findings into consultative problem-solving. When a consultant suggests the use of a principle such as modeling or shaping, he or she has taken the first step toward using scientific knowledge in consultation.

The strategies designated in plan design should, of course, be derived directly from the examination of conditions or skills conducted in the analysis phase of the problem analysis process. If, for example, conditions analysis suggested that parental reinforcement was probably a key variable controlling tantrum behavior in a child, then at least one of the strategies suggested for reducing tantrum behavior should include changes in parental reinforcement practices.

The presentation of psychological principles in the form of strategies enables the consultee to adapt general principles to specific problem requirements. When, for example, a consultant suggests the use of reinforcement, he or she offers the consultee a great deal of latitude in deciding how to incorporate reinforcement into plans to solve the specific problem under consideration. On the other hand, if the consultant were to say, "I think you should give Ted a piece of candy for every correct page of homework that he turns in," the consultee would have very little latitude in adapting the principle of reinforcement to his or her specific needs.

Developing Plan Tactics

After a strategy has been designated for use in plan design, the specific tactics to be used to implement the strategy must be specified. Thus, if the consultant has suggested that modeling be used to increase prosocial behavior, it is necessary to specify how modeling is to be incorporated into plan design.

Plan tactics should include a description of the procedures, the sequence of events, and the materials to be used in implementation. For instance, if reinforcement were to be used to motivate a child to complete her homework, it would be necessary to establish the kinds of reinforcers to be applied and how they would be delivered.

Tactics may also include a specification of who is to carry out the tactic. It is often implicitly assumed that the consultee will implement the tactics designed in problem analysis. However, there are many cases in which individuals other than the consultee will put the tactics into effect (see Chapter 5 for a discussion of implementation options). For example, when the consultee is a teacher, the teacher's aide, a parent, or the client may implement the plan tactics. When there is some doubt about who will carry out a tactic, it is necessary to include a specification of the individual(s) involved in implementation as part of the description of the tactic.

The specification of a plan tactic should always provide a description of the conditions under which implementation will occur. For example, it might be decided in problem analysis that reinforcement for completed homework will always be given in class immediately after collection of the milk money each morning.

Whereas strategies provide a vehicle for indicating what principles may be useful in consultation, tactics offer a way to translate principles into problem-solving practice. To be maximally effective, the translation effort should take into account the constraints operating in the client's environment that may limit the kinds of tactics that can be successfully applied.

One type of constraint on implementation includes practical factors such as limitations in material, time, money, or personnel (Kratochwill & Van Someren, 1985). For example, consultants must be particularly careful not to lead consultees into the development of plans that they do not have the time to implement. Consultees are generally very busy people who have a large number of responsibilities outside those associated with consultation. These responsibilities must be considered in plan design to maximize the likelihood of accurate plan implementation.

In addition to practical limitations, the consultant must consider the constraints on implementation associated with the attitudes and/or values of consultees and clients. For instance, it probably would not be advisable to suggest to a parent that he or she use candy as a reinforcer if the parent thinks that candy is bad for child's teeth, or that the use of candy is in effect bribing the child to emit behavior that she or he ought to emit simply because it is the right thing to do. Increasingly, it is being recognized that the acceptability of treatments plays a major role in their success (Elliott, 1988; Witt & Elliott, 1985).

In developing effective plan tactics, a consultant should consider the resources available for implementation as well as the constraints on implementation. Resources are the other side of the constraint coin. Like constraints, they may include the attitudes and values of the participants in consultation and factors such as material, time, money, and personnel. However, whereas constraints represent limitations on implementation, resources constitute possible alternative for use in implementation.

Among the consultant's principal tasks during plan design are to ascertain the resources available for implementation and to use these in the development of plan tactics. For example, teachers are often highly skilled in the generation of learning activities for children. Thus, in developing a plan with a teacher to teach the prerequisite skills underlying the mastery of a given academic area, the consultant might take advantage of the teacher's special competency in the design of interesting learning tasks for the child. The final plan established for the child, then, would be an amalgamation of the consultant's psychological knowledge and the teacher's skill in instruction.

Establishing Performance Assessment Procedures

The final step in plan design is to establish performance assessment procedures to be used during plan implementation. When the plan to be implemented is based on conditions analysis, the specification of the assessment procedures requires nothing more than reaffirming the baseline procedures established during problem identification.

If plan implementation involves skill development, the problem of establishing assessment procedures requires more than merely reaffirming the baseline assessment techniques. The assessment procedures used in skill cases should include provisions for collecting data on performance related to the terminal objectives to be achieved through consultation. In addition, they should involve plans for obtaining data on the acquisition of skills leading to the attainment of terminal objectives.

To obtain data on terminal objectives, the consultant should continue to use the baseline assessment procedures established during problem identification. For example, in the arithmetic problem discussed earlier in the chapter, the teacher continued to record Bob's addition performance in the same way she had recorded it during the baseline data-collection period.

The assessment procedures established for prerequisite skills should focus on indicating the point at which each of the various skills selected for instruction is mastered. There is generally no need to collect baseline data on prerequisite-skill performance because the major concern of the consultant and the consultee is establishing when skill acquisition has occurred.

The items used by the consultant during skill assessment can generally be adapted for use in measuring skill acquisition during plan implementation. For example, during plan implementation, Bob's performance was measured by assessing the percentage of the time that he was able to count forward correctly from numbers greater than 1, the percentage of the time that he was able to make the correct number of dots of the numerals presented, and the percentage of correct solutions to problems involving the addition of numbers and dots.

Prerequisite skills and performance related to terminal objectives should be graphed in the manner described in Chapter 3 for displaying data in skills cases. Figure 4-3 illustrates this graphing procedure for Bob's arithmetic behavior. As this figure shows, the tactic of graphing the skills and the performance related to the terminal objectives on the same graph provides a visual presentation that makes it possible to judge, at least in a rough way, the extent of the effectiveness of the skill training.

THE PROBLEM ANALYSIS INTERVIEW

The problem analysis process is implemented to a large extent through the problem analysis interview. In this interview, the consultant and the consultee decide whether a problem exists that warrants problem analysis. If they agree that there is a problem, they discuss the conditions and/or skills that may be influencing client behavior, and they design a plan to achieve problem solution.

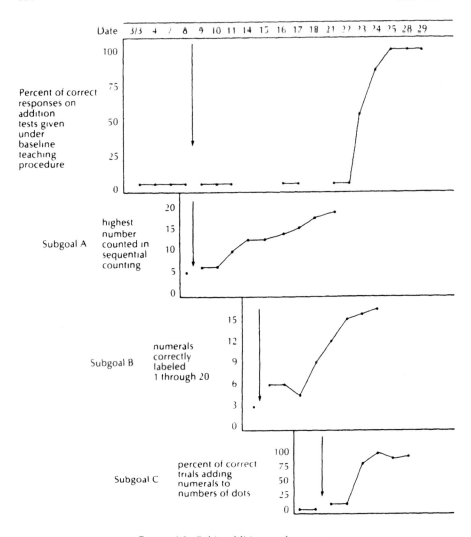

FIGURE 4-3. Bob's addition performance.

Interview Objectives and Strategies for Attaining Them

What the consultant says during the problem analysis interview should be guided by the objectives established for this kind of interview. As shown in Table 4-3, the problem analysis objectives include problem validation, analysis, plan design, and procedural goals.

Problem Validation Objectives

The first task to be accomplished during the problem analysis interview is to validate the existence of the problem to be solved in consultation.

TABLE 4-3. Objectives for the Problem Analysis Interview

Objective type	Interview type	
	Conditions interview	Skills interview
Problem validation	Determine the adequacy of baseline data.	Determine the adequacy of baseline data.
	Determine the discrepancy between existing and desired client performance.	Determine the discrepancy between existing and desired client performance.
	Establish agreement with the consultee on whether or not a problem exists.	Establish agreement with the consultee on whether or not a problem exists.
Analysis	Determine conditions that may influence client attainment of consultation goals.	Communicate results of skills assessment.
		Obtain information about techniques used to enhance client performance during the baseline period.
Plan design	Establish plan strategies.	Establish plan strategies.
	Establish plan tactics.	Establish plan tactics.
	Reaffirm assessment procedures established in problem identification.	Reaffirm baseline assessment of terminal objectives.
		Establish procedures for assessing skills that are prerequisite to terminal objective.
Procedure	Set the date for the problem evaluation interview.	Set the date for the problem evaluation interview.
	Make provisions for monitoring implementation.	Make provisions for monitoring implementation.
	Make provisions for training if required.	Make provisions for training if required.

In some cases, the baseline data reveal that a problem may not be as serious as it was thought to be. Parents may find that their child does not fight with children in the neighborhood as much as they thought, or a teacher may discover that a student is a more able reader than he had suspected. In such situations, either the consultation may be terminated or a new problem may be identified. Of course, in many instances consultation reveals a significant problem, and in these cases, further analysis of the problem validation determines the adequacy of the baseline data collected during problem identification. Early in the problem-analysis interview, the consultant should ask to see the baseline records collected by the consultee. The consultant usually graphs the data that have been collected so that he or she and the consultee have a visual picture of the client behavior of concern.

The examination of baseline records permits the consultant to make a rough judgment regarding the adequacy of the data that have been collected. If data have been collected for only 2 days and if 5 days of data collection had been planned, there may not be enough information to determine accurately the extent (the severity or frequency) of the problem under consideration. Thus, the consultant might say, "I think we should have a few more days of baseline data before we make a judgment about Bobby's pestering. Let's hope he isn't sick again this week."

The consultant's second objective with respect to problem validation is to determine the discrepancy between existing performance and desired performance of the client. The consultant takes steps to achieve this objective when the baseline data are sufficient to undertake problem validation.

To establish the discrepancy between the baseline and the desired performance, the consultant asks the consultee to compare the baseline level of performance with the goal established for performance. For example, the consultant might say, "You indicated that you felt that Bob should be able to perform the addition problems assigned to him correctly 100% of the time. The baseline data that you have collected indicate less than 5% accuracy."

In problem-centered consultation, the level of desired performance is often not precisely specified during problem identification. For example, it may have been established that a mother is concerned about her child's temper tantrums. However, the consultant may not have asked her to indicate the precise number of tantrums per day or week that would be acceptable. In these cases, it is necessary to specify level as part of the process of determining the discrepancy between existing and desired performance standards. Thus, while examining baseline data in the tantrum illustration, the consultant would ask the parent for an indication of what might be an acceptable number of tantrums.

The consultant's final objective with regard to problem validation is to ensure agreement between himself or herself and the consultee regarding the existence of the problem. In some cases, the discrepancy between what is observed and what is desired is so large that agreement is implicit. However, in other instances, the consultant may have to ask the consultee if he or she believes that the observed discrepancy between the existing and the desired performance is extensive enough to warrant saying that a problem exists. For example, the consultant might say, "Our baseline data indicate that Teddy is having tantrums about three times per week, and you have said that, as far as you are concerned, one tantrum is too many. Do we agree, then, that there is a real problem here?"

Analysis Objectives

In those cases involving conditions analysis, the consultant's central objective is to determine the conditions that may influence the client's attainment of the goals of consultation. The identification of conditions includes both the specification of the conditions currently existing in the client's environment and the conditions that, although not currently operative in the environment, may nonetheless affect client behavior.

The consultant identifies the conditions that are potentially relevant to problem solutions simply by asking the consultee to describe those antecedent, consequent, and sequential conditions related to client behavior during the period of baseline data collection. The consultant combines the information obtained regarding the conditions existing during baseline performance with what he or she has learned about the conditions during the problem identification interview to generate hypotheses about factors that may be controlling the client's behavior. For instance, suppose that, during problem identification, a consultant learns that a child who is overly aggressive in school emits most of her aggressive behaviors during the morning. In problem analysis, it is revealed that a great many changes in activity occur during transitional periods. Information of this kind may lead the consultant to advance the hypothesis that the transitional periods serve as cues for aggressive acts.

The identification of the conditions currently operative in the client's environment may lead to hypotheses involving the potential influence on behavior of factors not present in the immediate situation. For example, a discussion of antecedent conditions might reveal that a teacher is currently not using modeling techniques in circumstances in which such techniques may have a beneficial influence on learning. In such a situation, the consultant might well advance the hypothesis that modeling procedures may be a useful tool in solving the problem of concern to the teacher.

In those cases involving skills analysis, the central objective of the consultant is to communicate the results of his or her assessment of the client's skills to the consultee. For instance, a consultant might summarize the assessment of a child's addition skills by saying, "When I tested Bob, I found that he did not count forward from numbers other than 1. He also didn't correctly respond that numbers represented quantities of things. For example, I showed him some numerals and asked him to make as many dots as each numeral signified. He did not to do this correctly."

A consultant's second objective in a case involving skills analysis is to obtain information about the techniques used to enhance the client's performance of the terminal objectives during the baseline period. For example, in the case of Bob's addition difficulties, the consultant would want to know what instructional procedures were used to teach addition during the baseline period. The consultant will already have explored the topic of instructional procedures in some detail during problem identification. Thus, during problem analysis, the consultant would probably focus his or her efforts on discovering whether there had been any changes in procedure.

The consultant uses the same techniques to get information about instructional procedures as she or he uses to acquire information about other kinds of environmental influence on client behavior. Thus, the consultant asks about the antecedent, consequent, and sequential conditions that define the procedures that the consultee used during baseline to enhance client performance.

Plan Design Objectives

The first objective in the plan design phase of the problem analysis interview is to establish plan strategies for possible use in implementation. Because of his or her knowledge of the psychological principles that may influence goal attainment, the consultant should generally assume the major responsibility for specifying strategies that may be used in plan design. In some cases, strategies may be designated simply by indicating conditions or skills that the consultant believes may influence client behavior. For example, a consultant might say, "I found that Bob was unable to count forward from numbers greater than 1. I think that this is probably one of the skills that he will need to develop in order to learn to add." In other instances, the consultant may lead the consultee to the specification of a strategy to be used in consultation. For instance, a consultant might say, "You said that, when Ted masturbates in class, you generally make him sit next to you. Ted seems to like to be with adults, he seems to feel more secure when he is with you or with the reading teacher than when he is with the other children, and his masturbation is probably at least in part an effort to get your attention. How could you make use of these observations about Ted in designing a plan to eliminate his masturbation?"

The consultant should generally specify possible strategies for the consultee when the consultee lacks the necessary information to participate in the formulation of workable strategies for use in plan design. Strategies based on skills analysis provide an example. The consultant identifies prerequisite skills during his or her assessment of the client's capabilities. The consultee may not know what skills have been identified until it is time to specify strategies during the problem analysis interview.

The consultant should also provide strategies when the consultee specifically asks what should be done to solve the problem of concern. As indicated earlier, the task of making psychological principles available to the consultee is an important part of the consultant role. The consultee usually expects a consultant to have special knowledge of the relevant psychological principles, and he or she may call on the consultant to express this knowledge in a direct way during plan design.

Although the consultant often finds it necessary to specify the strategies to be used in plan design, there are advantages in eliciting strategies from the consultee. When the consultee specifies the strategies to be used in the plan design, the chances are high that he or she understands the strategies that have been identified and how they relate to the client's problem. It is also probable that he or she will support the use of the strategies that have been specified. A consultee is unlikely to suggest a strategy that he or she would not consider using to achieve a problem solution.

Regardless of who actually designates the strategies used in the plan design, the consultee has the final say concerning which strategies will be incorporated into the plan. Because of the central role that the consultee plays in the implementation process and because of his or her special responsibilities to the client, the strategies used in plan design should have the full endorsement of the consultee. For this reason, it is generally advisable for the consultant not to convince the consultee to agree to a strategy that he or she believes is inappropriate. The consultant's task is to find a strategy that is both workable and acceptable to the consultee.

The second objective to be achieved during the plan design phase of the problem analysis interview is to develop the tactics to be used in plan implementation. Whereas it is generally best for the consultant to assume the responsibility for specifying plan strategies, it is usually advisable for the consultee to indicate the tactics to be used in implementing strategies. One advantage of eliciting tactics from the consultee is that the consultee will often have special skills in implementing the plan tactics. For example, consider the familiar situation in which a consultant asks a teacher to identify ways in which reinforcement may be used to alter disruptive behavior in the classroom. The typical plan strategy used in this kind of situation is to ignore disruptive behavior and to reinforce desired behavior. One of the tactical questions related to this strategy is selecting the kind of reinforcer to use. In some cases, the teacher is in a much better position to make this selection than the consultant. Some teachers have a wide range of reinforcement techniques in their repertoire of instructional skills. Moreover, they are often able to apply these techniques in extremely creative ways. By requesting the teacher to specify reinforcement tactics, the consultant may take advantage of the skills that the teacher has.

Not only does a consultee often have special skills that can be used in implementing tactics, but he or she generally has knowledge about the clients that may determine which tactics are most likely to be effective. For example, a teacher attempting to control disruptive classroom behavior probably has a good idea of the kinds of consequences that are most likely to be reinforcing to the children in the class. Asking the teacher to specify plan tactics takes advantage of this knowledge.

A third advantage of eliciting tactics from the consultee is that it uses the consultee's knowledge of the constraints and resources in the client's environment that may influence the plan's effectiveness. For example, as indicated earlier, one highly important constraint on plan design is the acceptability to the consultee of the plan tactics. Consider further the use of reinforcement in the control of disruptive classroom behavior. There are some reinforcement techniques that teachers may feel uncomfortable applying. The specific kinds of reinforcement likely to generate antagonism vary from teacher to teacher. One may object to tangible rewards such as candy. Another may object to the use of activities such as free-choice periods, arguing that they interfere with the children's work schedule. Despite these kinds of reservations, virtually all teachers are familiar with a variety of reinforcement procedures, which they use in various ways daily in the classroom.

In recent years, there has been a growing body of empirical work devoted to treatment acceptability. *Treatment acceptability* is defined as "judgments by lay persons, clients, and others of whether treatment procedures are appropriate, fair, and reasonable for the problem or client" (Kazdin, 1981, p. 493). Conceptual models for understanding treatment acceptability have recently been advanced (Reimers, Wacker, & Koeppl, 1987; Witt & Elliott, 1985). Building on the work of Witt and Elliott (1985), Reimers *et al.* (1987) presented a model of treatment acceptability (see Figure 4-4). Based on the model, a treatment perceived to be low in acceptability will have low compliance in delivery and therefore will probably not be effective. If the treatment is not effective, there may be poor maintenance or other side effects.

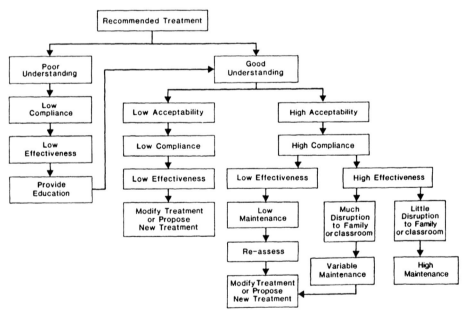

FIGURE 4-4. Proposed model for acceptability. [Source: T. M. Reimers, D. P. Wacker, & G. Koeppl. (1987). Acceptability of behavioral treatments: A review of the literature. *School Psychology Review, 16,* 212–227. Reproduced by permission.]

Recently, Elliott (1988) presented a range of variables that have been examined by researchers interested in pretreatment acceptability and its effects on treatment outcome (see Table 4-4). Based on the research documented in Table 4-4, Elliott (1988) came to four conclusions. First, a methodology exists for assessing consumers' and clients' perceptions of treatments (see below). Second, treatment acceptability is a complex construct and in consultation is influenced by consultant, consultee, and client variables. Third, generally, consumers evaluate positive treatments as more acceptable than negative or punishment treatments. Finally, a moderate to strong positive relation exists between pretreatment acceptability and perceived treatment effectiveness.

Treatment acceptability can be assessed by one of several rating scales. These scales are presented in the appendix to this chapter. We recommend that consultant-practitioners use a treatment acceptability measure whenever possible. An assessment of treatment acceptability is also essential in research on consultation (see Chapter 9).

The final plan-design objective to be achieved during the problem analysis interview is to establish the performance assessment procedures to be used in plan implementation. When the plan design is based on conditions analysis, the specification of assessment measures requires only that the procedures established during baseline assessment be reaffirmed. However, when the plan design is based on skills analysis, procedures should be devised to assess these skills during problem analysis.

When new assessment procedures have to be devised during problem analysis, the interview objectives discussed in Chapter 3 (under the heading of the problem analysis interview). Thus, for example, in establishing procedures for skills assessment during problem analysis, the consultant should attempt to meet the objectives described in Chapter 3 by establishing (1) the type of measures to be used in skills assessment; (2) what skills are to be assessed; (3) the amount of data to be collected on each skill; (4) the recording schedule to be used for each skill; and (5) the individual(s) who is to be responsible for the data collection.

As indicated in Chapter 3, the consultant should assume the major responsibility for establishing the performance assessment procedures to be used in consultation. Because of his or her special skills in the area of measurement and evaluation, the consultant is in an excellent position to offer suggestions that will enable the consultee to obtain accurate data with a minimum amount of time and effort.

Procedural Objectives

The first procedural objective in problem analysis is setting the date for the problem evaluation interview. The date selected should be determined largely by an estimate of the length of time that will be required to achieve

TABLE 4-4. Summary of Research on Treatment Acceptability

Authors	Year	Subjects	Type of study	Independent variable(s)	Dependent measure(s)	Major findings
Kazdin, A. E.	1980a	Undergraduate college students	Analogue	Four alternative behavior interventions	Treatment Evaluation Inventory (TEI); semantic differential	Interventions differed markedly in acceptability ratings, with positive treatments being rated more favorably than reductive.
Kazdin, A. E.	1980b	Undergraduate college students	Analogue	Four alternative behavioral interventions	Treatment Evaluation Inventory (TEI); semantic differential	In Exp. 1: Reinforcement of incompatible behavior and nonexclusionary forms of time-out were rated as more acceptable than isolation. In Exp. 2: Isolation was more acceptable when included in a contingency context, and when used to back up another form of time-out, than when used by itself.
Kazdin, A. E.	1981	Undergraduate college students	Analogue	Four alternative behavioral interventions	Treatment Evaluation Inventory (TEI); semantic differential	In Exp. 1: Effectiveness of treatments in altering behavior did not influence acceptability ratings, but did influence strength of treatment. In Exp. 2: Presence of adverse side effects markedly influenced acceptability ratings.
Kazdin, A. E. French, N. H. Sherick, R. B.	1981	Child psychiatric inpatients, parents, and staff members	Analogue	Four alternative behavioral interventions	Treatment Evaluation Inventory (TEI); semantic differential	Treatments varied in their overall acceptability, with positive treatments being rated as most acceptable. Children rated treatments as less acceptable than their parents.
Witt, J. C. Martens, B. K.	1983	Preservice and student teachers	Analogue	Six alternative behavioral interventions	Intervention Rating Profile (IRP)	Judgments of the acceptability of classroom interventions are comprised of one major and four secondary components. Results indi-

Author	Year	Subjects	Design	Variables	Instrument	Results
Witt, J. C. Elliott, S. N. Martens, B. K.	1984	Preservice and student teachers	Analogue	Intervention type (positive vs. reductive) teacher time involvement, and behavior problem severity	Intervention Rating Profile (IRP)	cated that positive interventions requiring low amounts of teacher time and applied to a mild behavior problem were viewed as most acceptable. Those interventions that were positive and required less teacher time were viewed as most acceptable. The severity of the behavior problem did not significantly influence ratings of acceptability.
McKee, W. T.	1984	Regular education teachers	Analogue	Teacher's knowledge of behavior principles, type of problem, and type of intervention	Treatment Evaluation Inventory (TEI); semantic differential	High-knowledge-group teachers rated treatments more acceptable than low-knowledge-group teachers. Treatments were rated differentially, with reinforcement significantly more acceptable than time-out and positive practice. Ratings were not different for the different problem cases.
Witt, J. C. Martens, B. K. Elliott, S. N.	1984	School teachers (K–12)	Analogue	Intervention type, teacher time involvement, and behavior problem severity	Intervention Rating Profile (IRP)	Interventions that required more time to implement were viewed as least acceptable to teachers.
Elliott, S. N. Witt, J. C. Galvin, G. Peterson, R.	1984	Regular and special-education teachers	Analogue	Intervention complexity and behavior problem severity	Intervention Rating Profile (IRP)	Acceptability ratings varied with severity of problem behavior. Interventions that required less time were viewed as most acceptable. Positive treatments were viewed as more acceptable than reductive techniques.

(continued)

TABLE 4-4. (*Continued*)

Authors	Year	Subjects	Type of study	Independent variable(s)	Dependent measure(s)	Major findings
Witt, J. C. Moe, G. Gutkin, T. B. Andrews, L.	1984	Regular and special-education teachers	Analogue	(Jargon of Tx) description, behavior problem severity, teacher experience	Intervention Rating Profile (IRP)	Pragmatic description was viewed as more acceptable than behavioral or humanistic descriptions. In erventions were rated as more acceptable when the problem was severe. Highly experienced teachers rated interventions as less acceptable.
Martens, B. K. Witt, J. C. Elliott, S. N. Darveaux, D.	1985	Regular and special-education teachers	Analogue	Behavior problem severity, interventionist, case intervention modality	Intervention Rating Profile-15 (IRP-15); semantic differential	Intervention requiring moderate amounts of time were viewed as most acceptable. Interventions were rated as more acceptable when the problem behavior was severe.
Witt, J. C. Robbins, J. R.	1985	Regular education, preschool, and Head Start teachers	Analogue	Type of intervention, behavior problem severity, teacher experience, and interventionist	Intervention Rating Profile (IRP)	Positive interventions were rated as more acceptable than reductive strategies. Teachers with less experience rated interventions as more acceptable than experienced teachers.
Cavell, T. A. Frentz, C. E. Kelley, M. L.	1986b	Middle- and high-school teachers	Analogue	Paradoxical treatments	Treatment Evaluation Inventory (TEI)	Teachers rated paradoxical procedures generally unacceptable and significantly lower than an unsuccessful contingency contract. Ratings of the four paradoxical conditions varied according to rationale.
Cavell, T. A. Frentz, C. E. Kelley, M. L.	1986a	Middle- and high-school teachers	Analogue	Withdrawal of treatments	Treatment Evaluation Inventory (TEI)	Acceptability of withdrawal conditions varied with respect to rationale.

Author	Year	Subjects	Design	Variables	Instrument	Findings
Epstein, M. H. Matson, J. L. Repp, A. Helsel, W. J.	1986	Regular and special educators	Analogue	Five alternative treatment approaches	Treatment Evaluation Inventory (TEI)	In two experiments, the results indicated that teachers could distinguish between treatments on the basis of their acceptability. No differences were found between regular and special-education teachers or between children labeled as mentally retarded or learning-disabled.
Frentz, C. Kelley, M. L.	1986	Mothers of children between the ages of 2 and 12	Analogue	Five alternative (reductive) interventions	Treatment Evaluation Inventory (TEI)	Treatments were rated as more acceptable when applied to a more severe behavior problem.
Von Brock, M. B. Elliott, S. N.	1987	Regular education teachers	Analogue	Behavior problem severity, intervention type, and outcome information	Behavior Intervention Rating Scale (BIRS); semantic differential	The BIRS reliably measures acceptability and effectiveness, and treatment outcome information was shown to influence ratings of treatments.
Elliott, S. N. Turco, T. L. Gresham, F. M.	1987	Regular education teacher	Analogue	Rater, behavior problem severity, intervention type, and sex of rater	Children's Intervention Rating Profile (CIRP); Intervention Rating Profile (IRP)	Children rated all three types of group contingencies acceptable, whereas teachers and psychologists rated dependent group contingencies unacceptable and independent and interdependent forms acceptable.
Clark, L. Elliott, S. N.	1986	Regular and special-education teachers	Analogue	Behavior problem type, intervention type, outcome information, and teacher's intervention knowledge	Behavior Intervention Rating Scale (BIRS); Teacher's intervention-use assessment	Teachers preferred modeling or coaching to overcorrection for social skills problems, and treatment outcome information significantly influenced ratings of both acceptability and effectiveness.

(continued)

TABLE 4-4. (*Continued*)

Authors	Year	Subjects	Type of study	Independent variable(s)	Dependent measure(s)	Major findings
Shapiro, E. S. Goldberg, R.	1986	Sixth-graders	Naturalistic	Type of group contingency	Children's Intervention Rating Profile (CIRP); spelling performance	Group contingencies did not differentially effect spelling performance; however, sixth-graders rated the independent group contingency more acceptable than the interdependent or dependent group contingency.

Source: S. N. Elliott (1988). Acceptability of behavioral treatments in educational settings. In J. C. Witt, S. N. Elliott, and F. M. Gresham (Eds.), *Handbook of behavior therapy in education* (pp. 121–150). New York: Plenum Press.

the goals established during problem identification. For example, if the goal of consultation is to alter a child's aggressive behavior believed to be under the control of environmental conditions, the amount of time required for goal attainment would probably be relatively small. Thus, the consultant might schedule the problem evaluation interview approximately a week after problem analysis. On the other hand, if the goal of consultation is to teach a group of first-grade children to identify 30 selected words from the Dolch list of sight vocabulary words, it would probably take a longer period to attain the goal. Thus, the consultant might set the problem evaluation interview 2 or 3 weeks after problem analysis.

Even though some goals may take a long time to achieve, it is generally not advisable to allow more than a few weeks to intervene between problem analysis and problem evaluation. Thus, in those cases involving long-term goals, it is best to break a problem down into component goals that can be achieved relatively quickly. For instance, cases of developmental consultation often require reiterative applications of the problem-solving process. The length of time needed to achieve any one of the goals of developmental consultation may be relatively brief, even though the attainment of the long-term objectives of consultation may take several months.

The principal reason for restricting the time interval between analysis and evaluation is that such a restriction ensures relatively frequent contact between the consultant and the consultee. The consultant's continuing interest in the case, manifested in frequent contacts with the consultee, may have a beneficial motivational influence on the consultee with respect to plan implementation. More important, when a plan is not effective, frequent contact minimizes the amount of time spent pursuing strategies that are not leading toward goal attainment.

The second procedural objective to be achieved during problem analysis is to make provisions to monitor the implementation process. The consultant should make arrangements to telephone the consultee or to make a short visit to the consultee at some point during the first few days of implementation. The first day is a good time to follow up. Monitoring of this kind enables the consultant to make sure that the plan established during problem analysis is being implemented as intended. In addition, such monitoring makes it possible for the consultant to assist the consultee to make minor revisions in the plan associated with circumstances that were unforeseen during problem analysis.

The final procedural objective associated with problem analysis involves consultee training. In some consultation cases, the consultant may train the consultee in the procedures to be used during implementation. For example, suppose that a plan developed during problem analysis calls for setting up a token economy in a classroom. To initiate plan implementation, the consultant may teach the consultee how to establish a token economy and how to deliver tokens and backup reinforcers. In cases involving training, the consultant must make arrangements with the consultee concerning when training is to take place and how it is to occur. More detailed information on training consultees (teachers and parents) is presented in Chapter 5.

Outlines for the Problem Analysis Interview

Outlines for problem analysis interviews involving conditions and skills analysis are given below. As pointed out in Chapter 3, the interview outlines are intended only as general guides for interviewing behavior and do not cover all possible cases.

An Interview Involving Conditions Analysis

The following interview outline details the steps involved in conducting a problem analysis interview involving conditions analysis. The outline below has been constructed along the same lines as the outlines presented in Chapter 3. Roman-numeral headings indicate the objectives to be achieved in the interview. Capital-letter headings designate the kinds of verbalizations required to achieve objectives, and arabic-number headings provide examples of verbalizations that a consultant might emit to achieve the interview objectives.

I. Validate the problem.
  A. Emit behavior specification elicitors to initiate an examination of the baseline data.
    1. "Let's look at the data on Ted's hitting."
    2. "Could you show me the baseline data you collected on Ted's behavior?"
  B. If the baseline data are inadequate for the purposes of problem validation, emit observation specification elicitors and/or emitters and observation positive-validation elicitors to establish adequate performance-assessment procedures.
    1. "As Ted was sick most of last week, we ought to have a few more days of baseline data before we proceed further."
    2. "I would suggest that you collect data on Ted's hitting for another 3 days."
    3. "Would it be possible for you to do that?"
  C. If the data are sufficient for problem validation, emit behavior specification elicitors and/or emitters describing baseline performance while graphing the data for the consultee.
    1. "How many times did Ted hit on Monday?"
    2. "On Tuesday, Ted hit nine times according to the data you have here."

  D. Emit behavior specification elicitors, behavior summarization emitters, and positive validation elicitors to establish agreement regarding the goals of consultation.
    1. "How much hitting per day by Ted would be acceptable to you?"
    2. "Then, if Ted hit no more, you would be satisfied?"
    3. "Right?"
    4. "You said last week that if Ted hit no more you would be satisfied."
    5. "Is that correct?"
  E. When there is a question about whether the discrepancy between the goals and the current behavior is large enough to warrant saying that a problem exists, emit behavior summarization emitters and positive validation elicitors to attain agreement regarding the existence of the problem.
    1. "We can see that Ted hits about three times a day on the average."
    2. "You indicated that you would like to eliminate hitting completely."
    3. "Do we agree, then, that there is a problem here?"
II. Conduct conditions analysis.
  A. Emit behavior-setting-specification elicitors to establish the antecedent conditions of the baseline performance.
    1. "What generally occurred right before Ted's hitting last week?"
    2. "What were the other children usually doing just before Ted started to hit?"
  B. Emit behavior-setting-specification elicitors to establish the consequent conditions of the baseline behavior.
    1. "How did you respond to Ted's hitting?"
    2. "How did the other children react?"
  C. Emit behavior-setting-specification elicitors to establish the sequential conditions of the baseline behavior.
    1. "When during the day did the hitting most often occur?"
    2. "At what times during the morning was the hitting most pronounced?"
  D. Emit behavior-setting-summarization emitters and positive validation elicitors to focus attention on those conditions that may be involved in plan design and to establish agreement regarding the presence of those conditions.
    1. "You said that sometimes you ignored Ted when he hit."
    2. "However, sometimes you reprimanded him."
    3. "Is that right?"

III. Design a plan to achieve problem solution.
   A. Emit plan specification elicitors and emitters to establish plan strategies and tactics.
      1. "Let's make a plan now to solve this problem."
      2. "One way to avoid reinforcing Ted for hitting would be to ignore him and to rescue his victim."
      3. "If he hits someone, you could go to the child who has been hit and take that child out of Ted's reach."
      4. "How might you reward Ted for appropriate interactions with his peers?"
   B. Emit plan summarization emitters and positive validation elicitors to establish agreement regarding the plan.
      1. "You said that you'll try to praise Ted for appropriate social interactions."
      2. "However, if he hits someone, you'll simply ignore him and rescue his victim."
      3. "Have I got it right?"
   C. Emit observation specification elicitors or emitters, observation summarization emitters and elicitors, and positive validation elicitors to reaffirm assessment procedures.
      1. "Let's talk about data for a minute."
      2. "You're going to continue tallying the number of times that Ted hits on the form that I gave you last week."
      3. "And if you can, you'll note what happens before and after Ted hits."
      4. "OK?"
IV. Make arrangements for subsequent contacts with the consultee.
   A. Emit other specification elicitors to arrange for the problem evaluation interview.
      1. "When could we meet next week to see how things have progressed?"
      2. "Where would it be convenient for us to get together?"
   B. Emit other specification elicitors or emitters to arrange for monitoring implementation.
      1. "I'll stop in on Tuesday to see how the plan is working."
      2. "When would be the best time for me to see the plan in operation?"
   C. In those cases involving training of the consultee, emit other specification elicitors to set up a time for training.
      1. "What would be the best time for me to come in to help you set up your token economy?"
      2. "When would it be most convenient for me to demonstrate the delivery of tokens?"

An Interview Involving Skills Analysis

The following example illustrates the problem analysis interview for a case involving skills analysis. This example illustrates a skills interview of an academic problem. However, the reader should keep in mind that the skills approach can also be used in cases involving social or emotional functioning.

 I. Validate the problem.
  A. Emit behavior specification elicitors to initiate a examination of the baseline data.
   1. "Show me how Bob did on his examination worksheets."
   2. "Let's look at what he did each day on his worksheets."
  B. If the baseline data are inadequate for the purposes of problem validation, emit observation specification elicitors and/or emitters and observation positive-validation elicitors to establish adequate performance-assessment procedures
   1. "As our focus is only on Bob's difficulties with addition, we need a few samples of his work in that area rather than in the area of subtraction."
   2. "Could you keep those worksheets that Bob turns in that involve addition for the next 3 days?"
   3. "Would you be able to do that?"
  C. If the data are sufficient for problem validation, emit behavior specification elicitors and/or emitters describing baseline performance while graphing the data for the consultee.
   1. "Let's see what percentage of problems Bob worked correctly on Monday."
   2. "And on Tuesday, he got none right."
  D. Emit behavior specification elicitors, behavior summarization emitters, and positive validation elicitors to establish agreement regarding the goals of consultation.
   1. "You indicated last week that you thought Bob should be able to work the addition problems that you give him correctly 100% of the time."
   2. "Right?"
   3. "How accurate do you think Bob's addition performance should be?"
   4. "Bob should be able to work these problems correctly 100% of the time."
   5. "Is that correct?"
  E. If there is a question about whether the discrepancy between goals and current behavior is large enough to warrant saying that a problem exists, emit behavior summarization emitters

and positive validation elicitors to achieve agreement concerning the existence of the problem.
1. "Bob worked 75% of his addition problems correctly."
2. "You said that he should work 100% correctly."
3. "Do we agree, then, that a problem exists here?"

II. Report the results of the skills analysis.
   A. Emit behavior specification emitters describing the results of the skills assessment.
      1. "When I worked with Bob, he could recognize numerals other than 1."
      2. "However, he was not able to count forward from numbers other than 1."
      3. "He also was unable to specify the number of things a numeral represented."
      4. "And he could not add even simple combinations involving numerals and groups of things."
   B. Emit behavior summarization emitters and behavior inference emitters to establish what skills the client needs to acquire.
      1. "In summary, then, Bob can't count up from numbers other than one."
      2. "He can't indicate the number of things that a numeral represents."
      3. "And he can't add numbers and things."
      4. "These are probably the things that he needs to learn in order to be able to add simple combinations of the type that you're concerned about."

III. Establish the procedures currently in use to promote the attainment of consultation goals.
   A. Emit behavior-setting-specification elicitors to establish the sequential conditions related to the goal behavior during the baseline period.
      1. "What steps did you go through in teaching addition this week?"
      2. "When during the day did you have arithmetic?"
   B. Emit behavior-setting-specification elicitors to establish the antecedent conditions of the goal behavior.
      1. "What do you do first, before Bob works an addition problem?"
      2. "What do you say when you introduce addition to Bob?"
   C. Emit behavior-setting-specification elicitors to establish the consequent conditions of the goal behavior.
      1. "What do you do when Bob works a problem incorrectly?"
      2. "What do you do when Bob gets one right?
   D. Emit behavior and behavior-setting-summarization emitters

and positive validation elicitors to establish agreement regarding the procedures used during baseline to promote goal attainment.

1. "You said that, each morning, you hand out worksheets to the children containing addition problems."
2. "You ask the children to work all of the problems on the sheets and to ask for help if they are having difficulty."
3. "When you ask Bob to work the problems, he always tries to comply."
4. "However, he gets almost every problem wrong."
5. "He never asks for help."
6. "But you often go over to him and demonstrate how to do problems."
7. "You generally ignore his wrong answers and praise him for the few right answers that he gives."
8. "Have I got it straight?"

E. Emit plan specification elicitor(s), plan positive-validation elicitors, and, if desired, plan evaluation emitters(s) and plan inference emitter(s) to ensure that the procedures used during baseline will be continued during the plan implementation.

1. "Next week, could you continue teaching Bobby just as you did last week?
2. "OK?"
3. "That will help us to see if the skills we have talked about are the ones he needs to learn to improve his addition."
4. "If the skills we have identified are critical, he should begin to improve, under the teaching procedure you have been using, as he acquires them."

IV. Design a plan to achieve problem solution.

A. Emit plan specification elicitors and emitters to establish plan tactics.

1. "We need to make a plan."
2. "How could you incorporate the teaching of those skills that Bob lacks into arithmetic instruction?"
3. "What steps would you go through to teach these skills?"
4. "When during the day would you give the instruction?"
5. "How much time would you spend on this?"

B. Emit plan summarization emitters and positive validation elicitors to establish agreement regarding plan tactics.

1. "To summarize then, you're going to work with Bobby for 5 to 10 minutes a day during free-choice period."
2. "You'll demonstrate how to count forward from numbers other than 1."
3. "You'll ask him to do it."

       4. "Then you'll praise him if he does it correctly."
       5. "And if he makes an error, you'll show him again."
       6. "You'll follow this same general pattern of demonstration, performance, and praise with the other two skills."
       7. "Have I got it?"
  C. Emit observation specification elicitors and/or summarization emitters and positive-validation elicitors to reaffirm the baseline assessment procedures.
       1. "We need to discuss recording for a moment."
       2. "Could you continue to record the percentage of addition problems that Bob works correctly just as you did last week?"
       3. "Would that be OK?"
  D. Emit observation specification elicitors and emitters and positive validation elicitors to establish skill assessment procedures.
       1. "We need also to get a record of Bobby's skill learning."
       2. "I would suggest that, for each skill, mark the number of correct responses that Bob makes."
       3. "You can use this form."
       4. "At the end of the week, we'll convert the scores for each day to percentages."
       5. "Are these recording plans OK with you?"
  V. Make arrangements for subsequent contacts with the consultee.
  A. Emit other specification elicitors to arrange for the problem evaluation interview.
       1. "When can we get together next week to check progress on this?"
       2. "Where shall we meet?"
  B. Emit other specification elicitors or emitters to arrange for monitoring implementation.
       1. "I'll drop in early next week to see how things are going."
       2. "When would be the most convenient time for you to let me see the plan in operation?"
  C. In those instances involving training of the consultee, emit other specification elicitors to set up a time of training.
       1. "When could I come in to go over the skill-training procedures with you?"
       2. "What day next week would be best for you?"

Assessing Interviewing Skills

At this point, the reader may want to try some problem-analysis interviews. It is recommended that the reader try at least one interview requiring conditions analysis with a problem involving social behavior; the reader might also try the approach with academic behavior. For example, the consultant could select a problem involving a large group of children having difficulty mastering an academic task. When beginning skills analysis, the consultant should try a problem involving social behavior. The interviews should be tape-recorded for evaluation by means of the procedures described, as follows:

Checklist Evaluation for Problem Analysis

Figure 4-5 lists the required verbalizations for an effective problem-analysis interview. This checklist can be used in interviews involving conditions or skills analysis. The checklist can be used to evaluate interviews by means of the scoring procedure discussed in Chapter 2.

Message Classification Analysis of Interviewing Skills

Indices of consultant effectiveness have been developed for analyzing messages in problem analysis interviews. In the event that the reader wishes to do an in-depth study of her or his use of the content, process, and control categories, the interviews should be coded by means of the consultation analysis record (CAR) illustrated in Figure 2-1 in Chapter 2.

In the problem-analysis interview, message content should be confined mainly to the *behavior*, *behavior setting*, and *plan categories*. In skills analysis cases, the *observation category* may also be used to a significant extent. A discussion of the behavior is required in problem validation and in the examination of client skills in skills analysis cases. Verbalizations in the behavior setting category are needed to conduct a conditions analysis. They also occur in skills analysis interviews in establishing the procedures to be used during baseline to promote goal attainment. Utterances in the *plan category* are needed in plan design. The *observation category* is used in specifying the skills assessment procedures and in reaffirming the baseline assessment techniques.

One significant error that a consultant can make with respect to content is to omit or minimize discussion of a relevant content category. Consider the following interview segment:

Consultant: Does Bob tend to get out of his seat in all centers, or is it just during math?

Consultee: More during math center.

Consultant: It looks as if it really makes a difference which center he's in because I noticed that, in the science center and the reading center, he tends to be good. Did you find the same thing?

Consultee: Yes.

CONSULTANT _____ CASE NUMBER _____

CONSULTEE _____ PAGE _____

Problem-Analysis Checklist

Required Verbal Units	Frequency of Unit Use

1. Behavior specification elicitors (to elicit baseline data examination) _____

2. Observation specification emitters and/or elicitors (to establish adequate assessment procedures if baseline data are inadequate) _____

3. Observation positive-validation elicitors (to establish adequate assessment procedures if baseline data are inadequate) _____

4. Behavior specification elicitors and/or emitters (to describe baseline data as you graph it) _____

5. Behavior specification elicitors (to establish agreement regarding goals) _____

6. Behavior summarization emitters (to establish agreement regarding goals) _____

7. Behavior positive-validation elicitors (to establish agreement regarding goals) _____

8. Behavior summarization emitters (to attain agreement regarding existence of a problem) _____

9. Behavior positive-validation elicitors (to attain agreement regarding existence of a problem) _____

10. Behavior-setting specification elicitors (to establish antecedent conditions) _____

11. Behavior-setting specification elicitors (to establish consequent conditions) _____

12. Behavior-setting specification elicitors (to establish sequential conditions) _____

13. Behavior-setting summarization emitters (to focus on conditions important to plan design or on skill training procedures used during baseline) _____

FIGURE 4-5. Consultation analysis checklist for the problem analysis interview.

Required Verbal Units	Frequency of Unit Use
14. Behavior-setting positive-validation elicitors (to establish agreement about conditions or baseline teaching procedures)	_____
15. Plan specification elicitors and emitters (to establish plan strategies and tactics, which in skills interviews, will include provision for continuing implementation of baseline teaching procedures)	_____
16. Plan summarization emitters (to summarize plan strategies and tactics)	_____
17. Plan positive-validation elicitors (to establish agreement concerning plan)	_____
18. Observation specification elicitors or emitters (to reaffirm assessment procedures)	_____
19. Observation summarization emitters and elicitors (to reaffirm assessment procedures)	_____
20. Observation positive-validation elicitors (to reaffirm assessment procedures)	_____
21. Other specification elicitors (to arrange for next interview)	_____
22. Other specification emitters and/or elicitors (to arrange monitoring)	_____
23. Other specification elicitors (to arrange for training)	_____
In the case of a skills interview include the following:	
24. Behavior specification emitters (to describe skill assessment results)	_____
25. Behavior summarization emitters (to establish skills needed by client)	_____
26. Behavior inference emitters (to establish skills needed by client)	_____

FIGURE 4-5. (Cont.)

Consultant: It looks as if the problem occurs more at the math center than at any other time. Can you think of some way that we might be able to control his behavior at the math center?

This consultant has jumped into plan design with very little information about the conditions under which the behavior of concern is occurring. The consultant has identified a sequential condition related to the behavior. However, he has not established the antecedent events that may serve as cues for the behavior or the consequent events that may be reinforcing the behavior.

The second major error that can occur with respect to content is talking too much in content categories that are not relevant in the analysis or planning phases of problem analysis. For example, excessive discussion of the individual characteristics or the background environment of the client may impair the effectiveness of a problem analysis interview. From the behavioral perspective, neither of these categories is likely to contribute to an analysis of the factors that may be altered to achieve the desired consultation goals.

To avoid the two kinds of content errors described above, the consultant should strive for a fairly even distribution of utterances in the behavior, behavior-setting, and plan categories. If the interview involves skills analysis, the verbalizations should be distributed evenly across the behavior, behavior-setting, plan, and observation categories.

As in the analysis of problem identification, the consultant's examination of interview content should include a consideration of the interview focus as well as the content type. The consultant should try to stay on one topic of discussion long enough to explore it in detail. As indicated in the Chapter 3, the consultant can get a rough indication of focus by visually scanning the pattern of the content changes that have been recorded on the CAR forms. If most of the verbalizations within each set of five utterances recorded are in the same content category, the focus is probably adequate.

The process categories suggested for use in problem analysis are precisely the same as those suggested for application in problem identification. As in problem identification, utterances in problem analysis should fall mainly in the specification, summarization, and validation categories. Specifications are used to call for information from the consultee regarding the topics under discussion. The verbalizations in problem analysis should be approximately evenly distributed across the specification, summarization, and validation categories. However, there will probably be a somewhat larger number of utterances in the specification category than in the other two classifications.

Throughout consultation, it is the consultant's responsibility to lead the consultee through the problem-solving process. Thus, in problem analysis as in problem identification, the consultant should emit more elicitors than emitters. As indicated in Chapter 3, the consultant can check the adequacy of elicitors simply by computing the percentage of utterances in the elicitor category.

APPENDIX

The Treatment Evaluation Inventory*

Please complete the items listed below. The items should be completed by placing a checkmark on the line under the question that best indicates how you feel about the treatment. Please read the items very carefully because a checkmark accidentally placed on one space rather than another may not represent the meaning you intended.

1. How acceptable do you find this treatment to be for the child's problem behavior?

| Not at all acceptable | | | Moderately acceptable | | | Very acceptable |

2. How willing would you be to carry out this procedure yourself if you had to change the child's problems?

| Not at all willing | | | Moderately willing | | | Very willing |

3. How suitable is this procedure for children who might have other behavioral problems than those described for this child?

| Not at all suitable | | | Moderately suitable | | | Very suitable |

4. If children had to be assigned to treatment without their consent, how bad would it be to give them *this* treatment?

| Very bad | | | Moderately | | | Not bad at all |

5. How cruel or unfair do you find this treatment?

| Very cruel | | | Moderately cruel | | | Not cruel at all |

*From A. E. Kazdin. (1980). Acceptability of alternative treatments for deviant child behavior. *Journal of Applied Behavior Analysis, 13,* 259–273. Copyright 1982 by *Journal of Applied Behavior Analysis.* Reprinted by permission.

6. Would it be acceptable to apply this procedure to institutionalized children, the mentally retarded, or other individuals who are not given an opportunity to choose treatment for themselves?

Not at all acceptable to apply this procedure	Moderately acceptable	Very acceptable to apply this procedure

7. How consistent is this treatment with common sense or everyday notions about what treatment should be?

Very different or inconsistent	Moderately consistent	Very consistent with everyday notions

8. To what extent does this procedure treat children humanely?

Does not treat humanely at all	Treats them moderately humanely	Treats them very humanely

9. To what extent do you think there might be risks in undergoing this kind of treatment?

Losts of risks are likely	Some risks are likely	No risks are likely

10. How much do you like the procedures used in this treatment?

Do not like them at all	Moderately like them	Like them very much

11. How effective is this treatment likely to be?

Not at all effective	Moderately effective	Very effective

12. How likely is it that this treatment makes permanent improvements in the child?

Unlikely	Moderately	Very likely

13. To what extent are *un*desirable side effects likely to result from this treatment?

| Many undesirable side effects likely | | Some undesirable side effects likely | | | No undesirable side effects would occur |

14. How much discomfort is the child likely to experience during the course of treatment?

| Very much discomfort | | Moderate discomfort | | | No discomfort at all |

15. Overall, what is your general reaction to this form of treatment?

| Very negative | | Ambivalent | | | Very positive |

*Intervention Rating Profile-20 (IRP-20)**

The purpose of this questionnaire is to obtain information that will aid in the selection of classroom interventions. These interventions will be used by teachers of children with behavior problems. Please circle the number that best describes your agreement or disagreement with each statement.

	Strongly disagree	Disagree	Slightly disagree	Slightly agree	Agree	Strongly agree
1. Teachers are likely to use this intervention because it requires few technical skills.	1	2	3	4	5	6
2. Teachers are likely to use this intervention because it requires little training to implement effectively.	1	2	3	4	5	6
3. Most teachers would find this intervention appropriate for behavior problem described.	1	2	3	4	5	6
4. Most teachers would find this intervention appropriate for behavior	1	2	3	4	5	6

*From J. C. Witt and B. K. Martens. (1983). Assessing the acceptability of behavioral interventions used in classrooms. *Psychology in the Schools, 20,* 510–517. Copyright 1983 by *Psychology in the Schools.* Reprinted by permission.

	Strongly disagree	Disagree	Slightly disagree	Slightly agree	Agree	Strongly agree
problems in addition to the one described.						
5. The child's behavior problem is severe enough to warrant the use of this intervention.	1	2	3	4	5	6
6. This intervention would be appropriate for use *before* making a referral.	1	2	3	4	5	6
7. This intervention would not be difficult to implement in a classroom with 30 other students.	1	2	3	4	5	6
8. This intervention is practical in the amount of time required for parent contact.	1	2	3	4	5	6
9. This intervention is practical in the amount of time required for contact with school staff.	1	2	3	4	5	6
10. This intervention is practical in the amount of time required for record keeping.	1	2	3	4	5	6
11. This intervention is practical in the amount of out-of-school time required for implementation.	1	2	3	4	5	6
12. This intervention would not be disruptive to other students.	1	2	3	4	5	6
13. It would not be difficult to use this intervention and still meet the needs of other children in a classroom.	1	2	3	4	5	6
14. This intervention should prove effective in changing the child's problem behavior.	1	2	3	4	5	6
15. This would be an acceptable intervention for the child's problem behavior.	1	2	3	4	5	6
16. This intervention would not result in negative side effects for the child.	1	2	3	4	5	6
17. This intervention would not result in risk to the child.	1	2	3	4	5	6
18. This intervention would not be considered a "last resort."	1	2	3	4	5	6

	Strongly disagree	Disagree	Slightly disagree	Slightly agree	Agree	Strongly agree
19. Overall, this intervention would be beneficial to the child.	1	2	3	4	5	6
20. I would be willing to use this intervention in the classroom setting.	1	2	3	4	5	6

Intervention Rating Profile-15 (IRP-15)*

The purpose of this questionnaire is to obtain information that will aid in the selection of classroom interventions. These interventions will be used by teachers of children with behavior problems. Please circle the number that best describes your agreement or disagreement with each statement.

	Strongly disagree	Disagree	Slightly disagree	Slightly agree	Agree	Strongly agree
1. This would be an acceptable intervention for the child's problem behavior.	1	2	3	4	5	6
2. Most teachers would find this intervention appropriate for behavior problems in addition to the one described.	1	2	3	4	5	6
3. This intervention should prove effective in changing the child's problem behavior.	1	2	3	4	5	6
4. I would suggest the use of this intervention to other teachers.	1	2	3	4	5	6
5. The child's behavior problem is severe enough to warrant the use of this intervention.	1	2	3	4	5	6
6. Most teachers would find this intervention suitable for the behavior problem described.	1	2	3	4	5	6
7. I would be willing to use this intervention in the classroom setting.	1	2	3	4	5	6
8. This intervention would *not* result in negative side effects for the child.	1	2	3	4	5	6

*From J. C. Witt and S. N. Elliott. (1985). Acceptability of classroom management strategies. In T. R. Kratochwill (Ed.), *Advances in School Psychology* (Vol. 4, pp. 251–288). Copyright 1985 by Lawrence Erlbaum Associates, Inc. Reprinted by permission.

	Strongly disagree	Disagree	Slightly disagree	Slightly agree	Agree	Strongly agree
9. This intervention would be appropriate for a variety of children.	1	2	3	4	5	6
10. This intervention is consistent with those I have used in classroom settings.	1	2	3	4	5	6
11. The intervention was a fair way to handle the child's problem behavior.	1	2	3	4	5	6
12. This intervention is reasonable for the behavior problem described.	1	2	3	4	5	6
13. I liked the procedures used in this intervention.	1	2	3	4	5	6
14. This intervention was a good way to handle this child's behavior problem.	1	2	3	4	5	6
15. Overall, this intervention would be beneficial to the child.	1	2	3	4	5	6

The Children's Intervention Rating Profile (CIRP)

                            I agree   I do not agree

1. The method used to deal with the behavior problem was fair. |------|------|------|------|------|

2. This child's teacher was too harsh on him/her. |------|------|------|------|------|

3. The method used to deal with the behavior may cause problems with this child's friends. |------|------|------|------|------|

4. There are better ways to handle this child's problem than the one described here. |------|------|------|------|------|

5. The method used by this teacher would be a good one to use with other children. |------|------|------|------|------|

6. I like the method used for this child's be- |------|------|------|------|------|
   havior problem.

7. I think that the method used for this |------|------|------|------|------|
   problem would help this child do better
   in school.   _____

$$5$$

Plan Implementation

The third stage in the consultative problem-solving process is plan imple
mentation. During this stage, the plan designed in problem analysis is put
into operation. Obviously, the effectiveness of consultation depends in a
very direct way on what is done during plan implementation. The best of
plans may not produce the desired results if they are not implemented
properly. The function of consultation during implementation is to maximize the likelihood that the plan put into effect will produce the desired
outcomes. In this chapter, we describe the implementation process and the
role of consultation in maximizing its effectiveness.

THE IMPLEMENTATION PROCESS

The process of implementing a plan designed in consultation may be
divided into two stages. The first involves making the necessary preparations to carry out the plan to be implemented. The second includes those
activities associated with putting the plan into operation.

Preparing for Implementation

The initial stage in the implementation process is making the necessary preparations for carrying out the plan designed during problem analysis. As noted in Chapter 4, a number of issues may require attention before
implementation can occur. It is usually necessary to assign people to various roles in the implementation process. If materials are required, someone must gather them together so that they will be available when needed.
Finally, in some cases, it may be necessary to develop specific implementation skills in those individuals responsible for carrying out the plan.

Assigning Implementation Roles

The first step to be taken in preparing for implementation is to facilitate the assignment of people to the various roles in carrying out the implementation plan. It may happen that one or a small group of individuals will each be responsible for enacting a number of roles. Under these circumstances, role assignments are often implicitly understood by the individuals involved in implementation. For example, in behavioral counseling or therapy in which the client and the consultee are the same person, it is generally implicit that the consultee-client will occupy most of the roles associated with implementation. On the other hand, there are circumstances in which several people may be involved in implementation, and it may be necessary to make role assignments explicit.

The various roles associated with plan implementation are summarized in Table 5-1. One role required for plan implementation is implementation director. As is evident from the table, the implementation director is responsible for overseeing the operations of the plan. He or she must make role assignments, specify the general types of materials to be used in the plan, schedule plan implementation activities, and specify the nature of the activities involved in carrying out the plan.

As indicated in Chapter 1, the consultee is generally responsible for directing implementation operations. The main reason is that the consultee typically has some measure of direct responsibility for the social, emotional, and/or intellectual development of the client. For example, if the consultee is a parent and the client a child, the consultee bears direct responsibility for the child.

Consultees often have little or no training in the application of psychological principles for the purpose of changing behavior. For example, parents often have little formal training in behavioral management. Teachers have surprisingly little preservice applied or practicum training in classroom management. An important question related to the viability of consultation as a problem-solving tool is whether people without extensive specialized training can direct implementation operations effectively. A

TABLE 5-1. Implementation Roles

Role labels	Role descriptions
Implementation director	Guides implementation: makes role assignments, specifies materials, schedules activities, and specifies nature of activities.
Plan executor	Implements consultation plans.
Observer	Observes client behavior targeted for change in consultation.
Skill developer	Develops plan executor skills necessary for implementation.

number of research studies have shown that they can (see reviews by Allen & Forman, 1984; Anderson & Kratochwill, 1988). For example, in an early study in this area, Hall, Cristler, Cranston, and Tucker (1970) reported on projects directed by teachers and parents involving successful attempts to effect changes in the behavior of children and adolescents. These studies involved the modification of behaviors related to intellectual development and relatively mild behavior problems such as being late to class. Subsequently, Hall, Fox, Willard, Goldsmith, Emerson, Owen, Davis, and Porcia (1971) showed that teachers could direct successful programs that modified disruptive classroom behavior. In addition, Hall, Axelrod, Tyler, Grief, Jones, and Robertson (1972) showed that parents can direct interventions that solve behavior problems occurring in the home. Since these early studies, there have been numerous others in the area of teaching teachers classroom management.

A second role in implementation is that of *plan executor*. Plan executors are responsible for actually carrying out the implementation plan. In some instances, there is only one plan executor. However, in other cases, many individuals are involved in the execution of a plan.

The consultee also typically assumes the role of plan executor. For example, parents and teachers, who often serve as consultees, generally assume the direct responsibility for carrying out the implementation plans intended to change the behavior of children in their charge. Although parents and teachers are quite capable of fulfilling this responsibility, research has also shown that other socializing agents may be effective as plan executors. For example, Copeland, Brown, and Hall (1974) demonstrated the effectiveness of a school principal in implementing behavioral change programs. In one of their studies, an elementary-school principal implemented a plan involving the use of praise to increase the school attendance of three young children. In a second study, the principal used praise to increase the academic performance of a small group of fifth-grade boys, and in a third investigation, he applied praise to accelerate the academic performance of two classrooms of third-grade children.

Although parents or teachers serving as consultees can be highly effective as plan executors, there are times when it may be beneficial to have individuals other than the consultee fulfill the executor role. For example, a teacher's busy schedule may not permit a commitment of time adequate to ensure effective implementation. In fact, Ponti et al. (1988) found that teacher time was one of the major barriers to establishing their prereferral consultation program.

One alternative to consultee plan implementation that is sometimes used in educational settings is to make use of paraprofessionals in plan execution (Guerney, 1969). Paraprofessionals can be effective plan executors providing adequate provisions are made for *supervising* their efforts.

Another possibility with respect to plan execution in educational settings is to use peers. Research indicates that the use of peers may produce beneficial results in the development of social skills in plan implementation (Sancilio, 1987; Strain, 1981). Sancilio (1987) noted that peer interaction can be used as a method of therapeutic intervention with children and can be either programmed or unprogrammed. Programmed interventions involve the use of peers as social reinforcers and as social initiators. Unprogrammed interventions involve group integration, peer pairing, and social skills training-plus-interaction. Based on this review of the literature, Sancilio concluded that active modification of the social environment to modify the behavior of a child's peers can be effective in changing the child-client's behavior. On the other hand, increasing the child's contacts with peers through unprogrammed interactions is an ineffective intervention unless the consultant combines it with improving the client's social skills.

Peer tutoring appears to be a programmed-interaction technique that can be used to change child-client behavior. For instance, Harris and Sherman (1973) found that fourth- and fifth-grade children were able to help one another learn to solve arithmetic problems. Johnson and Bailey (1974) showed that cross-age peer tutoring could also be effective. In their study, five fifth-grade students tutored five kindergarten children in basic counting and number recognition skills. The peer tutors produced dramatic increases in the children's learning. Moreover, the performance of the children who had received tutoring was substantially better than that of a control group who received regular classroom instruction but no tutoring. Gladstone and Sherman (1975) demonstrated that adolescent behavior managers could be taught to tutor severely mentally retarded children in tasks requiring the following of simple directions. In their investigation, high-school students learned basic behavior-modification skills such as cuing and reinforcing. Not only were the students able to apply their newly acquired skills to learning tasks on which they had been specifically trained, but they were also able to generalize their behavioral teaching competencies to instructional tasks for which they had received no direct training. Lancioni (1982, Exp. 1) used non-mentally-retarded fourth-grade children as tutors to assist socially withdrawn mentally retarded children to increase cooperative play, activities, and self-help skills. Greer and Polivstok (1982) trained junior-high-school students to be tutors of children needing remedial reading assistance.

A third alternative to consultee plan implementations is to have the client assume the role of plan executor. Client execution of implementation plans can be effective not only when the client is an adolescent or adult (Mahoney & Thoresen, 1974), but also when he or she is a relatively young child (Kazdin, 1989; Ollendick & Cerny, 1981). There are several advantages in using a self-control program (Ollendick & Cerny, 1981). First, research has shown that children can manage their own behavior. For example, Glynn, Thomas, and Shee (1974) demonstrated that 6- and 7-year-old children could use behavioral self-control procedures to maintain high rates of on-task behavior previously established by adult-imposed contingencies. Subsequently, Glynn and Thomas (1974) found that third-grade children were able to use self-control techniques to increase their on-task behavior when they were given teacher cues defining on-task behavior. Ballard and Glynn (1975) also showed that third-graders can use self-control techniques to teach themselves specific intellectual competencies important in written composition. The Ballard and Glynn study illustrates that plan implementation by child clients may substantially enhance the efficiency of the implementation process. Teaching children how to write well is a very time-consuming task. Insofar as the children in the Ballard investigation were able to teach themselves effective writing skills, a great deal of teacher time was made available for meeting other student needs. Second, through self-control procedures, children may be able to observe and change behaviors that would be missed by external adult observers or consultees. Third, adults who administer treatment may serve as discriminative cues for certain behaviors. When these adults are not around, the child may function quite differently and even inappropriately (Kazdin, 1975). Fourth, self-control strategies may lead to more efficient and more durable behavior change in that they can be used as a contingency-fading procedure to increase maintenance (Gardner, Cole, Berry, & Nowinski, 1983). Fifth, children's engagement in self-control activities may provide adults with time to engage in other child-oriented activities.

A third role generally required for plan implementation is *behavior observer*. In the many cases of consultation involving observations of behavior in natural settings, someone must be given the responsibility for carrying out the necessary observations for evaluations of treatment effects. The role of observer may have, of course, have been assigned during problem identification. As indicated in Chapter 3, the consultee is often responsible for observing behavior. However, as in the case of the other roles described to this point, individuals other than the consultee may sometimes assume observation responsibilities. Research cited in the previous paragraphs has shown that parents (Hall *et al.*, 1972), teachers (Hall *et al.*, 1971), and young children engaging in self-observation (Gardner & Cole, 1988) can be taught to observe reliably. Fixsen *et al.* (1972) showed that peer observers can also make reliable observations of behavior under reinforcement made contingent on observational accuracy.

A final role that is sometimes necessary for effective implementation is *implementation skill developer*. It may happen that the plan executors lack the necessary skills to effectively implement the plan intended to be used in consultation. When this occurs, someone must be assigned the responsibility of ensuring that the executors will acquire the needed skills to implement the plan as it was designed.

The consultant generally assumes the responsibility for skill development. The development effort typically takes the form of training sessions conducted before the plan is actually put into operation. However, in some instances, skill development may be effected during implementation. For example, the consultant may assist plan executors in educational settings to acquire implementation skills by cuing and/or reinforcing the use of these skills in the classroom during the time that a plan is in operation.

Assembling Implementation Materials

A second step that may be involved in preparing for implementation is assembling or organizing the necessary materials for carrying out the plan to be put into effect during the Problem Identification Interview (PII). A number of materials may be necessary for plan implementation. For example, if plan executors must be trained, it may be necessary to assemble training materials. These may range from instruction sheets describing implementation skills to videotapes illustrating implementation procedures. In cases involving academic goals, special instructional materials may be needed. For example, programmed reading texts may be used during plan implementation. Self-instructional audiovisual materials of a variety of types may also be required on occasion. Programs involving the use of tangible rewards represent yet another instance in which materials are used in consultation. Finally, procedures for assessing client behavior may require the use of special materials such as scoring sheets or mechanical or electronic recording devices. These, of course, should have been obtained during problem identification.

There are a number of factors that should be considered in assembling materials. One of these is to ensure that the materials will be available when needed. For example, if a training session involves the use of a videotape recorder, provisions must be made to ensure that a recorder will be available at the time the training is scheduled to begin. Failure to plan for a procedural detail of this kind may produce frustrating inconveniences for a consultee and a client that can damage the effectiveness of an intervention program.

When mechanical or electronic devices are involved in consultation, it is necessary to examine these devices before the time they are to be used to make sure they are in working order. It can be very frustrating indeed to be on the brink of plan implementation and to find that a mechanical or electronic device required for implementation is not functional.

Yet another consideration that must be planned for when machines are involved in consultation is the ability of the participants to operate the equipment they are expected to use. When there is a question of user competence, it is beneficial to have a trial operation and a training session.

In many cases, the consultant has little control over the gathering of the materials to be used in consultation. It is generally the consultee's responsibility to attend to this matter. In light of both the lack of consultant control over materials and the many complications that can occur in the process of gathering them, it seems clear that it is usually advisable to keep the use of materials in consultation to a minimum. Nevertheless, there are situations that require the extensive use of materials. When this is the case, the consultant should check with the consultee before implementation to ensure that adequate provisions have been made for the assembly of materials.

Developing Implementation Skills

In cases in which plan executors may lack the necessary skill for effective plan implementation, steps must be taken to develop the required skills. As mentioned earlier, the consultant generally assumes the responsibility for directing skill development activities and, in addition, may also implement the activities.

One frequently used mechanism for developing the skills of plan executors is the training session conducted outside the setting in which the plan implementation will take place. Although this type of skill training is often carried out before plan implementation occurs, in some cases it is done periodically during the implementation process.

Usually, training activities in consultation are directed toward teachers and parents because they most often serve in the role of consultee. In the following section, we review briefly some illustrations of both teacher and parent training. However, it must be emphasized that a detailed discussion of these areas is beyond the scope of the text. The reader interested in work in this area should review the original text sources cited in this book.

Teacher Training. In-service training for teachers and other school personnel is an extremely useful tool for facilitating consultation as a service delivery model and for increasing consultee intervention skills. There is a rather extensive teacher-training literature indicating that teachers can be trained in behavior management skills to intervene with children who are experiencing academic and behavioral problems (e.g., Allen & Forman, 1984; Anderson & Kratochwill, 1988; Bernstein, 1982). Several studies involving a variety of techniques have demonstrated that training can be effective in developing plan executor skills. For example, Horton (1975) conducted a study that illustrates the effectiveness of a very brief teacher-training program. In this investigation, two teachers were provided with discrimination training in the form of a videotape and an audiotape that demonstrated what the investigators in the study called "behavior-specific praise." Behavior-specific praise was defined as praise that identified a specific student behavior for which approval was being given. The statement "You worked that problem very well" is an example of behavior-specific praise. The teachers learned to code examples of behavior-specific praise from the tapes. They then attempted to apply what they had learned in their own classrooms. During applications, audiotapes were made of their behavior each day. The teachers coded these and thus attained feedback concerning the extent to which they used praise. Discrimination training involving the coding of praise related to specific subject-matter areas such as reading and mathematics was found to be effective in increasing the rate of teacher praise.

Several studies have demonstrated that training involving role playing can be effective in developing plan executor skills. For example, Gardner (1972) used a lecture method and role playing to train institutional attendants in a residential treatment center for severely mentally retarded individuals in the use of basic behavior-modification skills such as shaping and reinforcing. One group of attendants was exposed to an 8-hour lecture series presenting basic behavior-modification principles in everyday language. A second group participated in 6 hours of role playing. In the role-playing sessions, the trainer demonstrated various behavior-modification techniques to be used in teaching the institutional residents simple skills such as dressing, undressing, and eating with a spoon. The attendants then worked in pairs on the demonstrated skills. One played the role of attendant, and the other, the role of institutional resident. During role playing, the trainer provided corrective feedback to enhance skill development. Gardner found that the training procedure involving role playing was more effective than the lecture series in teaching the attendants to apply behavioral techniques. However, the lecture series was more effective than role playing in facilitating the acquisition of knowledge about behavioral principles.

Jones and Eimers (1975) described a skill-training package involving the use of role playing that they applied to train two third-grade teachers to control disruptive classroom behavior. The training procedure, which extended over six sessions, was quite similar to that used by Gardner. The skills, which were modeled by the trainer, included the early identification of instances of misbehavior and the use of low-intensity, nonpejorative verbalizations such as "That's enough" to signal the need to desist from further inappropriate action. After the skills were modeled by the trainer, the teachers engaged in role-playing activities in which they attempted to apply the demonstrated skills to control the disruptive activities of individuals playing the role of children engaged in inappropriate classroom behavior. Following role playing, feedback was given concerning the adequacy of the skill performance. When the teachers had performed a skill well, they were told that they had done a good job. When they failed to perform adequately, they were asked to give a critique of their own performance. The individuals playing the role of the student were also asked to give reactions to the performance. Finally, suggestions were made on how the skill might be enacted effectively. Data collected on classroom disruptions before, during, and after training indicated that the training procedure was effective in helping the teachers to reduce disruptive classroom behavior.

As indicated earlier, in some cases plan executors may be children or adolescents rather than adults. Research cited earlier in this chapter indicates that training involving role playing can be effective in teaching children and youths the necessary plan-implementation skills. For example, in the Johnson and Bailey (1974) study described earlier in the discussion of peer tutoring, role-playing techniques were used to train the tutors. Training consisted of three 30-minute sessions conducted on consecutive days before the onset of tutoring. During the first session, the tutoring program was described and appropriate teaching behaviors were modeled. During the second session, the materials to be used in tutoring were introduced, and the children were given the opportunity to role-play the skills that they had observed previously. The third session was devoted entirely to role playing, with a special emphasis on giving social reinforcement contingent on appropriate social and academic behavior of the student. Positive feedback was given by the experimenter for the correct enactment of skills. The training was shown to be effective by the fact that the children who were subsequently tutored by the trained peers showed a marked improvement in their counting and number recognition skills.

Although formal training sessions conducted outside the situation in which implementation occurs constitute a widely used technique for developing executor skills, sometimes training is conducted in the implementation setting during the time implementation takes place. Training of this kind generally takes the form of guiding implementation by procedures such as cuing the application of implementation skills and providing feedback following skill use.

Parsonson, Baer, and Baer (1974) conducted a study that illustrates the use of feedback as a device for training implementation skills in a classroom setting. In this study, two teachers responsible for a kindergarten-type program for institutionalized mentally retarded children were taught to attend to appropriate behavior of students and to ignore inappropriate behavior. The training procedure consisted of classroom observers' frequent feedback to the teachers regarding the extent to which they had attended to appropriate behavior. The observers coded such behaviors as praising a child for the correct use of language or complementing a child for following instructions. Every 3 to 5 minutes the observers provided a brief report to the teachers indicating the percentage of teacher behaviors involving attention to appropriate student responses. The training, which lasted for 5 days for one teacher and for 8 days for the other, resulted in a marked increase in the appropriate use of social contingencies in the classroom. The training effects were shown to be lasting. Moreover, the ability to apply the acquired skills generalized to a variety of different child behaviors.

Van Houten and Sullivan (1975) carried out an investigation that demonstrates the use of cuing as a training device during plan implementation. Their study examined the effects of self-recording and cuing on the rate of verbal praise given to students by their classroom teachers. A special-education teacher, a fourth-grade teacher, and a seventh-grade teacher participated in the investigation. In one experimental condition, two of the teachers were given a wrist counter of the type used to keep a golf score and were instructed to count each time they praised a child for his or her work. The teachers used the results of their counting to compute the rate per minute that they praised their students. The teachers were asked to use the feedback provided through self-observation to maintain a praise rate of two responses per minute. This procedure had little or no effect on the teachers' behavior. In a cuing treatment condition, all three teachers participated. Cues in the form of short auditory beeps presented through the classroom public address system were introduced on a variable schedule with a mean rate of two cues per minute. These cues produced an increase in the teachers' praise beyond the required level. This study is of interest not only because it illustrates the effectiveness of training plan executors through the use of cuing, but also because it demonstrates the use of materials indigenous to the consultee's environment. Public address systems are often available in public school classrooms. Van Houten and Sullivan (1975) demonstrated that they can be used effectively as a teacher-training device.

The results of the Van Houten and Sullivan (1975) study with respect to the effects of self-recording of teacher behavior are quite different from those of the Horton (1975) study described earlier in the chapter as an illustration of the effects of discrimination training on teacher praise. As the reader may recall, teachers participating in the Horton investigation coded their own rates of praise from audiotapes when they had finished teaching. Moreover, they observed videotapes and audiotapes to learn to discriminate instances of behavior-specific praise before applying self-observation to their own teaching. In the Van Houten and Sullivan study, self-observation was conducted during teaching with the assistance of a wrist counter, and no provisions were made for discrimination training before self-observation of behavior. One or more of these differences in method may account for the fact that self-observation in the Horton investigation was associated with beneficial changes in teacher behavior, whereas this was not the case in the Van Houten and Sullivan study.

Some researchers have examined the relation between training in behavior modification and consultation services to the classroom teacher (e.g., Anderson, Kratochwill, & Bergan, 1986; White & Pryzwansky, 1982).

In one of these studies (Anderson *et al.*, 1986), we evaluated the relative effectiveness of two teacher-training conditions under two consultation-dependent measures. The subjects in the study included elementary-school teachers ($N = 56$) in an urban school district. The conditions included training in classroom behavior modification and consultation, and training in consultative service-delivery procedures and general multi-disciplinary team processes (a nonspecial control). The consultation-dependent measures included specific and general problem identification, problem analysis, and problem-evaluation behavioral-consultation elicitors. The effectiveness of the four conditions was evaluated on knowledge of behavior modification principles and concepts, and on the frequency of specific categories of consultee (teacher) verbal behaviors. The results suggested that the training package was effective in increasing teacher knowledge of behavioral procedures and in increasing the frequency of teacher verbalizations regarding overt child behaviors, behavior observation techniques, and behavioral intervention plans during the problem identification and problem analysis phases of consultation. It was also found that, even after training, specific consultant questions were important in eliciting consultee statements related to the environmental conditions surrounding behavior. In contrast, the use of more general consultant verbal behaviors resulted in significantly more vague, unspecified, and irrelevant types of consultee verbalizations. Although this training project was a promising beginning, no real client services were involved, and therefore, the real value of this model of training remains untested.

The teacher-training research literature suggests a number of effective training options. Didactic instruction, modeling, role playing, cuing, and feedback have all been used effectively to train teachers in the use of classroom behavior-management techniques. Didactic instruction should be used in combination with other training methods (e.g., modeling, role playing, and feedback). Didactic instruction alone has been found to be effective in at least two studies (i.e., Andrews, 1970; Brown, Frankel, Birkimer, & Gamboa, 1966), but some studies that included didactic instruction as part of a component analysis did not find any evidence of its effectiveness (e.g., Bowles & Nelson, 1976; Cossairt *et al.*, 1973; Johnson & Sloat, 1980). It is probable that some form of didactic training is a prerequisite to other forms of successful teacher training (Anderson & Kratochwill, 1988). Cuing has been investigated relatively infrequently. In the Bowles and Nelson (1976) study, didactic instruction and cuing were effective during training.

Role playing and role playing combined with modeling have provided effective instructional procedures in a number of training studies. However, differences among studies, such as the amount of training time and the focus of the outcome measure, may be a factor in determining how successful these procedures are independently and in combination. In research on feedback procedures, there is considerable support, but most feedback is provided within the context of other components (e.g., didactic instruction and modeling). Modeling and feedback appear to be effective when used in isolation as well as in combination with other methods. The use of didactic instructional techniques (written materials, lectures, and discussions) in combination with modeling, role playing and feedback has been found effective (e.g., Carnine & Fink, 1978; Madsen, Madsen, Saudargas, Hammond, Smith, & Edgar, 1970).

Generally, few studies have used specific reinforcement procedures independently of other instructional procedures. This finding is surprising in view of the relative efficacy of this tactic in regard to a wide range of effective target responses, settings, and subjects. A limitation common to the teacher-training research overall appears to be a dearth of evidence of the generalization and maintenance of teacher-training effects. In a review of the generalization of behavioral teacher-training, Robinson and Swanton (1980) reported only six studies that established that the training had resulted in generalized change and three studies provided convincing evidence of that finding.

Koegel, Russo, and Rincover (1977) evaluated a training package that included the use of a written manual, videotaped modeling, and trainer feedback. This combination was found to be effective in training skills that generalized to a variety of children and target behaviors. The Horton (1975) study discussed above found increased rates of specific teacher praise through the use of feedback that generalized to subject areas other than that in which it was trained, and Parsonson, Baer, and Baer (1974) also used feedback to train preschool teachers to apply correct social contingencies to several classes of child behaviors. Generalization in these studies appeared to be related to two variables: the type of training provided and the teachers' attitudes toward the training. Generalization appeared to be prompted by extensive training involving a wide range of conditions in which skills can be learned. It was also found that the teachers whose training generalized to other situations and subjects held more favorable attitudes toward their training than those whose training did not generalize (Robinson & Swanton, 1980).

Parent Training. Relative to research on teacher training, the empirical work on parent management training is extensive and covers a broad range of children varying in age and type of problems or disorder (O'Dell, 1985). In work on parent training, three different formats have been used (Ollendick & Cerny, 1981), the first including "didactic instruction" (Johnson & Katz, 1973), "educational groups" (O'Dell, 1974), or "parent consultation" (Cobb & Medway, 1978). This first approach involves the consultant in a training role with the parent, but no direct contact with the child client. That is, the parent serves as the consultee and implements the procedures presented during training sessions and consultation. A second format involves an individual parent-training approach in which the consultant focuses on one set of parents at a time while providing direct training and supervision during program development and implementation. The parents and the children may both be involved in the training sessions. A third format focuses on group parent-training and combines features of both consultation and individual training formats. Parents are given group training and usually are supervised during application of the child management techniques.

Many parent-training programs are based on a group didactic strategy. Unfortunately, the effects of didactic workshop training are generally small and not durable. As an alternative, competency-based training (CBT) has been proposed. Although there is little research in the area of CBT, some researchers have presented data on the efficacy of the approach (Rickert, Sottolando, Parish, Riley, Hunt, & Pelco, 1988). In fact, in the study reported by Rickert and his associates, didactic training was insufficient to develop skills in the parents. In contrast, seven parents who participated in competency-based instruction in instruction-giving and time-out skills demonstrated skill proficiency (at least 90%).

The choice of a particular parent-training format depends on a number of variables. To begin with, the consultant's time and resources are a major factor. Does the consultant have the time and resources to engage parents in the intensive training that may be needed to assist their child as characterized in the second and third formats? This question is particularly relevant to the CBT approach. Second, as Ollendick and Cerny (1981) speculated, consultation formats may be sufficient for parent training only when child behaviors are not of a severe clinical nature, and when the goal is oriented to primary prevention. More serious clinical disorders may require *direct* client contact through the behavior therapy procedures. Third, empirical support for parent-training programs is generally good. With regard to research support, reviews of the parent-training literature are generally positive about showing parent and child change (Berkowitz & Graziano, 1972; Cobb & Medway, 1978; Dangel & Polster, 1984, 1988; Forehand & McMahon, 1981; Johnson & Katz, 1973; Kazdin, 1988; O'Dell, 1974; Patterson, 1982). Patterson and his colleagues, for example, provided extensive research on parent training designed to manage aggressive children between the ages of 3 and 12 years. In a review of work in this area, Kazdin (1988) noted several important findings, including positive change in child behavior to within a normative level when compared to nonreferred peers, maintenance of therapeutic gains 1 year following treatment, and some benefits of treatment more than 10 years later. Moreover, the effects of the treatment extend beyond the target behaviors, parents often generalize treatment to other children, and parent psychopathology (e.g., depression) decreases following parent training.

Several factors also appear to contribute to successful parent-training outcome according to Kazdin (1988). To begin with, brief training-session interventions (i.e., less than 10 hours) are less likely to have positive effects than more intensive programs (i.e., 50–60 hours) especially for severe clinical disorders. This finding also supports Ollendick and Cerny's (1981) statement that a "consultation" format for parent training may not be appropriate for more severe problems. Second, training in some very specific treatment components (social learning principles and time-out) improves the treatment effect. Third, the therapist's training and skills are related to the magnitude and durability of the treatment, but less is known in this area. Fourth, families that are experiencing many risk factors of childhood psychopathology (e.g., parent psychopathology) demonstrate fewer gains in treatment and less maintenance. Fifth, the mother's social support system outside the home appears to be related to successful outcome: more insular mothers show less positive response to treatment (see Wahler, 1975).

Nevertheless, a determination of long-term effectiveness and more knowledge of matching the format to the type of problem will be necessary for consultants to make informed decisions about what type of services to provide. In consultation, the consultant's decision to engage in training is based on a number of considerations, such as the need as perceived by the consultant for plan executor skill-development, the willingness of plan executors to participate in training, the likelihood that the training will produce the desired results, and the cost of the training in terms of time, materials, and human resources. Each of these factors is discussed later in this chapter.

Operating the Implementation Plan

After adequate preparations, the implementation plan is put into effect. During this period, plan executors carry out the intervention designed in the problem analysis. In addition, provisions must be made to monitor the implementation and to make revisions in the implementation procedures when required.

Monitoring Implementation

Two kinds of monitoring normally occur during plan implementation. One is the monitoring of client behavior. Provisions for assessing client behavior during the implementation will have been made during problem identification and problem analysis. As indicated in earlier chapters, procedures for measuring behavior related to the behavioral goals or the performance objectives are established during the problem identification interview. When the consultation involves skills analysis, procedures for assessing skill mastery are established during the problem analysis interview. As in the stages of consultation, during plan implementation the consultee is generally responsible for overseeing and, in many cases, for implementing the assessment procedures.

Another kind of monitoring that occurs during plan implementation is the monitoring of the operations involved in carrying out the implementation of the treatment plan. The major purpose of this kind of monitoring is to make sure the treatment is implemented as designed. The degree to which a treatment is implemented as intended is referred to as *treatment integrity* or *fidelity* (Yeaton & Sechrest, 1981). Few consultation research studies have involved a systematic assessment and monitoring of the treatment (Gresham & Kendall, 1987; Kratochwill, Sheridan, & Van Someren, 1988). There is, of course, no guarantee that plans designed in problem analysis, regardless of quality, will be implemented as intended. Whether a treatment will be implemented with integrity may be related to several factors, including (1) how complex the treatment is to implement; (2) the time needed to implement the treatment; (3) the resources needed to implement the treatment; (4) the number of consultees required to implement the treatment; (5) the perceived and actual effectiveness of the treatments; and (6) the motivation of the consultees. It is important, therefore, that the consultant become aware of discrepancies between what was planned and what was implemented and designed as quickly as possible so that steps may be taken to rectify any implementation inadequacies.

A second purpose of monitoring implementation is to ensure that an assessment of client performance is taking place. As pointed out previously, assessment procedures established during problem identification and used to collect the baseline data should be continued during plan implementation. When they are not, it is generally impossible to evaluate either plan effectiveness or goal attainment. Likewise, changes in recording procedures between the baseline and the implementation phases of consultation generally produce a dilemma analogous to the time-honored unsolvable problem of comparing apples and oranges. When changes in assessment occur during consultation, what typically happens is that a problem is defined in one way and the attainment of a solution to the problem is evaluated in another.

One might think that, in light of the obvious evaluation difficulties that changes in assessment procedures produce, they might never occur. The fact is that they do. Consider, for example, the situation in which an elementary-school teacher has decided during problem identification that, as an indication of off-task behavior, she will measure the number of times a boy leaves an arithmetic study committee during committee time. During plan implementation, the boy begins to show marked improvement. The teacher wishes to encourage the child by showing him the record of his progress, but she begins to realize that she has defined the problem in a basically negative way. At this point, she feels that both she and the child would be much more interested in knowing the amount of time spent on-task than in being made continuously aware of the number of instances of off-task behavior. Accordingly, in the midst of plan implementation, she changes her recording procedures. In such circumstances, it may be impossible to determine whether the goal of consultation has been attained. Moreover, there is no way to evaluate the effectiveness of the implementation plan because there can be no comparison between the baseline behavior and the behavior assessed during the implementation. Clearly, the consultant should take steps to become aware of possible changes in assessment procedures so that appropriate measures may be taken to forestall the unfortunate consequences that such changes may produce.

The monitoring of the operations involved in plan implementation may occur in a number of ways. One of these is to interview the plan executors. Shortly after initial plan implementation, a consultant might ask the observers for the data that have been collected or might talk with the plan executors about specific examples describing plan operations.

Christophersen, Arnold, Hill, and Quilitich (1972) conducted a study that illustrates the use of the interview in monitoring plan implementation. During office interviews, they taught two sets of parents to use a point system. During these sessions, the parents were shown a film and were given a written description of a point system. In addition, they were shown how to use point cards to tabulate the points earned by their children for appropriate behavior and the points lost as a result of inappropriate activities. Following training, the parents implemented the point system at home. During the evening of the first day of implementation, a consultant visited the homes to interview the parents with respect to the operation of the system. In this interview, the parents were asked to describe how they had used the system during the day. The information gained from the interview provided feedback indicating the extent to which the parents were using the system properly. In addition, it provided an opportunity for the consultant to encourage the parents to continue to use the system.

The interview has the advantage of being a relatively easy procedure to undertake when one is seeking information regarding implementation. Interviews can typically be arranged at the convenience of all the parties involved. Moreover, they usually do not require much time to conduct. The central disadvantage of the interview, of course, is that the information obtained through interviewing may not be entirely accurate.

Another procedure that may be used to monitor implementation is observation of the operation of the plan in the implementation setting. In some cases, self-observation may be used by plan executors in monitoring implementation. This tactic was illustrated in the Horton (1975) and Van Houten and Sullivan (1975) investigations described earlier in the chapter.

Recall that, in the Horton study, teachers coded tape recordings of their use of behavior-specific praise. In the Van Houten and Sullivan investigation, teachers used wrist counters to record their praise rates.

Information obtained through self-observation may be communicated to a consultant in written form. For example, coding sheets summarizing observations may be given to the consultant periodically to communicate the details of plan operations. Self-observation often combined with interviewing to facilitate the sharing of information about plan implementation.

Self-observation is advantageous from the consultant's point of view in that it takes a minimal amount of consultant time. Moreover, as discussed previously in the chapter, it may have the additional advantage of assisting plan executors to develop the skills needed for effective implementation. There are two disadvantages in the approach, however. One is that it requires plan executor time that might be spent in other ways. The second is the possibility that self-observations may be unreliable. If unreliability is a concern, steps must be taken to establish the fact that plan executors are recording the plan operations reliably (see Nelson, 1977a,b) by having another person also record the plan operations. Interrater agreement may then be computed to determine the reliability of the observations.

Another way in which the consultant may assess treatment integrity is to design a direct observational system that allows someone else to monitor the treatment components. For example, Gresham (1989) presented an example of how treatment integrity might be assessed in a response-cost lottery-intervention (Witt & Elliott, 1982). The response-cost lottery involves implementing a response-cost procedure within a point system. Basically, all the children in a class or group are under the same response contingencies, but specific consequences are applied for each individual based on her or his performance.

Figure 5-1 presents a hypothetical example of assessing the treatment integrity of 11 components of the response-cost lottery. The data presented in the figure show that the integrity over a 5-day period ranged from 20% to 100%, and that the integrity over time ranged from 64% to 91%.

Direct observational data of the type reported in Figure 5-1 can provide important information to the consultant on how treatment integrity is progressing. However, the cost of this type of assessment as well as the potential reactivity of observation may prove to be a problem (see Chapter 3). As an option, Gresham (1989) proposed that a rating system be used by the consultee and/or the consultant. Figures 5-2 and 5-3 show rating systems that may be used by the consultee and the consultant, respectively.

The consultant may also assume the role of trained observer in some cases. The consultant is afforded the opportunity of seeing the extent to which the plan is being implemented as designed and may gain new insights into factors that may be controlling client behavior. In these circum-

Components	Monday	Tuesday	Wednesday	Thursday	Friday	% Component Integrity
1 Describes system	X I	XI	X I	X I	X I	100%
2. Displays/Describes reinforcers	X I	I O	I O	X I	X I	60%
3. 3X5 card placed on desks	X I	XI	X I	X I	X I	100%
4 Card taped on 3 sides	X I	XI	X I	X I	X I	100%
5. 4 slips of colored paper placed in cards	X I	XI	X I	X I	X I	100%
6. Lottery in effect 1/2 hour	X I	I O	I O	I O	X I	40%
7. Slips removed contingent on rule violation	X I	I O	X I	I O	I O	40%
8. Restates rule contingently	I O	I O	I O	X I	X I	20%
9. Tickets placed in box	X I	XI	X I	X I	X I	100%
10. Drawing on Friday	NA I	NA I	NA I	NA I	X I	100%
11. Winner selects reinforcer	NA I	NA I	NA I	NA I	X I	100%
Daily Integrity ▪	91%	64%	73%	82%	82%	

FIGURE 5-1. Direct observation form for recording treatment integrity of the response-cost lottery. X, occurrence; O, nonoccurrence. $\bar{X}$ integrity = 78%. [Source: F. M. Gresham (1989). Assessment of treatment integrity in school consultation and prereferral intervention. *School Psychology Review*, 18, 37–50. Reproduced by permission.]

Consultee: _____ Date: _____ Consultant: _____

Response-Cost Lottery

	High integrity				Low integrity
1. Described system to students.	1	2	3	4	5
2. Displayed and described reinforcers.	1	2	3	4	5
3. Placed 3 × 5 cards on student's desks.	1	2	3	4	5
4. Card taped on three sides.	1	2	3	4	5
5. Four slips of colored paper inserted (different colors for each student).	1	2	3	4	5
6. Lottery in effect for one-half hour.	1	2	3	4	5
7. Slips removed contingent on rule violations.	1	2	3	4	5
8. Teacher restates rule contingent on violation.	1	2	3	4	5
9. Remaining tickets placed in box.	1	2	3	4	5
10. Drawing occurs on Friday.	1	2	3	4	5
11. Winner selects reinforcer on Friday.	1	2	3	4	5

FIGURE 5-2. Example of a self-report integrity assessment. [Source: F. M. Gresham (1989). Assessment of treatment integrity in school consultation and prereferral intervention. *School Psychology Review*, 18, 37–50. Reproduced by permission.]

Date: ___/___/___   Teacher _____   Day: M T W Th F

Response-Cost Lottery

Directions. Please complete this form each day *after* the period in which the intervention has been implemented in your classroom.

	Strongly disagree				Strongly agree
1. I described the response-cost lottery-system to the class.	1	2	3	4	5
2. I displayed and described the rewards that the students could receive in the lottery.	1	2	3	4	5
3. I placed a 3 × 5 card on top of each student's desk.	1	2	3	4	5
4. I taped the card on three sides with one side open.	1	2	3	4	5
5. I inserted four slips of colored paper inside each card, using different colors for each student.	1	2	3	4	5
6. I left the lottery in effect for one-half hour today.	1	2	3	4	5
7. I removed slips from each card whenever a student violated a class rule.	1	2	3	4	5
8. I restated the class rule whenever a student violated the rule.	1	2	3	4	5
9. I placed the remaining tickets in the lottery box after lottery time concluded today.	1	2	3	4	5
10. I conducted the drawing for the winner today (Friday only).	1	2	3	4	5
11. The winner was allowed to select a reward (Friday only).	1	2	3	4	5

FIGURE 5-3. Example of a behavior-rating scale for treatment integrity. [Source: F. M. Gresham (1989). Assessment of treatment integrity in school consultation and prereferral intervention. *School Psychology Review, 18*, 37–50. Reproduced by permission.]

stances, one advantage of the observation approach is that it provides firsthand information to the consultant on plan operations.

Whether observation is carried out by the consultant or by someone else, observation can be used to provide both cuing and feedback to the plan executors during implementation. The Parsonson *et al.* (1974) study described previously in the chapter illustrates how observer communications to plan executors during implementation produced beneficial results. Recall that, in this investigation, the observers provided frequent feedback to the teachers to influence their attention to appropriate student behavior.

The principal disadvantage of the observation technique is that it requires time on the part of the observer. In some cases, it may not be practical for a busy consultant to give time to observation purposes. One strategy that may be used as a partial solution to the time problem is to engage in intermittent observation. For instance, a consultant might observe for a short period on the first day of implementation and then again on the last day of plan operation before the problem evaluation interview.

The final approach to monitoring plan operations is to use observations of client behavior as an indicator of the extent to which the plan is being implemented as intended. The primary concern in consultation is generally whether client behavior is changing as desired. If it is, the consultant and the consultee may be willing to "assume" that the plan is being implemented adequately.

The Jones and Eimers (1975) study discussed earlier in the chapter provides one of many examples in the behavioral literature in which observations of client behavior are used to make inferences about plan operations. Again, Jones and Eimers trained teachers to use a behavior-management skill-package to control disruptive behavior in their classrooms. Jones and Eimers pointed out that the skill package was too complex to permit observational verification of the adequacy of its use in the classroom. As a result, they chose to measure the incidence of disruptive child behavior in an effort to show that skill training had been effective.

The Jones and Eimers study demonstrates the principal advantage of the strategy of using measures of client behavior as an indicator of plan operations: Client observations reduce the complexity of the task of monitoring implementation. The obvious disadvantage is that inferences made about plan implementation on the basis of client observations may be inaccurate (Gresham, 1989; Kratochwill et al., 1988).

As may be inferred from the above discussion, there is no way to monitor implementation that is adequate in all circumstances. In determining how to go about the monitoring task, one must consider the purposes to be achieved through monitoring and the cost, in terms of time and resources, of the various options available for carrying out monitoring. Considerations of this kind often will result in the use of combinations of the procedures described above to maximize the probability of obtaining the needed information and at the same time to minimize the cost of the information.

Revising Procedures during Implementation

In some instances, it may be advisable to revise implementation procedures during the implementation process when programs are not achieving their desired effects. If monitoring operations reveal that behavior is not changing as desired or that the treatment plan is not being implemented as designed, changes in implementation procedures may be warranted.

One type of change that may be made during implementation is a revision to make plan operations congruent with plan design (i.e., increase treatment integrity). If the plan calls for the consultee to reinforce appropriate client behavior and to ignore inappropriate behavior (if he or she has been ignoring desired behavior and reinforcing inappropriate actions), the consultant may wish to take steps to bring about a closer correspondence between plan execution and plan design than has been currently observed.

The decision to increase congruence between plan implementation and plan design is based, in part, on observed changes in client behavior during implementation. If client behavior is changing as desired, it may be decided not to alter implementation procedures even if there is a discrepancy between implementation and design. On the other hand, if the plan appears not to be working and there is a design implementation discrepancy, change should be considered.

The factors determined to control lack of implementation–design congruence influences to some degree, the decision to increase congruence. One such factor is the adequacy of communication between the consultant and the consultee during problem analysis. For example, it may happen that a consultee fails to implement a plan as the consultant thought it was designed because each party failed to comprehend fully what the other said during the problem analysis interview. The obvious course of action is to clarify communication regarding how the plan is to be implemented and then to do what is necessary to ensure that the implementation will be congruent with the design.

A second factor that may influence congruence is the skill of the plan executors. It may become obvious after plan implementation is initiated that the plan executors lack the necessary competencies to carry out the plan as it was constructed. For example, if peer tutors are involved in implementation, it may be discovered that, despite preimplementation training, some of the tutors lack the necessary plan-implementation skills. In such circumstances, further training may be instituted to achieve congruence, or additional tutors may be recruited and trained for participation in the plan implementation. If the latter course of action is followed, care must be taken to make sure that the tutors who lack skills are given an alternative learning experience that will benefit them educationally.

A third factor that can influence congruence is the set of contingencies operating on the plan executors during implementation. One especially important type of contingency that may affect executor behavior is the behavior of the client. A parent, for example, may find it impossible to implement an extinction procedure to eliminate tantrum behavior because the child destroys property in the home when extinction is in effect.

There may be a tendency not to recognize the influence of the client's behavior on the plan executor's behavior when the executor is an adult socializing agent. Nevertheless, there is evidence that children do affect the behavior of adult socializing agents. For example, in a classic review of child development literature, Bell (1968) presented findings that he interpreted as showing that, from the earliest days of life, the behavior of children influence the reactions of their parents to them. Yarrow, Waxler, and Scott (1971) demonstrated an association between behavior of very young children and the reactions of their teachers to them. These investigators found a relation between the extent to which preschool children reinforced their teachers and the amount of time the teachers spent with them.

When the contingencies operating on plan executors appear to be having a detrimental influence on the congruence between plan implementation and plan design, revision toward congruence may be difficult or impossible to achieve. Under these conditions, some other course of action must be taken.

A second type of revision that may be made during plan implementation is to alter the original plan. One reason for making an alteration of this kind is that contingencies operating on the plan executors may make it infeasible to implement the plan in its initial form. For example, suppose that a teacher implements a plan in which disruptive classroom behavior is to be controlled by praising behavior incompatible with disruptions. Disruptions may cause the teacher to become sufficiently angry so that praise for behavior incompatible with disruptions has an obviously insincere ring. Under these conditions, it may be advisable to change the initial plan.

One kind of alteration that may be made when client contingencies are making plan implementation difficult or impossible is to have the consultant change those behavior contingencies. For instance, in the previous example, it might be possible to change student behavior to affect teacher reactions to the students. The initial goal of eliminating disruptions would then be achieved through direct negotiations between the consultant and the students rather than through the plan implemented by the teacher. At the same time, the teacher's behavior would be changed in such a way as to increase the likelihood that the teacher would be able to maintain adequate classroom discipline.

Sherman and Cormier (1974) conducted a study that illustrates the approach of changing teacher behavior by changing student behavior. Two of the children in an elementary teacher's class were highly disruptive. Tangible rewards given by an experimenter were used to change the behavior of these students. The teacher's attention to appropriate and inappropriate behavior was measured during the study, and it was found that changes in student behavior resulted in changes in the teacher's treatment of the students. Moreover, a rating scale completed by the teacher indicated that she believed that she had become more positive in her attitude toward the students as a result of the intervention.

Sometimes, it is advisable to alter a plan that is being implemented according to the design because the plan obviously isn't working. Several examples of plan adjustments in consultation have been reported (e.g., Piersel & Kratochwill, 1979). In many cases, plan modifications made to enhance plan effectiveness require only minor adjustments. Knight and McKenzie (1974) carried out research on thumb sucking at bedtime that demonstrates the potential benefits of minor adjustments. The initial plan was to make story reading at bedtime contingent on non-thumb-sucking behavior. The parents read a bedtime story, and if the child started to suck her thumb, they stopped reading until the child stopped sucking. This procedure worked quite well for two of the children in the study, but not for a third child. The parents of this third child reported that the child was fascinated by items on some attractive shelves near her bed. The modification in the plan was to relocate the child's bed. When this was done, the plan was effective in controlling thumb-sucking behavior.

CONSULTATION DURING THE IMPLEMENTATION

One feature that sharply distinguishes consultation during plan implementation from consultation in other stages of the problem-solving process is that, during plan implementation, there is generally no formal interview between the consultant and the consultee. Nevertheless, several consultation tasks must be accomplished during plan implementation if the process is to proceed as intended. In this section, we detail the consultation goals that must be achieved during plan implementation and the consultation procedures that may be used to attain those goals.

Objectives of Consultation during Implementation

Consultation objectives during plan implementation are shown in Table 5-4. Consultation goals fall into those same categories. One of these objectives has to do with skill development; the second involves monitoring the implementation process; and the third deals with plan revision.

Skill Development Objectives

The first skill-development objective to be achieved during plan implementation is to determine whether the plan executors possess the skills needed to implement the plan effectively. For example, if modeling and reinforcement procedures are to be used, there must be some assurance that the people who are going to apply those techniques have the skills necessary to make the applications properly. The consultant is responsible for determining skill adequacy. To make this determination, the consultant must compare the plan implementation requirements that have been specified during the designation of plan tactics in the problem analysis inter-

TABLE 5-2. Consultation Objectives for Plan Implementation

Categories for objectives	Objectives
Skill development	Determine whether the plan executors possess the skills needed for implementation.
	Ascertain the feasibility of conducting skill training.
	Design procedures to enhance skill mastery.
	Implement procedures to enhance skill mastery.
	Evaluate skill training.
Implementation monitoring	Monitor data collection on client performance.
	Monitor plan operations.
Revision	Determine the need for plan revisions.
	Develop a revised plan when a need for revision exists.

view with information describing the prior knowledge and skill of the plan executors in the application of behavioral principles. When the plan executor is the consultee informal observations of skill adequacy are preferred over a formal assessment of competency. The consultant should take careful notes about how the consultee approaches the tasks of problem identification and analysis and the extent to which the consultee uses behavioral techniques effectively in working with individuals other than the client.

When the consultee is the executor, there may be no need of training, because the consultee is most likely to suggest plan tactics that are familiar and with which he or she is comfortable. However, a concern that might arise is whether the consultee can apply the tactics in the specific fashion required by the plan.

Although the determination of skills may often be based on informal observations made before plan implementation, there are circumstances in which this may not be the case. For example, when peer tutors are to be used in plan implementation, it is usually necessary to take steps to ascertain the skills of the tutors during the preparation stage of implementation. In some instances, tutors are children who have never done any tutoring, and it is safe to assume that they do not possess the needed skills. However, in other instances, tutors have had prior instructional experience. Under these conditions, it may be useful to assess their skills to determine the specific implementation techniques that should receive the most emphasis during tutor training.

If a need for skill development has been established, the second skill-development objective to be pursued during plan implementation is to ascertain the feasibility of implementing various types of training procedures to enhance development. One factor influencing the feasibility of training is obviously the willingness of the plan executors to participate. If the plan executor is a child serving as a peer tutor, he or she may be quite interested in acquiring the skills needed for plan implementation. In addition, willingness to participate in training can be a condition of being a tutor. On the other hand, if the executor is an adult with a busy schedule, interest may be tempered by concerns regarding the amount of time required for training. Research has shown that the willingness of adults to participate in training programs can pose a serious problem in behavioral intervention programs (Chamberlain & Baldwin, 1988; O'Dell, 1974). For example, Morrey (1970) described a parent-training program that began with 20 interested families and ended with only 6. Research on the factors that may influence willingness to participate in training is in its early stages. However, Chamberlain and Baldwin (1988) reported a number of procedures that can be used to assess and overcome resistance.

A second factor influencing the feasibility of training is the likelihood that training will produce the desired results. As the research described earlier illustrates, a variety of training techniques may be beneficial. Accordingly, it is generally reasonable to assume that training will be effective.

A final factor to consider when determining the feasibility of training is the cost of training in terms of time, materials, and human resources. Most of the training procedures described earlier require several hours to implement. Moreover, they typically require the participation of skilled personnel and, in some cases, involve expensive materials. In deciding whether to engage in training, the consultant must weigh the advantages to be gained through training against the cost involved in implementing a training package.

There are cases in which the consultant may find that it is simply not practical to deal with the problem of skill development through training. Under these unfortunate conditions, the consultant and the consultee must go back to problem analysis to devise a new plan if the goals of consultation are to be pursued further.

If the consultant determines that training is both needed and feasible, the third skill-development objective in plan implementation is designing procedures to enhance skill mastery. As indicated earlier in the chapter, the consultant is generally responsible for the design of skill-training procedures. He or she must select and gather the materials necessary for training, work out the procedures to be used in training, and assume the major responsibility for scheduling when and where training is to occur.

A fourth consultation objective related to skill development is implementing the procedures to be used in increasing plan executor skills. As pointed out earlier in the chapter, the consultant is responsible for directing skill-training procedures and, in most cases, for carrying out skill-training programs. However, on occasion, the actual task of carrying out training may be assigned to other people. For example, Henderson and Swanson (1974) conducted a study that involved training mothers to stimulate question asking in their children. The parents participating in the program were Papago Indians living on a reservation many miles from the researchers. Moreover, there were differences in cultural background between the researchers and the mothers. For these reasons, it was decided to train paraprofessionals indigenous to the Papago culture to conduct the parent training. Because they had the same cultural heritage as the parents, the paraprofessionals were able to relate the training to the particular cultural concerns of the Papago mothers. For example, in the Papago culture, it is often considered rude to ask an excessive number of questions. The paraprofessionals were sensitive to this fact and were able to show the Papago mothers how the skill of question asking might be used appropriately within the limitations imposed by Papago customs.

The final skill-development objective to be pursued during implementation is to evaluate skill-training outcomes and procedures. The evaluation is generally aimed primarily at determining whether the goals of training have been attained. Goal attainment may be judged in terms of the congruence between the performance objectives specifying the training goals and the measures of executor skill following training. In addition to the evaluation of goal attainment, it may be of interest to determine the effectiveness of the training procedures. In Chapter 6, we describe numerous designs and procedures that can be applied to the evaluation of training effectiveness.

Monitoring Objectives

One monitoring objective to be achieved during plan implementation is to determine whether the data collection is proceeding as intended. The consultant generally accomplishes this task by examining the records made on client performance. A cursory study of performance records usually indicates when the data are being gathered, how performance is being measured, and what behavior is being assessed. If the records include checks on interobserver agreement, it is also possible to make some judgments about consistency in recording client behavior.

A second monitoring goal to be attained during plan implementation is to ascertain whether the plan operations directed at changing client behavior are proceeding according to the design. Again, the consultant is responsible for seeing that this objective is achieved. However, as pointed out earlier, the actual implementation of monitoring operations may be carried out, on occasion, by individuals other than the consultant.

As indicated in a previous section, in many cases the monitoring of plan operations is based on inferences made from the data on client performance. When this inference occurs, the monitoring of plan operations takes place as part of the process of monitoring the data collection on client behavior. For example, suppose that a consultee is implementing a plan to increase the development of a specific set of language skills in a preschool child. Assume that the plan is one that has been used many times before and has been found to be effective. As a check on the adequacy of the plan implementation, the consultant might make arrangements to see the data on the child's behavior after the first 2 days in which the plan has been in effect. At this time, the consultant has the opportunity to make a judgment regarding whether the data are being collected properly. In addition, he or she may be able to make some reasonable inferences about whether the plan is being implemented according to the design. If the consultant observes little progress toward goal attainment, he or she will probably question the consultee about the manner in which the plan is being implemented, on the hunch that there may be some implementation inadequacies. On the other hand, if there is obvious progress toward the goal, the consultant may be willing to assume that the plan is being implemented properly.

Revision Objectives

The first consultation objective to be pursued in connection with plan revision is to determine whether there is a need to make any changes in the implementation of the plan that has been put into operation. The consultant is responsible for making sure that this objective is achieved. In this regard, the consultant generally attempts, first, to determine whether the client's behavior is changing as desired. If it is, in most cases there will be no need to give further consideration to the possibility of revision. However, if it is not, further steps must be taken to ascertain the need for revision. The consultant must find out whether the plan is being implemented as it was designed. If it is not, an effort must be made to ascertain the reasons for the discrepancy between implementation and design. If client behavior is not changing as desired and/or if there is a lack of implementation–design congruence that it is feasible to rectify, there is a demonstrated need for revision.

The second consultation objective related to revision is to make a revision plan. The consultant must assume the responsibility for assisting the consultee with the development of such a plan. Generally, this assistance requires the use of the plan-design interviewing-techniques discussed in Chapter 4. However, in most instances, it is not necessary to go into the detail required in problem analysis to construct the revision plan. As mentioned earlier in the chapter, revision quite often calls for only minor adjustments in the original plan.

Consultative Interactions during Implementation

Although there are generally no formal consultation interviews during plan implementation, a variety of other kinds of interactions may occur between the consultant and the various participants in consultation. These

Interactions are procedures by which the objectives of consultation are achieved during this phase of consultation.

The Brief Contact

One procedure for achieving implementation goals is the brief contact. A brief contact means an interaction between the consultant and one of the participants in plan implementation that lasts no more than a few minutes. Generally, brief contacts are about 5 or 10 minutes long. In most cases, the person with whom the consultant interacts in a brief contact is the consultee.

Sometimes, it is convenient to make a brief contact by telephone. For example, a consultant may call a parent to discuss some phase of plan implementation. The phone contact has the obvious advantage of saving a trip by the consultant to the place where the treatment implementation is occurring. In addition, it has the benefit of minimizing the amount of disruption of the consultee's daily routine that a visit may cause. For example, parents may feel obliged to take special care to ensure that their home will be immaculately clean when visitors come to the house. Thus, if the consultant has made arrangements for a visit, the parents may feel it necessary to change their plans for the day so that they will have time to clean the house. The central disadvantage of the phone contact is that some kinds of information are easier to communicate in person than they are over the telephone. For example, the consultee may wish to show the consultant how a piece of equipment such as a videotape recorder is being used in the implementation process. It is generally easier to communicate this kind of information through demonstration than through conversation.

Because there are many types of information regarding plan implementation that are best communicated in face-to-face contact, the consultant often makes brief contacts through a personal visit to the consultee in the setting in which implementation is taking place. Visits of this kind make it possible for the consultant to (1) see what kinds of data are being recorded; (2) examine the materials being used in implementation; (3) view the setting in which implementation is occurring; and, in some instances, (4) catch at least a glimpse of how the client operates in his or her natural environment.

One use of the brief contact is to assist in the monitoring of treatment implementation. A few minutes of conversation between the consultant and the consultee during the first day or two of implementation may provide information regarding how the data on client performance are being collected, how the plan is being implemented, and whether the client is making any progress toward attaining the goals of consultation.

A second function of the brief contact is to assist in making plan revisions. For example, if it is determined that there has been no progress toward the goal of consultation and that the plan is not being implemented as intended, conversation in the brief contact should turn to a discussion of possible alterations in plan operations.

The consultant should generally begin discussion in the brief contact by asking to see the data that are being collected on client performance. Data collection forms often provide sufficient information to show any gross errors that may be occurring in the data collection procedures. For example, if it has been agreed that the consultee will record the number of times a child makes self-deprecating remarks and if the recording form contains a frequency count of the number of times the child talks out of turn in class, then the consultant knows immediately that further discussion of the behavior to be recorded during implementation is required.

Another reason for initiating the brief contact by looking at the data on performance is that the data will show whether the client is making progress toward achieving the goal of consultation. Plans implemented during consultation often show their effects on client behavior very quickly. Thus, even though a plan has been in operation only for a day or two when a brief contact occurs, the data on client behavior may provide evidence of behavior change.

If the data on client performance suggest that behavior is changing as desired, the brief contact may terminate. However, if this is not the case, the consultant should turn the discussion to how the plan is being implemented. If the implementation operations are being monitored, the consultant should ask to see the data describing implementation. However, in the more typical situation in which there is no formal record of how the plan is being executed, the consultant should ask for specific examples illustrating the operation of the plan. For instance, a consultant might say, "Give me an example of what you did right after Carol made a disparaging remark about herself today."

If the discussion of client performance or plan implementation reveals a possible need for plan revision, the topic of conversation in the brief contact should turn to considerations of whether a revision should be made. For example, a consultant might say, "There may have been some misunderstanding about what you were to do after Carol made a self-deprecating remark. As her behavior is not changing as we would like it to, we ought to consider making some minor adjustments in the plan."

If it is decided that a revision should be made, the conversation should focus on the development of the specific alterations that need to be made in the plan. As mentioned earlier, the formulation of plan revisions often requires only a minimal amount of discussion. For instance, suppose that a consultant wanted to supplement intermittent reinforcement of desirable behavior with extinction. This might be done through the use of one or two elicitors, such as "What could you do to ignore Carol's disparaging comments?" When plan revisions have been specified, they should be summarized and validated in accordance with the procedures described in Chapter 4 in connection with the discussion of plan design. Thus, a consultant might say, "Then, from now on, you are going to ignore Carol's disparaging comments by immediately attending to one of the other students when Carol engages in self-deprecation. Is that correct?"

The brief contact should generally be terminated by reaffirming the scheduling of the next meeting between the consultant and the other party involved in the contact. For instance, a consultant might close a contact with a consultee by reminding him or her of the time and date of the problem evaluation interview.

The Observation

A second kind of interaction that may be used to pursue the goals of consultation during implementation is the observation. Observation may be conducted either by the consultant or by trained observers in the setting in which the implementation is taking place.

In many cases, observers have little involvement in the implementation process. They may sit unobtrusively several feet away from the center of the implementation action; or in a clinic where one-way observation rooms are available, observations may be conducted completely out of view of the participants in plan implementation. There are, however, some instances in which observers take an active part in implementation. For example, a consultant observing plan implementation in a classroom may take an active role in the instructional process. He or she may work with the children on specific tasks related to the implementation while making observations of the implementation effort.

The most obvious function of observation is monitoring the treatment implementation. Information gathered through the observation of implementation can indicate whether the plan is being applied properly. Observations generally reveal implementation–design discrepancies in a sufficiently precise way to indicate the specific changes required for implementation–design congruence.

Although monitoring is the main function of observation, observing can also assist in the development of plan executor skills. As pointed out earlier in the chapter, observers may cue plan executors during the course of implementation. Observer cues can serve as signals indicating the need to engage in a particular implementation activity. Observers may also model implementation skills for plan executors. For example, an observer might demonstrate how to deliver immediate reinforcement in the classroom by working with one of the children in the room. Finally, observers may provide feedback regarding the adequacy of implementation. As shown earlier in the chapter, feedback of this kind may increase the extent to which the plan executors make use of their implementation skills.

The observation is usually initiated by having someone involved in the implementation introduce the observer to the participants in consultation. The introduction should include an explanation in general terms of the purpose of the observation activities. However, it should *not* include statements that may clearly bias the behavior of the client or of the plan executors during the time in which the observations are made. For example, a teacher might say to a group of students, "Ms. Skinner is here to observe how I go about teaching math and how you go about learning it." A statement of this kind, although it communicates the purpose of the observation, does not indicate the kinds of changes in behavior expected to occur during the implementation.

After the introduction has been made, the observer should begin the observation task immediately. Delaying observation could disrupt plan implementation by focusing attention on the observer's presence rather than on the task at hand. For example, if the observer were to engage in lengthy conversation with the plan executors before beginning observations, the time allotted for implementation would be decreased.

The Training Session

The final type of interaction that may be used in pursuing implementation goals is the formal training session conducted outside the setting in which the implementation is to take place. As indicated earlier in the chapter, the consultant generally directs and implements training. However, in some cases, individuals under the consultant's supervision may conduct training sessions.

The central function of the training session is to develop plan executor skills. In most cases, the need for skill development is recognized before plan implementation is initiated, and training is started before the plan is put into operation. However, in some instances, the need for training may not become apparent until the plan is being implemented.

As discussed earlier in the chapter, a variety of types of training sessions have been found to be effective in assisting plan executors to develop implementation skills. Nevertheless, there are certain characteristics that it is reasonably safe to assume ought to be a part of an effective training program. One of these is a set of objectives specifying the goals of training. General, subordinate, and performance objectives, the characteristics of which were described in Chapter 3, may be specified for training sessions.

A second characteristic that generally should be included in a training sequence is a set of procedures indicating how the training is to occur. There may be substantial variation in training methods from program to program. Most of these variations involve some combination of cuing, modeling, role playing, and feedback, as well as reinforcement. The Henderson and Swanson (1974) parent-training study described earlier in the chapter is an illustration. As the reader will recall, the parents in that study were trained to stimulate question asking on the part of their children. Training with respect to a particular skill was initiated by a verbal description of the skill. The description was followed by a demonstration involving the modeling of skill execution. The parents were then given the opportunity to role-play skill enactment. During role playing, they were provided with feedback that indicated the adequacy of their skill performance and that offered suggestions for improving their performance.

The third characteristic that should be included in a training sequence is a set of procedures for evaluating the training. These should involve measures that can be applied to determine whether the training goals have been reached and may also involve the application of an evaluation design to establish the effectiveness of the training procedures.

The training sessions should generally be relatively short. In most cases, the training should last no longer than an hour. The reason for keeping sessions short is that brevity minimizes the inconvenience of training for plan executors. For example, when the plan executor is a teacher, extended training sessions are usually excessively burdensome unless they are scheduled as a regular part of in-service activities. Teachers have very busy schedules, and time sent in training is time that cannot be used for other purposes.

One key to brevity in the training session is organization. The material to be covered in the session should be organized clearly in advance of the session. Moreover, although in many instances it may be useful to provide some flexibility in the manner in which training is conducted, the trainers should attempt to follow the plan for the training session closely.

The training sessions should be started and ended on time. There may be a temptation to extend the session if the skills targeted for mastery during the session have not been acquired. Extending training sessions beyond the scheduled time may inconvenience the trainees and decrease their willingness to participate in further training.

It is often difficult to determine just how many sessions of training will be required to achieve the training objectives. For this reason, it is usually advisable not to specify in advance that there will be a certain number of training sessions. However, it may be necessary and useful to indicate a range within which the number of required training sessions is likely to fall.

At the close of each training session, it is often useful to provide feedback indicating the objectives that have been achieved during the session and the objectives that remain to be mastered. This information can be used to indicate the need for further training sessions and to specify, within a range, the probable number of sessions required.

As in consultation interviews, the final matter to be taken up in a training session is the scheduling of the next training meeting or, in the case of the last meeting, the announcement that no further training will occur. It is usually advisable to have a regular schedule for training meetings. When there is a schedule of this kind, the discussion of the next meeting is limited to a simple reaffirmation of the schedule.

Problem Evaluation

After an intervention plan has been in effect for a suitable period, problem evaluation is undertaken to determine whether the goals of consultation have been attained and whether the plan implemented has been effective. The information provided through problem evaluation makes it possible for the parties involved in the consultation process to determine what course of action to take next. Problem evaluation may indicate that consultation should be terminated and that a postimplementation plan should be put into effect. It may suggest that new goals should be identified, or it may point to the need to alter the plan previously in operation. The various courses of action suggested through problem evaluation relate the actions taken in consultation to the behavioral outcomes of the process. Problem evaluation is the central mechanism for producing feedback to ensure that the process will be responsive to the goals established during problem identification.

In addition to its role in guiding decision making through the provision of feedback, problem evaluation may involve the production of new knowledge of importance not only to the immediate participants in the consultation process, but also to the scientific and professional communities in the field of psychology and related disciplines. Behavioral research occurring over the last quarter century has shown clearly the essential contribution that scientific studies conducted in people's natural environments make to the advancement of knowledge. Thus, for example, the scientific principles on which behavioral consultation is based have been established not only through controlled laboratory experimentation, but also through analyses of behavior applied to human problems occurring in natural settings.

Applied behavioral research generally involves a blending of service to clients and artful experimentation (Barlow, Hayes, & Nelson, 1984). Behavioral consultation provides an ideal framework for producing a fruitful blending of service and experimentation. Consultation is, of course, aimed directly at meeting service needs. Yet, it also includes the necessary conditions for applied experimentation. The link between research and practice in behavioral consultation is the data on client behavior collected over time. Data are necessary for effective decision-making in consultation. At the same time, they can be used in the production of knowledge concerning the conditions governing behavior in the natural environment.

In this chapter, we discuss the problem evaluation process as it relates both to decisions made in consultation and to research generated through consultation. In addition, it describes the problem evaluation interview, in which consultation decision-making takes place.

THE EVALUATION PROCESS

The term *evaluation* has been defined in number of different ways in the psychological literature (Maher & Kratochwill, 1980). Stufflebeam (1971) described evaluation as "the process of delineating, obtaining, and providing useful information for judging decision alternatives" (p. 40). This definition is suitable for the purposes of the present chapter because it indicates that evaluation involves not only judgmental acts, but also the selection and gathering of data on which to base judgments.

Stufflebeam's definition suggests that, in consultation, the evaluation process actually begins with the first contact between the consultant and the consultee. During the initial phases of consultation, the consultant and the consultee determine what kinds of information to gather for evaluation purposes and how that information will be obtained. These early preparations, coupled with the data collection that occurs during consultation, make the judgmental acts that take place during the problem evaluation interview possible.

Evaluating Goal Attainment

The first step in problem evaluation is to determine whether the goals of consultation have been achieved. The evaluation of goal attainment provides the necessary information for making decisions concerning future actions to be taken with respect to client behavior.

Judging the Congruence of Objectives and Behavior

In consultative problem-solving, the evaluation of goal attainment is based on judgment concerning the congruence of objectives and current client behavior. The process of evaluating goal attainment begins during problem identification with the specification of objectives and of procedures for measuring their mastery. Data collected on client behavior during consultation provide the information needed to judge the congruence of objectives and performance.

In the case of problem-centered consultation, judgments of congruence are based on the examination of client data in relation to behaviorally defined goals established through problem identification. Judgments should include a consideration of the specific behavior being assessed, the conditions under which it occurred, and the level of performance achieved. For example, consider the case of a parent who sought consultation services for their girl because she was having difficulty getting enough sleep at night. Suppose that, during problem identification, it was decided that one measure of sleep behavior would be the number of hours slept each night. The onset of sleep would be determined by parental judgments of changes in breathing after the girl went to bed. The time that sleep terminated would be tallied by the girl on awakening to her alarm. In a case like this, the measure selected to assess sleep may provide useful data up to the time of implementation and yet may prove unsatisfactory during problem evaluation. For instance, suppose that the parent came to the problem evaluation interview and reported that, on a number of occasions during plan implementation, their daughter spontaneously awakened during the middle of the night long after the parents had gone to bed, that she had great difficulty getting back to sleep, and that they had no idea how long she remained awake on these occasions. In a case such as this, the measure of behavior change would have to be judged as inadequate, and it would have to be assumed that the goal of consultation had not been achieved regardless of the sleep onset and termination times reported by the girl.

To carry the above example a little further, suppose that, rather than reporting several sleepless nights, the parent indicated that, during 4 out of 5 days of plan implementation, she had slept well. However, on one occasion, her neighbors next door, contrary to years of established custom, had held a raucous party that kept everyone in the girl's family up for a good part of the night. If unusual conditions such as wild parties were not understood to be included in the specification of consultation objectives, it would be possible to conclude that the goal of consultation had been attained even though the girl did not rest well every night.

In the event that both the assessment of behavior and the conditions under which it occurs correspond to the specifications established during problem identification, the judgment of the congruence of objectives and behavior is based solely on the performance level of the client. Insofar as client behavior matches the standard established during problem identification, goal attainment has occurred. If behavior does not match the required performance level, then, of course, it cannot be assumed that the problem has been solved.

In the case of developmental consultation, judging the congruence of objectives and behavior requires an assessment of the extent to which the behavior exhibited by the client is congruent with the general, subordinate, and performance objectives established in problem identification. In the initial problem-evaluation interview, evaluation generally focuses primarily on judgments concerning the performance objectives. However, with reiterative applications of the consultative problem-solving process, the focus broadens to include a consideration of subordinate objectives and, in the last phases of consultation, general objectives.

Essentially, the same variables are involved in evaluating the attainment of performance objectives in developmental consultation as are associated with judgments of goal attainment in problem-centered consultation. Behavior, conditions, and competency must be considered in establishing the congruence of the objectives and the performance level.

The congruence of behavior and the subordinate objectives is established by determining whether the performance goals included within the subordinate objective have been achieved. For example, suppose that a parent has selected the development of self-care skills as a subordinate objective for a 6-year-old. Assume that this goal includes performance objectives involving the boy's skills in dressing himself, washing himself, brushing his teeth, picking up his room, and making his bed. The subordinate objective of having developed self-care skills would be regarded as having been achieved when each of the performance objectives falling within the category of self-care skills has been mastered.

The congruence of behavior and the general objective is achieved when all of the subordinate objectives included within the general objective have been mastered. For instance, suppose that the parent described in the last paragraph had chosen as a general objective the development of independence. Assume that the parent included as subordinate goals the acquisition of self-care skills, the skills necessary to move about freely in the neighborhood, and skills for completing schoolwork without adult help. Given these conditions, the general goal of achieving independence skills would be reached when the three subordinate objectives had been attained.

Making Decisions on the Basis of Congruence

A determination of the congruence of behavior and objectives produces the feedback necessary to guide decision making in consultation. Judgments of congruence may be described in terms of three categories: no progress toward the goal, goal partially attained, and goal attained. Each of these categories suggests a different course of action in consultation.

The most unfortunate outcome in consultation is, of course, no progress toward the goal. The first course of action suggested by this outcome is a return to problem analysis. Reanalysis of the problem should focus initially on determining whether the plan previously in effect was implemented as intended. For example, suppose that a teacher has implemented a plan involving the use of extinction to eliminate disruptive classroom behavior and that problem evaluation reveals that the goal of consultation has not been attained. A reanalysis of the problem might well include a close examination of the reactions of both classmates and the teacher to the child's disruptive actions. If it is found that disruptions were ignored on some occasions and reinforced by attention on others, the child has been inadvertently placed on an intermittent reinforcement schedule rather than on an extinction schedule. One possible reason for failure to achieve goal attainment, then, is that the plan was not implemented as designed. Recognition of this fact would probably lead to a discussion of the feasibility of implementing the original plan. If it is possible to implement the initial plan, it will probably be left unchanged. However, if conditions in the classroom situation suggest that it is unlikely that the plan can be carried out as intended, suitable alterations have to be made.

If the plan has been implemented satisfactorily, and the goal of consultation has still not been achieved, the focus of reanalysis should shift to a reconsideration of the factors that may be controlling the child's behavior. For example, suppose that the goal of consultation is to increase the frequency of a preschool child's positive interactions with her peers and that evaluation reveals that the goal has not been achieved. A reanalysis of the problem might reveal the previously undiscovered fact that the child is being reinforced by adult attention for failure to interact effectively with peers. A new plan would have to be devised to facilitate goal attainment.

In some cases in which there has been no progress toward goal attainment, consultation may terminate. Even after the implementation of one or more carefully devised plans, the client may fail to make any progress toward the goal, and the feasibility of goal attainment may be questioned. If it seems likely that the initial goal cannot be achieved, the consultee may decide that it is useless to proceed further.

Even when the goal of consultation seems impossible to achieve, there may be some value in returning to problem analysis rather than terminating services. The case of a 10-year-old mentally retarded girl who was unable to recognize letters or numerals illustrates this point. The goal of consultation was to teach the child to identify visually presented numerals from 0 through 9. A carefully designed plan involving the use of modeling and reinforcement in a simple discrimination-learning paradigm produced no progress toward the goal. The girl seemed to be trying to learn, and she and her teacher were becoming increasingly frustrated by her obvious lack of progress on the identification task. Finally, the consultant and the consultee decided that the girl simply did not have the skills to achieve the goal, so they reinitiated problem analysis. They hypothesized that, to identify numerals, the child would have to be able to identify shapes of less complexity than numerals. Consequently, they constructed a new set of stimuli that included the most elemental visual forms, for example, a circle and a straight line. The consultant and the consultee hoped eventually to achieve the original goal by working toward it through a series of subgoals. For instance, after the child mastered the identification of elemental forms, they planned to increase the form complexity by combining elemental shapes. Thus, the child might be asked to identify a circle with a line through it or one circle on top of another as occurs in the numeral 8.

Another alternative that may be pursued when there has been no progress toward goal attainment is to return to problem identification to redefine the goal of consultation. It may happen that even though the initial goal of consultation is apparently unattainable, a revised goal can be reached. For example, suppose that the initial aim of consultation is to assist a young boy to complete academic assignments within a given time. Problem evaluation reveals no progress toward goal attainment. Yet, problem analysis has revealed that the child has the skills necessary to do these assignments. His difficulty is simply that he cannot do the work as quickly as desired. Under such conditions, the consultant and the consultee may choose to revise the goal of consultation so that the child has some chance of reaching it. After the child has experienced some success with the revised goal, more stringent performance requirements may be introduced.

Sometimes, even though a goal of consultation is not attained, there is progress toward goal attainment. The course of action to be taken depends on the kind of objective with which one is dealing. In the case of a behavioral goal or a performance objective, partial goal attainment generally suggests a return to problem analysis. For example, suppose that the goal of consultation is to increase a child's percentage of completion of arithmetic workbook assignments to the level of 85%. Problem evaluation reveals that the child is currently completing 50% of the assignments. However, the data indicate a steady improvement in completing behavior throughout the course of plan implementation. In such circumstances, the consultant and the consultee would return to problem analysis to consider whether the initial plan should be left in operation or changed. Given the steady trend of behavior toward goal attainment, the initial plan might well be left in effect. If, on the other hand, progress toward goal attainment is minimal during the initial plan-implementation period, serious consideration should be given to altering the plan.

In the case of a subordinate objective, partial goal attainment is an important issue for consultation when not all performance objectives have been considered. This state of affairs indicates a need to return to problem identification. As indicated earlier in the book, during successive problem-evaluation interviews in developmental consultation, the consultant and the consultee must determine whether the subordinate goals have been achieved. If they have not, a return to problem identification is warranted.

Sometimes, the return to problem identification involves the formal specification of previously unidentified performance objectives. Developmental consultation does not require that all performance objectives for a particular subordinate goal be specified in the initial interview during which the subordinate goal is established. Thus, the consultee may have in mind a number of performance goals related to a subordinate objective that were not identified formally in earlier problem-identification interviews. To investigate this possibility, the consultant must ask the consultee during problem evaluation whether there are additional performance goals related to the subordinate goal under consideration that have not yet been determined. If there are, problem identification is undertaken to identify these goals.

In some cases of the partial goal attainment of subordinate objectives, all of the performance objectives related to the subordinate goal have been specified previously. However, data may not have been gathered indicating the level of client performance with respect to some of these goals. Under these conditions, problem identification is undertaken to gather data and thereby to validate whether problems exist with respect to the mastery of the remaining objectives.

As in the case of subordinate objectives, the partial goal attainment of a general objective usually calls for a return to problem identification. For example, suppose that a general objective has three subordinate objectives and that two of these have been mastered. In such a situation, problem identification would be undertaken to identify performance objectives for the third subordinate goal, or to gather data on the mastery of performance objectives if they have been specified previously.

In some instances, consultation terminates following the partial attainment of behavioral, subordinate, or general goals. The consultee may feel that continued improvement is likely following consultation and that, as a consequence, there is no need for further formal consultation sessions. Termination associated with partial goal attainment may also occur when it impractical to continue consultation. For example, in educational settings, partial goal attainment may occur at the end of the school year or just before the client or the consultee is transferred to another school district.

Happily, the goals of consultation are often achieved. In this fortunate state of affairs, the consultant and the consultee should proceed to the next phase in the problem evaluation process.

Evaluating Plan Effectiveness

The next step in the problem evaluation process is the evaluation of plan effectiveness. Information concerning plan effectiveness does not influence direct decision-making about the case at hand, but it may be useful fui solving future problems of a similar nature. For example, if an abrupt change in arithmetic performance follows plan implementation involving a certain kind of arithmetic skill instruction, the consultee has some evidence that the particular form of instruction may be useful in other cases involving similar deficits in arithmetic.

The central task to be accomplished in evaluating plan effectiveness is to select and implement an appropriate evaluation strategy and is usually accomplished through the use of a single-case research or evaluation design. An evaluation design allows the specification of when observations of client behavior will take place and when plan implementation will occur in relation to client observations.

Plan evaluation may involve any of the broad range of designs developed for use in experimental research and, more recently, adapted for use in empirical clinical practice (Barlow *et al.*, 1984). Single-case time-series designs can be useful in evaluating plan effectiveness in behavioral consultation. These designs involve the collection of data over a series of points in time. In this section of the chapter, we discuss some evaluation strategies that can be applied in behavioral consultation. No attempt will be made to cover all of the many possible options for constructing an evaluation scheme in consultation. More detailed discussions are presented elsewhere (see Barlow *et al.*, 1984; Kazdin, 1982b). Rather, the designs and evaluation schemes presented are intended to illustrate a range of techniques that may be implemented in consultation. As the consultant becomes familiar with the evaluation strategies, he or she should recognize that many different strategies may be used in combination to create unique methods of evaluating consultation services. The specific evaluation needs encountered in consultation service and research activities often require unique and creative strategies.

Case Study Methods

Case study methodology has been used relatively often in school-based consultation research and practice. Traditionally, the term *case study* has referred to the relatively uncontrolled and subjectively described study of a single case. However, as we describe in this section of the chapter, case studies need not be restricted to this type of methodology. Various strategies can be used by the consultant to improve on the inferences that are drawn from case study techniques. It is important to emphasize the contributions that case study methods can make to consultation research and practice. First, case study methods often provide knowledge about a particular technique or strategy that cannot be obtained by other methods. Case study methods are useful in this regard because they provide the practitioner with the option of conducting a study of a single case. Case study methods also allow practitioners to be involved in research activities in consultation (see Kratochwill, 1985). Case study methods may not involve some of the restrictions that often accompany more well-controlled single-case time-series research-activities (Kazdin, 1981c).

Case study methods also provide the consultation researcher with alternatives to traditional group designs. Group designs often involve various ethical and legal barriers when adapted to applied settings. In this regard, case study research often allows consultants to become involved directly in treatment activities without some of the usual barriers to the use of group designs.

Case study strategies as applied to the consultation process are typically focused on therapeutic or intervention activities. In this regard, the consultant is interested in evaluating the efficacy of some intervention program as implemented by the consultee. Usually, case study strategies are characterized by the absence of the variety of experimental controls that are associated with research (Kazdin, 1980d, 1981c). The absence of experimental control means that various sources of internal validity are not addressed within the usual case study. That is, the consultant is unable to rule out many rival interpretations of the observed or reported changes in the behavior of the client. Thus, these types of case study investigations are labeled *preexperimental* because they do not contain the experimental and statistical controls that would allow the consultant to draw firm conclusions from the study. Nevertheless, the consultants' ability to rule out various threats to validity is usually a matter of degree. In this regard, it should be noted that even well-controlled experimental studies may contain various sources of artifacts, bias, and invalidity that make rival alternatives plausible. Yet, when threats to validity can be assessed in case studies, there is a higher degree of inference that the intervention produced change in the client's behavior. In the sections that follow, we describe a variety of strategies that the consultation practitioner and researcher may consider when implementing a preexperimental case study to evaluate consultation services. More detailed information related to case study methodology generally, and to the contributions that this strategy can make to research and practice, are presented in Kazdin (1981c) and Kratochwill (1985).

Methodological Considerations

Table 6-1 provides a series of methodological factors that the consultant can take into account in order to draw valid inferences from case study investigations. Each of these dimensions is elaborated on briefly below.

Type of Data. Case studies can vary greatly in the type of data that the consultant gathers. Traditionally, case studies have involved the subjective description of client progress including, such things as reported impres-

TABLE 6 1.   Dimensions of Case Study Methodology[a]

Methodological factor	Dimension	
Type of data	Subjective	Objective
Assessment occasions	Pre-post	Repeated
Planned vs. *ex post facto*	Not manipulated	Manipulated
Projections of performance	Chronic	Transient
Effect size	Small	Large
Effect impact	Delayed	Immediate
Number of subjects	$N = 1$	$N > 1$
Diversity of subjects	Nondiverse	Diverse
Standardization of assessment and treatment	Nonstandardized	Standardized
Integrity of assessment and treatment	No monitoring	Monitoring
Impact of treatment	Single	Multiple
Formal design structure	No design	Minimal A/B
Social validation	No validation	Validation
Analysis of results	No analysis	Formal analysis
Generalization and follow-up	No assessment	Assessment

[a]From T. R. Kratochwill (1985). Case study research in school psychology *School Psychology Review*, *14*, 204–215. Reproduced by permission.

sions of self-report data from the consultee. As we noted in Chapter 3, the consultant or the consultee may be able to gather more objective data, such as direct observational measures in classroom or other naturalistic settings. A variety of measures can be used to conduct a continuous assessment over various phases of case study investigation. Those most readily applied include direct observation, self-monitoring, permanent product measures, and physiological recordings. Usually, the more traditional assessment devices that are used to assess personality and social functioning, such as IQ tests, projective tests, and self-report inventories, are not as readily adaptable to repeated assessment (Hersen & Barlow, 1976; Kazdin, 1982b).

A number of case study reports have been presented in the school-psychology consultation-literature in which very few data were gathered (e.g., Ajchenbaum & Reynolds, 1981; Randolph, 1979). In each of these investigations, the consultant relied primarily on a subjective description of the client's progress. Also, a characteristic of some of these studies is that the data are not presented in a formal way, and readers of the report must therefore rely on the investigator's description of the data to determine their credibility. Direct measures of progress should supplement more subjective data whenever possible.

Assessment Occasions. The number and timing of assessment occasions in a case study has a direct bearing on the consultant's ability to draw valid inferences. In some case studies, assessment occurs before and at the end of the intervention program. However, the case study can be greatly improved if assessment is conducted repeatedly over the course of the consultation. This type of continuous assessment allows the consultant to rule out a greater number of threats to validity then would be typical in a prepost assessment format. Usually, the assessment measures must be gathered for a long enough duration to allow the consultant and the consultee to determine whether the data are stable. For example, if the data display great variability and/or trend, the consultant and consultee will have difficulty determining whether the treatment effects are apparent. Strategies for the evaluation of data have been presented in the single-case research-design literature (e.g., Parsonson & Baer, 1978).

Planned versus Ex Post Facto Case Studies. The degree to which valid inferences can be drawn from a case study also relates to whether it is an *ex post facto* (i.e., a passive observational) strategy or one in which there is active manipulation of the treatment variable. Generally, active implementation of the treatment increases the evidence for concluding that this variable was responsible for the changes observed during the process of consultation. In contrast, in passive-observational case-studies, the consultant and the consultee have no direct control over the treatment, and the treatment is free to vary or is not subjected to the usual "experimental" manipulations (Cook & Campbell, 1979). For example, a consultee may implement a plan before the formal consultation process. Such a *post hoc* plan would not carry the same degree of validity as one that was planned and implemented during formal consultation.

Consider also an example from the consultation research literature. In a study by Miller and Kratochwill (1979) a parent terminated a time-out procedure during the treatment phase. After this unplanned return to baseline, the child's behavior returned to pretreatment levels. When the parent was instructed to reinstate the plan, the problem was again eliminated. This evaluation procedure can be construed as a passive observational paradigm because it was not part of the manipulation initially planned by the investigators. Nevertheless, the researchers did not directly manipulate this variable, and the evidence of its controlling effect was thus reduced.

Past and Future Projections of Performance. When a clinical disorder or problem is chronic, it is unlikely that change will occur without some type of formal intervention. If the consultant can demonstrate that the disorder was chronic before the implementation of the treatment plan and that dramatic change occurred once the treatment was implemented, inference of the effect is stronger than without this type of history. In contrast, some problems may be quite transient and are likely to respond to any mild intervention. Therefore, the history of the problem takes on importance in drawing inferences from the case study.

To take into account this aspect of the problem, the consultant must determine and report the history of the case. This report can be accomplished in at least four ways (Kratochwill, 1985). First, the consultant can examine case records or other information available to determine whether the case is a chronic problem. This information may be available from case research or in the referral data from the consultee. The point is that the consultant must examine some data to determine that the problem did not improve with the simple passage of time. A second way to determine whether the problem is a chronic one is to gather baseline data (see Chapter 3). Extended baseline assessment sometimes provides the consultant with evidence that the disorder does not change. Third, it may be possible for the consultant to examine the usual course of the disorder or problem. In some cases the empirical literature can provide information of this type. For example, children experiencing conduct disorder are unlikely to change without some potent treatment. Finally, the consultant may be able to draw more valid inferences if it can be demonstrated that previous attempts to treat the problem have been unsuccessful. For example, the consultee may report that several well-developed attempts made to change the child's behavior have met with a lack of success.

Effect Size. Once a treatment has been applied to the clinical problem by the measures selected for consultation, the consultant must take into account the effect size. When the effect size is relatively large, a greater degree of inference can be drawn than when rather small changes occur. A large effect can be determined by several visual analysis strategies (Parsonson & Baer, 1978). Also, an effect that is clinically important, such as reducing aggressive behaviors to zero levels, is likely to allow a greater degree of inference that the treatment was responsible for the change than if clinical criteria are not used (see the later section on social validity).

Effect Impact. In addition to the effect size, the consultant should take into account the specific impact of the treatment. If the consultant finds that the impact of the treatment is relatively immediate, a greater degree of inference can be drawn than if the treatment takes a considerable period of time (e.g., weeks or months) to show in effect. Essentially, the consultant hopes to rule out such effects as maturation or regression by taking into account the treatment impact. Again, an evaluation of the impact of the treatment must take into account various characteristics of the data that are gathered. For example, investigators should note score overlap, variability, and trends as compared to any baseline data series.

Number of Subjects. Case study investigations are not limited to one subject, although this is a common focus. When the consultant is able to implement treatment across a number of clients, a greater degree of inference for the treatment effect is possible than when the treatment is implemented on only one client. Generally, the greater the number of cases that show successful change with treatment, the more likely it is that extraneous events are not responsible for the change. The treatment can be implemented across single subjects in a replication series, or it can be implemented on an intact group of subjects at the same time. Both of these procedures will strengthen the study, but replication across individual subjects at different times is preferred. We realize that, in most situations, it is impossible to replicate consultation services across multiple cases. However, occasionally, the consultant may have an opportunity to replicate a package treatment program across clients who are experiencing similar problems (e.g., elective mutism, social withdrawal, conduct problems, or learning disabilities). When replication across multiple cases can be scheduled, and when the treatment is consistently effective, greater validity can be established.

Diversity of Subjects. In addition to the replication across similar clients experiencing similar problems, the consultant has the option of involving diverse clients in a replication series. Successful replications can occur across subjects when diverse characteristics, such as race, social class, age, and type of disorder, are taken into account (Hersen & Barlow, 1976). When replications demonstrate consistent effects of the intervention, inferences drawn about the intervention are stronger than when diversity is not apparent. Thus, validity threats can be reduced when diverse cases can be scheduled in the case-study replication series.

Standardization of Assessment and Treatment. Whenever possible, the consultant should use an assessment and treatment that are relatively standardized (see also the discussion of this issue in Chapter 9). The term *standardization* refers to a number of specific procedures. First, the assessment and the treatment need to be explicitly defined, and a protocol for their implementation must be developed (Kazdin, 1988). The protocol allows the consultee to implement the treatment consistently and also allows a check on implementation integrity during consultation (see below). Second, standardization allows for replication across other clients. As noted above, without a standardized assessment and treatment, exact replication is impossible. Third, standardization allows other practitioners to implement the assessment and the treatment in applied settings once they have been demonstrated to be successful.

Standardization may occur through procedures that have already been developed in existing programs (e.g., published instruments, parent training manuals, standardized audio cassettes, and comprehensive intervention programs for classrooms). As an example of a standardized treatment program, Sheridan, Kratochwill, and Elliott (1989) developed a treatment

program consisting of a manual, goal setting, self-monitoring, and a reinforcement strategy to facilitate social interactions among socially withdrawn children. The program was successfully implemented through a
teacher-only or a combination teacher–parent consultation format. Replication occurred across two client pairs within each consultation format. In
addition, the program involved a standardized assessment package for the
direct observation of school and home behaviors.

Integrity of Assessment and Treatment. Standardizing assessment and
treatment does not always guarantee that they will be implemented in the
way they were designed. To determine correct implementation, the consultant should establish the integrity of the implementation of assessment
and treatment (e.g., Johnston & Pennypacker, 1980; Peterson *et al.*, 1982;
Sechrest, West, Phillips, Wagner, & Yeaton, 1979; Yeaton & Sechrest,
1981). The usual observation of the dependent variable and checks on
accuracy and reliability are considered insufficient to allow conclusions
regarding the integrity of the implementation of the treatment. In addition,
the consultant must schedule separate and repeated checks on the implementation of the treatment to determine if there is a functional relation
between the target behavior and the treatment variable.

Several procedures can be used to check the integrity of the treatment
in case study investigations (see Chapter 9 for a more detailed discussion).
First, the investigator can check the integrity in the same way that the
accuracy and reliability of the dependent variable are assessed. Specifically, multiple observer checks can be scheduled to determine whether the
treatment is being implemented as specified. Although this procedure may
not be cost-efficient under some conditions, periodic checks may be scheduled by the consultant to determine whether the treatment has been implemented consistently across various phases of the project. Second, the consultant can continually check on the accuracy of the independent variable
after reviewing the protocol that has been standardized in the treatment
plan.

Impact of Treatment. In the usual case-study investigation, the effects of
the treatment are evaluated on one or few outcome measures. Typically, in
behavioral consultation, a single target behavior is chosen for treatment;
yet the inference that can be drawn from a case study can be increased
when multiple measures of client behavior are assessed. This point is
important because several dimensions of client functioning may be influenced by a particular treatment (Kazdin & Wilson, 1978). It is also very
desirable to know how pervasive the treatment effects are in improving
client functioning. Multiple assessment provides information about the
choice of a particular target behavior, which is sometimes guided by the
impact that the behavior has on other positive and negative behaviors

(Kazdin, 1982b; Voeltz & Evans, 1982). Finally, assessing the impact of treatment may be improved with multiple measures because the consultant can provide more information on both the theoretical and the conceptual underpinnings of the treatment.

An example of multiple measurement occurred in a case study by Bloom and Zimmerman (1981), who reported the successful application of a social learning approach to reduce the unpopularity of an 11-year-old girl in a summer camp. The target behaviors chosen were lack of contact with class members during free-choice time and a negative conversational style. The client improved her performance on both of these measure following implementation of the intervention program. The assessment of treatment effects on multiple measures improves the inferences that can be drawn from the case study investigation.

Formal Design Structure. Preexperimental case studies are usually distinguished from all controlled research strategies by the lack of a formal design structure. Case studies can be greatly improved if the consultant uses some type of baseline-and-treatment, or A/B, experimental-design format. Basic to drawing inferences from case study data is comparison. A baseline series allows the consultant to make some minimal statements regarding the effects of treatment when compared with this series. Thus, whenever possible, the consultant should consider structuring the study so that, at a minimum, an A/B design is used.

The A/B design is initiated by the collection of baseline data over a series of points in time. Intervention in the form of plan implementation then occurs, and a second set of observations is made. In some cases, the treatment occurs continuously throughout the second observational period. However, in other instances, the treatment plan takes place just once or twice, and behavior is measured at several points following plan implementation.

Figure 6-1 shows data from a consultation case that illustrates the A/B design. The case illustrated in the figure involved the familiar problem of excessive talking out of turn in the classroom. However, the case was somewhat unusual in that the child's peers, as well as the teacher, were concerned about this problem. The plan used to solve the problem included an agreement on the part of the teacher and the child's peers to ignore talking out. In addition, the consultant modeled the appropriate procedures for making verbal contributions in the classroom setting. For instance, the consultant showed the child how to raise his hand and how to wait to be acknowledged by the teacher before speaking. As indicated in the figure, his talking out decreased sharply during plan implementation.

The basic A/B time-series design is used widely in consultation because it is usually the easiest of the available designs to apply in investigating the effects of a single intervention on the behavior of one individual.

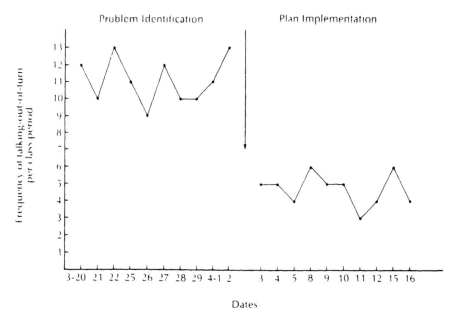

FIGURE 6-1. Modification of talking without permission.

The application of the design requires only that baseline data be collected following the problem identification interview and that the data collection continue during plan implementation.

The central problem of the design, as noted above, is that it does not control for the possibility that an event occurring at the same time as the intervention may have produced the observed changes in behavior. In the literature on evaluation, this problem is referred to as the failure to control for history involving events other than the intervention that may affect behavior. For example, in the case described below, some other event occurring simultaneously with plan implementation may have produced the observed changes in talking-out behavior.

Social Validation. Objective measures can be supplemented by subjective measures of behavior change in case study investigations. Such measures are being used increasingly in applied research and have generally been referred to as *social validation* (Kazdin, 1977b; Wolf, 1978). In social validation the behavior of a client can be compared to the behavior of peers who are not considered deviant. Another component of social validation refers to a subjective evaluation of the client's performance. Such measures are solicited from individuals in the natural environment. When the consultant finds that the behavior change has reached a clinical criterion, the program outcomes are evaluated according to this criterion.

Normative comparisons were reported by Tarpley and Saudargas (1981), who selected two preschool children to participate in a case study. The target child was a 4-year-old male who was referred by his teacher to the consulting school psychologist because of extreme social withdrawal and isolation. The comparison child was a 4-year-old female who was described by the teacher as being generally average in social behaviors. Following baseline measures on social interaction, crying, laughing and smiling, and social interaction with the teacher, an intervention program was established. The results suggested that there were marked differences between the two children during baseline in social interaction, crying, and laughing and smiling, but not in social interaction with the teacher. However, once the treatment was implemented, the data for the target child became indistinguishable from those for the comparison child, thereby indicating that normative data could be used as a criterion toward which to develop interventions in this setting. Generally, these procedures increase the inferences that can be drawn from a case study and improve it overall from a methodological standpoint.

Analysis of Results. When consultants present data from a case project, it is rare to find that the data have been subjected to any type of formal analysis. Nevertheless, a formal visual and/or statistical data analysis greatly improve the inferences that can be drawn from the program. In a formal data analysis, repeated measurement across at least the A and B phases is necessary (It is unlikely that pre- and posttest measurement will allow any type of formal data analysis to occur.)

Data analysis can occur on a number of different dimensions. In visual analysis, the magnitude of change revolves around score overlap, variability, and trend. If the behavior never occurs before baseline, a sudden change once treatment is implemented allows the researcher to assess the magnitude of change relatively easily. In addition, if the behavior occurs at a stable low frequency before treatment and shows a dramatic increase when treatment is implemented, a significant change is more easily discerned; however, when change in neither magnitude nor rate is significant, data interpretation through visual analysis must be approached with considerable caution. In such cases, a more formal statistical analysis may be considered (Kratochwill, 1978).

Generalization and Follow-Up. Intervention case studies can be greatly improved by the assessment and programming of the generalization and maintenance of the target behaviors (Stokes & Baer, 1977). Typically, generalization and follow-up are recommended in most outcome research in psychotherapy (Kazdin, 1988), and there is no need to exclude it as an important ingredient in drawing valid inferences in case study projects.

Generalization can be assessed across several dimensions, including

behaviors, settings, and subjects, as well as over time. In the latter case,
generalization is usually regarded as follow-up or maintenance assessment. Measures can be selected that are convenient for assessment generalization such as self-monitoring or self-report data (see Chapter 9).

Single-Case Designs

In some cases, the consultant may be able to adopt a formal single-case
research design to evaluate the effectiveness of the consultation services.
However, in most cases, this type of design strategy is used primarily in
empirical research (see Chapter 9 for a further discussion of the efficacy of
single-case designs in consultation research). The various designs to be
discussed in this section are summarized in Table 6-2. Basically, there are
three major classes of design types: within-series elements, between-series
elements, and combined-series elements (Hayes, 1981). Within each of

TABLE 6-2. Major Types of Time Series Designs and Associated Characteristics

Design type	Representative example	Characteristics
Within-series elements	Simple phase change (e.g., A/B, A/B/A, A/B/A/B) Complex phase change (e.g., interaction element: B/B + C/B, C/B + C/C, B + C/C/B + C, B + C/B/B + C; changing criterion element)	In these design elements, estimates of variability level and trend *within* a data series are assessed under similar conditions, the independent variable is introduced, and the concomitant changes are assessed in stability, level, and trend across the phases of a single data series.
Between-series elements	Alternating-treatments design	In these design elements, estimates of variability, level, and trend in a data series are assessed in measures within a specific condition and across time. Outcome is assessed by comparing two or more of the series.
Combined-series elements	Multiple baseline (e.g., across subjects, across behaviors, across situations)	In these design elements, comparisons are made both between and within a data series. Repetitions of a single, simple phase-change are scheduled, each with a new series, in which both the length and the timing of the phase change differ across repetitions. Changes in variability, level, and trend are assessed within phases across the repetitions.

these design types, data from a single subject or aggregated from a group (e.g., a classroom) can be used in the evaluation of consultation services. Within-series designs involve comparing data patterns across different conditions or phases of a single data series (e.g., consultant or consultee data in the baseline treatment phases). As noted in the table, there are three types of designs in this group.

Between-series designs provide the consultant and/or the consultee an evaluation strategy for comparing two or more treatment conditions within a single individual or group. The logic of this evaluation strategy rests on making comparisons within two or more data series measured over time. Although there are two forms of the design, the alternating-treatments design is the most commonly used procedure in applied settings.

Combined-series designs are named for the evaluation of client performance both within and between data series established by the consultant researcher. As can be observed in the table, the multiple-baseline design and its variations are the design type making up this class of experimental procedures.

Within-Series Designs. Several applied investigations illustrate the application of within-series designs; the A/B/A/B procedure offers the most straightforward illustration of this design logic. The A/B/A/B design offers a procedure for investigating the effects of one or more interventions on the same individual or group of individuals. In the simplest case, the A/B/A/B design involves one intervention replicated across phases of the experiment. Following a baseline period, the intervention is first introduced. Subsequently, the intervention is withdrawn and then reinstated so that there is a "replication" of the experimental procedure.

An investigation by Knight and McKenzie (1974) mentioned in Chapter 5 illustrates features of the A/B/A/B design. As the reader may recall, the purpose of the experiment was to determine the effectiveness of techniques that would be practical for parents to use to reduce thumb sucking at bedtime. The intervention in the study involved making parental story-reading contingent on the absence of thumb sucking. Thus, whenever thumb sucking started, the parent stopped reading. When thumb sucking ceased, reading would begin again. Three children participated in the study, a 3-year-old, a 6-year-old, and an 8-year-old. As shown in Figure 6-2, an A/B/A/B design was used to assess the effects of the contingent-reading intervention on thumb sucking in each of the children. In the case of Jennifer, whose behavior is summarized at the bottom of Figure 6-2, it was necessary to add another baseline treatment period to the design. According to the authors, Jennifer was distracted by items on bookshelves near her bed during the initial phase of intervention. Thus, it was necessary to relocate her bed before the experimental treatment could take effect.

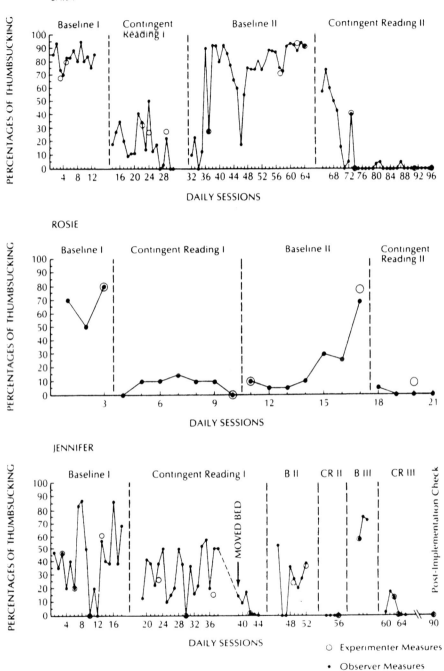

FIGURE 6-2. Thumb sucking behavior in three children. Each point represents the percentage of time the child sucked her thumb during daily bedtime reading sessions. The arrow in the graph for Jennifer indicates a relocation of the bed away from apparently distracting stimulus materials. [Source: M. K. Knight & H. S. McKenzie. (1974). Elimination of bedtime thumb-sucking in home settings through contingent reading. *Journal of Applied Behavior Analysis, 7,* 33–38.]

The principal advantage of the A/B/A/B design is that it reduces the likelihood that history in the form of extraneous influence occurring with the intervention are responsible for the observed changes in behavior. Note, however, that it is still possible for history to effect experimental outcome in the A/B/A/B design. Nevertheless, the chances of such an occurrence are reduced.

Several potential disadvantages are associated with the A/B/A/B design (Kazdin, 1982b). One disadvantage relates to the fact that many behaviors are not easily reversed or will return to the baseline levels once the treatment is withdrawn. Academic skills provide an obvious example. A child who had learned to add well is not likely to forget that skill. One may effect a reversal by withdrawing instruction before the skill has been thoroughly mastered. However, consultants and consultees working on problems involving academic skills would probably have little interest in pursuing this course of action.

A second problem in the A/B/A/B design is that it may not always be practical or ethical to reverse behavior even if it seems likely that it could be done. For example, if a consultant and a consultee have succeeded in reducing aggressive behavior in a child, they may not be willing to reinstate aggressive behavior if it poses a serious physical threat to the child's peers.

It may also happen in consultation that there will be an interest in determining the effects of more than one intervention on client behavior. For instance, the plan described above to illustrate the A/B design involved two variables: modeling and extinction in the form of ignoring talking-out behavior. It would, of course, have been possible to treat these two aspects of the plan as separate interventions and to evaluate the effects of each on behavior. Basically, this approach involves a complex interaction design. In this type of situation, two or more interventions can actually be compared.

A study by Wells, Conners, Imber, and Delamater (1981) illustrates both simple and complex phase changes in a design strategy. These researchers were interested in examining the effects of various psychoactive medications alone and in combination with a self-control program implemented for a 9-year-old child identified as hyperactive. Observational data were taken on the child's classroom behavior, on a psychiatric inpatient unit. The measures included an assessment of excessive gross-motor behavior, inappropriate vocalizations, off-task behavior, and on-task with no deviant behavior. The design and treatment sequence consisted of an A/B/A/C/CD/A_1D/CD design, where A was baseline, A^1 was pseudo medication, B was dextroamphetamine (Dexedrine) treatment, C was methylphenidate (Ritalin) treatment, and D was a behavioral self-control program. As presented in Figure 6-3, the data indicate the Dexedrine was unsuccessful in improving the child's performance. This finding, in turn, led the researchers to introduce Ritalin following a second baseline period.

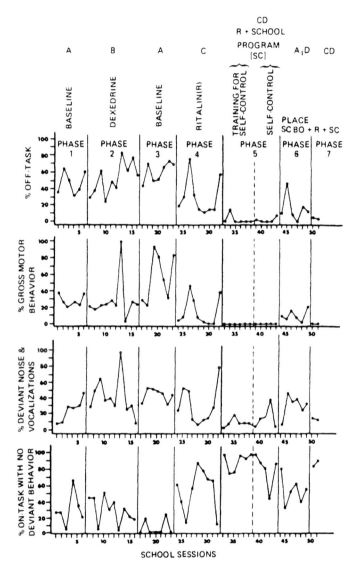

FIGURE 6-3. Percentage occurrence in the classroom of off-task behavior, gross motor behavior, deviant noise and vocalizations, and on-task behavior with no other deviant behavior recorded, measured across baseline, medication, and placebo phases. [Source: K. L. Wells, C. K. Conners, L. Imber, and A. Delamater. (1981). Use of single-subject methodology in clinical decision-making with a hyperactive child on the psychiatric inpatient unit. *Behavioral Assessment, 3,* 359–369. Copyright 1981 by Association for the Advancement of Behavior Therapy. Reproduced by permission.]

With the exception of Sessions 26 and 32, the child's response to Ritalin was generally positive across the selected outcome measures.

During the CD phase, Ritalin was combined with a self-control program involving self-monitoring of on-task behavior and a self-administered token system. As the data in the $C/CD/A_1D/CD$ sequence indicate, the Ritalin plus self-control treatment-combination appeared most effective. Neither Ritalin (C phase) nor behavioral self-control (A_1D phase) alone was as potent as the interactive effects.

Another within-series design procedure is the changing-criterion design. This design is used to evaluate the effects of a treatment on a single gradually acquired target behavior. Typically, this design is applied when the researcher is interested in evaluating the effectiveness of shaping behavior gradually across some time period. The effect of the intervention is demonstrated by showing that behavior changes gradually over the course of the treatment program. Rather than withdrawing or withholding the treatment, the design uses several subphases within the primary intervention phase. In this subphase, a different criterion for performance is specified. When performance meets the criterion level established by the investigator, more stringent criteria are established, and this process is repeated across the subphases of the design.

During the baseline phase a single target response is typically monitored until a stable response is achieved. Baseline data are used to establish initial criterion level, and treatment is initiated and continued until the behavior stabilizes at that level. Typically, the reinforcement schedules and the criterion levels are then increased. The remainder of the phases progress in a steplike manner, with criterion adjustment more closely approximating some terminal level. An example of the changing criterion design was presented by Hall and Fox (1977, Experiment 2), who modified the academic performance of two boys. The boys in the study had refused to complete their assignments or had completed them at rather low rates. In the project, each student was provided a worksheet that included math problems. The student was also required to work on the math problems before recess. Following the baseline phase indicating the number of problems completed correctly, a treatment program was implemented in which a child was told that he could go to recess and play basketball following the correct completion of a specified number of problems. If the child failed to complete the problems correctly, he remained in the room at recess until they were completed correctly. The investigators established the criterion for this first subphase of the intervention program by calculating the mean for the baseline and selecting the criterion at the next highest whole number. The effects of the program for one child, Dennis, are presented in Figure 6-4. The figure shows that the criterion-level performance as illustrated by the numbers at the top of each subphase was consistently met across the series of subphases. In the final phase, textbook problems were substituted for problems included in the previous phases. At that point, the criterion-level performance also remained in effect. Generally, Dennis's

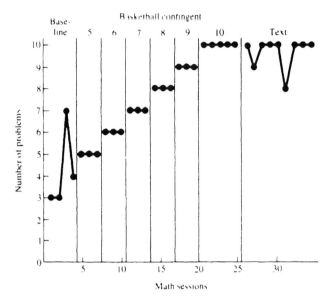

FIGURE 6-4. A record of the number of math problems correctly solved by Dennis, a "behavior-disordered" boy, during baseline, recess, and the opportunity-to-play-basketball contingent on changing levels of performance and return-to-textbook phases. [Source: Hall, R. V. & Fox, R. G. (1977). Changing criterion designs: An alternative applied behavior analysis procedure. In C. C. Etzel, J. M. LeBlanc, & D. M. Baer (Eds.), *New developments in behavioral research: Theory, methods, and applications. In honor of Sidney W. Bijou.* Hillsdale, NJ: Erlbaum.]

performance closely corresponded to the criterion shifts that were established during the final phase.

In the changing-criterion design, several specific aspects are important in drawing valid inferences, including the phase length, the number and magnitude of criterion shifts, the directionality of change, and potential ambiguity due to characteristics of the data. Clearly, the design appears to be most appropriate for behaviors that are acquired or shaped gradually and that do not require a withdrawal or reversal of treatment. Generally, only one behavior is selected for treatment, so that some inferences can be made about the change in that specific behavior. Further discussion of the changing criterion design can be found in Kazdin (1982).

Between-Series Designs. Between-series designs allow the researcher to compare two or more treatments or conditions and to examine their relative effectiveness on a given outcome measure. The alternating-treatments design is the most common between-series design strategy used in applied and clinical research (Barlow *et al.*, 1984). The alternating-treatments design involves a rapid alteration of two or more conditions, and it exposes the client to the separate treatment components for equal periods of time. The treatment is alternated from one session to another or across two sessions each day, the sequence of treatment administration being determined randomly or through counterbalancing. Differences between or among the treatments are examined, rather than differences over time within one condition. Gettinger (1985) used an alternating-treatments design to study the effects of teacher-directed versus student-directed instruction and cues versus no cues in improving spelling performance. In the study, nine children received four alternating experimental treatments during a 16-week spelling program. The two cuing procedures (cues versus no cues) were alternated weekly, and the student-directed and teacher-directed components were alternated biweekly. Mean pretest, posttest, and retention scores were retained for each treatment condition; they indicated improved spelling accuracy for all four conditions. Generally, the data demonstrated that a student-directed procedure incorporating visual and verbal cues produced the highest posttest accuracy scores.

Another example of the alternating-treatments design is presented in a study by Rose (1984), who investigated the relative effectiveness of two oral reading procedures consisting of reading preview, or prepractice, and procedures, including a silent condition in which the child read silently an assigned reading passage before reading the passage out loud, and a listening condition, in which the teacher read the assigned selection out loud and the student followed along silently before the student read the passage out loud. In the study, six elementary-school-aged learning-disabled students (three boys and three girls) participated. The session began with the student reading a 2-minute time-sample from the previous day's reading assignment. Instruction was not provided during these performance sessions. The words read correctly were determined by subtracting the error words from the total number of words read. The author took this number and divided it by 2 minutes to arrive at the rate measure of the words read correctly. The reading instruction under the two treatment conditions and the baseline control were then alternated across school days.

The results presented in Figure 6-5 shows that for the six children the author found that the systematic prepractice procedure generally corresponded to higher performance levels than no prepractice or baseline. Also, Rose found that the listening procedure resulted in a higher rate of words read correctly than the silent procedure. However, the results were not consistent for all the children, in that the differential effectiveness of the two treatment procedures were not clear for the third subject and another subject whose data are not shown in the figure.

The alternating-treatments design is being used increasingly in applied and clinical research. However, it does contain some potential problems. The interactive effects of two treatments or conditions are often difficult to determine, especially with some clinical problems. The carryover or generalization effects of one intervention may confound inferences that might be made with regard to the other treatment. Both alternating-treatments and other designs in this category depend on showing changes in a given behavior across sessions or time periods. The design

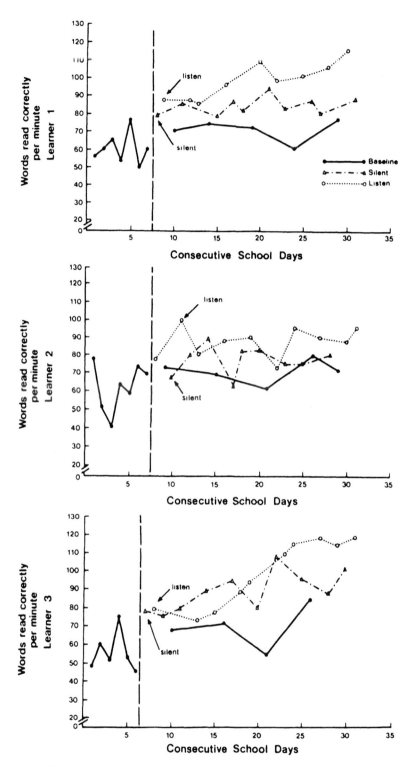

FIGURE 6-5. The effects of systematic prepractice procedures on the rates of correctly read words.

requires a rather dramatic shift in direction for interventions, and generally, interventions suitable for these designs need to show rapid effects when terminated. If the effects of the first intervention linger after it is no longer presented in a subsequent condition, the intervention that follows may be confounded by a prior effect.

Combined-Series Designs. Combined-series designs involve comparisons both between and within data series in the experiment. The researcher schedules repetitions of the simple phase change, but each series is staggered across different subjects, behaviors, or situations. The most common procedure in this category is the multiple-baseline design with replications across subjects, behaviors, or situations.

In some cases, it may be of interest to determine the effects of an intervention on more than one client behavior. The *multiple-baseline design across behaviors* can be used for this purpose. The multiple-baseline design across behaviors is initiated by collecting simultaneous baseline data on more than one behavior. After an initial baseline period, intervention occurs with respect to one of the behaviors being recorded. Data collection continues. Then intervention occurs with respect to another of the behaviors of concern. The strategy of periodic intervention on successive behaviors is followed until intervention has taken place for all of the behaviors of interest.

Ballard and Glynn (1975) conducted an investigation described in Chapter 5 illustrating a variation of the multiple-baseline technique across behaviors. The design of this investigation is illustrated in Figure 6-6. As the reader may recall, the study dealt with the application of self-management behaviors by students to improve their skills in story writing. The ability of students to direct their own learning is of obvious importance in any area of the curriculum, but it is particularly so in areas involving written composition because of the inordinate amount of teacher time that may be required to check themes and other written work. Ballard and Glynn investigated the hypothesis that, through the application of self-management techniques, students would be able to improve their own writing abilities.

Fourteen 8- and 9-year-old children participated in the study. The investigation began with a 12-day baseline period during which records were taken of the percentage of the allotted time that the children spent on the story-writing task, the number of complete sentences in the stories, the number of descriptive words (i.e., adverbs and adjectives) used in the stories, and the number of action words (i.e., verbs expressing action or movement) in the stories.

Following the baseline period, a self-assessment plus self-recording treatment was introduced. This treatment remained in effect throughout the rest of the experiment. To initiate self-assessment and recording, the

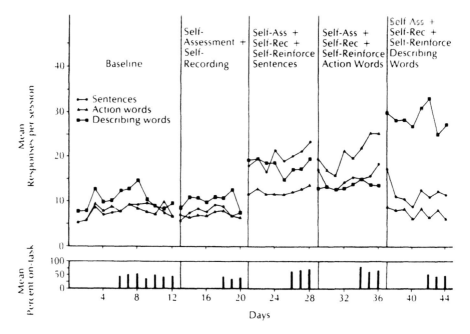

FIGURE 6-6. Mean number of sentences, different action words, and different describing words, and mean percentage of on-task behavior throughout the study. [Source: K. D. Ballard & T. Glynn. (1975). Behavioral self-management in story writing with elementary school children. *Journal of Applied Behavior Analysis, 8,* 393.]

children were taught to check their work against criteria presented in a "good-writing chart" displayed on the wall of the classroom and were given counting sheets for use in recording their own writing performance. The intent of this treatment was to separate whatever effects self-assessment and recording might have on behavior from the effects of self-reinforcement.

The multiple-baseline technique was introduced after self-assessment plus self-recording had been in effect for several days. The first behavior to be modified was the production of complete sentences in the stories. The intervention used to effect a change in sentence production involved having the children give themselves points for the sentences in their stories. The points could be used to purchase the privilege of engaging in a range of desirable activities in the classroom. After a number of days, the children gave themselves points for the production of action words. In the final phase of the study, points were administered for descriptive words.

The multiple-baseline design across behaviors has the advantage of reducing the likelihood that extraneous factors occurring at the time of intervention are responsible for the observed changes in behavior (Kazdin, 1982b). If it can be shown that an intervention affects only the behavior that it is targeted toward and that the same intervention can be used to influence other behaviors at different times, it is extremely unlikely that the observed behavioral changes are the result of extraneous influences.

A second advantage of the multiple-baseline technique is that, unlike the A/B/A/B design, it can be used in the study of behaviors that cannot be easily reversed or that consultants and consultees may not wish to reverse. The Ballard and Glynn (1975) study provides an example of a situation in which it would be unlikely that the individuals involved in the instructional program would want to reverse the behaviors. The teacher in this study undoubtedly felt that it was important for the children to learn to write in complete sentences and to make use of descriptive and action words in their writing. It seems unlikely that she would want to reverse the gains in these behaviors.

The central problem with the multiple-baseline design across behaviors is that it cannot be used effectively in situations in which changes in the behaviors under investigation tend to be correlated. The Ballard and Glynn study illustrates this problem. As shown in Figure 6-6, the intervention designed to affect sentence production also influenced the production of descriptive words. Fortunately, action words were not affected during the sentence intervention. Moreover, there were no correlated changes in behavior in either of the other two interventions. Thus, the investigation provides a convincing demonstration of treatment effects despite the one instance of correlated behavior change.

The assessment-plus-recording phase of the Ballard and Glynn (1975) investigation introduces a complication into the experimental design that requires further comment. In this study, there was a clear possibility that multiple-treatment interference effects were operative. For example, self-reinforcement may have influenced sentence production only because it was combined with self-assessment and self-recording. It is also possible that self-reinforcement influenced sentence production only because it followed a period of self-assessment and self-recording. Finally, self-reinforcement and self-assessment may have taken place. Each of these possibilities illustrates the fact that, even though the self-assessment plus self-recording intervention had no discernible effect on behavior by itself, it may have served as a catalyst influencing the effects of the self-reinforcement treatment.

Possible multiple-treatment interference effects in the Ballard and Glynn study do not render the study meaningless. They merely limit the conclusions that can be drawn from the investigation. Specifically, although the study does not conclusively show that self-reinforcement affects writing behaviors, it does show that, when self-assessment and self-recording were put into effect and were then combined with self reinforcement, there was an effect on the writing behavior of the children.

In some cases it may be of interest to determine whether intervention effects can be produced across situations. The *multiple baseline design across situations* can be used to investigate this kind of outcome. The multiple-baseline design across situations is initiated by a baseline period in which data are collected on the same behavior in more than one situation. Then, an intervention is introduced to modify behavior in one of the situations while data collection continues in both settings. After intervention effects have been demonstrated in the initial setting, the intervention is introduced in a second situation. Periodic intervention continues until the treatment effects have been investigated in all of the situations selected for study.

Hart and Risley (1975) conducted an investigation that illustrates the use of the multiple-baseline design across situations. These investigators assisted a preschool teacher to facilitate the language development of 11 economically disadvantaged preschool children. The goal to be achieved by the teacher was to teach the children to use compound sentences. The intervention involved the use of an "incidental-teaching" procedure that had the following characteristics: Play materials were placed out of reach of the children so that to get the materials they had to ask the teacher for them. The children were prompted to use compound sentences in making their requests, and they were reinforced by verbal praise for correct responses. The results of the investigation are shown in Figure 6-7.

The study was initiated by a baseline period in which incidental instruction was used to teach the children the names of the materials. For example, on observing that a child wished to obtain an out-of-reach toy, the teacher might ask, "What do you want?" If the child responded, "I want that," the teacher might model the name of the object and then ask the child to imitate her behavior.

After 36 days of baseline, incidental teaching of compound sentences was introduced in the first situation. The initial situation involved verbal interactions between the teacher and a child. The goal during this phase of the experiment was to teach the children to use compound sentences in requesting play materials from the teacher. To cue the use of compound sentences, the teacher responded to requests for materials by asking the children why they wanted the materials for which they had asked. For instance, if a child said, "I want that truck," the teacher might respond, "What for?" If the child emitted a compound sentence, the teacher would give the child the truck and praise her or him. If a compound sentence was not forthcoming, the teacher would engage in further cuing or would model a compound utterance and request the child to imitate the utterance.

An issue of obvious importance in language instruction is whether the linguistic skills acquired through teacher assistance generalize to other situations. For example, for skill in the production of compound sentences to be useful to children, they have to be able to apply that skill in verbal

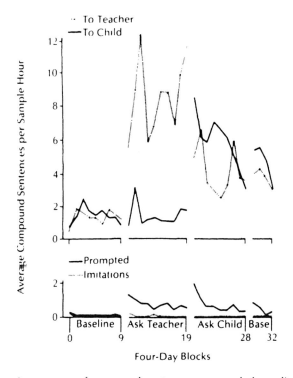

FIGURE 6-7. Top: Average use of compound sentences per sample hour directed by all 11 children to teachers (dotted line) and to children (solid line). Bottom: Average number of statements by all 11 children that were prompted (solid line) by a teacher statement and that were imitations (dotted line) of an immediately preceding teacher statement. Experimental conditions were baseline, blocks 1–9 (Days 1–36); incidental teaching of compound sentences directed to teachers, blocks 10–19 (Days 37–76); incidental teaching of compound sentences directed to children, blocks 20–28 (Days 77–112); and baseline blocks 29–32 (Days 113–128). Each point represents four 15-minute verbalization samples, that is, 4 consecutive days of observation. [Source: B. Hart & T. R. Risley. (1975). Incidental teaching of language in the preschool. *Journal of Applied Behavior Analysis, 8,* 417.]

interactions with people other than their teacher. As a step toward enabling the children in the study to use compound sentences in a variety of situations, Hart and Risley included a phase in the experiment in which the children were taught to use compound sentences in interacting with their peers. In this part of the experiment, the response to requests for materials was giving the desired materials to another child and telling the first child to ask the second for the materials. Cuing and modeling were used by the teacher as in the previous phase of the experiment in the event that the child did not initially emit a compound sentence.

In the final phase of the experiment, the incidental-teaching intervention was withdrawn. As indicated in Figure 6-7, the children continued to emit a moderately high rate of compound sentences even in the absence of the intervention.

The multiple-baseline design across situations has the advantage of reducing the likelihood that the conclusions of an experiment will be invalid because of the effects of history. An extraneous influence may occur precisely at the time of intervention in each of the situations under investigation, but the probability of such an occurrence would be low.

An additional advantage of the multiple-baseline procedure applied across situations is, of course, that it increases the generality of the findings. For example, in the Hart and Risley study, incidental teaching was shown to affect not only teacher–child interactions but also child–child interactions.

The principal difficulty that may be encountered in using the design involves the fact that behavior change in one situation may be correlated with change in another situation. For example, increasing the use of compound sentences in teacher–child interactions might have produced an increase in such utterances in child–child interactions in the absence of any specific intervention to modify verbal interchanges between children. Had this occurred, intervention in the second situation would have been pointless, and the design would have been reduced to an A/B/A design involving baseline, followed by intervention, followed by the withdrawal of intervention.

The *multiple-baseline design across individuals or groups* involves assessment across groups or individuals and, at the same time, minimizes the effects of history confounding on experimental validity. In this design, baseline data are collected simultaneously across a number of groups or individuals. Then, an intervention is introduced for one of the experimental units. At a subsequent time, the intervention is put into effect for a second experimental unit. This process continues until all groups or individuals have received the experimental treatment.

Research by Copeland *et al.* (1974), mentioned in Chapter 5, illustrates a variation of the multiple-baseline design across individuals. The general plan to be evaluated in the research involved the use of praise by a school principal to modify the behavior of elementary-school children. In one experiment, praise by the principal was used to increase the rate of school attendance in three young children, Elbert, Yolanda, and Lynette. As shown in Figure 6-8, the study was initiated by collecting 7 weeks of baseline data on the daily rate of attendance of the three children. In the 8th week, the principal initiated a praise treatment for Elbert that consisted of going up to Elbert, patting him on the back, and praising him for school attendance. At the beginning of the 10th week, the praise treatment was put into effect for Yolanda, and in the 13th week, it was instituted for Lynette. The principal initiated a second intervention involving the use of intermittent praise in the 20th week. During this intervention, the principal

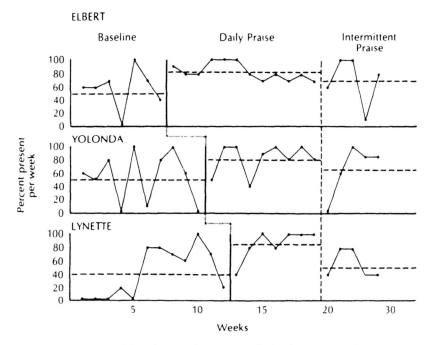

FIGURE 6-8. Percentage of time three students attended school. Baseline: before experimental procedures. Daily principal praise: principal entered subjects' classrooms daily and delivered praise for school attendance. Intermittent: principal entered classrooms two or three times a week and delivered praise for school attendance. [Source: R. E. Copeland, R. E. Brown, & R. V. Hall. (1974). The effects of principal-implemented techniques on the behavior of pupils. *Journal of Applied Behavior Analysis, 7,* 79.]

praised each of the children two or three times a week for school attendance.

The Copeland *et al.* study demonstrated that principal praise constituted an effective intervention for three individuals, thereby extending the generality of the findings over what would have been the case if only one child had participated in the study. In addition, by staggering the interventions across time, Copeland and his colleagues minimized the likelihood that history would be a significant source of invalidity in the experiment.

The intermittent-praise condition introduced a multiple-intervention component to the study. The use of the second intervention provided an economical way to answer the very practical question of whether high attendance rates could be maintained with only occasional praise. Given the time demands ordinarily made on the principal, this was a very important question to answer in consultation. The data in Figure 6-8 indicate that the intermittent-praise treatment was not very effective in maintaining attendance. However, all that can be concluded from these data is that, when intermittent praise followed a period of continuous praise, it was not a particularly effective technique for maintaining school attendance.

Had intermittent praise been applied in the absence of a daily-praise condition, different results might have been attained. The multiple-intervention component in this study represented a compromise in which a gain in economy in carrying out the study was balanced by a loss of information with respect to the effects of the intermittent-praise condition.

Sources of Invalidity in Evaluation Designs

If a single-case design has been selected and implemented, the evaluation of plan's effectiveness involves making a judgment of whether the plan produced the desired changes in client behavior and whether the observed changes generalize to other settings or persons. Resolution of these issues should be based on a consideration of the possible sources of invalidity in the particular evaluation design selected for implementation.

In discussing the uses, advantages, and disadvantages associated with the various evaluation designs presented above, we pointed out some of the major sources of invalidity in different designs. In addition to the major sources already mentioned, there are a number or other sources of invalidity that the consultant should be aware of to get a general picture of the validity problems that may occur in time series designs used in plan evaluation. In a classic article, Campbell and Stanley (1963) identified two categories of validity, which they called "internal validity" and "external validity." We shall use their categorization system, as well as some suggestions by Glass, Wilson, and Gottman (1975) and by Cook and Campbell (1979), as a basis for describing the sources of invalidity that may arise in the use of time series designs for purposes of plan evaluation.

Internal validity, as the term applies to consultation, refers to concluding that plan implementation produced observed changes in client behavior. For example, suppose that, after implementing a carefully devised plan, a mother observes a marked change in her daughter's temper-tantrum behavior. To what extent would it be justifiable for her to conclude that the change is due to the implementation of the plan? This is a question related to internal validity.

External validity refers to the degree to which the results of plan evaluation can be generalized to other consultants, consultees, clients, and situations. For instance, suppose that plan evaluation reveals that a plan is highly effective in assisting a particular child to increase his reading skills. Would it be justifiable to assume that this plan will work with other children? This is a question of external validity.

Several possible sources of internal invalidity may be associated with time series designs. One that has already been mentioned is *history*. An extraneous event occurring at the time of intervention, rather than the intervention itself, may be responsible for producing a change in client behavior. For instance, if an intervention involves teacher reinforcement to increase a child's academic productivity, and if the instructions indicating the desired performance occur at the same time as the intervention, these instructions may be, at least in part, responsible for changes in the child's academic accomplishment.

Maturation represents another source of internal invalidity that may affect the evaluation of plan effectiveness, particularly in developmental consultation. When consultation takes place over a relatively long time, significant changes may occur in client behavior that are not the result of a particular intervention, but that accrue as a consequence of developmental processes in the child.

Testing represents a third potential source of internal invalidity. The very act of testing a client may influence behavior independently of whatever intervention may be put into effect. For example, repeated exposure to a particular testing format or type of test item may produce changes in client behavior that are independent of those associated with the intervention.

Another source of internal invalidity is *instrumentation.* Instrumentation is the manner in which client behavior is scored when it is being measured. Any changes occurring in scoring can, of course, pose a serious threat to the internal validity of an evaluation. Some early research by O'Leary and his associates demonstrates how instrumentation problems pose a threat to the validity of a study. Romanczyk, Kent, Diament, and O'Leary (1973) demonstrated that observers may change their criteria for scoring behavior during the course of an experiment. O'Leary et al. (1975) found that changes in scoring criteria may be related to observer expectations regarding the desired experimental outcomes. Thus, it is possible that, when an observer knows that a consultant and a consultee desire and expect a particular behavioral outcome, observations will be biased in the direction of the expectations.

Another potential source of internal invalidity is *regression* associated with unreliability of behavioral measures. When measures are unreliable (that is, when there are inconsistencies in measures due to the random inaccuracy of measurement), scores change or regress toward the mean (average) over time. When change due to regression occurs in the same direction as that expected through intervention, the validity of the plan evaluation is jeopardized.

In time series evaluations in which different individuals are observed at successive points in time, the *selection* of individuals for purposes of observation may constitute a source of internal invalidity. For example, suppose that a consultant is working with a principal and a group of first-grade teachers to evaluate a plan involving the use of an innovative method of teaching arithmetic. The group decides that they want to use a time series design to evaluate the plan's effectiveness. However, they want to avoid excessive testing of the children. One way out of this dilemma is to test a different group of children at each of a number of successive points in time. However, if this strategy is followed, it is necessary to ensure that the various groups of children selected for testing will not differ from one another in any systematic way. This may be done by assigning the children randomly to different testing groups.

In time series evaluations involving groups of individuals, *a change in unit composition* may jeopardize internal validity. For example, suppose that a consultant and a consultee evaluate a plan involving the use of an innovative method of reading instruction and that assessments of reading performance reveal that there has been marked change in reading level between the beginning of the year and the end of the year. Suppose further that the composition of the group of students involved in the reading program has changed during the year: during the early part of the year, the program included a number of children from migrant-worker families. Let's assume that these children had little formal schooling and that they lacked the necessary language skills to do well in reading. Under these conditions, changes in performance from the beginning of the year to the end of the year might be due to the fact that the children from migrant-worker families left the program as their parents found employment in other areas.

Instability of time series data is a potential source of invalidity in time series designs. In those cases in which behavior varies substantially across a series of observations, a consultant and a consultee may mistakenly assume that an observed change in client behavior has occurred as a result of plan implementation when, in fact, the change reflects simply unaccountable fluctuations in the behavior under study. The problem of instability is a particular concern in applied behavioral work because both researcher and practitioner applications of behavioral principles involving time series designs do not generally include the use of statistical tests to aid in determining whether an intervention has produced a significant change in behavior (Kratochwill, 1978). Statistical tests are available for this purpose (see Kazdin, 1982; Kratochwill, 1978). However, the problem of instability may also be approached by achieving sufficient control over behavior to reduce unaccounted-for variability to the point where it becomes obvious that the observed changes in performance cannot be explained in terms of instability (Johnston & Pennypacker, 1980).

In time series evaluations involving more than one group, the selection of the individuals to be assigned to the different groups may interact with other sources of invalidity to jeopardize the validity of the plan evaluation. By way of illustration, consider the possibility of an interaction involving selection and instrumentation in a multiple-group, multiple-baseline-across-subjects design. Suppose that a consultant and a teacher acting as consultee are evaluating a plan to improve the reading skills of nine children in the teacher's class. The plan involves an intervention applied to each of three groups. Suppose that observations of oral reading are made by the teacher's aide. Interobserver agreement is established during baseline by calculating the extent of agreement between the aide's observations and observations made by the teacher. Suppose that two of the three groups of children are extremely well behaved in class, whereas the children in the third group are a constant source of disruption. Assume further that the aide expects the first two groups to profit from the intervention plan but has serious doubts about the likelihood of the plan's effectiveness for the third group. Under circumstances such as these, the aide's observations during plan implementation may be biased with respect to the unruly children to the extent that intervention effects are obscured in the disruptive group.

In addition to the various sources of internal invalidity described above, a number of threats to external validity must be considered in connection with the use of time series designs. One of these is *multiple-intervention interference*. The discussion of many of the designs presented in the previous section illustrated the fact that multiple-intervention interference may be a source of internal invalidity in time series evaluations. When an evaluation involves the use of more than one intervention, the first intervention may influence the effects of the second intervention. Unless provisions are made to control for this problem, external validity may be affected. More specifically, in the absence of provisions for control, there would be no justification for concluding that the observed effects of the second intervention would occur for individuals who had not experienced the first intervention.

Another source of external invalidity is the *interaction of testing and intervention*. A particular client whose behavior is under study in consultation may react differently to an intervention than another client would because of repeated testing experiences occurring during consultation. For example, a student who in the course of baseline data collection gains extensive experience in taking multiple-choice tests may react differently to an intervention designed to improve academic skills as measured by multiple-choice performance than a student who has little experience with the multiple-choice format. When there is the possibility of a testing-intervention interaction, it would probably not be advisable to conclude that results demonstrating plan effectiveness can be generalized to other clients. One of the reasons for using time series designs to study the behavior of individuals rather than using traditional procedures involving comparisons between experimental groups and control groups is that traditional statistical techniques may obscure differences in the way individuals react to intervention (Barlow *et al.*, 1984).

Reactive effects of experimental arrangements are another potential source of external invalidity threats in time series evaluations. Reactive arrangements are conditions influencing behavior that occur in the particular environment in which the intervention takes place. Reactive conditions include those cues in the environment that indicate to a client that a particular experimental or evaluation outcome is desired. When reactive arrangements are present, the evaluation results cannot be generalized to other occasions, groups, and settings. Reactive arrangements constitute a threat to validity in applied behavioral practice. Applied behavioral research and evaluation generally involve observations of client behavior. These observations in themselves may affect client performance. For example, although the evidence is far from conclusive, there are data to suggest that self-observation may affect behavior (Nelson, 1977a,b; Shapiro, 1984). Thus, if a child is asked to make observations of his own behavior independently of plan implementation, a change in behavior may occur independently of the intervention (see Piersel & Kratochwill, 1979, for an example of this outcome in consultation research). Observations made by persons other than the client may also affect behavior. If, for example, a child becomes aware that her teacher is recording her behavior, the child may change in the absence of intervention.

As the discussion in this section and the previous section implies, the selection of an appropriate evaluation design must include a consideration of both the uses to be made of the evaluation and the sources of invalidity associated with the various designs. For example, if a consultant and a consultee are seeking a design that can be used to evaluate the effects of multiple interventions, there are a number of possibilities from which to choose. In making their final selection of a design, they should consider carefully the potential sources of invalidity associated with each of the designs that they have singled out for consideration.

Postimplementation Planning

The final step in the problem evaluation process is postimplementation planning. A postimplementation plan is put into operation after the consultation goal has been attained and consultation for the problem currently being evaluated has terminated formally. Postimplementation planning is undertaken to forestall problem reoccurrence and to ensure that the consultant will be alerted to reappearances of the problem if they should happen to take place.

Postimplementation Plan Alternatives

There are basically three alternatives available in designing a postimplementation plan: (1) leaving the plan implemented during consultation in effect; (2) introducing a new plan; and (3) removing the plan implemented during consultation. A factor that should be taken into account in considering these alternatives is the reversibility of client behavior (Voeltz & Evans, 1983). If client behavior is likely to be reversed easily, the consultee may wish to leave the consultation plan in operation. For example, suppose that a well-designed plan has resulted in the total elimination of aggressive behavior in a child. Even though the goal of consultation has been attained, there is a clear possibility that aggressive behavior may return after the treatment is terminated. Therefore, the consultee might decide to leave the plan implemented during consultation in effect.

Another issue that should be considered in determining whether to leave a consultation plan in operation is the feasibility of implementing the plan for a prolonged period. For instance, suppose that the plan selected to eliminate aggressive actions in the example described in the last paragraph involved the use of tangible reinforcers to increase behavior incompatible with aggression. Tangible rewards tend to be expensive and may not be part of the natural ecology of the applied setting. Thus, it may not be practical to implement the plan long after the termination of consultation. By contrast, consider the case in which a plan involves the use of reinforcers already available in the client's natural environment. For instance, suppose that a first-grade girl is being inadvertently reinforced by teacher attention for inaccurate problem-solving behavior in arithmetic. The obvious plan in a case like this would be to make teacher attention contingent on accurate problem-solving. Teacher attention will be available after consultation, and presumably, there would be no advantage in discontinuing attention following accurate problem-solving. Moreover, the teacher would surely not want to return to his/her former practice of rendering attention as a consequence of inaccuracy.

A second alternative in postimplementation planning is to introduce a new plan after consultation has terminated. A new plan may be called for to maintain behavior change when the behavior of concern is reversible and it is impractical to leave the original consultation plan in operation. For instance, if it is impractical to continue a plan that uses tangible rewards after the termination of consultation, it would probably be useful to consider installing an alternative plan based on the application of reinforcers available in the child's natural environment.

Another circumstance that typically calls for the implementation of a new plan following consultation is that in which there is a need to ensure that behavior changed during consultation will generalize to new settings. A number of studies have shown that, unless a specific plan is designed to ensure generalization to new settings, generalization is not likely to occur (Stokes & Baer, 1977). For example, in an early investigation, Wahler (1969) studied the generalization of newly acquired academic and social behaviors from the home to the school and found no behavioral transfer across these settings. A 5-year-old boy and an 8-year-old boy participated in Wahler's investigation. These two children were referred by their teachers to an outpatient clinic because they manifested psychological problems. Consultation with the boys' parents revealed that the children presented serious problems at home that were similar to those encountered at school. One of the children, Steve, displayed behavior described as oppositional both at home and at school. The goal of consultation for Steve was to replace this behavior with cooperative actions. The other child, Louis, was described as highly disruptive both at home and at school. The goal of consultation for Louis was to replace his disruptive acts with study behavior. The plan developed in consultation to achieve the goals specified for the two children involved training the children's parents to provide positive forms of attention for the desired behaviors and to ignore the undesirable behaviors. In addition to these above techniques, Steve's parents were instructed in the use of a time-out procedure that involved isolating Steve in his bedroom immediately following oppositional behavior. As shown in Figure 6-9, the plans were effective in changing the children's home behavior but did nothing to alter their school behavior. However, changes were effected by initiating plans at school similar to those used at home.

The importance of the home in affecting both the learning of academic skills and social behaviors has become increasingly well documented in recent years (Ollendick & Cerny, 1981). However, as the Wahler study indicates, altering behavior in the home provides no guarantee that behavior will change as desired in the school setting. Two strategies can be followed in designing a postimplementation plan to ensure the maintenance or generalization of behavior changed during the course of consultation. One approach is to alter antecedent and/or consequent conditions operating in the client's natural environment. Walker and Buckley (1972) conducted a study that illustrates this technique. Their investigation involved elementary-school children whose behavior was so disruptive that it could not be coped with in the regular classroom. The 44 children who participated in the study were place in an experimental classroom 6 at a time during successive periods lasting 2 months each. A token economy was implemented in the classroom activity. After the children had spent 2 months in the experimental classroom, they were returned to the regular classroom, whereupon they were each assigned at random to one of a number of treatments designed to produce generalization to the regular classroom of the behaviors acquired in the experimental classroom. The second strategy involved making cues such as academic materials and reinforcers such as verbal praise in the regular classroom similar to those used in the experimental room. Both of these plans were effective in producing a generalization of appropriate classroom behavior from the experimental setting to the regular classroom.

The second strategy that can be used to promote the maintenance and generalization of behavior changes effected through consultation is to de-

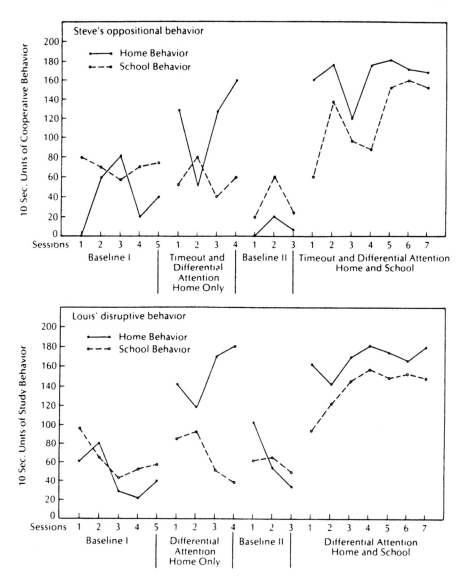

FIGURE 6-9. The modification of oppositional and disruptive behaviors in the home and in the school. [Source: R. G. Wahler (1969). Setting generality: Some specific and general effects of child behavior therapy. *Journal of Applied Behavior Analysis*, 2, 243, 245.]

vise a postimplementation plan to place the behaviors dealt with during consultation under client control. When a plan implemented during consultation involves the manipulation of antecedent or consequent events under the control of the consultee, it cannot necessarily be assumed that a change in client behavior will be accompanied by a change in client ability to control behavior. For instance, a teacher may implement a successful plan to reduce a child's aggressive actions without increasing the child's control over the aggressive response.

Postimplementation planning to place behavior under client control can be accomplished by repeating problem identification, problem analysis, and problem evaluation, with the client serving as his or her own consultee. Self-management requires awareness of the occurrence of behavior to be controlled and of the conditions influencing it (Mahoney & Thoresen, 1974). In addition, there must be a plan to produce the conditions influencing client behavior under the client's direction and an evaluation to enable the client to determine whether the desired changes in behavior are being maintained or generalized to new situations. Problem identification can be used to establish the necessary awareness of the incidence of the behavior to be controlled. The precise specification of the behavior afforded by problem identification and the designation and implementation of procedures for measuring the behavior make it possible for the client to become fully cognizant of the extent of the occurrence of the behavior to be subsequently placed under self-management. Problem analysis offers a way to make the client aware of the conditions controlling the behavior and to help him or her establish a plan to maintain the desired behavior or to generalize it to new settings. Problem evaluation provides a means by which the client can judge whether the behavior is being maintained or is being applied in new situations as desired.

The consultee generally assumes the role of consultant in postimplementation planning to enhance the self-management of behavior by the client. For example, a teacher may assist a child to establish a self-recording procedure to increase the child's awareness of failure to complete assignments, or parents may help their child to identify the stimulus conditions controlling study behavior at home (see Hallahan, Lloyd, Kauffman, & Loper, 1983, for examples of the use of self-monitoring as an intervention).

When the consultee does function as a consultant to increase self-management, it may be useful to provide some training to the consultee in procedures for consultation with the client. Training of this kind need not be extensive. For instance, it may be possible to provide sufficient consultation skills simply by role playing with the consultee the kinds of things that he or she might say in conducting problem identification, problem analysis, or problem evaluation.

The extensiveness of postimplementation planning to place behavior under client control usually varies as a function of the degree to which the client has been involved in the earlier phases of consultation. If the client has participated actively in problem identification and problem analysis, he or she probably has a good grasp of the problem and the conditions relevant to solving it. Under these circumstances, postimplementation planning is often confined to establishing specific procedures for transferring full control of the behavior to the client. For example, suppose that a mother and a daughter have been working on a plan to increase the daughter's self-care skills. During problem identification, they established that the girl needed to be more regular with respect to brushing her teeth and washing her face in the morning. Suppose that they have developed and implemented a successful plan in which the mother has cued and reinforced the desired self-care skills. Postimplementation planning to enhance self-management would probably focus on finding ways in which the child can cue and reinforce her own self-care behavior.

When client involvement in the prior phases of consultation has been minimal, postimplementation planning may have to be quite detailed. Minimal client involvement may occur when the consultee feels that the client cannot contribute effectively to the consultation process. For example, a parent seeking consultation regarding the behavior of a very young child is probably less likely to want to involve the child in consultation decision-making than a parent seeking services regarding the behavior of an older child.

If it is decided during postimplementation planning that it is possible to increase self-management even though the client has not participated actively in the earlier phases of consultation, a detailed plan involving problem identification, problem analysis, and problem evaluation is generally required. For example, suppose that a mother has been concerned about increasing the incidence of sharing behavior in her pre-school-aged daughter. A successful plan has resulted in the desired change in sharing activities, but the plan requires constant supervision by the mother. As a result, the mother and the consultant decide to place sharing behavior under the child's control. In a situation like this, steps would have to be taken to make sure that the child can discriminate sharing behavior from other behavior. In addition, the child will have to be assisted to formulate goals with respect to sharing and to implement procedures to achieve control over the conditions governing sharing. Finally, steps will have to be taken to make sure that the child can evaluate the adequacy of her sharing behavior.

The final alternative available in postimplementation planning is to remove the plan implemented during consultation. This may be done gradually or all at once. A father may implement a plan to develop certain social competencies in his child. When the child acquires the competencies, the father and the consultant may decide that continued implementation of the plan is no longer necessary. Accordingly, they may remove it at the termination of consultation. However, as noted above, a problem that may be encountered is a rapid performance decrement when the treatment is withdrawn abruptly (Cuvo, 1979). Gradual withdrawal of treatment may be more helpful in treatment maintenance and generalization. For example, suppose that a mother is implementing a plan involving positive reinforcement given on a continuous schedule for behavior incompatible with aggression. Assume that the reinforcement delivery is taking an excessive amount of the mother's time and that she would like to terminate the plan. However, she is afraid that, if she does, the aggressive behavior will return. In a situation like this, the consultant and the mother may decide to thin the reinforcement schedule gradually to the point where the plan is eventually entirely withdrawn. It is well established that extinction of behavior occurs more slowly when behavior has been maintained previously by an intermittent schedule of reinforcement than it does when behavior has been reinforced continuously (Bandura, 1969). Thus, if the mother changes from continuous reinforcement to intermittent reinforcement and then gradually thins the schedule, it will probably be possible for her to remove the plan without ill effects.

The safest circumstance under which one may opt for the total removal of a plan may be that in which the behaviors of concern are not easily reversed. For example, if a plan has been implemented successfully to increase a child's arithmetic skills, it is probably safe to remove the plan when the skills have been thoroughly mastered, as the behaviors generally required in the performance of arithmetic problems are not easily eliminated once they have been attained. However, this option may not address the issue of skill generalization.

A second circumstance that may suggest the removal of a plan is that in which there is some likelihood that contingencies operating in the natural environment will maintain the behavior changed during the course of consultation. For instance, a teacher's implementation of a successful plan to reduce a child's hitting behavior may inadvertently produce previously unavailable reinforcers for behavior that is incompatible with hitting. Peers, for example, may reinforce positive social interactions on the part of the previously aggressive child and thereby forestall the recurrence of aggressive behavior.

In many instances, desired behavior is maintained in society by reinforcers in the natural environment. However, reinforcers are not equally available to everyone, nor are they applied to the same behaviors for every individual. Inappropriate behaviors may arise when reinforcers maintaining appropriate behavior are not available to the individual. An implicit purpose of most behavior-change programs is to increase the availability of reinforcement for desired behaviors. When this is accomplished through consultation, it is often possible to remove the plan implemented during consultation without producing problem recurrence.

Postimplementation Recording

Regardless of the alternative selected with respect to a postimplementation plan, it is generally useful to include some provision in the plan for postimplementation recording. Postimplementation records provide the data necessary for judging whether the behavior changes occurring during consultation have been maintained or generalized to new settings.

Postimplementation recording procedures should be designed to provide the needed information to the participants in consultation. However, they must also be constructed so that the record-keeping demands on the consultee and the client are kept to a minimum.

One strategy for providing the needed information and for keeping the recording demands at a low level is to use the probe technique for assessing behavior following consultation (Cuvo, 1979; Horner & Baer, 1978). The probe technique involves the periodic measurement of behavior under a particular set of conditions. In consultation, the conditions are specified by the postimplementation plan. For example, suppose that a postimplementation plan for maintaining accuracy in oral reading called for a teacher to reinforce accurate oral reading responses and to ignore inaccurate responses. A postimplementation probe of reading behavior might involve the measurement of accuracy in oral reading under the conditions specified by the postimplementation plan for a 3-day period a month after the termination of consultation.

One way to use the probe technique is to assess behavior over a fixed sequence of times. For instance, oral-reading behavior might be measured once a month for 6 months. The principal function served by a periodic assessment of this kind is to verify the durability of the behavior changes effected during consultation.

A second way to use the probe technique is to assess behavior under varying conditions at several different points in time. For instance, the level of disruptive classroom behavior following successful plan implementation might be measured during periods involving transition from one classroom activity to another on one occasion. On a second recording occasion, the level of disruption might be measured right before lunch. The purpose of probes of this kind is to assess the extent to which behavior changes are being maintained under varying sets of conditions.

A third way to probe is to conduct periodic assessments of behavior, each assessment being linked to the acquisition of other behaviors on the part of the client. For example, a teacher might use periodic review sessions to assess a child's mastery of basic sight vocabulary in reading. The purpose of this type of probe is to determine whether the acquisition of new behaviors is associated with decrements in the level of previously acquired skills. It is well known that learning something new may interfere with the retention of previously acquired information (Kintsch, 1970). The probe technique can be used to check for decrements in performance that may be associated with interference effects.

Postimplementation and Problem Recurrence

If recurrences of target problems are not handled effectively, the prior consultation will obviously have been of only limited value to the consultee and to the client. Not only will the consultee and the client have to cope with the same problem they faced before consultation was initiated, but they may also become disillusioned regarding the effectiveness of consultation. Thus, there is a risk that they will be cut off from the benefits that consultation may afford as an avenue for achieving problem solution.

The ill effects of problem recurrence can generally be forestalled if steps are taken to ensure the formulation and implementation of a new plan to deal with the new problem. A key factor influencing whether proper steps will be taken to ensure the construction and implementation of such a plan is the communication between the consultant and consultee following the formal termination of consultation. If there are no provisions in the postimplementation plan for contact between the consultant and the consultee after consultation is ended, then obviously, the probability that a new plan will be constructed and put into effect is reduced.

In the case of developmental consultation, the issue of contact concerning a problem previously dealt with is, for the most part, easily handled. All that is generally necessary is to schedule periodic postimplementation evaluations during problem evaluation interviews conducted in reiterative applications of the consultative problem-solving process. For example, if one of the early goals of developmental consultation involves increasing a child's sharing behavior, postimplementation evaluations of sharing can be conducted during problem evaluation interviews aimed primarily at the evaluation of the goals dealt with after sharing in the consultation process. Of course, this strategy does not work during the later phases of developmental consultation, as a point comes at which all of the various developmental goals have been considered in problem evaluation interviews. At this point, there may still be a need for some postimplementation evaluations, particularly for those behaviors handled in the final reiterative applications of consultative problem-solving. However, by this time, the pattern of postimplementation evaluations will have been well established. Thus, in most cases, it is relatively easy to arrange for additional evaluations following the termination of consultation. The consultee is quite familiar with the conduct of postimplementation evaluations and probably feels free to call for them when they are needed.

Contact regarding postimplementation evaluations may be more difficult to ensure in problem-centered consultation. Difficulties are particularly likely to arise when the consultant and the consultee do not know each other well and are not likely to have any contact with one another in connection with matters other than those taken up in consultation for the case at hand. For example, consider a situation in which a consultant is called in on a temporary basis to conduct problem-centered consultation with a teacher. For example, assume that the consultant does not know the teacher and that she has no interactions other than consultation with the teacher or with other school personnel in that school building. Under circumstances like these, opportunities for communication outside consultation are minimal. If communication is to occur, it must be planned for systematically. By contrast, consider a situation in which a consultant routinely provides services in a particular school building and has contact with the various teachers in the building with respect to several cases. Under these conditions, there are many opportunities for the consultant to become aware of postimplementation problems if they happen to occur.

Regardless of whether a consultant is involved in developmental or problem-centered consultation, and regardless of whether opportunities for postconsultation contact are good or bad, arrangements for contact should be made explicit during problem evaluation. One way to arrange for postconsultation contact is simply for the consultant to encourage the consultee to make contact in the event that the problem dealt with during consultation happens to recur. This approach will probably be adequate in those instances in which opportunities for postconsultation interaction between the consultant and the consultee are relatively good. For example, if the consultee is a teacher and the consultant regularly visits the school where the teacher works, the teacher will have ample opportunity to bring up discussion of problem recurrences.

When opportunities for postconsultation contact are not optional, simple encouragement to make contact may not be sufficient to ensure that contact will be likely to take place. An obvious alternative is for the consultant to initiate contact. This strategy has two advantages. First, it ensures that contact will be made. Second, it is a sign to the consultee that the consultant is concerned about the client and is ready to give his or her assistance if required. The advantages of consultant-initiated contact are partially counterbalanced by two disadvantages. First of all, there is no guarantee that the consultant will initiate contact at the right time. The consultant may call the consultee just before problem recurrence takes place. In these circumstances, the consultee will be in the position of having just informed the consultant that everything is going well only to find that this is no longer the case. The second disadvantage of consultant-initiated contact is that it requires the consultant to spend time on the case when there may no need for further involvement in it.

In most cases in which opportunities for postconsultation contact are limited, the advantages of consultant-initiated contact outweigh the disadvantages. The expenditure of time is small, and the potential ill effects of making contact at the wrong time are minimal. Thus, when there is a likelihood that the consultee will fail to make contact when it is needed, consultant-initiated contact should be given serious consideration.

In many cases, it may be useful to augment the provisions for subsequent contact by making a contingency plan during problem evaluation. The contingency plan should specify the procedures to be implemented in the event of problem recurrence. For example, consider a situation in which a plan is removed at the termination of consultation. An obvious contingency plan in such a situation is to reinstate the original plan in the event of problem recurrence. Then, after the behavior of concern is once again under control, the plan may be withdrawn gradually. The contingency plan has the advantage of not requiring total reliance on postconsultation contact in dealing with problem recurrence. Despite this fact, contingency plans should always be combined with provisions for postconsultation contact, as there is always a possibility that the contingency plans will be ineffective.

THE PROBLEM EVALUATION INTERVIEW

The problem evaluation process culminates in the problem evaluation interview. In this interview, the consultant and the consultee determine whether the goals of consultation have been attained and whether the plans implemented to achieve those goals have been effective. On the basis of their evaluation of goal attainment, they decide whether there is a need for further problem identification or analysis. Finally, if goal attainment has occurred, they establish postimplementation plans to reduce the likelihood of problem recurrence and to deal with recurrence if it should happen to take place.

Evaluation Interview Objectives and Strategies for Attaining Them

Consultant verbalizations during the problem evaluation interview should be guided by the objectives established for this type of interview. Problem evaluation objectives for both developmental and problem-centered consultation are shown in Table 6-3. As indicated in the table, the interview objectives fall into five categories: goal attainment, consultation guidance, plan effectiveness, postimplementation planning, and procedure.

Goal Attainment Objectives for Developmental Consultation

The first task of the consultant in the problem evaluation interview is to establish the extent to which the goals of consultation have been achieved. In the case of developmental consultation, this requires a consideration of the general, subordinate, and performance objectives. In the initial stages of developmental consultation, evaluation may be restricted largely to consideration of the performance and subordinate objectives. The judgment that the general objectives have not been achieved is usually implicit in the first few evaluation interviews.

The consultant should initiate the evaluation of goal attainment by considering those performance objectives that have been targeted for mas-

TABLE 6-3. Objectives for the Problem Evaluation Interviews

Objective type	Interview type	
	Developmental interview	Problem-centered interview
Goal attainment	Evaluate performance objectives. Evaluate subordinate objectives. Evaluate general objectives.	Evaluate behavioral goals.
Consultation guidance	Signal the need to return to an earlier phase of consultation when required. Signal the need to progress to the next phase in the evaluation interview when appropriate.	Signal the need to return to an earlier phase of consultation when required. Signal the need to progress to the next phase in the evaluation interview when appropriate.
Plan effectiveness	Establish sources of internal invalidity bearing on the evaluation of plan effectiveness. Evaluate plan effectiveness with reference to possible sources of internal invalidity. Establish sources of external invalidity bearing on the evaluation of plan effectiveness. Evaluate plan effectiveness with reference to possible sources of external invalidity.	Establish sources of internal invalidity bearing on the evaluation of plan effectiveness. Evaluate plan effectiveness with reference to possible sources of internal invalidity. Establish sources of external invalidity bearing on the evaluation of plan effectiveness. Evaluate plan effectiveness with reference to possible sources of external invalidity.
Postimplementation planning	Establish postimplementation strategies and plan tactics. Establish postimplementation recording procedures. Establish procedures for handling postimplementation problems.	Establish postimplementation strategies and plan tactics. Establish postimplementation recording procedures. Establish procedures for handling postimplementation problems.
Procedure	Schedule the next interview. Terminate consultation.	Schedule the next interview. Terminate consultation.

tery during the plan implementation period immediately preceding the evaluation interview. Each objective should be dealt with separately. The consultant should begin by asking to see the data describing performance during plan implementation for the first objective to be considered. Then, he or she should summarize the objectives as it was established during problem identification. The summary should include a description of the goal in behavioral terms, a specification of the conditions under which performance was to occur, and the required level of competency. Next, the consultant should summarize the data collected during plan implementation. Finally, the consultant generally asks the consultee for his or her judgment of the extent of goal attainment.

After the consultee has made a judgment concerning goal attainment, the consultant may decide to advance to the next step in the evaluation process for the objective just evaluated, or he or she may decide to initiate conversation about another objective. The former of these alternatives is generally preferable. There is a danger that an interview will become disorganized when the format requires repeated switching of the topic of conversation from one objective to another.

When all phases of evaluation have been taken up for the first performance objective, an evaluation of goal attainment is initiated for another objective. This process is continued until all performance objectives have been considered.

After the performance objectives have been discussed, an evaluation of goal attainment is undertaken for the subordinate objectives. The evaluation of a subordinate objective is generally initiated by summarizing the objective as it was stated during problem identification. For example, the consultant might say, "During problem identification, you indicated that one of your subordinate goals for Bob was for him to be able to initiate positive contacts with others." Next, the consultant recounts the performance objectives included within the subordinate goal. He or she then asks the consultee to specify any additional performance objectives that should be included within the subordinate objective. As indicated in Chapter 3, it is typically the case that not all performance objectives related to a particular subordinate goal will have been specified during the initial problem-identification interview. Thus, it is necessary to take up the issue of additional performance objectives falling within a subordinate goal during evaluation interviews following the initial problem identification. After determining whether there are additional performance objectives, the consultant summarizes the status of the previously specified performance goals with respect to goal attainment. Finally, if the data suggest that the subordinate goal has been attained, the consultant asks the consultee for his or her judgment on whether the subordinate goal has been achieved.

When goal attainment has been established for a particular subordinate objective, discussion may turn to the consideration of a second subordinate goal. The evaluation of goal attainment for the second subordinate objective should, of course, be handled essentially the same way as for the first goal. Consideration of more than two subordinate goals in an evaluation interview is extremely rare. In all likelihood, the discussion will reveal that the second goal has not been attained. Under these circumstances, the major share of interview time for the second objective is usually taken up in establishing performance objectives that fall within the second subordinate goal.

During the later stages of developmental consultation, consideration must be given to evaluating the attainment of the general objectives. To evaluate the attainment of a general objective, the consultant begins by summarizing the objective as it was stated during problem identification. For example, he or she might say, "During problem identification, we said that one of our general goals was for Bob to become effective in his interactions with other children." Then, the consultant would list the subordinate objectives defining the general goal. Thus, he or she might say, "We said that, in order for Bob to be effective in his interactions with other children, he would have to learn to share toys with them, to initiate positive contacts with them, and not to engage in aggressive behavior in his play with others." The consultant would then summarize the status of each of the subordinate goals with respect to goal attainment. Finally, he or she would ask the consultee to render a judgment on the attainment of the general goal.

Goal Attainment Objectives for Problem-Centered Consultation

There is only one goal-attainment objective for problem-centered consultation: to determine the extent to which the behavioral goals established during problem identification have been achieved. To evaluate goal attainment, the consultant begins by selecting for discussion one of the behavioral goals that has been the focus of the consultation efforts. Of course, in some cases, there is only one goal, and selection is obviated. The consultant should ask to see the data for the goal selected. The next step is to summarize the goal as it was established during problem identification. The summary should include a description of the goal in behavioral terms, a detailing of the conditions under which the behavior must occur or not occur if the goal is to be achieved, and a specification of the desired level of strength of the behavior. For example, a consultant might say, "We established at the beginning of consultation that Ted's immaturity manifested itself mainly in his hitting other children. You also said that your goal for Ted was to eliminate hitting behavior completely in situations calling for sharing." After summarizing the previously established goal, the consultant should summarize the data collected during plan implementation. Thus, he or she might say, "I see from the data you collected last week that Ted hit other children three times during the week, once on Monday and twice on Wednesday." The final step in evaluating goal attainment is to ask the consultee for a judgment regarding the extent to which the goal under consideration has been achieved. Thus, in the example given above, the consultant might ask, "On the basis of the data that you collected on Ted's hitting behavior, to what extent would you say that he has achieved the goal of eliminating hitting?"

After goal attainment has been evaluated for the first goal selected, the focus of discussion should shift to the next phase of the evaluation interview. When all phases of evaluation of the initial goal have been completed, another goal should be considered. Evaluation should proceed exactly as before. When all of the behavioral goals to be evaluated have been dealt with, the interview is terminated.

Consultation Guidance Objectives

As pointed out earlier in the chapter, information regarding the extent of goal attainment provides feedback that can be used to guide the consultant and the consultee in selecting a future course of action with respect to the behaviors being considered in the evaluation process. If goal attainment has not occurred, it may be decided that it is necessary to return to problem identification to define a new problem. On the other hand, further problem analysis may be indicated. The phrase "consultation guidance objectives" indicates interview goals related to the task of guiding the consultation process on the basis of feedback concerning goal attainment.

One of the tasks of the consultant at this point in the problem evaluation interview is to signal the need either to progress to the next phase in the evaluation interview, or to go back to an earlier stage in the consultation process when the evaluation of goal attainment suggests that such a course of action might be useful. Signaling of this kind should be done immediately following judgment of the extent to which the goal under consideration has been achieved. For example, in dealing with a behavioral goal in problem-centered consultation, a consultant might say, "As our goal of eliminating Bob's hitting has been only partially attained, we need to conduct a further analysis of the conditions that may be controlling the occurrence of Bob's aggressive acts." Similarly, in handling a subordinate objective in developmental consultation, a consultant might suggest, "Insofar as we have not fully attained the broad goal of assisting Bob to initiate positive interactions with his peers, we'll need to go back to problem identification to establish the remaining specific objectives that fall within the category of positive interactions."

Plan Effectiveness Objectives

One of the major purposes of the evaluation interview is to determine the effectiveness of the plans implemented to achieve specific behavioral goals or performance objectives. Formal evaluation of plan effectiveness is undertaken when efforts to achieve the particular goal associated with the plan being evaluated have ceased. When there has been no progress toward the goal, it is understood implicitly that the plan has not been effective. Thus, there is no need for formal plan evaluation. However, in those instances in which partial goal attainment or goal attainment has occurred, an evaluation of plan effectiveness is useful.

The first interview objective to be achieved in evaluating plan effectiveness is for the consultant to communicate his or her judgments (inferences) regarding plan effectiveness in light of the sources of internal invalidity associated with the evaluation design used for the plan under consideration. The communication of such judgments assists the consultee in making a decision about whether the changes in behavior occurring during consultation should be attributed to the particular plan that was implemented. Judgments based on a recognition of sources of internal invalidity may protect the consultee from drawing unwarranted conclusions about the benefit of a particular intervention. For example, suppose that a teacher implemented a plan involving the use of tangible reinforcement to increase the percentage of assignments completed by a child. The intervention was implemented following a baseline phase, making an A/B design format. The consultant might point out to the teacher that the observed changes in assignment completion may result from events other than the tangible reinforcement that occurred during intervention. For instance, the child's parents may have decided to implement a reinforcement plan of their own.

The second interview objective involved in evaluating plan effectiveness is to elicit a judgment concerning effectiveness from the consultee. Basically, this is a form of social validation involving a subjective judgment by the consultee regarding whether the data are perceived as clinically significant (Kazdin, 1977b; Wolf, 1978). For example, a consultant might ask, "Do you feel that our plan made a difference in Bob's tendency to complete assignments?" The consultee's response to a question of this kind provides the consultant with information concerning the extent to which there is agreement regarding plan effectiveness. If there is not agreement, further discussion should be undertaken to identify and resolve the sources of disagreement. A variety of forms or rating scales may also be used to obtain data on the social validity of the program.

Following the discussion of plan effectiveness related to internal validity, the consultant should generally shift the topic of conversation to the issue of external invalidity. The consultant should begin by giving his or her judgments regarding generalization to other clients and/or settings based on a recognition of sources of external invalidity relevant to the evaluation of the plan. Judgments of this kind help the consultee in making judgments regarding the extent to which the results of consultation can be applied to other persons or situations. For example, when a plan implemented during consultation is successful, the consultant should indicate to the consultee that conclusions regarding the generalizability of the intervention effects may be limited by the various situational and environmental factors in the applied setting.

After the consultant has explained the sources of external invalidity associated with the plan under discussion, he or she should ask the consultee for a judgment regarding external validity. As in the evaluation of internal invalidity, the consultee's judgment indicates to the consultant the extent to which information regarding invalidity has been applied by the consultee to the plan evaluation.

Postimplementation Planning Objectives

When the plan evaluation has been completed, postimplementation planning is initiated. The first interview goal to be achieved in postimplementation planning is to select a postimplementation plan alternative from among the three possible types that may be put into operation following the termination of consultation.

The consultant generally takes the lead in introducing the discussion of postimplementation plan alternatives. A discussion of alternatives may be initiated simply by alerting the consultee to the need to make a decision concerning the advisability of leaving the previously implemented plan in effect, removing the plan, or constructing a new plan. For example, a consultant might say, "We need to make some decisions regarding the plan that you implemented to eliminate Ted's aggressive behavior. You may decide to leave the plan in effect; you may want to alter it in some way; or you may want to remove it entirely."

After the consultee has been alerted to the need to consider the postimplementation alternatives, the consultant may wish to point out factors that may influence the likelihood of problem recurrence. This should be done when there is a likelihood that potentially significant influences on problem recurrence will go unrecognized if they are not mentioned. For example, if withdrawal of the reinforcement used during plan implementation is likely to cause the behavior of concern in consultation to revert to baseline level, the consultant would probably choose to call this fact to the consultee's attention.

When in the consultant's judgment all of the factors relevant to problem recurrence have been discussed, the consultant asks the consultee to select a postimplementation plan alternative. It is not always necessary for the consultee to consider all three possible alternatives in making a selection. In some instances, the choice is obvious and requires little discussion. For example, if the goal of consultation involved the acquisition of a new academic skill and if it is likely that the skill will be used continually without special planning for review sessions, the consultee would probably suggest removing the previously implemented plan without much discussion of other alternatives.

If the consultee chooses either to leave the previously implemented plan in effect following consultation, or to remove the plan immediately, the discussion of the postimplementation plan is complete. However, if the choice is to construct a new plan, or to gradually withdraw the old plan, the details of the new plan or of the gradual withdrawal must be specified. In either case, the consultant must establish both plan strategies and plan tactics following the procedures described in Chapter 4. For example, a consultant might ask a parent, "How could you use the social approval provided at home to help maintain the improvements in Ted's study behavior that you have helped him to achieve?" In this question, the consultant suggests the strategy of using reinforcement available in the natural environment to maintain behavior and, at the same time, calls for the specification of a tactic by the consultee, indicating precisely what reinforcers to use and how to apply them.

When the construction of a new plan involves placing the behavior under client control, post implementation plan strategies almost invariably include some provision for the consultee to interview the client to establish the postimplementation goals, the procedures for measuring the behavior related to the goals, the plans to achieve the goals, and the methods of assessing goal attainment. As in other instances of the construction of a new plan, the consultant usually takes the lead in specifying the necessary strategies, and the consultee is often largely responsible for the designation of the plan tactics. For example, a consultant might say, "If Alice is going to assume responsibility for maintaining her own self-care behavior, you'll need to spend some time discussing with her how she might remind herself of the need to brush her teeth and wash her face in the morning. You'll also need to help her to devise some way to reinforce herself for appropriate self-care behavior, as you'll no longer be rewarding her for it. How do you want to go about discussing these issues with Alice?"

When a postimplementation plan has been established, provisions must be made for postimplementation recording. Because of the consultant's special knowledge regarding assessment, he or she should take the lead in suggesting a postimplementation recording procedure. In pointing out the various possibilities for recording, the consultant should keep in mind consultee concerns and expectations regarding the maintenance and generalization of behavior. For example, if the consultee is concerned only about the durability of the behavior change, the consultant may suggest the use of the probe technique at successive points in time. On the other hand, if generalization is an issue of importance, the consultant may advise that a probe measure be used across different situations.

After the issue of the type of procedure to be used has been settled,

the consultant must establish the specific details of the recording pro
cedure. The accomplishment of this task should follow the procedures
described in Chapter 3 regarding the specification of recording techniques.
For example, in the many instances in which observations of behavior are
needed, the consultant must establish what to record, how to record, how
many data to take, when to record, how many times to record, and who is
to carry out the data collection.

The final objective in postimplementation planning is to establish procedures specifying what to do in the event of problem recurrence. The
central task of the consultant in establishing procedures for handling problem recurrence is to ensure contact between the consultant and the consultee in the event of recurrence. The consultant may plan to establish
contact either by requesting the consultee to initiate contact if the problem
should reappear, or by suggesting a consultant-initiated contact for follow-
up in the case. When the consultant feels that the consultee may fail to
make contact when it is needed, the consultant may suggest a contingency
plan to augment postconsultation contacts. As in the design of other types
of plans in consultation, the construction of a contingency plan requires
the designation of plan strategies and plan tactics.

Procedural Objectives in Problem Evaluation

Two kinds of procedural details may have to be attended to in the
problem evaluation interview. One is to schedule additional interviews
and the other is to terminate consultation. If one or more goals of consultation have not been attained, it is necessary for the consultant to schedule
the next meeting to deal with the objectives that have not been achieved.
For example, in developmental consultation involving reiterative applications of the consultative problem-solving process, the problem evaluation
interview is typically combined with problem identification. Under these
conditions, the consultant schedules a problem analysis interview to follow
the combined evaluation identification interview.

If all goals have been achieved, the consultant should formally terminate consultation. Termination should generally include an invitation to
seek further consultation services should the need for such services arise.
For example, the termination of problem-centered consultation typically
involves an invitation to call for services in the event that additional problems of concern to the consultee occur. The main reason for extending
invitations to seek further service is that it indicates a willingness on the
part of the consultant to provide assistance when needed.

Outline for the Problem Evaluation Interview

Outlines of problem evaluation interviews for developmental and
problem-centered consultation are presented below. Like the interview

outlines given in earlier chapters, the outlines of evaluation interviews are intended only as general guides. They do not cover all possible cases.

The Developmental Evaluation Interview

The following interview outline illustrates the steps generally followed in conducting a problem evaluation interview for developmental consultation. The procedure of indicating objectives by roman-numeral heading, types of verbalizations of capital letters, and examples by arabic numbers is followed here as in previous outlines.

Evaluate goal attainment:

    I. Emit behavior specification elicitors to initiate evaluation of goal attainment of the performance objectives.
        A. "Let's look at the data on Carol's disparaging remarks concerning her grades."
        B. "Show me the data on student accuracy in listing occupations related to distributive careers."
    II. If there are sufficient data to evaluate goal attainment, emit behavior specification elicitors and/or emitters describing client performance during intervention while graphing the intervention data for the consultee.
        A. "The data show that Carol didn't make any disparaging remarks about her grades last week."
        B. "I see that the sample of students you tested on Monday were able to name occupations in the distributive category with 90% accuracy."
   III. Emit behavior and behavior-setting-summarization emitters to establish recall of the performance objectives specified during problem identification.
        A. "During our initial meeting, you indicated that your first goal was to eliminate completely Carol's disparaging comments about her grades."
        B. "You said that you wanted her to stop making critical comments about her grades at home, in informal social gatherings with her friends, and to her teachers."
        C. "You indicated that, for the unit on distributive occupations, you wanted the students to be able to list 10 occupations in the distributive category."
        D. "You said that the students could show mastery of these goals through either oral or written test performance."
   IV. Emit behavior summarization emitters and positive validation elicitors to evaluate the extent to which the objective under consideration has been attained.

A. "The data indicate that Carol made no disparaging remarks about her grades in any of the settings in which observations were made."
B. "The data show that each of the students you tested was able to name distributive occupations with 90% accuracy."
C. "Do we agree that this goal has been attained?"

V. After the evaluation of goal attainment of the performance objectives previously targeted for intervention, emit behavior summarization emitters to initiate the evaluation of goal attainment of the subordinate objectives. The verbalizations that initiate the evaluation should summarize the subordinate goal under discussion as it was specified in problem identification and should recount the performance objectives designated as falling within the domain of the subordinate goal.

A. "During our first session, you indicated that one of your broad goals for Carol was to assist her to show self-confidence through the kinds of things that she says about herself."
B. "One specific goal falling within the broad category of verbal behavior demonstrating self-confidence was to eliminate Carol's disparaging remarks about grades."
C. "In our first meeting, you said that one of the major goals of your career education program was for students to become knowledgeable about the broad categories of occupations from which they may choose a career."
D. "One of the specific goals that we established within the category of knowledge of occupations was for students to be able to list 10 occupations in the distributive category."

VI. Emit behavior specification elicitors to identify previously unspecified performance objectives falling within the class of objectives defined by the subordinate objective under discussion.

A. "In addition to eliminating disparaging remarks about grades, what are some other specific goals that you have relating to the broad goal of increasing Carols' verbal manifestations of self-confidence?"
B. "What are some other specific objectives that you have for your students regarding knowledge of occupations?"

VII. Emit behavior summarization emitters to summarize the status of goal attainment of the performance objectives falling within the domain of the subordinate objective discussion.

A. "Within the broad goal of assisting Carol to display self-confidence verbally, we have attained the goal of eliminating her disparaging remarks about her grades."

B. "However, we have not yet established specific goals with respect to Carol's tendency to criticize her physical appearance and her social skills."

C. "In the area of knowledge of occupations, your students have demonstrated knowledge of occupations in the distributive category."

D. "However, they have not demonstrated knowledge of occupations in any other of the career categories that you specified."

VIII. Emit behavior positive-validation elicitors to evaluate the extent of goal attainment of the subordinate objectives.

A. "Do we agree that the broad goal of assisting Carol to display self-confidence has been only partially attained?"

B. "Do we concur that we have only partially reached the objective of assisting your students to become knowledgeable about occupational categories?"

IX. During the later stages of developmental consultation, emit behavior summarization emitters to initiate the evaluation of goal attainment of the general objectives. Verbalizations used to initiate the evaluation should summarize the general objective under consideration as specified during problem identification. In addition, subordinate objectives falling within the general objective should be recounted.

A. "When we first started consultation, you said that your main goal for Carol was to help her to display self-confidence in social situations."

B. "You also indicated that, for Carol to show self-confidence, she would have to display confidence through both what she said and how she acted."

C. "You indicated that one of the major goals of your career education program was to enable students to attain knowledge about vocational and avocational activities."

D. "You said that, in the area of knowledge about careers, students ought to know the broad categories of occupations from which they may choose a career, the kinds of activities associated with those occupations, the societal functions served by the various occupations, the educational requirements for entry into the various occupations, and the range of income levels associated with different occupational areas."

E. "You indicated that, in the area of knowledge about avocational activities, students should display awareness of the broad categories of avocational interest from which they may

select their leisuretime activities, of the societal functions
served by avocational interests, and of the role of avocational
activities in enhancing social and personal development."

X. Emit behavior summarization emitters and positive validation
elicitors to evaluate the extent of goal attainment of the general
objective under discussion.

A. "As we agreed earlier, Carol has demonstrated self-confidence both in her physical acts and in her verbal behavior."

B. "Can we say, then, that your overall goal of assisting Carol
to achieve self-confidence in social situations has been
attained?"

C. "We have shown that your students have achieved all of the
subordinate goals falling within the major objective of attaining knowledge concerning vocational and avocational
activities."

D. "Do we agree, then, that this general goal of your career
education program has been achieved?"

On the basis of information derived from the evaluation of goal attainment, guide the consultation either to the next phase of the evaluation
interview or to earlier stages in the consultation process:

I. If the information derived from the evaluation of goal attainment
suggests the desirability of progressing to the next phase in the
evaluation interview, emit plan specification elicitors to signal
the need to move to the next phase.

A. "Let's talk for a minute about the effectiveness of the plan
that was implemented to eliminate Carol's critical comments
about her grades."

B. "Let's consider the effectiveness of the teaching procedure
that you used to assist the students to learn the names of
occupations in the distributive category."

II. If information derived from the evaluation of goal attainment
suggests the need to return either to problem identification or to
problem analysis, emit behavior or plan specification elicitors to
signal the need to go back to an earlier stage in the consultation
process.

A. "Let's identify precisely those objectives that we have not
yet considered and establish procedures for assessing behavior related to them."

B. "Let's spend a little time reanalyzing the problem of how to
teach for mastery of the objective of specifying the educational requirements for entry into distributive occupations."

Evaluate plan effectiveness:

I. Emit plan inference emitters to evaluate plan effectiveness in light of sources of internal invalidity.
   A. "As our plan for Carol was in effect for only a single time period, and as other events occurring during that time might have produced the desired changes in Carol's behavior, it is possible that the plan did not change Carol's actions."
   B. "As your teaching procedure was in effect for the same time period for all students, it is possible that our plan was not the only factor influencing student learning of types of occupations."

II. Emit plan positive-validation elicitors to evaluate whether, in the consultee's judgment, the plan implemented was responsible for the observed changes in client behavior.
   A. "Do we agree that we cannot say for sure that the plan to eliminate Carol's disparaging remarks about her grades was effective?"
   B. "In your judgment, can we say with a reasonable degree of confidence that your plan to teach recall of activities associated with the category of distributing goods was effective?"

III. Emit plan inference emitters to evaluate plan effectiveness in light of possible sources of external invalidity related to the evaluation design under consideration.
   A. "Because observations made on a person's behavior may affect the behavior, our plan for Carol may not work in situations in which observations of her behavior do not occur."
   B. "Even though your plan for teaching the recall of activities associated with occupations involving the distribution of goods was effective, it is possible that it may not work with other students having different abilities."

IV. Emit behavior and/or plan positive-validation elicitors to evaluate the likelihood that plan effects will generalize to other clients or situations.
   A. "Do we agree that it is not necessarily safe to assume that the changes that have taken place in Carol's behavior will generalize to situations in which observations of her behavior, either by her or by you do not occur?"
   B. "Do we concur that, in the absence of any marked changes in the student population from year to year, your plan will probably be effective with other students who have acquired information regarding distributive occupations."

Carry out postimplementation planning:

    I. Emit plan specification elicitors to initiate a consideration of postimplementation plan alternatives.

       A. "We need to consider whether to keep the plan you used to change Carol's behavior in effect or to alter it or to remove it."

       B. "Let's talk for a minute about the kinds of plans we might make to maintain the knowledge that your students have acquired regarding distributive occupations."

   II. Emit inference emitters in various content categories (e.g., behavior, behavior setting, plan, and observation) to describe factors that may influence problem recurrence.

       A. "It is conceivable that an abrupt cessation of Carols' observations of her own behavior may eventuate in a return of the problem."

       B. "It is possible that interference from things learned after the unit on occupations related to the distribution of goods may cause the students to forget the information that they acquired regarding occupations in the distributive category."

  III. Emit plan specification elicitors and emitters to establish plan strategies and tactics for the postimplementation plan.

       A. "Following consultation, do you want to keep your plan in effect, alter it, or remove it?"

       B. "How would you like to change the plan?"

       C. "One procedure that could be used to avoid possible ill effects of the abrupt cessation of observations of Carol's behavior would be to withdraw observation gradually."

       D. "We need to make some plans to ensure that your students won't forget what they have just learned."

       E. "What kinds of provisions could you make to have them review the material on distributive occupations periodically?"

  IV. Emit plan summarization emitters and positive validation elicitors to establish agreement regarding the postimplementation plan.

       A. "You said that you were going to leave all aspects of the plan for controlling disparaging remarks in effect with the exception of Carol's observations of her own behavior."

       B. "Observations will be withdrawn gradually during the next month by a progressive reduction in the number of days that observations are made during the week."

       C. "Is that correct?"

       D. "You indicated that you intended to set aside two self-study

periods each month for the next 2 months to give your students a chance to review what they have learned about occupations related to the distribution of goods."

  E. "Have I summarized your plan accurately?"

V. Emit observation specification and/or, if desired, evaluation elicitors and emitters and positive-validation elicitors to establish
postimplementation recording procedures.

  A. "We need to establish some procedures for a periodic assessment of Carol's critical comments about her grades."

  B. "Periodic recording will give us a record of problem recurrence if it should happen to take place."

  C. "I would suggest that you record Carol's behavior for 2 days
each month for the next 3 months, using the same procedures that you have been using."

  D. "It would be advisable for Carol to record her own behavior
at school and with her friends just as she has been doing."

  E. "However, as we discussed earlier, she should gradually
reduce the number of days per week that she has been recording her behavior."

  F. "During the second and third months, Carol ought to record
2 days a month, using the same recording schedule that you
will follow."

  G. "Do these suggestions meet with your approval?"

  H. "We need to set up some procedures to measure forgetting
in your students with respect to the material that they have
mastered."

  I. "I would suggest that you include two or three items on
distributive occupations in the unit test that you give during
the next 3 or 4 months."

  J. "Does that idea meet with your approval?"

VI. Emit other specification elicitors or emitters to arrange for
postconsultation contact related to problem recurrence.

  A. "When we evaluate Carol's progress toward her next consultation goal, let's take a few moments to check on any
recurrence of disparaging remarks about grades."

  B. "In a couple of months, let's plan to discuss how well your
students have retained the information that they acquired on
distributive occupations."

  C. "We can discuss retention along with the evaluation of performance for some of the other goals that we will be dealing
with at that time."

VII. If advisable, emit plan specification elicitors to initiate establishment of a contingency plan to be used in the event of problem
recurrence. The initiation of contingency planning should be

followed by the specification of plan strategies and plan tactics as discussed in Chapter 4.
  A. "Let's make a plan specifying what you can do if Carol's tendency to make critical remarks about her grades should recur."
  B. "Let's establish a plan indicating what you can do if an inordinate amount of forgetting should occur regarding knowledge of distributive occupations."

Terminate the consultation, or make arrangements for subsequent interviews:

  I. In the event that all objectives have been dealt with in developmental consultation, emit other specification elicitors and emitters and positive evaluation emitters to terminate the consultation.
    A. "As we have dealt with all of the goals that you specified for Carol, this will be our last interview."
    B. "I have enjoyed working with you."
    C. "If other problems come up, don't hesitate to call."
    D. "Insofar as we have considered all of the objectives that you have established for the career education program, our work is finished."
    E. "It has been a rewarding experience for me to work with you on the program."
    F. "If I can be of further assistance, don't hesitate to contact me."
  II. In the event that some objectives have not yet been considered in developmental consultation, emit other specification elicitors and/or emitters to schedule the next interview.
    A. "When shall we meet again to discuss plans for achieving the next goal for Carol?"
    B. "When can we get together to discuss plans for objectives related to building a value system to guide vocational and avocational decisions?"

The Problem-Centered Evaluation Interview

The outline below illustrates the typical structure of the problem-centered evaluation interview. The format of the outline is the same as that used to illustrate the developmental interview.

  I. Evaluate goal attainment.
    A. Emit behavior specification elicitors to initiate the evaluation of goal attainment.

1. "Show me the data that you collected last week on Alice's hitting."
2. "Let's look at the data on Ted's oral reading for last week."

B. If the data are sufficient to warrant an evaluation of goal attainment, emit behavior specification elicitors and/or emitters describing client behavior during plan implementation while graphing the intervention data for the consultee.
   1. "Alice didn't hit other children at all last week."
   2. "Ted made three errors on Tuesday and five on Wednesday."

C. Emit behavior and behavior-setting-summarization emitters to establish recall of the specific behavioral goal under discussion.
   1. "In our first meeting, you indicated that Alice used to hit other children in the classroom."
   2. "You further stated that because the behavior was so disruptive you wanted it eliminated completely."
   3. "In our first session, you indicated that Ted continually misread words during oral reading."
   4. "Subsequently, you indicated that you would be satisfied if he could reduce his error rate to five errors per day."

D. Emit behavior summarization emitters and positive validation elicitors to evaluate attainment of the goal under consideration.
   1. "Alice did not hit children last week."
   2. "Do we agree that the goal of eliminating Alice's hitting behavior has been achieved?"
   3. "Ted made an average of three errors per session in oral reading last week."
   4. "Can we say, then, that the goal of reducing Ted's errors to five per day has been attained?"

II. On the basis of information obtained in the evaluation of goal attainment, guide consultation either to the next phase of the evaluation interview or to earlier stages in the consultation process.

A. If information obtained in the evaluation of goal attainment suggests the advisability of progressing to the next phase in the evaluation interview, emit plan specification elicitors to signal the need to move to the next phase.
   1. "We need to discuss the effectiveness of the plan implemented to eliminate Alice's hitting."
   2. "Let's discuss the effectiveness of the procedures used to reduce Ted's errors in oral reading."

B. If information obtained in the evaluation of goal attainment indicates a need to go back either to problem identification or to problem analysis, emit behavior and plan specification elicitors to signal the need to return to an earlier stage in the consultation process.

1. "As Alice hit a considerable number of children last week, we need to reconsider our plan for controlling her aggressive behavior."
2. "Insofar as Ted is still making a large number of errors in oral reading, we need to take another look at our plan for increasing his oral reading accuracy."

III. Evaluate plan effectiveness.

A. Emit plan inference emitters to evaluate plan effectiveness in light of sources of internal invalidity.

1. "Our plan for Alice may not have been what changed her behavior."
2. "As it is possible that events that we were not aware of occurred at the same time that the plan was implemented and could have produced the changes that took place in Alice's behavior, our plan for Alice may not have been effective."

B. Emit plan positive-validation elicitors to evaluate whether, in the consultee's judgment, the plan implemented was responsible for the observed changes in behavior.

1. "Do we concur that there is some doubt about whether the plan implemented to eliminate Alice's hitting was entirely responsible for the disappearance of that behavior?"
2. "In your opinion, was the plan implemented to reduce Ted's errors in oral reading effective?"

C. Emit plan inference emitters to evaluate plan effectiveness in light of possible sources of external invalidity associated with the plan design.

1. "Even though our plan worked with Ted, it might not have worked with another student."
2. "If Ted had not had the skills to read accurately, our plan probably would not have worked."

D. Emit behavior and/or plan positive-validation elicitors to evaluate the likelihood that plan effects will generalize to other clients or situations.

1. "Because, as I have indicated, the basic plan that we used with Alice has been applied many times, in your judgment would the plan work with other children with whom you are having discipline problems?"

    2. "Do we concur that it would probably not be safe to conclude that the plan implemented for Ted would work with other students who have different skills?"

IV. Carry out postimplementation planning.

  A. Emit plan specification elicitors to initiate a consideration of postimplementation plan alternatives.

    1. "Let's make some plans to ensure that Alice won't start hitting again."

    2. "We need to think about things that can be done to ensure that Ted will maintain his low error rate in oral reading."

  B. If necessary, emit inference emitters in various content categories (e.g., behavior, behavior setting, plan, and observation) to describe factors that the consultee may have failed to consider and that may influence problem recurrence.

    1. "You probably will want to stop using tangible rewards to maintain behavior other than hitting because of the expense involved in using this type of reward."

    2. "However, it is possible that if you were to withdraw the rewards, Alice's hitting would emerge once again under the control of peer attention."

  C. Emit plan specification and/or inference elicitors and emitters to establish plan strategies and tactics for the postimplementation plan.

    1. "It might be useful to replace tangible rewards gradually with social approval for activities other than hitting."

    2. "Give me some examples of things that you could do to replace tangible incentives with social approval."

    3. "What changes, if any, would you make in your plan for Ted following consultation?"

  D. Emit plan summarization emitters and positive validation elicitors to establish agreement regarding the postimplementation plan.

    1. "You have said that you are going to remove tangible rewards for Alice and replace them with social approval."

    2. "You indicated that you would do this by increasing the time period between instances of tangible reinforcement, and by increasing the number of instances of social approval between the times that tangible incentives are given."

  E. Emit observation specifications and/or, if desired, evaluation elicitors and emitters and positive validation elicitors and emitters to establish postimplementation recording procedures.

1. "We need to make some provisions for documenting hit
   ting, should it occur in the future."
2. "I would suggest that, for the next couple of months, you
   make a record at the end of each month of any instances
   of hitting that you recall during the month."
3. "Would that be agreeable to you?"
4. "We need to have a periodic record of Ted's oral reading
   so that we will be aware of any recurrence of his problems
   in this area."
5. "I would suggest that you set aside 2 days each month for
   the next couple of months to record his errors in oral
   reading."
6. "You can apply the same recording procedures that you
   have been using."
7. "Is it OK with you?"

F. Emit other specification elicitors or emitters to arrange for
   postimplementation contact concerning problem recurrence.
   1. "I'll call you in a couple of months to see how Alice is
      doing."
   2. "Be sure to contact me if Ted's error rate in oral reading
      increases."

G. If advisable, emit plan specification elicitors to initiate the
   construction of a contingency plan to be used in the event of
   problem recurrence. The initiation of the contingency plan
   should be followed by the establishment of plan strategies
   and tactics in accordance with the procedures described in
   Chapter 4.
   1. "We need to make a plan indicating what you can do if
      Alice returns to her hitting ways."
   2. "Let's discuss what you might do if Ted started to make a
      lot of errors in oral reading again."

V. Terminate the consultation or make arrangements for subsequent interviews.

A. If the goals of problem-centered consultation have been attained, or if no further interventions are planned with respect to the goals under consideration, emit other
   specification elicitors and evaluation emitters to terminate
   consultation.
   1. "As our goal for Alice has been achieved, this will be our
      last meeting."
   2. "It has been a pleasure working with you."
   3. "If other problems arise in your classroom, please give me
      a call."

4. "Our work with Ted is finished."
5. "I have enjoyed our discussions."
6. "If you have additional concerns about ways to help Ted or any of the other children, please give me call."

B. If the goals of consultation have not yet been met, emit other specification elicitors and/or emitters to schedule the next interview.

1. "When can we meet again to evaluate Alice's progress under our new plan for her?"
2. "Where shall we get together?"

Assessing Evaluation Interview Skills

After having read through the above outlines, the reader may want to try conducting some problem-evaluation interviews. Obviously, it would be beneficial to try both a developmental and problem-centered interview before attempting a developmental interview, as the developmental interview tends to be more complex than the problem-centered evaluation session. The reader should tape-record these interviews so that they can be evaluated by means of the procedures described in the following paragraphs.

Checklists for the Problem Evaluation Interview

Figures 6-10 and 6-11 illustrate checklists that can be used in evaluating developmental and problem-centered interviews. As in earlier chapters, the reader should apply the scoring procedures described in Chapter 2 in using the checklists.

Message Classification Analysis in Problem Evaluation

The reader wishes to do an in-depth study of his or her verbalizations in the evaluation interview should use the consultation analysis record (CAR) described in earlier sections of the book. As discussed previously, coding with the CAR will enable the reader to analyze her or his use of the content, process, and control categories during interviewing sessions.

As should be clear from the discussion of the problem evaluation interview presented in the previous section, there is quite a bit of flexibility in the conduct of the interview. For example, as we have indicated, the interview may be combined with either problem identification or problem analysis. The procedures for assessing interviewing effectiveness to be described in subsequent paragraphs apply only to those portions of the interview concerned directly with evaluation. Should it be necessary to

CONSULTANT _____ CASE NUMBER _____

CONSULTEE _____ PAGE _____

**Problem-Evaluation Checklist
for Developmental Consultation**

Required Verbal Units	*Frequency of Unit Use*
1. Behavior specification elicitors (to initiate examination of plan implementation data)	_____
2. Behavior specification elicitors or emitters (to describe client performance)	_____
3. Behavior summarization emitters (to recall performance objectives and summarize client performance)	_____
4. Behavior-setting summarization emitters (to recall performance objectives)	_____
5. Behavior positive-validation elicitors (to evaluate goal-attainment for performance objectives)	_____
6. Behavior summarization emitters (to recall subordinate and general objectives being evaluated)	_____
7. Behavior specification elicitors (to identify previously unspecified performance objectives)	_____
8. Behavior summarization emitters (to summarize the goal-attainment status of performance objectives related to subordinate goals under discussion)	_____
9. Behavior positive-validation elicitors (to evaluate attainment of subordinate and/or general objectives)	_____
10. Behavior specification elicitors (to identify previously unspecified performance objectives)	_____
11. Behavior summarization emitters (to summarize status of performance objectives)	_____

Required Verbal Units	Frequency of Unit Use
12. Behavior or plan specification elicitors (to guide the consultation process)	
13. Plan inference emitters (to evaluate plan effectiveness in light of sources of invalidity)	
14. Behavior and/or plan positive validation elicitors (to evaluate likelihood that plan effects will generalize to other clients or situations)	_____
15. Plan specification elicitors and emitters (to establish a post-implementation plan)	_____
16. Inference emitters (to describe influences in problem reoccurrence)	_____
17. Plan specification elicitors and emitters (to establish post-implementation plan strategies and tactics)	_____
18. Plan summarization emitters (to summarize the post-implementation plan)	_____
19. Plan positive-validation elicitors (to establish agreement concerning the post-implementation plan)	_____
20. Observation elicitors and emitters (to establish post-implementation recording procedures)	_____
21. Observation positive validation elicitors (to affirm agreement regarding post-implementation recording)	_____
22. If necessary, plan specification elicitors and emitters (to establish a contingency plan)	_____
23. Other specification elicitors and emitters (to terminate consultation or schedule additional contacts)	_____

FIGURE 6-10. Consultation analysis checklist for a developmental problem-evaluation interview.

CONSULTANT _____ CASE NUMBER _____

CONSULTEE _____ PAGE _____

Problem-Evaluation Checklist
for Problem-Centered Consultation

Required Verbal Units	*Frequency of Unit Use*
1. Behavior specification elicitors (to initiate examination of plan-implementation data)	_____
2. Behavior specification elicitors or emitters (to describe client behavior)	_____
3. Behavior summarization emitters (to recall behavioral goal and summarize client performance)	_____
4. Behavior-setting summarization emitters (to recall behavioral goal)	_____
5. Behavior positive-validation elicitors (to evaluate goal attainment)	_____
6. Behavior and/or plan specification elicitors (to guide the consultation process)	_____
7. Plan inference emitters (to provide inferences concerning plan effectiveness)	_____
8. Plan positive-validation elicitors (to evaluate role of plan in behavior change)	_____
9. Behavior and/or plan positive-validation elicitors (to establish agreement regarding plan effectiveness)	_____

FIGURE 6-11. Consultation analysis checklist for a problem-centered problem-evaluation interview.

return to problem identification or to problem analysis, the reader should apply the indices of interviewing effectiveness for those interviews in evaluating segments that do not focus on evaluation.

In both developmental and problem-centered evaluation interviews, message content should include mainly the behavior, plan, and observation categories. The use of the behavior category occurs, for the most part, in the evaluation of goal attainment. More attention is usually given to this task in developmental interviews than in problem-centered interviews. Thus, the reader should expect to find a somewhat greater proportion of verbalizations falling in the behavior category in developmental evaluation interviews than in problem-centered interviews. Plan verbalizations tend to occur most often in connection with the evaluation of plan effectiveness.

Required Verbal Units	Frequency of Unit Use
10. Plan specification elicitors and emitters (to establish a post-implementation plan)	_____
11. Inference emitters (to describe influences on problem reoccurrence)	_____
12. Plan specification and/or inference elicitors and emitters (to establish post-implementation plan strategies and tactics)	_____
13. Plan summarization emitters (to summarize the post-implementation plan)	_____
14. Plan positive-validation elicitors (to establish agreement concerning the post-implementation plan)	_____
15. Observation specification elicitors and emitters (to establish post-implementation recording procedures)	_____
16. Observation positive-validation elicitors (to affirm agreement regarding post-implementation recording)	_____
17. If necessary, plan specification elicitors and emitters (to establish a contingency plan)	_____
18. Other specification elicitors and emitters (to terminate consultation or schedule additional contacts)	_____

FIGURE 6-11. (Cont.)

However, plan verbalizations are also used in postimplementation planning. Observation verbalizations are used mainly in the discussion of postimplementation recording procedures. However, they may also occur occasionally in conversation about the data collected during plan implementation.

The reader is undoubtedly familiar with the two kinds of errors that can be made with respect to interview content. One is to omit discussion within a particular content category entirely. The other is to slight one of the categories. In either case, there is a failure to communicate needed information, and it is possible that the effectiveness of the consultation may be damaged. For example, a failure to include adequate discussion in the observation subcategory of message content may lead to a failure to develop an adequate set of procedures for postimplementation recording. If this were to happen, the consultee would probably be deprived of the data necessary to assess the durability of goal attainment or the generalization of goal behavior to new settings.

To avoid the errors of slighting or omitting important content, one should strive for a relatively even balance of utterances in the relevant content categories. Thus, in the problem evaluation interview, verbalizations in the behavior, plan, and observation categories should be fairly evenly distributed. However, as we indicated above, in the case of the developmental interview, there may be greater representation in the behavior classification than in the other two categories.

As in both the problem identification and the problem analysis interviews, the reader should strive not only for content balance, but also for content focus. Generally, the reader should try to explore one topic of conversation in detail before turning to other matters and should use the same procedures for judging focus that were used for the problem identification and analysis interviews. The pattern of content changes will show up on the CAR form. If the majority of verbalizations within each set of five utterances fall within the same category, the focus is probably adequate.

With one exception, the process categories used in problem evaluation are the same as those used in problem identification and problem analysis. The preponderance of verbalizations should fall in the specification, summarization, and validation categories. However, in the problem evaluation interview, there should also be a number of inferences. These, as the reader will recall, are used mainly in the discussion of sources of invalidity related to plan effectiveness. In addition, they should occur in the description of factors that may influence problem recurrence. Verbalizations in the specification, summarization, validation, and inference categories should be relatively evenly distributed during the problem evaluation interview. However, inferences may be slightly underrepresented without significant damage to interviewing effectiveness.

In all interviews, it is the consultant's responsibility to guide the consultee through the problem-solving process. Thus, in problem evaluation, as in other interviews, the percentage of consultant elicitors should outweigh the percentage of emitters. However, the consultant is required to provide more direct information to the consultee during the evaluation interview than in the other interviews. For example, he or she generally emits inferences about plan effectiveness and about factors influencing problem recurrence. Accordingly, the balance between elicitors and emitters may be closer in the evaluation interview than is typically the case in the other interviews.

III

Applications of Consultation in Applied Settings

7

Case Studies in Behavioral Consultation

This chapter contains three case studies illustrating applications of the consultative problem-solving model. Much of the material is in the form of verbatim transcripts of actual consultation interviews. They have been edited slightly to increase readability. The editing has been limited to the deletion of redundancies, irrelevant interjections, and other similar utterances that contributed nothing to the substance of the recorded discussions. The cases were selected to represent a variety of different types of problems and to illustrate some of the ways in which what a consultant says during an interview may produce desirable or undesirable outcomes in consultation.

An Example of a Developmental Problem-Identification Interview

The first consultation example to be presented is a developmental problem-identification interview. With respect to interview structure, developmental consultation differs from problem-centered consultation mainly in the manner in which the problem identification interview is conducted. The case presented below illustrates the use of the developmental approach in formulating goals for increasing the social competency of a second-grade girl.

The Problem Identification Interview[1]

Consultant: (1) Jody, what are your general concerns regarding Candy's behavior? (2) In very general terms, tell me about her behavior.

[1]Numbers in parentheses refer to the units of observation coded on CAR forms for interviews discussed in the chapter.

07

Consultee: She is a very complicated child. She has had quite a difficult background. Mainly, I guess it's her adjustment to her new home, her adjustment to the new class situation, and being able to get along with her peer group.

Consultant: (3) OK.

Consultee: All of these things are based on what has been happening to her in the past.

Consultant: (4) As far as adjustment to her classroom situation is concerned, what are some of the things you are talking about?

Consultee: Her behavior is inappropriate in that she has a hard time staying in her seat. She has a hard time knowing when to speak out and when not to. She does a lot of blurting out of things when she shouldn't. She has been taking things from other children but wants very much to be their friend and to be my friend.

Consultant: (5) The general area then appears to be social, getting along with other children.

Consultee: Right. Rather than academics.

Consultant: (6) Academic behavior is not uppermost in your mind?

Consultee: She does quite well.

Consultant: (7) In the area of social concerns, it would be adjustment to the classroom situation, staying in the seat, speaking at appropriate times, and taking things from others that are the concerns you have about her social behavior.

Consultee: She just doesn't know how to go about getting along with other people. There are a lot of little things that happen that cause her not to be liked by the other children. Yet, they are trying, in part, to overlook things. She doesn't seem to be willing to try to work things out by herself, nor does she seem to understand what is necessary. She just seems to go down her own little path.

Consultant: (8) So that the major goals that you have, or the direction that you would like to move in, is for her to be able to get along better with others and to adjust to the classroom situation better. (9) You see those as two separate areas: adjusting to the classroom and getting along better with others?

Consultee: Separate, yes. But it is important to work on them together.

Consultant: (10) As far as getting along better with others is concerned, what are some of the things you would like her to do?

Consultee: I would like for her to learn to understand others. What are some of the necessary social skills she needs to have? She needs to know when children want to be her friend. She often puts the children in a position where she demands this friendship. When she doesn't get it, she turns kind of vengeful instead of trying to figure out what she is going to do in order to get them to be her friend.

Consultant: (11) All right, she demands friendship, and (12) what exactly does she do in these kinds of situations?

Consultee: When she is wanting to have friends?

Consultant: (13) Yes.

Consultee: She will pull at them physically, handle them in trying to get them away from other children. She often trys to give things to the children and then expects them to turn around and be her friend because she has given something to them. She trys to get up and be by a particular person at a time when she shouldn't be out of her seat. The other child knows that what is going on is wrong and trys to ignore it or tells her to sit down or something. She still stays right there.

Consultant: (14) Then, in getting along with peers, it is to know when she is with friends not to demand their friendship or to get them away from other children or to try to bribe them into being her friend, but to understand the ways in which she can get other children to like her. (15) Is that right?

Consultee: Yes.

Consultant: (16) In the area of adjustment to the classroom, what are some of the skills that you would like her to have?

Consultee: I would like her to stay in her seat when it is the appropriate time to be in her seat. I would like her to listen when I say, "Please go sit down," rather than have to get to the point that I am having to get mad at her. I don't like to get to that point. She won't listen at first. She won't listen a second time and so on. I would like her to raise her hand instead of just blurting out in class. These are the main things she needs to work on, I think.

Consultant: (17) Our two major areas of concern are getting along with other children and adjusting to the classroom situation. (18) Which of these areas would you want to concentrate on?

Consultee: I think working on the classroom behavior. I think that if that can begin to come around, the children would in turn understand and like her better.

Consultant: (19) Under classroom behavior, what do you want to work on first? (20) You mentioned staying in her seat, listening when spoken to, and raising her hand to be called on. (21) Which of those would you like to work on first?

Consultee: I would like to work on the one that I think we could remedy the fastest and easiest so that the other things could come around. So I would say following directions.

Consultant: (22) The situation we would like her to follow directions in is in the classroom. (23) Is there any particular time?

Consultee: During direct teaching time. During the time that they do independent work. I think it would be mostly when it is teacher-directed.

Consultant: (24) So, whenever you are doing direct teaching to the group, you would like her to follow whatever directions you give to the group?

Consultee: No. Wait a minute. I think I want to change that. I would say, actually, that we have the most trouble in between subjects, while we are changing over, when we are changing the activity or something. That is when she has the hardest time.

Consultant: (25) So, whenever you are changing from one activity to another and you give a direction to the class, you would like her to follow the direction immediately. (1) Would you be able in the next few days, until I get back here on Tuesday, to keep track of how many times you give a direction and it is not followed by her? (2) It could simply be just keeping a running tally during these times.

Consultee: Shall I keep track of what the specific direction is?

Consultant: (3) If you can, because there may be one type of direction that she is not following rather than another. (4) The type of direction and whether she follows it would be a simple thing. (5) Record every time you give a direction and whether she follows it so we have a percentage.

Consultee: OK. Sure.

Consultant: (6) Then, our goal is to get her to adjust to the classroom, (7) and our first step is to get her to follow directions. (8) Once we have helped that, we can concentrate on staying in her seat and that sort of thing.

Consultee: I think that is good.

Consultant: (9) Can we get together, then, next Tuesday, look at the data, and go from there?

Consultee: Yes. This same time?

Consultant: (10) Fine. (11) Thanks.

Discussion of the Interview Transcript

The consultation analysis record shown in Figure 7-1 reveals that the consultant in this case was, for the most part, effective in his use of the content, process, and control message-classification categories. As is appropriate, the content of the consultant's verbalizations was limited largely to the behavior, behavior-setting, and observation subcategories. In accordance with expectations for a developmental interview, the largest number of utterances was in the behavior subcategory. Verbalizations in this content area reflected the consultant's efforts to establish general, subordinate, and performance objectives in the case. Utterances in the behavior-setting subcategory dealt with establishing the conditions under which performance had to occur to satisfy the requirements of the objective of following directions, which was the goal selected as the initial focus in consultation. Verbalizations in the observation subcategory had to do with establishing procedures for collecting baseline data. There probably should have been more utterances in both the behavior-setting and the observation subcategories. It would have been useful to have additional information about the specific kinds of situations in which following directions was expected to occur. In addition, it would have been helpful to have more information regarding how recording was to occur.

The consultant was effective in his use of the process category as well as the content category. His verbalizations fell mainly in the specification, summarization, and validation subcategories. This is the general pattern hoped for in behavioral consultation. However, there should have been a more equal distribution than there was across process subcategories. Specifications far outweighed summarizations and validations.

The consultant's use of the control category was adequate. His use of elicitors gave him control of the interview. He was able to guide the consultee through the discussion of a large number of topics by using elicitors to gain information from the consultee and by restricting his use of emitters mainly to summaries.

The consultant said a number of specific things that produced beneficial consequences in the interview. First of all, he initiated the interview by attempting to elicit general objectives from the teacher. His first question was "What are your general concerns regarding Candy's behavior?" After eliciting general goals from the consultee, he attempted to link the general objectives that had been established to subordinate goals. For example, in an effort to establish subordinate objectives, he remarked, "As far as adjustment to her classroom situation is concerned, what are some of the things you are talking about?" A little later in the interview he asked, "As far as getting along better with others is concerned, what are some of the things you would like her to do?"

When the subordinate objectives had been established, the consultant provided further direction in the interview by asking the consultee to select a particular goal as the initial focus of consultation. A major problem occurred in the interview at this point. The consultee selected following directions in the classroom as the objective of initial concern in consultation. This was an objective that had not been specifically mentioned previously in the interview. To define following directions in performance terms, the consultant should have used an elicitor such as "What would Candy have to do to demonstrate that she was following directions?" The consultant might also have said, "Give me some examples of the ways in which Candy could show that she was following directions." Questions such as these would have increased the likelihood of agreement between the consultant and the teacher regarding what was meant by the phrase "following directions." The questions would also have had a beneficial influence on the accuracy of baseline recording in that they would have assisted the consultee to specify precisely the behaviors to be recorded. Finally, questions calling for a behavioral specification of following directions would have helped to set the stage for an examination in problem analysis of the conditions related to following directions. For example, suppose that, during problem analysis, the consultant had explored the consequences of not following directions. In the absence of a clear specification of the phrase "following directions," he might have asked a question such as "How did you react when Candy did not follow a direction?" A question of this kind would probably yield less information than a question such as "What did you say to Candy when she failed to start working on her math problems after you had told her to do so?" To be able to ask a

CONSULTATION-ANALYSIS RECORD

	Message Source		Message Content							Message Process							Message Control	
	Consultee	Consultant	Background Environment	Behavior Setting	Behavior	Individual Characteristics	Observation	Plan	Other	Negative Evaluation	Positive Evaluation	Inference	Specification	Summarization	Negative Validation	Positive Validation	Elicitor	Emitter
1		/			/								/				/	
2		/			/								/				/	
3		/			/											/		/
4		/			/								/				/	
5		/			/							/						/
6		/			/											/	/	
7		/			/									/				/
8		/			/									/				/
9		/			/									/			/	
10		/			/								/				/	
11		/			/									/				/
12		/			/								/				/	
13		/			/											/		/
14		/			/									/				/
15		/			/											/	/	
16		/			/								/				/	
17		/			/									/				/
18		/			/								/				/	
19		/			/								/				/	
20		/			/									/				/
21		/			/								/				/	
22		/		/									/					/
23		/		/									/				/	
24		/			/									/			/	
25		/			/									/				/

FIGURE 7-1. Message classification analysis of consultant verbalizations in a developmental problem-identification interview.

CONSULTANT Milton CASE NUMBER 1

CONSULTEE Jody INTERVIEW TYPE PII

PAGE 2

CONSULTATION-ANALYSIS RECORD

	Message Source		Message Content							Message Process							Message Control	
	Consultee	Consultant	Background Environment	Behavior Setting	Behavior	Individual Characteristics	Observation	Plan	Other	Negative Evaluation	Positive Evaluation	Inference	Specification	Summarization	Negative Validation	Positive Validation	Elicitor	Emitter
1		/					/						/				/	
2		/					/						/					/
3		/					/									/		/
4		/					/					/						/
5		/					/						/				/	
6		/			/									/				/
7		/			/									/				/
8		/			/								/					/
9		/						/								/	/	
10		/						/								/		/
11		/						/			/							/
12																		
13																		
14																		
15																		
16																		
17																		
18																		
19																		
20																		
21																		
22																		
23																		
24																		
25																		

FIGURE 7-1. (Cont.)

question of the latter type, the consultant would need to have a behavioral description of the phrase "following directions."

The major strength that the consultant displayed in conducting the problem identification interview was his ability to elicit information from the consultee in an organized way. He moved in a smooth and logically concise fashion from the specification of general objectives to the designation of subordinate objectives, and then to the selection of a performance objective to be the immediate focus of consultation. One result of the consultant's highly organized approach was that he was able to conduct the interview quite quickly. Even though this was a developmental interview involving the specification of a number of objectives, the conversation lasted only about 10 minutes. One of the major points illustrated by this interview is that consultants can provide long-term developmental consultation for children without making excessive interview-time demands on consultees.

AN EXAMPLE OF A PROBLEM-CENTERED CONSULTATION

The second case to be discussed illustrates the use of a problem-centered consultation to increase the number of times during each school day that a preschool boy talked to his teacher and to other adult socializing agents in the school setting. The initial plan, which was unsuccessful, involved the use of positive reinforcement in the form of teacher attention to increase the child's verbal behavior. A second plan, which included the use of cuing, reinforcement, and extinction, was effective in increasing the child's talking behavior.

The Problem Identification Interview

Consultant: (1) Who's the child who is of concern to you?

Consultee: His name is Walter. He's been coming to our school for about 2 years.

Consultant: (2) And what concerns you about Walter?

Consultee: Ah, he seems to be rather shy. He doesn't talk a lot.

Consultant: (3) Uh-huh, what does he do that shows you that he's shy?

Consultee: Well, when he comes in the morning, and we all say hello to him, he seems shy and won't say hello back. Things like that.

Consultant: (4) What other things show you that he's shy?

Consultee: Well, if he wants his shoe tied, he seems to be reluctant to ask us to tie his shoe, so he'll do something like just put his foot out, you know, for us to tie his shoe, and he won't ask for his shoe to be tied. Things like that. Or if we're having some kind of project or we're working on something at a table, and other kids are talking to us about what they're doing—"Teacher look at what I did," things like that—he doesn't do that. He'll just sit there, and he won't ask us to look at what he's done, or anything like that.

Consultant: (5) Then, what concerns you is that Walter doesn't talk to you?

Consultee: Yes, right.

Consultant: (6) Are there any other things you mean when you say he's shy?

Consultee: I don't think so. I think that it's just that he won't talk to us when we talk to him or ask him questions. And then, he won't ask for things like materials that he needs. He'll just point or something like that.

Consultant: (7) OK. Does he talk to other kids? (8) Does he talk to kids?

Consultee: Yes. He does talk to kids some.

Consultant: (9) So you're concerned that Walter doesn't talk to you. (10) And he doesn't talk to you when you ask him questions.

Consultee: Uh-huh, he doesn't talk to any of the teachers.

Consultant: (11) OK, and he doesn't talk, for example, in group time when other kids   (12) he doesn't show you his work.

Consultee: Uh-huh.

Consultant: (13) Talk and show you his work.

Consultee: Right.

Consultant: (14) And he doesn't ask for things.

Consultee: Right.

Consultant: (15) Okay, how often would you say he does talk to you?

Consultee: It's hard to say. Very little, almost never.

Consultant: (16) How often did he talk to you today?

Consultee: I don't think he talked to me at all today.

Consultant: (17) How often would you say, in a week, he talks to you?

Consultee: Oh, maybe a few times, maybe a couple times, not more than that. Maybe a couple times a week.

Consultant: (18) So he's only talking to you a couple of times a week?

Consultee: Yes.

Consultant: (19) When is it, could you describe for me when it is that you expect him to talk, or you would expect him to talk and he doesn't talk?

Consultee: Ah, well, as I said, when he comes in the morning, or when we talk to him, he doesn't talk back.

Consultant: (20) Uh-huh.

Consultee: Ah, when the teachers just make comments to him, he doesn't talk back, or when we ask him questions in group time and the other kids are talking and answering questions, Walter doesn't want to answer questions. And as I said, he doesn't ask for materials.

Consultant: (21) What do you do when he doesn't talk or when he doesn't ask for materials?

Consultee: When he doesn't ask for materials, I guess what we do is go ahead and give him what he needs, you know, what he is pointing to. For a while, we did try ignoring him when he was pointing to materials, but most of the time, I guess we go ahead and tie his shoe or give him the scissors that he needs, or whatever.

Consultant: (22) OK, what do you do when you, say, ask him a question in the group and he doesn't answer it?

Consultee: Ah, let me see. I sometimes ask the question more than once. I might ask him again or ask it in a different way or something like that.

Consultant: (23) Uh-huh.

Consultee: But when he doesn't say anything, usually, I guess, I go on to something or maybe ask another child to answer the question. If he can go ahead and do whatever I'm asking without talking, then that's fine. He does that, and then we go in the building.

Consultant: (24) So Walter's not talking when he wants materials. (25) Rather, he points. (1) In group, when you ask him questions, he doesn't talk. (2) And then, just as you said, he doesn't just spontaneously talk to you.

Consultee: Uh-huh.

Consultant: (3) And when you ask him something . . . When there's a situation when maybe he should talk and he doesn't, you either give him what he wants or you just go on to someone else.

Consultee: Uh-huh.

Consultant: (4) The first thing we need to do is to get some baseline data. (5) We need to record Walter's behavior. (6) Do you know what baseline data are?

Consultee: Yes.

Consultant: (7) OK, good. (8) It will be helpful to get some baseline data so that we know exactly what's happening. (9) And it will also help us to evaluate whether the plan that we figure out next time will work.

Consultee: OK.

Consultant: (10) You are basically concerned with how often Walter talks, (11) is that right?

Consultee: Yes.

Consultant: (12) Could you count how often Walter talks?

Consultee: Sure.

Consultant: (13) OK, good. (14) You can do that by writing down a mark on a piece of paper whenever he talks to you.

Consultee: So, just count whenever he does talk?

Consultant: (15) Right.

Consultee: Write that down?

Consultant: (16) Something else that would be really useful is if you could count how often some normal child—I mean some child who talks as often as you would like Walter to talk—how often that child talks to you. (17) Is there some child who, say, if Walter talked as often as that child, you'd be happy with him?

Consultee: Well, Walter does play with a little boy he does talk to some, named Dewey. I could count how many times Dewey talks.

Consultant: (18) That'd be real helpful.

Consultee: Uh-huh.

Consultant: (19) So you're going to count how often Walter talks to you.

Consultee: Uh-huh.

Consultant: (20) And how often Dewey talks to you.

Consultee: Uh-huh.

Consultant: (21) Do you know how to graph?

Consultee: Uh-huh, we've done that.

Consultant: (22) Could you graph the data? (23) Every day, could you graph how often Walter talks to you and how often Dewey talks to you?

Consultee: OK, I could do that.

Consultant: (24) OK, great. (25) Now, what time of the day could you do this recording?

Consultee: I don't know what you mean.

Consultant: (1) I mean, could you do it, do you want to do it, all day?

Consultee: Oh, well I couldn't do it all day because they're not both there all day. I could do it in the mornings when they're both there.

Consultant: (2) That'd be really good.

Consultee: OK, so when I graph, I'll put each day and how many times each of them talked.

Consultant: (3) Right.

Consultee: Something like that?

Consultant: (4) Right. (5) Can I call you sometime next week and see how this data collection is going?

Consultee: Sure.

Consultant: (6) Well, let me call you on Tuesday or Wednesday.

Consultee: Fine.

Consultant: (7) So probably Tuesday or Wednesday, when I call, we can set up another meeting.

Consultee: That will be fine.

Consultant: (8) OK, great.

Discussion of the Problem Identification Interview

The consultant's verbal behavior in the problem-identification-interview transcript presented above was coded on consultation-analysis-record forms and is shown in Figure 7-2. The data in the figure indicate that the consultant was effective in her use of the content, process, and control message-classification categories. As should be the case, the bulk of the interview content fell in the behavior, behavior-setting, and observation subcategories. Moreover, the consultant maintained a high degree of focus in discussing various topics. Most of the utterances in the initial part of the interview were in the behavior subcategory. Then, the consultant shifted the focus of discussion to the behavior-setting classification. During the later stages of the interview, most of the utterances fell in the observation category.

The effectiveness of the consultant's interviewing skills is revealed in her use of the process category. As is appropriate, her utterances were restricted, for the most part, to the specification, summarization, and validation subcategories. The use of the control category in the interview was also effective. There were a large number of elicitors. Moreover, the use of emitters was restricted mainly to giving summaries and to specifying recording procedures.

It may be instructive to look at some of the specific things that the consultant said that made the interview effective. Early in the interview, the consultant asked the consultee what it was about Walter's behavior that concerned her. The consultee responded that Walter was rather shy. Then, the consultant asked, "What does he do that shows you that he's shy?" This question and other similar elicitors that followed it revealed that what the consultee really meant by the term *shy* was that Walter did not converse with adults in the school environment. If the series of behavior specification elicitors that the consultant emitted early in the interview had not occurred, the problem would probably never have been defined in behavioral terms.

The failure to obtain a behavioral description of a subordinate goal is illustrated below. The following excerpt illustrates the consequences of a lack of behavioral specificity in a case involving problem-centered consultation:

Consultant: Tell me about Jeffrey.

Consultee: Jeffrey started school in January, so it took him a while to get used to it and to the kids and the routine. He's pretty much used to that right now, but he still has a pretty big problem on the rug. He has an extremely difficult time focusing his attention, particularly when there are a lot of other children around. He tends to be a follower. If someone else is doing something, he feels he needs to do it, in order to be in, to be accepted. He'll follow whatever they're doing. So, to me at least, right now, the biggest problem is his focusing attention on the rug when there are a lot of children around. He is pretty good at listening and responding individually, but it's when there's a group of four or more or especially the whole group together.

Consultant: The behavior you would like to zero in on, then, is paying attention?
Consultee: Yes.
Consultant: What generally happens before Jeffrey isn't paying attention?

The consultant in this brief interview excerpt accepted the consultee's vague description of Jeffrey's behavior. She never did get a precise specification of what concerned the consultee. As a result, she could not determine the conditions surrounding the behavior and could not be sure of what the consultee was recording when data were collected.

Now, let's return to Walter's case. After having elicited a behavioral description of Walter's shyness from the teacher, the consultant was in an excellent position to explore the conditions surrounding Walter's behavior. Her handling of the specification of antecedent conditions was particularly effective. Recall that the teacher said that Walter's problem was that he did not talk. Obviously, it would have made no sense for the consultant to attempt to establish the antecedents of not talking by saying, "What generally happens right before Walter doesn't talk?" She realized this, and yet she was also aware that antecedent conditions might be important in the case. The consultant recognized that an implicit aspect of the teacher's complaining that Walter did not talk was an assumption on the teacher's part that Walter should have been responding verbally to certain environmental cues. To determine the nature of those cues, the consultant asked, "When is it, could you describe for me when it is that you expect him to talk, or you would expect him to talk and he doesn't talk?" As will be discussed later, the consultant could have used the information that she obtained from this question during problem analysis in the design of a plan to increase talking. Ironically, after having recognized the importance of the question, she failed to follow up on it during problem analysis; that is very likely one reason that the initial plan failed to achieve the desired results.

The decision to ask the consultee when Walter was expected to talk not only produced useful information regarding the available cues signaling the need to verbalize but also set the stage for establishing the consequences that followed not talking. Having identified the particular situation in which talking was expected to occur, the consultant was able to ask the teacher what she did following Walter's failure to speak in those situations. The information obtained in response to the consultant's query regarding the consequences of Walter's failure to speak was quite revealing. Recall that the teacher indicated that, when Walter failed to request materials verbally or when he refused to ask the teacher in words to tie his shoe, she generally attempted to respond to his needs on the basis of the nonverbal communications that served as substitutes for verbal behaviors.

During the discussion of recording procedures, the consultant made a decision that may have had a marked effect on the subsequent phases in

CONSULTANT __Susan__ CASE NUMBER __2__

CONSULTEE __Jane__ INTERVIEW TYPE __PII__

PAGE __1__

CONSULTATION-ANALYSIS RECORD

#	Message Source		Message Content							Message Process							Message Control	
	Consultee	Consultant	Background Environment	Behavior Setting	Behavior	Individual Characteristics	Observation	Plan	Other	Negative Evaluation	Positive Evaluation	Inference	Specification	Summarization	Negative Validation	Positive Validation	Elicitor	Emitter
1	/								/				/				/	
2	/					/							/				/	
3	/				/								/				/	
4	/				/								/				/	
5	/				/									/				/
6	/				/										/		/	
7	/				/										/		/	
8	/				/										/		/	
9	/				/									/				/
10	/				/									/				/
11	/				/								/					/
12	/				/								/					/
13	/				/								/					/
14	/				/									/				/
15	/				/								/				/	
16	/				/								/				/	
17	/				/								/				/	
18	/				/									/				/
19	/			/									/				/	
20	/			/											/			/
21	/			/									/				/	
22	/			/									/				/	
23	/			/												/		/
24	/			/										/				/
25	/				/									/				/

FIGURE 7-2. Message classification analysis of consultant verbalizations in a problem-centered problem-identification interview.

CONSULTATION-ANALYSIS RECORD

	Message Source		Message Content							Message Process							Message Control	
	Consultee	Consultant	Background Environment	Behavior Setting	Behavior	Individual Characteristics	Observation	Plan	Other	Negative Evaluation	Positive Evaluation	Inference	Specification	Summarization	Negative Validation	Positive Validation	Elicitor	Emitter
1		/		/										/				/
2		/			/									/				/
3		/		/										/				/
4		/					/						/				/	
5		/					/						/				/	
6		/							/								/	/
7		/							/			/						/
8		/					/					/						/
9		/					/					/						/
10		/		/												/		/
11		/		/												/	/	
12		/					/									/	/	
13		/					/					/						/
14		/					/						/					/
15		/					/									/		/
16		/					/					/						/
17		/							/							/	/	
18		/					/					/						/
19		/					/							/				/
20		/					/							/				/
21		/						/								/	/	
22		/					/						/					/
23		/					/										/	
24		/					/					/						/
25		/					/						/				/	

FIGURE 7-2. (Cont.)

CONSULTATION-ANALYSIS RECORD

	Message Source		Message Content							Message Process							Message Control	
	Consultee	Consultant	Background Environment	Behavior Setting	Behavior	Individual Characteristics	Observation	Plan	Other	Negative Evaluation	Positive Evaluation	Inference	Specification	Summarization	Negative Validation	Positive Validation	Elicitor	Emitter
1	/						/									/	/	
2	/						/				/							/
3	/						/								/			/
4	/						/								/			/
5	/								/						/		/	
6	/								/				/					/
7	/								/			/						/
8	/								/			/						/
9																		
10																		
11																		
12																		
13																		
14																		
15																		
16																		
17																		
18																		
19																		
20																		
21																		
22																		
23																		
24																		
25																		

FIGURE 7-2. (Cont.)

the case. The teacher had indicated that Walter's problem was that he did not talk. However, in the discussion of recording, the consultant shifted the focus of conversation from Walter's failure to speak to a discussion about how to assess the number of times that he actually did speak. In this connection, the consultant said, "You're basically concerned with how often Walter talks, is that right?" After receiving an affirmative response to this question, the consultant went on to say, "OK, could you count how often Walter talks?"

Two beneficial consequences followed the decision to record talking rather than lack of talking. First of all, talking was a very low-rate behavior for Walter. As a result, it was easy for the teacher to record it. Second, recording Walter's verbalizations focused the evaluation on a positive accomplishment (the acceleration of Walter's verbal behavior) rather than on the elimination of something negative (Walter's failure to speak). Despite these advantages, one very unfortunate consequence was associated with the recording plan adopted. That is, it provided no information that could be used to establish the conditions surrounding Walter's failure to speak. For example, the data provided no occasion for the consultant to ask the teacher during problem analysis what she did when Walter was expected to speak and did not. There was no record of the times when Walter ought to have spoken but did not do so. Consequently, as will be discussed further in the chapter, the consequences of Walter's not talking in situations in which he was expected to talk were not discussed.

The consultant could have solved the recording problem by tabulating the percentage of occasions during each school day on which Walter talked when he was expected to talk. This measure would have provided a record of positive accomplishment and, at the same time, would have presented data that might have stimulated a discussion of the events surrounding Walter's failure to communicate verbally. For example, the consultant might have asked the teacher to make a note of the types of situations in which Walter failed to respond verbally and of her reactions to Walter's lack of speech.

The Problem Analysis Interview

Consultant: (1) Let's look at the data, (2) OK?

Consultee: Yes.

Consultant: (3) So Walter's only spoken to you twice in all this time. (4) Right?

Consultee: Uh-huh.

Consultant: (5) So it really looks as if there's a problem.

Consultee: Yes, only twice, that's all.

Consultant: (6) What happened those two times when Walter did talk to you?

Consultee: One of them was when he wanted his shoe tied.

Consultant: (7) And what did he do? (8) Describe for me what happened.

Consultee: Well, he came up to me . . . I was just sitting at the table. He started to put his foot out to have his shoe tied, and he said something like, "Shoe." And I was real pleased to hear that, and I tied his shoe, of course. But it was really soft. You know, he still seemed shy, but he did say something; he said, "Shoe."

Consultant: (9) What about the other time?

Consultee: The other time was when, after school was over, he was going home, and I said, "Bye, Walter," and he did say good-bye.

Consultant: (10) Let's take yesterday. (11) Dewey spoke to you six times. (12) Would you describe a couple of those.

Consultee: Well, when he came in the morning he said hello. He asked me when snack time was, I remember—you know, "Is is time for snacks yet?" or something like that. Let me think. I remember that he told me that he wanted to paint. He wanted to do some painting. I can't really think of any others right now.

Consultant: (13) OK.

Consultee: I can't remember.

Consultant: (14) So, in the last 3 weeks, Walter's only talked twice, and (15) those were when he wanted something and when you said something to him.

Consultee: Uh-huh.

Consultant: (16) OK. And Dewey's talking to you. (17) He's asking you questions. And he's . . .

Consultee: Uh-huh, like when is snack time.

Consultant: (18) asking for materials and . . .

Consultee: He said hi.

Consultant: (19) Right.

Consultee: And I can't remember what else he was saying yesterday.

Consultant: (20) What we need to so is to make up a plan, to see if we can't get Walter talking to you. Is there some kind of . . . (21) What does Walter like? (22) What does Walter like to do around school?

Consultee: Well, he doesn't play on the equipment a lot, so you don't see him playing on the equipment. He does like to play cowboys; it is what he likes to do. Yes, he does like to play cowboy, but not on the equipment.

Consultant: (23) Is there some way that you could attend to Walter, give Walter some attention if he did talk?

Consultee: Yes. I think if we paid too much attention to him, I think he would kind of draw back. You know, if we paid a lot of attention to him when he said something I think he just might withdraw.

Consultant: (24) What would be likely to happen if Walter were playing cowboy and he said something to one of the other kids and you praised him for talking?

Consultee: Things like that have happened before, and usually, what he does is hide or turn away or something like that. I don't think that would be too good.

Consultant: (25) OK.

Consultee: He just seems to be too shy when we pay too much attention to him. I think if we overload with a lot of attention, I think he would just be too shy.

Consultant: (1) Is there some other way you could pay attention to him?

Consultee: Well, I could do things like seeing that his shoes are tied. He brings that up a lot. It seems as if he wants to get attention by getting his shoes tied. So, I could certainly do that kind of thing. Check his shoes, see if he needs a Kleenex, or something like that. See that he has materials. Something that's not real obvious, that wouldn't require a whole pouring on of attention. I could do something like that.

Consultant: (2) Could you do it when he talks to other children?

Consultee: Uh-huh. I don't see why not, sure.

Consultant: (3) OK. Well, let's try that.

Consultee: OK. I might not be able to catch all the times that he is talking.

Consultant: (4) Oh, sure.

Consultee: But when I see him, I could do that.

Consultant: (5) OK, good. (6) So you are going to pay attention to Walter, for instance by checking his shoe . . .

Consultee: Uh-huh.

Consultant: and checking things . . .

Consultee: Yes.

Consultant: (7) Right?

Consultee: Right.

Consultant: (8) Can you continue to collect the same kind of data that you've been collecting?

Consultee: Uh-huh. The same thing, when he's talking to me.

Consultant: (9) Right.

Consultee: Uh-huh, sure. I can keep doing that.

Consultant: (10) OK, well let's try that, see if that works.

Consultee: OK.

Consultant: (11) I'd like to call . . . What do you . . . (12) Thursday's Thanksgiving. (13) When do you have classes here?

Consultee: We do come back on Friday.

Consultant: (14) Well, I'm going out of town so I won't . . . (15) I mean, there's not a whole lot of point calling you tomorrow.

Consultee: Yes.

Consultant: (16) I won't be here Friday. (17) We could just get together next week and see how it's going.

CONSULTATION-ANALYSIS RECORD

	Message Source		Message Content							Message Process							Message Control	
	Consultee	Consultant	Background Environment	Behavior Setting	Behavior	Individual Characteristics	Observation	Plan	Other	Negative Evaluation	Positive Evaluation	Inference	Specification	Summarization	Negative Validation	Positive Validation	Elicitor	Emitter
1		/			/								/				/	
2		/			/											/	/	
3		/			/									/				/
4		/			/									/				/
5		/			/							/						/
6		/		/									/				/	
7		/			/								/				/	
8		/		/									/				/	
9		/		/									/				/	
10		/			/								/				/	
11		/			/								/					/
12		/			/								/				/	
13		/		/												/		/
14		/			/									/				/
15		/		/										/				/
16		/			/									/				/
17		/			/									/				/
18		/			/									/				/
19		/			/											/		/
20		/						/					/				/	
21		/			/								/				/	
22		/			/								/				/	
23		/						/								/	/	
24		/						/				/					/	
25		/						/						/				/

FIGURE 7-3. Message classification analysis of consultant verbalizations in a problem-centered problem-analysis interview.

CONSULTATION-ANALYSIS RECORD

	Message Source		Message Content							Message Process							Message Control	
	Consultee	Consultant	Background Environment	Behavior Setting	Behavior	Individual Characteristics	Observation	Plan	Other	Negative Evaluation	Positive Evaluation	Inference	Specification	Summarization	Negative Validation	Positive Validation	Elicitor	Emitter
1		/						/								/	/	
2		/						/								/	/	
3		/						/					/				/	
4		/						/								/		/
5		/						/			/							/
6		/						/						/				/
7		/						/								/	/	
8		/					/									/	/	
9		/					/									/		/
10		/						/					/					/
11		/							/		/							/
12		/						/					/					/
13		/						/					/					/
14		/						/					/					/
15	/							/		/								/
16	/							/					/					/
17	/							/					/					/
18	/							/					/			/		
19	/							/						/				/
20	/							/							/		/	
21	/						/							/				/
22	/						/					/						/
23																		
24																		
25																		

FIGURE 7-3. (Cont.)

Consultee: OK.

Consultant: (18) When's good for you?

Consultee: How about Tuesday? Would that be good for you?

Consultant: OK, so we'll get together Tuesday. (20) Here at three?

Consultee: OK, that's fine.

Consultant: (21) And you're going to collect that same kind of data.

Consultee: Uh-huh, right. And pay attention with the shoes when he's talking.

Consultant: (22) Good.

Discussion of the Problem Analysis Interview

The consultation analysis record shown in Figure 7-3 reveals a major error in the conduct of the problem analysis interview. The number of statements in the behavior-setting subcategory was less than half the number of utterances in either the behavior or the plan subcategories. As indicated in Chapter 4, the consultant should strive to make the number of utterances in these three classifications about equal during problem analysis.

The main consequence of slighting the behavior-setting subcategory in problem analysis is usually that the consultant and the consultee fail to consider the conditions associated currently with the client's behavior in constructing a plan to change behavior. This is precisely what happened in Walter's case. The formulation of a plan to change Walter's behavior did not follow from an analysis of the conditions recognized as potential sources of influence on Walter's speaking. After signaling the need to make a plan, the consultant initiated conversation about that topic by asking what kinds of things Walter liked to do around school. It became apparent shortly after this comment that her plan strategy was to introduce a new reinforcer or set of reinforcers into the situation in an effort to increase the frequency of Walter's verbalizations.

As pointed out above, it seems probable that the consultant's failure to consider the conditions currently associated with Walter's verbal behavior stemmed, at least in part, from the decision that she made regarding the recording of behavior during problem identification. If the teacher had included in her record of Walter's verbalization information regarding the occasions on which Walter was expected to speak but did not, the discussion of the baseline data might have involved some specification of the kinds of situations in which Walter failed to verbalize and an indication of precisely what the teacher did in response to Walter's failure to speak. If information on these matters had been elicited, it might have been incorporated into the plan to change Walter's behavior.

Although the consultant did fail to link conditions analysis to the plan design, she was highly effective in eliciting plan tactics from the consultee. For example, at one point, the consultant said, "Is there some way that you could attend to Walter, give some attention to Walter if he did talk?" A few sentences later the consultant asked, "What would be likely to happen if Walter were playing cowboy and he said something to one of the other kids and you praised him for talking?"

The consultant's use of elicitors in establishing the plan tactics served a useful purpose. It brought into the open constraints and resources in the consultee's environment that might affect plan design. For example, when asked whether paying attention to Walter for speaking would be feasible, the consultee responded, "You know, if we paid a lot of attention to him when he said something, I think he just might withdraw." The consultant might never have become aware that the teacher had this reservation about the use of attention if she had simply told the teacher to use attention rather than asking for her views on the subject. A little later in the conversation, the consultee indicated the kinds of reinforcers that, in her view, could be applied to increasing Walter's speech. In this regard she said, "Well, I could do things like seeing that his shoes are tied." It is interesting that the reinforcers that the teacher mentioned for use in the plan design fell in the same categories as those consequent conditions discussed during problem identification. As was pointed out in the discussion of the problem identification interview, those conditions may have been serving as reinforcers for nonverbal substitutes for speech behaviors. It is particularly significant that the plan formulated in the problem analysis interview did nothing to preclude the possibility that those consequent conditions would continue to reinforce nonverbal communication patterns.

During the final stages of the problem analysis interview, an unfortunate circumstance arose that added to the difficulties involved in achieving a solution to Walter's problem. The consultant wanted to contact the teacher after the plan had been put into effect for a brief period. However, she was unable to do this. Consequently, even though the plan did not work, it remained in operation for an extended period of time.

The Problem Evaluation Interview

Consultant: Okay, how did it go?

Consultee: Well, it's not working.

Consultant: It's not working. What do the data look like?

Consultee: It looks as if it hasn't made any difference in the number of times that he's talking.

Consultant: How often? Did he talk any more last week? How often did he talk?

Consultee: Just about three times. That's about it.

Consultant: Three times in the whole week?

Consultee: Yes.

Consultant: So it's . . .

Consultee: It looks as if it's not having any effect.

Consultant: OK, we have to do something else. I think that we need to try something that's more powerful.

Consultee: Uh-huh.

Consultant: What we did was indirect. I think we need to try something that's more powerful. Is there anything around the school that Walter especially likes?

Consultee: You mean activities or something like that?

Consultant: Are there any privileges around school or special materials that he likes?

Consultee: We do let different children start the line. That's a privilege that the children usually like. And then, there are different chores we let the children do, and we change it so that different ones get a turn. Everybody gets a turn to do them.

Consultant: Does Walter like to do those things? Does he like to do the chores?

Consultee: Well, he does when we ask him to. I'm not really sure if he likes it or not. It's hard to tell. He does it, but I'm not sure if he likes it that much.

Consultant: What about lining up first?

Consultee: I think he likes that. The problem with that would be that, if we let him do it all the time, I don't think that would be good for the other children because they all like it so much. I don't think that would be a good idea.

Consultant: Is there anything else around school, something that Walter could get or have, say, if he talked?

Consultee: Well, those are about the only privileges, and they're all rotated. I could do something like give him a piece of candy or something like that when he talks.

Consultant: You could do that? You could give him candy?

Consultee: Sure.

Consultant: That would be really good. Maybe you could do this. I'm thinking that what we need to do is more teaching. Could you do this: a couple of times during the day—say, when Walter comes to school—could you go up to Walter and say, "Walter, if you say hi, I'll give you whatever, a piece of candy or a raisin or a piece of popcorn or a sunflower seed? A lot of children like sunflower seeds. I mean, it doesn't have to be candy. A lot of children like other things besides candy. Sometimes, people don't like to use candy, but there are lots of things like that.

Consultee: Sure, we could try that.

Consultant: Okay, say five times a day?

Consultee: That I should go up to him an ask him to say something and give him a piece of candy, you mean?

Consultant: Right.

Consultee: I don't think five times a day would be a problem. I'd be able to do that, I think.

Consultant: Okay. Let's do that. Let's practice that.

Consultee: Okay. When should I do it? Should I go ahead and tell him that he's going to get the candy when he says something, or should I just give him the candy when he says it?

Consultant: You might want to explain it to Walter ahead of time, then go up to Walter and say, "Walter, if you say . . ." and I would stick to one word. Other children say, "Teacher, look at what I have." You could say . . .

Consultee: You mean just ask him to say one word?

Consultant: Right.

Consultee: But not the same word all the time.

Consultant: No, right, different words. But say, "Walter, if you say *look*, I'll give you a raisin."

Consultee: Uh-huh. OK.

MDUL/Consultant: OK?

Consultee: Yes.

Consultant: And then you could do the same thing when he comes up to get some kind of materials.

Consultee: Uh-huh.

Consultant: When he comes up and wants his shoes tied.

Consultee: When he points to something.

Consultant: Right. When he points, you could say, "Walter, if you say *paint*, I'll give you the paint . . .

Consultee: OK.

Consultant: . . . and I'll give you a raisin." OK, let's practice that.

Consultee: OK.

Consultant: OK. I'll be you and you be Walter.

Consultee: All right. I'll be Walter.

Consultant: Right, you be Walter, and why don't you come up and you want your shoes tied. OK? Walter, if you say *tie*, I'll give you a raisin.

Consultee: Tie.

Consultant: Good, Walter, that's good. Here's your raisin.

Consultee: OK. Should I tell him that's good when I do it?

Consultant: Yes, why don't you do that?

Consultee: What if he doesn't do it, you know, what if he doesn't do it the first time? What should I do?

Consultant: Just go back to your work.

Consultee: And what if he comes and shows me his shoe again?

Consultant: Just . . .

Consultee: Same thing?

Consultant: Same thing.

Consultee: OK.

Consultant: What you don't want to get into is "Walter, say *tie;* Walter, say *tie;* Walter, say *tie,* and I'll give you a raisin. Do you want a raisin, Walter?" That's what you don't want to do.

Consultee: So you just want me to say it once, and if he doesn't do it, forget it?

Consultant: Right.

Consultee: OK.

Consultant: Now you be you and I'll be Walter.

Consultee: All right.

Consultant: OK?

Consultee: Walter, if you say *tie,* I'll give you a raisin. (*No response.*) Walter, if you say *tie,* I'll give you a raisin. (*No response.*) Now I don't know what to do with that.

Consultant: Just ignore it. Go back to your work.

Consultee: OK.

Consultant: You go ahead and ignore it.

Consultee: OK.

Consultant: OK?

Consultee: All right.

Consultant: OK. And can you continue to collect the same kind of data?

Consultee: Counting how many times, yes.

Consultant: Right.

Consultee: Do you want me to still take it on Dewey?

Consultant: Yes. Can I call you on Friday and see how it's going?

Consultee: Yes, Friday would be fine.

Consultant: Then I'll call on Friday, and we can set up another meeting if it looks as if we need one.

Consultee: OK. So I should forget about the other thing and just do this asking him to say just one word?

Consultant: OK?

Consultee: Uh-huh. Hope it works.

Discussion of the Problem Evaluation Interview

The problem evaluation interview revealed immediately that the goal of consultation had not been achieved. The data collected by the consultee did not show any improvement in the child's performance. Accordingly, the consultant had to decide what to do next. As discussed in Chapter 6, when there has been no progress toward goal attainment, the first course of action that the consultant·should consider is a return to problem analysis. The consultant elected this option in Walter's case.

The plan formulated during the return to problem analysis took into consideration the information gleaned about the conditions surrounding Walter's lack of speech during problem identification. During the second problem analysis, the consultant realized that, as talking was a low-rate behavior for Walter, it would have to be cued in order to occur. It may be very difficult to increase low-rate response when no procedures other than reinforcement are used to elicit the responses of interest (Kazdin, 1989). When the consultant took this fact into account, she began to look for cues that could be used to elicit verbal behavior from Walter. The teacher had mentioned a number of these during problem identification. For example, she pointed out that requests for materials and requests for assistance in tying his shoes were situations that the teacher regarded as cues for Walter to speak. The teacher had previously emitted verbal cues to Walter requesting speech in these situations, but to no avail. Nevertheless, the consultant realized that these verbal and situational cues could be used as part of a plan to increase the frequency of Walter's verbalizations. For example, the consultant suggested that, when Walter wanted materials such as paints, the consultee ask him to make this request in words.

During the first problem-analysis interview, the consultant had taken the position that it would be necessary to reinforce speech behavior to increase it. The major differences between the first plan and the second was that, in the second plan, reinforcement was coupled with cuing. In addition, Walter was told that positive consequences would follow verbal behavior. For instance, the consultant suggested that the teacher might say, "If you say *paint*, I'll give you the paint . . . and I'll give you a raisin."

The reinforcers selected to increase Walter's speaking behavior included the consequences that the teacher had mentioned as consequent conditions during problem identification. In addition, to the consultant's surprise, the teacher suggested the use of food as a reinforcer. It might have been possible to produce the desired changes in Walter's behavior without using food. There would have been some advantage to avoiding the use of food, as the other reinforcers in the situation were ones that were typically associated with cues for Walter to speak. The use of food required that the teacher carry raisins or other goodies with her. This would not have been necessary if only the reinforcers already available in the situation had been applied. Parents might also object to the use of food as a reinforcer.

A particularly significant feature of the second plan was that it required the teacher to ignore nonverbal communications aimed at eliciting the reinforcers that were being used to increase verbal behavior. For example, the teacher was advised to ignore Walter's nonverbal request for materials or assistance in tying his shoes. Thus, whereas during problem identification Walter had been able to get the things that he wanted through the use of gestures, during the implementation of the second plan he had to speak if he was to get what he wanted.

The second analysis is of interest not only because it demonstrates the construction of a plan that was far superior to the plan initially put into effect, but also because it illustrates the use of role playing as a technique for training plan executors in consultation. As pointed out in Chapter 5, role playing has been found to be an effective tool for training the individuals responsible for carrying out a plan to implement the plan correctly. The consultant in this case demonstrated that role playing can be incorporated directly into a consultation interview when desired.

A second problem-evaluation interview revealed that the goal of consultation had been attained and suggested that the plan designed to achieve the goal had been effective. As is often the case in consultation, an A/B design was used to evaluate the treatment program. Thus, the conclusion that the plan had produced the desired outcome is subject to the reservations discussed in Chapter 6 with respect to validity. Of particular importance in this regard is the fact that history cannot be ruled out as a possible source of influence on Walter's behavior. It is possible that some extraneous event occurring at the time of plan implementation was responsible for the observed increase in Walter's verbalizations.

Concluding Comments Regarding the Case Studies

The case studies presented in this chapter illustrate consultation techniques that the reader can use to improve her or his consultation skills. As the case studies show, it is often useful to begin an examination of consultation effectiveness with a message classification analysis using consultation analysis records. Message classification analysis provides a convenient way to pinpoint interviewing errors that may lead to a negative outcome in consultation. For example, message classification analysis of the problem-identification and problem-analysis interviews may reveal a lack of verbalization in the behavior-setting subcategory. Similarly, an examination of the problem-analysis interview regarding Walter's lack of verbal behavior also revealed a shortage of verbalizations in the behavior-setting subcategory.

As the case studies show, it is often useful to follow message classification analysis with an in-depth examination of the consequences associated with variations from expected verbalization patterns in interviews. For example, the lack of behavior-setting verbalizations in the problem analysis interview regarding Walter's speech was shown to be associated with inadequate specification of the conditions controlling Walter's verbalizations.

The failure to specify these conditions adequately in all likelihood contributed to the failure to develop an effective plan to change his behavior.

In addition to examining the consequences associated with variations from expected verbalization patterns in interviews, it is important to consider the probable cause of such variations. For instance, the discussion of Walter's case revealed that the lack of behavior-setting verbalizations in problem analysis could be traced, at least in part, to the procedures specified for observing behavior during problem identification. The decision to record talking, an extremely low-rate behavior, produced only two examples of behavior that could be subjected to conditions analysis during problem analysis. Had the consultant made provisions to record occasions during which Walter was expected to talk but did not, it would have been much easier for her to explore the conditions associated with Walter's failure to verbalize.

The identification of the causes of variations from expected verbalization patterns in consultation interviews may lead directly to increased consultation effectiveness. When consultants know what their mistakes have been and what has caused them, they are in an excellent position to make beneficial changes in the manner in which they function as consultants.

8

The Use of Consultative Problem-Solving to Advance Knowledge

Applications of consultation such as those described in Chapter 7 generally occur as activities of an ongoing consultative problem-solving system linked in one way or another to the socialization efforts of the family, the school, and other institutions responsible for guiding the development of the young. A consultative problem-solving system may be thought of as a group of elements or components serving interrelated functions, all of which contribute to the goal of achieving problem solutions in consultation. In some instances, systems of this kind are quite elaborate, involving several people occupying highly specialized roles. In other instances, system structure is very simple. In simple structure, a small group of individuals assumes a broad range of responsibilities.

SOCIALIZATION, KNOWLEDGE UTILIZATION, AND CONSULTATION

From a behavioral perspective, the analysis of the socialization process begins with the assumption that the child-rearing practices of parents, teachers, and other socializing agents are behavioral patterns that, like other forms of behavior, are controlled by contingencies operating in the environment (Kratochwill & Bijou, 1987). The *environment* from our perspective is defined broadly as encompassing ecological perspectives that relate complex interdependencies among clients, consultees, and consultants with social-environmental variables (Elliott, Witt, & Kratochwill, 1990; Martens & Witt, 1988). Thus, behavioral consultation should involve a focus that views problem behavior within a system's framework (Petrie,

337

Brown, Piersel, Frinfrock, Schelble, LeBlanc, & Kratochwill, 1980), where child problems can be perceived as solvable through change in the system rather than in the child. Examples were presented in the context of changing teacher behavior as it relates to affective classroom instruction (Gettinger, 1988).

Scholars from a variety of theoretical perspectives have asserted that the environmental forces shaping socialization practices not only produce temporary positive consequences for those who guide development but are also responsible in a very direct way for cultural survival. In this connection, Skinner (1971) argued that the operation of environmental contingencies with respect to socialization practices has created a cultural evolution analogous to the evolution of species described by Darwin (1859). Practices that contribute to survival are reinforced, and those that do not are either punished or subjected to extinction. An analysis of child-rearing practices in 107 different cultures by Barry, Child, and Bacon (1959) provides some empirical support for the idea that socialization practices do play a role in furthering cultural survival. These investigators found that obedience tended to be emphasized in those societies in which economic subsistence depended to a large degree on agriculture. Barry and his colleagues argued that, in the agrarian society, conscientious adherence to the behavioral patterns associated with crop care is essential to survival. In contrast to the findings for agrarian cultures, Barry and his associates found that hunting-and-fishing societies stressed initiative and independence in children rather than obedience.

Although adventitious contingencies may have played an important role in shaping socialization practices that fostered cultural survival in the past, there are many who doubt that they will necessarily continue to do so in the future. Indeed, it seems possible that the uncontrolled operation of environmental influences on socialization and other societal practices will lead to the destruction of the technological culture in which we live. In this regard, Albert Bandura (1974) remarked:

> When the aversive consequences of otherwise rewarding life-styles are delayed and imperceptibly cumulative, people become willful agents of their own self-destruction. Thus, if enough people benefit from activities that progressively degrade their environment, then, barring contravening influences, they will eventually destroy their environment. (p. 869)

One reason for the current distrust of the benefits of adventitious contingencies in socialization is that technological advancements in contemporary culture have provided human beings with destructive power over their environment and over one another on an unprecedented scale. Regarding this point, Skinner (1975) wrote, "I am proceeding on the assumption that nothing less than a vast improvement in our understanding of human behavior will prevent the destruction of our way of life or of mankind" (p. 42). The basis for Skinner's dark pronouncement was his assertion that the ability of human beings to control their behavior has not kept pace with the power provided by technological developments (Skinner, 1971). Thus, Skinner reasoned that there is a clear possibility that people will not use their technological capabilities wisely.

Another source of skepticism regarding the benefits of adventitious environmental influences on socialization has to do with the speed of cultural change in contemporary society (Toffler, 1970). The rapidity of cultural change has placed new social, emotional, and intellectual demands on people. It seems doubtful that the socialization practices shaped by the cultural conditions of the past are effective in preparing today's children for the world of the future.

Distrust of adventitious socialization has suggested the need to make scientific knowledge related to child rearing systematically available to socializing agents and to the children in their charge so that they may achieve greater control than has previously been possible over socialization practices and thereby over the outcomes of socialization. Substantial progress has already been made toward the goal of making scientific knowledge systematically available to socializing agents. During recent decades, what may be thought of as a large knowledge-utilization system has begun to emerge in society. The central function of this system is to provide socializing agents with the knowledge and the technology necessary to produce the desired socialization outcomes. In fact, the technology of behavioral psychology has been proposed for dealing with a large variety of environmental problems, including, for example, litter, noise, recycling, and water conservation (Cone & Hayes, 1980).

When viewed from a knowledge utilization perspective, consultation may be described in the main as a tool facilitating the communication of scientific knowledge by knowledge producers to knowledge consumers. Consultation for children and youths, then, can be seen as a device for promoting the socialization of the young by assisting socializing agents to apply scientific knowledge in the socialization process.

The Knowledge Utilization System in Socialization

As suggested above, knowledge utilization in socialization can be described as a process involving the operation of a large knowledge-utilization system in which the interrelated components function in a coordinated way to achieve knowledge utilization goals. The concept of a knowledge utilization system offers a useful metaphor for describing knowledge utilization because it provides a way to delineate clearly the differentiated functions of and interrelationships among the individuals and institutions involved in the utilization of scientific knowledge in socialization. For example, it is helpful to be able to differentiate those individuals and organizations whose primary role in the knowledge utilization process relates to the production of knowledge from those persons and groups who function in the main as consumers of knowledge.

Despite the utility of the systems concept, it should be kept in mind that it is an imperfect metaphor for characterizing the knowledge utilization process. As Guba and Clark (1975) pointed out in their description of knowledge utilization in education, the knowledge utilization process differs in significant ways from what is generally thought to characterize the functioning of a system. One difference is that the operation of system components is typically described as being directed exclusively toward the achievement of common system goals. By contrast, the functioning of the components of a knowledge utilization system is not governed by a common set of goals. The goals of a research center may be quite different from the objectives of a public school or a mental health clinic. Yet, all three of these institutions may be heavily involved in the problem of knowledge utilization. A second difference is that system components are generally related in a formal way. That is, when the systems metaphor is applied in the description of societal organizations, it generally implies a set of authority relationships that specify that some groups in the system have power over others. This is not the case in a knowledge utilization system. The components tend to function independently of one another, and one component usually has no direct control over the operation of another. For instance, a parent, as a knowledge consumer, has no direct authority over a book publishers who produces materials on child-rearing practices, nor does the book publisher have any direct control over the parent.

The unique characteristics of the knowledge utilization system in socialization imply a need for special procedures to enhance the likelihood that the system components will function in a complementary way. For example, as producers have no authority over consumers, there is no guarantee that useful scientific information will be applied to the socialization process. Application cannot be mandated by authority. If it is to occur, consumers must be persuaded that beneficial consequences will follow.

Knowledge Production and Socialization

As indicated in the above discussion, one major category of activity involved in the utilization of knowledge in socialization is knowledge production. It is convenient to describe the individuals and organizations involved in generating knowledge for use in socialization as belonging to a production component that functions as part of a larger knowledge-utilization system. A variety of organizations may be involved in the production process. Among these are colleges and universities that encourage their facilities to pursue research interests, research laboratories associated with industrial or military organizations that have an interest in education and training, and research corporations supported primarily through government contracts.

The operations of the knowledge production component influence knowledge utilization in socialization in a number of ways. One obvious source of influence is the kind of research pursued by knowledge producers. Knowledge consumers are limited in their applications of scientific findings by the kinds of findings that are available. There are many illustrations of this fact in contemporary society. One of the most widely recognized involves the elaborate testing technology developed through research on individual differences in cognitive abilities and applied in the classification of the intellectual competencies of children (Reynolds & Willson, 1985). It is now widely held that intelligence in children is described as it is in schools and other socializing institutions at least in part because of the kinds of tests available for measuring intelligence (Henderson & Bergan, 1976).

Insofar as the type of research pursued by producers has an effect on the utilization of knowledge, it is important to determine what influences the kinds of research endeavors undertaken by producers. There are a number of possible sources of influence. One is the particular interests of the investigators conducting research. A second is the set of research priorities established by the government agencies funding research. A third is the specific needs of potential consumers. A fourth is scientific theory.

Scientific theory has long been regarded as a major determinant of research activity. Theories have typically been thought of as dispassionate attempts to organize the objectively determined facts of science into a coherent body of knowledge and to establish hypotheses for guiding research aimed at the acquisition of knowledge. However, a number of scholars have indicated that the social and economic conditions within a culture play a major role in determining the nature of specific theories (e.g., see Buss, 1975; Riegel, 1972). For instance, as pointed out by Henderson and Bergan (1976), behaviorism may be described as a point of view shaped, at least to some extent, by cultural conditions:

> The cultural origins of behaviorism can be found in the rise of science and technology in Western Europe. Behaviorism shares the faith, which spread across Western culture during the last 500 years, that science coupled with technology holds the key to the betterment of human life. . . . Behaviorism is an extension of the cultural belief that humans can gain control over nature through scientific study linked to the development of technological products designed to control environmental conditions. (p. 38)

The cultural heritage described above as underlying behavioral theory is consistent with the kinds of research produced by behavioral psychologists for use in socialization. As the many examples of behavioral research given in previous chapters show, behavioral studies related to socialization deal, for the most part, with the problem of increasing what is known about the ways in which socializing agents and children can control the environment to increase their control over behavior.

A second characteristic of knowledge production operations that has an effect on the use of scientific knowledge in socialization involves the time required to produce research knowledge and to make it known to knowledge consumers. Garvey and Griffith (1971) conducted an extensive investigation of the process of generating psychological knowledge through research. The results of their project indicated that several years usually elapse between the time research is initiated and the time the results are first made available to the lay public.

The result of the long time between research production and knowledge availability is inevitably that the utilization of knowledge in socialization lags far behind existing knowledge about the socialization process. For this reason, there is continuing pressure on organizations within the knowledge production component to make information available more quickly than it has been made available in the past. Likewise, there is considerable interest among individuals and groups in the consumer component in finding ways to gain access to new information.

A third feature of knowledge production that has a significant impact on knowledge use involves the credibility of research findings and the interpretations made of them. As Garvey and Griffith (1971) pointed out, one of the reasons it generally takes a long time for research findings to become available to the public is that the process of evaluating the significance and the validity of findings is laborious and time-consuming. The evaluative process is essential if potential consumers are to be saved from misguided actions based on erroneous findings or unjustifiable interpretations of findings. Unfortunately, because evaluation does take a long time, there is ample opportunity for what might be described as knowledge leaks that allow the public to become aware of and act on information that has not been adequately evaluated within the scientific community. There are numerous examples involving research related to socialization. Research knowledge regarding the attention deficit disorder or the "hyperactive child" is a case in point. Little is known about the variables controlling the behavior of the hyperactive child, and numerous assessment measures have been used on the basis of inadequate research information (Ostrom & Jenson, 1988). Consequently, it is not surprising that large numbers of treatment programs designed to deal with the problem of hyperactivity have been ineffective.

A fourth aspect of knowledge production activities that affects the application of knowledge in socialization is the so-called knowledge explosion. Although the time required for communicating research information is relatively long, the amount of new information available at any given time is enormous. As an illustration, Nelson (1974) pointed out that, within the period of a single year, there were 24,000 citations in the *Psychological Abstracts* and 55,000 citations in the *Educational Index*. In addition to these two major sources of summaries of research relevant to socialization, Nelson listed a number of other journal-abstracting and -indexing services containing more than 85,000 citations. Moreover, he pointed out that there is very little overlap in the coverage of the various existing services.

The large quantities of available research information create a formidable problem for both producers and consumers of research knowledge related to socialization. Because there is so much information, it is virtually impossible for anyone associated in any way with the knowledge utilization process to keep up with new developments. As a result, there is a substantial need in all components of the knowledge utilization system to find ways to select only the information that is relevant to the particular socialization needs of direct concern to the person(s) seeking information.

A final characteristic of knowledge production activities that may have an influence on knowledge use in socialization is the form in which knowledge is made available by producers. Garvey and Griffith (1971) indicated that the first formal communication of research findings generally occurs through journal publication. Two or three years following journal publication, research may be incorporated into an evaluative review. Finally, the findings may be presented in a book or a major theoretical publication such as a presidential address to the American Psychological Association. Clearly, the vast majority of socializing agents have very little access to any of these forms of publication. Therefore, there is a need to translate research information into forms that are usable by those involved in the socialization process.

Knowledge Consumption in Socialization

A second major category of activity involved in knowledge utilization is knowledge consumption. Within the systems metaphor for conceptualizing knowledge utilization, the various individuals and institutions that apply research knowledge in the socialization of the young may be thought of as belonging to a knowledge consumption component. The consumption component imposes limitations on knowledge utilization in that it invariably contains barriers or constraints that impede the flow of scientific information from the production component to potential users (Havelock, 1969). The problem of dealing with constraints in consultation was discussed in Chapter 4. As indicated in that chapter, constraints related to time, money, material, the availability of personnel, and the attitudes and values of the individuals involved in consultation impose limitations on the kinds of plans that may be implemented in consultation. When viewed from the standpoint of knowledge utilization, it becomes clear that, by imposing limitations on plan design, constraints may impede the flow of scientific information to the knowledge consumers in consultation, who are, of course, the consultee and the client.

Reppucci and Saunders (1974) listed a number of specific constraints or barriers that may be encountered in consultation and gave examples of how these barriers impede the utilization of behavioral principles in socialization (see also Kratochwill & Van Someren, 1985; Piersel & Gutkin, 1983; Witt & Martens, 1988). One of these is external pressure. Individuals and organizations involved in the socialization process may be under pressure from outside agencies and groups to implement policies and programs that are contraindicated by scientific information. As an illustration of external pressure, Reppucci and Saunders described one of the problems they encountered in implementing a behavior change program in a training school for delinquent boys. When the number of runaways in the school increased, there was pressure from the news media, politicians, and police to tighten security with respect to the activities of the boys. The response of the institution to this pressure was to lengthen the time spent by runaways in the maximum security unit after being caught. Although this response did have the effect of reducing the probability of escape from the institution, it also severely curtailed the availability of positive reinforcers that could be used to change the boys' behavior.

A second potential barrier to knowledge utilization in behavior change programs is the set of organizational constraints governing the possible activities of potential knowledge consumers. Reppucci and Saunders cited a case described by Tharp and Wetzel (1969) to illustrate how organizational constraints may impede knowledge utilization. In this example, it was suggested to a school administration that an intervention plan for a particular child include making participation in an after-school football program contingent on good behavior during school in the morning. The administration objected to this plan primarily because there was no convenient opportunity for the teacher who provided instruction during the morning to communicate information about the child's behavior to the coach. This constraint on communication within the school made the plan impractical to implement.

A third barrier that may affect knowledge utilization in socialization is the language used by consumers and by those individuals responsible for conveying knowledge to consumers. For example, knowledge consumers may object to the scientific jargon associated with a particular theory or research finding (Witt, Moe, Gutkin, & Andrews, 1984). In this connection, Reppucci and Saunders pointed out that a number of the staff members of the training school in which they were functioning as consultants objected to the jargon of behavior modification. As a consequence it was decided not to use behavioral terminology in conveying knowledge to the staff. However, the relation between technical language and acceptability is complex. In a recent study, we explored the influence of consultative involvement and consultant language in an analogue consultation study (Rhoades & Kratochwill, 1989). Two levels of consultee involvement (involved/not involved in the intervention) and two levels of language (technical jargon/nonjargon) were crossed to create four videotaped scenarios. Elementary-school teachers were exposed to one of the conditions and rated the tape on acceptability. We found a significant intersection: teachers experienced a preference for technical jargon, but only when the consultant took the directive role in developing the intervention and did not involve the teacher.

A fourth barrier to knowledge utilization that Reppucci and Saunders identified is that the conveyors of scientific knowledge usually have no direct control over the application of the knowledge. Socializing agents such as parents and teachers generally serve as mediators in the application of scientific knowledge. As a consequence, there is always the possibility that, because of inexperience with the principles being used, they will apply them incorrectly.

A fifth barrier identified by Reppucci and Saunders is the problem of limited resources. As indicated in Chapter 4, the resources available to socializing agents functioning as consumers of scientific information limit the kinds of applications they can make of the information provided. Perhaps the most common illustration of the resource problem is the effective program that must be discontinued because the necessary funds are not available to support it.

A sixth barrier described by Reppucci and Saunders involves the manner in which activities and environmental conditions are conceptualized by knowledge consumers. If consumers conceptualize an activity or a condition as a scientific principle, then the consumers may not be able to make use of the principle in socialization. As an illustration, Reppucci and Saunders described a situation in the training school where they were working in which an activity—namely, a field trip—that might well have functioned as a reinforcer was labeled as an educational experience rather than as a reinforcer. Because the staff of the school conceptualized the field trip as an educational activity required for all students, they were able to make use of it as a reinforcer for appropriate school behavior.

A seventh barrier specified by Reppucci and Saunders is associated with the fact that consumers may perceive conveyors of scientific knowledge as inflexible in their adherence to scientific principles. In connection with this point, these authors remarked, "behavior modifiers working in the natural environment must struggle constantly to ensure the basic integrity of the programs they develop while at the same time not becoming unduly and unrealistically rigid; that is, they must strive for *flexibility but within theoretical context*" (pp. 656–657). A common example of the problem of perceived inflexibility in consultation is the situation in which a consultant is particularly insistent that data be collected on client behavior. A consultee may not understand the importance of data collection and therefore may object to it on the grounds that it is a waste of time. If the consultant does not acquiesce in at least some measure with respect to the data collection requirements, he or she may be perceived as inflexible. The consultee's judgment that the consultant is inflexible may impair the consultant's ability to communicate scientific information to the consultee effectively. Insofar as the consultee regards the consultant as a rigid individual, he or she may be unwilling to accept information that the consultant has to offer.

The final barrier to knowledge utilization discussed by Reppucci and Saunders is the set of contingencies that knowledge consumers impose on consultants. The contingencies operating on a consultant in the consultee environment may work against the communication of scientific information to be applied in socialization. Under these conditions, the consultant may compromise himself or herself by ignoring scientific information and acquiescing to the environmental contingencies in the situation. For example, a consultant may hesitate to suggest the use of modeling to increase intellectual behavior if he or she has heard the consultee make several derisive comments describing imitation as a "monkey see, monkey do" phenomenon.

Production–Consumption Linkage in Socialization

A third major type of operation required in knowledge utilization is transmitting information between knowledge producers and knowledge consumers. Individuals and organizations involved in linking activities related to knowledge utilization in socialization can be described as belonging to a production–consumption linkage component. Some of the more familiar examples of organizations representing this component include educational institutions that communicate information regarding socialization to consumers through instructional programs; publishers of books and other types of written materials containing information about socialization; groups using television, films, and other electronic communication devices to disseminate information about socialization; and psychological consultants communicating information to consumers by procedures such as those described in this book.

Sashkin, Morris, and Horst (1973) described three kinds of linking activities that may affect knowledge utilization. The first they called "input linking." Input-linking activities are operations that assist consumers to obtain and to apply scientific information articulated to their specific needs. Input-linking procedures include diagnosing consumer needs for information, providing scientific information to users, and recommending uses for the information that has been provided. Input linking affects knowledge utilization by influencing the application of scientific principles in the solution of specific problems faced by knowledge users.

The second type of linking activity specified by Sashkin and his colleagues is "throughput linking." Throughput-linking activities are procedures that assist the consumer to learn how to acquire and apply scientific information in the solution of problems. The emphasis in throughput linking is not on the solution of a specific problem. Rather, it is on the development of generalizable skills that can be applied to the solution of large numbers of problems.

The principal vehicle suggested by Sashkin and his associates for achieving throughput linking is training. Training is applied to help the consumer to learn to use knowledge retrieval methods to obtain needed information. It may be used to assist the consumer to learn to use data in developing plans to solve problems. First, it may be applied in helping the consumer to learn new skills for implementing and evaluating the effects of innovative plans.

The third type of linking activity identified by Sashkin *et al.* (1973) is "output linking." Output linking involves research and evaluation activities conducted within the knowledge consumption component and communicated to the production component to become part of the scientific knowledge base.

Consultation as a Knowledge-Linking Tool

Having examined knowledge utilization as it relates to socialization, the consultant now might reasonably ask for a detailed account of what part consultation plays in the knowledge utilization process. Consultation is an activity of the production–consumption linkage component. In the following sections, we discuss the linking functions that consultation serves in knowledge utilization, the characteristics of consultation that make it particularly well suited to fulfilling a linking role, and the requirements for making consultation an effective knowledge-linking tool.

The Linking Functions of Consultation

Consultation serves three linking functions in the knowledge utilization process. These are represented by the three types of linking identified by Sashkin *et al.* (1973) and discussed in the previous section.

The major linking function of consultation is input linking. Consultation provides a means of making the knowledge generated by producers available to consumers for use in achieving solutions to specified socialization problems. The consultant initiates input linking by assisting the consultee to identify problems during problem identification. In problem analysis, the consultant links the consultee or knowledge-consumer to the scientific knowledge base by assisting him or her to use psychological principles in the development of a plan to solve the problem presented in consultation. For example, recent research suggests that a variety of instructional strategies can be used to promote effective classroom management without necessarily focusing on disruptive behavior contingencies (see Gettinger, 1988).

Although input linking is the principal function of consultation, consultation also plays a role in output linking. One output-linking activity associated with consultation is generating research knowledge within the consumption component. As indicated in Chapter 6, consultation provides a mechanism for conducting applied research (see also Barlow *et al.*, 1984). If consultative problem-solving reveals new information that may be of interest to the scientific and professional community in psychology and related disciplines, output linking may be effected by communicating the results of consultation to the research community through such procedures as journal publication.

Another output-linking activity that may occur through consultation is the communication of consumers needs to knowledge producers. Consultation identifies the types of problems of concern to socializing agents functioning as knowledge consumers. Information regarding the kinds of problems that consumers have identified as being important in socialization may assist knowledge producers in selecting socialization problems on which to conduct research. There are no well-established formal mechanisms that we know of by which consultants may communicate consumer needs to knowledge producers. This is no doubt unfortunate. Nonetheless, information regarding consumer needs is communicated through informal channels. For example, a consultant may have friends or acquaintances who are involved in knowledge production and may communicate information concerning needs during conversations with them.

The third linking function of consultation is facilitating throughput linking. Most of the examples of consultation given in this book are not directly concerned with throughput linking. However, consultation offered to knowledge consumers may be aimed at showing consumers how to use knowledge in the solution of problems. The central function served by consultation of this kind is promoting throughput linking. Problem identification in consultation related to throughput linking is directed at identifying the discrepancy between current capability and desired capability in order to gain direct access to and to use scientific information in the solution of socialization problems. Problem analysis is concerned with identifying the conditions and skills of consumers that may affect throughput linking. In addition, problem analysis is directed toward the formulation of plans to increase throughput-linking capabilities. Problem evaluation is, of course, concerned with evaluating the attainment of the throughput-linking goals and the effectiveness of the plans designed to achieve them.

Characteristics of Consultation That Facilitate Linking Activities

There are several features of consultation that make it particularly well suited to the task of fulfilling linking functions. All of these are related to the fact that consultation is primarily a form of face-to-face oral communication. Face-to-face communication has been the principal vehicle for conveying information from one person to another since the beginning of human culture. Moreover, even today, it is the most widely applied of the available mechanisms for exchanging ideas. The elaborate communications technology existing in contemporary culture tends, to some degree, to obscure the role that face-to-face communication plays in the exchange of information. This is particularly so in the area of knowledge utilization. Within the field of knowledge utilization, there has been great emphasis on the communication of scientific information to socializing agents through the development of products (e.g., books, audiovisual materials, manuals, and computers) to be applied in socialization. It is important to point out that there are advantages in oral communication as a knowledge-linking tool that may not be associated with other means of transmitting information.

One feature of consultation as a form of oral communication that makes it particularly well suited to fulfill a knowledge-linking role is the speed with which it communicates information. If a consultant is aware of a particular piece of scientific information that may be useful in consultation, he or she may communicate that information to a consultee without delay whenever it is desirable to do so. By contrast, Sashkin *et al.* (1973) pointed out that it may take between 20 and 40 years to convert research into a usable technological product. One reason for this long time lag is that product developers may not have access to research findings for several years after the findings have first become available. Consultants, of course, face a similar problem. However, much of the delay involved in applying research through product development is associated with the time necessary to create the product. This type of delay is circumvented when research information is applied through consultation.

A second feature of consultation that makes it a useful knowledge-linking tool is that it presents information in a form that facilitates the broad-scale diffusion of the information. When a consultant describes a scientific principle to a consultee within the context of a language tradition shared by both of them, the consultee is able to communicate that information to another by word of mouth. Communications of this kind may result in broad-scale dissemination of the information.

The ability to communicate to a large audience is, of course, not unique to consultation. Moreover, other forms of communication are better suited than consultation to the task of broad-scale information dissemination. Mass-communication media and computers provide an obvious example. Nonetheless, it is worth noting that consultation may produce wide dissemination of information. Recall that, in societies lacking a written language and other modern forms of communication, culture, including knowledge, customs, traditions, values, and attitudes, is transmitted from one generation to the next largely through oral communication. The transmission of culture from generation to generation in nontechnological societies illustrates just how broad the dissemination of information obtained in face-to-face interactions can be.

A third aspect of consultation that makes it an advantageous procedure in knowledge linking is that it provides a convenient and inexpensive way to alter the form in which research is communicated to consultees, and thus, it facilitates consumer use of research-generated knowledge. As indicated earlier in the chapter, the first formal communication of a research finding is typically a journal publication. Some years later, the finding may appear in an evaluative review or a scholarly text. These forms of communication are not accessible to many socializing agents. Moreover, it would be difficult for some socializing agents to extract information from journal publications, reviews, or highly technical books even if these were readily available. Consultation provides a means of changing the technical language of the research publication into a common language shared by the consultant and the consultee.

A final characteristic of consultation that facilitates knowledge linking is its responsiveness to consumer communications. Consultation brings research information to bear on the solution of specific problems presented by the consultee. The consultee is not a passive knowledge consumer. By specifying the nature of the problem to be solved through consultation and by participating in the design of a plan to achieve problem solution, the consultee imposes requirements on the selection of information from the scientific knowledge base for use in consultation and plays a role in the determination of how that information will be applied. Face-to-face oral communication makes it possible for the consultant to make information obtained from knowledge producers responsive to the individual needs and requirements specified by the consultee.

The ease with which responsibility is handled in consultation is best illustrated by contrasting the adaptiveness of consultation to the product development approach to handling responsibility. When knowledge is packaged as a technological product such as a set of instructional materials, responsivity must be handled by creating alternate versions of the product to meet known variations in consultee needs. For example, an educator may complain that the social content of a particular set of basic reading materials is inappropriate for the children with whom he or she is working.

The only way to deal with a complaint of this kind is to construct alternative versions of the materials appropriate for children growing up in different social settings. The construction of alternative versions of socialization products is possible, but it is both expensive and difficult to achieve. Adequate individualization has not yet been accomplished by developers of socialization products and probably will not be for some time to come.

Requirements for Effective Knowledge-Linking through Consultation

Even though consultation has a number of inherent attributes that make it a potentially useful knowledge-linking mechanism, certain requirements must be met before it can be an effective linking tool. One of these is rapid access for the consultant to up-to-date, accurate information from the scientific knowledge base. The effectiveness of consultation as a knowledge-linking device is directly limited by the quality of the information communicated to the consultee. If the information communicated is out-of-date or inaccurate, whatever benefits may have been attained through the utilization of scientific information in consultation is lost or severely curtailed.

The consequences of using out-of-date, inaccurate information are revealed in what can be described as psychological fossilism in socialization. When consultants are cut off from the continuous surge of new information being generated by knowledge producers, vestiges of bygone psychological principles appear in socialization practice with frequency. For example, in this age of unprecedented technological achievement, we find psychologists musing over differences in intellectual subtest scores involving subscales that have never been shown to measure discrete abilities, and we still find children who, on the basis of primitive diagnostic tools, are labeled as brain-damaged and are prescribed medication.

A second requirement for effective knowledge linking is a means of overcoming the barriers to knowledge utilization that operate within the knowledge consumption component. Very little research is available that deals with the issue of circumventing barriers (Giacquinta, 1973; Kratochwill & Van Someren, 1985; Piersel & Gutkin, 1983). However, among theorists concerned with social and organizational change, it is regarded as axiomatic that overcoming resistance to the utilization of new information requires that knowledge consumers play an active role in the knowledge utilization process (Giacquinta, 1973). That is, they must have some control over the kinds of changes introduced into their lives through knowledge utilization. The consultative problem-solving model was designed to actively involve knowledge consumers (i.e., consultees and clients) in knowledge utilization. As indicated earlier in this book, the consultee and, in some cases, the client define the problems to be considered in consultation and make the final decision regarding data collection, plan design, and evaluation. The role of the consultee in plan design is particularly important in overcoming barriers to knowledge utilization. As pointed out in Chapter 4, the consultee's participation in the development of plan tactics makes it possible to construct a plan that takes into account both the constraints and the resources available for knowledge utilization in the client's environment. The consultee is likely to be aware of existing constraints and resources. Thus, his or her participation in the specification of plan tactics may make it possible to circumvent barriers and to use resources of which the consultant may have no knowledge.

A third necessity for making consultation an effective knowledge-linking tool is a mechanism for communicating information from knowledge consumers to knowledge producers. Consultation may eventually result in the production of applied research findings that should be communicated to the production component of society's knowledge utilization system. In addition, consultation may reveal important consumer needs that ought to be addressed by knowledge producers.

The final requirement for making consultation an effective knowledge-linking device is a means of evaluating the effects of knowledge utilization in the consultation process. The central question to be answered through this kind of evaluation is whether the goals of consultation are being achieved through the utilization of scientific information. Answering this question requires an assessment of the outcomes of consultation as they relate to the kinds of psychological principles being applied and the manner in which principles are used in consultation.

THE DESIGN OF CONSULTATIVE PROBLEM-SOLVING SYSTEMS

It seems doubtful that the requirements outlined above for making consultation an effective knowledge-linking tool can be met without embedding consultation activities in the framework of a comprehensive problem-solving system of some kind. The main advantage of a systems approach is that it makes provisions for the differentiated roles and functions necessary to effective knowledge utilization. A consultant operating alone cannot possibly assume the total responsibility for meeting all of the requirements of effective knowledge-linking. No single individual can ensure rapid access to information from knowledge producers, can be effective in communicating information from consumers to producers, and can conduct a comprehensive evaluation of consultation services. This is not to say that consultants should not continue in many instances to function independently of socializing institutions. Consultation services should be linked in some way to a consultative problem-solving system capable of serving knowledge utilization functions.

In this section of the book, we offer some suggestions for the construction of consultative problem-solving systems. Some of these suggestions are futuristic in that their implementation would require conditions that do not now exist. However, most of the suggestions are derived from procedures that have been tried in research and demonstration projects and have been found to be useful in the provision of effective consultation services.

The suggestions are based on the assumption that a consultative problem-solving system should serve three broad functions: information management, service implementation, and evaluation. Each of these functions may be thought of as representing the activities of a separate component of the overall system. In some cases, the components may be linked to one another formally. For example, a large community-mental-health center might construct a consultative problem-solving system involving information management, service implementation, and evaluation components coordinated by an administrative component responsible for governing overall system operations. In some instances, there may be no formal ties among system components. For instance, a consultant in private practice might gain access to up-to-date scientific information from an information management service to which the consultant has no formal ties other than subscribing to the service.

Information Management

Gathering Information

The problem of gathering information for the information management component is formidable, but by no means insurmountable. First, it is necessary to devise procedures for gathering information from the scientific knowledge base. Because the first formal presentation of scientific findings generally takes the form of journal publication, adequate coverage of the scientific knowledge base can probably be achieved by monitoring those journals publishing research findings of relevance in socialization. Information from relevant journals may be summarized by abstracts indicating the nature of the research, the methods used to conduct it, and the results obtained.

There are a number of journal-abstracting services currently in operation that monitor psychological journals in the manner described in the preceding paragraph. For example, the American Psychological Association produces a number of abstracting services that are useful to consultants (e.g., *Psychological Abstracts* and *Psyc SCAN: Clinical Psychology*). The existence of current abstracting services demonstrates that the technology for a comprehensive service covering the field of socialization is available. This system is highly useful in constructing an information management

component for a consultative problem-solving system. However, even
without it, it is possible to use the existing abstracting services to gather
much of the available information on socialization from the scientific
knowledge base.

In addition to gathering information from research, it is necessary to
bring together information describing the operation of consultation services by individuals and groups making use of the information management component. This information can be disseminated to knowledge producers to make them aware of consumer needs and consultation practices.
In addition, it can be shared by consultants using the information management component.

In 1973, the first author was involved in a research and demonstration
program that illustrates how information from consultants providing psychological services can be gathered by an information management component (Bergan, Curry, Currin, Haverman, & Nicholson, 1973). The project
was supported by the Follow Through Implementation Program, a large,
federally funded research and demonstration program aimed at assessing
the effects of variations in educational programming on the social, emotional, and intellectual development of children.

Psychological services were provided through the project to 13 communities widely dispersed across the nation. A variety of cultural back-
grounds and social conditions were represented in these communities. For
example, one community was located on a small island off the coast of
Alaska. Rural communities in the Midwest and in the South also participated. In addition, some large urban centers in the Midatlantic region, the
Midwest, and the Southwest were represented. Psychological consultants
functioning in schools in these communities provided information on case-
reporting forms to an information management component housed in the
Arizona Center for Educational Research and Development at the University of Arizona. The case-reporting forms were designed so that they could
be completed by a consultant during consultation interviews. They generally took less than 5 minutes to complete. Thus, the amount of paperwork
required to communicate information to the information management
component was kept at a minimum. The forms were forwarded quarterly
to the information management component at the Arizona center. Much of
the information was in the form of numerical codes that could be easily
transformed into computer input. In addition to the numerical information, a description of the problem, the plan used to solve it, and a graph
showing client behavior were provided. Research assistants working in the
information management component summarized the information from
case-reporting forms. Summaries like the one shown in Figure 8-1 were
made available as computer output accessible to consultants in the various
communities as well as to researchers at the Arizona Center.

The following case terminated with status goal partially attained: change agent decision.

01800   Goal—Working cooperatively with others.
         Before center begins, child told to be attentive and nondisruptive. Successful completion of center earns job of teacher's helper (collect papers, take notes to office).

The following case terminated with status goal attained.

02110   Goal—Staying in group for group activities.
         Onset of group activity remove child's toys during group activity. Teacher sits near child and praises him when attending.

The following case terminated with status goal partially attained: change of goal.

02170   Goal—Attending to academic class.
         Reduce academic assignments—5 problems per 5 pages instead of 25 problems per page. Other assignments cut comparably. When child distractible-may, with child's OK, be isolated, or a "quiet" earphone may be worn. Immediate social reinforcement at completion of each assignment.

The following case terminated with status plan unsuccessful: child moved.

02420   Goal—Listening to directions.
         Teacher cues child as to desired activity and verbally reinforces listening. Tells child she wants him to treat other children nicely. Reinforce.

The following case terminated with status goal attained.

03750   Goal—Enter classroom voluntarily and immediately upon arrival.
         Teacher will meet child at bus to encourage voluntary entrance to class. At arrival, child will assist teacher in getting snack ready.

FIGURE 8-1. An illustration of intervention plan summaries that could be retrieved as computer output from the Follow Through information-management component. These plans were retrieved by calling for plan summaries involving problems related to the control of attention.

Storing and Retrieving Information

It is beyond the scope of this book to go into the technical details of how information can best be stored and retrieved. However, it will be useful to make some general comments about the organization of information for storage and retrieval. The comments made presuppose that some form of computer-based storage and retrieval system is used in the classification of information.

A major factor that should govern the organization of information in storage is how the information is to be used after retrieval. In consultative problem-solving, information is applied within a behavioral perspective to facilitate the solution of socialization problems. Accordingly, information intended for use in consultative problem-solving should be organized to reflect a behavioral approach to the problem-solving process.

Scientific information disseminated through professional journals, evaluative reviews, and texts is generally not rendered in a form that is usable for solving socialization problems from a behavioral perspective. As noted previously in the chapter, the technical language of scientific publications is likely to be unfamiliar to most socializing agents and is therefore not readily comprehended by them. A more serious problem, however, is that research findings that might be applied within a behavioral approach to socialization may be ignored because they are linked to a contending theoretical and/or philosophical position. For example, the practitioner who subscribes to a behavioral viewpoint is likely to make use of such principles as modeling, cuing, reinforcement, and extinction. However, it is by no means certain that he or she would apply the vast quantity of research data that have been accumulating during this century on the conditions influencing verbal learning and memory even if the problem to be solved involves the recall of verbal information.

Regardless of the theoretical perspective from which one is working, it would be beneficial to have access to all information that might be useful in consultation. In large systems involving consultants operating from a variety of theoretical positions, an information management component should have the flexibility to organize information in accordance with a number of different points of view. In any case, information should be classified in a form that separates it from its theoretical origins and that translates it into the theoretical framework within which it is to be applied.

In the case of consultative problem-solving occurring within a behavioral perspective, four broad categories may be used in the organization of information for storage and retrieval purposes: individual characteristics, competency area, goal direction, and stimulus conditions influencing behavior. This list is not intended to represent all of the possible categories to be used in storing and retrieving information, but it does encompass some major types of information useful to the behavioral consultant.

Information falling within the individual-characteristics category would be organized in accordance with attributes of the individuals whose behavior is under study in research investigations or consultation cases stored in the information management component. Some of the more familiar examples of individual characteristics that are of interest in consultation are age and sex.

The individual-characteristics category would be particularly useful in assisting a consultant to locate information describing conditions affecting the behavior of individuals similar to the client(s) with whom the consultant is working. For example, a consultant working with an 8-year-old boy described as hyperactive might be interested in retrieving information on research studies dealing with the control of attention deficit behavior in males under the age of 10. The reason that the consultant might limit the search to young males is that behavior may not generalize across individuals who vary markedly in individual characteristics. Thus, by limiting the research information being considered to individuals similar to the client, the consultant increases the probability that the information will be useful in achieving a problem solution.

A second category within which information might be organized for storage and retrieval purposes is competency area. The term *competency area* refers to the type of behavioral capability dealt with in research studies or consultation cases. For example, information might be classified in terms of cognitive competencies, social competencies, emotional competencies, and physical competencies.

Classification by competency would be useful in assisting consultants to obtain information regarding the control of particular types of behavior. For instance, a consultant working with a teenage girl on weight control might be interested in finding out about various procedures applied by other consultants using the information management component to control weight. Similarly, a consultant working with a young child having reading difficulties might want to know what recent research had to say about increasing reading competency.

The third and fourth categories for classifying information, goal direction and conditions, were discussed at some length in Chapter 4. As the reader will recall, consultation goals may be divided into three classes: those involving attempts to increase behavior, those concerned with maintaining behavior at its current level, and those aimed at reducing the occurrence of behavior. Conditions may also be conceptualized in terms of four classes: setting events, antecedent conditions, consequent conditions, and sequential conditions.

Disseminating Information

The final problem that must be considered regarding the operation of the information management component is the dissemination of information to component users. If information in the component is to be useful in consultation, component users must have ready access to it. The main problem of information dissemination in a consultative problem-solving system is to find ways to ensure rapid access to information at a reasonable cost.

The dissemination of information in the Follow Through project described earlier in the chapter illustrates one way of ensuring component users of access to knowledge stored in an information management component. As indicated above, consultants participating in the Follow Through program forwarded information about their cases to the Arizona center, where they were placed in computer storage. Dissemination occurred in a three-stage process. First, a request for information was sent to the Arizona center by a consultant using the component. Second, a computer terminal at the center was used to retrieve the specific information requested. The final step was to send the computer printout to the individual who initially requested the information.

The dissemination procedure used in the Follow Through project had the advantage of being very inexpensive to implement. However, it was rather slow. If each community participating in the project had had its own computer terminal, dissemination would have occurred much more quickly than it did. Microcomputer terminals are now available at very reasonable prices. Moreover, they can be connected by telephone line to information systems in virtually any geographic location.

Because of the availability of microcomputers, information can be disseminated almost instantaneously. For example, in the Follow Through project, information on consultation cases was retrieved through the terminal by means of a computer program. The program provided almost immediate access to a wide variety of information. Information was retrieved by using a numerical code representing the various categories of data stored in the machine. Suppose that a consultant was interested in obtaining information on cases involving attempts to decrease aggressive behavior in 7-year-old boys. To obtain this information, the consultant would type three numbers on the terminal, one representing aggressive behavior, one representing 7-year-olds, and one representing boys. Within seconds, the printer would produce all of the cases in storage falling within these three categories. The major function served by a consultative problem-solving system should be, of course, providing services to consultees and clients in the system.

Service Implementation

The service implementation component of a consultative problem-solving system fulfills this function. The principal problems associated with providing adequate services are to ensure that a match between consultee and client needs and the services rendered and to ensure that the services that are provided will be effective.

Matching Services to Needs

A major task to be accomplished in matching services to needs is to make potential consultees and clients aware of the kinds of services that are available. The problem of ensuring awareness is most critical when new services are being installed in a socialization setting. However, even when services have been available in a setting for a long period of time, there is a need to make sure that socializing agents know what kinds of services they can expect to receive. For example, in a school setting, there are usually a considerable number of changes in personnel from year to year. Moreover, technological advancements may eventuate in the offering new kinds of services. Factors such as personnel changes and technological innovations make it necessary to update information about services periodically.

One way to initiate awareness is through face-to-face contacts with people who are in a position to influence the use of consultation services. These can often be accomplished through organization development consultation (Schmuck et al., 1972). For example, if services focused on a school system, the consultant would focus initially on the available service options as negotiated with the school administrators. The consultant might then describe the scope of the services offered and might give some examples of specific cases. By contrast, if services are to be offered mainly to parents through a private clinic, initial contacts explaining the services might be made with pediatricians or other individuals likely to have contact with large numbers of parents who are potential service users.

Contacts with individuals having the potential to influence service use should generally be followed by discussions with socializing agents who are likely to avail themselves of the services. For example, following initial contacts with administrators, a consultant might discuss services with the teachers in the schools to receive the services. Generally, it is best to conduct discussions of this kind individually or in small groups. Individual or small-group contacts make it easy for potential consultees to raise questions about the nature of the services and to make suggestions regarding the offering of the services.

Initial contacts describing the nature of services to the individuals influencing service use and to socializing agents who might want the services may be followed by selective demonstrations of service effectiveness. For instance, after having talked with several pediatricians and small groups of parents, a consultant might offer to work with one or two parents to demonstrate the effectiveness of the consultation services. If the services are demonstrated to be effective, there is a good chance that information regarding the efficacy of consultation will travel quickly by word of mouth throughout the community.

In some cases, it may be useful to augment individual contacts and demonstrations of service effectiveness with presentations of information regarding the services to large groups. For example, after having established credibility with the teachers in a school system, a consultant might conduct a large in-service training program designed to provide information about some new aspect of consultation services.

If consultees have been made aware of the various kinds of consultation services available to them, an attempt should be made to assess the general needs of the consultees with respect to the services. For example, if consultation services are being provided in a school district, one or more individuals representing the consultative problem-solving system should establish with the school administration what their objectives are with respect to the services offered by the system.

There is a rather large and growing literature on the applications of organization development consultation (ODC), including applications for the diagnosis of the organization (e.g., Harrison, 1987) and program evaluation in special education (e.g., Maher & Bennett, 1984). Various aspects of ODC, as outlined by Maher and Bennett (1984), have been applied to the special problems faced by a consultant in implementing behavioral programs in schools. Specifically, Maher and Bennett outlined a framework with seven components that can facilitate program implementation. The acronym for these factors is *DURABLE: Discussing, Understanding, Reinforcing, Acquiring, Building, Learning, and Evaluating.*

Discussing. This is a component that occurs before program implementation. The consultant meets with program staff (e.g., teachers and parents) and considers the purpose, goals, and objectives of the program; the nature and scope of the activities of the program; program timelines, dates, and consultee responsibilities; and staff supervision guidelines.

Understanding. This component also involves an activity that occurs before program implementation. The primary purpose of this activity is to clarify the extent to which the organization is ready to implement a program. Maher and his associates have recommended the AVICTORY strategy (Davis & Salasin, 1975) for obtaining readiness information. With this strategy, the consultant can obtain information within eight dimensions: *Ability* (e.g., Do staff have the skills to implement the program?), *Values,* (e.g., Do the staff share the same program values as the consultant?), *Idea* (e.g., Do staff understand the nature and scope of the program?), *Circumstances* (e.g., Are current administrative guidelines conducive to program implementation?), *Timing* (e.g., Is it the right time to implement a program?) *Obligation* (e.g., Is the program need apparent?), *Resistance* (e.g., Is active resistance among the staff apparent?), and *Yield* (e.g., Are positive outcomes apparent to staff?). The information from AVICTORY can be used to facilitate the understanding of the staff in order to maximize program implementation.

Reinforcing. An important part of the program implementation is arranging the environment to reinforce the staff for their part in this process.

Acquiring. Certain program preconditions must be met for a program to be implemented, including, for example, making sure that program goals and activities have been communicated to the staff, acquiring materials, and establishing a budget.

Building. This component involves relationship building among consultant(s), consultees, and administrators. It may involve developing positive expectations of the program among these individuals.

Learning. This component is a supervisory component in which the staff are provided knowledge and skills related to program implementation and become more aware of their roles in the program.

Evaluating. Program evaluation functions are an important part of developing a consultation program. The reader is referred to Maher and Bennett (1984) for a comprehensive discussion of program evaluation activities, goals, and methods.

Example Applications. A number of examples of the AVICTORY model have appeared in the literature, including applications to a behavioral group-counseling program an the development of a system for managing individualized education programs (Maher, 1984). More recently, Ponti, Zins, and Graden (1988) described system-level activities that the authors were involved in during the implementation of a consultation-based service-delivery system to decrease referrals for special education. The application represents an example of a system of consultation services rather than individual case applications. The model of services is presented in Figure 8-2. It can be observed that the consultant provides service when a problem is observed. Consultation activities involve work with teachers, special services staff, and parents. Assessment activities may focus on the curriculum as part of problem identification. As in other prereferral intervention models (e.g., Graden, Casey, & Bonstrom, 1985; Graden, Casey, & Christenson, 1985; Gutkin, Henning-Stout, & Piersel, 1988), extensive psychoeducational assessment is not undertaken unless consultation services are ineffective.

The prereferral program was implemented in an elementary school serving approximately 500 children. The system-level issues that were addressed through specific aspects of the DURABLE framework are presented in Table 8-1. Generally, the program was considered successful in terms of expanding the range of service delivery, the rates of referrals, and the requests for consultation services. Despite the positive results of the program, the authors did identify several barriers (see our discussion of this and other research on prereferral consultation programs in Chapter 9). First, there were difficulties due to the lack of staff training in consultation,

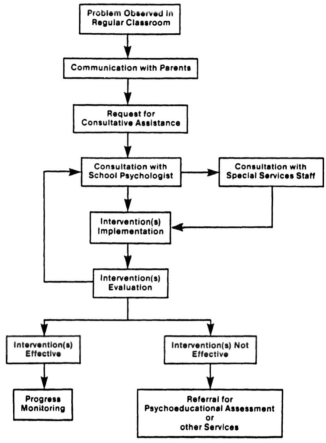

FIGURE 8-2. Flowchart for prereferral consultation process. [Source: C. R. Ponti, J. E. Zins, & J. L. Graden. (1988). Implementing a consultation-based service delivery system to decrease referrals for special education: A case study of organizational considerations. *School Psychology Review, 17,* 89–100. Reproduced by permission.]

of team meetings, and of coordination. Second, there were some problems associated with curricular modifications and evaluation methods. Third, some problem emerged over the promotion of students who displayed academic difficulties. A fourth, and major concern was the amount of time that teachers needed to implement the interventions. Finally, as the number of requests for consultation increased, the psychologist-consultant had difficulty meeting service requests.

Over a period of several years, Bergan also conducted a program through the Office of Psychoeducational Research at the University of Arizona that illustrates one way of establishing service objectives in a school system. The Office of Psychoeducational Research program was designed to demonstrate the effectiveness of the consultation services ren-

TABLE 8-1. Application of DURABLE Framework to Prereferral
Consultation Programs

Component	Examples of application activities
Discussing	Goal of making assistance available to all students and teachers in a more timely manner
	Intended outcome of reducing special education referrals
	Practical issues regarding record keeping, meeting times, incentives for staff participation
Understanding	Why consideration is being given to implementing the consultation program at this time
	Concerns that funding may decrease if there are fewer special-education placements, possibly resulting in a need for fewer staff
Reinforcing	Staff efforts in expanding their roles to include more consultation
	Participation by providing release from other activities to engage in consultation process
Adapting	School policy to require that interventions be attempted before a referral for assessment
	Job descriptions of special services staff to include consultation
Building	Efficacy expectations in staff by emphasizing the success that other organizations have had with consultation programs
	Commitment to carry out the change successfully by involving staff in program implementation
Learning	That special services staff require in-service training in consultation and teaming strategies in order to be able to participate in the pre-referral process
	That before and after school hours are inconvenient for many teachers to engage in prereferral consultation
Evaluating	Whether most staff used the consultative assistance
	If requests for consultation increased
	If the roles of special-services staff changed
	Whether student behaviors changed

Source: Ponti, C. R., Zins, J. E., & Graden, J. L. (1988) Implementing a consultation-based service delivery system to decrease referrals for special education: A case study of organizational considerations. *School Psychology Review*, 17, 89–100. Reproduced by permission

dered to local school districts through a consultative problem-solving system. Within the program, the objectives for services to a particular school district are established by a "field services coordinator" who provides consultation at the administrative level for that district. To formulate objectives, the field services coordinator conducts a modified problem-identification interview with the school administration at the beginning of the school year. The content of the interview is restricted mainly to a discussion of program objectives. The field service coordinator initiates the interview by specifying the categories of objectives within which the service goals may be established. Objectives for the program are divided into five categories: program effectiveness, program efficiency, extent of program use, types of procedures used to solve problems, and types of problems dealt with by consultants. After indicating the general categories established for objectives, the coordinator elicits specific program goals from administrators within these categories.

The establishment of objectives for services makes it possible to match the services to needs and to evaluate whether a match has been achieved. For instance, in the psychoeducational research program, the goals established with the school administration serve as guidelines for delivering services within the system. In addition, they make it possible to evaluate whether the system has provided the kinds of services desired.

Providing Effective Services

The skills and efficiency of consultants are variables of critical importance in ensuring the provision of effective services to consultees and clients. Bergan and Tombari (1976) investigated the effectiveness of consultation services in 806 cases obtained from 10 communities participating in the Follow Through project. Effectiveness was defined in terms of the extent to which the consultation goals were obtained. Service efficiency was defined by the amount of time between the receipt of a referral and the first interview between the consultant and the consultee. There were several measures of consultant skill. One of these was the consultant's "flexibility" in using psychological principles. Flexibility was assessed in terms of the variety of psychological principles applied by the consultants. The authors assumed that the consultants who applied a broad range of psychological principles in consultation were more effective than the consultants who used a narrow range of principles repetitively. In addition to the measure of flexibility, the researchers used the measures of interviewing skill discussed in earlier chapters in the book. Included among these was a measure of the extent to which the consultants used elicitors to control verbalizations in consultation; a measure of the extent to which they applied specification, summarization, and validation verbalizations; a measure of the relevance of the interview content; and a measure of the extent to which the consultants maintained interview focus by staying on one topic of conversation for an extended period rather than switching back and forth across topics.

Evaluation

The inclusion of an evaluation component within a consultative problem-solving system may have beneficial effects on the services offered (Maher & Bennett, 1984). In such a component, the consultant should be responsible for collecting, analyzing, interpreting, and reporting data on the operation of the services rendered within the service implementation component. The purposes of this evaluation are to make the overall program of services offered through the system accountable to the people using the system and to provide a basis for future planning to maximize effectiveness.

Evaluation is particularly useful when consultation services are being offered through an institution such as a community-mental-health center or a public school. Programmatic evaluations of services rendered through institutions can be used to determine whether the services provided correspond to the objectives established for services. Moreover, program evaluations may reveal unanticipated problems resulting from services. Information of this kind may be useful in improving the quality of future services. Evaluation data may also be of interest to individuals in private practice. For example, broad-scale evaluations conducted within a community can be used to identify the extent to which community needs for services are being met. Information of this type may help the private practitioner to determine within his or her capabilities what types of services should be offered within the community.

Evaluating the Attainment of Service Goals

The major function of evaluation component is to determine the extent to which the objectives established for the service implementation component have been achieved. The first task to be accomplished in determining the implementation goals is establishing categories for describing the goals. The categories used in the Office of Psychoeducational Research program mentioned above illustrate some kinds of classifications that may be used to describe service objectives. As the reader may recall, the objectives were divided into five broad categories. Information given within the category of program effectiveness detailed the percentage of successful problem solutions for the various types of cases. The data on efficiency included such information as the amount of time between the initial referral and the start of consultation as well as the time between the beginning of consultation and the attainment of problem solution. The information regarding program use involved a description of the types of personnel using consultation services. Data on the kinds of procedures used in consultation involved a description of the plans implemented in consultation in terms of categories of psychological principles such as modeling, cuing, and reinforcement. The information concerning the types of problems involved a description of cases in terms of classes of behavior such as aggression, disruption, and academic performance.

The second task to be accomplished in evaluating the attainment of the service implementation goals is to set up procedures for collecting the data to be used in assessing the achievement of the goals. Case-reporting forms completed by consultants as they provide services can be used to meet many data-collection needs. Examples of case-reporting forms used in the psychoeducational research program, as well as procedures for coding the data obtained from them, are given in Appendix C.

A case-reporting form should include identifying information such as the names of the consultees and the clients involved in the case, the name of the institution within which the services are being rendered (if there is an institution), the age and sex of the clients, and the individual or individuals who made the initial referral. If the information is to be stored in a computer, it is useful to assign an identification number to the case. The identification number not only facilitates retrieval but also helps to protect the privacy of the clients and the consultees involved in the case. When an ID number is assigned, it is possible to use information for evaluation purposes without communicating the names of clients and consultees to persons involved in the evaluation. Moreover, the likelihood is reduced that the information will inadvertently fall into the hands of individuals and groups not authorized by clients and consultees to possess the information.

In addition to identifying information, case-reporting forms should allow a description of the amount of time spent on the case. For example, the form may include information on the date of referral, the date of the problem identification interview, and the date that the case was closed. It also may detail the number of interviews and other contacts necessary to complete the case. Information regarding the time spent on the case can be used in evaluating service efficiency. Of course, we don't mean to imply that those cases involving the fewest number of contacts are necessarily the most efficient. Other factors such as the complexity of the case must be considered in making judgments concerning efficiency (see the discussion of this issue in Chapter 9).

A third type of information that should be included on a case-reporting form is the status of the case at the time that the consultation services were terminated. Information regarding status and the explanation of it may be used in evaluating program effectiveness. For example, data indicating that the goal of consultation has been attained and that the plan designed to achieve the goal was successful provide information indicating that services have been effective.

A fourth type of data that should be included on a case-reporting form is a specification of the problem to be solved through consultation. As discussed in earlier chapters, problem definition should include a behavioral specification of the goal(s) to be achieved through consultation and a description of the procedures to be used in measuring the attainment of the goals.

The final type of information that should be included on a case-reporting form is a description of the plan designed during problem analysis. Information regarding the plan should specify the plan executors and the procedures used to effect changes in client behavior.

The process of evaluating the attainment of service goals can be quite burdensome when the amount of service being offered through a consultative problem-solving system is large. The use of microcomputers is an obvious solution to the problem of conducting large-scale evaluations (Kratochwill, Doll, & Dickson, 1985). To use the computer effectively in the evaluation of service implementation goals, a generalized program must be written that will process the various kinds of data that may be collected in the evaluation process. The program should be flexible enough to accommodate minor changes in priorities and data collection strategies without requiring extensive rewriting of the program. In addition to a flexible program, procedures must be established for entering data into the machine. As the forms presented in Appendix C illustrate, it is possible to establish a numerical code for all of the categories of information described above as being necessary on a case-reporting form. The use of a numerical code enables the evaluators to enter data from the form directly into the computer.

The final task to be accomplished in evaluating the attainment of service implementation goals is to report the results of the evaluation to the individuals offering services through the system and to consultees using the services of the system. An example of an evaluation report for a psychoeducational research program is given in Appendix D. The task of reporting may be simplified greatly by including within the computer evaluation program the capability of printing the data in a form that is directly usable in the report. For example, in the report reproduced in Appendix D, all of the tables were printed by the computer in the same form as that used in the report. The tables not only provided a summary of the data described in the report but also served as guides for the written discussion in the report.

It is generally advisable for someone to interpret the evaluation report to those individuals who receive a copy. For instance, when services are provided within a school setting, evaluation reports should probably be sent to the school superintendent and the other administrative officials in the district. It is often useful to interpret the results of the evaluation in interviews with administrative personnel. Meetings arranged for the purpose of reviewing the evaluation of services not only serve to clarify questions that may arise about the evaluation but may also serve as a catalyst for the discussion of needs and priorities with respect to future services.

Evaluating Unanticipated System Effects

In recent years, the science of ecology has made it increasingly apparent that changes intended to produce one outcome in a particular environmental setting often eventuate in other, unanticipated outcomes. For example, people are now painfully aware that, although the automobile

has afforded useful transportation services, it has also made an unanticipated contribution to the pollution of the environment. Similarly, cities
have provided housing and employment opportunities for large masses of
people, but they have also produced once-unanticipated increases in
crime. As these examples imply, human beings exist within large ecosystems involving interrelated elements that influence one another. Thus,
a change in a particular element in the system tends to produce a change in
one or more of the other elements in the system.

Edwin Willems (1974) argued persuasively that behavior modification
programs, like other technological intrusions into existing ecosystems,
may produce unanticipated consequences of substantial significance. More
recently, Martens and Witt (1988) argued that an ecological perspective
should guide behavioral-consultation problem-solving efforts to reduce the
negative side effects of such programs (see also Lentz, 1988, for example).
In some cases, the unanticipated outcomes of behavioral interventions may
be beneficial. However, behavioral programs may also produce unforeseen
consequences that are detrimental to the individuals assumed to profit
from the programs. Moreover, in some instances, a single intervention
may produce both desirable and undesirable outcomes that have not been
anticipated. For example, Sajwaj, Twardosz, and Burke (1972) reported an
investigation that demonstrated that unanticipated positive and negative
outcomes may accompany a behavioral intervention. In their study, a preschool teacher used an extinction procedure to reduce a boy's attempts to
engage her in conversation during a free-play period. The teacher was
concerned about the excessive number of interactions the child initiated.
To reduce this excessive conversation, she ignored the child's efforts to
start conversations with her. The extinction procedure was quite successful. However, it produced a number of unanticipated outcomes. Two
positive effects were that the child's interactions with other children increased and the amount he played with inappropriate things during free
play decreased. The negative outcomes included a decline in appropriate
behavior during group sessions devoted to academic learning and an increase in classroom disruptions. In an effort to control the undesirable
outcomes of the initial intervention, an additional intervention was introduced. The second intervention, which involved removing the child from
the class for a 2-minute period following inappropriate behavior or classroom disruptions, was successful in eliminating the undesirable outcomes
resulting from the first treatment.

Petrie et al. (1980) presented an example of the possible (and plausible)
unintended effects that can occur as a consequence of establishing a token
program designed to increase student engaged time. Some possible types
of unintended effects on behaviors not directly targeted for intervention by
the psychologist are depicted in Figure 8-3. For example, an undesirable
behavior such as stealing, may increase, may affect children within the

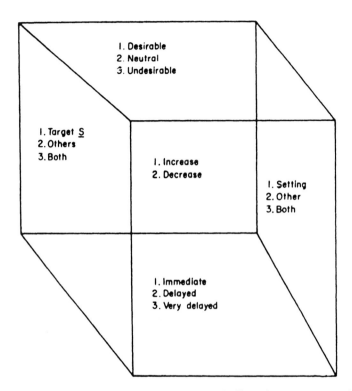

FIGURE 8-3. Classification of some kinds of unintended effects that may occur in behaviors that are not manipulated directly by the psychologist. [Source: P. Petrie, K. Brown, W. C. Piersel, S. R. Frinfrock, M. Schelble, C. P. Leblanc, & T. R. Kratochwill (1980). The school psychologist as behavioral ecologist. *Journal of School Psychology, 18,* 222–233. Reproduced by permission.]

program or children within another program, may extend into the home setting, or may occur after the token program is terminated. As can be observed in the figure, there are 162 (i.e., $3 \times 2 \times 3 \times 3 \times 3$) possible kinds of side effects. The point is that the number of other changes can occur in addition to the changes in the target behaviors.

One conclusion to be drawn from the ecological perspective on behavioral consultation is that steps must be taken to evaluate unplanned outcomes associated with behavior modification programs. Evaluation procedures should include not only procedures for detecting unforeseen outcomes when they occur but also strategies for anticipating such outcomes before they take place (Locatis & Gooler, 1975; Petrie *et al.*, 1980). There are certain general guidelines for conducting technology evaluations that can be usefully incorporated into the evaluation component of a consultative problem-solving system.

Some Technology Assessment Strategies for the Behavioral School Psychologist[1]

Given the probability that unanticipated system effects may produce negative consequences, what options are available? There seem to be four (Petrie *et al.*, 1980). First, they can be ignored. This option is becoming less commonplace than has been true in the past. A second option proposed from time to time is to call a moratorium on certain behavioral intervention strategies until all negative influences are determined. About this option, Baer (1974) pointed out:

> caution in the assessment of ecological consequences of any new technology is in itself disaster prone. Some societies waiting for a complete understanding of the modification programs they might be applying to their behaviorally dispossessed citizens may find themselves burned down by those citizens, in the name of caution. (p. 169)

A third option, presented by Willems (1974), involves actual research on unanticipated side effects. Such research might best be conducted in naturalistic settings, such as schools, and deserves consideration in future endeavors in applied behavior analysis. In this regard, Lentz (1988) provided a conceptual guideline to examining the relations among materials that have been used to measure the outcomes of classroom intervention studies (see Figure 8-4). The first level of measurement represents the most inclusive categories, in which behavior is dichotomized as desirable or undesirable. A time-sampling strategy may be used to assess on-task or off-task behavior. The subsequent levels involve dividing the wide categories into components with increasing the specificity of measurement (on dimensions of more restrictive and specific topography and measurement precision). As can be observed in the figure, time sampling with increasing differentiation is involved in Levels 1–3, and Level 4 involves "real true" data assessment.

A fourth option involves following some guidelines for appraising and conducting individual assessments or the evaluation of second-order consequences (cf. Locatis & Gooler, 1975). Second-order consequences are the unanticipated side effects of technology. As Locatis and Gooler (1975) noted, a movement toward technology assessment has emerged to reduce the probability of being surprised by such effects. In reviewing those aspects of technology assessments relevant to education, these authors' 14 guidelines pertain to the constitution of individual assessments and are specifically relevant to school psychologists operating within the behavioral paradigm. Some specific guidelines for school psychologist-consultants are presented from these 14 points.

---

[1]This section is adapted from Petrie *et al.* (1980, pp. 225–230).

Desirable Behaviors	Undesirable Behaviors
LEVEL I[a] (Time sampled — inclusive)	
On-task	Off-task
(Appropriate behavior)	(Inappropriate behavior)
(Attention)	(Inattention?)
(Academic Engagement)	(Nonengagement?)
(Study behavior)	Nonstudy behavior?)
LEVEL II[b] (Time sampled — global)	
On-task	Passive off-task
	Disruptive behavior
LEVEL III[c] (Time sampled — specific)	
Writing, academic questions, reading aloud, reading silently, attend, raise hand, look for materials	gross motor, noise, orient, blurt, talk, aggression
LEVEL IV[d]	
(Rate or percentage correct:)	(Rate or count:)
answer correctly written responses	hits verbals concompliance
(math, reading, spelling, etc.)	looks approaches interactions

[a](e.g., Hay, Hay, & Nelson, 1978; Winett & Roach, 1973)
[b](e.g., Ferritor, Buckholdt, Hamblin, & Smith, 1972)
[c](e.g., Hall et al., 1982; Becker et al., 1967)
[d](e.g, Shapiro & Lentz, 1986; Lentz & Shapiro, 1985 for discussions)

FIGURE 8-4. Relationships among levels of measurement of common classroom-intervention targets. [Source: F. E. Lentz. (1988). On-task behavior, academic performance, and classroom disruptions: Untangling the target selection problem in classroom interventions. *School Psychology Review, 17*, 243–257. Reproduced by permission.]

The application of these 14 guidelines is exemplified in the Petrie *et al.* (1980) example of a school psychologist who was asked to intervene in a classroom of second-grade students. The teacher reported to the school psychologist that her students continually exhibited disruptive behaviors and infrequently completed assignments. In this example, the school psychologist recommended the implementation of a token economy as a likely solution to the target problems. Although the implementation of token economies is a frequently used intervention program in educational settings (e.g., Kazdin, 1989), it is only one of numerous examples that can be cited to assess the relevance of the following guidelines:

1. *Use a broad range of criteria.* When multiple and broad-range criteria

are used, the probability of detecting second-order consequences is increased. For example, in our token program, the psychologist can use Willems's (1974) interactive items and develop others to anticipate pervasive second-order consequences. Further, parents, administrators, and teaching staff can be directed to serve in the role of second-order observers and could be cued for positive and negative effects (e.g., reduction of disruptive behavior in the home as a second-order positive outcome or excessive critical comments made by the principal as a negative outcome in the school). Not only does this role encourage more options in the search for second-order consequences, but it supports a variety of perspectives that, in turn, allow for criteria more diversified than those that may be proposed by a single consultant.

2. *Utilize adversary proceedings.* Depending on the type of intervention considered, individuals from the natural environment can be assembled to debate the pros and cons of the treatment program. Winett (1976) noted that a child welfare program in Kentucky was based on the concept that citizens representative of a particular community can assess community needs, design solutions to problems, and assist with the implementation of strategies for change. The consultant recommending implementation of the system in a second-grade classroom to reduce high levels of disruptive behavior can likewise use an adversary-proceedings approach. A fellow colleague-psychologist may play the "devil's advocate" in discussing the application of the token program by raising the objections commonly expressed by school staff and parents. A principal or counselor can also serve in the adversary role, suggesting issues that may be a problem from an administrator's perspective. For example, a plausible issue that they may suggest is that the parents of children not enrolled in the classroom targeted for intervention may demand that their children receive the same treatment services. Further, it may be noted that parents who have children in the classroom may express their concern about potential student dependence on external rewards. Thus, such individuals can assist in monitoring the initial concerns within the context of the token economy.

3. *Assemble multidisciplinary teams.* Although states now mandate multidisciplinary teams for special-education placement, such teams can also be used in an assessment strategy for interventions not specifically affiliated with special education (e.g., Ponti *et al.*, 1988). In our token program example, the consultant can assemble a teacher, an administrator, and perhaps another specialist to plan the program and to develop a communication system regarding program efficacy. Such a team allows input from professionals outside psychology and is likely to be useful in gauging second-order consequences and planning for them in multifaceted ways. In addition, such a team can provide "social validation" of the effectiveness of the token economy (cf. Kazdin, 1977; Wolf, 1978). In summary, the notion of conventional "staffing" can be reconceptualized as a team ap-

proach to technology evaluation, perhaps existing throughout the duration of the program.

4. *Use the empirical data and scientific theories.* The available research reveals many examples of unanticipated effects of behavioral interventions (e.g., LaVigna & Donnellan, 1986; Lentz, 1988; Martens & Witt, 1988). To prevent adverse side effects and to maximize constructive behavior change, the psychologist should have a thorough knowledge of the relevant behavioral research. In the school psychology literature, examples are available of problems of unanticipated effects when certain target behaviors are chosen (Lentz, 1988). Furthermore, examples of why and how token systems fail can be beneficial to psychologists implementing token program treatments (e.g., Drabman & Tucker, 1974). In our example, the psychologist implementing a token economy to reduce student disruptive behaviors should peruse related studies and review token economy research (e.g., Kazdin, 1989) before implementing the program.

5. *Conduct experiments.* Although the school psychologist's role is not formally conceptualized in the context of research, many practitioners have methodological skills that need not atrophy (see a discussion of this issue in Chapter 6). Thus, the token program, especially if it involves novel components, can be conceptualized as applied research, and any novel features can be shared with other professionals if a credible methodology is formulated. For example, the teacher can record the daily levels of disruptive behavior and assignment completion over the duration of the program. Such data would document program effectiveness and promote accountability. Methodologies emphasizing time series experimentation can further provide a vehicle for the direct evaluation and assessment of technological intervention consequences (Barlow *et al.*, 1984; Kratochwill & Bergan, 1978a). With the emphasis on nearly continuous measurement and analysis, flexibility in design, and potential application to single subject(s) or groups, single case designs can be used to respond productively to Willems's suggestion (1974) that research must be conducted to assess unanticipated system effects. Finally, consultants can become involved in the "experimental ecology of education" and can further the understanding of socialization processes in ecological systems (Bronfenbrenner, 1976).

6. *Structure the assessment so as to separate multiple issues and variables.* Assessments of behavior change, especially second-order consequences, typically involve multiple issues and variables (see also Martens & Witt, 1988). To identify agents of second-order behavior change requires consultants to structure evaluative mechanisms so as to isolate multiple issues and variables. The consultant implementing a token system to reduce incidents of disruptive behavior may benefit from recording other student or teacher behavior. For example, the consultant might collect data on *teacher* data collection. If it is determined that the teacher has discontinued recording student behavior on prescribed record forms, the multiple issues in-

volved in this second-order consequence may be analyzed. While evaluating the recording system, it may be determined that the record forms require excessive time to complete. Then, the psychologist must revise the recording system to ensure future teacher data-recording. Administering acceptability questionnaires to students, teacher, and parents may also assist the school psychologist to determine the levels of consumer satisfaction with the token system, and to identify problem areas (see Elliott, 1988). Such measures allow for the isolation of multiple issues and variables related to the implementation of a token program.

7. *Estimate priorities.* In the context of everyday service activities, consultants are unable to assess every possible second-order consequence that occurs as a result of some intervention program. Thus, priorities as to which variables to examine must be set before the intervention occurs or must be continually reevaluated as the program evolves. A negative consequence of a behavioral program for delinquent youth reported by Reppucci and Saunders (1974) suggests an example. As noted previously, the program ran into difficulty when the news media, politicians, and police pressured the institution for tight security measures when the number of runaways increased. The resulting tightened security severely curtailed the reinforcers used in the program. Such a negative consequence may be more important than the negative consequences of staff failing to collect data initially.

In our token program example, the consultant must also estimate priorities in second-order assessment. It may be more productive to channel efforts into determining how second-grade teachers will react to implementing the token system, rather than to spend excessive time measuring students' disruptive behavior in the home. Undue pressure from teachers-peers may lead to a termination of the teacher's involvement in the program.

8. *Examine in detail the inherent characteristics of the action being assessed.* Assessing the inherent characteristics of a behavioral program can involve a thorough analysis of the relation between the program and the environment in which it is implemented. For example, such an assessment may focus on the physical environment and its relation to the program as well as on the usual analysis of social situations. Thus, in response to Willems's focus (1974) on the linkup of behavior and the physical environment, consultants can broaden their assessment base by determining how such factors as the physical structure of the setting (e.g., the classroom, the home, the playground, the school bus, or wherever a behavioral program is implemented) contributes to the success or failure of the program. For example, if a second-order negative consequence of the token program is that the teacher is ineffective in the contingent delivery of the tokens, it may be determined that the seating arrangement used in the classroom precludes an effective contingent-delivery system. Some assessment of this problem must occur with the intent of solving it. The solution may be simply to

rearrange the classroom furniture (see Dunn, 1987, for a review of instructional environments).

9. *Explore a broad range of potential consequences.* Exploring a broad range of consequences is necessary but may be difficult with novel interventions. One strategy that can be used in identifying unanticipated consequences of behavioral interventions is brainstorming (Bergan, 1977; Osborn, 1963). For example, Bergan (1977) suggested that behavioral consultants and consultees be asked to participate in a series of short brainstorming sessions to identify the specific alternative consequences that may be produced by an intervention. In our token program, such individuals can brainstorm typical as well as potential novel consequences in the context of the school system into which the program is being introduced. Thus, a brainstorming session in the context of our token program may determine that small tokens and the fact that the children may mouth them is dangerous.

10. *Investigate the support systems.* A comprehensive examination of the environments into which interventions are introduced may be productive in gauging the influence of potential unanticipated effects. Referring to our example, the consultant may find that parents are requesting the establishment of a supportive environment for a contingency program based on naturalistic reinforcers such as parent–child activities. The teacher may, however, favor a token economy in which the children receive a specific tangible reward in the classroom. The consultant exploring the nature of these two environments and treatment options may recommend combining reinforcement strategies with the token intervention program and may divert disagreement among teachers and parents.

11. *Explore possible abuses.* There is increasing concern about possible abuses of behavioral programs and the implications that these abuses have in both ethical and legal areas (cf. Koocher & Farber, 1976; Martin, 1975; Stoltz, 1978; Tryon, 1976), especially with the application of punishment (see LaVigna & Donnellan, 1986). Unanticipated negative consequences of a token program may place the consultant in both ethical and legal jeopardy (see also Bersoff, 1975). For example, our psychologist implementing a token program that has as one component a punishment procedure must ensure that one of the second-order consequences will not be abuse of this punishment. Abuse can come from a teacher who uses the procedure for certain behaviors not deemed appropriate by the psychologist. Also, the psychologist implementing the program must be sure that it represents the "least restrictive" alternative treatment procedure.

Some excellent guidelines that can be followed in the implementation of behavioral programs in applied settings were presented by the Association for Advancement of Behavior Therapy and are reproduced in Table 8-2. Consultants will find that adherence to these procedural considerations greatly improves the probability of decreasing unanticipated effects provides quality behavioral interventions.

12. *Calculate the magnitude of the action or activity being assessed.* Some

TABLE 8-2. Guidelines for Assessment and Intervention in Behavior Therapy[a]

A. Have the goals of treatment been adequately considered?
 1. To insure that the goals are explicit, are they written?
 2. Has the client's understanding of the goals been assured by having the client restate them orally or in writing?
 3. Have the therapist and client agreed on the goals of therapy?
 4. Will serving the client's interests be contrary to the interests of other persons?
 5. Will serving the client's immediate interests be contrary to the client's long-term interest?
B. Has the choice of treatment methods been adequately considered?
 1. Does the published literature show the procedure to be the best one available for that problem?
 2. If no literature exists regarding the treatment method, is the method consistent with generally accepted practice?
 3. Has the client been told of alternative procedures that might be preferred by the client on the basis of significant differences in discomfort, treatment time, cost, or degree of demonstrated effectiveness?
 4. If a treatment procedure is publicly, legally, or professionally controversial, has formal professional consultation been obtained, has the reaction of the affected segment of the public been adequately considered, and have the alternative treatment methods been more closely reexamined and reconsidered?
C. Is the client's participation voluntary?
 1. Have possible sources of coercion on the client's participation been considered?
 2. If treatment is legally mandated, has the available range of treatments and therapists been offered?
 3. Can the client withdraw from treatment without a penalty or financial loss that exceeds actual clinical costs?
D. When another person or an agency is empowered to arrange for therapy, have the interests of the subordinated client been sufficiently considered?
 1. Has the subordinated client been informed of the treatment objectives and participated in the choice of treatment procedures?
 2. Where the subordinated client's competence to decide is limited, have the client as well as the guardian participated in the treatment discussions to the extent that the client's abilities permit?
 3. If the interests of the subordinated person and the superordinate persons or agency conflict, have attempts been made to reduce the conflict by dealing with both interests?
E. Has the adequacy of treatment been evaluated?
 1. Have the quantitative measures of the problem and its progress been obtained?
 2. Have the measures of the problem and its progress been made available to the client during treatment?
F. Has the confidentiality of the treatment relationship been protected?
 1. Has the client been told who has access to the records?
 2. Are records available only to authorized persons?
G. Does the therapist refer the clients to other therapists when necessary?
 1. If treatment is unsuccessful, is the client referred to other therapists?
 2. Has the client been told that if dissatisfied with the treatment, referral will be made?
H. Is the therapist qualified to provide treatment?
 1. Has the therapist had training or experience in treating problems like the client's?
 2. If deficits exist in the therapist's qualifications, has the client been informed?
 3. If the therapist is not adequately qualified, is the client referred to other therapists, or has supervision by a qualified therapist been provided? Is the client informed of the supervisory relation?
 4. If the treatment is administered by mediators, have the mediators been adequately supervised by a qualified therapist?

[a]Source: *Association for Advancement of Behavior Therapy*. Ethical issues for human services *Behavior Therapy*, 1977, 8. v–vi. Reproduced by permission

behavioral interventions have relatively little probability of unanticipated effects, whereas the magnitude of effects of other programs may be quite substantial. However, effects can be immediate, delayed, or both. Thus, the assessment of an intervention must be multidimensional with respect to its magnitude of effects and should occur over time. The magnitude of second-order consequences is typically greater in a token program than in a system that relies on social consequences. Whereas it is possible that children may steal tokens from other children, this negative consequence is impossible in a social reinforcement system.

13. *Estimate the controllability of the hypothesized adverse effects.* Once the potential adverse effects have been identified, or their probability has been determined, the consultant should hypothesize how the effects may be controlled. Control procedures may be conceptualized most parsimoniously as another behavioral intervention where the problem is targeted for change. For example, if our consultant predicts that token stealing will occur but is a manageable problem, he or she is still likely to recommend implementation of the token economy. However, the consultant may abandon the token project if he or she estimates that the program will be terminated by the school superintendent because of the excessive parental pressure already exhibited with regard to other treatment projects.

14. *Indicate the amount of uncertainty associated with each hypothesized impact.* If aforementioned recommendations are followed, some degree of "error variance" will still be associated with the program designed to evaluate and predict unanticipated effects. The amount of uncertainty can be usefully determined by exploring past programs of a similar nature and personal experience in school settings, by brainstorming with other professionals in the schools, and by surveying the natural environment carefully. For example, the consultant assessing the peer pressure that may be exerted on the teacher implementing the token program is likely to have less uncertainty when a thorough knowledge of the school system is available. As this knowledge is unlikely in more instances, an element of flexibility must be maintained in assessing the possible negative impact.

Conclusions

Consultants involved in the application of behavioral technology to educational systems must increasingly attend to the ecological impact of such interventions (Martens & Witt, 1988). An ecological orientation that emphasizes systemlike interdependencies among environment, organism, and behavior can provide a vehicle for research that both evaluates behavioral technology (Willems, 1974) and indicates the second-order consequences of implementing behavioral programs. In this section, we have presented some examples of problems in implementing behavioral technology in the schools as well as some options for future practice. The option of conducting some individual assessments of potential and second-order consequences (Locatis & Gooler, 1975) extends the behavioral consultant's role into determining what the consequences may be and developing strategies to cope with them. The 14 assessment options offer consultants some strategies for evaluating second-order consequences. Increased attention to this ecological orientation by the behavioral consultant adds both a broader scope to psychological services and credibility in the implementation of behavioral programs.

The decision to implement or not to implement a new technological tool requires an analysis of the positive and negative consequences that may be associated with both the introduction of the innovation and the failure to implement the innovation. Recent history shows that a failure to anticipate the unplanned consequences of technological innovation may produce serious problems. Yet, the decision not to intervene may have unfortunate consequences, too. A society that seriously curtails the use of technology to solve its problems will in all likelihood lose the power to mount a technology that will be effective in meeting societal needs. Technological innovation, like other social activities, must be nurtured through use. Inaction leading to the disuse of psychological innovations in socialization would ultimately render society largely incapable of producing innovations to solve its socialization problems.

Methodological and Conceptual Issues in Behavioral Consultation Outcome Research

As we have noted throughout the text, research and practice in behavioral consultation have expanded rapidly during the past several years. Research on the process and outcome effectiveness of consultation is becoming a high priority in school psychology for several reasons. A first issue relates to whether consultation and associated interventions designed for clients are effective. Especially, there is growing interest in the question of how behavioral consultation compares to other models of consultation (Gresham & Kendall, 1987). Currently, the school psychology field is represented by mental health consultation (Meyers, 1981; Meyers *et al.*, 1979), organizational development consultation (Schmuck, 1982) problem-centered consultation (Gutkin & Curtis, 1982) and behavioral consultation (Bergan, 1977; Tharp & Wetzel, 1969). As noted in Chapter 1, other "models" have been identified as well (West & Idol, 1987), but as we shall discuss later in this chapter, there are problems with the model conceptualization of consultation. Nevertheless, interest stems from determining whether one particular form or type of consultation is better than another and the implications for practice.

Previous reviews of the research literature suggest that consultation is generally an effective form of intervention in applied settings (Mannino & Shore, 1975; Medway, 1979b, 1982; Medway & Updyke, 1985). Specifically, Mannino and Shore (1975) suggested that 69% of the studies that they reviewed showed positive change in the consultee, the client, or the system level, or some combination of these. Subsequently, Medway (1979b) noted that 76% of investigations reported at least one or more positive

effects from consultation interventions. Medway (1979b, 1982) also reported that behavioral consultation was particularly effective, given certain
methodological limitations of work in this area. Meta-analysis has also
been applied to the consultation outcome literature. Medway and Updyke
(1985) conducted a meta-analysis of 54 consultation studies representing
mental health, behavioral, and organizational development models. The
authors found that consultation was generally effective in changing consultee behavior and attitude (an effect size of .55) and, to a lesser extent,
the behavior and attitudes of clients (an effect size of .39). In contrast to
previous reviews, no differences were found in the effectiveness of the
three major models of consultation, although behavioral consultation was
generally effective (an effect size of .47). Sibley (1986) reviewed 63 investigations and found that the effect size for clients was .91 and for consultees
.60, a finding in contrast with those of Medway and Updyke (1985). Sibley
did find an overall mean effect size of .75 for behavioral consultation.
These findings have very likely piqued interest among the proponents of a
particular model of consultation and have raised questions about the criteria applied in the evaluation of comparative outcome research.

A second reason for careful scrutiny of behavioral consultation is that
it is often recommended as an alternative to traditional assessment and
intervention practices in educational settings (Conoley & Gutkin, 1986;
Reschly, 1988a,b; Zins, Curtis, Graden, & Ponti, 1988). Increasingly, consultation has been proposed as an alternative to testing or assessment that
usually accompanies traditional service-delivery models—a strategy sometimes labeled prereferral intervention (e.g., Graden, Casey, & Christenson,
1985; Graden, Casey, & Bonstrom, 1985; Gutkin et al., 1988; Ponti et al.,
1988). However, behavioral consultation is not designed to replace assessment practices that may lead to understanding the problem under consideration. Behavioral consultation has been proposed as an alternative to
some of the biased assessment practices that have been most scrutinized
recently in the school psychology literature (Kratochwill, Alper, & Cancelli, 1980; Reschly, 1988a,b).

A third reason for a careful consideration of consultation relates to the
increased emphasis on formalized training in consultation in school psychology programs. Increasingly, psychologist-trainers have emphasized
consultation as a major part of the curriculum (Brown & Minke, 1986).
Training individuals in consultation has obvious implications for the future
practice of consultation. If training is empirically based and practitioners
use procedures that have a high probability of success in the schools, a
major impact may be made on children and teachers receiving these psychological services.

Fourth, consultation has also been considered an important part of
major secondary-prevention programs (Durlak & Jason, 1986). For example, the Primary Mental Health Project (PMHP) in Rochester, New York

(Cowen, Trost, Izzo, Lorion, Dorr, & Isaacson, 1975), emphasizes, as one of its major components, program development, consultation, and evaluation as an alternative to direct therapeutic activity. Various programs that are offspring of the PMHP (e.g., Kirschenbaum, 1979; Rickel, Smith, & Sharp, 1979) also incorporate consultation as a program component. Although these programs have developed within a "community psychology" framework, it is important to emphasize that they are based in schools and involve school mental-health professionals in consultation with teachers and/or parents.

Fifth, increasingly in the mental-health field, there has been interest in the development and implementation of brief therapies as an efficient and cost-effective form of intervention. Consultation can be considered a form of brief intervention for the client, as in the problem-solving approaches in behavioral consultation. Behavioral techniques (e.g., cognitive mediation, outside therapy assignments, and monitoring interventions) often facilitate attaining goals in a very short time.

The points raised above convey something of the current interest in behavioral consultation. A number of methodological and conceptual issues are important to consider in consultation outcome research. In this section of the chapter, we provide an overview of some of the issues that appear most salient in drawing conclusions from the existing consultation-outcome literature as well as in planning future research in the area. The methodological and conceptual issues raised below are a basic minimum that need to be addressed in future research in this area. They also serve as a yardstick for measuring the quality of the existing knowledge base in the consultation literature.

We confine our discussion primarily to issues of outcome studies and do not review extensively concerns about consultation process variables. Although the review is designed to supplement earlier empirical reviews of this literature, our purpose is to examine the literature critically from a number of perspectives that have not yet been used. The reader interested in this area should read several reviews that consider these issues (e.g., Gresham & Kendall, 1987; Idol & West, 1987; West & Idol, 1987).

DEFINITION OF CONSULTATION AND CONSULTATION MODELS

Nature of the Problem

Consultation is generally portrayed as an indirect service-delivery model (e.g., Alpert, 1976; Caplan, 1970; Medway, 1979b). One can typically find a general consensus that consultation involves a problem-solving activity between the psychologist-consultant and one or more consultees (usually teachers or parents) who take the primary responsibility for providing services to a client (usually a child) Virtually all consultation approaches embrace an *indirect* mode of service delivery, in which the consultant works through a consultee to deliver psychological services. Working through a consultee or mediator is a major distinguishing characteristic of the triadic model of consultation (Tharp, 1984). This approach, of course, contrasts with many behavioral intervention programs that are delivered directly by a trained professional or with the direct assistance of the professional who works along with the service provider to help the child client.

A major problem in the existing definitions of consultation is that they are quite broad and allow a large variety of strategies to be considered "consultation." For example, it is difficult to exclude any procedure in which there is an indirect involvement of a consultant with a consultee, the latter being primarily responsible for the client's service program. An appraisal of the published literature in behavior therapy attests to the enormous number of studies that involve this format. Even if one were to take a very strict definition of no direct consultant involvement with the client (such as in modeling the treatment program or carrying out some part of the treatment protocol), a very large number of studies would have to be defined as describing behavioral consultation. Ironically, many of these studies have *not* been included in consultation-outcome literature-reviews. An appraisal of the studies published in the *Journal of Applied Behavior Analysis,* for example, attests to the indirect service-delivery approaches that are often used in behavior modification or therapy.

This "indirect" approach generally embraces a model in which the primary-care provider for the child is directly involved in the treatment procedure. One of the more salient illustrations is the parent-training literature (e.g., Ollendick & Cerny, 1981). For example, as noted in Chapter 5, Ollendick and Cerny (1981) presented three basic training formats that have been used to teach parents behavior modification techniques to use on children's behavior. The first of these techniques is labeled "didactic instruction" (Johnson & Katz, 1973), "educational groups" (Odell, 1974), or "parent consultation" (Cobb & Medway, 1978). The procedure involves providing parents with information about behavioral principles and techniques via a variety of formats (e.g., reading material, films or videotapes, and demonstrations). Parents may be seen individually or in a group.

A second procedure involves training parents in individual intervention approaches. In this case, the trainer of the parents meets with one parent at a time and provides not only direct training, but also direct supervision of the parents while they carry out a treatment program for their children. The supervised practice in using behavior change procedures and hands-on experience during training is a major distinguishing characteristic of this focus.

A third format combines both the consultation and the individual formats: groups of parents are given instruction in behavioral management skills and are given supervised practice in techniques and applied settings. Parents may come into clinical settings and receive supervised experience before working with their children at home.

The point that we are making is that all three of these techniques may be considered a consultation approach. Any specific conclusions made about the efficacy of consultation have to take into account this rather extensive parent-training literature. Of course, the same might be said about the teacher-training literature, which in many areas runs parallel to the kinds of formats used in parent training (see Anderson & Kratochwill, 1988).

The difficulty of defining behavioral consultation extends beyond the format issue and relates to the different approaches or models within applied psychology. Specifically, several different approaches to behavioral consultation have been explicitly identified in the professional literature. An early model proposed by Tharp and Wetzel (1969) was defined within a triadic format in which the consultant works with a mediator, who, in turn, works with the client. This conceptual framework was presented in the school psychology literature by Tharp (1984), who outlined this triadic model of consultation in a consultation training module (Tucker, 1984). The model basically adheres to the consultant–consultee–client approach and can be conceptualized as similar to the parent-training approaches that are used in community settings.

More recently, Brown and Schulte (1987) outlined a social-learning-theory consultation-approach. These authors noted that the model is based on Bandura's social learning theory (1977b) and embraces the philosophical assumptions of reciprocal determinism during the consultation process. These writers suggested that the model involves relationship building, assessment, problem statement, goal setting, intervention, and evaluation. They also noted that the model differs from the more traditional model of consultation as described by Bergan (1977) in that it incorporates current research and theory regarding the role of cognitions in behavior change. Of course, the earlier work of Bergan embraced social learning principles and procedures that are clearly within the domain of behavioral consultation and intervention strategies as outlined in this text.

Recommendations

The term *consultation* has been used in a variety of ways both across and within various theoretical models. In effect, little has changed since Reschly's analysis of consultation (1976) in which he noted major problems of definition. A major dilemma for the researcher examining outcome studies of behavioral consultation is how to define that literature base. If one uses a very broad definition, a large variety of behavioral intervention programs that were very likely never conceptualized as part of a "consulta-tion model" can be included. This broad definition may be beneficial in future research. The benefit of this definition is that it increases the knowl-edge base for the efficacy of what are really indirect service-delivery ap-proaches within the field of school, clinical, counseling, and other applied areas of psychology and education.

At the other end of the spectrum are those studies that have been conducted within a specified model or approach, such as the model out-lined in this text. In this case, there are relatively few studies that have embraced the four-stage problem-solving process with any high degree of integrity. We advocate that individuals reviewing the behavioral-consulta-tion research-outcome area embrace a broad perspective and incorporate the large and ever-growing number of indirect service-delivery approaches that have been used in the field of behavior therapy or behavior modifica-tion. We also advocate that, in the future, researchers define more specifi-cally the *processes* occurring during actual consultation. In this regard, the procedures outlined in the current text will be most helpful, and specific recommendations are presented in the following sections of the chapter.

STANDARDIZATION OF CONSULTATION

A priority in future research in the behavioral consultation field is to use standardized procedures and formats. Standardization requires the development and use of formal interview guidelines, response protocols, and training manuals, among other features. Virtually none of the existing research studies that we have examined in the consultation literature have used a standardized format for the provision of consultation services. However, in future research, this should be a high priority for several reasons (Kratochwill, 1985; Kratochwill & Van Someren, 1985; Kratochwill *et al.*, 1988). First, the standardization of consultation will allow a replica-tion of the procedures used in future research activities. The replication of consultation procedures across research studies is especially important as researchers address the efficacy of consultation strategies and generalize successful outcome techniques across problem behavior settings, thera-pists, and other dimensions.

A second reason for recommending standardization of the consulta-tion process is that training in specific consultation skills will be possible. A major shortcoming of consultation research is that researchers do not often outline specific procedures for training individual consultants and con-sultees in the skills that are a part of the consultation process. Neverthe-less, like other therapeutic skills, consultation skills can be taught (Gar-field, 1977). A growing number of empirical studies support the finding that a standardized approach based on competency-based criteria can be used to train school psychologists in behavioral consultation (Bergan, Kratochwill, & Luiten, 1978; Kratochwill & Bergan, 1978b; Kratochwill *et al.*, 1981). Competency-based training approaches have been used to train school psychology students in problem-identification interview-skills (e.g., Brown, Kratochwill, & Bergan, 1982) and have recently been applied to the full spectrum of the behavioral consultation process in a training paradigm (Kratochwill *et al.*, 1989). A major reason for emphasizing standardized approaches is that consultants can be trained in consultation procedures and implement them in a way that will allow the integrity of the consultation process to be monitored over the course of the research investigation.

Third, once standardized approaches are documented in research, consultation may be more readily used by practitioners in applied settings. The lack of standardized approaches in the practice of consultation is part of the more general difficulty of behavior assessment and the treatment procedures for which standardized formats are often unavailable to practitioners (Kratochwill, 1985). The use of standardized formats to implement consultation would also appear to be essential in the empirical development of psychotherapeutic techniques that are eventually disseminated in practice to assist consultees and clients (Kazdin, Kratochwill, & Vanden Bos, 1986).

Finally, standardization of consultation process would appear to have an important bearing on legal and ethical issues in the delivery of psychological services in applied settings. The proliferation of behavioral consultation approaches that are not standardized raises potential ethical and legal concerns in terms of addressing standards for practice such as the most recent *Standards for Educational and Psychological Testing* (1985). Whether we will ever be at the stage of establishing technical standards for intervention procedures is unclear. Nevertheless, empirically based procedures that have been procedurally standardized at least set the stage for research that can address the current and emerging ethical and legal issues in applied settings for the delivery of psychological services.

Standardizing the consultation process at some global level may assist in defining the nature of behavioral consultation as a process. However, it must be recognized that there will still be large differences in process variables across individual consultants. This difference across consultants is quite apparent when the reader examines the transcripts of typical consultation sessions. Moreover, there will be differences across consultants at the level of words and phrases the tone of voice, and the body posturing used by the consultant, just to name a few variables. In this regard, it remains to be determined what factors are associated with successful consultation outcomes. Descriptive analysis of the successful consultant and the successful process of consultation is needed to advance our understanding of this issue.

It should also be recognized that it is possible for consultants to follow

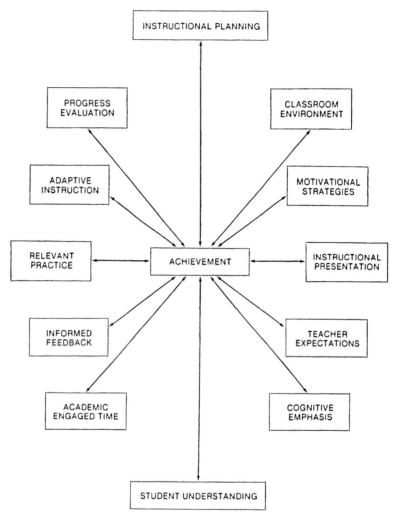

FIGURE 9-1. Components of the instructional environment. [Source: J. E. Ysseldyke, & S. Christenson. (1987). *The Instructional Environment Scale*. Austin, TX: Pro-Ed. Reprinted by permission.]

the prescriptions of standardized behavioral consultation and still be "poor" consultants in term of unsuccessful consultee- and client-related outcomes. For example, with the current level and type of consultation standardization, it is still possible for a consultant to select or recommend interventions that may not be effective. This selection can occur in three ways. First, to increase the acceptability of the intervention, the consultant may agree to a procedure that is selected by the consultee, but that is unlikely to yield major benefits for the child. Second, a consultant may select a treatment procedure that is not supported in the empirical literature. Third, adherence to a standardized process does not guarantee the selection of certain components of a treatment that may have a broad impact on the instructional environment. Nevertheless, even in this third issue, some level of standardization might occur to facilitate the consideration of a broad range of components of the instructional environment. For example, the consultant might use The Instructional Environment Scale (TIES; Ysseldyke & Christenson, 1987). Figure 9-1 shows components of the instructional environment that might be assessed by the consultant. The point is that some level of standardization in the assessment phase, such as through the TIES, may facilitate the selection of a range of variables that are likely to differ from those used by a consultant unfamiliar with the TIES.

Another concern to be raised about a standardized approach to consultation is that, because the consultant follows an established procedure, the major goal is to control consultee behavior. In fact, a unidirectional influence has been documented in the research on relational control in behavioral consultation (Erchul, 1987). However, recognition must occur that the consultee also influences the consultant in a variety of ways, particularly through the teacher's expertise in classroom intervention strategies. Some teachers, such as special-education teachers, have extensive educational background and experience in classroom management. In fact, bidirectional control may occur when consultees are trained in consultation procedures and behavior management (Anderson *et al.*, 1986) or when parents are trained in skills designed to improve their communication with professionals. For example, Kohr, Parrish, Neef, Drieseen, and Hallinan (1988) identified and experimentally validated the skills required of parents for effective communication with professionals. Table 9-1 lists the skills included in the researchers' program. It is quite likely that parents trained in the skills listed in Table 9-1 would be more effective consultees than those without such training.

PSYCHOMETRIC CONSIDERATIONS

As noted above, there are several advantages in the development of a standardized approach to consultation. A standardized approach may serve as a first step in facilitating the development of various psychometric characteristics of the interview technology applied in the consultation process. Consultation is viewed as a series of interviews (i.e., problem identification, problem analysis, and plan evaluation). Our perspective is similar to that of others in the field who have argued for endorsing standardized, school-oriented interviews from which various psychometric charac-

TABLE 9-1. Social Validation of Task Analysis of Parent Communication Skills

	Mean	Range
Preparation		
Parent thanks the professional for taking the time to meet with him or her.	2.8	1–4
Parent states that he or she is willing to actively participate in the meeting by providing information, feedback, and/or helping in the decision-making process.	4.4	3–5
Parent states how he or she has prepared for the meeting by bringing relevant materials (e.g., "I have brought my child's report cards") and/or stating that he or she has given thought to his or her child's behavior.	4.4	3–5
Parent brings to the meeting a list of the evaluators and their disciplines.	3.4	1–4
Parent brings to the meeting materials necessary to record information.	3.6	3–4
Complete communication		
Parent states a summary of what the professional has said at least at the conclusion of the professional's report (i.e., summary must include same topic area as that of professional's report).	4.5	4–5
Parent states his or her general observations of the child in the natural environment with regard to the topic at hand.	5.0	5–5
Parent asks for feedback from his or her partner (if present).	4.8	4–5
If there is a discrepancy between parent's and professional's observations, then parent requests clarification of the professional's statements of observation(s) just given.	5.0	5–5
Clarification		
Parent asks questions about what has been discussed, or states that he or she has no questions about (understands) information given.	4.8	4–5
Parent states a summary of the professional's response to his or her question(s) (i.e., a summary must include same topic area) or states that he or she understands.	4.6	3–5
Consensus		
Parent compliments the professional, the evaluation, or the meeting and/or makes a statement to acknowledge appropriateness of some aspect of professional's suggestion or report.	3.0	1–4
Parent states specific area(s) of agreement with the professional (i.e., uses I statements) or states there are no areas of agreement.	4.3	3–5
Identification of issues		
Parent states area(s) of disagreement with the professional (i.e., using I statements) without stating that the professional is incorrect or states that there are no areas of disagreement.	4.5	4–5
If disagreement, parent states his or her understanding of the professional's concern for the child.	3.9	3–5
If the parent was mistaken about the disagreement or the professional's statement(s), he or she admits mistake.	4.0	3–5
Suggestion of options		
Parent states or requests the possible options based on areas of agreement and/or disagreement.	4.5	4–5
Parent summarizes all options that have been presented.	4.5	4–5

(continued)

Table 9-1. (Continued)

	Mean	Range
Parent asks for or states the advantages and disadvantages of each option listed.	4.4	4–5
Parent states options in descending order of preference.	3.4	2–5
If there is a disagreement regarding most preferred option, parent makes a statement allowing the professional to "own" the parent's most preferred option (e.g., using you, your).	3.4	2–4
If there is a disagreement, parent states the more positive aspect of his or her chosen option.	3.9	3–5
Decide on action to be taken		
Parent states or asks who will deliver services.	4.9	4–5
Parent states or asks what services are to be delivered.	4.9	4–5
Parent states or asks where services will be delivered.	4.9	4–5
Parent states or asks when services will begin.	4.9	4–5
Parent states or asks the time and day of week that services will be delivered.	4.8	4–5
Parent states or asks how much the services will cost and/or if insurance will cover cost.	4.8	3–5
Parent states or asks how long the services will need to be provided.	4.8	4–5
Parent states chosen option or states why option is not feasible.	4.8	4–5
If necessary, parent states his or her next preferred option.	4.6	4–5
Feedback and acknowledgment		
Parent compliments the professional, the evaluation, and/or the meeting.	3.3	1–4
Parent states or asks who will make the next contact.	4.9	4–5
Parent states or asks when the next contact is to made.	4.9	4–5
Parent asks or states how the contact person may be reached.	4.8	3–5

Source: Kohr, M. A., Parrish, J. M., Neef, N. A., Driessen, J. R., & Hallinan, P. C. (1988). Communication skills training for parents: Experimental and social validation. *Journal of Applied Behavior Analysis, 21*, 21–30. Reproduced by permission.

teristics can be well documented (e.g., Burke & DeMers, 1979; Gresham, 1984). Concerns about the psychometric adequacy of the consultation process generally fall into the areas of reliability and validity (Gresham, 1984).

Reliability and Agreement Measures

One of the first considerations in establishing the psychometric standards of the interview relates to determining interrater reliability on the verbalizations that occur during the process of consultation. In this regard, the researcher must demonstrate that verbalizations can be assigned reliably to various categories included in the consultation interview (e.g., content, process, and control domains). Several studies have demonstrated that relatively high measures of interobserver agreement can be established during consultation interviews (e.g., Bergan, Burnes, & Kratochwill,

1979; Bergan & Neumann, 1980; Bergan & Tombari, 1976; Brown, Kratoch-will, & Bergan, 1982; Curtis & Watson, 1980; Kratochwill *et al.*, 1989; Tombari & Bergan, 1978). For example, in the Bergan and Tombari (1975) study, two observers coded randomly selected verbalizations from consultation interviews. The raters were able to achieve 96% agreement in assigning the verbalizations to the units of observation, including behavior, behavior setting, observation, specifications, and summarization. Generally, the use of a consultation analysis record (CAR) has demonstrated that verbalizations can be operationally defined and reliably assessed across time. Future research must address a broader spectrum of reliability concerns, including multiple raters and test–retest reliability, among other important dimensions.

Validity Considerations

Several different dimensions of validity are important in the behavioral consultation process. Generally, these fall within the areas of content validity, criterion-related validity, construct validity, and treatment validity.

Content Validity. The term *content validity* refers to how well the conditions under which the individual behaviors are assessed actually represent the sets of conditions that one is interested in generalizing (Livingston, 1977). Generally, content validity requires an adequate and unambiguous specification of the universe of interest, a representative sampling from the universe, and a specification of the method of evaluating responses and forming a score (Cronbach, 1971).

Within behavioral consultation, the CAR, as presented in Chapter 2 of the text, is designed to assess verbalizations in consultation and allows certain domains to be elicited and analyzed within the context of behavior, behavior setting, observation, and plan. The content validity of this process seems useful within the context of establishing effective intervention programs related to behavior analysis. One priority for future research is determining whether a more refined coding system will be necessary in the analysis of behavior. Several alternative coding systems are now available for use in the analysis of behavioral consultation (e.g., Erchul, 1987). In the Erchul (1987) study, the role of interpersonal power (control) was assessed by means of a variation of the Rogers and Farace (1975) "relational communication coding system." In the study, eight consultants worked with one consultee each across three interviews. Measures of relational control, domineeringness and dominance, and perceptions were obtained. The results of the study indicated that the consultants controlled the dyadic relationship across all stages of consultation. Also, the consultants who had high dominance scores were judged as more effective by the consultees, and the consultees with higher domineeringness scores were judged by the consultants to be better at gathering baseline data.

Criterion-Related Validity. Criterion-related validity is typically determined by an examination of correlations from behavior interviews with other diverse assessment criteria. In the case of consultation interviews, some data support the criterion-related validity of the interview process across the various phases of consultation (e.g., Bergan & Newman, 1980; Bergan *et al.*, 1979; Bergan & Tombari, 1976; Curtis & Watson, 1980; Tombari & Bergan, 1978). One important issue in the development of criterion-related validity is whether behavioral consultation interviews are more predictive of a consultee's ability to define a target behavior and a consultee's expectations concerning her or his ability to solve behavior problems in other interview formats (Gresham, 1984). Tombari and Bergan (1978) conducted a study involving 60 teachers who participated in a behavioral or medical model consultation interview format. During an interview, the teachers were given either specific behavioral cues (e.g., "When does this behavior typically occur in your classroom?") or medical model cues (e.g., "When does John's problem typically manifest itself?"). The authors found that the type of cue used by the consultant exerted a strong influence on teacher expectations concerning their actual abilities to solve a problem as rated on a 7-point Likert scale from 7 = probable to 1 = improbable. Also, the authors found that expectancy influences the teacher's ability to define the problem (which involved a written definition of the child's problem categorized as behavioral or medical model approaches.) Thus, the results of the study indicate that the actual verbalizations of the consultant during the process of consultation can predict a consultee's ability to define the problems and may even lead to more positive expectations.

As noted by Gresham (1984), there has been little research on the relation between consultation interview reports of dimensions of behavior (e.g., frequency, intensity, and duration) and actual observer assessment of behavior in the classroom. Extensive research in this area is needed because of the heavy reliance on verbal behavior description during the consultation process.

Construct Validity. Generally, the term *construct validity* refers to the extent to which a test measures some psychological construct or trait (Sattler, 1988). Construct validity in behavioral consultation can be evaluated by determining how the items in the consultation interview relate to the general features that the interview is designed to assess, such as specific processes occurring within consultants and consultees. As an example, Tombari and Bergan (1978) demonstrated that behavioral model and medical model cues delivered during the interview differentially affected the consultee's problem definition and expectations regarding the ability to solve the problem in the classroom. Likewise, in the Bergan et al. (1979) study, it was demonstrated that teachers who participated in a behavioral consultation interview were more successful in using the appropriate teaching skills than teachers in a medical-model-interview condition.

In the Curtis and Watson (1980) study, teachers exposed to behavioral interviews by skilled consultants were better able to define problem behaviors, spent more time in describing behaviors, and had a greater proportion of verbalizations based on factual rather than inferential information than were consultees exposed to individuals who were not as well skilled. In this regard, consultees' descriptions of the target behaviors were discriminated on the basis of high- versus low-skilled behavioral consultants.

Treatment Validity. Major goals of the behavioral consultation process are (1) to have the consultant and the consultee select target behaviors, and (2) to design an appropriate treatment as well as evaluate the treatment. Once a target behavior has been selected during the consultation process, the client should improve over and above what he or she would have if one selected an inappropriate target response. Moreover, if the appropriate treatment has been selected, the client should improve more than when an inappropriate treatment is selected (Hayes, Nelson, & Jarrett, 1986, 1988). When these two goals are met, behavioral consultation can be said to contribute to improved treatment outcome or to demonstrate treatment validity or utility. Treatment validity addresses a functional approach to evaluating aspects of the consultation process. Treatment validity is a relatively new psychometric standard and has not been investigated extensively in the field of behavioral assessment.

A variety of strategies have been designed to establish the treatment validity of investigations, and the reader is referred to Hayes et al. (1986, 1988) for a review of these procedures. Table 9-2 lists the types of treatment utility studies, the questions asked, and the methods used for research in this area. We believe that at least one of the early studies in behavioral consultation meets the criteria for a treatment validity investigation. (The study has often been referred to as a study of criterion-related validity— e.g., see Gresham, 1984, and Gresham & Davis, 1988.) In the study, Bergan and Tombari (1976) trained 11 behavioral consultants to provide services to 806 children (Grades K–3) who had been referred for psychological services by teacher-consultees. The problem behaviors included a wide range of difficulties, including physical assault, disruption, following classroom rules, and academic and social deficits. Using multiple-regression procedures, the authors found that the single best predictor of implementing a treatment plan was the problem identification interview ($R = .776$). More than 60% of the variance in plan implementation was accounted for by identifying the problem to be solved during a problem identification

TABLE 9-2. Types of Treatment Utility Studies, Questions Asked, and Methods Used

Type of study	Question	Typical group comparison	Time-series (single case)	
			Main question between subject	Main question within subject
Post hoc studies	What is the relation between client characteristics and treatment outcome?	Pre-post correlational.	Time-series design, then correlational.	Not applicable.
A priori single-dimension studies				
Manipulated assessment	What is the effect of the administration of, or data from, different assessment devices or methods on treatment outcome?	Two or more groups randomly assigned. Assessment taken or made available differs. Use of information in treatment stays the same.	Two or more groups randomly assigned. Assessment taken or made available differs. Use of information in treatment stays the same. Treatment assessed in series of time-series designs.	Assessment taken or made available differs. Use of information in treatment stays the same. Treatments compared within subject using time-series designs.
Manipulated use	What is the effect of different uses of available assessment data on treatment outcome?	Two or more groups randomly assigned. Assessment the same. Use of assessment in treatment differs.	Two ore more groups randomly assigned. Assessment the same. Use of assessment in treatment differs. Treatment assessed in series of time-series design.	Assessment the same. Use of assessment in treatment differs. Treatments compared within subject using time-series designs.
Obtained differences	What is the relation between distinct patient types and treatment outcome?	Two or more known groups based on pre-treatment differences. Same treatment.	Two or more known groups based on pre-treatment differences. Treatment assessed in series of time-series designs.	Not applicable.

(continued)

TABLE 9-2. (*Continued*)

Type of study	Question	Typical group comparison	Main question between subject	Main question within subject
A priori multiple-dimension studies				
Manipulated assessment/manipulated use	What is the effect of different assessment devices or methods when the information from them is used in different ways to design treatment?	Factorial groups randomly assigned. Assessment taken or made available differs. Use of assessment data in treatment differs.	Factorial groups randomly assigned. Assessment taken or made available differs. Use of assessment data in treatment differs. Treatment assessed in series of time-series designs.	Assessment taken or made available differs. Use of assessment data in treatment differs. Treatments based on different combinations of above compared within subject using time-series designs
Manipulated assessment/obtained differences	What is the effect of different assessment devices or methods on treatment outcome for two or more distinct patient types?	Groups randomly assigned within known groups. Assessment taken or made available differs. Use of data in treatment stays the same.	Groups randomly assigned within known groups. Assessment taken or made available differs. Use of data in treatment stays the same. Treatment assessed in series of time-series designs.	Assessment taken or made available differs. Use of data in treatment stays the same. Treatments compared within subject using time-series designed in each o two or more known groups.

The column header "Time-series (single case)" spans the last two columns (Main question between subject / Main question within subject).

Manipulated use/obtained differences	What is the effect of different uses of available assessment data on treatment outcome for two or more distinct patient types?	Groups randomly assigned within known groups. Use of assessment data differs. Assessment taken or made available stays the same.	Groups randomly assigned within known groups. Use of assessment data differs. Treatment assessed in series of time-series designs.	Use of assessment data differs. Treatments compared within subject using time-series designs in each of two or more known groups.
Manipulated assessment/manipulated use/obtained differences	What is the effect of different types and uses of available assessment data on treatment outcome for two or more distinct patient types?	Groups randomly assigned within known groups. Use of assessment data differs. Assessment taken or made available differs.	Groups randomly assigned within known groups. Use of assessment data differs. Assessment taken or made available differs. Treatment assessed in series of time-series designs.	Nature and use of assessment data differ. Treatments compared within subject using time-series designs in each of two or more known groups.
Obtained differences/two or more treatments	What is the effect of different treatments on outcome for two or more distinct patient types?	Two or more known groups of subjects randomly assigned to two or more treatments.	Two or more known groups of subjects randomly assigned to two or more treatments. Treatment assessed in series of time-series designs. Each subject receives one type of treatment.	Two or more known groups of subjects. Two or more treatments compared within subject using time-series designs.

Source: Hayes, S. N., Nelson, R. O & Jarrett, R. B. (1987). The treatment utility of assessment. *American Psychologist, 42,* 963–974. Reproduced by permission.

interview. The authors also found that the correlation between plan imple mentation and problem solution was .977. This information, which we regard as an important finding about treatment validity, demonstrates that implementing a plan for a problem behavior accounted for 95% of the variance in problem solution. Interestingly, consultants' interviewing be- haviors demonstrated the greatest impact on the problem-solving process during the problem identification phase. When consultants lacked specific consultation skills, a definition of the problem and related problem-solving activities often did not occur. Future research of this kind is greatly needed in the area of behavioral consultation.

Future Directions

Research in behavioral consultation is plagued by some important conceptual disagreements on what the appropriate standards should be for establishing reliability, validity, and other psychometric features. Specifi- cally, there has been controversy surrounding the appropriateness of the psychometric concepts used in this research process (Cone, 1981, 1986, 1988). For example, Cone (1981) argued that work in the behavioral assess- ment field must focus on a paradigm radically different from the traditional trait psychometric procedures that are often used to establish validity and generalizability. Cone (1988) argued that behavioral assessment must gen- erally embrace a conceptual model of individual variability different from the traditional psychometric standards. As an alternative, Cone proposed that accuracy be the primary method of establishing the psychometric di- mensions of behavioral assessment.

Gresham and Davis (1988) argued that the two divergent approaches to validation can be resolved by clearly specifying the different approaches to assessment in consultation. They noted that, if the purpose of an inter- view is to screen potential clients for an intervention, traditional psycho- metric criteria may be applied. In contrast, they suggested that, when the interview is designed to conduct a functional analysis of behavior and to design an intervention program for an individual client, the functional criteria of accuracy be applied to the data. Currently, research on both of these psychometric dimensions seems to be a high priority. Which model will results in the most effective and useful information in future consulta- tion practice remains to be determined.

TRAINING BEHAVIORAL CONSULTANTS

Conceptually related to establishing the psychometric adequacy of consultation is the importance of training consultants. One of the major issues in the training area is that there are relatively few studies focusing on behavioral interviewing skills (Gresham, 1984; Gresham & Davis, 1988). Reviews of the literature on training psychologists as consultants (e.g., Gallessich, McDermott, & Jennings, 1986) indicate that researchers have generally failed to specify the skills or master criteria for teaching consultation. We believe that behavioral consultation has been explicitly linked to a competency-based approach (see Kratochwill & Bergan, 1978b; Kratochwill & Van Someren, 1985) and therefore lends itself to the development of specific skills in teaching and assessment. Throughout the text, these objectives have been operationalized and focus on the consultant's ability to elicit specific information during each phase of the consultation process. As a result, the training of consultants to a minimal level of competence can be documented during training activities.

As noted above, the development of standardized protocols in consultation, as through the CAR, may facilitate training activities in that the consultant and/or an independent rater in research can identify when specific interview goals have been met. Moreover, in this format, the consultant can self-monitor the criteria for a successful interview and improve her or his performance over time. In fact, the development of standardized consultation formats should facilitate the training of consultants in applied settings generally (Verberg & Reppucci, 1986).

Research in behavior modification provides some interesting leads on how consultants may be trained in successful behavioral-consultation skills. Generally, the findings support the notion that didactic training alone is inadequate for effective training (Allen & Forman, 1984; Ford, 1979). A recent study by Miltenberger and Fuqua (1985) documents that a training manual is as effective as individualized instruction that includes modeling, rehearsal, and feedback in teaching behavioral assessment interview skills. In another study, Whang, Fletscher, and Fawcett (1982) used a training program consisting of written instructions, practice, and performance feedback to train a low-income community-service staff in counseling skills. This study also demonstrated generalization across clients, behaviors, and time. Also, Iwata, Wong, Riordan, Dorsey, and Lau (1982) showed that a training program of written materials, classroom instruction, practice, and quizzes improved therapists' interviewing skills in both analogue and follow-up clinical settings.

Research has also been conducted on competency-based models in the administration of intelligence tests. Some work in this area by Fantuzzo and his associates supports the competency-based training approach. Fantuzzo, Sisemore, and Spradlin (1983) developed an instrument to provide criteria for the documentation of a minimal level of competence in the administration of the Wechsler Intelligence Scale for Children–Revised (WISC-R). They used a three-component training package consisting of a didactic lecture, observations of the model, and rehearsal with feedback (to train graduate students to use the WISC-R). They used this package to bring their students to a minimal (90%) level of competence. In a more recent study by Moon, Fantuzzo, and Gorsuch (1986), the competency-based training program noted earlier was found to be more effective and cost-efficient than the existing training models used in internship.

A few studies have been conducted by the present authors to develop a competency-based training model for behavioral consultation. In one of the first studies, in this area Brown et al. (1982) developed a program designed to train problem-identification-interview skills. Four graduate students were trained in problem-identification-interview skills and ana-lyzed before and after training in analogue situations. The training compo-nents in the study included written outlines, a videotaped model with prompts, explanations, and feedback sessions. The training package was effective for all the subjects and generalized across a 2-month follow-up assessment.

In a more recent study, Kratochwill et al. (1989) conducted an investi-gation in order to extend the work by Brown et al. and to examine the application of a competency-based model to all phases of the consultation process in actual cases. These goals were accomplished in three separate experiments. In the first experiment, four subjects were exposed to a train-ing manual and viewed videotaped interview models. In the second study, the videotapes were not used, but all of the components of the training process remained intact. The third study used the training manual to teach skills to practicing school psychologists, who then used the interview guidelines and format presented in the manual in an actual case. The results of all these studies indicated that the training package and its varia-tions were effective and cost-efficient in providing interview training. Gen-erally, the study suggested that training in specific consultation skills can be achieved successfully through the use of a standardized training format and formal interview guides (see Kratochwill & Bergan, 1990). In fact, the authors found that, after comparing the data from all three studies, the percentage of criterion objectives met was equivalent to or higher for sub-jects using the procedures in natural settings. The research extended the existing knowledge base, indicating that the training manuals are effective in teaching interview skills (e.g., Miltenberger & Fuqua, 1985). The skills were also found to generalize to actual cases in the natural environment.

Recommendations

Little empirical research has occurred on training effective behavioral consultants. In the future, training research in this area will be a high priority, as it is likely that training individuals to use standardized inter-view formats will generally enhance the psychometric characteristics of the consultation process (Gresham, 1984; Gresham & Davis, 1988). As Hay, Hay, Angle, and Nelson (1979) noted, standardized interview formats can reduce specific input variables, such as the range and number of areas discussed, and output variables, such as the loss of interview data through informal recording or memory problems.

Basically, three major formats can be used to train school psychology practitioners in consultation and prereferral intervention: individual competency-based training, workshop-based training, and self-instructional training. Each of these procedures has been used occasionally in professional training activities and research. Of course, these procedures may be used in combination to present a fourth option in training activities.

Individual competency-based training is training for specific objectives within each phase of behavioral consultation in order to maximize consultant success in identifying, analyzing, and evaluating a problem and the related intervention. The techniques that have been developed to train behavioral consultants have typically used conventional formats to facilitate the didactic instruction of discrete verbalization skills and the use of standardized interview protocols. Competency-based-training materials have been developed by Kratochwill and his associates and typically consist of a training package used by individual consultants to promote the development of the competencies associated with each of the kinds of interviews in the consultation process. This package usually includes reading materials (Kratochwill & Bergan, 1990), videotaped models, simulated role-play situations, group discussions, self-monitoring, and performance feedback. As noted above, empirical work in this area suggests that students can be trained quite effectively through such opportunities for guided practice and immediate feedback.

Training in this competency-based format is very expensive and time-consuming and typically requires a period of many months to implement. Therefore, this approach, which has been very useful and successful in the past, is probably best suited to graduate programs for students in professional training where there are a low faculty-to-student ratio and the resources to handle this type of training commitment.

A second kind of training uses *workshops* of varying lengths and formats in which consultation strategies are presented. This approach has typically been used at professional conferences at the state and national level. The workshops are accompanied by reading materials and other resources that facilitate the training. Workshops have been used extensively in the project "Re-Aim" in the state of Iowa, a project run by the Iowa Department of Public Instruction and implemented by Jeff Grimes and Dan Reschly and their associates. In Project Re-Aim, workshops are provided on consultation and on the background and importance of this service-delivery model. Some empirical work has been published in this area. McDougall, Reschly, and Corkery (1988) evaluated the effectiveness of a 1-day in-service workshop focused on behavioral consultation. In this project, 16 school psychologists submitted audiotapes of prereferral interviews with teachers before and after the workshops. The audiotapes were analyzed through Bergan's consultation analysis record of a problem identification interview. Although McDougall *et al.* found that each of six problem-identification-interview objectives increased significantly, few were significant, and the authors pointed to the need for broad-based training in objectives rather than discrete verbal segments. The shortcoming of this and other research has been that only the problem identification interview has been examined for the effectiveness of training on interviewer skills. Moreover, individual-child-outcome data have not been assessed. This type of training format has also been expensive, and the outcome data have not been very promising.

The final kind of training is *self-instructional*. Self-instructional training has been implicit in much of professional training and especially in continuing-education activities. Despite the importance of this format, we know of no research that has focused on an evaluation of self-instructional approaches to the training of consultants, school psychologists, and other professionals in prereferral intervention and consultation. Research and demonstration projects in this area seem to be a high priority, in view of the need to evaluate models that are alternatives to programs run outside of university-based training programs. Indeed, it is likely that most practicing professionals would find an approach based on self-instruction an acceptable training strategy.

One question that extends through all training formats relates to whether the CAR strategy is necessary to use to promote reliable and valid consultation interview formats. In the Kratochwill *et al.* study (1989) the subjects were trained with a manual (Kratochwill & Bergan, 1990) that did not include the CAR, but consultant verbalizations generally conformed to the appropriate categories during the actual consultation process. (Table 9-3 shows the objectives that the consultants were trained in over each phase of consultation.) Nevertheless, it is possible that training specifically on the CAR may further facilitate appropriate verbalizations during consultation.

Future research should explore how consultation differs from other service-delivery approaches such as counseling. In previous research, Henning-Stout and Conoley (1987) demonstrated the procedural divergence of consultation and counseling techniques by analyzing the verbal behaviors of consultants and counselors with Larrabee's recording technique (1980). Research focusing on the use of the CAR could help in analyses of the similarities between consultation and counseling approaches and the implications that these similarities have for training.

Generally, research in the training area is in its very early stages. For example, a limited number of subjects have been involved in training studies, and many of the formats have had an analogue focus. In the behavioral consultation area, only the Kratochwill *et al.* study (1989) involved an actual field-testing phase with a clinical replication format. Nevertheless, this

TABLE 9-3. Training Objectives for Each Phase of Consultation

Problem identification interview	Problem analysis interview	Treatment evaluation interview
1. Opening salutation	1. Opening salutation	1. Opening salutation
2. General statement	2. General statement	2. Outcome questions

3. Behavior specification
  a. Specify examples
  b. Specify priorities
	3. Behavior strength	3. Goal attainment questions

4. Behavior setting
  a. Specify examples
  b. Specify priorities
	4. Behavior conditions
	  a. Antecedent
	  b. Sequential
	  c. Consequent
		4. Internal validity

5. Identify antecedents	5. Summarize and validate	5. External validity
6. Identify sequential conditions	6. Interpretation	6. Plan continuation
7. Identify consequents	7. Plan statement	7. Plan modification validation
8. Summarize and validate	8. Summarize and validate	8. Generalization and maintenance
9. Behavior strength	9. Continuing data collection	9. Follow-up assessment
10. Summarize and validate	10. Establish date of next appointment	10. Future interviews
11. Tentative definition of goal	11. Closing salutation	11. Termination of consultation
12. Assets question		12. Closing salutation
13. Questions re: existing procedures		
14. Summarize and validate		
15. Directional statement re: data recording		
16. Data collection procedures		
17. Summarize and validate		
18. Date to begin data collection		
19. Establish date of next appointment		
20. Closing salutation		

Source: Kratochwill, T. R., Van Someren, K. R., & Sheridan, S. M. (1989). Training behavioral consultants: A competency-based model to teach interview skills *Professional School Psychology, 4*, 41–58 Reproduced by permission.

research focus is most likely to yield valuable data for future modifications in training.

A related issue is the importance of data on teacher- or parent-consultee verbal behavior during the consultation process. An analysis of these kinds of data in training—specifically, discovering whether consultees prepared in consultation service delivery do better than those not prepared—is an important area for future investigation (Anderson *et al.*, 1986).

REPRESENTATIVENESS OF CONSULTATION

Consultation is increasingly being taught in training programs in school psychology. Presumably, a variety of formats have been developed for teaching consultation and for integrating practicum experiences into this process (see, for example, Carlson & Tombari, 1987). An important issue in behavioral consultation is determining whether consultation as practiced in research activities is representative of practices in applied and clinical settings. That is, is behavioral consultation in the research literature really like what practitioners engage in during practice in applied settings? Our experience suggests that there may not be a good match between research activities and practice, although this question certainly needs to be answered empirically. An example will illustrate this point.

From our own training research, we have developed relatively standardized formats for teaching behavioral consultation skills to specified criteria (see the earlier discussion). Individuals read a standardized manual and perform consultation interviews with scrip formats that specify the questions to be asked, the appropriate interview sequence, and the recording procedures for the entire consultation process. Indeed, a rather elaborate monitoring system has been established. Individuals are trained in this procedure and then enter applied settings to work on actual cases referred for psychological services. The question, of course, is whether studies this consultation process will be "fairly and faithfully" represented in future consultation-outcome studies (Kazdin, 1988). In other words, the question of interest is whether research of this type will reflect what practitioners engage in in consultation practice.

Future Research Directions

It is important that the representativeness of behavioral consultation be addressed before major outcome studies are designed, and this representativeness can be accomplished empirically. Several options for testing the representativeness for treatments have been recommended (Kazdin, 1988). First of all, descriptive data may be obtained on the current practices of consultants in applied settings. Some research exists that provides data on the daily activities of school psychologists (e.g., Lacayo, Sherwood, & Morris, 1981). These data indicate that school psychologists engage in consultation, but this research does not answer the question of what type of consultation procedures are actually practiced in applied settings.

Second, as some procedurally standardized materials described in the consultation process are available (e.g., Kratochwill & Bergan, 1990), practitioners may be presented this written material and asked to rate its utility or representativeness in actual practice. Within this procedure, it is also possible to assess the acceptability of the consultation process. A growing literature on the acceptability of various treatments has focused on consultees and clients (Elliott, 1988; Witt & Elliott, 1985). We know of no research that has assessed the consultant's acceptability of consultation procedures.

One of the major difficulties in matching consultation practices in research and service is that it is very hard for people to agree on what makes up the consultation process. Thus, it is important to develop standardized materials, so that various critical dimensions of consultation can be varied. For example, questions related to the actual interview contents, the length of the interviews, and the sequencing of the question, as well as the mode of operation in the consultation process, all influence the relation of representativeness of consultation in research to representativeness in practice.

Another important direction in future research will be to have consultation investigators specify the features of the consultation process that are likely to vary from standard practice in applied settings (Kazdin, 1988). Unfortunately, as Kazdin (1988) noted, there are no standard procedures for evaluating whether a treatment faithfully represents the intervention of interest.

INTEGRITY OF BEHAVIORAL CONSULTATION

A major issue that must be addressed in behavioral consultation research is whether behavioral consultation is, in fact, being practiced. As currently conceived of, consultation is usually defined as an indirect service model in which a consultant works with a consultee to provide some type of direct psychological-educational assistance to a client. Within our behavioral consultation model four stages of problem solving are delineated: problem identification, problem analysis, treatment implementation, and treatment evaluation. Although this conceptual organization of behavioral consultation serves to organize research generally, it falls considerably short of what is needed at the methodological level to define actual consultation practices.

Future Research Directions

In psychotherapy research, there has been a major emphasis on evaluating treatment programs to ensure their integrity. Researchers have emphasized that, when a treatment is evaluated, it must be carried out as originally intended (e.g., Peterson *et al.*, 1982; Yeaton & Sechrest, 1981). That is, in consultation, investigators must evaluate the implementation of the consultation process and the associated treatments to make sure that what has been specified is actually being carried out. Integrity in the consultation process is required in research so that the readers of published reports will know exactly what was occurring in the investigation. Moreover, from a scientific standpoint, integrity must be demonstrated so that replication can occur. In comparative outcome studies, it is important to distinguish treatment integrity from treatment differentiation. The term *integrity* refers to a comparison of a treatment as it actually is with how it should be conducted. *Differentiation* refers to identifying whether differences can be delineated in how two or more treatments are conducted. For example, we would expect consultation to differ from counseling (Henning-Stout & Conoley, 1987). Treatments may differ from each other in how they are conducted, but may not have high integrity (Kazdin, 1988).

Traditionally, integrity as a methodological criterion has been linked to specific treatments as implemented directly with clients. However, in behavioral consultation, integrity must be expanded to several different components or levels. To begin with, the researcher must ensure the integrity of the *consultation process*. At this first level, it must be demonstrated that the consultant is following a specific consultation model or approach with integrity. Typically, the integrity of this process is checked by direct observation of the actual consultation components during the problem identification, problem analysis, and treatment evaluation interviews. Specifically, Peterson and her associates (1982) note that failure to monitor an intervention can threaten the reliability and validity of studies. Some consultation investigations have demonstrated integrity monitoring of the consultation process. For example, Jason and Ferone (1978) taped and coded all consultation sessions. Usually, some type of coding procedure is necessary in behavioral consultation research. In the behavioral consultation model presented in this text, a coding strategy has been developed (i.e., the CAR) that may be used to ensure the integrity of the consultation process.

An interesting issue related to the integrity of the consultation process pertains to whether the four stages are necessary to produce positive results in students (clients). Fuchs, Fuchs, Bahr, Fernstrom, and Stecker (1989) reported the results of a study designed to assess the effects of three increasingly inclusive versions of behavioral consultation on student problem behavior in mainstream classrooms. In the least inclusive variation (BC_1), the consultant and the teacher identified and analyzed the problem (problem identification and problem analysis). In this condition, the consultant did not assist in the teacher's implementation of the treatment, and there was no formal evaluation of the treatment.

The second variant (BC$_2$), included problem identification, problem analysis, and plan implementation. In the plan implementation stage, the consultant made a minimum of two classroom visits, during which time the teacher was provided corrective feedback while implementing the intervention. No formal evaluation occurred. The most inclusive version (BC$_3$) included the first three stages and also required the consultant and the teacher to evaluate the intervention program. The preintervention, postintervention, and follow-up observations of student behavior indicated that the more inclusive BC versions (BC$_2$ and BC$_3$) had exerted stronger effects than the least inclusive variant (BC$_1$) in reducing problem behavior. The authors noted that variations in student outcome were due to the consultation *process* and not to quantitative or qualitative differences in classroom interventions. The implications for the integrity of consultation are that the four-stage process may be necessary to ensure favorable client outcome.

A challenge for future consultation researchers is to specify consultation-specific ingredients that occur *in addition* to the usual components of behavioral consultation. In this regard, three classes of variables are important to consider (Kazdin, 1988). The first includes those variables that are usually held constant so as not to cause confounds in group outcome research. These variables include such factors as the number of consultation contacts, the duration of the contacts, and the spacing between the consultation interviews.

Second, an analysis of consultant verbalizations should be conducted to determine the extent of statements that may not relate to the focus of the consultation. For example, high frequencies of verbalizations may occur in the background characteristics category of behavioral consultation. Consultation may lead to successful outcomes for the clients; these outcomes may not correspond to the usual focus of consultation, but over time with the accumulation of cases, it may be learned that the discussion of background characteristics leads to an expanded focus on target behaviors, or that a discussion of teachers' personal concerns leads to better working relationships.

The third class of variables is not usually identified as part of consultation. These variables are a class of "nonspecific treatments factors" and include therapeutic relationship and expectancy effects, among others. In consultation, these variables may operate at the consultant, consultee, and client levels.

Little is known about the so-called consultation input variables in consultation research generally, and specifically in behavioral consultation. West and Idol (1987) concluded that investigations of the influence of consultation input variables, including consultant and consultee characteristics and the nature of the problem presented, have provided mixed and contradictory results. Nevertheless, data on these dimensions of be-

Parent Checklist

Name: _____

Date: _____

Directions

    At the end of each day, complete the following checklist. Specifically, indicate on the line to the left of each item whether or not you covered the content in adequate detail. If there are certain things that you are unsure of, please contact the consultant before continuing. The consultant will be available to provide feedback and suggestions. Thank you!

Goal-Setting

_____ Involved your child in setting a goal for neighborhood play situations.

_____ Your child could control this goal.

_____ Your child could be successful at this goal.

_____ The goal told your child what to do.

_____ The goal was very specific and concrete.

_____ The goal was recorded on the home chart.

Self-Reporting

_____ Inquired about play upon child's return.

_____ Inquired about goal attainment.

_____ Provided praise for positive, appropriate interactions.

_____ Allowed your child to record successful goal attainment on the goal sheet.

Positive Reinforcement

_____ Allowed your child to choose a reward to work towards when establishing the daily goal.

_____ Provided specific, genuine verbal praise for goal attainment.

_____ Provided the reward soon following goal attainment.

(continued)

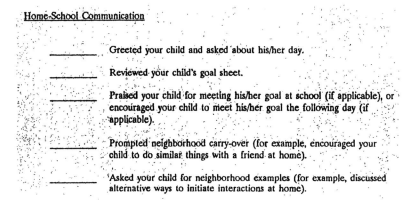

FIGURE 9-2. Integrity-monitoring form for parents. [Source: S. M. Sheridan. (1988). *Conjoint behavioral consultation: A link between home and school settings.* Unpublished doctoral dissertation, University of Wisconsin–Madison.]

havioral consultation should routinely be assessed wherever possible because they can provide information related to the representativeness of consultation. Moreover, once these variables are identified they can become part of training manuals and integrated into training activities.

Demonstrating the integrity of the consultation process is only the first step in ensuring integrity. At the next level, it must be demonstrated that the consultee is, in fact, carrying out the program as intended by the consultant or through mutual agreement, as in collaborative problem-solving consultation-strategies. This dimension of integrity is basically the type that is focused on in psychotherapy research. Unfortunately, in the consultation area, demonstrations of treatment integrity have been rare.

Examples of treatment-integrity-monitoring forms were presented in Chapter 6 (see Gresham, 1989). Another kind of treatment-integrity-rating form was used in a study by Sheridan *et al.* (1989) and is presented in Figure 9-2. As can be observed in the figure, parents were required to complete the checklist at the end of each day, checking the specific components associated with goal setting, self-reporting, positive reinforcement, and home–school communication.

Finally, if a child is involved in implementing an intervention program, particularly one that involves a self-control strategy, treatment implementation and its integrity should be monitored at this level as well. Although few studies have reported the monitoring of both the consultee and the client, in a study reported by Workman, Kendall, and Williams (1980) both the teacher and the student were assessed by observers, who provided a check on the reliability of the independent and dependent variables.

Thus, a priority in future research is monitoring the integrity of consultation. As we have noted above, there are three potential dimensions of integrity that have generally been neglected. First, it must be demonstrated that consultation is actually being practiced, through an assessment of the process of consultation. Second, consultee implementation of the intervention program must be monitored to make sure that it is being implemented as intended. Finally, client adherence to the program, especially in regard to the application of self-control strategies, must be assessed. Future researchers should model this tripartite approach to ensure that consultation is taking place under conditions intended by the researcher.

MODELS OF CONSULTATION OUTCOME RESEARCH

In addition to the multiple variables and factors we have mentioned in previous sections of this chapter, a major issue in consultation research is the investigator's conceptualization of what consultation is designed to address. Presumably, the issues in consultation are similar to the issues in traditional psychotherapy research in terms of the model of outcome that the investigator embraces (Kazdin, 1988). In consultation, some ambiguity has surrounded what types of clinical problems consultation is designed to address, and as has been true in psychotherapy research, consultation research is sometimes limited by the restricted model that has been applied. Like some traditional psychotherapy research outcome studies, a "conventional treatment model" has been applied. In the typical consultation-outcome study, a specific intervention study program is implemented by the consultee for some specific type of problem with a child for a limited time. Typically, outcomes are evaluated after the treatment is removed, over a follow-up period. It is assumed that consultation with a professional has been useful for a wide range of clinical disorders in classrooms. Specifically, a variety of teacher-as-consultee treatment procedures have been implemented with little or no analysis of the purposes of the consultation. As Kazdin (1988) noted from a review of traditional models of psychotherapy evaluation, there may be problems in the scientific yield in this line of research, so major questions may be raised at the conceptual level about the future direction of behavioral consultation approaches:

> The yield from the conventional model of psychotherapy evaluation has not been particularly great for the development of child psychotherapies. Yet, the model and manifold questions that it can address should not be faulted. Relatively few studies have taken advantage of the conventional model. Of the many studies, methodological flaws have often interfered with the range of inferences that can be drawn. For example, the patient sample and the treatment are often poorly specified, randomization of children to groups is sacrificed, and treatment is not implemented as intended. The yield of an investigation of any treatment strategy requires that basic methodological

requirements are met. Because of methodological limitations, the different strategies embraced by the conventional model have not been thoroughly mined. (p. 92)

Yet, alternative models of treatment outcome research should be considered in the study of behavioral consultation. These models can facilitate an understanding of what problems behavioral consultation is effective with. These models include the high-strength intervention model, the amiability-to-treatment model, the broad-based intervention model, and a chronic disease model. Each of these models provides some specific guidelines for how consultation research might be focused in the future.

The High-Strength Intervention Model

Consultation researchers have generally failed to make explicit how potent the consultation services are designed to be. In determining what behavioral consultation is designed to do, the first issue that the researcher must address is what is the most potent application of the consultation process and what impact it will have on the client? These questions are designed to address the applications of consultation to relatively severe problems experienced in educational settings. For example, in a project by Kratochwill and his associates (Kratochwill, 1988), behavioral consultation was applied to work with teachers serving children who were classified as severely emotionally handicapped and who had been placed in special-education classes. The application of behavioral consultation in this context deviated somewhat from its usual applications to relatively mild classroom problems and its use in a "prereferral" intervention context. In our project, it was assumed that behavioral consultation involves not just a problem-centered consultation process but a developmental consultation with individual teachers over a relatively long period of time. In fact, in some cases, consultation occurred over periods of months because of the nature and the severity of the children's problems. In such cases, consultation would be expected to be ongoing and to serve multiple purposes.

Another way in which researchers may conceptualize the strength of treatment relates to the nature and the scope of consultation services to consultees. For example, a child's problem might be treated exclusively by the teacher at school, or one might use a conjoint consultation process in which both teacher and parents served in complementary roles to implement a treatment program for the child. The conjoint behavioral-consultation process supports the notion that consultation involving both teacher and parent is more effective than consultation with only the teacher, at least in the cases of the treatment of social withdrawal (Sheridan et al., 1989).

Treatment strength may be conceptualized in a variety of ways, but the reason for mentioning this issue here is that high-strength tests of consultation have rarely been conducted. Even when they are, there are several problems (Kazdin, 1988). To begin with, there is no set agreement on what constitutes strength of treatment. It is not clear whether it means more time with the consultee, longer sessions with the client, the engagement of multiple consultees in the process, the components of the treatment program, and so on. It is difficult to know how to maximize the strength of treatment because it involves multiple criteria, often without clear empirical guidelines. We do have some important information from the Fuchs *et al.* (1989) study that the four-stage process may be necessary to ensure successful behavior change.

Second, in applied settings, especially when practicing school psychologists implement behavioral consultation, there are practical problems in increasing the strength of treatment. In fact, many consultation approaches are designed, paradoxically, to be relatively low-strength treatments that will serve to facilitate documentation that more extensive treatment is needed, especially in the context of "prereferral intervention programs."

Third, it is not always feasible or desirable for consultation to replace direct treatment programs, in which a professional implements the intervention with the client. That is, many treatments are better placed in the hands of mental-health professionals who are trained in the use of certain therapy techniques rather than in the hands of professional consultees or nonprofessional consultees, such as parents. Nevertheless, comparative outcome studies in which this issue has been addressed are not widely available, so that this is more of a conceptual than empirical issue.

The Amenability-to-Treatment Model

Conceptually related to the issue of matching consultation services to the nature of the problem is the amenability to treatment of certain clients. In this regard, behavioral consultation approaches may be selected based on identified factors related to amenability to treatment. For example, certain types of behavior consultation may be found effective in dealing with minor or relatively minor classroom-management issues and not in dealing with rather severe clinical problems. The reason may be the nature of the treatments identified as appropriate to that population or the consultee's lack of expertise in implementing such treatments. For example, it is unlikely that relatively brief problem-solving-directed behavioral consultation will have a large impact on severe conduct disorders and antisocial behaviors of children because of the difficulties in the treatment of this clinical disorder (see Kazdin, 1985). Nevertheless, a major focus of future research should be identifying how amenable consultation approaches are to clients with various school-based disorders. The point is that consultation may be used with those clients who are likely to be responsive to a treatment and to the consultees implementing the treatment.

The Broad-Based Intervention Model

A related model involves implementing an intervention designed to affect broad aspects of a child's functioning. For example, one may consider how pervasive and broad-based consultation services need to be for a child diagnosed as having attention deficit disorder with hyperactivity. Such an intervention may have to focus on management of the child's behavior at home and school and his or her academic functioning and social skills, as well as on training the parents to deal with the problem, and it may also extend to medical intervention. Effective treatment may therefore involve a component of consultation, but may need to be supplemented by other broad-based intervention techniques. As Kazdin (1988) noted, treatment may be conceived of in a "modular fashion" in which separate components of the treatment program are incorporated into an overall treatment regime. In such cases, consultation may be supplemented with other effective and high-strength intervention approaches to provide a more comprehensive treatment. The point is that consultation as an independent intervention may fall considerably short of what is needed to deal effectively with the severity of the clinical problem faced by the child. Indeed, consultation may be regarded as relatively narrow in scope and focus and may be doomed to failure without a broader based model of intervention. Thus, researchers need to consider this issue when evaluating the efficacy of behavioral consultation in applied settings.

The Chronic Disease Model

Behavioral consultation has been applied to a variety of child problems. Indeed, its application to more severely handicapped youngsters suggests that it can be implemented within the context of a medical model of deviant behavior. Our experience and even some empirical evidence suggest that certain types of childhood difficulties, such as conduct disorder, are relatively severe and long-lasting. In this regard consultation may need to occur over a period of many years and to reflect the chronic nature and course of a specific childhood disorder. Treatment may be focused on multiple care providers as well as multiple consultees, especially as the child progresses through school. Thus, consultation may not always be conceptualized as a relatively brief form of intervention approach. Reiterative applications of the problem-solving process are important to consider within the context of the chronic nature of many childhood problems.

CONSULTATION OUTCOME MEASURES

A major concern in research in consultation is the assessment criteria for measuring outcome in clients and consultees. There is a rather extensive literature on this subject. Generally, the evidence suggests that traditional tests and global ratings can be quite misleading in the assessment of therapeutic outcomes (e.g., Kazdin, 1980d; Kazdin & Wilson, 1978). Nevertheless, there is growing agreement that an assessment of outcomes, involving multifaceted approaches to examining the different functioning domains of the client, the methods of assessment, and the setting, is needed for the comprehensive evaluation of treatment programs implemented through consultation.

An important first issue in outcome studies is defining the nature of the dysfunction or the problem of the child. In this regard, there has been considerable debate over the application of formal diagnostic systems. Although we do not intend to engage in the debate over whether standardized diagnostic systems are beneficial, wherever possible in consultation research investigators should report clinically derived psychiatric diagnoses, information from multivariate statistical procedures, and specific special-education assessment criteria. In addition to the diagnosis, the information provided on the clinical problem and the characteristics of the children, the consultee, and the parents may be helpful in future research.

Special information can be derived from the multiaxial assessment of children proposed by Achenbach and his colleagues (e.g., Achenbach, 1985; Achenbach, McConaughy, & Howell, 1987; McConaughy & Achenbach, 1989). Data provided in a number of studies have suggested that there is typically a low correspondence between reports from children, parents, and teachers and other mental-health workers when they are evaluating clinical dysfunction in children. Generally, these studies suggest that individual care-providers typically provide internally consistent data and that these data correlate with other criteria and may actually indicate that the child's functioning varies across settings, situations, and the individuals providing the data (Mischel, 1968). Table 9-4 demonstrates that, for multiaxial assessment, five different axes can be used for different age ranges of children. The data include parents' and teachers' reports, cognitive assessment, physical assessment, and a direct assessment of the child. In consultation research, this type of information is extremely valuable in identifying general areas of functioning and in assisting in the evaluation of treatment outcome. The model provides a comprehensive evaluation of child functioning and can help to demonstrate whether a treatment has had a specific impact or has had a more general impact on broad areas of functioning. Readers interested in a specific case application of empirically based assessment should review McConaughy and Achenbach (1989).

TABLE 9-4. Examples of Multiaxial Assessment

Age range	Axis I Parent reports	Axis II Teacher reports	Axis III Cognitive assessment	Axis IV Physical assessment	Axis V Direct assessment of child
0–2	Minnesota Child Development Inventory Developmental history Parent interview		Developmental testing, e.g., Bayley Infant Scales	Height, weight Medical exam Neurological exam	Observations during developmental testing
2–5	Child Behavior Checklist (CBCL) Developmental history Parental Interview	School records Teacher interview	Intelligence tests, e.g., McCarthy Scales of Children's Ability Perceptual-motor tests Speech and language tests	Height, weight Medical exam Neurological exam	Observations during play interview Direct-observation form (DOF)
6–11	CBCL Developmental history Parent interview	Teacher's report form (TRF) School records Teacher interview	Intelligence test e.g., WISC-R Achievement tests Perceptual-motor tests Speech and language tests	Height, weight Medical exam Neurological exam	DOF Semistructured Clinical Interview for Children (SCIC) SCIC–Observation Form
12–18	CBCL Developmental history Parent interview	TRF School records Teacher interview	Intelligence tests e.g., WISC-R, WAIS-R Achievement tests Speech and language tes s	Height, weight Medical exam Neurological exam	SCIC–Self-Report Form Youth Self-Report (YSR) Clinical interview Self-concept measures Personality tests

Source: T. M. Achenbach. (1985) *Assessment and taxonomy of child and adolescent psychopathology.* Beverly Hills, CA. Sage.

Although the multiaxial model presented by Achenbach and associates can be very helpful in identifying problems and can provide descriptive information on the case, we recommend that direct observational assessment methods be used whenever possible. Direct measures are
assessment strategies that incorporate self-monitoring or direct observation of the client's observable behavior. Several specific advantages of direct outcome-assessment measures may be noted. First, direct outcome
measures facilitate comparisons across different studies. Specific direct
measures are typically less affected by various methodological problems
than traditional outcome measures such as global ratings and subjective
self-report descriptions. We are not suggesting that direct observational
assessment techniques are free of methodological problems. Indeed, researchers have now noted a variety of methodological factors that are
known to bias or influence direct outcome measures (Hartmann, 1982).
Second, direct observational measures typically lend themselves easily to
repeated measurement across various phases of the consultation process, a
process that has already been linked very closely to single-case and case-
study research-design technologies. A repeated measurement of client performance is desirable in documenting the effectiveness of the treatment.
Third, the use of direct assessment measures can provide information on
the differential efficacy of different therapeutic techniques (Kazdin &
Wilson, 1978).

CONSULTATION RESEARCH DESIGN

The empirical basis for behavioral consultation has been associated
with a wide variety of research paradigms. In fact, the full spectrum of
research methods, including surveys, descriptive procedures, and passive
observational and experimental research paradigms, has been used to
study various aspects of behavioral and other models of consultation. In
this section of the chapter, we review several specific research methods
that have been used to study consultation outcome. Specifically, three
domains of research designs have been used, including large-N and between-group designs, single-case or time-series studies, and case study
methodology. We provide a review of the advantages and limitations of
these strategies within the context of the consultation outcome literature.

Traditional Large-N and Between-Group Studies

The research literature in the area of behavioral consultation contains
several studies that have used large-N between-group comparisons. Both
experimental, randomized designs and quasi-experimental procedures
have been used. In the case of randomized experimental designs, random
assignment serves as a basis for inferring consultation outcome. To begin

with, the researcher should draw random samples that are representative of some known or defined population. Second, the samples should be drawn so that the groups are comparable in the sense that every subject has an equal probability of going into the various conditions constructed by the experimenter. In contrast to the true experiment that involves randomization, group quasi-experimental designs do not use the randomization scheme to draw inferences about an intervention effect (Cook & Campbell, 1979).

Within the randomized experimental and quasi-experimental domains, a variety of specific design types are possible. Although it is beyond the scope of this chapter to review the strategies in detail (the reader should consult Kazdin, 1980d, and Cook & Campbell, 1979, for a review of these designs), we should indicate that between-group randomized designs are generally preferred because the researcher is able to control many major threats to internal validity. Also, randomized experimental designs allow the consultation researcher to investigate the effect of some treatment procedure or some dimension of consultation independent of a particular group having experienced the treatment previously. This strategy contrasts with single-case time-series methodology (reviewed below), in which the subjects typically serve as their own control and in which it is impossible to implement multiple treatments without prior contamination or sequence effects.

Several studies are often cited as examples of group comparative-outcome designs in the consultation field. Several researchers have compared various forms of behavioral consultation with other models of or approaches to psychological service delivery in the schools. In an early study, Randolph and Hardage (1972) attempted to differentiate the effects of classroom behavioral consultation from group counseling of potential school dropouts. Thirty fifth- and sixth-grade students in southern Mississippi were assigned to each of the aforementioned conditions. The consultation-group teacher received training in behavioral techniques. The group-counseling programs involved having the children meet in groups of six for weekly sessions.

The dependent measures included observation of time on-task, grade-point average, and school attendance rates. The results indicated increases in on-task behavior and in grade-point average in the consultation group. No differences were found in students in the counseling group. No changes were found in the attendance rates of either group involving clarifying, supportive, and reflective responses to help the teacher understand difficulties and to enhance her or his ability to work with problem children. The children of the teacher receiving behavioral consultation demonstrated change; however, a major limitation of this study was that there was only one teacher in each condition. Moreover, the fact that different consultants served in the two groups further potentially confounds this interesting study.

Two comparative outcome studies have been reported by Jason and his associates (Jason & Ferone, 1978; Jason, Ferone, & Anderegg, 1979). In the first study, the authors compared process and behavioral consultation in a program designed to assist teachers in managing disruptive first-grade children. The behavioral approach included discussions of behavior management, feedback concerning contingent praise, and the planning of individual behavioral programs.

In a subsequent investigation, Jason *et al.* (1979) examined the effectiveness of ecological, behavioral, and process approaches in a problem-solving consultation framework. The dependent measures in the study were (1) observational indexes; (2) the teachers' perceptions of targets, cues, and class environment; (3) achievement measures; and (4) the teachers' overall impression of the program's usefulness. Four inner-city parochial schools were assigned randomly to one of three treatment groups for 2 months. A fourth school served as a control. The first- and third-grade teachers in each school were asked to select four or five children who were the most disruptive in their classes. The treatment procedures consisted of weekly meetings for 15 minutes at each school (eight sessions) with the meetings following instructions for their treatment conditions. Consultants were assigned randomly to the consultation approaches.

The authors found that the children in the behavioral consultation group demonstrated significant improvement in conduct measures. The process consultation children made significant gains in academic areas. Virtually no changes were reported for the targeted children in the ecological or control groups. Consumer satisfaction measures also indicated that the consultants in all three programs were generally well liked. The teachers rated behavioral and process consultation as most beneficial and helpful. They also indicated a willingness to recommend the program to other colleagues.

Moracco and Kazandkian (1977) evaluated the effectiveness of behavioral counseling and consulting techniques with non-Western children identified as having behavior problems in school. The authors selected 60 first-, second-, and third-graders from an elementary school in Beirut. The children were selected by teacher referral and with the use of a behavior-rating scale. The children were then assigned randomly to one of four groups: a group that received behavioral counseling with the children (their teachers received consultation), a group that received behavioral consultation (the children had no contact with the consultants), a group in which the children received behavioral counseling and the teachers nothing, and a control group.

The dependent variable in the project was a change score from pre- to posttest on a child behavior-rating scale. Although all four groups showed some gain on this measure, the first group had the highest gain, followed by Groups 2, 3, and 4.

In another study, Goodwin and Coates (1972) used a consultation approach to effect change in psychologist (consultant), teacher (consultee), and student (client). Consultant change was measured in terms of increased theoretical knowledge and preference for solutions to classroom problems (both assessed by questionnaire measures). Teacher behavior change was measured by a classroom observation instrument; and pupil change was measured by direct observation on all measures. Teacher behavior change was noted on some measures (e.g., amount of engaged time) and not on others (e.g., overall percentages of teaching behaviors). Pupil behavior showed significant improvements.

King, Cotler, and Patterson (1975) focused on the absentee rates in a Mexican-American school in a study that involved the 50 children with the poorest attendance rates. To improve the children's attendance, the psychologists used a consultation approach, primarily with the parents. Letters were sent home with half the children in the experimental group and half in a control group. The control group letters asked for the parents' help in the area of attendance. The experimental group letter offered the parents a reward if their children attended for 14 of the next 15 days. In addition, the children in the experimental group received a daily reward for coming to the school. Three 15-day phases were used. The results of this study showed no difference between the groups.

Ponti et al. (1988) provide a case example that demonstrates the implementation of a consultation-based service-delivery system to decrease referrals for special education. This report was designed primarily to illustrate the organizational considerations that were involved in implementing the consultation system (see discussion in Chapter 8). Nevertheless, the data were gathered in the context of a pre-posttest design. The study indicated that an increased range of services was provided, including more consultation and counseling, and that the psychoeducational assessments were reduced by approximately 40% following the program's implementation. The authors also reported that the number of consultation cases increased following the program and that more students were assisted through the consultation approach than through the individual assessment services. Self-report data from the project also supported the benefits of the consultation model.

In a project with a similar focus, Gutkin et al. (1988) evaluated the impact of a district-wide prereferral group on patterns of school psychological-service delivery. The program was implemented in a semirural school district with a K–12 student population of approximately 2,800. Approximately 50% of the children were of Hispanic descent. During the 2 years before the program, there had been 1.8 Full Time Equivalents (FTEs) of school psychological service providers, and during the 4 years in which the prereferral intervention services were provided, the FTE was 2.0. Within the context of a pretest–posttest design, the authors evaluated the program by comparing data from 2 years before the program with data from the 4 years during implementation of the prereferral model. The authors reported that, during the time in which the program was in effect, more children were served by the school psychologists and a higher proportion of referred children achieved educational objectives in the regular classrooms. Like Graden *et al.* (1985) and Ponti *et al.* (1988), these authors found that a lower proportion of the referred children were tested for special-education services. Gutkin and his associates also found that a higher proportion of the children who were tested were found eligible for special-education program services. The study by Gutkin and associates does have several limitations, including the lack of a control group, a change in the philosophy of the psychologists at the time of the intervention, and lack of detail on the consultation program.

As the above studies illustrate, a number of limitations are associated with research paradigms involving groups. To begin with, among the more well-controlled group designs, there tend to be a number of analogue characteristics that are associated with the research procedures. Researchers who use group designs may embrace the rigor of the laboratory but sacrifice the inclusion of information and characteristics that are likely to reflect the realities of consultation practice. For example, the Bergan, Byrnes, and Kratochwill (1979) study has sometimes been cited as an example of a successful consultation-outcome investigation (e.g., Medway, 1979b). Yet, the study illustrates the extreme of analogue dimensions in that hypothetical subjects were involved on the client dimension.

Other problems with between-group designs can be identified as well (Barlow *et al.*, 1984; Kratochwill, 1978). First, there may be an ethical problem associated with withholding a treatment in a no-treatment control group or in providing subjects with a condition that is known to be less effective than another condition. Of course, this issue is especially worrisome when the subjects are experiencing rather severe clinical problems.

Second, in consultation outcome studies in applied settings and especially schools, there is the practical difficulty of finding subjects who are experiencing a homogeneous problem. Even in single-case research design, we have found difficulties in recruiting enough subjects homogeneous on a certain clinical problem, such as social withdrawal, to have enough subjects to make a multiple-baseline design. As is apparent in the discussion some of the consultation studies, there is the difficulty of mixing many different types of problems (e.g., academic and behavioral) within a particular study. This mixture is likely to increase variance and may wipe out between-group effects.

A third problem that often occurs in group research is that individual data on specific subjects may not be reported. Of course, researchers have the option of presenting data on individual subjects, but traditionally, this has not been routine, nor has it occurred often in the consultation outcome literature. Data from the group studies reported here on individual subjects would have been quite informative in terms of the effect on client outcomes. Unfortunately, none of the studies reviewed provided these kinds of data.

A fourth issue is that, in group research, finding statistical significance has sometimes taken priority over achieving differences that are clinically meaningful. Groups may differ across the various conditions in the statistical analyses, but without information on clinical meaningful change, it is difficult to establish the real success of consultation outcomes.

A fifth problem with group designs is that they sometimes lock investigators into portraying a particular model of consultation as homogeneous. Portraying behavioral consultation as a relatively homogeneous model may, in part, result from the way in which comparative-outcome research is framed. Comparative-outcome researchers often frame questions in an either-or fashion, a strategy that tends to maximize the differences between approaches even though the approaches may contain common ingredients. For example, an investigator may compare a behavioral consultation model or approach with another model of consultation. Yet, the two different models of consultation may include many common features, such as a problem-solving process and relationship building between the consultant and the consultee.

Finally, the results of a group study often cannot be easily generalized to individual clients. As Hersen and Barlow (1976) noted, when data are not provided on individual clients, the researcher may not know to what extent a given client is similar to clients who improved or perhaps deteriorated within the context of overall group improvement. Also, in cases of homogeneous groups, there is some loss of information when the researcher attempts to make generalizations to populations that were not included in the homogeneous sample. Findings cannot be generalized beyond the specific group of clients who were sampled in the experiment. Of course, because researchers infrequently draw random samples from a population, there will continue to be difficulties in generalizing the results of group investigations.

Single-Case Time-Series Designs

As noted in Chapter 6, single-case time-series designs have been used extensively in applied and clinical settings. As we have already discussed the variations in single-case research designs, we will not elaborate on them here. The interested reader is referred to Table 9-5 for a number of original works in the area. Generally, these designs cannot be regarded as true experiments in that randomization is not a part of treatment implementation. However, it is possible to introduce sequences of the designs randomly, as well as to intervene at random times. Typically, however, this is not done in most applications of these procedures.

A wide variety of single-case research designs have been used in re-

TABLE 9-5. Major Textbooks in the Area of Single-Case Research Design and/or Analysis

Date	Author	Textbook title
1977	Bailey, J. S.	*A handbook of research methods in applied behavior analysis.* Gainesville: University of Florida.
1984	Barlow, D. H., Hayes, S. C., & Nelson, R. O.	*The scientist-practitioner: Research and accountability in clinical and educational settings.* New York: Pergamon Press.
1985	Barlow, D. H., & Hersen, M.	*Single case experimental designs: Strategies for studying behavior change* (2nd ed.). New York: Pergamon Press.
1985	Behling, J. H., & Merves, E. S.	*The practice of clinical research: The single-case method.* Lanham, MD: Univ. Press of America.
1986	Bromley, D. B.	*The case-study method in psychology and related disciplines.* New York: Wiley.
1979	Cook, T. D., & Campbell, D. T. (Eds.)	*Quasi-experimentation: Design and analysis issues for field settings.* Chicago: Rand McNally.
1986	Cryer, J. D.	*Time series analysis.* Boston: Duxbury Press.
1969	Davidson, P. O., & Costello, C. G. (Eds.)	*N = 1: Experimental studies of single cases.* New York: Van Nostrand/Reinhold.
1978	Fischer, J.	*Effective casework practices: An eclectic approach.* New York: McGraw-Hill.
1975	Glass, G. V., Willson, V. L., & Gottman, J. M.	*Design and analysis of time-series experiments.* Boulder: Colorado Associated University Press.
1981	Gottman, J. M.	*Time-series analysis: A comprehensive introduction for social scientists.* Cambridge: Cambridge University Press.
1973	Jayaratne, S., & Levy, R. L.	*Emprirical clinical practice.* Irvington, NY: Columbia University Press.
1980	Johnson, J. M., & Pennypacker, H. S.	*Strategies and tactics of human behavioral research.* Hillsdale, NJ: Erlbaum.
1980	Kazdin, A. E.	*Research design in clinical psychology.* New York: Harper & Row.
1982	Kazdin, A. E.	*Single-case research designs: Methods for clinical and applied settings.* New York: Oxford University Press.
1982	Kazdin, A. E., & Tuma, A. H. (Eds.)	*Single-case research designs.* San Francisco: Jossey-Bass.
1978	Kratochwill, T. R. (Ed.)	*Single-subject research: Strategies for evaluating change.* New York: Academic Press.
1980	McCleary, R., & Hay, R. A., Jr.	*Applied time-series analysis for the social sciences.* Beverly Hills, CA: Sage.
1980	McDowall, D., McCleary, R., Meidfinger, E. E., & Hay, R. A., Jr.	*Interrupted time-series analysis.* Beverly Hills, CA: Sage.
1983	McReynolds, L. V., & Kearns, K. P.	*Single-subject experimental designs in communicative disorders.* Baltimore: University Park Press.
1986	Poling, A., & Fuqua, R. W. (Eds.)	*Research methods in applied behavior analysis: Issues and advances.* New York: Plenum Press.
1979	Robinson, P. W., & Foster, D. F.	*Experimental psychology: A small-n approach.* New York: Harper & Row.

(continued)

TABLE 9-5. (Continued)

Date	Author	Textbook title
1960	Sidman, M.	*Tactics of scientific research.* New York: Basic Books.
1984	Tawney, J. W., & Gast, D. L.	*Single subject research in special education.* Columbus, OH: Merrill.
1986	Valsinger, J. (Ed.)	*The individual subject and scientific psychology.* New York: Plenum Press.
1981	Wodarski, J. S.	*The role of research in clinical practice: A practical approach for human services.* Baltimore: University Park Press.
1984	Yin, R. K.	*Case study research: Design and methods.* Beverly Hills, CA: Sage.

Source: Kratochwill, T. R., & Williams, B L (1988) Personal perspectives on pitfalls and hassles in the conduct of single-subject research. *Journal of The Association of Persons with Severe Handicaps, 13,* 147–154 Reproduced by permission.

search identified as "behavioral consultation." Several studies that have reported the use of behavioral consultation have used single-case time-series research designs with replication to evaluate the efficacy of the intervention. In one project reported by Piersel and Kratochwill (1979), and discussed in Chapter 3, case-study and single-case research designs were used to evaluate the effect of a consultation approach combined with a direct intervention strategy on four elementary-school children. Self-monitoring was used as a method of assessment in each of the cases, but it demonstrated a reactive effect and improved the target behavior to which it was applied. In each of the four cases, the classroom teacher served as the consultee. Two of the cases involved academic problems (completing assignments), and two involved behavior problems (disruptiveness).

Another project, reported by Farber and Mayer (1972), used behavioral consultation in a secondary school in which average 10th-grade English-class students served as clients. The target behavior selected was assignment completion. Interviews were held with the teacher to determine the terminal goals, the criterion levels of performance, and the baseline measures. Data were collected from three sources: cumulative records, the teacher's role book, and direct observations. A list of appropriate behaviors was agreed on by the teacher and the consultant. The reinforcement available for use by the teacher included praise, small tangibles, and privileges such as record playing and an unlimited hall pass.

The study used a within-series replication-design format. Following a 3-day baseline period, a 7-day training phase occurred in which the psychologist taught the teacher various behavioral skills. The treatment phase, which followed, used reinforcement and extinction principles. The second baseline and treatment series was implemented and concluded with a maintenance stage (i.e., gradual withdrawal of the intervention). The results demonstrated that assignments reached a criterion level (60%) only during the two treatment and maintenance phases.

Also using a replication design, Bornstein, Hamilton, and Quevillon (1977) demonstrated the effect of behavioral consultation on a 9-year-old male child who was referred because of inappropriate out-of-seat behavior. In this study, the teacher conducted all the observations and implemented the treatment. All contact with the psychologist was via telephone or mail. Thus, this consultation study deviates from others in that there was no face-to-face contact with a psychologist-consultant.

Following the baseline phase, a positive-practice technique was used. The final phase involved a reinforcement system in which the child could earn extra recess time. The results indicated the desired change in the child's behavior during the intervention phase, with an appropriate return to baseline levels when the program was withdrawn. Follow-up at 6 months showed a much lower level of out-of-seat behavior than the earlier baseline periods.

Heron and Catera (1980) implemented a consultation approach in three classrooms. In the first, an A/B/C/A design was used and a treatment scheme was implemented to increase the work completion rate of a first-grade child. After a 5-week baseline period, a punishment phase was instituted. When the student failed to complete assignments, he had to complete it the next day during recess. The third phase involved a token system in which the student received a card on which was punched the completion notice of his work. When meeting the weekly criteria, he received an "achievement award." A completion rate of 50% occurred during baseline, 25% during the punishment phase, and up to 90% during the punch card phase. In a return to baseline phase, the rate dropped to 75%.

The second study was of an 11-year-old male with similar work-completion problems. The authors used an A/B/A/B design. Following a baseline measure, an intervention was implemented in which the student received verbal praise from a teacher and the principal for all work completed. The third condition involved a return to baseline, and this was again followed by the intervention. During the baseline, 50% of the assignments were completed; 82% were completed during intervention, and 75% in the reversal phase.

Study 3 involved five male students with identical problems. The study used an A/B design combined with a delayed multiple baseline on one of the students. The intervention phase involved self-recording in which the students recorded their work on a raised scheme board. No specific reinforcers were used. Baseline percentages of 41%, 63%, 60%, 36%, and 43% were obtained. During the intervention phase, the averages rose to 68%, 89%, 91%, 84%, and 80%.

In another study, Workman et al. (1980) compared the effects of praise plus ignoring with praise plus verbal reprimand on a student who was off-task in a classroom setting. Using six male junior-high-school students and their female science teacher, a consultation approach was used to increase on-task behavior. Using a time-sampling technique, observers recorded the behavior of the six students as appropriate, off-task, or disruptive. A multiple baseline with reversals was used and included four conditions: baseline, praise plus ignoring, reversal, and praise plus reprimand. The sequence of conditions was given in two orders, as the subjects were in two classes, forming an A/B/A/C/A/B/A/C design.

The results indicated similar effects in the two classes. The praise-plus-reprimand condition was generally more effective in supporting appropriate behavior than was praise plus ignoring. However, in terms of generalizability, the ignoring phase was found to be more effective. The reprimand phase also had a faster initial effect on the students' behavior. Both groups had a significantly higher rate of absenteeism than a third group of 25 students, who were deemed representative of the school as a whole.

Numerous single-case research-design projects have been used to evaluate the efficacy of consultation. The increasing popularity of single-case time-series designs on behavioral consultation research is likely to continue. These designs can usually be structured so that rigorous inferences can be established. Nevertheless, these designs have a number of limitations that should be taken into account when they are used in behavioral consultation research (Kratochwill & Williams, 1988). Single-subject research is often plagued by a number of methodological, conceptual, and philosophical problems that have a bearing on the efficacy of these design strategies in applied settings, generally, and in behavioral consultation research, specifically. Baseline trends, variability in data, and duration of phases are serious issues that researchers must address when conducting these investigations. In addition, conceptual issues include the range of outcome questions that single-case designs need to address as well as how the researcher establishes the generalizability of the findings. A number of other pitfalls and hassles are likely to emerge, including philosophical objections to single-case research designs, replication problems, using measurement paradigms that are compatible with the design assumptions, and the integration of these strategies into practice. The interested reader is referred to Barlow et al. (1984) and Kazdin (1982b) for a detailed discussion of these issues.

Case Study Methods

Case study methods have continued to play a major role in the investigation of behavioral consultation outcomes. As noted in Chapter 6, case studies have traditionally been construed as lacking the usual controls that are imposed on experimental research. In this regard, case study investigators are unable to rule out major threats to the validity of the experiment In cases where such controls are absent, the investigator cannot make firm statements about the effect of a treatment.

A number of investigations that have studied behavioral consultation outcomes have involved case study methodology. In this section, the term *case studies* refers to investigations that involve a single client, group, or social system (see Yin, 1984). These procedures are typically characterized by the absence of most of the experimental controls that are used in single-case and group-outcome investigations (Kazdin, 1981a; Kratochwill, 1985). In an early study in this area, Hops (1971) investigated the efficacy of consultation in dealing with problems in special classes and the outcomes of introducing behavioral techniques through untrained teachers. In the study, 22 out-of-control boys in a special class for emotionally disturbed children were treated through a token reinforcement system. The results of the investigation suggested an increase in task-oriented behavior and academic productivity. For appropriate behavior, the boys were allowed to spend time in a special room with comics, models, toys, and games. A second program implemented by two of the teachers was based on a token system in which the boys received points for appropriate behavior that they could exchange for candy. During this phase, the appropriate behavior rose to approximately 80%. The consultant did not enter the classroom until the 13th week of the program, when he acted as an independent observer and recorder to provide a reliability check on the teachers' ratings.

In an interesting project, Canter and Paulson (1974) reported the use of consultation as a college credit seminar for 10 elementary-school teachers. The teachers were trained in behavior analysis, and for practice, each chose one child from her or his class to use as a client in consultation with the psychologist. The results of this project included data taken from one of the case studies, in which a 10-year-old boy was frequently involved in fights with his peers. The intervention involved a contract stipulating positive reinforcers and time-out periods and was evaluated through an A/B design. Also reported were the results of a questionnaire completed by all the teachers on their feelings about changes that they had made in several areas of teaching, motivation, and controlling student behavior.

Selective mutism was also the focus of a consultation approach in two case studies (Colligan, Colligan, & Dilliard, 1977; Piersel & Kratochwill, 1981). In the Colligan *et al.* study, the treatment focused on a 5-year-old boy who was mute, and it followed three specific steps. In the first step, the consultant created a positive social reinforcer through the relationship of the child and his teacher. The second stage involved a shaping process. The third stage was a generalization of verbal interactions with just his teacher to verbal interactions with his classmates. By the end of the program, the student was speaking normally, and a 12-month follow-up showed that this progress had been maintained.

Randolph (1979) reported that training of a school counselor to act as a consultant to the teachers in a school district. The author indicated that the teachers changed their behavior through consultation in a relatively short period of time, and that, with more time, this change produced a definite impact on the pupils. Some support is given to the efficacy of the consultation process.

Gresham and Nagle (1981) and Nagle and Gresham (1979) reported a successful application of behavioral consultation in the school setting. In the first project, behavioral consultation was used with seven mentally retarded public-school students (IQ = 30–59). An $A/B_1/B_2$ design was used to evaluate a classroom program consisting of compliance and change in the nature of teacher commands. During baseline, observers counted the number of words in each teacher command and whether the command was compiled with. In the first treatment phase, one of the authors modeled commands before the beginning of the observer recordings. In the second phase, the modeling continued, and the teacher was given feedback after the class period. The length of teacher commands dropped from the baseline (8.2) through the treatment phase (4.7). At the same time, the compliance rate rose from 28% to 72% during these two phases, respectively. In the second intervention phase, there were very small decreases in both the length of the command and the rate of the compliance. The authors noted that a floor effect may have occurred.

In the other report (Nagle & Gresham, 1979), the authors used behavioral consultation to treat a "school phobia." Following a problem identification interview with the child's teacher, the target behaviors of crying and whining were identified. A 5-day baseline period was followed by the implementation of a time-out procedure coupled with a DRO technique. There was a decrease in the duration of tantrums from 18 minutes per day during baseline to total elimination after 5 days of treatment. A 5-day follow-up was scheduled after the 10-day intervention phase and indicated that the change had been maintained.

Ajchenbaum and Reynolds (1981) used a behavioral consultation approach to assist an elementary-school teacher to work with a 7-year-old child who often had his fingers in his mouth and that lead frequently to the destruction of books and worksheets. Using stickers as a positive reinforcer, the consultant and the teacher developed a "report card" in order to keep track of the boy's finger-sucking behavior. After an informal baseline period, the program was implemented during morning sessions, but the finger sucking still occurred in the afternoon sessions. A similar program was established with the boy's afternoon teacher and his parents. By the end of the second week, the problem had been eliminated, and the student was given a new book.

Graden and her associates (Graden, Casey, & Christenson, 1985; Graden, Casey, & Bonstrom, 1985) implemented a prereferral intervention program and provided program evaluation data on the consultation outcomes. The prereferral intervention was implemented in three schools and used a consulting teacher model to provide services. In a second set of three schools, the system was implemented by a school psychologist. The authors monitored (1) requests for consultation services; (2) referrals into the special-education process; (3) testing rates; and (4) placement rates.

The results of the program were mixed. Positive results were observed in four of the six schools. Consultation use was high in four schools, and there was a decline in testing and placement rates. Unfortunately, implementation of the prereferral program in two schools was not successful during the second year of the program and in the postimplementation year (the third year of the project); these schools displayed an increase in the number of students tested and placed. The authors suggested that system-level factors provided constraints on the successful implementation of the model.

In summary, several case studies have been reported in the behavioral consultation literature, but most focus on relatively simple classroom-deportment behaviors; the authors have often reported success during these projects. Success has also been reported in the treatment of more serious problems such as school phobia and selective mutism. Nevertheless, a major limitation of case study investigations is that the usual kinds of experimental controls are lacking, so that interpretations of these studies raise problems. However, it must be emphasized that not all of the case studies discussed are equally lacking in methodological rigor. Some of the case studies were better than others, especially those that maintained a formal design and a repeated measurement of the dependent variable (e.g., Gresham & Nagle, 1981; Hops, 1971).

Despite the major limitations of the case studies discussed, there are several reasons that case study investigation in the behavioral consultation literature should be supported in the future. First, case studies often provide hypotheses about certain types of consultation strategies that may be useful. Often, during a case study, an investigator can examine outcomes that form a unique or interesting data base that might not occur otherwise. In this regard, case studies serve as sources of information on various therapeutic techniques that have been applied in natural settings, such as schools, where other research strategies, such as group designs and single-case experimental techniques, are impossible to implement. Second, case studies may also be helpful in the study of rare disorders or problems. Often, consultants face unique types of clinical disorders in applied settings and therefore can report on a particular application in professional journals. Third, case studies often provide a counterinstance of a consultation treatment. Consultation may be unsuccessful under certain conditions, and reporting this information works against the typical bias of publishing only positive results.

We would also note that case study strategies are often applied in naturalistic conditions. A major reason for the continued support of these methodological strategies is that they are often used for clients experiencing severe problems. Such reports provide a contrast to the typical group designs in which the studies are made in conditions that reflect more well-controlled laboratory-analogue conditions.

DIRECTIONS FOR FUTURE BEHAVIORAL-CONSULTATION RESEARCH

The research methodologies reviewed above have allowed researchers to make major contributions to the consultation outcome literature. Yet, there is the question of what type of research should be conducted in the future and on what methodologies (e.g., group versus single-subject). Although consultation writers have come down on the side of both group designs (e.g., Medway, 1979) and single-case designs (e.g., Gresham & Kendall, 1987), no general conclusion can be reached in response to this question. A number of different methodological strategies are appropriate at different stages of knowledge development in an area. Moreover, there are many restrictions on certain types of research, and compromises will always be necessary.

Several perspectives on clinical and applied research are relevant to our discussion here (e.g., Agras & Berkowitz, 1980; Kazdin, 1981a; Ross, 1981). Agras and Berkowitz (1980) presented a "progressive model of clinical research" (see Figure 9-3) that can be adapted to empirical research in consultation. For example, applied outcome research in consultation can be perceived as an accumulation of studies that, when disseminated, will shape the future course of consultation research. The beginning of the Agras and Berkowitz model is the development of a novel intervention. Research may then involve short-term between-group comparisons of treatments for various clinical problems. Next, both analogue and single-case studies emerge. Such studies may be particularly valuable in defining which components of consultation are useful. The model then moves into short-term comparative-outcome studies that address aspects of treatment and treatment generalization. The next step is long-term outcome studies. These authors noted:

> By this time the procedure may have become quite complex, perhaps taking the form of a decision tree, in which a particular response to therapy calls for one procedure to be applied while another response leads to the application of a different procedure. Issues such as the relative cost effectiveness of different treatments or reductions in mobility (and even mortality if appropriate) may become salient at this point in research. Such studies, since they may require large numbers of participants, may have to be carried out in several centers, denoting the phase of the multicenter clinical trial. (p. 479)

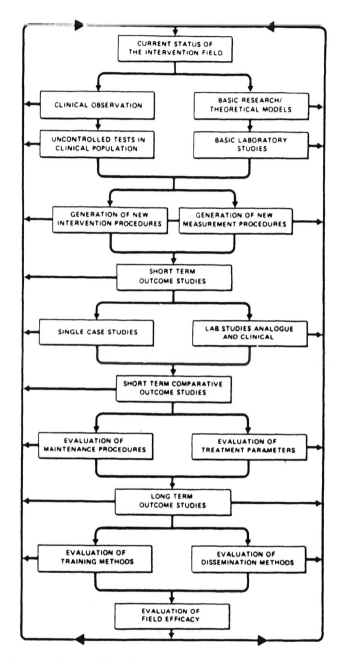

FIGURE 9-3. A progressive model of clinical research. [Source: W. S. Agras & R. Berkowitz. (1980). Clinical research in behavior therapy: Halfway there? *Behavior Therapy, 11,* 472–487. Copyright 1980 by the Association for Advancement for Behavior Therapy. Reproduced by permission.]

This idealized model is seldom represented in actual consultation research. Research may be going on at each stage, sometimes carried out by independent researchers. Researchers may or may not influence other researchers. The important point is that the interrelations of different types of research must be used to evaluate the state of knowledge in an area.

An important issue in this model is the dissemination of findings to practitioners so that treatments can be used. A critical issue here is whether the treatment is effective in actual clinical practice (Kazdin, Kratochwill, & VandenBos, 1986). Ross (1981b) advocated that clinical research be both rigorous and relevant to clinical practice. He suggested that an approach that combines a detailed study of individual cases with group comparison studies in the context of comprehensive research programs would be most useful. He also advocated a "tracer method," a procedure for gathering extensive information on each individual client after the data from group comparison studies have been analyzed. A "deviant case analysis" is then conducted. Ross noted:

> To do this, one first investigates a research question with one of the traditional experimental designs that employs groups of subjects and requires data analysis by appropriate statistical methods. Immediately after the data have been analyzed, while the subjects can still be identified and contacted, the results are examined for deviant cases, that is, for subjects whose performance did not "fit" the tested hypothesis. Depending on how many of these deviant cases are found, either all, or a sample, or the most extreme of them are then called back to the laboratory where they are examined by whatever case-study method is appropriate. Given time and resources, one can even go one step further and subject individuals whose performance was close to the mean of the group to similar individual scrutiny. By doing this, one can seek an answer to the question in what ways the deviant cases differed from the group. I suspect that this approach would generate new and interesting hypotheses that could then once more be tested in a well-controlled group design, thus leading to an ever greater refinement in our knowledge. (pp. 325–326)

Although this approach has the potential to advance knowledge in consultation, neither it or the Agras and Berkowitz model completely addresses the issue of the efficacy of a treatment in actual practice. As a further alternative, Kazdin et al. (1987) proposed "clinical replication" to obtain information on treatment efficacy. In a clinical replication, a treatment is introduced into an actual clinical setting without the typical controls imposed in research (e.g., design, therapist training, and monitoring of the treatment and the client). It is assumed that internal validity in the research on a particular treatment will already have been established. Clinical-replication case studies focus on establishing the generalizability or the external validity of a particular treatment. The clinical-replication case-study procedure is itself subject to empirical evaluation as a method of outcome evaluation.

Criteria for Evaluation of Outcomes

The traditional criteria for the evaluation of therapeutic outcomes in consultation have included a rather limited range of measures (Kratochwill et al., 1989). In this text, and specifically in this chapter, we have argued for measures that take into account broad areas of client functioning. Yet, even when these are used in research, they represent a rather limited source of information on the efficacy of consultation. Recently, several criteria have been recommended that take into account a broader conceptual and methodological picture of behavior change in clinical research (Kazdin, 1988; Kazdin & Wilson, 1978; Rachman & Wilson, 1980). These criteria include experimental and therapeutic criteria, client-related criteria, efficiency- and cost-related criteria, and criteria for generalization and follow-up.

Experimental and Therapeutic Criteria

In consultation research, two criteria should be used in outcome research. Experimental criteria are used in both group and single-case research, but they differ in some respects in the two methodologies.

In group research, appropriate inferential statistical tests are used to establish that the intervention had an effect. The choice of an appropriate data-analysis technique is a statistical-conclusion-validity issue (Cook & Campbell, 1979), and researchers should adhere to assumptions of the tests used. An important issue in group research is the power and the sample size needed to determine a treatment effect (Cohen, 1970; Levin, 1975). Although it is beyond the scope of this presentation to deal fully with the methodological and conceptual aspects of statistical power, we recommend the following steps in future group-consultation research. First, researchers should report the power and the desired effect size for their study. For example, a power $(1 - \beta)$ of .80 means that the Type II error rate is .20. The effect size is the magnitude of the difference relative to variability. When the effect size is large, the probability of finding a significant difference is increased. However, no formal statement can be made about what the power should be, as it depends on such factors as variability in the measures, differences between groups, the sample size used, the design, the number of conditions compared, the statistical test used (e.g., *a priori* tests are more powerful), and the alpha level chosen (.05 vs. .01). When the effect size is small, variability is large, and a small sample is used, the findings may be doomed to nonsignificance. Questions should then be raised about the feasibility of conducting the study. If few subjects are available, the researcher should consider a different type of methodology (e.g., single-case research-design). Finally, a meaningful effect size has implications for the therapeutic significance of the results. Small effects obtained through large sample sizes may be statistically significant, but not clinically meaningful.

In single-case research, the typical method of establishing the experimental criteria has been visual data analysis (Kazdin, 1982b; Kratochwill, 1978). When visual analysis is used, several guidelines that make the method more formal may be invoked (Parsonson & Baer, 1978). Although advances have been made in visual analysis, a major problem with the approach has been its unreliability (Kratochwill & Levin, 1979). As a supplement of visual analysis, statistical tests for time series experiments can be used (e.g., Kratochwill, 1978). Traditional techniques that do not take into account the autocorrelated nature of time series data (e.g. ANOVA and regression) are usually inappropriate. Procedures that take into account this potential problem include time series analysis (Gottman, 1981; McCleary & Hay, 1980) and a class of nonparametric randomization tests (Edgington, in press; Levin, Marascuilo, & Hubert, 1978). However, each of these techniques may add a degree of inflexibility to the research (e.g., design and measurement restrictions), and this should be balanced against other factors surrounding the research. Also, statistical criteria may be redundant if large effects are found that are visually evident.

In addition to experimental criteria, therapeutic criteria should be invoked in consultation outcome research. Therapeutic criteria are usually conceptualized within the context of social validation (Kazdin, 1977b; Wolf, 1978). First, the selection of certain therapeutic criteria presupposes that the behavior selected for change is meaningful and addresses a wide range of criteria used to select target behaviors (Mash & Terdal, 1988). When treatment outcomes are evaluated, there are two considerations. First, the behavior of the client is compared with that of his or her peers. As an alternative, consultation researchers may use data from peer ratings to help establish a therapeutic goal. A second procedure involves subjective evaluations of the child's behavior by socialization agents in the natural environment (e.g., teachers and parents). Therapeutic changes in the child can be viewed as therapeutically important to the degree that the intervention brings the child's behavior within a range of socially acceptable levels when compared to the peer group and based on qualitative ratings from socialization agents in applied settings.

In behavioral consultation, there is also the option to focus social validation criteria on the consultee. For example, the teacher-consultee may be compared to other teachers who are regarded as especially competent in managing children's behavior, or ratings may be obtained from supervisors.

In addition to these conceptual issues, social validation procedures may have important methodological implications. Such procedures are likely to allow the researcher to focus on clinically meaningful changes in addition to the usual experimental criteria. Generally, therapeutic or clinical criteria should far surpass experimental criteria. The major criterion in behavioral consultation research is clinically significant change in the client and, under some conditions, in the consultee.

Client-Related Criteria

Several client related criteria have a direct bearing on future investigations in behavioral consultation. Usually, the primary means of measuring improvement in clients receiving consultation services has been a single target measure that is evaluated by some experimental criteria. Of course, a single target is relevant because consultation researchers are interested in determining if the treatment altered the problem behavior of interest. In addition, the breadth of the changes produced can be used to differentiate treatments or to expand the understanding of the effects of treatment (Kazdin & Wilson, 1978). That is, two treatments may be equally effective, but one may have more desirable side effects than the other. Even if one form of treatment has demonstrated superiority over another, the alternative may be preferred when severe side effects are possible with the superior treatment. One treatment may also produce either positive or negative behaviors that should be monitored. Formal measures of academic and social competence would help describe the breadth of changes in a particular consultation program (Lentz, 1988).

Efficiency- and Cost-Related Criteria

The foregoing criteria greatly expand the possible ways in which a behavioral consultation program can be evaluated. In addition to these, future researchers should consider efficiency in the duration of consultation, efficiency in the administration of consultation, client costs, and cost-effectiveness. Each of these criteria can help the researcher make better decisions about the relative efficiency of two or more treatments or to examine the efficiency of a particular treatment.

Efficiency in the duration of consultation implies that treatment procedures that reach a desirable level of outcome in a relatively short time are generally preferred (when other criteria are considered).

Another relevant variable is the way in which the treatment is implemented. Treatment may be administered to groups, through reading materials, or by paraprofessionals rather than trained professional teachers. Some behavioral treatments cannot be widely disseminated because of their mode of service delivery (e.g., individual therapy) or the training required (learning) psychotherapy may take many years. An important consideration is the cost of the professional training required to conduct the treatment (Kazdin & Wilson, 1978). Some treatments can be carried out by individuals in the natural environment with minimal training (see Chapter 5). However, this type of treatment delivery usually necessitates careful monitoring by a skilled professional consultant, which must be included in any costs (see the discussion of treatment integrity). Nevertheless, approaches that rely on a triadic model, in which the consultant works through a consultee, are likely to be more cost-efficient than approaches that are not triadic. However, we know of no empirical data to support this assumption.

Various client costs, monetary or "emotional," should also be monitored in consultation research. Monetary costs are influenced by such factors as the cost of the professional training of the consultant or the consultee and the disseminability of the treatment. Emotional costs to the client should be monitored in each case but are especially important in programs that use punishment. The important issue here is that clients may actually refuse treatment (or consultees may refuse to administer the treatment) if they perceive the "cure" as being worse than the problem.

Finally, cost-effectiveness is an important issue in consultation research and should be considered with the other outcome measures. Fuchs *et al.* (1989) presented information on the *time* involved in their project. Consultants using the BC$_2$ and BC$_3$ strategies needed 6 hours per pupil to complete the treatment. They compared their time commitment to that typically required to complete a single psychological evaluation, which they estimated took twice as long. Data such as these should be routinely incorporated into consultation outcome studies to provide a cost index. Several additional features of a cost analysis may also be included (see Yates, Haven, & Thoresen, 1977). A cost-effectiveness analysis requires measuring the resources consumed and the outcomes produced, and developing an "input" to "output" ratio (Yates *et al.*, 1977). A number of different variables can be included in the cost analysis, including such factors as personnel, facilities, equipment, and material, in addition to the "costs" described above.

Unfortunately, no study in the consultation literature has conducted a comprehensive cost analysis that includes all of the variables described above. We strongly encourage consultation researchers to provide this type of information in future investigations. The following guidelines may be useful for conducting such an analysis (McMahon & Forehand, 1980):

1. The researcher should provide information on the amount of professional time required to:
   a. Train consultants to serve the case.
   b. Assess the problem.
   c. Develop the treatment material (e.g., a manual or recording formats).
2. The researcher should provide information on the amount of time

needed by caretakers or consultees (e.g., parents, teachers, and paraprofessionals) for:
   a. Training to treat the case.
   b. Assessment of the problem.
   c. Actual contact with the client in treatment.
   d. The "emotional" costs associated with treatment delivery.
3. Finally, the researcher should provide information on the amount of time needed by the client to:
   a. Train in the implementation of the treatment (e.g., self-control).
   b. Assess herself or himself (e.g., self-monitoring).
   c. Actually participate in the treatment program.
   d. Manage the negative emotional factors that stem from participation in the treatment program.

Generalization and Follow-Up Criteria

In recent years, the increased attention that behavioral researchers have devoted to generalization and follow-up measures has prompted critical examinations of these concepts and has resulted in several methodological advances (e.g., Drabman, Hammer, & Rosenbaum, 1979; Karoly & Steffen, 1980; Mash & Terdal, 1980; Stokes & Baer, 1977). Each of these issues has an important bearing on future research in consultation as well as on the conclusions that can be drawn from the existing literature.

Generalization. Generalization has several dimensions, including generalization across time, across settings, across behaviors, and across subjects. Generalization across time is usually conceptualized as maintenance or follow-up. A conceptual framework called the *generalization map* was presented by Drabman *et al.* (1979). In this framework, the various generalized effects of intervention programs can be categorized into 16 different classes (see Figure 9-4).

A number of issues have a bearing on generalization measurement (Drabman *et al.*, 1979, pp. 213–216). First, various designs can be used to assess generalization. In single-case research the investigator can study generalization systematically (see Kazdin & Kopel, 1975; Kendall, 1981; Rush & Kazdin, 1981). Generalization can also be studied in large-number between-group studies. For example, if the researcher includes two control groups, children who come into contact with treated children and/or treated parents can be assessed to determine if there is any generalization to "nontreated" subjects. Further, the specific assessment of individual subjects through the "trace" method advocated by Ross (1981b) can further help to determine the degree of generalization.

Second, generalization should be assessed across multiple measures. A number of unresolved issues remain in the area of treatment generaliza-

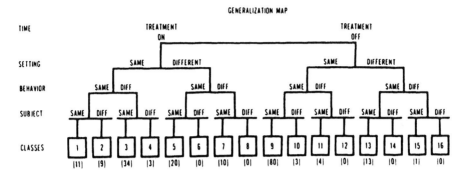

FIGURE 9-4. The generalization map, depicting the 16 different classes of generalized treatment effects. The numbers in parentheses indicate the number of studies found (in the Drabman *et al.*, 1979, review) that illustrate a particular class of generalization. [Source: R. S. Drabman, D. Hammer, & M. S. Rosenbaum. (1979). Assessing generalization in behavior modification with children: The generalization map. *Behavioral Assessment*, 1, 203–219. Copyright 1979 by the Association for Advancement of Behavior Therapy. Reproduced by permission.]

tion from one measure to another. For example, it is not clear whether treatment success as measured by overt behavior generalizes to the child's self-report or other measures. Generally, we prefer direct measures (e.g., observational measures) wherever possible. The measures should probably be qualitative as well as quantitative (Drabman *et al.*, 1979). As Drabman *et al.* noted, generalization typically occurs not only in frequency of response, but also in quality of performance, which may possibly be measured through ratings or even self-report.

Finally, generalization has typically been viewed as a passive phenomenon. Growing evidence suggests that it must be specifically programmed if it is to occur (e.g., Stokes & Baer, 1977). For example, Stokes and Baer (1977) presented a technology for programming generalization that is most useful in consultation research.

Follow-Up and Maintenance. Follow-up is recognized as an important feature of consultation research. Yet, considerable disagreement exists on the actual conceptual and methodological practices of follow-up assessment. The questions usually associated with follow-up measurement are: Does the treatment have a lasting impact? Are the effects of the treatment durable? And Does the client remain cured? Implicit in the concept of follow-up is the measurement of some client variable at two or more points in time, that is, one following the implementation of the program and one following its termination. Yet, the passage of time between the formal treatment program and the follow-up measure(s) is only one dimension of follow-up.

Several different purposes of follow-up can be distinguished (Mash & Terdal, 1980):

1. *Evaluative follow-up (E-FU)*. This type of follow-up assessment is aimed at determining whether changes have occurred in relation to some interventions, and whether they continue to occur. No attempt is made to intervene.
2. *Diagnostic follow-up (D-FU)*. This type of follow-up assessment is directed at making program changes when it is determined that revised interventions could improve the services to the client.
3. *Therapeutic follow-up (T-FU)*. This type of follow-up is therapeutically oriented and is directed at enhancing therapeutic effects on the client.
4. *Investigate follow-up (I-FU)*. In this type of follow-up, assessment is directed toward answering some type of research question. Longitudinal studies of intervention programs would be an example of this. (pp. 109–112)

Which type of follow-up is best in consultation research cannot be determined in the abstract. The type of follow-up assessment used depends on the type of problem and the nature of the study, among other features. Usually, however, in consultation research, D-FUs and T-FUs are used. In some respects, this is an ethical issue because a determination that the client is not doing well usually results in some type of consultee intervention.

An important issue that emerges in the model of follow-up recommended here relates to the question of how treatment and generalization are distinguished (Morris & Kratochwill, 1983). For example, it is arbitrary to suggest that, at some point, treatment terminates and generalization begins. Various strategies that promote generalization may be included in the treatment program (e.g., reinforcement and self-monitoring). The client may also be instructed to begin the treatment program again (e.g., with positive self-statements) if the problem recurs. In this regard, follow-up assessment needs to focus on what is occurring and in what treatment context.

Procedures for Computing Indices of Interview Effectiveness

This appendix contains procedures for computing content, process, control, and focus indices of interview effectiveness. As all but one of these indices require converting data from consultation analysis records into bits of information, a table for making the necessary conversions is included in the appendix. As indicated in the body of the book, the indices of interview effectiveness are intended to be used mainly for research purposes. There are no established standards for specifying precise scores defining effectiveness or ineffectiveness. However, for each of the indices, it is the case that the higher the score is, the more effective the interview is.

THE INDEX OF CONTENT RELEVANCE

As discussed in Part II of the book, each of the three interviews conducted in consultative problem-solving is designed to focus on a specific set of topics. These topics should make up the bulk of the interview content in consultation. During problem identification, the content should fall mainly in the behavior, behavior-setting, and observation subcategories. During problem analysis, content should be limited primarily to the behavior, behavior-setting, and plan categories, whereas in problem evaluation, the content should focus on the behavior, observation, and plan categories.

An index of content relevance has been designed to determine the extent to which consultant verbalizations represent a balanced coverage of appropriate interview content. In computing indices of content relevance, the consultant should implement the following steps:

1. Calculate the proportion of verbalizations falling within each of the

content subcategories relevant to the interview being evaluated. For exam
ple, in the consultation analysis record for a hypothetical problem-identification interview shown in Figure A-1, there are 5 consultant utterances in
the behavior subcategory, 5 in the behavior-setting subcategory, 5 in the
observation subcategory, and 10 in the other subcategory. To compute the
proportions of verbalizations in the behavior, behavior-setting, and observation subcategories (the relevant subcategories in the problem identification interview), divide the total number of statements in each relevant
subcategory by the total number of statements in the interview. Each of the
three relevant subcategories contains 5 utterances. The total number of
statements in the interview is 25.5/25 = .20.

2. Convert the proportions computed in Step 1 to bits by using Table
A-1. In the example given in Step 1, the behavior, behavior-setting, and
observation subcategories each contain .200 of the consultant verbalizations in the interview. Table A-1 indicates that the proportion .200 equals
.4644 bits.

3. Sum the bits computed in Step 2. This sum gives the index of
content relevance. For the example given here, the index of content relevance would be .4644 + .4644 = 1.3932 bits.

High values in the index of content relevance reflect a balanced use of
relevant content subcategories. For instance, a problem identification interview with many verbalizations in the behavior and behavior-setting subcategories would receive a lower score than an interview in which behavior, behavior-setting, and observation subcategories were equally represented. The conversion of raw scores to bits has the unique advantage of
reflecting not only the amount of usage of relevant content subcategories,
but also the balance achieved across subcategories.

The Index of Process Effectiveness

Achieving the goals of consultative problem-solving requires the specification, summarization, and validation of information. In addition, during the problem evaluation interview, there is generally a need to make
inferences about sources of invalidity relevant to the evaluation of plan
effectiveness. Indices of process effectiveness indicate the extent to which
the consultant uses process subcategories appropriately in the achievement of consultation goals. In the problem identification and problem analysis interviews, effective use of the process category requires an evenly
balanced distribution of utterances in the specification, summarization,
and validation subcategories. In the problem evaluation interview, the
distribution of utterances should be evenly spread across the specification,
summarization, validation, and inference subcategories.

CONSULTATION-ANALYSIS RECORD

	Message Source		Message Content							Message Process							Message Control	
	Consultee	Consultant	Background Environment	Behavior Setting	Behavior	Individual Characteristics	Observation	Plan	Other	Negative Evaluation	Positive Evaluation	Inference	Specification	Summarization	Negative Validation	Positive Validation	Elicitor	Emitter
1		/			/								/				/	
2		/			/								/				/	
3		/					/			/								/
4		/					/			/								/
5		/					/			/								
6		/			/									/				/
7		/			/									/				/
8		/			/											/	/	
9		/		/										/			/	
10		/		/											/			/
11		/			/					/							/	
12		/			/					/							/	
13		/		/										/				/
14		/			/											/	/	
15		/			/											/	/	
16		/					/							/			/	
17		/					/								/			/
18		/					/									/	/	
19		/						/						/			/	
20		/						/		/								/
21		/						/		/								/
22		/						/		/							/	
23		/						/		/							/	
24		/						/		/							/	
25		/						/								/	/	

FIGURE A-1. Consultation analysis record of consultant verbalizations in a hypothetical problem-identification interview.

TABLE A-1   Values in Bits for Proportions from .000 to .9991ᵃ

How to use this table:

Example: To find the value of .200 in bits,

1. Find the first two digits of the proportion in the first column of the table. Thus, you would locate .20 in Column 1.
2. Find the closest number in column 2 that is above the proportion you located in column 1. For the proportion .20, this would be 0.4. This is the first digit you will use in expressing .200 bits.
3. Read across from Column 1 to the third digit in the proportion; that in the example given is 0. The entry, which in this case is 644, gives the second, third, and forth digits in the answer you are seeking. Thus, the proportion .200 equals .4644 bits. The value in bits of the proportion 1.000, which is not given in the table, is 0.
4. When the table entries are in italics and are underlined, the first digit of the answer is to be read from the line below the one in which the proportion is located. For instance, the number of bits corresponding to the proportion .147 is .4066.

P		0	1	2	3	4	5	6	7	8	9
.00	0.0	000	100	179	251	319	382	443	501	557	612
.01		664	716	766	814	862	909	955	999	*043*	*086*
.02	0.1	129	170	211	252	291	330	369	407	444	481
.03		518	554	589	624	659	693	727	760	793	825
.04		858	889	921	952	983	*013*	*043*	*073*	*103*	*132*
.05	0.2	161	190	218	246	274	301	329	356	383	409
.06		435	461	487	513	538	563	588	613	637	662
.07		686	709	733	756	780	803	826	848	871	893
.08		915	937	959	980	*002*	*023*	*044*	*065*	*086*	*106*
.09	0.3	127	147	167	187	207	226	246	265	284	303
.10		322	341	359	378	396	414	432	450	468	485
.11		503	520	537	555	571	588	605	622	638	654
.12		671	687	703	719	734	750	766	781	796	811
.13		826	841	856	871	886	900	915	929	943	957
.14		971	985	999	*012*	*006*	*040*	*053*	*066*	*079*	*092*
.15	0.4	105	118	131	144	156	169	181	194	206	218
.16		230	242	254	266	278	289	301	312	323	335
.17		346	357	368	379	390	401	411	422	432	443
.18		453	463	474	484	494	504	514	523	533	543
.19		552	562	571	581	590	599	608	617	626	635
.20		644	653	661	670	678	687	695	704	712	720
.21		728	736	744	752	760	768	776	783	791	798
.22		806	813	821	828	835	842	849	856	863	870
.23		877	883	890	897	903	910	916	923	929	935
.24		941	948	954	960	966	971	977	983	989	994
.25	0.5	000	006	011	017	022	027	032	038	043	048
.26		053	058	063	068	073	077	082	087	091	096
.27		100	105	109	113	118	122	126	130	134	138
.28		142	146	150	154	158	161	165	169	172	176
.29		179	183	186	189	192	196	199	202	205	208
.30		211	214	217	220	222	225	228	230	233	235

TABLE A-1. (*Continued*)

P		0	1	2	3	4	5	6	7	8	9
.31		238	240	243	245	248	250	252	254	256	258
.32		260	262	264	266	268	270	272	273	275	277
.33		278	280	281	283	284	286	287	288	289	291
.34		292	293	294	295	296	297	298	299	300	300
.35		301	302	302	303	304	304	305	305	306	306
.36		306	306	307	307	307	307	307	307	307	307
.37		307	307	307	307	307	306	306	306	305	305
.38		305	304	304	303	302	302	301	300	300	299
.39		298	297	296	295	294	293	292	291	290	289
.40		288	287	285	284	283	281	280	278	277	276
.41		274	272	271	269	267	266	264	262	260	258
.42		257	255	253	251	249	247	244	242	240	238
.43		236	233	231	229	226	224	222	219	217	214
.44		212	209	206	204	201	198	195	193	190	187
.45		184	181	178	175	172	169	166	163	160	157
.46		153	150	147	144	140	137	133	130	127	123
.47		120	116	112	108	105	102	098	094	090	086
.48		083	079	075	071	067	063	059	055	051	047
.49		043	039	034	030	026	022	018	013	009	004
.50	0.5	000	996	991	987	982	978	973	968	964	959
.51	0.4	954	950	945	940	935	930	926	921	916	911
.52		906	901	896	891	886	880	875	870	865	860
.53		854	849	844	839	833	828	823	817	812	806
.54		801	795	789	784	778	772	767	761	755	750
.55		744	738	732	726	720	714	709	702	697	691
.56		684	678	672	666	660	654	648	641	635	629
.57		623	616	610	604	597	591	584	578	571	565
.58		558	551	545	538	532	515	518	511	505	498
.59		491	484	477	471	464	457	450	443	436	429
.60		422	415	408	401	393	386	379	372	365	357
.61		350	343	335	328	321	313	306	298	291	283
.62		276	268	261	253	246	238	230	223	215	207
.63		200	192	184	176	168	160	152	145	137	129
.64		121	113	105	097	089	081	072	064	056	048
.65		040	032	023	015	007	998	990	982	973	965
.66	0.3	957	948	940	931	923	914	906	897	888	880
.67		871	862	854	845	836	828	819	810	801	792
.68		783	774	766	757	748	739	730	721	712	703
.69		694	685	675	666	657	648	639	630	621	611
.70		602	593	583	574	565	556	546	537	527	718
.71		508	499	489	480	470	461	451	441	432	422
.72		412	403	393	383	373	364	354	344	334	324
.73		315	305	295	285	275	265	255	245	235	225
.74		215	204	194	184	174	164	154	144	133	123
.75		113	102	092	082	072	061	051	040	030	020
.76		009	999	988	978	967	957	946	935	925	914

(*continued*)

TABLF A-1 (Continued)

P	0	1	2	3	4	5	6	7	8	9
.77 0.2	903	893	882	872	861	850	839	828	818	807
.78	796	785	774	764	752	742	731	720	708	697
.79	686	676	665	654	642	631	620	609	598	587
.80	576	564	553	542	530	519	508	497	485	474
.81	462	451	440	428	417	405	394	383	371	359
.82	348	336	325	313	301	290	278	266	255	243
.83	231	219	208	196	184	172	160	148	137	125
.84	113	101	089	077	065	053	041	029	017	005
.85 0.1	993	981	969	957	944	932	920	908	896	884
.86	871	859	847	834	822	810	798	785	773	760
.87	748	735	723	712	698	686	673	661	684	635
.88	623	610	598	585	573	560	547	534	522	509
.89	496	484	471	458	445	432	420	407	394	381
.90	368	355	342	329	316	303	290	277	264	251
.91	238	225	212	199	186	173	159	146	133	120
.92	107	094	080	067	054	040	027	014	000	987
.93 0.0	974	960	947	934	920	907	893	880	866	853
.94	839	826	812	799	785	771	758	744	730	717
.95	703	689	675	662	648	635	621	607	593	579
.96	565	552	538	524	510	496	482	468	454	441
.97	426	412	398	384	370	356	342	328	314	300
.98	285	271	257	243	229	215	200	186	172	158
.99	144	129	115	101	086	072	058	043	029	014

"From E. B. Newman. (1951). Computational methods useful in analyzing series of binary data. *American Journal of Psychology, 54,* 252–262. By permission of the University of Illinois Press. Copyright 1951 by Karl M Dallenbach. Printed in USA

The following steps are required to compute the index of process effectiveness:

1. Group consultant utterances for the interview under consideration are divided into sets of 25 utterances each. The last set may not have 25 utterances. If it contains 12 or more utterances, it should be included. If it contains fewer then 12 verbalizations, it should be dropped from further consideration. The selection of the number 25 is somewhat arbitrary. It was based on the need to establish sets of verbalizations long enough to reflect patterns of utterances in an interview involving all relevant process subcategories. For example, in the problem identification interview, within a span of 25 utterances by a consultant it is reasonable to expect that there will be an even distribution of utterances in the specification, summarization, and validation subcategories.

2. Compute the proportion of utterances falling in each relevant process subcategory. For example, in Figure A-1 there are 5 specifications, 5

summarizations, 5 positive validations, and 10 positive evaluations. The proportions for the specification, summarization, and validation subcategories are each .200.

3. Convert the proportions computed in Step 2 into bits by using Table A-1. As indicated in the discussion of the index of content relevance, the proportion .200 turns out to equal .4644 bits.

4. The fourth step is to sum the number of bits computed in Step 3 across relevant process subcategories and then across each set of utterances being analyzed. In the example given in Figure A-1, the number of bits in the specification, summarization, and validation subcategories is .4644 + .4644 + .4644 = 1.3932 bits. There are only 25 utterances in this example. Had there been another 25 utterances, the number of bits associated with the second set of 25 would have been added to the sum obtained for the initial set of 25 verbalizations.

5. The final step is to compute the average number of bits for sets of 25. For example, if there were two sets of 25, the sum obtained in Step 4 would be divided by 2. The result obtained in Step 5 is the index of process effectiveness.

As in the case of the index of content relevance, high scores for the index of process effectiveness reflect a balanced use of relevant subcategories. Thus, a problem identification interview with many specification utterances, but few summarizations and validations, would receive a lower score than an interview involving balanced coverage of all three relevant process subcategories.

THE INDEX OF INTERVIEW CONTROL

As pointed out in the body of the book, the consultant guides the consultee through the problem-solving process by using elicitors. Thus, the proportion of elicitors should tend to be rather large. The index of interview control is intended to reveal the extent to which elicitors are used in an interview. The index is computed by calculating the proportion of consultant utterances falling in the elicitor subcategory. In the consultation analysis record shown in Figure A-1, there are 15 elicitors and 10 emitters. Thus, the proportion of elicitors is 15/25 = .60.

THE INDEX OF CONTENT FOCUS

Consultant verbalizations may determine the extent to which interview content shifts from one topic to another. As indicated earlier in the book, it is generally useful for the consultant to maintain a relatively high degree of focus in the interviews. The index of content focus reveals the extent to which the consultant tends to stay on one topic of conversation for brief sets of consultant verbalizations.

The following steps are necessary in the computation of the index of content focus:

1. Group consultant verbalizations into sets with five utterances in each set. The last set is dropped if it contains less than five verbalizations.

2. Compute the proportions of verbalizations falling in the various content subcategories for each set. For example, for the consultation analysis record shown in Figure A-1, the proportions are .40 in the behavior subcategory and .60 in the other subcategory for the first set of five. In the second set, the proportions are .60 in the behavior subcategory and .40 in the behavior-setting subcategory. In the third set, they are .40 in the observation subcategory and .60 in the behavior-setting subcategory. In the final set, they are 1.00 in the other subcategory.

3. Convert the proportions computed in Step 2 bits by using Table A-1. The bits associated with the proportions in each of the five sets described in Step 2 are:

    Set 1   .400 = .5288
              .600 = .4422
    Set 2   .600 = .4422
              .400 = .5288
    Set 3   .400 = .5288
              .600 = .4422
    Set 4   .600 = .4422
              .400 = .5288
    Set 5   1.000 = .0000

4. Sum the bits computed in Step 3. For the example given here, the sum is 3.840.

5. Compute the average number of bits in a set by dividing the total number of bits established in Step 4 by the number of sets being considered. For the example, given here there are five sets: 3.840/5 = .768.

6. Compute the maximum number of bits that could be in each set. The number of bits would be at a maximum if each of the five utterances in a set fell in a different content category. This means that, for each set of five utterances, there would have to be five proportions, each of which would be .200: .200 = .4644 bits. The maximum possible number of bits in a set of five utterances is .4644 × 5 = 2.322.

7. Subtract the average number of bits in a set from the maximum possible number of bits to obtain the index of content focus. For the example given here, the answer would be 2.322 − .768 = 1.5540.

The index of content focus gives high scores when there is very little shifting across subcategories. For instance, suppose that only one content subcategory were used in an interview. The second term in the subtraction problem in Step 7 would be 0 instead of .768. The measure of content focus would then be 2.322 bits, which is the highest possible average number of bits for sets of five verbalizations. On the other hand, if there were continuous shifting, the second term would be 2.322 and the index of content focus would be 0.

Appendix B

Tables Listing Conditions That Have the Potential to Affect Behavior

This appendix contains three tables[1] listing conditions that experimental studies have shown to have the potential to affect behavior. Table B-1 specifies the kinds of changes that can be made in antecedent, consequent, and sequential conditions to increase behavior. Table B-2 gives alterations in antecedent and sequential conditions that can be applied to maintain behavior at a particular level of strength. Table B-3 specifies changes in antecedent, consequent, and sequential conditions that can be used to reduce the strength of a behavior.

---

[1]Tables B-1, B-2, and B-3 from J. R. Bergan and J. A. Dunn (1976). *Psychology and education: A science for instruction* (pp. 434–439). Copyright 1976 by John Wiley & Sons. Reprinted by permission of John Wiley & Sons, Inc.

TABLE B-1. Environmental Changes for Producing Increases in Performance

---

Changes in antecedent conditions
  Stimulus alterations
  1. Exaggerate distinctive features of the stimulus. For example, color variations can be used to make the desired stimulus features stand out.
  2. Reduce the overall number of features to be considered in the stimulus. For example, base word identification on a selected subset of letters rather than on all of the letters in a word.
  3. Reduce the number of common characteristics among stimuli presented simultaneously. For example, in compiling a list of spelling words, select words that have the smallest number of letters in common.
  4. Reduce the overall number of stimuli presented on a given occasion. For example, in a concept-learning task such as learning the sound *og* in *dog*, *log*, and *fog*, keep the number of words presented simultaneously small.
  5. Increase stimulus complexity to increase attention. For example, provide visual stimuli that are detailed and that have color.
  6. Rearrange stimuli according to a logical or grammatical order. For example, in the learning of a set of facts, it is useful to group them into sentences.
  7. Reduce the number of different stimulus categories considered on a given occasion. For example, on a free-recall task, minimize the number of categories of verbal information.
  8. Increase the strength of stimulus presentation to increase attention. For example, present letters to be learned in bright and well-saturated colors.
  9. Make stimuli move to increase attention. For instance, move flash cards toward the child on a reading or arithmetic task.
  10. Vary the rate of stimulus presentation. To a point, increased rate of stimulus presentation may be beneficial. For example, reading speed and comprehension may be improved by increases in rate. However, there is a point at which further increases in rate of stimulus presentation result in performance decrements.
  Response alterations
  1. Decrease the strength of a competing response that is interfering with learning. Aggressive or disruptive behaviors that interfere with classroom activities are prime examples of competing responses requiring elimination to promote learning.
  2. Reduce the number of components in a desired response. For example, reduce the number of steps involved in carrying out directions for completing an assignment.
  3. Reduce the number of responses called for in a stimulus situation. For example, in a serial-learning task (such as learning to count), use only a small number of items in the series.
  4. Reduce the number of categories from which the learner may select a response. For example, in learning to identify the letter *m*, a child might use two response categories: *m* or *not m*.
  5. Reduce the number of common characteristics among responses. For example, sets of verbal responses that sound alike or have similar meanings may be easily confused and therefore paired incorrectly with stimuli in verbal-learning tasks.
  6. Sequence responses to a given stimulus that are emitted in a series in a logical or grammatical order. For example, if a set of words to be learned can be arranged in sentence form, acquisition occurs more readily than if the words are presented in nongrammatical order. Similarly, if words can be grouped into categories, they are more easily acquired than if categorization is not used.

TABLE B-1. (*Continued*)

7. Reduce the number of constraints on the order of responding to a given stimulus. For example, more units of information can be acquired on free-recall tasks than on serial-learning tasks.

Alterations in information given about stimuli or responses

1. Provide cues (e.g., instructions) specifying learner performance.
2. Provide a verbal statement of relevant rules in tasks calling for rule application. For example, when teaching children to use the articles *an* and *a*, teach them the verbal rule.
3. Provide cues about stimulus conditions. For example, tell the learner what kinds of environmental events may signal the occurrence of reinforcement.
4. Model responses to be emitted by the learner. For instance, demonstrate appropriate social interactions for a child.
5. Reduce the number of responses modeled for the learner on a given occasion. For example, model only portions of a skill at any one time. If teaching question-asking behavior, begin by modeling single, simple questions.
6. Reduce the number of component parts of a modeled response. If teaching proper classroom behavior, concentrate on a single aspect (such as listening behavior) at a time.
7. Reduce the rate of response modeling. For example, when teaching a physical skill, model the component parts in slow motion.
8. Provide cues to signal the occurrence of a response to be emitted. For example, the teacher might say the first word of a verbal chain to be emitted by a learner.
9. Provide cues giving verbal or pictorial associations to a response to be emitted. For example, provide word cues such as *a, apple, a* when teaching letter identification.
10. Provide physical response guidance. For example, move a learner's hand in such a way as to form letters when teaching her or him how to print or write.

Changes in consequent conditions

1. Provide negative reinforcement. For example, remove a negative reinforcer following the occurrence of a desired response.
2. Provide positive reinforcement.
3. Increase the immediacy of reinforcer delivery.
4. Alter the type of reinforcer to increase motivation.
5. Increase the magnitude of a reinforcer.

Changes in sequential conditions

1. Reduce the similarity—that is, the number of common characteristics—among stimuli presented and among responses required over a series of learning trials. For example, when teaching the alphabet, begin by teaching letters that are highly dissimilar both in appearance and in letter sound.
2. Increase the amount of repetition of stimuli and of responses over trials to enhance discrimination learning. Repetition provides the learner with an opportunity to discover distinctive features and patterns. For example, repetition enhances letter discrimination.
3. Use a continuous reinforcement schedule during the early phases of acquisition and an intermittent reinforcement schedule during the later phases of acquisition.
4. Differentially reinforce discrimination responses. That is, reinforce correct responses and do not reinforce incorrect responses.
5. Use shaping procedures. When a desired response is not in the child's repertoire, reinforce successive approximations of the correct response.

TABLE B-2. Environmental Changes for Promoting the Maintenance
of Performance Capability

Changes in antecedent conditions
1. Increase the meaningfulness of stimuli. For example, provide a large number of verbal associations with stimuli to be recalled.
2. Increase the concreteness of verbal stimuli by selecting stimuli that stand for concrete objects.
3. Choose stimulus–response pairs that have high associative strength. For instance, when possible, enhance retention by presenting information in words that seem to go together (e.g., *reward* or *punishment*).
4. Reduce similarities among verbal stimuli. For instance, in word identification, choose dissimilar words.
5. Provide mediators. For instance, in letter naming, the identification of the symbol *a* can be mediated by the covert response *apple*.
6. Provide a set of verbal classes for categorizing into classes the stimuli presented. For instance, group pieces of information to be recalled from a chapter in a text.
7. Provide instructions to remember. If the objective of a lesson is to acquire new information, mention this to the students before the lesson begins.
8. Present verbal stimuli in rhythmic patterns. For instance, use the "alphabet song" to teach the order of the letters in the alphabet.
9. Arrange verbal stimuli in grammatical order, for example, in sentences.
10. Provide stimulus chunking. That is, rearrange stimuli in terms of a small number of categories that include smaller stimulus units as, for example, placing letters in words.
11. Provide multisensory cues—for example, both visual and auditory cues—to facilitate recall.
12. Reduce interfering tasks between acquisition and recall. For instance, if a student is attempting to retain the meanings of a set of words, do not introduce an additional set of similar words.
13. Provide cues signaling probable reinforcement for recall. For instance, tell a student what value to him or her there may be in retaining a given piece of information.

Changes in sequential conditions
1. Increase opportunities for practice, for instance, by providing study periods.
2. Increase opportunities to rehearse responses covertly. For example, provide instructions to rehearse and allow time for rehearsal.
3. Encourage the learner to label the characteristics of the visual stimuli to be recalled verbally. If teaching letter discrimination, have the student say the defining characteristics of the letter being learned.
4. Reduce the number of different types of responses that the learner must make over a series of learning trials. For instance, in letter identification instruction, a child might respond to one or two letters (e.g., *g*) by name. Other letters could be temporarily called *not g*.
5. Provide massed practice in situations in which there is a high degree of stimulus or response similarity. Have long review sessions with substantial repetition to enhance the retention of highly similar verbal knowledge.
6. Provide distributed practice in situations in which the learner has acquired the ability to distinguish clearly among stimuli or responses. Space review sessions over time for verbal material that students can comprehend without confusion.
7. Keep interfering tasks between learning sessions to a minimum. For instance, use a variety of types of learning experiences during the school day. Dissimilar learning tasks are not likely to produce interference.
8. Provide overlearning (e.g., additional trials beyond the initial acquisition). For example, after a student has demonstrated knowledge of the verbal information in a chapter, encourage additional review to enhance long-term retention.
9. Provide periodic reinforcement to maintain the motivation to respond. For example, periodically praise a student for maintaining newly acquired social skills.

TABLE B-3. Environmental Changes for Producing Decreases
in Rate of Performance

Changes in antecedent conditions
  1. Remove cues that may elicit the response to be reduced. For example, if a student
     creates disruption when he is sitting near a particular classmate, the students may be
     separated.
  2. Classically condition a new response to the cue eliciting the response to be reduced.
     This involves introducing an unconditioned stimulus that will produce a new response
     in the presence of the cue previously eliciting the undesirable response. For example,
     make a child laugh in the presence of cues previously associated with tantrum behav-
     ior.
  3. Increase response effort. For example, for a disruptive child, arrange for strenuous
     physical activity during recess.
  4. Increase a competing response. For instance, it may be difficult for a child to be disrup-
     tive if she is working ~n her assignment. Procedures that may promote working on the
     assignment (for example, reinforcment) may serve to eliminate disruption.
  5. Reinforce the absence of the response to be reduced. This, in effect, is the reinforcement
     of any behavior other than that which is the response to be eliminated. For instance,
     praise a child for not engaging in undesirable acts.
Changes in consequent conditions
  1. Implement extinction; that is, remove a contingent reinforcer maintaining the response
     to be reduced. If poor performance is maintained because of the extra attention re-
     ceived, eliminate the attention.
  2. Implement punishment by withdrawing a positive reinforcer not previously maintain-
     ing the response of conern. For example, if playing outdoors is a positive reinforcer,
     make its use contingent on the elimination of undesirable behavior.
  3. Implement punishment by adding an aversive stimulus following the behavior to be
     reduced. For example, to eliminate self-injurious behavior in a severely emotionally
     disturbed child, it may be necessary to use a mild form of physical punishment.
  4. Increase the strength of the aversive stimuli used in punishment. For instance, in
     working with a severely disturbed child who injures himself, it may in some cases be
     necessary to increase the degree of aversive stimulation.
  5. Add an aversive stimulus before the response to be punished has been completed. For
     instance, a verbal reprimand may be effective if given while a misdeed is occurring.
  6. Minimize the punishment delay following the response to be reduced. For example, a
     verbal reprimand will probably be more effective if it is given immediately following
     undesirable behavior than it will be after a substantial delay.
Changes in sequential conditions
  1. If punishment is to be used, provide a continuous schedule. In order for punishment to
     be maximally effective, it must be administered consistently. For instance, if a student is
     to be reprimanded for a given act, reprimands should be given every time the act
     occurs.
  2. Increase the number of occasions on which punishment is applied. For example, a
     teacher might help a student eliminate an undesirable mannerism by increasing the
     number of occasions on which the student displays the mannerism and an aversive
     consequence ensues.
  3. If extinction is used, provide a continuous schedule. The positive reinforcer that pre-
     viously followed behavior should never be introduced. If it is, the individual is, in
     effect, placed on a partial reinforcement schedule.

Appendix C

Case-Reporting Forms and Coding Instructions

This appendix contains two case-reporting forms used in a consultation research program at the University of Arizona. One illustrates the type of form used in coding cases involving social and/or emotional problems. The second form illustrates the type of form used in describing problems related to academic competence. In addition to the case-reporting forms, a set of instructions for coding the form is included.

A FORM FOR CODING CASES INVOLVING SOCIAL AND EMOTIONAL PROBLEMS

DO NOT WRITE IN THIS SPACE

I.D. _____

No. of previous cases _____

Child's name _____

Sex (circle one):

1—Girl 2—Boy 3—Group of girls 4—Group of boys 5—Mixed group

Community _____ Psychologist _____

School _____

Teacher _____

Child's birth date _____

Grade (circle one):

8—Kindergarten   9—Head start   Grades 1, 2, 3, 4, 5, 6, 7, 8, 9, 10, 11, 12

____—Special education (specify category)

Referred by (circle one; if more than one *actually* referred the case, circle applicable ones):

01—Child's teacher   10—Social worker
02—Other teacher   11—Counselor
03—Principal   12—Teacher's aide
05—Special-services coordinator   13—Nurse
08—Parent   37—Child (self-referral)
09—Psychologist   47—Other _____

Nature of problem:

Psychologist's remarks:

Referral date: ____ / ____ / ____
                Month   Day   Year

PII date: ____ / ____ / ____
           Month   Day   Year

Closing date: ____ / ____ / ____
               Month   Day   Year

Total conferences by psychologist _____
Total contacts with:

Teacher   _____   Parent involvement _____

Principal _____   Child   _____

Parent _____ Teacher's aide _____

Program _____ Social worker _____

Assistant _____ Counselor _____

Other _____

Case termination (circle *one* under "Case status" and then circle the *one* principal reason* for terminating the case under "Explanation of status"):

Case status (circle one):

1—Problem not defined—No PII—Case not opened (circle 2, 3, 4, 5, 6, 7, or 9, below)
2—Plan not implemented—No PAI or plan in PAI not implemented (circle *one* of 1–3 below)
3—Goal attained (circle 0 below)
4—Goal partially attained (circle 1, 3, 4, 5, 6, 7, or 8, below)
5—No progress toward goal (circle 1, 3, 4, 5, 6, 7, or 8, below)

Explanation of status (circle only *one*):

0—Plan successful
1—Procedure not affecting behavior as desired
2—Behavior improved without intervention
3—Change agent decision (will not take data, decides behavior not really a problem, etc.)
4—Child moved from class
5—Referred to other services
6—Irregular school attendance
7—School year ended
8—Revised goal strength or change of target behavior
9—Testing, staffing, consultation only (applies to No. 1 case status)

Problem Identification Interview (Adjustment Case)

Date: _____

1. a) What is the target behavior?
   Behavior _____
   Conditions (cues) _____
   _____

b) Circle or check below the *one* most applicable target classification (review your copy of the instructions for definitions):

01—Physical assault
02—Destruction
03—Construction
04—Disruption
11—Verbalization: general
12—Verbal dysfluency
13—Inappropriate verbalizations
14—Verbal: language
12—Group involvement
22—Task production
23—Following rules or directives
24—Interpersonal relationships
31—Personal habits
32—Honesty
41—Physical skill
42—Psychophysiological reaction
43—Physical dysfunction

2. Measurement procedures:
   a) Strength measure (circle *one*):

      1. Frequency

      2. Duration (specify): _____

      3. Quality: _____

      4. By-products of behavior: _____

   b) Recording technique:
      1. Event recording
      2. Duration recording
      3. Momentary time-sampling
      4. Interval recording

Problem Analysis Interview (Adjustment Case)

Date: _____
What is the desired strength of target behavior (goal)?

Modification plan

Is the child told about the plan?   ( ) yes   ( ) no
Who are the change agents?

1—Teacher	5—Parent
2—Counselor	6—Tutor(s)
3—Aide	7—Child
4—Psychologist	8—Principal

9—Other (specify) _____

Target behavior modification

Are any changes to be made in the "preceding environment"? If so, *what are the changes?*

Are any changes to be made in the "consequent environment"? If so, *what are the changes?* How will the plan be implemented?

1. Goal of plan is to (circle one):

   0—Maintain target behavior
   1—Increase target behavior
   2—Decrease target behavior

2. *Antecedent events* (refer to your copy of the instructions for definitions and circle all of the following that define the procedure previously described).
3. *Consequent events* (refer to your copy of the instructions for definitions and circle all of the following that define the procedure previously described).

    1—Add positive reinforcer
    2—Remove positive reinforcer
    3—Add an aversive stimuli
    4—Remove aversive stimuli
    5—Extinction
    6—DRO
    7—Counseling

4. Positive reinforcers used (list below any positive reinforcers that are mentioned in the plan you previously described; use the following list and give the numbers in the appropriate blanks):

    1—Consumable (M & M, dessert)
    2—Object (doll, rabbit)
    3—Activities (typing, playing football, graphing)
    4—Position, location (first in line for lunch)
    5—Physical (hug)
    6—Verbal (praise, verbal acknowledgment in front of class)
    7—Token (stars, chips)

    List the numbers of any positive reinforcers used, using numbers from the list above and listing no more than three; leave blank if not applicable.

    _____ _____ _____

    List the numbers of any aversive stimuli used, using numbers from the list above and listing no more than three; leave blank if not applicable.

    _____ _____ _____

    List the number of any reinforcers for which tokens are exchanged, using numbers from above and listing no more then three; leave blank if not applicable.

    _____ _____ _____

5. Graph data below or attach a separate graph.

A FORM FOR CODING CASES INVOLVING PROBLEMS RELATED TO ACADEMIC COMPETENCE

DO NOT WRITE IN THIS SPACE

I.D. _____

No. of previous cases _____

Child's name _____

Sex (circle one):

1—Girl 2—Boy 3—Group of girls 4—Group of boys 5—Mixed group

Community _____ Psychologist _____

School _____

Teacher _____

Child's birth date _____

Grade (circle one):

8—Kindergarten 9—Head start Grades 1, 2, 3, 4, 5, 6, 7, 8, 9, 10, 11, 12

_____—Special education (specify category)

Referred by (circle one; if more than one *actually* referred the case, circle applicable ones):

01—Child's teacher	10—Social worker
02—Other teacher	11—Counselor
03—Principal	12—Teacher's aide
05—Special-services coordinator	13—Nurse
08—Parent	37—Child (self-referral)
09—Psychologist	47—Other _____

Nature of problem:

Psychologist's remarks:

Referral date: ____ / ____ / ____
            Month   Day   Year

PII date: ____ / ____ / ____
         Month   Day   Year

Closing date: ____ / ____ / ____
             Month   Day   Year

Total conferences by psychologist _____
Total contacts with:

Teacher   _____   Parent involvement _____

Principal   _____   Child   _____

Parent   _____   Teacher's aide   _____

Program   _____   Social worker   _____

Assistant   _____   Counselor   _____

                                   Other   _____

Case termination (circle *one* under "Case status" and then circle the *one* principal reason for terminating the case under "Explanation of status"):

Case status (circle one):

1—Problem not defined—No PII—Case not opened (circle 2, 3, 4, 5, 6, 7, or 9, below)

2—Plan not implemented—No PAI or plan in PAI not implemented (circle *one* of 1–8 below)

3—Goal attained (circle 0 below)

4—Goal partially attained (circle 1, 3, 4, 5, 6, 7, or 8, below)

5—No progress toward goal (circle 1, 3, 4, 5, 6, 7, or 8, below)

Explanation of status (circle *only one*):

0—Plan successful

1—Procedure not affecting behavior as desired

2—Behavior improved without intervention

3—Change agent decision (will not take data, decides behavior not really a problem, etc.)

4—Child moved from class

5—Referred to other services

6—Irregular school attendance

7—School year ended

8—Revised goal strength or change of target behavior

9—Testing, staffing, consultation only (applies to No. 1 case status)

Problem Identification Interview (Adjustment Case)

Date: _____

1. a) What is the target behavior? _____
   Major area (circle *one* appropriate number):

   1—Reading
   2—Writing
   3—Arithmetic
   4—Concept learning
   5—Other

   Content (circle *one* or two—no more—numbers most appropriate for primary target behavior):

1—Letters
2—Words
3—Numbers
4—Shapes
5—Objects
6—Concepts (position, directions)
7—Colors

Target response (circle *one* number identifying the desired response to the above content subarea; review the instructions for all that is included in each category):

1—Labeling
2—Reproducing
3—Serial reproducing
4—Performing combinations
5—Comprehension

6—Discrimination and matching

7—Generalization

2. For subgoals in intellectual skills cases, give the numbers describing them below, use the numbers listed above (leave blank those not needed):

> Subgoal 1 _____   _____
>
> Subgoal 2 _____   _____
>
> Subgoal 3 _____   _____

(Part 2 may not be completed until the problem analysis interview, but it is included here for convenient reference to numbers.)

3. Measurement procedures:

Strength: 1—Frequency   Conditions: 1—Event recording
         2—Duration   2—Duration recording
           (specify) _____   3—Momentary time-
         3—Quality   sampling
         4—By-products of   4—Interval recording
           behavior

Problem Analysis Interview (Academic)

Date: _____

Goal: What is the desired strength of the target behavior?

Modification plan

Is child told about the plan?   ( ) yes   ( ) no

Who is (are) the change agent(s)? Circle no more than three:

1—Teacher   5—Parent

2—Counselor   6—Tutor(s)

3—Aide   7—Child

4—Psychologist   8—Principal

                   9—Other (specify) _____

Teaching procedure for primary target behavior (please describe, giving stimuli used, conditions of presentation, instructions, task of child, reinforcement used, etc.):

For intellectual skills cases, use subgoal sheets to describe the teaching procedures of subgoals.

Problem Analysis Interview (Academic Skill)

Subgoal #_____

Subgoal conditions: Given _____

Subgoal behavior: The child will be able to _____

_____

Subgoal strength: At a level of _____
    Training procedure (describe, giving stimuli conditions of presentation, instructions, reinforcement, task of child, etc.):

		( ) day
		( ) week
		( ) hour
When does training occur?: _____ times per		( ) other (specify)

(Use as many of these sheets as there are subgoals. Let Subgoal 1 be the subgoal initially taught.)

1. Goal of remediation is to (circle one):

0—Maintain behavior
1—Increase behavior
2—Decrease behavior

2. Teaching procedures for primary target *and* all subgoals (if there are any) will be "lumped together" for coding. Please circle below numbers most applicable to coding the teaching procedures you described on the previous page(s). Refer to your copy of the instructions for definitions of the terms.

a) Antecedent events (circle all, remembering to combine teaching procedures for primary target and any subgoals):

1—Modeling
2—Prompting
3—Establishing, altering, or removing an S^D
4—Physical response guidance
5—Contingent application of hypothesized reinforcer
6—Task alteration
7—Other

b) Response types used in teaching procedures (circle any appropriate numbers):

1—Labeling
2—Reproducing
3—Serial reproducing
4—Performing combinations
5—Comprehension
6—Discrimination and matching
7—Generalization
8—Other

c) Consequent events (circle all used):

1—Add positive reinforcer
2—Remove positive reinforcer
3—Add an aversive stimulus
4—Remove aversive stimuli
5—Extinction
6—DRO

7—Counseling

8—Other

3. Reinforcers used:

1—Consumable (M & M, dessert)

2—Object (doll)

3—Activities (typing)

4—Position, location (first in line for lunch)

5—Physical (hug)

6—Verbal (praise)

7—Tokens (stars, chips)

8—Other

List the numbers of any positive reinforcers used, using numbers from the list above; leave blank if not applicable.

_____   _____   _____

List the numbers of any aversive stimuli used, using numbers from the list above; leave blank if not applicable.

_____   _____   _____

List the numbers of any reinforcers for which tokens are exchanged using numbers from above and listing no more than three; leave blank if not applicable.

_____   _____   _____

4. Graph data below or attach separate sheets.

INSTRUCTIONS FOR CODING CASE-REPORTING FORMS

Adjustment Cases

Referral Section

The first section of the coding form is self-explanatory, but the following remarks may be helpful:

1. If the case is a group problem, for small group of children (5 or less), list names; for a whole classroom, give the teacher's name instead of the children's names.
2. Under "Nature of problem," describe the problem as the teacher originally described it (or let the teacher use this form for referral).

3. When counting contacts and conferences, count a group conference (for example, a conference with a teacher, a child, and a parent) as 1 under "Total conferences." However, this same conference would be counted as 1 *each* under teacher, child, and parent in the "Total contacts" section. Therefore, all "contacts" totaled may be greater than "total conferences."

4. Under "Case status," please follow the guidelines for choosing an "Explanation of status." Certain "explanations" don't fit with certain case status designations. For example, "No progress toward goal" and "Plan successful" are not compatible descriptions.

Problem Identification Interview

1. a) Target behavior: Describe the behavior as completely as you can. Specify the *particular* behavior being focused on, as well as any condition or cues applicable.
Examples: Behavior—hitting
Examples: Conditions (cues)—during recess
Examples: Behavior—tying shoes
Examples: Conditions (cues)—without teacher assistance once each day

   b) Target class: Please study carefully the examples below and circle the number of the classification *most* applicable to the target behavior. Please avoid allowing "disruption," "following rules or directives," and "group involvement" to become catchall categories.
Target class (what is being recorded):
01—Physical assault (hitting, kicking, or other aggressive behavior directed toward another)
02—Destruction (burning, cutting, smashing, tearing, etc.)
03—Construction (making something, assembling puzzles, picture completion)
04—Disruption (target behavior tends to disrupt the ongoing activities and *is not appropriately classified elsewhere*)
11—Verbalization: general (increase or decrease amount of talking)
12—Verbal dysfluency (stuttering, stammering)
13—Inappropriate verbalizations (unnecessary yelling, screaming, whispering, swearing, bragging, crying)
14—Verbal: language (speaking English as opposed to another language)
21—Group involvement (physical location, social interaction, not participating in group task, hanging onto adults, stay-

ing in room and/or committees, participating in committees)

22—Task production (*individual*: attending to task, completing assignments, change way of completing task, doing more arithmetic problems, etc.)

23—Following rules or directives (given before a behavior occurs; latency in doing something: time it takes to line up, etc.; obedience, doing as told, not cleaning up after committee)

24—Interpersonal relationships (consideration for others, good sportsmanship, respect for others)

31—Personal habits (toilet training, nose picking, masturbation, inappropriate body movements; child can do something but does not, for example, clothes hanging, tongue hanging out, wearing glasses)

32—Honesty (lying, stealing)

41—Physical skill (cannot or has not learned to do something: bike riding, clothes hanging, eating correctly, etc.)

42—Psychophysiological reaction (rash, ulcer, vomiting)

43—Physical dysfunction (poor eyesight, hearing problem, cerebral palsy)

2. Measurement procedures: Circle appropriate numbers to tell how the data will be recorded.

Problem Analysis Interview

Remember to fill in the date!

When describing the modification plan, remember to describe it in enough detail so that another psychologist could use it for ideas (from a data bank!).

1. Goal of plan: This part is self-explanatory. To code the modification plan you must think of the procedures as either occurring *before* the target behavior or *after* the target behavior.

2. Antecedent events: Code the parts of the plan that take place before the target behavior occurs. Study the following list of antecedent events, their definitions, and examples. Choose any that apply to this case. If none apply, don't circle anything under antecedent events. If some apply, circle the appropriate numbers. Several portions of the plan can be coded the same way, for example, "Tell Johnny to stay in his seat during committee, and let him sit by Susie (whom he has been visiting) during committee." There are two changes in the preceding environment, but both are establishing or altering an S^D. Number 3 should be circled and only once.

1—Modeling. Give the complete response in words. Say, "This is an A." Act out the complete response. Demonstrate physically.

2—Prompting. Give a hint or a partial response. Draw attention to part of the stimulus: "This word is an a . . ." for *apple.* Show a picture of an apple. Write the word *apple* to get the verbal response *apple.*)

3—Establishing, altering, or removing S^D (discrimination stimulus). Ask the child to do something: "What is this letter?" "Throw the ball." Give the signal for a response: Point to a child to signal him or her to be quiet. Change a child's seat so he can't talk to a another student. Have the teacher sit next to the child to discourage hitting.

4—Physical response guidance. Help the child make the response. For example, take the child's hand and form the letter with him.

5—Contingent application of hypothesized reinforcer. Give a positive reinforcer before the response occurs. For example, hug and attend to Susie when she comes to school in hopes of preventing her from wanting to leave the classroom.

6—Task alteration. Change the stimulus, change the number of responses, reorder the presentation of stimuli, break a large task into several smaller ones.

3. Consequent events: Now code the parts of the plan that occur after the target response, using the same instructions as for antecedent events.

1—Add positive reinforcer. Reward the response. Praise, candy, and tokens are examples of reinforcers.

2—Remove positive reinforcer. Take away a positive reinforcer. Whenever Susie grabs from another student, she will not be permitted to play with the doll. When Joe hits, he will not be allowed to go to recess. Time-out is the removal of the child from an activity.

3—Add an aversive stimulus. Verbal reprimands are an example.

4—Remove aversive stimuli. Take away something negative that was there *before* the modification plan. To increase Susie's talking, stop the other children from teasing her when she talks.

5—Extinction. Ignore the response or take away positive reinforcement directly related to the response. The teacher stops putting her arm around a child while correcting him. She doesn't answer the child when a question is asked in a whining tone.

6—DRO (differential reinforcement of other behavior). Reinforce after a period of time in which the response did not occur. Johnny can paint at 10:30 if he has not hit all morning.

7—Counseling. This category includes discussions of the problem with the child where not codable in any other way.

4. Positive reinforcers and aversive stimuli used: If no reinforcers or aversive stimuli are mentioned in your plan, leave this section blank. If positive reinforcers were used, take the numbers from the list and put them (no more than three numbers) in the blanks under positive reinforcers. If aversive stimuli were used, choose numbers from the same list, and put them in the blanks under aversive stimuli. If the child was given tokens, indicate what the tokens were exchanged for to reinforce the child. List these numbers (still from the same list) in the blanks under reinforcers for which the tokens were exchanged.
5. Now graph the data. Remember to separate clearly baseline, intervention, and postintervention data. Clearly label the graph. Include what you are counting (dates, response strength units, etc.).

INSTRUCTIONS FOR CODING CASE-REPORTING FORMS

Academic Cases

Referral Section

The first section of the coding form is self-explanatory, but the following remarks may be helpful:

1. If the case is a group problem: for a small group of children (5 or less), list names; for a whole classroom, give the teacher's name instead of the children's names.
2. Under "Nature of Problem," describe the problem as the teacher originally described it (or let the teacher use this form for referral).
3. When counting contacts and conferences, count a group conference (for example, a conference with a teacher, a child, and a parent) as 1 under "Total Conferences." However, this same conference would be counted as 1 *each* under teacher, child, and parent in the "Total Contacts" section. Therefore, all "contacts" totaled may be greater than "total conferences."
4. Under "Case Status," please follow the guidelines for choosing an "Explanation of Status." Certain "explanations" don't fit with certain case status designations. For example, "No progress toward goal" and "plan successful" are not compatible descriptions.

Problem Identification Interview

1. Classify the target behavior by circling one number from each of the following: major area, content, and target response.

a) Major area·
1—Reading (letter identification, labeling words, reading out loud, word comprehension, etc.)
2—Writing (letter reproduction, etc.)
3—Arithmetic (addition, subtraction, set theory, etc.)
4—Concept learning (left-right/top-bottom, if not subgoal for letter identification; the concept of *dog*, etc.)
5—Other (everything else: sequencing, etc.)
b) Content is self-explanatory. Always circle only one unless a combined content is treated as one case, for example, letter and number recognition.
c) Target response: Circle only one number. Anytime two responses are handled, the target response should be two cases. We use these terms in the following way:
1—Labeling (identifying and recognizing: "What is this letter?" "Which letter is *A*?)
2—Reproducing (copying: "Say *cat*." "Write an *a*.)
3—Serial reproducing (saying the alphabet, counting to *10*, telling a story in order, spelling, etc.)
4—Performing combinations (adding, subtracting, etc.)
5—Comprehension ("What was the story you just read about?" "What is a *dog*?")
6—Discrimination and matching (use when the target is obviously the ability to discriminate or match rather than to label correctly or identify)
7—Generalization (use when the target is to have the child learn a concept and to be able to apply it to new examples of the same concept)
2. When the case includes subgoals (academic skills cases) identify them in the same way you identified the primary target. Insert the appropriate numbers in the blanks. As the subgoals are in the same major area as the primary goal, there is no need to recode the area. Code only the content and the response.
3. Circle the appropriate numbers, one under measurement procedures and one under conditions to describe how the data will be recorded.

Problem Analysis Interview

Remember the date.
The first section here is self-explanatory. Describe the goal and the modification plan. When describing the teaching procedure, be as complete as possible. Give the form of the stimuli, directions, child's response,

and so on. Remember that this description is what might be included in the data bank.

If there are no subgoals, omit the subgoal section. Use a separate form for each subgoal.

Describe the teaching procedure and the response desired from the child as completely as possible.

1. Goal of remediation: Circle the appropriate goal designation.
2. To code the teaching procedure, read over the descriptions of the procedures on *all* the primary target and subgoal sheets, and use the following definitions to choose any applicable antecedent events, response types, and/or consequent events to circle. Circle, on the report forms, the numbers of any and all that apply to the teaching procedures described.

   a) Antecedent events:

      1—Modeling. Give the complete rsponse in words: "This is an A." Write the word *apple* to get the verbal response *apple.* Act out or demonstrate the complete response.

      2—Prompting. Give a hint or a partial response, draw attention to part of the stimulus or show a picture of a stimulus.

      3—Establishing, altering, or removing S^D (discriminative stimulus). Ask the child to do something: "What is this letter?" "Throw the ball." Give a signal for a response: Point to the child to signal him to be quiet. Change the child's seat so she cannot talk to a best friend. Have the teacher sit next to the child to discourage hitting.

      4—Physical response guidance. Help the child perform the response. For example, take child's hand and form the letter with him.

      5—Contingent application of hypothesized reinforcer. Give a positive reinforcer before the response occurs. For example, hug and attend to Susie when she comes to school in hopes of preventing her from wanting to leave the classroom.

      6—Task alteration. Change the stimulus, change the number of responses, reorder the presentation of stimuli, break a large task into several smaller ones.

   b) Response types used in teaching procedures:

      1—Labeling (identifying and recognizing: "What is this letter?" "Which letter is *A*?")

      2—Reproducing (copying: "Say *cat.*" "Write an *a.*")

      3—Serial reproducing (saying the alphabet, counting to *10*, telling a story in order, spelling, etc.)

      4—Performing combinations (adding, subtracting, etc.)

      5—Comprehension ("What was the story you just read about?" "What is a dog?")

6—Discrimination and matching (use when the target is obviously the ability to discriminate or match rather than to label correctly or identify).

7—Generalization (use when the target is to have the child learn a concept and to be able to apply it to new examples of the same concept).

c) Consequent events:

1—Add positive reinforcer. Reward the response. Praise, candy, and tokens are examples of reinforcers.

2—Remove positive reinforcer. Take away a positive reinforcer. Whenever Susie grabs from another student, she will not be permitted to play with the doll. When Joe hits, he will not be allowed to go to recess.

3—Add an aversive stimulus. Verbal reprimands are an example.

4—Remove aversive stimuli. Take away something negative that was there *before* the modification plan. To increase Susie's talking, stop the other children from teasing her when she talks.

5—Extinction. Ignore the response or take away positive reinforcement directly related to the response. The teacher stops putting her arm around a child while correcting him. She doesn't answer the child when a question is asked in a whining tone.

6—DRO (differential reinforcement of other behavior). Reinforce after a period of time in which the response did not occur. Johnny can paint at 10:30 if he has not hit all morning.

7—Counseling. This category includes discussions of the problem with the child where not codable in any other way.

3. Reinforcers and aversive stimuli used: If no reinforcers or aversive stimuli are mentioned in your plan, leave this section blank. If positive reinforcers were used, take the numbers from the list and put them (no more than three) in the blanks under positive reinforcers. If aversive stimuli were used, choose numbers from the same list and put them in the blanks under aversive stimuli. List the numbers of any reinforcers that were available through token exchange.

4. Now graph you data. Remember to separate clearly baseline, intervention, and postintervention data. Clearly label the graph. Include what you are counting (dates, response strength units, etc.). Be sure to line up any subgoal data correctly with primary target data, showing any transfer.

Appendix D

Evaluation of Psychoeducational Services in a Local School District

Appendix D contains a report[1] prepared for the Tombstone Public Schools illustrating the evaluation of consultation services rendered by two half-time consultants to a school district through a consultative problem-solving system. The report was prepared by Drs. Margaret Ronstadt and Richard Koussa. Computer programming used in the analysis of data for the report was done by Dr. Sara Currin.

PROGRAM EVALUATION

The evaluation component of this past year's psychoeducational services at Tombstone Public Schools will be discussed in the following areas: program effectiveness, program efficiency, and program implementation. Behavioral objectives data are included under academic cases involving alterations in teaching procedures.

The primary purpose of this evaluation is the planning of services for the following year.

Program Effectiveness

Information related to the effectiveness of the program is presented in Table D-1. This table describes the effect that psychoeducational services

---

[1]This report is reprinted here through the kind permission of Joel T. Tudor, Superintendent, Tombstone Public Schools.

TABLE D-1. Status of Cases on Termination

School	1	2	3	4	Total
Number of cases	52	9	22	209	292
No problem identification interview					
Change agent decision	1	0	1	5	7
Percentage	.02	0.00	.05	.02	.02
Child moved from class	2	0	0	1	3
Percentage	.04	0.00	0.00	.00	.01
Referred to other services	1	0	0	2	3
Percentage	.02	0.00	0.00	.01	.01
School year ended	0	0	1	0	1
Percentage	0.00	0.00	.05	0.00	.00
Testing, staffing evaluation, or counseling	14	5	3	43	65
Percentage	.27	.56	.14	.21	.22
Plan not implemented					
Behavior improved without intervention	1	0	0	8	9
Percentage	.02	0.00	0.00	.04	.03
Change agent decision	2	1	2	13	18
Percentage	.04	.11	.09	.06	.06
Child moved from class	0	1	3	4	8
Percentage	0.00	.11	.14	.02	.03
Referred to other services	1	0	0	4	5
Percentage	.02	0.00	0.00	.02	.02
School year ended	1	0	0	2	3
Percentage	.02	0.00	0.00	.01	.01
Goal attained					
Plan successful	24	1	10	105	140
Percentage	.46	.11	.45	.50	.48
Revised goal strength or change of goal	0	0	0	0	0
Percentage	0.00	0.00	0.00	0.00	0.00
Goal partially attained					
Plan not affecting behavior as desired	1	0	1	10	12
Percentage	.02	0.00	.05	.05	.04
Change agent decision	0	0	0	5	5
Percentage	0.00	0.00	0.00	.02	.02
Child moved from class	0	0	1	0	1
Percentage	0.00	0.00	0.05	0.00	.00
School year ended	0	0	0	2	2
Percentage	0.00	0.00	0.00	.01	.01
Revised goal strength or changed goal	1	0	0	2	3
Percentage	.02	0.00	0.00	.01	.01
No progress made toward goal					
Plan not affecting behavior as desired	1	0	0	2	3
Percentage	.02	0.00	0.00	.01	.01
Change agent decision	0	0	0	1	1
Percentage	0.00	0.00	0.00	0.00	0.00
School year ended	1	0	0	0	1
Percentage	.02	0.00	0.00	0.00	.00

had on the referred cases during the 1974–1975 school year. All possible alternatives for a case—including cases for which no problem was identified, or no plan implemented, in addition to those cases in which the goal was attained or partially attained—are presented. The various reasons for the status of the case are also included. Such alternatives as behavior improved without intervention and change agent decision are a part of this category.

Although consultation services included responsibilities for testing children for possible placement in special-education programs, Table D-1 shows that a relatively small percentage of the total services provided

TABLE D-2. Successful Status by Case Type

School	1	2	3	4	Total
Adjustment	19	1	9	112	141
Goal attained					
Plan successful	19	1	9	98	127
Percentage	1.00	1.00	1.00	.88	.90
Goal partially attained					
Plan not affecting behavior as desired	0	0	0	10	10
Percentage	0.00	0.00	0.00	.09	.07
Revised goal strength or goal change	0	0	0	2	2
Percentage	0.00	0.00	0.00	.02	.01
No progress toward goal					
Plan not affecting behavior as desired	0	0	0	2	2
Percentage	0.00	0.00	0.00	.02	.01
Academic—Teaching procedures	4	0	2	7	13
Goal attained					
Plan successful	3	0	1	7	11
Percentage	.75	0.00	.50	1.00	.85
Goal partially attained					
Plan not affecting behavior as desired	1	0	1	0	2
Percentage	.25	0.00	.50	0.00	.15
Academic—Intellectual skills	4	0	0	0	4
Goal attained					
Plan successful	2	0	0	0	2
Percentage	.50	0.00	0.00	0.00	.50
Goal partially attained					
Revised goal strength or goal change	1	0	0	0	1
Percentage	.25	0.00	0.00	0.00	.25
No progress toward goal					
Plan not affecting behavior as desired	1	0	0	0	1
Percentage	.25	0.00	0.00	0.00	.25

called for testing and relating staffing and evaluation services. The "No problem identification—testing, staffing evaluation, or counseling" classification included 27% of the 52 cases reported in Table D-1 for School 1, 56% of the 9 cases for School 2 (the junior high school), 14% of the 22 cases reported for School 3 (the high school), and 21% of the 209 cases reported for School 4. The primary purpose of the testing program was to classify children for special-education services.

The percentage of cases processed through all phases of the consultation process is presented in Table D-2. The goal-attained rate for adjustment cases was 100% for Schools 1, 2, and 3. For School 4, this rate was 88%. The average across all was 90%. The goal-attained rate for academic—teaching procedures (cases involving a change in teacher strategy) was 85%. Only a very limited number of intellectual skills cases were reported during the past year. Of the cases reported, 50% were concluded successfully.

It does seem apparent, however, especially for adjustment cases, that if a problem is identified, a plan implemented, and the plan evaluated, the plan will be successful.

Efficiency of the Psychoeducational Services Program

Information related to psychologists' contacts is presented in Table D-3. School 4 generated the largest number of contacts (1,106) and also the largest number of cases (208). School 1 had a fewer number of contacts (180) and cases (52), followed by the high school (79 contacts and 22 cases),

TABLE D-3. Psychologists' Contacts

School	1	2	3	4	Total
Number of cases reporting contacts[a]	52	9	22	208	291
Minimum conferences[b] per case	1	1	1	1	1
Maximum conferences per case	8	11	10	18	18
Total conferences	180	31	79	1,106	1,396
Teacher contacts	97	15	7	396	515
Principal contacts	1	1	15	23	40
Parent contacts	11	1	2	53	67
Counselor contacts	0	1	9	0	10
Parent involvement contacts	1	0	0	1	2
Child contacts	47	6	31	481	565
Teacher aide contacts	8	0	0	57	65
Social worker contacts	0	0	1	0	1
Other contacts	16	6	23	91	136

[a]Contact is an individual within a conference.
[b]Conference may represent several contacts with one or more individuals present.

and the junior high (31 contacts and 9 cases). School 4 is serviced by two psychological specialists one day a week, which may account for the greater number of cases and subsequent contacts, whereas both the junior high and high school request psychological services through the counselor.

The majority of the contacts were with teachers and children. It may be expected that, in all situations, the teacher is the one most contacted by the psychologists. This was not the case at School 4, where 481 contacts were with children and 396 contacts were with teachers. A similar situation was evident at the high school, where children were contacted in 31 instances and teachers in only 7. Overall, teacher contacts were slightly lower (515) than child contacts (565).

A total of 1396 conferences were reported, an extremely high number when compared with conferences with a traditional psychologist and also when compared with conferences from the previous year (554). This information reflects the increased availability of the psychologist to work not only with the educational personnel but also with various others (e.g., parents, children, and principals) who seek help.

Information concerning the amount of time it took to process a case as well as the amount of time a teacher waited for an initial interview after a referral was made is an additional aspect of program efficiency. The days represented in Tables D-4 and D-5 include weekends, holidays, so for every 7 days, one should subtract approximately 2 days to get an accurate representation of the actual school-day time.

As shown in Table D-4, the longest time from the referral to the first interview for adjustment cases was 28 days at School 1, 21 at the junior high school, 8 at the high school, and 28 at School 4. At all schools, except the junior high, the median was 0, which means that cases were serviced

TABLE D-4. Time from Referral to Problem Identification Interview

School	1	2	3	4	Total
Adjustment	24	2	15	140	181
Minimum	0	7	0	0	7
Maximum	28	21	8	28	28
Median	0.0	14.0	0.0	0.0	0.0
Academic—Teaching procedures	6	1	2	11	20
Minimum	0	0	· 0	0	0
Maximum	7	0	14	28	28
Median	0.0	0.0	7.0	7.0	3.5
Academic—Subskills	4	0	0	0	4
Minimum	13	0	0	0	13
Maximum	27	0	0	0	27
Median	17.5	0.0	0.0	0.0	0.0

Table D-5. Time from Referral to Closing

School	1	2	3	4	Total
Adjustment	20	1	10	120	151
Minimum	0	42	0	0	42
Maximum	56	42	49	105	105
Median	21.0	42.0	19.5	28.0	24.5
Academic—Teaching procedures	5	0	2	7	14
Minimum	21	0	30	30	21
Maximum	57	0	48	49	57
Median	21.0	0.0	39.0	35.0	35.0
Academic—Subskills	4	0	0	0	4
Minimum	35	0	0	0	35
Maximum	55	0	0	0	55
Median	55.0	0.0	0.0	0.0	35.0

the day they were referred, a statistic that would be very difficult to improve.

For teaching procedure cases in the academic area, the longest a teacher waited was 28 days, and the median for all schools was 3.5 days, indicating again that cases were serviced very quickly.

Time from referral to closing (Table D-5) also indicates how quickly the psychologist serviced cases. For adjustment cases, the longest case was 56 days at School 1, 42 days at the junior high, 49 at the high school, and 105 at School 4. The medians, however, are extremely low and show that, generally, cases were serviced (from referral to closing) within an average of 24.5 days.

Academic cases, which generally take longer than adjustment cases, were usually serviced (median days) within 5 weeks.

Program Implementation

The information presented in the tables under program implementation includes the type of case referred (Table D-6), the type of adjustment (Table D-7) or academic problem referred (Tables D-8 and D-9), the type of intervention procedures implemented (Tables D-10, D-11, D-12, and D-13), the types of positive reinforcers and aversive stimuli used (Table D-14), data collection (Tables D-15 and D-16), and the source of referral (Table D-17).

The types of cases most often referred in each school are presented in Table D-6. The great majority of cases fell in the adjustment category (181), representing achievement of the school district's objective of emphasizing service to children with adjustment problems. This number also represents

TABLE D-6. Type of Case Referred

School	1	2	3	4	Total
Total cases	52	9	22	209	292
Adjustment	24	2	15	140	181
Percentage	.46	.22	.68	.67	.62
Academic—Target conditions	6	1	2	11	20
Percentage	.12	.11	.09	.05	.07
Academic—Intellectual skills	4	0	0	0	4
Percentage	.08	0.00	0.00	0.00	.01
Behavioral objectives—Adjustment	0	0	0	0	0
Percentage	0.00	0.00	0.00	0.00	0.00
Behavioral objectives—Academic	0	0	0	0	0
Percentage	0.00	0.00	0.00	0.00	0.00
Testing for special education	18	6	5	58	87
Percentage	.35	.67	.23	.28	.30

an increase of over 100% from the previous year in the number of cases falling in this category. A decrease in the proportion of academic and behavioral-objective cases is also evident when one compares this year's data with those from the previous year. Testing for special education comprised a total of 87 cases.

Table D-7 indicates the various types of adjustment problems referred. They are described under the following headings:

Physical assault: The referred behavior was usually reported as aggressiveness toward another that, more specifically, included hitting, kicking, biting, pushing, and so on.

Destruction: Behaviors in this category include burning, cutting, smashing, and tearing.

Disruption: The behavior of the child serves to disrupt the ongoing activity in the classroom or elsewhere. Behaviors in this class cannot be classified under another more specific class of behaviors, such as destruction, physical assault, or verbalizations.

Verbalization—General: This involves an increase or decrease of general verbalization (e.g., talking). A modification of specific forms of verbalization (e.g., stuttering) would not be included within this category.

Verbal dysfluency: Behaviors such as stuttering or stammering would be classified as verbal dysfluency.

Inappropriate verbalizations: Classified here would be such undesirable or unnecessary verbalizations as yelling, swearing, whispering, screaming, bragging, and crying.

Group involvement (social participation): This is a classification of behaviors that would include not participating in a group task, hanging onto

TABLE D-7. Type of Adjustment Problems Referred

School	1	2	3	4	Total
Total cases	24	2	15	140	181
Physical assault	1	0	0	22	23
Percentage	4	0	0	15	12
Destruction	0	0	1	0	1
Percentage	0	0	6	0	0
Construction	1	0	0	5	6
Percentage	4	0	0	3	3
Disruption	5	1	0	26	32
Percentage	20	50	0	18	17
Verbalization—General	1	0	2	2	5
Percentage	4	0	13	1	2
Verbal dysfluency	1	0	0	1	2
Percentage	4	0	0	0	1
Inappropriate verbalizations	0	0	3	23	26
Percentage	0	0	20	16	14
Group involvement	2	0	4	7	13
Percentage	8	0	26	5	7
Task production	5	1	1	33	40
Percentage	20	50	6	23	22
Following rules or directives	2	0	0	5	7
Percentage	8	0	0	3	3
Interpersonal relationships	0	0	3	8	11
Percentage	0	0	20	5	6
Personal habits	4	0	0	2	6
Percentage	16	0	0	1	3
Honesty	0	0	0	5	5
Percentage	0	0	0	3	2
Psychophysiological reaction	2	0	1	4	7
Percentage	8	0	6	2	3

adults, not staying in the room and/or location, and not socially interacting (includes leaving room or building and being overly attentive to an adult).

Task production: This category involves the individual behaviors of attending to a task, completing an assignment, changing the way of attacking a task, doing additional tasks, and so on.

Following rules or directives: This category involves requests by a change agent (e.g., teacher) for a child to perform various types of behavior.

Interpersonal relationships: This category involves behaviors such as consideration for others, good sportsmanship, and respect for other people and for their property.

Personal habits: Toilet training, nose picking, masturbation, and inappropriate body movements are examples of this category. Responses that a child can perform but does not are also included (e.g., clothes hanging, tongue hanging out, or wearing glasses). Obviously, these are specific to a particular child.

Honesty: Classified here would be behaviors such as lying or stealing.

Psychophysiological reaction (e.g., rash, ulcer, vomiting): With respect to type of adjustment problem referred (Table D-7), the largest single category was task production (22%), which represents a concern on the part of the teacher about students who are not producing work up to capacity. The second largest category was disruption (17%), followed by inappropriate verbalizations (14%) and physical assault (12%). The remainder of the adjustment categories had less than 10% of the total cases in each.

Tables D-8 and D-9 present the major area of academic problems. These two tables list the major educational areas in which cases were referred, and an additional specification of the content and the response required of the child.

Major area categories include:

Reading: This item covers such categories as word recognition, letter recognition, reading skills (e.g., comprehension and oral reading).

Writing: The child was referred because of difficulties with the physical response (with or without a model) of writing (cursive or printing).

Arithmetic: The referral was made in an effort to help the child with arithmetic concepts and computation (e.g., addition, subtraction, and set theory).

Concept learning: This category includes concepts such as left-right and top-bottom (if not a subgoal for letter identification).

Other: Everything else that is not included in the previous categories is found here (e.g., sequencing).

Academic difficulties are specified further by the content areas. More than one type of content can be specified for one case (the titles are self-explanatory): "Letters," "Words," "Numbers," "Shapes," and "Concepts."

Target response categories specify the performance required to show that the child is learning the specified goal behavior. More than one type of behavior may be required in the task:

Labeling: The child is required to verbalize the name of an object or concept. This category includes such behaviors as identifying.

Reproducing: The target behavior is the verbal or manipulative production of a sound, an object, a label, a word, a letter, or some other item that has been presented or modeled previously.

Performing combinations: The child is required to combine two or more elements to obtain a product. The target response generally occurs within the arithmetic area. However, it might also be listed in the area of reading.

Comprehension: The target response is a verbal or written response to a question or directive that shows whether the child has synthesized the material presented.

Discrimination and matching: The target response is selecting a correct response from two alternative stimuli. When matching, the child is required to find another example of the first stimulus presented.

The number of cases referred under academic problems involving alterations in teaching procedures (Table D-8) indicates that the psychologist was involved primarily in the area of reading (40% of the cases) followed by the area of arithmetic (25% of the cases). Both the writing and concept-learning areas comprised 15% of the cases, and the "other" category con-

TABLE D-8. Type of Academic Problems Referred
(Cases Involving Alterations in Teaching Procedures)

School	1	2	3	4	Total
Total cases	6	1	2	11	20
Major area					
Reading	2	0	1	5	8
Percentage	33	0	50	45	40
Writing	0	1	0	2	3
Percentage	0	100	0	18	15
Arithmetic	3	0	0	2	5
Percentage	50	0	0	18	25
Concept learning	1	0	0	2	3
Percentage	16	0	0	18	15
Other	0	0	1	0	1
Percentage	0	0	50	0	5
Content					
Letters	0	0	0	5	5
Percentage	0	0	0	45	25
Words	2	1	1	3	7
Percentage	33	100	50	27	35
Numbers	1	0	0	2	3
Percentage	16	0	0	18	15
Shapes	1	0	0	0	1
Percentage	16	0	0	0	5
Concepts	2	0	1	4	7
Percentage	33	0	50	36	35
Target response					
Labeling	2	0	0	4	6
Percentage	33	0	0	36	30
Reproducing	0	1	0	4	5
Percentage	0	100	0	3	25
Performing combinations	2	0	0	2	4
Percentage	33	0	0	18	20
Comprehension	1	0	2	0	3
Percentage	16	0	100	0	15
Discrimination and matching	1	0	0	1	2
Percentage	16	0	0	9	10

tained only 5% of the cases. When these data are compared with data from the previous year, it appears that the psychologist has been involved in a greatest number of areas.

A very limited number of cases (only 4) were referred under "Academic Problems—Intellectual Skills" (Table D-9). An endeavor should be made to increase teachers' awareness of the psychologist's expertise in this area. Objectives and methods should be developed to increase the number of referrals. We are not recognizing the important need to teach children the skills that will help them to cope with intellectual tasks.

The types of procedures used to increase behavior and decrease behavior are presented in Tables D-10 and D-11. The procedures used are described as antecedent and consequent events. The following classifications were used for antecedent events (Tables D-10, D-11, D-12, and D-13):

Modeling: The complete response required for the child is provided (verbal or physical), for example, "This is an *A.*"

Prompting: This category involves a hint or partial response or drawing attention to a part of the stimulus: "This is *a* . . . " (*apple*). This category also involves showing a picture of an apple or writing the word *apple* to get the required verbal response of *apple*.

TABLE D-9. Type of Academic
Problems Referred—Intellectual

School	1	2	3	4	Total
Total cases	4	0	0	0	4
Major area					
Reading	1	0	0	0	1
Percentage	25	0	0	0	25
Arithmetic	1	0	0	0	1
Percentage	25	0	0	0	25
Other	2	0	0	0	2
Percentage	50	0	0	0	50
Content					
Letters	3	0	0	0	3
Percentage	75	0	0	0	75
Words	2	0	0	0	2
Percentage	50	0	0	0	50
Numbers	1	0	0	0	1
Percentage	25	0	0	0	25
Target response					
Labeling	3	0	0	0	3
Percentage	75	0	0	0	75
Reproducing	1	0	0	0	1
Percentage	25	0	0	0	25

TABLE D-10. Type of Intervention Procedures Implemented
(Adjustment—Decrease Behavior)

School	1	2	3	4	Total
Antecedent events					
Modeling	1	0	0	29	30
Prompting	1	0	0	8	9
Establishing, altering, or removing S^D	3	0	3	52	58
Physical response guidance	2	0	0	3	5
Incontingent application of hypoth- esized reinforcement	0	0	0	1	1
Task alteration	2	0	0	10	12
Consequent events					
Add positive reinforcer	3	0	1	51	55
Remove positive reinforcer	3	1	0	14	18
Add an aversive stimulus	3	0	1	24	28
Remove aversive stimuli	0	0	1	3	4
Extinction	2	0	0	22	24
DRO	4	0	2	12	18
Counseling	0	0	2	23	25

Establishing, altering, or removing S^D (discriminative stimulus): In order to obtain the desired response, the change agent may give a stimulus that initiates behavior without providing any part of the actual response (such as the case with prompting): "Tell me the name of this letter," "Throw the ball." The change agent may give a signal for a response such as pointing

TABLE D-11. Type of Intervention Procedures Implemented
(Adjustment—Increase Behavior)

School	1	2	3	4	Total
Antecedent events					
Modeling	3	0	0	13	16
Prompting	4	0	3	10	17
Establishing, altering, or removing S^D	9	0	7	28	44
Physical response guidance	0	0	0	1	1
Task alteration	3	0	6	4	13
Consequent events					
Add positive reinforcer	8	0	3	41	52
Remove positive reinforcer	2	0	0	2	4
Add an aversive stimulus	0	0	2	9	11
Remove aversive stimuli	0	0	0	2	2
Extinction	0	0	0	18	18
DRO	0	0	0	3	3
Counseling	0	0	1	11	12

TABLE D-12. Types of Intervention Procedures Implemented (Intellectual Skills)

School	1	2	3	4	Total
Antecedent events					
Modeling	4	0	0	0	4
Prompting	4	0	0	0	4
Establishing, altering, or removing S^D	4	0	0	0	4
Physical response guidance	1	0	0	0	1
Task alteration	3	0	0	0	3
Consequent events					
Add positive reinforcer	4	0	0	0	4
Response types					
Labeling	3	0	0	0	3
Reproducing	4	0	0	0	4
Discrimination and matching	2	0	0	0	2

to a child as a signal for him or her to quiet down. The change agent may alter cues by reordering the environment so that the target response cannot be made, such as changing a child's seat so he can't talk to a peer or having the teacher sit next to a child to discourage hitting. The change agent may alter discriminative stimuli by doing something to instigate a child's behavior, such as giving the child tasks to do. In order for this classification to be used to describe antecedent events, the cue must occur immediately before

TABLE D-13. Types of Intervention Procedures Implemented
(Cases Involving Alterations in Teaching Procedures)

School	1	2	3	4	Total
Antecedent events					
Modeling	5	0	0	7	12
Prompting	3	0	0	7	10
Establishing, altering, or removing S^D	4	0	0	5	9
Physical response guidance	1	0	0	5	4
Task alteration	3	0	2	2	7
Consequent events					
Add positive reinforcer	5	0	1	9	15
Remove aversive stimuli	1	0	0	0	1
Extinction	1	0	0	2	3
Response types					
Labeling	4	0	2	5	11
Reproducing	0	0	1	5	6
Serial reproducing	0	0	0	1	1
Performing combinations	1	0	0	2	3
Comprehension	3	0	2	0	5
Discrimination and matching	2	0	1	3	6

the desired response. Instructions given to a child at some time before the desired response would not be included.

Physical response guidance: This category is defined as guiding the desired response, for example, actually taking the child's hand and forming the letter for him or her.

In *contingent application of hypothesized reinforcer:* This category includes instances in which the positive "reinforcer" is given before the response occurs, for example, hugging and attending to Susie when she comes to school in hopes of preventing her leaving the classroom. The change agent may praise everything the child does well.

Task alteration: Changing the stimulus or the number of responses to be made, reordering the presentation of stimuli, and breaking a large task into several smaller ones are examples of the alteration of a task.

The following classification descriptions were used for consequent events (Tables D-10, D-11, D-12, and D-13):

Add positive reinforcer: The response is rewarded with positive consequences (e.g., praise, candy, or stars).

Remove positive reinforcer: A reinforcer that is known to be positive is taken away; for example, (1) whenever Susie grabs from another student, she will not be permitted to play with the doll during free choice, and (2) when Joe hits, he will not be allowed to go to recess. Removal of the child from an activity is called time-out.

Add an aversive stimulus: This category involves the presentation of an aversive stimulus.

Remove aversive stimuli: This category includes taking away something unpleasant.

Extinction: This class involves pairing a previously rewarded behavior with neutral stimuli. Plans involving extinction require the removal of a reinforcer that is maintaining a behavior to be eliminated through consultation.

DRO (differential reinforcement of other behavior): An example of this procedure is reinforcing the absence of a response or reinforcing after a period of time in which the response has not occurred (e.g., Johnny can paint at 10:30 if he has not hit all morning).

Counseling: Counseling involves general discussions of a problem with a child that cannot be coded in any other way.

More than one intervention procedure may be used for the antecedent and consequent event, and the plan may also include the modification of both or of only one event. The combined totals of 10 and 11 demonstrate the frequent practice of altering, establishing, or removing a discriminative stimulus when attempting either to increase (44 instances) or to decrease (58 instances) behavior. Providing cues is an effective aid to successful change in behavior. The data demonstrate that cues were provided in many instances. Other antecedent events used to modify behavior were the following: modeling (46 instances), prompting (26 instances), task alteration (25 instances), physical response guidance (6 instances), and contingent application of hypothesized reinforcer (1 instance).

The combined totals also demonstrate that the technique used most often to alter consequent events was to add a positive reinforcer (107 instances). Positive techniques made up the total plan or were part of a more comprehensive plan using additional techniques.

When used in the modification of environmental events, a positive reinforcement is usually directed on a planned schedule. Thus, it becomes a powerful technique; however, it does depend on the occurrence of the desired response. This strategy would explain the high frequency of the procedures of establishing, altering, or removing a discriminative stimulus that would result in providing a cue antecedent to response occurrence.

Extinction (ignoring) is also an effective technique for decreasing an undesirable behavior (used in 24 instances). It may also be used to increase desirable behavior (used in 18 instances) by aiding in the elimination of responses interfering with desired behavior.

Table D-14 presents data concerning the types of positive reinforcers and aversive stimuli used. It is not surprising to discover that verbal praise

TABLE D-14. Types of Positive Reinforcers
and Aversive Stimuli Used

School	1	2	3	4	Total
Positive reinforcers					
Consumable	3	0	0	26	29
Objects	1	0	0	6	7
Activities	6	0	3	59	68
Position	4	1	0	4	9
Physical	0	0	0	18	18
Verbal	20	0	3	95	118
Tokens	3	0	0	18	21
Aversive stimuli					
Objects	1	0	0	0	1
Activities	1	0	4	16	21
Position	2	0	2	11	15
Physical	0	0	0	3	3
Verbal	1	0	1	8	10
Tokens	1	0	0	1	2
Reinforcers for which tokens were exchanged					
Consumable	4	0	0	14	18
Objects	0	0	0	4	4
Activities	1	0	0	2	3
Position	0	0	0	1	1
Verbal	0	0	0	11	11

was the most frequently used (118 instances). The other type used frequently (68 instances) was the application of reinforcement via activities such as painting, using the typewriter, an being made chairperson of a committee.

Two types of procedures are generally followed in planning for the solution of academic problems. One is to focus the intervention on making alterations in teaching techniques. The other is to develop intellectual skills that may facilitate subsequent learning. The decision about which procedure to follow is made by the psychologist during the problem identification interview and is based on certain clues gleaned from the statements made by the change agent. For instance, the change agent may give support to the possibility that (because of the inconsistent level of academic performance) the child is able to perform the instructional task in question but chooses not to do so. As a result of this type of information, the psychologist would use interviewing techniques that would lead to alterations in teaching procedures after baseline data have been obtained.

Descriptive information concerning the implementation of such teaching-procedure planning is provided in Table D-13. Tables D-12 and D-13, which present the procedures implemented in the academic cases, include the specific modification of the antecedent and consequent events previously described in this report. In addition, information about the child's behavior during teaching is provided.

When either antecedent or consequent events have been altered, the responses are essentially the same as the responses indicated in Tables D-8 and D-9. The control of antecedent and consequent events is directed toward increasing the desired target behavior, and some alteration is planned in the ongoing teaching procedure.

When intellectual-skill training is directed toward increasing learning, the response required of the child during skill training may not be the same as the ultimate performance desired.

As shown in Tables D-12 and D-13, modeling was the most popular antecedent procedure, with 16 instances. Other frequently used procedures occurring before the target response were establishing, altering, or removing a discriminative stimulus and prompting.

The response most often required during alterations in teaching-pro-

TABLE D-15. Baseline Data Collected

School	1	2	3	4	Total
Number of cases reporting data	32	2	13	139	186
Median number days, data per case	4.00	5.00	4.00	4.00	4.00
Minimum number days, data per case	2	5	2	1	1
Maximum number days, data per case	47	5	6	50	27

TABLE D-16. Intervention Data Collected

School	1	2	3	4	Total
Number of cases reporting data	29	1	10	129	169
Median number days, data per case	5.00	4.00	5.00	6.00	5.00
Minimum number days, data per case	3	4	2	2	2
Maximum number days, data per case	41	4	6	70	30

cedure cases (Table D-13) was labeling. The addition of positive reinforcers was again the most popular consequent event (15 instances).

An area of great importance is the collection of records. Baseline data are essential to an understanding of the nature of the problem. Data allow concrete definitions of problems to be formulated and enable the completion of problem analysis to determine the environmental conditions controlling behavior. Data are also required as a benchmark against which to evaluate any plan that has been implemented.

Table D-15 presents statistics describing the length of time during which baseline data were usually taken. The median days were included in order to show whether a high maximum number of days was the usual case or a reflection of one extreme case (see Schools 1 and 4). The median for all schools was approximately 4 days.

Table D-16 presents information on the number of days during which intervention data were collected. It should be understood that, although the intervention plan for the alteration of environmental factors may be ongoing, there may not be a continual taking of data. It is more efficient to

TABLE D-17. Source of Referral

School	1	2	3	4	Total
Child's teacher	37	4	5	110	156
Other teacher	8	4	1	39	52
Principal	0	0	6	6	12
Parent	3	0	2	14	19
Psychologist	0	0	0	5	5
Counselor	0	0	1	0	1
Teacher aide	1	0	0	7	8
Nurse	0	0	0	5	5
Teacher and principal	2	0	0	2	4
Teacher and parent	1	0	0	6	7
Child's teacher and other teacher	0	0	0	1	1
Child	0	0	5	11	16
Principal and psychologist	0	0	1	0	1
Other	0	0	1	3	4

take periodic data to spot-check progress. Therefore, we cannot make the assumption that the number of days during which intervention data were taken is also indicative of the number of days during which the intervention plan was in effect.

Table D-17 provides information about the sources of referrals. As would be expected, the child's teacher generated the largest number of cases (156), largely because of the amount of time the teacher spends with the child. Other teachers submitted the next largest number of referrals (52), followed by parents (19), children (16), and principals (12). These latter figures represent a considerable increase over the previous year.

References

Achenbach, T. M. (1985). *Assessment and taxonomy of child and adolescent psychopathology*. Beverly Hills, CA: Sage.

Achenbach, T. M., McConaughy, S. H., & Howell, C. T. (1987). Child/adolescent behavior and emotional problems: Implications of cross-informant correlations for situational specificity. *Psychological Bulletin, 101*, 213–232.

Adler, A. (1964). *Social interest: A challenge to mankind*. New York: Capricorn Books.

Agras, W. S., & Berkowitz, R. (1980). Clinical research in behavior therapy: Halfway there? *Behavior Therapy, 11*, 472–487.

Ajchenbaum, M., & Reynolds, C. R. (1981). A brief case study using behavioral consultation for behavior reduction. *School Psychology Review, 10*, 407–408.

Alessi, G. J., & Kaye, J. H. (1983). *Behavior assessment for school psychologists*. Kent, OH: National Association of School Psychologists Professional Development Publications.

Allen, C. T., & Forman, S. G. (1984). Efficacy of methods of training teachers in behavior modification. *School Psychology Review, 13*, 26–32.

Allport, G. W. (1937). *Personality: A social interpretation*. New York: Holt.

Alpert, J. L. (1976). Mental health consultation. *Professional Psychology, 7*, 619–625.

American Educational Research Association, American Psychological Association, and National Council on Measurement in Education. (1985). *Standards for educational and psychological testing*. Washington, DC: American Psychological Association.

Anastasi, A. (1976). *Psychological testing* (4th ed.). New York: Macmillan.

Anderson, T. K., & Kratochwill, T. R. (1988). Dissemination of behavioral procedures in the schools: Issues in training. In J. C. Witt, S. N. Elliott, & F. M. Gresham (Eds.), *Handbook of behavior therapy in education* (pp. 217–244). New York: Plenum Press.

Anderson, T. K., Kratochwill, T. R., & Bergan, J. R. (1986). Training teachers in behavioral consultation and therapy: An analysis of verbal behaviors, *Journal of School Psychology, 24*, 229–241.

Andrews, J. K. (1970). The result of a pilot program to train teachers in the classroom application of behavior modification techniques. *Journal of School Psychology, 8*, 37–42.

Argyris, C. (1964). *Integrating the individual and the organization*. New York: Wiley.

Armbruster, B. B., Stevens, R. J., & Rosenshine, B. V. (1977). *Analyzing content coverage and emphasis: A study of three curricula and two tests* (Technical Report No. 26), Urbana-Champaign: Center for the Study of Reading, University of Illinois.

Association for Advancement of Behavior Therapy. Ethical issues for human services. *Behavior Therapy*, 1977, *8*, v–vi.

491

Ayllon, T., Layman, D., & Kandel, H. J. (1975). A behavioral educational alternative to drug control of hyperactive children. *Journal of Applied Behavior Analysis, 8,* 137–146.

Baer, D. M. (1974). A note on the absence of a Santa Clause in any known ecosystem: A rejoinder to Willems. *Journal of Applied Behavior Analysis, 7,* 167–168.

Baer, D. M., Wolf, M. M., & Risley, T. R. (1968). Some current dimensions of applied behavior analysis. *Journal of Applied Behavior Analysis, 1,* 91–97.

Bailey, J. S. (1977). *A handbook of research methods in applied behavior analysis.* Gainesville: University of Florida.

Bales, R. F. (1950). *Interaction process analysis.* Cambridge, MA: Addison-Wesley.

Ballard, K. D., & Glynn, T. (1975). Behavioral self-management in story writing with elementary school children. *Journal of Applied Behavior Analysis, 8,* 387–398.

Bandura, A. (1969). *Principles of behavior modification.* New York: Holt, Rinehart & Winston.

Bandura, A. (1974). Behavior theory and the models of man. *American Psychologist, 29,* 859–869.

Barlow, D. H., & Hersen, M. (1985). *Single case experimental designs: Strategies for studying behavior change* (2nd ed.). New York: Pergamon Press.

Barlow, D. H., Hayes, S. C., & Nelson, R. O. (1984). *The scientist-practitioner: Research and accountability in clinical and educational settings.* New York: Pergamon Press.

Barnard, J. D., Christopherson, E. R., & Wolf, M. M. (1974). Supervising paraprofessional tutors in a remedial reading program. *Journal of Applied Behavior Analysis, 7,* 481.

Barrett, B. H., Johnston, J. M., & Pennypacker, H. S. (1986). Behavior: Its units, dimensions, and measurement. In R. O. Nelson & S. C. Hayes (Eds.), *Conceptual foundations of behavioral assessment* (pp. 156–200). New York: Guilford Press.

Barry, H., Child, I. L., & Bacon, M. K. (1959). Relation of child training to subsistence economy. *American Anthropologist, 61,* 51–63.

Bell, R. Q. (1968). A reinterpretation of the directions of effects and studies of socialization. *Psychological Review, 75,* 81–95.

Bennis, W. G. (1969). *Changing organizations.* New York: McGraw-Hill.

Bennis, W. G. (1970). *Beyond bureaucracy.* New York: McGraw-Hill.

Bergan, J. R. (1970). A systems approach to psychological services. *Psychology in the Schools, 8,* 315–319.

Bergan, J. R. (1972). Effects of verbal pretraining on letter identification under variations in response number. *Proceedings of the Annual Convention of the American Psychological Association,* Honolulu.

Bergan, J. R. (1977). *Behavioral consultation.* Columbus, OH: Charles E. Merrill.

Bergan, J. R. (1980). Path-referenced assessment. In T. R. Kratochwill (Ed.), *Advances in school psychology* (pp. 255–280). Hillsdale, NJ: Erlbaum.

Bergan, J. R. (1988). Latent variable techniques for measuring development. In R. Langeheine & J. Rost (Eds.), *Latent trait and latent class models.* New York: Plenum Press.

Bergan, J. R., & Caldwell, T. (1967). Operant techniques in school psychology. *Psychology in the Schools, 4,* 136–141.

Bergan, J. R., & Dunn, J. A. (1976). *Psychology and education: A science for instruction.* New York: Wiley.

Bergan, J. R., & Newman, A. (1980). The identification of resources and constraints influencing plan design in consultation. *Journal of School Psychology, 18,* 317–323.

Bergan, J. R., & Smith, A. N. (Eds.). (1986). *Head Start Measures Battery.* Tests developed for the National Head Start Organization through the Administration for Children, Youth, and Families, Department of Health and Human Services, under Contract No. HHS-105-81-C-008.

Bergan, J. R., Curry, D. R., Currin, S., Haverman, K., & Nicholson, E. (1973). *Tucson early education psychological services.* Tucson: Arizona Center for Educational Research and Development, University of Arizona.

Bergan, J. R., Kratochwill, T. R., & Luiten, J. (1978). Competency-based training in behavioral consultation. *Journal of School Psychology, 18*, 91–97.

Bergan, J. R., Byrnes, I. M., & Kratochwill, T. R. (1979). Effects of behavioral and medical models of consultation on teacher expectancies and instruction of a hypothetical child. *Journal of School Psychology, 17*, 307–316.

Bergan, J. R., & Tombari, M. L. (1975). The analysis of verbal interactions occurring during consultation. *Journal of School Psychology, 13*, 209–226.

Bergan, J. R., & Tombari, M. L. (1976). Consultant skill and efficiency and the implementation of outcomes of consultation. *Journal of School Psychology, 14*, 3–14.

Bergan, J. R., Stone, C. A., & Feld, J. K. (1985). Path-referenced assessment of individual differences. In C. R. Reynolds & V. L. Willson (Eds.), *Methodological and statistical advances in the study of individual differences* (pp. 425–466). New York: Plenum Publishing.

Berkowitz, B. P., & Graziano, A. M. (1972). Training parents as behavior therapists: A review. *Behaviour Research and Therapy, 10*, 297–317.

Bernstein, G. S. (1982). Training behavior change agents: A conceptual review. *Behavior Therapy, 13*, 1–23.

Bersoff, D. N. (1975). Professional ethics and legal responsibilities: On the horns of a dilemma. *Journal of School Psychology, 13*, 359–376.

Black, I. J. (1965). *The Bank Street Reading Series*. New York: Macmillan.

Bloom, D. E., & Zimmerman, B. J. (1981). Enhancing the social skills of an unpopular girl: A social learning intervention. *Journal of School Psychology, 19*, 295–303.

Bock, R. D., & Aitkin, M. (1981). Marginal maximum likelihood estimation of item parameters: Application of an algorithm. *Psychometrika, 46*, 443–459.

Bornstein, P. H., Hamilton, S. B., & Quivillon, R. P. (1977). Behavior modification by long distance: Demonstration of functional control over disruptive behavior in a rural classroom setting. *Behavior Modification, 1*, 369–380.

Bourne, L. E., Jr., & Dominowski, R. L. (1972). Thinking. *Annual Review of Psychology, 23*, 105–130.

Bower, G. H. (1974). Selective facilitation and interference in retention of prose. *Journal of Educational Psychology, 66*, 1–8.

Bowles, P. E., & Nelson, R. O. (1976). Training teachers as mediators: Efficacy of a workshop versus the bug-in-the-ear technique. *Journal of School Psychology, 14*, 15–26.

Brigance, A. (1977). *Brigance Inventory of Basic Skills*. North Billerica, MA: Curriculum Associates.

Brigance, A. (1980). *Brigance Diagnostic Inventory of Essential Skills*. North Billerica, MA: Curriculum Associates.

Briggs, L. J. (1970). Handbook of procedures for the design of instruction. *American Institutes for Research Monograph No. 4*.

Bronfenbrenner, U. (1976). The experimental ecology of education. *Educational Researcher, 5*, 5–15.

Broskowski, A. (1973). Concepts of teacher-centered consultation. *Professional Psychology, 4*, 50–58.

Brown, D., & Minke, K. M. (1986). School psychology graduate training: A comprehensive analysis. *American Psychologist, 41*, 1328–1338.

Brown, D., & Schulte, A. C. (1987). A social learning model of consultation. *Professional Psychology: Research and Practice, 18*, 283–287.

Brown, D., Wyne, M. D., Blackburn, J. E., & Powell, W. C. (1979). *Consultation: Strategy for improving education*. Boston: Allyn & Bacon.

Brown, D. K., Kratochwill, T. R., & Bergan, J. R. (1982). Teaching interview skills for problem identification: An analogue study. *Behavioral Assessment, 4*, 63–73.

Brown, J. H., Frankel, A., Birkimer, J. C., & Gamboa, A. N. (1966). The effects of a classroom management workshop on the reduction of children's problematic behavior. *Cor-*

rective and Social Psychiatry and Journal of Behavior Technology, Methods and Therapy, 22, 39–41.

Brown, J. S., & Burton, R. R. (1978). Diagnostic models for procedural bugs in basic mathematical skills. *Cognitive Science, 2*, 155–192.

Buchanan, C. D. (1968). *Sullivan Associates Programmed Reading* (Series 2, rev. ed.). New York: McGraw-Hill.

Burke, J. P., & DeMers, S. T. (1979). A paradigm for evaluating assessment interviewing techniques. *Psychology in the Schools, 16*, 51–60.

Buss, A. R. (1975). The emerging field of the sociology of psychological knowledge. *American Psychologist, 30*, 988–1002.

Cancelli, A. A., & Kratochwill, T. R. (1981). Criterion-referenced assessment. In T. R. Kratochwill (Ed.), *Advances in school psychology* (pp. 217–254). Hillsdale, NJ: Erlbaum.

Canter, L., & Paulson, T. (1974). A college credit model of in-school consultation: A functional behavioral training program. *Community Mental Health Journal, 10*, 268–275.

Caplan, G. (1970). *The theory and practice of mental health consultation.* New York: Basic Books.

Carnine, D. W., & Fink, W. J. (1978). Increasing the rate of presentation and use of signals in elementary classroom teachers. *Journal of Applied Behavior Analysis, 11*, 35–46.

Cavell, T. A., Frentz, C. E., & Kelley, M. L. (1986a). Acceptability of paradoxical interventions: Some nonparadoxical findings. *Professional Psychology: Research and Practice, 17*, 519–523.

Cavell, T. A., Frentz, C. E., & Kelley, M. L. (1986b). Consumer acceptability of the single case withdrawal design: Penalty for early withdrawal? *Behavior Therapy, 17*, 82–87.

Chamberlain, P., & Baldwin, D. V. (1988). Client resistance to parent training: Its therapeutic management. In T. R. Kratochwill (Ed.), *Advances in school psychology* (Vol. 6), pp. 131–171). Hillsdale, NJ: Erlbaum.

Chesler, M. A., Bryant, B. I., Jr., & Crowfoot, J. E. (1981). Consultation in schools: Inevitable conflict, partnership, and advocacy. In M. J. Curtis & J. E. Zins (Eds.), *The theory and practice of school consultation.* Springfield, IL: Charles C Thomas.

Christie, L., McKenzie, H., & Burdett, C. (1972). The consulting teacher approach to special education: Inservice training for regular classroom teachers. *Focus on Exceptional Children, 5*, 1–10.

Christopherson, E. R., Arnold, C. M., Hill, D. W., & Quilitch, H. R. (1972). The home point system: Token reinforcement procedures for application by parents of children with behavior problems. *Journal of Applied Behavior Analysis, 5*, 485–497.

Clark, L., & Elliott, S. N. (1988). The influence of treatment strength information of knowledgeable teachers' pretreatment evaluations of social skills training methods. *Professional School Psychology, 3*, 241–251.

Clymer, T. (1969). *Reading 360.* Boston: Ginn & Co.

Cobb, D. E., & Medway, F. J. (1978). Determinants of effectiveness in parent consultation. *Journal of Community Psychology, 6*, 229–240.

Cohen, J. (1970). *Statistical power analysis for the behavioral sciences.* New York: Academic Press.

Colligan, R. W., Colligan, R. C., & Dilliard, M. K. (1977). Contingency management in the classroom treatment of long-term elective mutism: A case report. *Journal of School Psychology, 15*, 9–17.

Cone, J. D. (1981). Psychometric considerations. In M. Hersen & A. Bellack (Eds.), *Behavioral assessment: A practical handbook* (2nd ed., pp. 38–68). Elmsford, NY: Pergamon Press.

Cone, J. D. (1986). Psychometric considerations and the multiple models of behavioral assessment. In M. Hersen & A. S. Bellack (Eds.), *Behavioral assessment: A practical handbook* (3rd ed., pp. 42–66). New York: Pergamon Press.

Cone, J. D. (1988). Psychometric considerations and the multiple models of behavioral assessment. In M. Hersen & A. S. Bellack (Eds.), *Behavioral assessment: A practical handbook* (3rd ed., pp. 42–66). New York: Pergamon Press.

Cone, J. D., & Hayes, S. C. (1980). *Environmental problems/behavioral solutions.* Monterey, CA: Brooks/Cole.

Conoley, J. C., & Conoley, C. W. (1982b). *School consultation: A guide to practice and training.* New York: Pergamon Press.

Conoley, J. C., & Gutkin, T. B. (1986). Educating school psychologists for the real world. *School Psychology Review, 15,* 457–465.

Cook, T. D., & Campbell, D. T. (Eds.). (1979). *Quasi-experimentation: Design and analysis issues for field settings.* Chicago: Rand McNally.

Copeland, R. E., Brown, R. E., & Hall, R. V. (1974). The effects of principal-implemented techniques on the behavior of pupils. *Journal of Applied Behavior Analysis, 7,* 77–86.

Cowen, E. L. (1973). Social and community interventions. *Annual Review of Psychology, 24,* 423–472.

Cowen, E. L., Trost, M. A., Izzo, L. D., Lorion, R. P., Dorr, D., & Isaacson, R. V. (1975). *New ways in school mental health: Early detection and prevention of school maladaptation.* New York: Human Sciences Press.

Cronbach, J. (1971). Test validation. In R. L. Thorndike (Ed.), *Educational measurement.* Washington, DC: American Council on Education.

Curtis, M. J., & Watson, K. L. (1980). Changes in consultee problem classification skills following consultation. *Journal of School Psychology, 18,* 210–221.

Cutts, N. E. (1955). *School psychologist at mid-century.* Washington, DC: American Psychological Association.

Cuvo, A. J. (1979). Multiple-baseline design in instructional research: Pitfalls of measurement and procedural advantages. *American Journal of Mental Deficiency, 84,* 219–228.

Dalis, G. T. (1970). Effect of precise objectives upon student achievement in health education. *The Journal of Experimental Education, 39,* 20–23.

Dangel, R. F., & Polster, R. A. (Eds.). (1984). *Parent training: Foundations of research and practice.* New York: Guilford Press.

Dangel, R. F., & Polster, R. A. (1988). *Teaching child management skills.* New York: Pergamon Press.

Darwin, C. (1859). *The origin of species.* London: Murray.

Davis, H. T., & Salasin, S. E. (1975). The utilization of evaluation. In E. L. Struening & M. Guttentag (Eds.), *Handbook of evaluation research* (Vol. 1). Beverly Hills, CA: Sage.

Deno, S. L., & Mirkin, P. (1977). *Date-based program modification: A manual.* Minneapolis: Leadership Training Institute/Special Education, University of Minnesota.

Deno, S. L., Marston, D., & Tindal, G. (1986). Direct and frequent curriculum based measurement: An alternative for educational decision making. *Special Services in the Schools, 2,* 5–27.

Dollard, J., & Mowrer, O. H. (1947). A method of measuring tension in written documents. *Journal of Abnormal and Social Psychology, 42,* 3–32.

Drabman, R. S., Hammer, D., & Rosenbaum, M. S. (1979). Assessing generalization in behavior modification with children: The generalization map. *Behavioral Assessment, 1,* 203–219.

Dreikurs, R. (1948). *The challenge of parenthood.* New York: Duell, Sloan & Pearce.

Dreikurs, R. (1967). *Psychology in the classroom* (2nd ed.). New York: Harper & Row.

Dubin, S. S. (1972). Obsolescence or lifelong education: A choice for the professional. *American Psychologist, 27,* 486–498.

Duchastel, P. C., & Merrill, P. F. (1973). The effects of behavioral objectives on learning: A review of empirical studies. *Review of Educational Research, 43,* 53–70.

Dunn, L. M., & Markwardt, F. C. (1970). *Peabody Individual Achievement Test.* Circle Pines, MN: American Guidance Services.

Duncan, O. (1975). *Introduction to structural equation models.* New York: Academic Press.

Edgington, E. S. (in press). Nonparametric tests for single-subject experiment. In T. R. Kratochwill & R. Levin (Eds.), *Single case data analysis.* Hillsdale, NJ: Erlbaum.

Elliott, S. N. (1988). Acceptability of behavioral treatments in educational settings. In J. C. Witt, S. N. Elliott, & F. M. Gresham (Eds.), *Handbook of behavior therapy in education* (pp. 121–150). New York: Plenum Press.

Elliott, S. N., Turco, T. L., Gresham, F. M. (1987). Consumers' and clients' pretreatment acceptability ratings of classroom-based group contingencies. *Journal of School Psychology, 25,* 145–154.

Epstein, M. H., Matson, J. L., Repp, A., & Helsel, W. J. (1986). Acceptability of treatment alternatives as a function of teacher status and student level. *School Psychology Review, 15,* 84–90.

Erchul, W. P. (1987). A relational communication analysis of control in school consultation. *Professional School Psychology, 2,* 113–124.

Fantuzzo, J. W., Sisemore, T. A., & Spradlin, W. H. (1983). A competency-based model for teaching skills in the administration of intelligence tests. *Professional Psychology: Research and Practice, 14,* 224–231.

Farber, H., & Mayer, G. R. (1972). Behavior consultation in a barrio high school. *Personnel and Guidance Journal, 51,* 273–279.

Ferster, C., & Skinner, B. F. (1957). *Schedules of reinforcement.* New York: Appleton-Century-Crofts.

Fixsen, D. L., Phillips, E. L., & Wolf, M. M. (1972). Achievement place: The reliability of self-reporting and peer-reporting and their effects on behavior. *Journal of Applied Behavior Analysis, 5,* 19–30.

Flanagan, J. C. (1970). Individualizing education. *Education, 90,* 191–206.

Ford, J. D. (1979). Research on training counselors and clinicians. *Review of Educational Research, 49,* 87–130.

Forehand, R. L., & McMahon, R. J. (1981). *Helping the non-compliant child: A clinician's guide to parent training.* New York: Guilford Press.

Frentz, C., & Kelley, M. L. (1986). Parents' acceptance of reductive treatment methods: The influence of problem severity and perception of child behavior. *Behavior Therapy, 17,* 75–81.

Freud, S. (1927). *The ego and the id.* London: Hogarth Press.

Freud, S. (1938). *The basic writings of Sigmund Freud* (A. A. Brill, Ed., & Trans.). New York: Random House.

Fuchs, D., Fuchs, L. S., Bahr, M. W., Fernstrom, P., & Stecker, P. M. (1989). Exploring effective and efficient prereferral interventions: A component analysis of behavioral consultation. *School Psychology Review, 18,* 260–279.

Gagné, R. M. (1968). Contributions of learning to human development. *Psychological Review, 75,* 182.

Gagné, R. M. (1970). *The conditions of learning* (2nd ed.). New York: Holt Rinehart & Winston.

Gagné, R. M. (1974). Task analysis: Its relation to content analysis. *Educational Psychologist, 2,* 11–18.

Gagné, R. M., & Briggs, L. J. (1974). *Principles of instructional design.* New York: Holt, Rinehart & Winston.

Gagné, R. M., & Weigand, V. K. (1970). Effects of a superordinate context on learning and retention of facts. *Journal of Educational Psychology, 61,* 406–409.

Gallessich, J. (1982). *The profession and practice of consultation.* San Francisco: Jossey-Bass.

Gallessich, J. (1985). Toward a meta-theory of consultation. *The Counseling Psychologist, 13,* 336–354.

Gallessich, J., McDermott, L. K., & Jennings, S. (1986). Training of mental health consultants. In F. V. Mannino, E. J. Trickett, M. F. Shore, M. G. Kidder, & G. Levin (Eds.), *Handbook of mental health consultation* (pp. 279–317). Washington, DC: National Institute of Mental Health.

Gardner, J. M. (1972). Teaching behavior modification to nonprofessionals. *Journal of Applied Behavior Analysis, 5,* 517–521.

Gardner, N. (1974). Action training and research: Something old and something new. *Public Administration Review, 34,* 106–115.

Gardner, W. I., & Cole, C. (1988). Self-monitoring. In E. S. Shapiro & T. R. Kratochwill (Eds.), *Behavioral assessment in the schools* (pp. 206–246). New York: Guilford Press.

Gardner, W. I., Cole, C. L., Berry, D. L., & Nowinski, J. M. (1983). Redirection of disruptive behaviors in mentally retarded adults: A self-management approach. *Behavior Modification, 7,* 79–96.

Garfield, S. L. (1977). Research on the training of professional psychotherapists. In A. S. Garman & A. M. Razin (Eds.), *Effective psychotherapy: A handbook of research* (pp. 63–83). Oxford: Pergamon Press.

Garvey, W. D., & Griffith, B. C. (1971). Scientific communication: Its role in the conduct of research and creation of knowledge. *American Psychologist, 26,* 349–362.

Gelfand, D. M., & Hartmann, D. P. (1984). *Child behavior analysis and therapy* (2nd ed.). New York: Pergamon Press.

Gesell, A. (1940). *The first five years of life.* New York: Harper.

Gettinger, M. (1985). Effects of teacher-directed versus student-directed instruction and cues versus no cues for improving spelling performance. *Journal of Applied Behavior Analysis, 18,* 167–171.

Gettinger, M. (1988). Methods of proactive classroom management. *School Psychology Review, 17,* 227–242.

Giacquinta, J. B. (1973). The process of organizational change in schools. In F. N. Kerlinger (Ed.), *Review of research in education.* Itasca, IL: Peacock.

Gladstone, B. W., & Sherman, J. A. (1975). Developing generalized behavior-modification skills in high-school students working with retarded children. *Journal of Applied Behavior Analysis, 8,* 169–180.

Glaser, R. (1963). Instructional technology and the measurement of learning outcomes: Some questions. *American Psychologist, 18,* 519–521.

Glaser, R., & Nitko, A. J. (1971). Measurement in learning and instruction. In R. L. Thorndike (Ed.), *Educational measurement* (2nd ed.). Washington, DC: American Council on Education.

Glass, G. V., Wilson, V. L., & Gottman, J. M. (1975). *Design and analysis of time-series experiments.* Boulder: Colorado Associated University Press.

Glynn, E. L., & Thomas, J. D. (1974). Effects of cueing on self-control of classroom behavior. *Journal of Applied Behavior Analysis, 7,* 299–306.

Glynn, E. L., Thomas, J. D., & Shee, S. M. (1973). Behavioral self-control of task behavior in an elementary classroom. *Journal of Applied Behavior Analysis, 6,* 105–113.

Goh, D. S., Teslow, C. J., & Fuller, G. B. (1981). The practice of psychological assessment among school psychologists. *Professional Psychology, 12,* 696–706.

Good, R. H., & Salvia, J. (1988). Curriculum bias in published, norm-referenced reading tests: Demonstrable effects. *School Psychology Review, 17,* 51–60.

Goodwin, D. L., & Coates, T. J. (1973). Increasing teacher effectiveness through social systems change: Training school psychologists as change agents. *California Journal of Educational Research, 25,* 147–156.

Goodwin, D. L., Garvey, W. P., & Barclay, J. R. (1971). Microconsultation and behavior analysis: A method of training psychologists as behavioral consultants. *Journal of Consulting and Clinical Psychology, 37,* 355–363.

Gottman, J. M. (1981). *Time-series analysis: A comprehensive introduction for social scientists.* Cambridge: Cambridge University Press.

Graden, J. L., Casey, A., & Bonstrom, O. (1985). Implementing a prereferral intervention system: Part 2. The data. *Exceptional Children, 51,* 487–496.

Graden, J. L., Casey, A., & Christenson, S. L. (1985). Implementing a pre-referral intervention system: Part 1. The model. *Exceptional Children, 51,* 377–384.

Greer, R. D., & Polivstok, S. R. (1982). Collateral gains and short-term maintenance in reading and on-task responses by inner-city adolescents as a function of their use of social reinforcement while tutoring. *Journal of Applied Behavior Analysis, 15,* 123–139.

Gresham, F. M. (1989). Assessment of treatment integrity in school consultation and prereferral intervention. *School Psychology Review, 18,* 37–50.

Gresham, F. M., & Davis, C. J. (1988). Behavioral interviews with teachers and parents. In E. S. Shapiro & T. R. Kratochwill (Eds.), *Behavioral assessment in schools: Conceptual foundations and practical application* (pp. 455–493). New York: Guilford Press.

Gresham, F. M., & Kendall, G. K. (1987). School consultation research: Methodological critique and future research directions. *School Psychology Review, 16,* 306–316.

Gresham, F. M., & Nagle, R. J. (1981). Treating school phobia using behavioral consultation: A case study. *School Psychology Review, 10,* 104–107.

Guba, E. G., & Clark, D. L. (1975). The configurational perspectives: A new view of educational knowledge and production. *Educational Researcher, 4,* 6–9.

Guilford, J. P. (1967). *The nature of human intelligence.* New York: McGraw-Hill.

Gutkin, T. B., & Curtis, M. J. (1982). School-based consultation. In C. R. Reynolds & T. B. Gutkin (Eds.), *The handbook of school psychology* (pp. 796–828). New York: Wiley.

Gutkin, T. B., Henning-Stout, M., & Piersel, W. C. (1988). Impact of a district-wide behavioral consultation prereferral intervention service on patterns of school psychological service delivery. *Professional School Psychology, 3,* 301–308.

Hall, R. V., & Fox, R. G. (1977). Changing criterion designs: An alternative applied behavior analysis procedure. In C. C. Etzel, J. M. LeBlanc, & D. M. Baer (Eds.), *New developments in behavioral research: Theory, methods, and applications. In honor of Sidney W. Bijou.* Hillsdale, NJ: Erlbaum.

Hall, R. V., Cristler, C., Cranston, S. S., & Tucker, B. (1970). Teachers and parents as researchers using multiple baseline designs. *Journal of Applied Behavior Analysis, 3,* 247–255.

Hall, R. V., Axelrod, S., Foundopoulos, M., Shellman, J., Campbell, R. A., & Cranston, S. S. (1971). The effective use of punishment to modify behavior in the classroom. *Educational Technology, 2,* 24–26.

Hall, R. V., Fox, R., Willard, D., Goldsmith, L., Emerson, M., Owen, M., Davis, R., & Porcia, E. (1971). The teacher as observer and experimenter in the modification of disputing and talking-out behaviors. *Journal of Applied Behavior Analysis, 4,* 141–149.

Hall, R. V., Axelrod, S., Tyler, L., Grief, E., Jones, F. C., & Robertson, R. (1972). Modification of behavior problems in the home with a parent as observer and experimenter. *Journal of Applied Behavior Analysis, 5,* 53–64.

Hallahan, D. P., Lloyd, J. W., Kauffman, J. M., & Loper, A. B. (1983). Academic problems. In R. J. Morris & T. R. Kratochwill (Eds.), *The practice of child therapy* (pp. 113–141). New York: Pergamon Press.

Harris, T., & Creekmore, M. (1972). *Keys to reading.* Oklahoma City: Economy Press.

Harris, V. W., & Sherman, J. A. (1973). Effects of peer tutoring and consequences on the math performance of elementary classroom students. *Journal of Applied Behavior Analysis, 6,* 587–597.

Harrison, M. I. (1987). *Diagnosing organizations: Methods, models, and processes.* Beverly Hills, CA: Sage.

Hart, B., & Risley, T. R. (1975). Incidental teaching of language in the preschool. *Journal of Applied Behavior Analysis, 8,* 411–420.

Hartmann, D. P. (Ed.). (1982). *Using observers to study behavior: New directions for methodology of social and behavioral science.* San Francisco: Jossey-Bass.

Havelock, R. G. (1969). *Planning for innovation through dissemination and utilization of knowledge.* Ann Arbor, MI: Institute for Social Research.

Hawkins, R. P., & Dobes, R. W. (1975). Behavioral definitions in applied behavior analysis:

Explicit or implicit. In B. C. Etzel, J. M. LeBlanc, & D. M. Baer (Eds.), *New developments in behavioral research: Theory, methods, and applications. In honor of Sidney W. Bijou.* Hillsdale, NJ: Erlbaum.

Hawkins, R. P., & Dotson, V. A. (1975). Reliability scores that delude: An Alice in Wonderland trip through the misleading characteristics of interobserver agreement scores in interval recording. In E. Ramp & G. Semb (Eds.), *Behavior analysis: Areas of research and application.* Englewood Cliffs, NJ: Prentice-Hall.

Hay, W. H., Hay, L. R., Angle, H. V., & Nelson, R. O. (1979). The reliability of problem identification in the behavioral interview. *Behavioral Assessment, 1,* 107–118.

Hayes, S. C. (1981). Single case experimental design and empirical clinical practice. *Journal of Consulting and Clinical Psychology, 49,* 193–211.

Hayes, S. C., Nelson, R. O., & Jarrett, R. B. (1986). Evaluating the quality of behavioral assessment. In R. O. Nelson & S. C. Hayes (Eds.), *Conceptual foundations of behavioral assessment* (pp. 463–503). New York: Guilford Press.

Hayes, S. C., Nelson, R. O., & Jarret, R. B. (1987). The treatment utility of assessment. *American Psychologist, 42,* 963–974.

Haynes, S. N., & Jensen, B. J. (1979). The interview as a behavioral assessment instrument. *Behavioral Assessment, 1,* 97–106.

Hebb, D. O. (1949). *The organization of behavior.* New York: Wiley.

Henderson, R. W., & Bergan, J. R. (1976). *The cultural context of childhood.* Columbus, OH: Merrill.

Henderson, R. W., & Garcia, A. B. (1973). The effects of a parent training program on the question-asking behavior of Mexican-American children. *American Educational Research Journal, 10,* 193–201.

Henderson, R. W., & Swanson, R. (1974). The application of social learning principles in a field setting: An applied experiment. *Exceptional Children, 41,* 53–55.

Henning-Stout, M., & Conoley, J. C. (1987). Consultation and counseling as procedurally divergent: Analysis of verbal behavior. *Professional Psychology: Research and Practice, 18,* 24–27.

Heron, T. E., & Catera, R. (1980). Teacher consultation: A functional approach. *School Psychology Review, 9,* 282–289.

Hersen, M., & Barlow, D. H. (1976). *Single case experimental designs: Strategies for studying behavior change.* New York: Pergamon Press.

Hetherington, E. M., & McIntyre, C. W. (1975). Developmental psychology. *Annual Review of Psychology, 26,* 97–136.

Homans, G. C. (1950). *The human group.* New York: Harcourt Brace.

Hops, H. (1971). The school psychologist as a behavior management consultant in a special class setting. *Journal of School Psychology, 9,* 473–483.

Horner, R. D., & Baer, D. M. (1978). Multiple-probe techniques: A variation on the multiple baseline. *Journal of Applied Behavior Analysis, 11,* 189–196.

Horton, G. O. (1975). Generalization of teacher behavior as a function of subject matter specific discrimination training. *Journal of Applied Behavior Analysis, 8,* 311–320.

Hughes, J. N. (1986). Ethical issues in school consultation. *School Psychology Review, 15,* 489–499.

Hughes, J. N. (1988). *Cognitive behavior therapy with children in schools.* New York: Pergamon Press.

Idol, L., Paolucci-Whitcomb, P., & Nevin, A. (1986). *Collaborative consultation.* Rockville, MD: Aspen.

Idol, L., & West, J. F. (1987). Consultation in special education: Part 2. Training and practice. *Journal of Learning Disabilities, 20,* 474–497.

Idol-Maestas, L. (1981). A teacher training model: The resource/consulting teacher. *Behavioral Disorders, 6,* 108–121.

Iwata, B. A., Wong, S. E., Riordan, M. M. Dorsey, M. F. & Lau, M. M. (1982). Assessment and training of clinical interviewing skills: Analogue analysis and field replication. *Journal of Applied Behavior Analysis, 15,* 191–203.

Jason, L. A., & Ferone, L., (1978). Behavioral versus process consultation interventions in school settings. *American Journal of Community Psychology, 6,* 531–543.

Jastak, J., & Jastak, S. (1978). *Wide Range Achievement Test.* Wilmington, DE: Jastak.

Jenkins, J. R., & Pany, D. (1978). Standardized achievement tests: How useful for special education? *Exceptional Children, 44,* 448–453.

Johnson, C. A., & Katz, R. C. (1973). Using parents as change agents for their children: A review. *Journal of Child Psychology and Psychiatry, 14,* 181–200.

Johnson, J. L., & Sloat, K. C. (1980). Teacher training effects: Real or illusory? *Psychology in the Schools, 77,* 109–115.

Johnson, M., & Bailey, J. S. (1974). Cross-age tutoring: Fifth graders as arithmetic tutors for kindergarten children. *Journal of Applied Behavior Analysis, 7,* 223–232.

Johnston, J. M., & Pennypacker, H. S. (1980). *Strategies and tactics of human behavioral research.* Hillsdale, NJ: Erlbaum.

Jones, F. H., & Eimers, R. C. (1975). Role playing to train elementary teachers to use a classroom management "skill package." *Journal of Applied Behavior Analysis, 8,* 421–433.

Kaplan, R. (1974). Effects of learning prose with part versus whole presentation of instructional objectives. *Journal of Educational Psychology, 66,* 787–792.

Kaplan, R., & Rothkopf, E. Z. (1974). Instructional objectives as directions to learners: Effects of passage length and amount of objective-relevant content. *Journal of Educational Psychology, 66,* 448–456.

Kaplan, R., & Simmons, F. G. (1974). Effects of instructional objectives used as orienting stimuli or as summary/review upon prose learning. *Journal of Educational Psychology, 66,* 614–622.

Karoly, P., & Steffen, J. J. (Eds.). (1980). *Improving the long-term effects of psychotherapy.* New York: Gardner.

Kaufman, R. A. (1971). A possible integrative model for the systematic and measurable improvement of education. *American Psychologist, 26,* 250–256.

Kazdin, A. E. (1975). *Behavior modification in applied settings.* Homewood, IL: Dorsey.

Kazdin, A. E. (1977). Assessing the clinical or applied significance of behavior change through social validation. *Behavior Modification, 1,* 427–452.

Kazdin, A. E. (1978). *History of behavior modification: Experimental foundations of contemporary research.* Baltimore: University Park Press.

Kazdin, A. E. (1979). Fictions, factions, and function of behavior therapy. *Behavior Therapy, 10,* 629–654.

Kazdin, A E. (1980a). Acceptability of alternative treatments for deviant child behavior. *Journal of Applied Behavior Analysis, 13,* 259–273.

Kazdin, A. E. (1980b). Acceptability of timeout from reinforcement procedures for disruptive child behavior. *Behavior Therapy, 11,* 329–344.

Kazdin, A. E. (1980c). *Behavior modification in applied settings* (2nd ed.). Homewood, IL: Dorsey.

Kazdin, A. E. (1980d). *Research design in clinical psychology.* New York: Harper & Row.

Kazdin, A. E. (1981a). Acceptability of child treatment techniques: The influence of treatment efficacy and adverse side effects. *Behavior Therapy, 12,* 493–506.

Kazdin, A. E. (1981b). Behavior modification in education: Contributions and limitations. *Developmental Review, 1,* 34–57.

Kazdin, A. E. (1981c). Drawing valid influences from case studies. *Journal of Consulting and Clinical Psychology 49,* 183–192.

Kazdin, A. E. (1981d). Uses and abuses of behavior modification in education: A rejoinder. *Developmental Review, 1,* 61–62.

Kazdin, A. E. (1982). *Single-case research designs: Methods for clinical and applied settings.* New York: Oxford University Press.

Kazdin, A. E. (1985). Selection of target behaviors: The relationship of the treatment focus to clinical dysfunction. *Behavioral Assessment, 7,* 33–47.

Kazdin, A. E. (1988). *Child psychotherapy: Developing and identifying effective treatments.* New York: Pergamon Press.

Kazdin, A. E. (1989). *Behavior modification in applied settings* (rev. ed.). Homewood, IL: Dorsey.

Kazdin, A. E., & Kopel, S. A. (1975). On resolving ambiguities of the multiple baseline design: Problems and recommendations. *Behavior Therapy, 6,* 601–608.

Kazdin, A. E., & Wilson, G. T. (1978). *Evaluation of behavior therapy: Issues, evidence and research strategies.* Cambridge, MA: Ballinger.

Kazdin, A. E., Silverman, N. A., & Sittler, J. L. (1975). The use of prompts to enhance vicarious effects of nonverbal approval. *Journal of Applied Behavior Analysis, 8,* 279–286.

Kazdin, A. E., French, N. H., & Sherick, R. B. (1981). Acceptability of alternative treatments for children: Evaluations by inpatient children, parents, and staff. *Journal of Consulting and Clinical Psychology, 49,* 900–907.

Kazdin, A. E., Kratochwill, T. R., & VandenBos, G. R. (1986). Beyond clinical trials: Generalizing from research to practice. *Professional Psychology: Research and Practice, 17,* 391–398.

Kendall, P. C. (1981). Assessing generalization and the single-subject strategies. *Behaviour Research and Therapy, 5,* 307–319.

King, L. W., Cotler, S. B., & Patterson, K. (1975). Behavior modification consultation in a Mexican-American school. *American Journal of Community Psychology, 3,* 229–235.

Kirschenbaun, D. S. (1979). Social competence intervention and evaluation of the inner city: Cincinnati's Social Skills Development Program. *Journal of Consulting and Clinical Psychology, 47,* 778–780.

Knight, M. F., & McKenzie, H. S. (1974). Elimination of bedtime thumbsucking in home settings through contingent reading. *Journal of Applied Behavior Analysis, 7,* 33–38.

Knight, M. F., Meyers, H. W., Paolucci Whitcomb, P., Hasazi, S. E., & Nevin, A. (1981). A four-year evaluation of consulting teacher service. *Behavioral Disorders, 6,* 92–100.

Knoff, H. M. (1986). Supervision in school psychology: The forgotten or future path to effective services. *School Psychology Review, 15,* 529–545.

Koegel, R. L., Russo, D. D., & Rincover, A. (1977). Assessing and training teachers in the use of behavior modification with autistic children. *Journal of Applied Behavior Analysis, 10,* 197–205.

Kohr, M. A., Parrish, J. M., Neef, N. A., Drieseen, J. R., & Hallinan, P. C. (1988). Communication skills training for parents: Experimental and social validation. *Journal of Applied Behavior Analysis, 21,* 21–30.

Koocher, G. P., & Farber, S. (Eds.). (1976). *Children's rights and the mental health professions.* New York: Wiley-Interscience.

Krasner, L., & Ullmann, L. P. (1965). *Research in behavior modification: New developments and implications.* New York: Holt, Rinehart & Winston.

Krathwohl, D. R., & Payne, D. A. (1971). Defining and assessing educational objectives. In R. L. Thorndike (Ed.), *Educational measurement* (2nd ed.). Washington, DC: American Council on Education.

Kratochwill, T. R. (Ed.). (1978). *Single-subject research: Strategies for evaluating change.* New York: Academic Press.

Kratochwill, T. R. (1982). Advances in behavioral assessment. In C. R. Reynolds & T. B. Gutkin (Eds.), *Handbook of school psychology* (pp. 314–350). New York: Wiley.

Kratochwill, T. R. (1985). Selection of target behaviors in behavioral consultation. *Behavioral Assessment, 7*, 49–61.

Kratochwill, T. R. (1988). *Preparation of school psychologists to serve as consultants for teachers of emotionally disturbed children.* United States Department of Education, Office of Special Education and Rehabilitative Services (1986–88 funding period).

Kratochwill, T. R., & Bergan, J. R. (1978a). Evaluating programs in applied settings through behavioral consultation. *Journal of School Psychology, 16*, 375–386.

Kratochwill, T. R., & Bergan, J. R. (1978b). Training school psychologists: Some perspectives on a competency-based behavioral consultation model. *Professional Psychology, 9*, 71–82.

Kratochwill, T. R., & Bergan, J. R. (1990). *Behavioral consultation in applied settings: An individual guide.* New York: Plenum Press.

Kratochwill, T. R., & Bijou, S. W. (1987). The impact of behaviorism on educational psychology. In J. A. Glover & R. R. Rouning (Eds.), *A history of educational psychology* (pp. 131–157). New York: Pergamon Press.

Kratochwill, T. R., & Levin, J. R. (1979). What single subject-single group research has to offer education now. *Contemporary Educational Psychology, 3*, 273–329.

Kratochwill, T. R., & Morris, R. J. (Eds.) (1990). *The practice of child therapy* (2nd ed.). New York: Pergamon Press.

Kratochwill, T. R., & Van Someren, K. R. (1985). Barriers to treatment success in behavioral consultation: Current limitations and future directions. *Journal of School Psychology, 23*, 225–239.

Kratochwill, T. R., & Williams, B. L. (1988). Personal perspectives on pitfalls and hassles in the conduct of single subject research. *Journal of the Association of Persons with Severe Handicaps, 13*, 147–154.

Kratochwill, T. R., Demuth, D. V., & Conzemius, W. D. (1977). The effects of overlearning on preschool children's retention of sight vocabulary words. *Reading Improvement, 14*, 223–228.

Kratochwill, T. R., Alper, S., & Cancelli, A. A. (1980). Nondiscriminatory assessment in psychology and education. In L. Mann & D. A. Sabatino (eds.), *Fourth review of special education* (pp. 229–286). New York: Grune & Stratton.

Kratochwill, T. R., Bergan, J. R., & Mace, F. C. (1981). Practitioner competencies needed for implementation of behavioral psychology in the schools: Issues in supervision. *School Psychology Review, 10*, 434–444.

Kratochwill, T. R., Doll, E. J., & Dickson, W. P. (1985). Microcomputers in behavioral assessment: Recent advances and remaining issues. *Computers in Human Behavior, 1*, 277–291.

Kratochwill, T. R., Sheridan, S. M., & Van Someren, K. P. (1988). Research in behavioral consultation: Current status and future directions. In F. J. West (Ed.), *School consultation: Interdisciplinary perspectives on theory, research, training, and practice* (pp. 77–102). Austin, TX: Association of Educational and Psychological Consultants.

Kratochwill, T. R., Van Someren, K. R., & Sheridan, S. M. (1989). Training behavioral consultants: A competency-based model to teach interview skills. *Professional School Psychology, 4*, 41–58.

Kreuger, W. C. F. (1929). The effect of overlearning on retention. *Journal of Experimental Psychology, 12*, 71–78.

Krumboltz, J. D., & Thoresen, C. E. (1969). *Behavioral counseling: Cases and Techniques.* New York: Holt, Rinehart & Winston.

Kubany, E. S., & Sloggett, B. B. (1973). Coding procedures for teachers. *Journal of Applied Behavior Analysis, 6*, 339–344.

Kurpius, D., & Robinson, S. E. (1978). Overview of consultation. *Personnel and Guidance Journal, 56*, 321–323.

Lacayo, N., Sherwood, G., & Morris, J. (1981). Daily activities of school psychologists: A national survey. *Psychology in the Schools, 18*, 184–190.

Lambert, N. M. (1974). A school-based consultation model. *Professional Psychology, 5,* 267–276.

Lancioni, G. E. (1982). Normal children as tutors to teach social responses to withdrawn mentally retarded school mates: Training, maintenance, and generalization. *Journal of Applied Behavior Analysis, 2,* 195–198.

Larrabee, M. J. (1980). *Counselor verbal behavior analysis definitions.* Unpublished manuscript, Texas A & M University.

LaVigna, G. W., & Donnellan, A. M. (1986). *Alternatives to punishment: Solving behavior problems with non-aversive strategies.* New York: Irvington.

Leinhardt, G., & Seewald, A. (1981). Overlap: What's tested, what's taught. *Journal of Educational Measurement, 18,* 85–96.

Lentz, F. E., Jr. (1988). On-task behavior, academic performance, and classroom disruptions: Untangling the target selection problem in classroom interventions. *School Psychology Review, 17,* 243–257.

Lentz, F. E., & Shapiro, E. S. (1985). Behavior school psychology: A conceptual model for the delivery of psychological services. In T. R. Kratochwill (Ed.), *Advances in school psychology* (Vol. 4, pp. 191–232). Hillsdale, NJ: Erlbaum.

Levin, J. R. (1975). Determining the sample size for planned and post hoc analysis of variable comparisons. *Journal of Educational Measurement, 12,* 99–108.

Levin, J. R. (1985). Educational applications of mnemonic pictures: Possibilities beyond your wildest imagination. In A. A. Sheikh & K. S. Sheikh (Eds.), *Imagery in education: Imagery in the educational process* (pp. 63–87). Farmingdale, NY: Baywood.

Levin, J. R., Marascuelo, L. M., & Hubert, L. N. (1978). Nonparametric randomization tests. In T. R. Kratochwill (Ed.), *Single subject research: Strategies to evaluate change* (pp. 167–196). New York: Academic Press.

Lewin, K. (1951). *Field theory in social science.* New York: Harper.

Lindsay, C. A., Crowe, M. B., & Jacobs, D. F. (1987). Continuing professional education for clinical psychology: A practice-oriented model. In B. A. Edelstein and E. S. Berler (Eds.), *Evaluation and accountability in clinical training* (pp. 331–363). New York: Berkeley Publishing.

Lindsley, O. R. (1964). Direct measurement and prosthesis of retarded behavior. *Journal of Education, 147,* 62–81.

Lippitt, G. L. (1969). *Organizational renewal.* New York: Appleton-Century-Crofts.

Livingston, S. A. (1977). Psychometric techniques for criterion-referenced testing and behavioral assessment. In J. D. Cone & R. P. Hawkins (Eds.), *Behavioral assessment: New directions in clinical psychology* (pp. 308–329). New York: Brunner/Mazel.

Locatis, C. N., & Gooler, D. D. (1975). Evaluating second-order consequences: Technology assessment and education. *Review of Educational Research, 45,* 327–353.

Lord, F. M. (1980). *Application of item response theory to practical testing problems.* Hillsdale, NJ: Erlbaum.

Mace, F. C., & West, B. J. (1986). Unresolved theoretical issues in self-management: Implications for research and practice. *Professional School Psychology, 1,* 149–163.

Madsen, C. H., Madsen, C. K., Saudargas, R. A., Hammond, W. R., Smith, J. B., & Edgar, D. E. (1970). Classroom RAIS (Rules, Approval, Ignore, Disapproval): A cooperative approach for professionals and volunteers. *Journal of School Psychology, 8,* 180–185.

Mager, R. F. (1961). *Preparing objectives for programmed instruction.* Palo Alto, CA: Fearon.

Maher, C. A., & Bennett, R. E. (1984). *Planning and evaluating special education services.* Englewood Cliffs, NJ: Prentice-Hall.

Maher, C. A., & Kratochwill, T. R. (1980). Program evaluation and school psychology: Issues and implications. *School Psychology Monograph, 4*(1), 1–24.

Mahoney, M. J., & Thoresen, C. E. (1974). *Self-control: Power to the person.* Monterey, CA: Brooks/Cole.

Mannino, F. V., & Shore, M. F. (1975). The effects of consultation: A review of the literature. *American Journal of Community Psychology, 3,* 1–21.

Marsh, G., Desberg, P., & Farwell, L. K. (1974). Stimulus and response variables in children's learning and grapheme-phoneme correspondence. *Journal of Educational Psychology, 66,* 112–116.

Martens, B. K., & Witt, J. C. (1988). Expanding the scope of behavioral consultation: A systems approach to classroom behavior change. *Professional School Psychology, 3,* 271–281.

Martens, B. K., & Witt, J. C. (in press). Ecological behavior analysis. In M. Hersen, R. M. Eisler, & P. M. Miller (Eds.), *Progress in behavior modification,* (Vol. 22). Beverly Hills, CA: Sage.

Martens, B. K., Witt, J. C., Elliott, S. N., & Darveaux, D. X. (1990). Teacher judgments concerning the acceptability of school-based interventions. *Professional Psychology.*

Martin, F. (1975). Increasing teachers' positive actions in the classroom. *Psychological Reports, 37,* 335–338.

Mash, E. J., & Terdal, L. G. (1980). Follow-up assessments in behavior therapy. In P. Karoly & J. J. Steffen (Eds.), *Improving the long term effects of psychotherapy.* New York: Gardner.

Mash, & Terdal, L. (Eds.). (1988). *Behavioral assessment of childhood disorders.* (2nd ed.). New York: Guilford Press.

McCleary, R., & Hay, R. A., Jr. (1980). *Applied time series analysis for the social sciences.* Beverly Hills, CA: Sage.

McConaughy, S. H., & Achenbach, T. M. (1989). Empirically-based assessment of serious emotional disturbance. *Journal of School Psychology, 27,* 91–117.

McDougall, L. M., Reschly, D. J., & Corkery, J. M. (1988). Changes in referral interviews with teachers after behavioral consultation training. *Journal of School Psychology, 26,* 255–232.

McGinnis, E., & Goldstein, A. P. (1984). *Skill-streaming the elementary school child: A guide for teaching prosocial skills.* Champaign, IL: Research Press.

McKee, W. T. (1984). *Acceptability of alternative classroom treatment strategies and factors affecting teachers' ratings.* Unpublished master's thesis, University of British Columbia, Vancouver, Canada.

McLaughlin, T. F. (1975). An analysis of the scientific rigor and practicality of the observational and recording techniques used in behavior modification research in public schools. *Corrective and Social Psychiatry and Journal of Behavior Technology Methods and Therapy, 21,* 13–16.

McMahon, R. J., & Forehand, R. (1980). Self-help behavior therapies in parent training. In B. B. Lahey & A. E. Kazdin (Eds.), *Advances in clinical child psychology* (Vol. 2, pp. 149–176). New York: Plenum Press.

McNamara, J. R., & Diehl, L. A. (1974). Behavioral consultation with a head start program. *Professional Psychology, 2,* 352–357.

Medway, F. J. (1979a). Causal attributions for school-related problems: Teacher perceptions and teacher feedback. *Journal of Educational Psychology, 71,* 809–818.

Medway, F. J. (1979b). How effective is school consultation: A review of recent research. *Journal of School Psychology, 17,* 275–282.

Medway, F. J. (1979c). School consultation research: Past trends and future directions. *Professional Psychology, 13,* 422–430.

Medway, F. J., & Updyke, J. F. (1985). Meta-analysis of consultation outcome studies. *American Journal of Community Psychology, 13,* 489–505.

Meyers, J. (1981). Mental health consultation. In J. C. Conoley (Ed.), *Consultation in schools: Theory, research, and procedures* (pp. 35–58). New York: Academic Press.

Meyers, J., Parsons, D., & Martin, R. (1979). *Mental health consultation in the schools.* San Francisco: Jossey-Bass.

Miller, A. J., & Kratochwill, T. R. (1979). Reduction of frequent stomachache complaints by a time-out. *Behavior therapy, 10,* 211–218.

Miltenberger, R. G., & Fuqua, R. W. (1985). Evaluation of a training manual for the acquisition of behavioral assessment interviewing skills. *Journal of Applied Behavior Analysis, 18,* 323–328.

Mischel, W. L. (1968). *Personality and assessment.* New York: Wiley.

Moon, G. W., Fantuzzo, J. W., & Gorsuch, R. L. (1986). Teaching WAIS-R administration skills: Comparison of the MASTERY model to other existing clinical training modalities. *Professional Psychology: Research and Practice, 17,* 32–35.

Moracco, J., & Kazandkian, A. (1977). Effectiveness of behavior counseling and consulting with non-Western elementary school children. *Elementary School Guidance and Counseling, 11,* 244–251.

Morrey, J. G. (1970). *Parent training in precise behavior management with mentally retarded children.* Doctoral dissertation, Utah State University. Ann Arbor, MI: University Microfilms, No. 7-27011.

Morris, R. J. & Kratochwill, T. R. (1983). *Treating children's fears and phobias: A behavioral approach.* New York: Pergamon Press.

Morris, R. J., & Kratochwill, T. R. (1984). *The practice of child therapy.* New York: Pergamon Press.

Nagle, R. J., & Gresham, F. M. (1979). A modeling based approach to teacher consultation: A case study. *Psychology in the Schools, 16,* 527–532.

Neel, R. S. (1981). How to put the consultant to work in consulting teaching. *Behavioral Disorders, 6,* 78–81.

Nelson, C. E. (1974). Abstract and information retrieval services in educational research: Current status and planned improvement. *Educational Researcher, 3,* 16–18.

Nelson, R. O. (1977a). Assessment and therapeutic functions of self-monitoring. In M. Hersen, R. M. Eisler, & P. M. Miller (Eds.), *Progress in behavior modification* (Vol. 5). New York: Academic Press.

Nelson, R. O. (1977b). Methodological issues in assessment via self-monitoring. In J. D. Cone & R. P. Hawkins (Eds.), *Behavioral assessment: New directions in clinical psychology.* New York: Brunner/Mazel.

Nelson, R. O. (1985). Behavioral assessment in school psychology. In T. R. Kratochwill (Ed.), *Advances in school psychology* (Vol. 4, pp. 45–87). Hillsdale, NJ: Erlbaum.

Nelson, R. O., & Wein, K. S. (1974). Training letter discrimination by presentation of high-confusion versus low-confusion alternatives. *Journal of Educational Psychology, 66,* 926–931.

Newman, E. B. (1951). Computational methods useful in analyzing series of binary data. *American Journal of Psychology, 54,* 252–262.

O'Dell, S. (1974). Training parents in behavior modifications: A review. *Psychological Bulletin, 8,* 418–433.

O'Dell, S. (1985). Progress in parent training. In M. Hersen, R. M. Eisler, & P. M. Miller (Eds.), *Progress in behavior modification* (Vol. 9, pp. 57–108). New York: Academic Press.

O'Leary, K. D., & Wilson, E. T. (Eds.) (1987). *Behavior therapy: Application and outcome.* Englewood Cliffs, NJ: Prentice-Hall.

O'Leary, K. D., Kaufman, K. F., Kass, R. E., & Drabman, R. S. (1970). The effects of loud and soft reprimands on the behavior of disruptive students. *Exceptional Children, 37,* 145–155.

O'Leary, K. D., Kent, R. N., & Kanowitz, J. (1975). Shaping data collection congruent with experimental hypothesis. *Journal of Applied Behavior Analysis, 8,* 43–51.

O'Leary, K. D., Romancyzyk, R. G., Kass, R. E., Dietz, A. T., & Santogrossi, D. (1979). *Procedures for classroom observation of teachers and children* (2nd ed.). Unpublished manuscript, State University of New York at Stony Brook.

Ollendick, T. H., & Cerny, J. A. (1981). *Clinical behavior therapy with children.* New York: Pergamon Press.

Osborn, A. F. (1963). *Applied imagination: Principles and procedures of creative problem solving* (3rd rev. ed.). New York: Scribners.

Ostrom, N. N., & Jenson, W. R. (1988). Assessment of attention deficits in children. *Professional School Psychology, 3*, 253–269.

Parsonson, B. S., & Baer, D. M. (1978). The analysis and presentation of graphic data. In T. R. Kratochwill (Ed.), *Single subject research: Strategies for evaluating change* (pp. 101–165). New York: Academic Press.

Parsonson, B. S., & Baer, D. M. (1986). The graphic analysis of data. In A. Poling & R. W. Fuqua (Eds.), *Research methods in applied behavior analysis* (pp. 157–186). New York: Plenum Press.

Patterson, G. R. (1971). Behavioral intervention procedures in the classroom and in the home. In A. E. Bergan & L. Garfield (Eds.), *Handbook of Psychotherapy and Behavior Change* (pp. 751–775). New York: Wiley.

Patterson, G. R. (1982). *Coercive family process.* Eugene, OR: Castalia.

Patterson, G. R., Ray, R. W., Shaw, D. A., & Cobb, J. A. (1969). *A manual for coding family interactions* (6th rev). New York: ASIS National Auxiliary Publications Service, CCM Information Services, Document No. 01234.

Pearl, A. (1974). The psychological consultant as a change agent. *Professional Psychology, 5*, 292–298.

Peterson, L., Homer, A. L., & Wonderlich, S. A. (1982). The integrity of independent variables in behavior analysis. *Journal of Applied Behavior Analysis, 15*, 477–492.

Petrie, P., Brown, K., Piersel, W. C., Frinfrock, S. R., Schelble, M., LeBlanc, C. P., & Kratochwill, T. R. (1980). The school psychologist as behavioral ecologist. *Journal of School Psychology, 10*, 222–233.

Phillips, B. N. (1982). Reading and evaluating research in school psychology. In C. R. Reynolds & T. B. Gutkin (Eds.), *Handbook of school psychology* (pp. 24–47). New York: Wiley.

Piersel, W. C., & Gutkin, T. B. (1983). Resistance to school-based consultation: A behavioral analysis of the problem. *Psychology in the Schools, 20*, 311–320.

Piersel, W. C., & Kratochwill, T. R. (1979). Self-observation and behavior change: Applications to academic and adjustment problems through behavioral consultation. *Journal of School Psychology, 17*, 151–161.

Piersel, W. C., & Kratochwill, T. R. (1981). Classroom assessment and treatment of selective mutism. *Behavioral Assessment, 3*, 371–382.

Pinkston, E. M., Reese, N. M., LeBlanc, J. M., & Baer, D. M. (1973). Independent control of a preschool child's aggression and peer interaction by contingent teacher attention. *Journal of Applied Behavior Analysis, 6*, 115–124.

Ponti, C. R., Zins, J. E., & Graden, J. L. (1988). Implementing a consultation-based service delivery system to decrease referrals for special education: A case study of organizational considerations. *School Psychology Review, 17*, 89–100.

Popham, W. J. (1968). *Probing the validity of arguments against behavioral goals.* Symposium presented at the Annual Meeting of the American Educational Research Association, Chicago, February.

Porter, E. H. (1943). The developmental and evaluation of a measure of counseling interview procedures: 1. The development. *Educational and Psychological Measurement, 3*, 215–238.

Rachman, S. J., & Wilson, G. T. (1980). *The effects of psychological therapy* (2nd ed.). Oxford, England: Pergamon Press.

Randolph, D. L. (1979). The behavioral consultant in the school. *American Journal of Community Psychology, 7*, 353–356.

Randolph, D. L., & Hardage, N. C. (1972). Behavioral consultation and group counseling with potential drop-outs. *Elementary School Guidance and Counseling, 7*, 204–209.

Rasmussen, D., & Goldbert, L. (1970). *The SRA reading program: Basic reading series.* Chicago: Science Research Association.

Reimers, T. M., Wacker, D. P., Koeppl, G. (1987). Acceptability of behavioral treatment interventions: A review of the literature. *School Psychology Review, 16*, 212–227.

Reppucci, N. D., & Saunders, J. T. (1974). Social psychology of behavior modification: Problems of implementation in natural settings. *American Psychologist, 29*, 649–660.

Reschly, D. J. (1976). School psychology consultation: Frenzied, faddish, or fundamental? *Journal of School Psychology, 14*, 457–464.

Resnick, L. B., Wang, M. C., & Kaplan, J. (1973). Task analysis in curriculum design: A hierarchically sequenced introductory mathematics curriculum. *Journal of Applied Behavior Analysis, 6*, 679–710.

Reynolds, C. R., & Willson, V. L. (Eds.). (1985). *Methodological and statistical advances in the study of individual differences.* New York: Plenum Press.

Reynolds, C. R., Gutkin, T. B., Elliot, S. N., & Witt, J. C. (1984). *School psychology:* Essentials of theory and practice. New York: Wiley.

Rhoades, M. M., & Kratochwill, T. R. (1989). Teacher acceptability of behavioral consultation: An analysis of language and involvement. *Manuscript submitted for publication.*

Rhodes, W. C. (1974). Principles and practices of consultation. *Professional Psychology, 5*, 287–291.

Rickel, A. U., Smith, R. L., & Sharp, K. C. (1979). Description and evaluation of a preventive mental health program for preschoolers. *Journal of Abnormal Child Psychology, 7*, 101–112.

Rickert, V. I., Sottolando, D. C., Parish, J. M., Riley, A. W., Hunt, F. M., & Pelco, L. E. (1988). Training parents to become better behavior managers: The need for a competency-based approach. *Behavior Modification, 12*, 475–496.

Riegel, K. F. (1972). Influence of economic and political ideologies on the development of developmental psychology. *Psychological Bulletin, 78*, 129–141.

Risley, T. R., & Hart, B. (1968). Developing correspondence between the non-verbal and verbal behavior of preschool children. *Journal of Applied Behavior Analysis, 1*, 267–281.

Robinson, V., & Swanton, C. (1980). The generalization of behavioral teacher training. *Review of Educational Research, 50*, 486–498.

Rogers, C. R. (1942). *Counseling and psychotherapy.* Boston: Houghton-Mifflin.

Rogers, C. R. (1951). *Client centered therapy.* Boston: Houghton-Mifflin.

Rogers, C. R. (1959). A theory of therapy, personality and interpersonal relationships, as developed in the client-centered framework. In S. Koch (Ed.), *Psychology: A study of science: Vol. 2. Formulations of the personal and social concept.* New York: McGraw-Hill.

Rogers, L. E., & Farace, R. V. (1975). Analysis of relational communication in dyads: New measurement procedures. *Human Communication Research, 1*, 222–239.

Romanczyk, R. G., Kent, R. N., Diament, C., & O'Leary, K. D. (1973). Measuring the reliability of observational data: A reactive process. *Journal of Applied Behavior Analysis, 6*, 175–184.

Rose, T. L. (1984). The effects of two prepractice procedures on oral reading. *Journal of Learning Disabilities, 17*, 544–548.

Rosenfield, S. A. (1987). *Instructional consultation.* Hillsdale, NJ: Erlbaum.

Ross, A. O. (1981b). Of rigor and relevance *Professional Psychology, 12*, 318–327.

Rush, F. R., & Kazdin, A. E. (1981). Toward a methodology of withdrawal designs for the assessment of response maintenance. *Journal of Applied Behavior Analysis, 14*, 131–140.

Sajwaj, T., Twardosz, S., & Burke, M. (1972). Side effects of extinction procedures in a remedial preschool. *Journal of Applied Behavior Analysis, 5*, 163–175.

Salvia, J., & Yesseldyke, J. E. (1988). *Assessment in special and remedial education* (4th ed.). Boston: Houghton Mifflin.

Samuels, S. J. (1973). Effect of distinctive feature training on paired-associate learning. *Journal of Educational Psychology, 64*, 164–170.

Sancilio, M. F. M. (1987). Peer interaction as a method of therapeutic intervention with children. *Clinical Psychology Review, 7*, 475–500.

Sarason, S. B. (1982). *The culture of the school and the problem of change* (2nd ed.). Boston: Allyn & Bacon.

Sashkin, M., Morris, W. C., & Horst, L. (1973). A comparison of social and organizational change models: Information flow and data use processes. *Psychological Review, 80,* 510–526.

Sattler, J. M. (1988). *Assessment of children's intelligence and special abilities* (3rd ed.). Brandon, VT: CPPC.

Saudargas, R. A. (1983). *State-event classroom observation code.* Knoxville: University of Tennessee, Department of Psychology. (Available from author.)

Saudargas, R. A., & Creed, V. (1980). *State-Event Classroom Observation System.* Knoxville: University of Tennessee, Department of Psychology.

Schein, E. H. (1969). *Process consultation: Its role in organizational development.* Reading, MA: Addison-Wesley.

Schmuck, R. A. (1982). Organization development in the schools. In C. R. Reynolds & T. B. Gutkin (Eds.), *Handbook of school psychology* (pp. 829–857). New York: Wiley.

Schmuck, R. A., & Runkel, P. J. (1972). Organizational training. In R. A. Schmuck (Ed.), *Handbook of organizational development in schools.* Palo Alto: Mayfield.

Schmuck, R. A., Runkel, P. J. Saturen, S. L., Martell, R. T., & Derr, C. B. (1972). *Handbook of organization development in schools.* Palo Alto, CA: National Press.

Shapiro, E. S. (1984). Self-monitoring procedures. In T. H. Ollendick & M. Hersen (Eds.), *Child behavioral assessment: Principles and procedures* (pp. 148–165). New York: Pergamon Press.

Shapiro, E. S. (1987). *Behavioral assessment in school psychology.* Hillsdale, NJ: Erlbaum.

Shapiro, E. S., & Goldberg, R. (1986). A comparison of group contingencies for increasing spelling performance among sixth grade students. *School Psychology Review, 15,* 546–557.

Shapiro, E. S., & Kratochwill, T. R. (Eds.). (1988). *Behavioral assessment in schools.* New York: Guilford Press.

Shapiro, E. S., & Lentz, F. E., Jr. (1986). Behavioral assessment of academic skills. In T. R. Kratochwill (Ed.), *Advances in school psychology* (Vol. 5, pp. 87–139). Hillsdale, NJ: Erlbaum.

Sheridan, S. M. (1988). Conjoint behavioral consultation: A link between home and school settings. Unpublished doctoral dissertation, University of Wisconsin–Madison.

Sheridan, S. M., Kratochwill, T. R., & Elliott, S. N. (in press). *Behavioral consultation with parents and teachers of socially withdrawn children. School Psychology Review.*

Sherman, T. M., & Cormier, W. H. (1974). An investigation of the influence of student behavior on teacher behavior. *Journal of Applied Behavior Analysis, 7,* 11–22.

Shinn, M. R. (Ed.). (1988). *Curriculum-based measurement and special services for children.* New York: Guilford Press.

Sibley, S. (1986). *A meta-analysis of school consultation research.* Unpublished doctoral dissertation, Texas Women's University, Denton.

Skinner, B. F. (1953). *Science and human behavior.* New York: Macmillan.

Skinner, B. F. (1957). *Verbal behavior.* New York: Appleton-Century-Crofts.

Skinner, B. F. (1971). *Beyond freedom and dignity.* New York: Knopf.

Skinner, B. F. (1975). The steep and thorny way to a science of behavior. *American Psychologist, 30,* 42–49.

Stephens, T. (1977). *Teaching skills to children with learning and behavior disorders.* Columbus, OH: Merrill.

Stokes, R. F. & Baer, D. M. (1977). An implicit technology of generalization. *Journal of Applied Behavior Analysis, 10,* 349–368.

Stolz, S. B., & Associates (1978). *Ethical issues in behavior modification.* San Francisco, CA: Jossey-Bass

Strain, P. S. (Ed.). (1981). *The utilization of classroom peers as behavior change agents*. New York: Plenum Press.

Stufflebeam, B. (1971). (Ed.). *Educational evaluation and decision making*. Itasca, IL: Peacock.

Sulzer-Azaroff, B., & Mayer, G. R. (1977). *Applying behavior analysis procedures with children and youth*. New York: Holt, Rinehart & Winston.

Sulzer-Azaroff, B., & Mayer, R. E. (1986). *Achieving educational excellence: Using behavioral strategies*. New York: Holt, Rinehart, & Winston.

Surratt, P. R., Ulrich, R. E., & Hawkins, R. P. (1969). An elementary student as a behavioral engineer. *Journal of Applied Behavior Analysis, 2*, 85–92.

Tarpley, B. S. & Saudargas, R. A. (1981). An intervention for a withdrawn child based on teacher recorded levels of social interaction. *School Psychology Review, 10*, 409–412.

Tharp, R. G. (1975). The triadic model of consultation: Current considerations: In C. A. Parker (Ed.), *Psychological consultation: Helping teachers meet special needs* (pp. 133–155). Reston, VA: Council for Exceptional Children.

Tharp, R. G. (1984). The triadic model. In J. A. Tucker (module developer), *School psychology in the classroom: A case study tutorial*. Minneapolis: National School Psychology Inservice Training Network.

Tharp, R. G., & Wetzel, R. J. (1969). *Behavioral modification in the natural environment*. New York: Academic Press.

Thorndike, R. L. (Ed.). (1971) *Educational measurement* (2nd ed.). Washington, DC: American Council on Education.

Tindal, G., Wesson, C., Deno, S. L., Germann, G., & Mirkin, P. K. (1985). The Pine County model for special education delivery: A data-based system. In T. R. Kratochwill (Ed.), *Advances in school psychology* (Vol. 4, pp. 223–250). Hillsdale, NJ: Erlbaum.

Toffler, A. (1970). *Future shock*. New York: Bantam Books.

Tombari, M. L., & Bergan, J. R. (1978). Consultant cues and teacher verbalization, judgments and expectations concerning children's adjustment problems. *Journal of School Psychology, 16*, 212–219.

Tomlinson-Keasey, C., Crawford, G. G., & Miser, A. L. (1975). Classification: An organizing operation for memory. *Developmental Psychology, 11*, 409–410.

Trabasso, T. R. (1963). Stimulus emphasis and all-or-nothing learning in concept identification. *Journal of Experimental Psychology, 65*, 398–406.

Tryon, W. W. (1976). Behavior modification therapy and the law. *Professional Psychology, 1*, 468–474.

Tucker, J. A. (Module Developer). (1984). *School psychology in the classroom: A case study tutorial*. Minneapolis: National School Psychology Inservice Training Network.

Underwood, B. J. (1961). An evaluation of the Gibson theory of verbal learning. In C. N. Cofer (Ed.), *Verbal learning and verbal behavior*. New York: McGraw-Hill.

Van Houten, R., & Sullivan, K. (1975). Effects of an audio cueing system on the rate of teacher praise. *Journal of Applied Behavior Analysis, 8*, 197–202.

Vernberg, E. M., & Reppucci, N. D. (1986). Behavioral consultation. In F. V. Mannino, E. J. Trickett, M. F. Shore, M. G. Kidder, & G. Levin (Eds.), *Handbook of mental health consultation* (pp. 49–80). Washington, DC: National Institute of Mental Health.

Voeltz, L. M., & Evans, I. M. (1982). The assessment of behavioral interrelationships in child behavior therapy. *Behavioral Assessment, 4*, 131–165.

Voeltz, L. M., & Evans, I. M. (1983). Educational validity: Procedures to evaluate outcomes in programs for severely handicapped learners. *Journal of the Association of the Severely Handicapped, 8*, 3–15.

von Bertalanffy, L. (1950). The theory of open systems in physics and biology. *Science, 111*, 23–28.

Von Brock, M. B., & Elliott, S. N. (1987). The influence of treatment effectiveness information on the acceptability of classroom interventions. *Journal of School Psychology, 25*, 131–144.

Wahler, R. G. (1969). Setting generality: Some specific and general effects of child behavior therapy. *Journal of Applied Behavior Analysis, 2,* 239–246.

Wahler, R. G. (1975). Some structural aspects of deviant child behavior. *Journal of Applied Behavior Analysis, 8,* 27–42.

Wahler, R. G. (1980). The insular mother: Her problems in parent-child treatment. *Journal of Applied Behavior Analysis, 13,* 207–219.

Wahler, R. G., & Graves, M. G. (1983). Setting events in social networks: Ally or enemy in child behavior therapy? *Behavior Therapy, 14,* 19–36.

Wahler, R. G., House, A. E., & Stambaugh, E. E. (1976). *Ecological assessment of child problem behavior: A clinical practice for home, school, and institutional setting.* New York: Pergamon Press.

Walker, H. M., & Buckley, N. K. (1972). Programming generalization and maintenance of treatment effects across time and across settings. *Journal of Applied Behavior Analysis, 5,* 209–224.

Walters, R. H., Parke, R. D., & Cane, V. A. (1965). Timing of punishment and the observation of consequences to others as determinants of response inhibition. *Journal of Experimental Psychology, 2,* 10–30.

Wang, M. C. (1973). Psychometric studies in the validation of an early learning curriculum. *Child Development, 44,* 54–60.

Weiner, K. B. (1982). *Child and adolescent psychopathology.* New York: Wiley.

Wells, K. C., Conners, C. K., Imber, L., & Delamater, J. (1981). Use of single-subject methodology in clinical decision-making with a hyperactive child on the psychiatric inpatient unit. *Behavioral Assessment, 3,* 359–369.

West, J. F., & Idol, L. (1987). School consultation: Part 1. An interdisciplinary perspective on theory, models, and research. *Journal of Learning Disabilities, 20,* 388–405.

Wetzel, R. J., & Patterson, J. R. (1975). Technical developments in classroom behavior analysis. In B. C. Etzel, J. M. LeBlanc, & D. M. Baer (Eds.), *New developments in behavioral research: Theory, methods, and applications. In honor of Sidney W. Bijou.* Hillsdale, NJ: Erlbaum.

Whang, P. L., Fletcher, R. K., & Fawcett, S. B. (1982). Training counseling skills: An experimental analysis and social validation. *Journal of Applied Behavior Analysis, 15,* 325–334.

White, G. W., & Pryzwansky, W. B. (1982). Consultation outcome as a result of in-service resource teacher training. *Psychology in the Schools, 19,* 495–501.

White, O., & Haring, N. (1980). *Exceptional teaching.* Columbus, OH: Merrill.

White, R. T. (1973). Learning hierarchies. *Review of Educational Research, 43,* 361–375.

White, R. T. (1974). The validation of a learning hierarchy. *American Educational Research Journal, 11,* 121–136.

White, R. T., & Gagné, R. M. (1974). Past and future research on learning hierarchies. *Educational Psychologist, 2*(1), 19–28.

Willems, E. P. (1974). Behavioral technology and behavioral ecology. *Journal of Applied Behavior Analysis, 7,* 151–166.

Winett, R. A. (1976). Environmental design: An expanded behavioral research framework for school consultation and educational innovation. *Professional Psychology, 1,* 631–636.

Witt, J. C., & Elliott, S. N. (1982). The response cost lottery: A time efficient and effective classroom intervention. *Journal of School Psychology, 20,* 155–161.

Witt, J. C., & Elliott, S. N. (1985). Acceptability of classroom management strategies. In T. R. Kratochwill (Ed.), *Advances in school psychology* (Vol. 4, pp. 251–288). Hillsdale, NJ: Erlbaum.

Witt, J. C., & Martens, B. K. (1988). Problems with problem-solving consultation: A re-analysis of assumptions, methods and goals. *School Psychology Review, 17,* 211–226.

Witt, J. C., & Martens, B. K. (1983). Assessing the acceptability of behavioral interventions. *Psychology in the Schools, 20,* 510–517.

Witt, J. C., & Robbins, J. R. (1985). Acceptability of reductive interventions for the control of inappropriate child behavior. *Journal of Abnormal Child Psychology, 13,* 59–67.

Witt, J. C., Moe, G., Gutkin, T. B., & Andrews, L. (1984). The effect of saying the same thing in different ways: The problem of language and jargon in school-based consultation. *Journal of School Psychology, 22,* 361–367.

Witt, J. C., Elliott, S. N., & Martens, B. K. (1984). Acceptability of behavioral interventions used in classrooms: The influence of amount of teacher time, severity of behavior problem, and type of intervention. *Behavioral Disorders, 10,* 95–104.

Witt, J. C., Martens, B. K., & Elliott, S. N. (1984). Factors affecting teachers' judgments of the acceptability of behavioral interventions: Time involvement, behavior problem severity, and type of intervention. *Behavior Therapy, 15,* 204–209.

Wolf, M. M. (1978). Social validity: The case for subjective measurement or how applied behavior analysis is finding its heart. *Journal of Applied Behavior Analysis, 11,* 203–214.

Wolf, M. M., Risley, T. R., & Mees, H. I. (1964). Application of operant conditioning procedures to the behavior problems of an autistic child. *Behavior Research and Therapy, 1,* 305–312.

Workman, E. A., Kendall, L. M., & Williams, R. L. (1980). The consultative merits of praise-ignore versus praise-reprimand instruction. *Journal of School Psychology, 18,* 373–380.

Yarrow, M. R., Waxler, C. Z., & Scott, P. M. (1971). Child effects on adult behavior. *Developmental Psychology, 5,* 300–311.

Yates, B. T., Haven, W. G., & Thoresen, C. T. (1977). Cost-effectiveness analyses at Learning House: How much changes for how much money? In J. S. Stumphauzer (Ed.), *Progress in behavioral therapy with delinquents* (Vol. 2). Springfield, IL: Charles C Thomas.

Yeaton, W. H. & Sechrest, L. (1981). Critical dimensions in the choice and maintenance of successful treatments: Strength, integrity, and effectiveness. *Journal of Consulting and Clinical Psychology, 49,* 156–167.

Yin, R. K. (1984). *Case study research: Design and methods.* Beverly Hills, CA: Sage.

Ysseldyke, J. E., & Christenson, S. (1987). *The Instructional Environment Scale.* Austin, TX: Pro-Ed.

Ysseldyke, J. E., Reynolds, M. C., & Weinberg, R. A. (1984). *School psychology: A blueprint for training and practice.* Minneapolis: National School Psychology Resource Training Network.

Zins, J. E., Curtis, M. H., Graden, J. L., & Ponti, C. R. (1988). *Alternatives to special education referral: Prereferral consultation and intervention systems.* San Francisco: Jossey-Bass.

Index

Basic concepts, viii, 3–42

Case-reporting forms
  academic competence, 459–465
  emotional problems, 453–458
  instructions for coding
    academic cases, 469–472
    adjustment cases, 465–469
Case studies in behavioral consultation,
    viii, 307–335
Coding process
  coding instruments
    analysis checklist, 69–71
    analysis record, 66–69
    use of, 66–71
  what to code
    incomplete verbalization, 65
    independent clause, 64
    interrupted verbalization, 65
    unit of observation, 64
Conditions that can affect behavior
  environmental changes, table of
    decreases in performance, 451
    increases in performance, 448–449
    maintenance of performance ca-
      pability, 450
Consultation during implementation
  interactions
    brief contact, 224–226
    observation, 226–227
    training session, 227–229
  objectives
    monitoring, 222–223
    revision, 223

Consultation during implementation (cont.)
  objectives (cont.)
    skill development, 219–222
Controlling verbal behavior
  production practice
    segment production, 77
    unit production, 76
    verbal subcategories, 76
    verbal subcategory sequence, 77
  recognition practice
    analysis of PEI segment, example of,
      75
    analysis of PII segment, example of,
      74
    interview segment, in, 73
    sample units of observation, 72
    segment of PEI, 73
    segment of PII, 72
    unit recognition, 71

Definition and models of consultation
  nature of problem, 381–383
  recommendations, 383–384
Design of consultative problem-solving
    systems
  evaluation
    attainment of service goals, 365–367
    unanticipated system effects, 367–370
  information management
    disseminating information, 358–359
    DURABLE framework, 356
    gathering information, 354–355
    retrieving information, 355–358
    storing information, 355–358

513

Printed in the United States
98105LV00001B/106-108/A

9 780306 433450